A Companion to Martin Buber

A Companion to Martin Buber

EDITED BY PAUL MENDES-FLOHR

The University of Chicago Press
Chicago and London

The University of Chicago Press, Chicago 60637
The University of Chicago Press, Ltd., London
© 2025 by The University of Chicago
All rights reserved. No part of this book may be used or reproduced in any manner whatsoever without written permission, except in the case of brief quotations in critical articles and reviews. For more information, contact the University of Chicago Press, 1427 E. 60th St., Chicago, IL 60637.
Published 2025

34 33 32 31 30 29 28 27 26 25   1 2 3 4 5

ISBN-13: 978-0-226-83889-2 (cloth)
ISBN-13: 978-0-226-83891-5 (paper)
ISBN-13: 978-0-226-83890-8 (e-book)
DOI: https://doi.org/10.7208/chicago/9780226838908.001.0001

Library of Congress Cataloging-in-Publication Data

Names: Mendes-Flohr, Paul R., editor.
Title: A companion to Martin Buber / edited by Paul Mendes-Flohr.
Description: Chicago : The University of Chicago Press, 2025. |
  Includes bibliographical references and index.
Identifiers: LCCN 2024041045 | ISBN 9780226838892 (cloth) |
  ISBN 9780226838915 (paperback) | ISBN 9780226838908 (ebook)
Subjects: LCSH: Buber, Martin, 1878–1965. | Jewish philosophy—20th century.
Classification: LCC B3213.B84 C65 2025 | DDC 296.3092—dc23/eng/20240912
LC record available at https://lccn.loc.gov/2024041045

Tamar Goldschmidt and Aya Kaniuk
faithful companions in dialogue

You should first understand the silence before you try to understand one's words.
ANONYMOUS GRAFFITI, Chania, Crete

Contents

PROLOGUE: Martin Buber: Philosopher of Dialogue
  Paul Mendes-Flohr   1

PART 1 Philosophy of Dialogue

Introduction
  Paul Mendes-Flohr   17
1 Exodus from Monological Modernity
  Christoph Schmidt   19
2 Martin Buber and Philosophical Anthropology
  Asher Biemann   33
3 "The Between": Martin Buber's Transformation of Consciousness
  Michael Fishbane   53
4 Imaging the Imageless, Making Present, and Coming to Light of the Other: Imagination and Buber's Dialogical Thinking
  Elliot R. Wolfson   67
5 To Hallow the Everyday
  Paul Mendes-Flohr   84
6 Martin Buber's Ethics of Perception
  Sarah Scott   97

PART 2 Language and Hermeneutics

Introduction
  Paul Mendes-Flohr   115
7 Buber and Language
  Joachim Oberst   117
8 Martin Buber and the Philosophy of Communication
  Johan Siebers   129
9 Buber and Expressionism
  Bernhard Lang   142

10 Buber's Hermeneutical Biblical Theology
   Steven Kepnes   156
11 Buber's Relational Ontology and Dialogical Listening
   Claudia Welz   166

PART 3   Psychology and Education

Introduction
   Paul Mendes-Flohr   187
12 Buber's Concept of the Soul
   Cornelia Muth   189
13 Buber on Solitude
   Michal Bizoň   194
14 Buber on Psychotherapy and Psychoanalysis
   Henry Abramovitch   206
15 Martin Buber: Education toward Humanism
   Aslaug Kristiansen   215

PART 4   Interfaith Dialogue

Introduction
   Paul Mendes-Flohr   225
16 Buber and Christianity
   Karl-Josef Kuschel   227
17 Martin Buber and Eastern Wisdom
   Hune Margulies   239
18 Buber Meeting and Not-Meeting Islam
   Khaled Furani   251

PART 5   Judaism

Introduction
   Paul Mendes-Flohr   263
19 Martin Buber on Israel's Divine Election
   Manuel Duarte de Oliveira   265
20 Buber and Hasidism
   Sam S. B. Shonkoff   271
21 Buber and the Holocaust
   David Barzilai   287

PART 6   Politics

Introduction
   Paul Mendes-Flohr   297

22 Buber's Concept of Theopolitics
   Samuel Hayim Brody   299
23 Buber's Concept of *Gemeinschaft* (Community)
   Inka Sauter   309
24 The Ethical View of the Palestinian Other
   Amal Jamal   323
25 Feminism and Buber's Legacy: A Critical Reception
   Yemima Hadad   335

PART 7 Reception

Introduction
   Paul Mendes-Flohr   353
26 Buber in France: From Gaston Bachelard to Emmanuel Levinas
   Dominique Bourel   355
27 Buber's Philosophy of Dialogue: A Japanese Perspective
   Fumio Ono   360

Glossary 375
List of Contributors 381
Index 387

PROLOGUE

Martin Buber: Philosopher of Dialogue

PAUL MENDES-FLOHR

Inaugurated with the publication of *Ich und Du* (I and Thou) in 1923, Martin Buber's philosophy of dialogue has enjoyed a ramified resonance in diverse academic disciplines, from anthropology to architecture, comparative religion to Jewish studies, psychotherapy to pedagogy, hermeneutics to political science, religious existentialism to the philosophy of language.[1] Each of the compendious twenty-one volumes of the recently completed German critical edition of Buber's writings is devoted to a distinctive subject that engaged his capacious intellect.[2]

As conceived by Buber, dialogue is not a synonym for convivial conversation or earnest negotiations. It rather constitutes a radical critique of the regnant epistemological and methodological presuppositions of the study of social life. Indeed, as the French historian of philosophy Rémi Brague has noted, Buber "sought a new way of being in the world" and thereby "opened a new field of investigation."[3]

The seeds of Buber's philosophy of dialogue may be traced back to his doctoral dissertation of 1904, "On the History of the Problem of Individuation: Nicholas of Cusa and Jakob Böhme."[4] He asked together, as it were, with these two late Renaissance Christian thinkers, how we are to understand every individual as distinctively singular and unique. In addressing this question, it was Böhme who focused Buber's attention on individuation as manifest in a person's desire to meet and interact with others. In his early, pre-dialogical writings, however, Buber followed the German mystic in viewing individuation, fraught as it is with the imponderables of interpersonal relations, as a problem to overcome.

Buber thus sought to unite, as he would later confess, "the self with the all-self," untrammeled by the divisive pull of individuation. In the course of twenty years, he came to realize that when the mystic perforce returns to life "in the world and with the world, he is naturally inclined from then on to regard everyday life as an obscuring of the true life."[5] To be sure, individuation entails existential isolation and vulnerability, but as Buber affirmed in *I and Thou*, it is not to be overcome by withdrawal into the inner precincts of the self—be that construed as religious spirituality or otherwise. Nor is one's individuated existence to be overcome by allowing oneself to be swallowed up in the whirl of a universe governed by collective identities (buttressed by ethnocentric nationalism and political ideologies putatively attuned to the drumbeats of the cunning of historical necessity). Buber refers to these delusory palliatives to the existential anxieties of individuation as *psychologism* and *cosmologism*, respectively.[6] Rather, he contends, "the fundamental fact of human existence is neither the individual as such nor the aggregate as such. [...] The individual is a fact of existence in so far as he steps into a living relation with other individuals."[7] Buber duly called this intersubjective realm of human-being-in-the-world "the between" (*das Zwischen*) and accordingly spoke of his philosophy of dialogue as the ontology of the between man and man (*die Ontologie des Zwischenmenschliche*).[8]

When individuals enter an I-Thou relationship of mutual recognition and confirmation of each other's distinctive and unique being (*Dasein*), they attain the fullness of being (*Sein*). But, alas, the trials and tribulations of life deflect one from realizing the ontological ideal, "the true life," that unfolds in the dialogical meeting between individuals. Interpersonal and intercommunal conflict are real and engender an understandable mistrust. One's perceived opponents are thus to be held at bay, cast in objectified adversarial categories, subject to what Buber calls "I-It" relations—relations that are regarded to be primed and guided by a sober realism. (In the political realm, such realism is defiantly upheld as *Realpolitik*.) In response, Buber presented "I-Thou dialogue" as "a more penetrating realism, a greater realism, the realism of a greater reality!" In dialogue, the other

> is not to be seen through [an adversarial lens], but to be perceived ever more completely in his openness and hiddenness and in the relation of the two to each other. We wish to trust him, not blindly indeed but clear-sightedly. We wish to perceive his manifoldness and his wholeness, his proper character, without any preconceptions about this or that background, and with the intention of accepting and confirming him to the extent that this perception will allow.[9]

In the modern era, the prevailing social and political mistrust is ever greatly deepened by a miasmic "loss of confidence in human existence in general."[10] With the eclipse of traditional social structures and metaphysical affirmations, humanity is increasingly adrift in the world without any sure sense of the meaning of life. One finds oneself to be "a stranger and solitary in the world."[11] Humanity's "homelessness" compounds the mistrust that confounds social and political relations with a deep-seated existential mistrust. Dialogue thus takes on an urgency to restore what Buber regarded as the primordial trust in human relations and in life.[12] In accord with his "greater realism," Buber was cognizant that it is an imperative fraught with untoward "risk." To be dialogically present to the other, we must discard the "armor" constructed to secure our "inner integrity" from what is perceived to be a threatening reality. To meet the other is thus to cross a "narrow ridge," suspending our defensive postures, and to bare our existential vulnerability to the other with the risk that it might not elicit a corresponding openness. "Mismeetings" define the risk, but it is a "holy risk."[13] It is a risk we must bear if we are to overcome the existential mistrust that gnaws at our confidence in being. We each secretly wish to be confirmed in our very being, a confirmation that can only come from fellow humans:

> Sent forth into the hazard of the solitary category, surrounded by the air of a chaos which came into being with him, secretly and bashfully he watches for a Yes which allows him to be, and which can come only from one human person to another.[14]
>
> The unavowed secret of man [*Mensch*] is that he wants to be confirmed in his being and his existence by his fellow men and he wishes to make it possible for them to confirm him ... to confirm his presence [*Gegenwart*]. This is the indispensable minimum of humanity.[15]

The reciprocity of the dialogical I-Thou relation echoes the biblical injunction "to love your fellow as yourself: I am the Lord" (Lev. 19:18).[16] Hilary Putnam notes that Buber's concept of dialogical reciprocity is in accord with Aristotle, "who taught us that to love others one must be able to love oneself." He thus found Emmanuel Levinas's critique of Buber to be mistakenly based on a "one-sided" phenomenology of ethics. "It is because it is one-sided [. . . that] Levinas's relation to Buber is fundamentally a competitive one,"[17] consequent to a profoundly different conception of the I-Thou relation.

For Levinas, the encounter with the other "disrupts" the solitude of the self-centered ego, opening one to "the dimension of height," transcendence, soliciting an ethical response. He thus found Buber's face-to-face dialogical meeting wanting. For it is born of a quest for reciprocal "intimacy," of mutual "hospitality," hence, Buber's Thou is "not the You (*le Vous*) of the face that reveals itself in a dimension of height," a transcendent ethical imperative "exterior" to the self. It is precisely because Buber's Thou (*le tu*) is the language of familiarity that it is "a language without teaching, a silent language, and understanding without words, an expression without secret. The I-Thou in which Buber sees the category of interhuman relationship is the relation not with the interlocutor but with *feminine* alterity."[18]

La Femme denotes in Levinas's lexicon the welcoming "interiority" by an "exterior" ethical command. But it was precisely the feminine (*frauenhaft*) tenor of Buber's thought, even prior to the crystallization of his philosophy of dialogue, that Gustav Landauer (1870–1919) hailed as an ethical and political virtue. Eschewing purely abstract philosophical discourse, Landauer noted, Buber "awakens and advocates a specific feminine form of thought without which our exhausted and collapsed culture cannot be renewed and replenished. Only when all thoughts, which abide in human beings as spirit, when abstract thought is conjoined and submerged in the depths of feeling, will our thought engender deeds, will a true life emerge from our logical desert. Towards that objective women will help us." As a philosopher who is attuned to the poetic cadences and emotional ground of life, Landauer exults, Buber belongs to the spiritual family of the feminine.[19]

Nor is the "silent language, understanding without words" of the "feminine," intimate embrace bereft of ethical significance for Buber: As a mutual dialogical affirmation, a wordless I-Thou encounter is a metaethical moment that constitutes the existential ground of a genuine ethical response to the other. Dialogue is, indeed, ultimately beyond the spoken word, but precisely therein lies its ethical (and political) import. The soundless speech of dialogue is thus not even that of the "tender silence" of lovers, "resting in one another," sharing a gaze, "rich in inward relations." Nor is Buber "thinking of the mystical shared silence, such as reported of the Franciscan Aegidius and [King] Louis of France [. . .] who, meeting once, did not utter a word, but 'taking their stand in the reflection of the Divine Face' experienced one another. For here too there is the expression of a gesture, of the physical attitude of the one to the other."[20] Mediated by neither words nor gestures, dialogue is not an interpretative, cognitive act. It is simply the felt acknowledgment and thus mutual confirmation of the existential presence of the partners in the dialogical encounter. Words and gestures are, in fact, to be transcended, for they carry a range of meanings that bear the stamp of cultural and personal inflections which are liable to hinder dialogue.[21] "The relation to the [Thou] is unmediated. Nothing conceptual intervenes between I and [Thou], no prior knowledge and no imagination. [. . .] Every means is an obstacle" to dialogue. "Only where all means have disintegrated [do] encounters occur." Nor is dialogue a purposeful act. The Thou "encounters me by grace—it cannot be found by seeking"—hence, it is not akin to negotiations or prompted by a desire to engage in a conversation. The Thou encounters one, to which one may respond dialogically. The I-Thou relationship is thus one of "election and electing, passive and active at once." As unmediated response to the existential presence of the other, dialogue "approaches passivity," without "any sense of action."[22]

Buber's concept of passive action is informed by his understanding of the Taoist concept of *wúwéi*—non-action, a non-intentional, non-calculating, non-deliberative manner of being in the world. In adhering to the "path" of *wúwéi*, one is spontaneously and wholly open to the moment, to the here and now.[23] In accord with the teachings of the Chinese Taoist sage Tschuang-Tse, Buber would distinguish the dialogical response to the other, one's Thou, from an empathetic identification with the feelings and experience of others as analogous to what one has experienced or imagines as experiencing. For empathy, by its very nature, entails a projection of meaning that may not be consonant and consistent with the experience and feelings of others—and thus in effect denies the existential integrity of their experience and feelings.[24] To escape this hermeneutical circle, Buber spoke of dialogical inclusion (*Umfassung*): to listen to the other's voice, muffled in silence or otherwise, without interpretation, and simply allow it to resonate, as it were, aside one's own "story," one's own inner voice.[25] To listen to the voice of the other is to be attuned to a shared experience "from the other side": One "actively participates" in the other's experience "without forfeiting anything of [one's own] felt reality [...] and lives through a common event from the standpoint of the other. [...] Not only is the shared silence of two such persons in a dialogue, but also their dialogical life continues, even when they are separated in space, as the continual potential of the presence of the one to the other." Genuine ethical and political life "springs from an experience of inclusion."[26]

As a radically "new way of being in the world,"[27] dialogue, as Christoph Schmidt observes in his contribution to this volume, is "man's emergence from self-imposed [intellectual and spiritual] immaturity," determined by a monological conception of truth as a transtemporal, subject-object, I-It logos. To be sure, to let go of the monological conceptual and cultural categories entails a risk, but it is a "holy risk," for it is the path from "the cradle" to the fullness of life.[28]

*

In consonance with the polymathic, interdisciplinary scope of Buber's philosophical and cultural interests, his writings have enjoyed a global resonance. The scholarly voices represented in this volume attest to the planetary reach of the reception accorded Buber's teachings, with essays contributed by scholars from Japan, India, Denmark, Norway, France, Germany, Slovenia, Portugal, England, Israel, Palestine, and the United States.

Buber proudly regarded himself as an "atypic thinker," who could not be easily cast as a "philosopher or theologian or something else." He readily conceded that he had no teaching in a conceptually rigorous sense: "I only point to something . . . in reality that had not or had too little been seen. I take him who listens to me by the hand and lead him to the window. I open the window and point to what is outside. I have no teaching but carry on a conversation."[29] This volume seeks to continue the conversation inspired by Buber.

Notes

1. See *Dialogue as a Trans-Disciplinary Concept*, ed. Paul Mendes-Flohr (Berlin: Walter de Gruyer Verlag, 2016). The essays in this *Companion to Martin Buber* reflect on Buber's seminal contributions to the study of Arab-Jewish relations (Jamal Amal), Islam (Khalid Furani), Eastern religions (Hune Margolis, Fumio Ono), ethics (Sarah Scott), education (Aslaugh Kristiansen), existentialism (Michal Bizon, Cornelia Muth), feminism (Yamima Haddad), Hasidism (Sam Berrin Shonkoff), hermeneutics (Stephen Kepnes, Elliot Wolfson), Jewish-Christian understanding (Hans-Josef Kuschel), language and communicative reason (Joachim Oberst, Johan Siebers), literary and poetic expressionism (Bernhard Lang), philosophical anthropology (Asher D. Biemann), philosophy (Michael Fishbane, Claudia Welz, Christoph Schmidt, Fumio Ono), political theology (Samuel H. Brody, Christoph Schmidt), psychotherapy and psychoanalysis (Henry Abramovich), and theology (Hans-Josef Kuschel, Manuel Durate de Oliveria, Paul Mendes-Flohr, Sam Berrin Shonkoff).

2. *Martin-Buber Werkausgabe*, ed. Paul Mendes-Flohr and Peter Schäfer (2001–10), Bernd Witte (2010–19) (Gütersloh: Gütersloher Verlagshaus, 2001–19), 21 vols. (26 bks.). Sponsored by the Berlin-Brandenburg Academy of the Sciences and the Israel Academy of Sciences and the Humanities.

3. Rémi Brague, "How to Be in the World: Gnosis, Religion, Philosophy," in *Martin Buber: A Contemporary Perspective*, ed. Paul Mendes-Flohr (Syracuse, NY: Syracuse University Press, 2002), 144, 146.

4. Sarah Scott discerns in the dissertation the seeds of Buber's philosophy of dialogue. Buber took "from the Renaissance Neoplatonic philosophers Nicholas of Cusa and Jakob Böhme a new way of thinking about the process of individuation, in which . . . individuation and community further one another," noting that the theme of individuation so understood runs throughout Buber's ramified writings. As Buber himself noted, "individuation is [. . .] the presupposition of dialogical life." Martin Buber, "Hope for This Hour," in Buber, *Pointing the Way*, ed. and trans. Maurice S. Friedman (New York: Harper, 1963), 224. See Sarah Scott, "The Ethics of Perception: Martin Buber's Study of Nicolas of Cusa and Jakob Böhme, Art and Aesthetics" (PhD diss., New School for Social Research, 2011), and her contribution to this volume.

5. Buber, foreword to *Pointing the Way*, ix.

6. Martin Buber, "Von der Verseelung der Welt," in Buber, *Nachlese* (Heidelberg: Verlag Lambert Schneider, 1965), 149.

7. Martin Buber, *Between Man and Man*, trans. Ronald Gregor Smith (London: Routledge, 2002), 239. In *I and Thou* he adumbrated phylogenetic and anthropological explications of this thesis, which he later elaborated as the basis of a philosophical anthropology. See *I and Thou*, trans. Walter Kaufmann, 100th anniversary reissue (New York: Free Press, 2023), 70–80; and Martin Buber, *The Knowledge of Man: Selected Essays*, trans. Maurice Friedman (New York: Harper & Row, 1965). Buber originally contemplated calling this collection of essays *We: Studies in Philosophical Anthropology*. See Asher D. Biermann's essay in this volume.

8. Martin Buber, "Elemente des Zwischenmenschlichen," in Buber, *Das dialogische Prinzip* (Heidelberg: Verlag Lambert Schneider, 1979), 290. As Buber himself acknowledged, his ontology shared in Heidegger's rejection of the Cartesian dualism of mind and body, and the epistemological presupposition of subject-object dualism, which Buber characterized as the I-It relation. See Michael A. Fishbane's essay in this volume.

9. Buber, "Hope for This Hour," 227. On Buber's political thought, see in this volume the essays by Samuel Hayyim Brody and Christoph Schmidt.

10. Buber, "Hope for This Hour," 224.

11. Buber, *Between Man and Man*, 150. Cf. Martin Heidegger, "Die Heimatlosigkeit wird in Weltschicksal" (Homelessness is becoming the fate of the world), in Heidegger, *Briefe über Humanismus*, Gesamte Ausgabe (Frankfurt: Verlag Vittorio Klostermann, 1986), 9:339.

12. Buber embroidered throughout writings a critique of gnostic ontological denigration of the "created order." See Orr Scharf, "A Tale of Light and Darkness: Martin Buber's Gnostic Canon and the Birth of Theo-politics," *Religions* 10, no. 4 (2019): 1–18. Cf. "The basic word I-It does come from evil—as much as matter—comes from evil." *I and Thou*, Kaufmann translation, 95. Cf. "What saved Judaism is not, as the Marcionites imagine, the fact that it failed to experience 'the tragedy,' the contradictions are the world's process, deeply enough, but rather it experienced 'that tragedy' in the dialogical situation, they experienced the tragedy as a *theophany*. This very world, this very contradiction, unabridged, unmitigated, unsmoothed, unsimplified, unreduced, this world shall not be overcome—but consummated. [. . .] It is not a redemption from evil, as the power which God created for this service and the performance of his work." Martin Buber, "The Faith of Israel" (1928), in *Israel and the World: Essays in a Time of Crisis*, trans. Olga Marx et al. (New York: Schocken Books, 1948), 26. Also see my essay in this volume, "The Redemption of the It-World: Hallowing the Everyday," and Sam Berrin Shonkoff's essay on Hasidism.

13. Martin Buber, *I and Thou*, centennial ed., trans. Ronald Gregor Smith (New York: Scribner Classics, 2023), 9. A year after the publication of *Ich und Du*, Buber published "Drama and Theater" in a German journal on the thespian arts, which expatiated on the inextricable risks attendant on dialogue. "Regarded as a species of poetry, drama is [. . .] the formation of the *word* as something that moves *between beings*, the mystery of word and answer. Essential to it is the fact of the *tension* between word and answer—the fact, namely, that two men never mean the same things by the words they use, that there is, therefore, no pure reply, that at each point of the conversation [. . .] understanding and misunderstanding are [inevitably] interwoven— from which comes the interplay of openness and closeness, expression, and reserve. [. . .] If the play as poetry is thus grounded in the fact that man seeks to communicate to men through speaking, and across all barriers of individuation actually succeeds in communication, if only in tension, the play also belongs to a more natural level. It originates in the elemental impulse to leap [. . .] over the abyss between I and Thou that is bridge[d] through speech." Buber, "Drama und Theater," *Masken. Zeitschrift für deutsche Theaterkultur*, 18 Jg., Erstes Oktoberheft 1924, S. 3–5. Translated in *Martin Buber and the Theater*, ed. and trans. Maurice Friedman (New York:

Funk & Wagnalls, 1969), 83f. (Buber's italics). Also see the essays in this *Companion to Martin Buber* by Joachim Oberst and Johan Siebers.

14. Buber, *Knowledge of Man*, 71.

15. Martin Buber, "Community and Environment," in Buber, *A Believing Humanism, 1902–1965*, trans. Maurice Friedman (New York: Simon & Schuster, 1967), 95.

16. The Jewish Publication Society Tanakh translation: *The Jewish Study Bible* (New York: Oxford University Press, 1989/1999). The Hebrew term *re'ah* is usually translated as "neighbor." In his translation of the Hebrew Bible, Buber similarly rendered the term "companion" (*Genosse*). Cf. "Halte lieb deinen Genossen, dir gleich," *Er Riefe* [Lev.] 19:18, in *Die fünf Bücher der Weisung*, trans. Martin Buber with Franz Rosenzweig (Heidelberg: Verlag Lambert Schneider, 1981), 326. For an exegetical and hermeneutical analysis of the commandment, see Paul Mendes-Flohr, *Love, Accusative and Dative: Reflections on Leviticus 19:18* (Syracuse, NY: Syracuse University Press, 2007).

17. Hilary Putnam, "Levinas and Judaism," in *The Cambridge Companion to Levinas*, ed. Simon Critchley and Robert Bernasconi (Cambridge: Cambridge University Press, 2002), 57.

18. Emmanuel Levinas, *Totality and Infinity: An Essay on Exteriority*, trans. Alphonso Lingris (Pittsburgh: Duquesne University Press, 1969), 155 (emphasis added).

19. Gustav Landauer, "Martin Buber," *Neue Blätter des Festspielhaus Hellerau* 3, nos. 1–2 (1913): 90–107; Gustav Landauer, *Werkausgabe*, vol. 3, *Dichter, Ketzer, Außenseiter. Reden zu Literatur, Philosophie, Judentum*, ed. Hanna Delft (Berlin: Akademie Verlag, 1997), 165.

20. Laudauer, "Martin Buber," 4.

21. Buber, "Drama und Theater"; see n. 13 above.

22. Buber, *I and Thou*, Kaufmann translation, 63, 64, 62.

23. See Martin Buber, "Die Lehre von Tao," Nachwort, *Reden und Gleichnisse des Tschuang-Tse*, ed. Buber (Leipzig: Insel Verlag, 1910); "The Teaching of the Dao," in Buber, *Pointing the Way*, 31–36.

24. Martin Buber, "Education," in *Between Man and Man*, 114f.

25. Buber, "Education," 114f. As an act of embracing, without interpretation, the experience of another, Buber thus asks what, then, does one learn of the other when one relates to him or her in the sacred stance of an I-Thou relation? "Nothing at all" (*I and Thou*, Kaufmann translation, 61). It does, however, inform one's intersubjective and hence ethical sensibilities.

26. Buber, "Education," 115.

27. See Brague, "How to Be in the World."

28. Buber, *I and Thou*, Smith translation, 9.

29. Martin Buber, "Replies to My Critics," in *The Philosophy of Martin Buber*, Library of Living Philosophers, vol. 12, ed. Paul Arthur Schilpp and Maurice Friedman (LaSalle, IL: Open Court, 1967), 693.

Bibliographies of Buber's Writings and Articles on Him

Brody, Samuel H. "Martin Buber." Philosophy. *Oxford Bibliographies*.

This bibliography is organized by the same categories as the Mendes-Flohr volume below, but with greater attention to Buber's philosophy of dialogue and his political thought and aesthetics. Both Oxford bibliographies are periodically updated and accessible online.

These two appendices to the last volume of the German critical edition of Buber's publications, numbering more than a thousand pages, provide a comprehensive chronological and alphabetical register of the books, essays, and contributions included in the twenty-one volumes (in twenty-six books) of the *Martin Buber Werkausgabe*.

Buber, Raphael, and Margot Cohn. *Martin Buber: A Bibliography of His Writings*. Jerusalem: Magnes Press/Munich: K. G. Saur, 1980.

Prepared jointly by Buber's son Raphael and the director of the Martin Buber Archive, who also served as Buber's private *secretary* for the last eight years of his life, this bibliography lists more than 1,400 entries. A detailed index gives the reference to the entries by subject and language.

Chronologisches Gesamtregister der Werke, Aufsätze und Beträge Martin Bubers, Martin Buber Werkausgabe, vol. 21 (2019), 776–812; *Alphabetisches Gesamtregister de Werk, Aufsätze und Beiträge Martin Bubers, Martin Buber Werkausgabe*, vol. 21 (2019), 813–32.

Heuer, Renate, ed. *Lexikon deutsch-jüdischer Autoren. Archiv Bibliographia Judaica*. Munich: K. G. Saur, 1996. Volume 4: 251–303, edited by R. Heuer (1928–2014) and Rashmi Arora. Berlin: Walter de Gruyter, 2019.

This bibliographical essay contains not only the most comprehensive account of Buber's publications in German (until 2018) but also for each entry pertinent reviews, often summarized. It provides an extensive survey of secondary German literature, with concise summaries of the principal arguments.

Mendes-Flohr, Paul. "Martin Buber." Jewish Studies. *Oxford Bibliographies*.

This annotated bibliography is organized according to the following: introductory biography; general surveys of Buber's thought; biographies; Buber's collected works in German; Buber's philosophical writings in English; Buber's other writings in English; Buber's editorial work; secondary scholarship on Buber. This and the Brody bibliography above are both periodically updated and accessible online.

Moonan, Willard. *Martin Buber and His Critics: An Annotated Bibliography of Writings in English through 1978*. New York: Garland Publishing, 1981.

This volume is divided between English translations of Buber's writings (377 in total until 1975) and *secondary* literature in English (667 in number until 1978). It contains a comprehensive title and subject index.

Critical Evaluations

Friedman, Maurice, ed. "Interrogation of Martin Buber." In *Philosophical Interrogations*, edited by Sydney Rome and Beatrice Rome. New York: Holt, Rinehart & Winston.

An incisive exchange between some fifty scholars and Buber on his philosophy of dialogue, theory of knowledge, philosophy of education, social philosophy, philosophy of religion, the Bible and biblical Judaism, and his conception of evil.

Mendes-Flohr, Paul, ed. *Dialogue as a Trans-Disciplinary Concept: Buber's Philosophy of Dialogue and Its Contemporary Reception*. Berlin: Walter de Gruyter, 2015.

A collection of thirteen essays attesting to the seminal role that Buber's concept of dialogue has had on literary studies, philosophy, political theory, Jewish mysticism, Christianity, anthropology, psychotherapy, family therapy, memory studies, and the sociology of identity.

———, ed. *Martin Buber: A Contemporary Perspective*. Syracuse, NY: Syracuse University Press, 2002.

Proceedings of an international conference held at the Israel Academy of Sciences and Humanities, of which Buber was the first president.

Schilpp, Paul Arthur, and Maurice Friedman, eds. *The Philosophy of Martin Buber*. LaSalle, IL: Open Court, 1967.
   For this volume of the Library of Living Philosophers, the editors solicited thirty scholars to offer critical essays on virtually every aspect of Buber's thought and scholarship. In response to these probing analyses, see Buber's "Replies to My Critics."
Scott, Sarah, ed. *Martin Buber: Creaturely Life and Social Form*. Bloomington: Indiana University Press, 2021.
   A collection of nine essays that seek to decenter the overarching importance of Buber's I-Thou dialogue so as to focus on Buber as a thinker who nurtured relationships of mutual trust to promote spiritual, social, and political change. Buber thus emerges as a thinker characterized primarily by aesthetics and politics rather than by ontology or questions of religious faith.
Shonkoff, Sam B., ed. *Martin Buber: His Intellectual and Scholarly Legacy*. The Hague: Brill, 2018.
   A collection of sixteen essays organized according to dialogues with Christianity; dialogues with the political; dialogues with philosophy and philosophers; and dialogues with Jewish sources.
Zank, Michael, ed. *New Perspectives on Martin Buber*. Tübingen: Mohr Siebeck, 2006.
   Sixteen essays analyzing Buber's place in philosophy, biblical studies, the academic study of religion, and politics.

Collections of Buber's Writings and Correspondence

Biemann, Asher D., ed. and annotator. *The Martin Buber Reader: Essential Writings*. New York: Palgrave Macmillan, 2002.
   A judicious selection with detailed explanatory notes. The *Reader* is divided into seven sections: the Bible; Judaism and Jewish religiosity; Hasidism; dialogue; philosophy and education; community and individual; and Zionism.
Buber, Martin. *Briefwechsel aus sieben Jahrzehnten*. Edited by Grete Schaeder. 3 volumes. Heidelberg: Lambert Scheider, 1973.
———. *Buber Korrespondenzen digital*: https://www.adwmainz.de/projekte/buber-korrespondenzen-digital/beschreibung.html.
   Drawn from various archives, Buber's correspondence of more than 50,000 extant letters is in the process of being digitized with commentary by a team of scholars at the Universities of Frankfurt and Jena, Germany, headed by Dr. Heike Breitenbach.
———. *On Intersubjectivity and Cultural Creativity*. Edited and introduced by Samuel Noah Eisenstadt. Chicago: University of Chicago Press, 1992.
   Edited by Buber's first doctoral student as a professor of the philosophy of society (sociology) at the Hebrew University of Jerusalem, the volume focuses on Buber's writings as they bear on the relation between social interaction, or intersubjectivity, and the process of human creativity.
———. *Martin Buber Werkausgabe* (*MBW*). Im Auftrag der Berlin-Brandenburgischen Akademie der Wissenschaften (until 2009), der Israel Academy of Sciences and Humanities und der Heinrich-Heine-Universität Düsseldorf (since 2010). Edited by Paul Mendes-Flohr, Peter Schäfer, and (since 2010) Bernd Witte. 21 volumes. Gütersloh: Gütersloher Verlagshaus, 2001–19.

Buber Agassi, Judith. *Martin Buber on Psychology and Psychotherapy: Essays, Letters, and Dialogue.* Syracuse, NY: Syracuse University Press, 1999.

Glatzer, Nahum N., and Paul Mendes-Flohr, eds. *The Letters of Martin Buber: A Life of Dialogue.* New York: Schocken Books, 1991.

Lang, Bernhard, ed. *Ich und Du.* Ditzingen: Reclam, 2021.

This is a richly annotated edition of Buber's most seminal work. The editor also provides a detailed glossary, "Bubers Begriffswelt," and a "Literaturhinweis" of primarily German critical evaluations of Buber's writings. The volume concludes with a synoptic overview contextualizing *Ich und Du* in cultural and scholarly debates of the time as well as its critical reception.

Smith, Gilya G., ed. and trans. *The First Buber: Youthful Zionist Writings of Martin Buber.* Syracuse, NY: Syracuse University Press, 1999.

An anthology of forty essays and poems documenting Buber's early involvement in Zionism as an advocate of a "Jewish Renaissance" as an intellectually and spiritually engaging culture.

Biographies

Bourel, Dominique. *Martin Buber. Sentinelle de l'humanité.* Paris: Albin Michel, 2015. German translation by Horst Brühmann. Gütersloh: Gütersloher Verlagshaus, 2017.

Friedman, Maurice S. *Martin Buber: The Life of Dialogue* (1955). 4th ed., revised and expanded. London: Harper Torchbooks, 2002.

———. *Martin Buber's Life and Work: The Early Years, 1878–1923.* New York: E. P. Dutton, 1981. Paperback edition, Detroit: Wayne State University Press, 1988. *Martin Buber's Life and Work: The Middle Years, 1923–1945.* New York: E. P. Dutton, 1983. Paperback edition, Detroit: Wayne State University Press, 1988. *Martin Buber's Life and Work: The Later Years, 1945–1965.* New York: E. P. Dutton, 1984. Paperback edition, Detroit: Wayne State University Press, 1988.

Kohn, Hans. *Martin Buber. Sein Werk und seine Zeit. Ein Beitrag zur Geistesgeschichte Mitteleuropas 1880—1930.* Berlin, 1930; Nachwort: 1930–60, by Robert Weltsch. Cologne: J. Melzer, 1961.

Mendes-Flohr, Paul. *Martin Buber: A Life of Faith and Dissent.* New Haven, CT: Yale University Press, 2019.

Schaeder, Grete. *The Hebrew Humanism of Martin Buber.* Translated by Noah J. Jacobs. Detroit: Wayne State University Press, 1973.

Scott, Sarah. "Martin Buber." *Internet Encyclopedia of Philosophy* (2020). https://iep.utm.edu/martin-buber/.

Zank, Michael. "Martin Buber." *Stanford Encyclopedia of Philosophy* (updated by Zachary Braiterman, 2020).

Buber's Writings in English

A Believing Humanism: My Testament. Translated by M. Friedman. New York: Simon & Schuster, 1967.

Between Man and Man. Translated by Ronald Gregor-Smith, with an introduction by Maurice Friedman. London: Routledge, 2002.

Chinese Tales: Zhuangzi, Sayings and Parables and Chinese Ghost and Love Stories. Translated by Alex Page, with an introduction by Irene Eber. Atlantic Highlands, NJ: Humanities Press International, 1991.

Daniel: Dialogues on Realization. New York: Holt, Rinehart & Winston, 1964; Syracuse, NY: Syracuse University Press, 2019.

Eclipse of God. New York: Harper & Brothers, 1952; 2nd edition, Westport, CT: Greenwood Press, 1977.

Ecstatic Confessions. Edited by Paul Mendes-Flohr, translated by Esther Cameron. San Francisco: Harper & Row, 1985.

Encounter: Autobiographical Fragments. LaSalle, IL: Open Court, 1970.

The First Buber: Youthful Zionist Writings of Martin Buber. Edited and translated by Gilya G. Schmidt. Syracuse, NY: Syracuse University Press, 1999.

Gog and Magog: A Novel. Translated by Ludwig Lewisohn. Syracuse, NY: Syracuse University Press, 1999.

I and Thou. Translated by Ronald Gregor Smith. Edinburgh: T. & T. Clark, 1937; 2nd edition, New York: Charles Scribner's Sons, 1958; Scribner Classics edition, New York: Scribner, 2000; Centenary edition with introduction by Paul Mendes-Flohr, New York: Simon & Schuster, 2023; Jubilee edition, New York: Free Press, 2023.

I and Thou. New translation with a prologue, "I and You," and notes by Walter Kaufmann. New York: Charles Scribner's Sons, 1970; Jubilee edition, introduced and annotated by P. Mendes-Flohr, New York: Free Press, 2023.

The Knowledge of Man. Translated by Ronald Gregor Smith and Maurice Friedman. New York: Harper & Row, 1965; 2nd edition, New York, 1966; Amherst, MA: Prometheus, 1998.

A Land of Two Peoples: Martin Buber on Jews and Arabs. Edited with commentary by Paul R. Mendes-Flohr. New York: Oxford University Press, 1983; 2nd edition, Gloucester, MA: Peter Smith, 1994, Chicago: University of Chicago Press, 2008; 2025, with two new forewords by P. Mendes-Flohr and Raef Zreik.

The Legend of the Baal-Shem. Translated by Maurice Friedman. London: Routledge, 2002.

Mamre: Essays in Religion. Translated by Greta Hort. Westport, CT: Greenwood Press, 1970.

Martin Buber and the Theater, including Martin Buber's "Mystery Play" Elijah. Edited and translated with three introductory essays by Maurice Friedman. New York: Funk & Wagnalls, 1970.

Martin Buber on Psychology and Psychotherapy: Essays, Letters, and Dialogue. Edited by Judith Buber Agassi. Syracuse, NY: Syracuse University Press, 1999.

The Martin Buber Reader: Essential Writings. Edited by Asher D. Biemann. New York: Palgrave Macmillan, 2002.

Meetings. Edited with an introduction and bibliography by Maurice Friedman. LaSalle, IL: Open Court, 1973; 3rd edition, London: Routledge, 2002.

On Intersubjectivity and Cultural Creativity. Edited and with an introduction by S. N. Eisenstadt. Chicago: University of Chicago Press, 1992.

On Judaism. Edited by Nahum Glatzer and translated by Eva Jospe and others. New York: Schocken Books, 1967.

On the Bible: Eighteen Studies. Edited by Nahum Glatzer. New York: Schocken Books, 1968.

On Zion: The History of an Idea. Translated by Stanley Godman, with a new foreword by Nahum N. Glatzer. New York: Schocken Books, 1973.

The Origin and Meaning of Hasidism. Translated by M. Friedman. New York: Horizon Press, 1960.
Paths in Utopia. Translated by R. F. Hull. Syracuse, NY: Syracuse University Press, 1996.
Pointing the Way. Translated by Maurice Friedman. New York: Harper, 1957; 2nd edition, New York: Schocken Books, 1974.
Scripture and Translation. By Martin Buber and Franz Rosenzweig. Translated by Lawrence Rosenwald with Everett Fox. Bloomington: Indiana University Press, 1994.
Tales of the Hasidim. Foreword by Chaim Potok. New York: Schocken Books, 1991.
Ten Rungs: Collected Hasidic Sayings. Translated by Olga Marx. London: Routledge, 2002.
Two Types of Faith. Translated by Norman P. Goldhawk, with an afterword by David Flusser. Syracuse, NY: Syracuse University Press, 2003.
The Way of Man: According to the Teaching of Hasidim. London: Routledge, 2002.
The Way of Response: Martin Buber: Selections from His Writings. Edited by N. N. Glatzer. New York: Schocken Books, 1966.

PART ONE

Philosophy of Dialogue

Introduction

PAUL MENDES-FLOHR

Abjuring the traditional method of philosophical discourse—*apodeixis*—of logical reasoning and demonstration, Buber regarded his task to be that of *deixis*—pointing and eliciting recognition—the acknowledgment of the trials and tribulations of interpersonal relations that constitute everyday life. Christoph Schmidt characterizes Buber's radical break with traditional "monological" forms of philosophical discourse in favor of dialogical conversation and encounter with the infinite otherness of our fellow human beings and God as "the emergence from self-imposed [philosophical] immaturity."

Buber understood his "liberation" from monological philosophical reasoning, as Asher Biemann details, as addressing a question that Kant posed but did not manage to address: What is man? (*Was ist der Mensch?*). When once asked about his profession, Buber accordingly replied, "Philosophical anthropology."

On yet another occasion, Buber was prodded to define his philosophical teaching, which he was reluctant to label because he feared it would foreclose the ongoing conversation he sought to promote. He yielded and said what he probed in his ramified writings on dialogue was "die Ontologie des Zwischenmenschlichen"—the ontology of the between (*das Zwischen*) human beings when they meet in a reciprocal I-Thou relationship. Michael Fishbane explores the existential and theological inflections of Buber's conception of the intersubjective "between."

Buber was also loathe to speak of himself as a theologian, for he claimed that he had no access to God's logos and infinite otherness. The infinite God—the Eternal Thou—is imageless but nevertheless not beyond our imagination. Elliot Wolfson probes how Buber contended with the aporia of the imageless God and one's necessarily anthropomorphic imagination of the divine.

The aporia is inherent in Buber's concept of dialogue as a meeting with our fellow human beings and God in their existential presence (*Gegenwart*) in a given moment (the temporal presence) unmediated by concepts by which we generally perceive others (concepts drawn, as they are, from the past). Suspending these concepts, one acknowledges the infinite otherness of the other (the Thou). Dialogue may thus be regarded as metaethical, responding to the presence of the other without the guidance of normative concepts and principles. Here too we are enjoined, as Sarah Scott explains, to exercise our imagination—a moral imagination of the lived reality of the other. Dialogical ethics honors the unique reality of the other, not as an act of empathetic feeling but, indeed, as a "decision" to imagine how the other perceives and experiences life in a shared relational context. Buber's ethics of perception, Scott duly notes, also bears on his political ethos.

1

Exodus from Monological Modernity

CHRISTOPH SCHMIDT

Enlightenment is man's emergence from his self-imposed immaturity.
IMMANUEL KANT

The dialogical encounter "has no alphabet, each of its sounds is a new creation and [it] would have to be grasped as such." Dialogue is a living event in the present, which cannot be subsumed under any system of rules, a fixed grammar, or a theory of communication. Since it is inscribed in a horizon of utter openness, dialogue unfolds as an "infinite conversation," which points to its divine dimension, namely to God as the "eternal Thou." God, like the human other, steps out of his traditional theological objectifications—constituting a doctrinally determined I-It relation or subject-object logic—and addresses man in the here and now as a Thou. In response one is beckoned to address God as a Thou. "The word of him, who wishes to speak with men without speaking with God is not fulfilled: but the word of him who wishes to speak with God without speaking with men goes astray."[1]

With these two dimensions of dialogical communication—the human and the divine—Buber adopts an asystematic, anarchist manner of thinking necessarily bereft of an alphabet. Whereas Buber can only point to the phenomenon of the dialogue, in promoting it he understood it as a response to the crisis of modern European and Jewish-Christian culture. Buber describes this crisis as "the eclipse of God," namely as the historical epoch of absence of the Thou in human existence, community, politics, and theology. Buber aims then at a revolutionary turn of a single individual's relation to self and the other as the condition of possibility for an exit from the self-inflicted monological immaturity of modernity, which indeed wishes both to follow the path of humanistic emancipation and to secure its utopia. In this sense Buber's dialogical thinking combines the eschatological tradition of Gotthold Ephraim Lessing, Friedrich Hölderlin, and Gustav Landauer, aiming at the creation of the kingdom of God as the true realm of human freedom "here and now," with the forerunners of dialogical thinking, Ludwig Feuerbach and Søren Kierkegaard, as the basis of his radical post-traditional theology.[2]

From this perspective Nietzsche's "God is dead" appears as a central symptom of the crisis and eclipse of dialogical life[3] closing itself as autonomous self in its various formations in modern secular culture. But inasmuch as this death represents the collapse of the god in metaphysical and orthodox theology, which either fixes him as objective ground of being in an I-It (*Ich-Es*) relation or in a legal system, this eclipse opens in fact the horizon for the revelation of the "totally other" God as Thou. Beyond and behind the metaphysical and orthodox idolatries, that is, their constructions and projections in a talk "about God," this God reveals his being only in direct address as the ultimate Thou. The diagnosis of the eclipse of God does not aim then at a restoration of premodern forms of theology (in metaphysics or doctrinal orthodoxy) but at the true origin of dialogical existence in a post-traditional theology, which Buber—among others—recognizes in the very primordial foundations of biblical theology.

Buber's universal principle of dialogue thus finds its Jewish correspondence and parallel in the original biblical revelation of the covenant as the ultimate ethical phenomenon which radically transcends rabbinic legal theology. Both the intersubjective and the human-divine relation reveal themselves in their immediacy in the everyday encounter that precedes legal codification, so that the primordial revelation of God in the covenant, with its immediate address to man, represents the "spirit" prior to and transcending the proclamation of divine law. In conceiving of the foundational dialogical event of the divine covenant as constituted by the two commandments of love (of God and the other), Buber is in accord with the Pentateuch, the prophets, the Jewish Jesus, and eighteenth-century Hasidism. Expressly rejecting the classical Christian view that the law is fulfilled and thus abrogated with Jesus the Christ, Buber understands the divine covenant as an ongoing task of creating dialogical relations for a just and equitable community. This conception of the divine commandments to love allowed Buber to align eschatological politics, from Lessing[4] and Hölderlin[5] to Landauer,[6] with what he calls "biblical theopolitics," as represented by Gideon, Samuel, and the prophets.[7] So conceived, theopolitics is presented as the radical critique of all monological politics, driven as they are by the I-It perceptions of the world order, be they of the European species of political theology or of Zionist politics.

In defining the two fundamental word pairs of "I-Thou" and "I-It" as denoting the two fundamental attitudes whereby one relates to others and the world, Buber wishes to point to the fact that, in the I-Thou dialogue, one abides in the metaspace of the "*between*," which cannot be defined or measured. This original mode of the relation in the *between*, which comprises the three dimensions of the relation to nature, the human other, and God, consists of the direct encounter, which resists the conceptual mediation of the It-World (*Es-Welt*). "The Thou meets me. But I step into direct relation with it. [...] I become through my relation to the Thou: as I become I, I say thou."[8]

The self perforce continuously alternates between I-Thou and I-It attitudes. Ideally the self can find a balance between the two attitudes, which Buber describes with Goethe's distinction between the "diastole and systole" in breathing. This alternation of the two attitudes is grounded already in the temporality of the self, since the present event of the encounter must move into the past, so that address and response become reshaped in the perspective of memory and reflection. The event of the I-Thou has to turn unavoidably into an I-It relation, which Buber interprets as the fundamental "sublime melancholy of our fate."[9]

With this necessary regress into the I-It attitude, the danger arises of the solidification and stabilization of this attitude, which can lead to the self's renouncing its original freedom and dialogical openness toward others and their vulnerability. The initial consciousness of the original relatedness of the self nevertheless remains receptive for the original "spirit" of the self, and thus the self can liberate itself always from this regress and "respond to his Thou."[10]

But the self finds itself not only threatened by its vulnerability to temporality and the proximity of the other, when it retreats into itself, to protect itself by embracing a defensive I-It attitude. Buber speaks of the effect of this enclosure of the self in the protective shield of the It-World (*Es-Welt*) as the self's alienation from its true self. One's paradoxical dependence on nature (the It-World) and vulnerability to its fateful decrees, *Ananke*, necessitate self-preservation through work, and its social and economic organization leads to other forms of distance from one's true self.

The self thus seeks "refuge" in ideal social constructions or superstructures, such as a "ground of being" or the idea of "humankind,"[11] to fend off the inevitable decrees of Ananke through conceiving a rational "order of things," but by so doing reduces the I and the other to mere functional attributes of the "fixed" It-World. From this perspective, religion, metaphysics, theology, and science, by constructing the order of things on the ground of a primal absolute principle (God, Being, Subject, Substance, etc.), do not only explain this order but fix it in an eternal logic of the I-It, which extends its domination on existence, culture, society, and politics. When the self has thus reified itself and the other in the realm of It, it finds its absolute correlation in the objectification of God as the ground of the It-World, which provides a postulated ontological legitimation of the existent social and political order. The

It-World of self and the other is thus removed from the flow and flux of life, and from a fortiori dialogue as an ever recurring *event* of an I-Thou relation of the self and the other, and of self and God.

If existence, culture, society, and politics presuppose a vital form of dialogical equilibrium as their adequate form of government, a culture, which is no longer centered "in a living, continually renewed relational event," courts the danger of "freezing" in the It-World. The It-World can, however, only be interrupted occasionally "by the glowing deeds of solitary spirits," which "only spasmodically break through." In "times of illness" the It-World is no longer "penetrated and fructified by the inflowing world of the Thou as by living streams" but in fact "overpowered" by the sphere of the I-It.[12] In this case, the equilibrium between the two spheres—that of the I-Thou and the I-It—is destroyed and so are adequate forms of government and, if they are grounded in a theological orientation, its original relation to God.

The dialogical life of freedom presupposes the relation between free and equal persons, who can debate their social inclinations and interests in a democratic and solidaric mode of communication and mutuality, undistorted by power relations. The I-It relation generates in the best case an anonymous order of functioning persons, which can easily be turned into an authoritarian system under the rule of a sovereign power, instrumentalizing this functioning order. When the dialogical form of the open society finds its ideal correlation in a dialogical relation with the Absolute Thou—the God of dialogue—the anonymous and authoritarian order derives its legitimacy from a religious, metaphysical, or scientific system. This system fixes the ontological order in an objective I-It relation and an absolute ground or principle of the It as God, substance, or subject.

Under the ever-present and pressing threat of the It-World, and the attendant impulse for self-preservation, society and politics appear as necessary formations that yield to destiny, an unavoidable fate, or as a dialectical necessity. But Ananke's decree, Buber contends, should not be mistakenly deemed an ineluctable "doom" (*Verhängnis*), for it can be challenged by the courageous intervention of conscious social groups and especially by single persons who dare to question and resist the regnant social and political order.

Buber stresses the importance of the individual, who in the state of progressive alienation acts to bond with others and to create a genuine community and fraternal forms of government. It is the individual's resolute resistance to the dictates of the It-World that enables a "return" to an original calling, to take responsibility for one's own life, with one's fellow human beings, to initiate a new beginning. Buber occasionally describes this process using Hölderlin's theopoetical vision of "Salvation," which grows in response to "expanding danger."

In extreme "emergency situations," the single individual may have to lead a "hidden subterranean and, as it were, cancelled existence" in the underground.[13] But even under totalitarian rule and its pressures, one might find the courage to question publicly the seemingly eternal order with its mechanisms of oppression and its absolute legitimation of power (through religion, metaphysics, or ideology) and to break through its monological structures of power.

The exit from self-inflicted monological immaturity thus always presupposes an act of responsible freedom by every individual, who will step out of that anonymous, hidden form of existence, to instantiate a new dialogical and therapeutic act. This single individual might initially be totally alone in responding to the call of the divine spirit—as had the prophets of Israel, who were fully cognizant that they might likely find themselves and their words rejected by the ruling political and social order. At the same time, they were aware that there could be no external change of social and economic conditions unless this change originated in every single individual.

To be sure, as Buber noted, not every I-It relation is immediately translatable into an I-Thou relation. Nevertheless, he held that all I-It relations are basically pathological and should be regarded as "a vibrant self-contradiction" in which each individual betrays an "inborn Thou," the primal a priori dialogical disposition. "If a man does not represent the *a priori* of relation in his living with the world, if he does not work out and realize the inborn-Thou on what meets it, then it strikes inwards. It develops on the unnatural, impossible object of the I, that is, it develops where there is no place at all for it to develop. Thus, confrontation of what is over against him takes place within himself, and this cannot be relation, or presence, or streaming interaction, but only self-contradiction."[14]

The struggle to overcome this contradiction in one's inner being and emerge from self-encapsulation raises what Buber calls the problem of the existential singularity of the one—the Single-One—who is true to one's own primal dialogical self. At the same time, the struggle also reveals the radical otherness of the other precisely through the opposition to the other.

The Single-One is thus in a seemingly paradoxical situation: One understands oneself primarily from the encounter with the other, while at the same time as a Single-One one is supposed to be the beginning of the radical return to the dialogical origin and to initiate an exit from the systems of power and domination, the revolution of the circumstances against all resistances and power structures. In "The Question to the Single-One," Buber discusses the problem in light of the genesis of radical existentialist protest against the Hegelian system as the ultimate system of subject-object. Both Max Stirner[15] and Søren Kierkegaard[16] turned against the Hegelian system of the object's absolute identity with the subject and toward an individual existence liberated from the metaphysical essence and idea and their material manifestations in state and society. Their exit from the system epitomized the alternatives of the liberation of the Single-One: between a dialogical return and a chimera of existential solitude:

STIRNER: "The man who belongs to himself alone is by origin free, for he acknowledges nothing but himself. [. . .] True is what is Mine."[17]
KIERKEGAARD: "And indeed a man can have dealings with God only as a single One, as man, who has become a Single One."[18]

Whereas Stirner represents the exit of the self into absolute encapsulation, isolated from the collective and all religious and ethical principles, Kierkegaard restored the dialogical relation with God and thus severed the monological claims of (Hegelian) metaphysics. But Buber contends that Kierkegaard renewed this dialogue with God by isolating it in fact from the everyday ethical dimension. "But thereby the category of the Single-One, which has scarcely been properly discovered[,] is already fatefully misunderstood."[19]

From Kierkegaard's early statements regarding his severance of his engagement with Regina Olsen, Buber concludes that the existentialist theologian in effect was beholden to the Protestant Lutheran acosmic relation to God. According to this theological disposition, "God wants Thou to be truly said only to him, and to all others only an unessential and fundamentally invalid word—that God demands of us to choose between him and his creation."[20] With this reproach Buber brings Kierkegaard's supposedly exclusive relation to God beyond the ethical closure of Stirner's Single-One with his general denial of the ethical sphere.

By limiting his reading to Kierkegaard's *Fear and Trembling*, Buber misconstrued the Danish philosopher's ultimate position.[21] For Kierkegaard perfectly understood the responsibility of the Single-One for the public weal and the danger one faced when addressing the truth to the *parrhesia*.[22] Like the prophets of Israel, one attested to the truth with one's life. Although Buber himself opposes the Greek (and Heideggerian) concept of truth as *aletheia* to the Hebrew concept of *emet* as "testimony,"[23] he failed to appreciate the full meaning of Kierkegaard's idea of the singular existence as testimony. Contending with the fact that most of his contemporaries had become totally estranged from religious life, Kierkegaard's Single-One had to lead a life of loneliness and thus, through personal sacrifice, attest to religious truth.

Like Buber, Kierkegaard understood the biblical commandments to "love God with all your might" and "to love the neighbor as you love yourself" as imperatives for a theopolitics that opens a dialogical horizon for mobilizing philosophy and religious faith to oppose all monological metaphysics and politics. In opposing monological politics—ideological formations of religion and state—Buber enjoined the Jewish Jesus as a paradigmatic theopolitical teacher. He presented Jesus, whom Buber embraced as his "great brother," as a prophet who was dialogically attentive and responsive to "the significance of a situation as it is lived, and nothing but lived, continually, ever anew, without foresight, without forethought, without prescription."[24]

In the *Kingdom of God*, Buber explicates dialogical, metanomian politics with the neologism *Geistern*, which denotes the spirit (*Geist*) as the continuous event of revelation qua presence/absence of God's emergence from the monological constructions which humanity imposes on divinity. It is the monological conception of God whose death Nietzsche's madman bemoaned. The declaration of the death of God is an ironic eulogy for the passing of the substantive God of metaphysics and traditional orthodoxy, delimiting God as "Being," "Ground," or "Substance" in their conceptual or legal systems. God, for Buber, is not, however, an object of predication and deduction, but the Thou of the direct address, revealing himself as a *Geistern* beyond all fixed representations as a metaphysical reification or "idol." Understanding divine revelation as a historically and existentially recurring event, Buber provides the foundation for a post-traditional theology, which, focusing on the dialogical event in the *between* as its ethical center, has jettisoned all religious certainties, so typical of classical orthodox traditions and metaphysical theology. "The word of God crosses my vision like a falling star to whose fire the meteorite will bear witness without making it light up for me, and I myself can only bear witness to the light but not produce the stone and say, 'This is it.'"[25]

This post-traditional theology, beyond all fixed legal systems or final linguistic codes, prompts us to renew our modes and conceptions of understanding as a concrete hermeneutics in every new situation. In its openness and constitutive "weakness," it participates in the event of revelation as a dialogical creation and renewal of man and society through their liberation from closed and codified experience and captivity of selfhood, ergo redemption.

Thus, the age of darkness following the death of God is possibly always already the age of a radical renewal of faith, not a sign of its attenuation. As such, this age of renewal adopts a new relation to the word of tradition, which is clarified by the dialogical experience. "The situation of the word itself, in the most serious sense, more precisely, the relation between God and man, has changed. And this change is certainly not comprehended in its essence by our thinking only of the darkening, so familiar to us, of the supreme light, only of the night of our being, empty of revelation. It is the night of an expectation—not of a vague hope, but of an expectation. We expect a theophany of which we know nothing but the place, and the place is called community."[26]

Buber consistently underlined the inner connection between this universal post-traditional theology beyond all national, philosophical, and religious languages and the primordial and original experience of Israel's encounter with God in the desert. He would thereby dislodge traditional Judaism from its moorings in orthodox rabbinical dogmatics, legal exegesis, and nationalist interpretations. Jewish prophecy from Moses to Jesus and up to Hasidism of the eighteenth century, he held, exemplified primordial dialogical spirituality as paradigmatic for the modern existential and political experience as articulated in the eschatological politics of Lessing, Hölderlin, and Landauer, and the Protestant religious socialists Leonard Ragaz and Paul Tillich.

But rather than an adoption of Protestant Christianity in the wake of St. Paul's critique of the law, of which he was often accused, Buber aimed at a revolution of Judaism from within its original dialogical spirit, which, of course, could not be normatively codified. Rabbinic law was a rather later and secondary effort to translate the primordial ethical message of the dialogical event into ethical deeds. If the primordial event could be formulated in terms of law at all, it would have to be defined in the two metaprinciples of love (to the other and to God) as the two central dimensions of the dialogical event. Buber seems to acknowledge only these principles as the trajectory of Jewish tradition from the Torah to the prophets, from Jesus's life and teaching to the eighteenth-century Hasidic way of life. "The relation with man is the real simile of the relation with God; in it true address receives true response: except that in God's response everything, the universe, is made manifest as language."[27]

Thus, the dialogical response to the other and thus also to God as the Eternal Thou not only emancipates man and society from their captivity and self-encapsulation but also liberates them from all fixed vocabularies; it opens them for themselves and others through an "unalphabetic" experience. Dialogical encounters redeem man from all the forms of self-encapsulation in fixed conceptual constructs, be they existential, social, or political conventions and customs, or purely ideational. As viewed from the Hebrew Bible, the dialogical event unfolds as creation, revelation, and redemption of human relations, which Buber interprets with reference to the Mosaic account of the Exodus from political oppression in Egypt and the revelation of God's unique name as the name of all names, which Buber translates as "I am there as who I am there." Rendered in the present tense, the divine name is in accord with Buber's metanomian conception of God's eternal presence.

Buber further relates his phenomenology of the dialogue to the concept of place or space—in Hebrew, *makom*—pointing to the concrete situation of the *between*, "here and now." He thus in effect evoked yet another name of the biblical God without explicitly noting it, namely *makom*. The abstract presence/absence of God as the revelation of the source of language can thus actualize itself only in the concrete situation of the *between*, the metaspace in the here and now, where the two dimensions of dialogical relation coincide and complement each other.

When Buber translates the post-traditional religion of dialogue into the spirit of the biblical revelation, instantiating the covenant of Israel with God, he finds the explicit expression of this primordial revelation in the early Israelite theopolitics as exemplified by the judge Gideon and the prophet Samuel. He cites the famous passage in which Gideon resists the demand of the people to be appointed king, as both a kind of ethical and primal constitution of all dialogical theopolitics:

> His No, born out of the situation, is meant for all historical times as an unconditional No, since it leads to an unconditional Yes, i.e., to a declaration of the eternal kingdom. I, Gideon, shall not rule over you. This includes: no man shall rule over you, because it follows: JHWH God himself and Him alone will rule over you.[28]

Gideon acts as the responsible Single-One, who vouches for the dialogical community in the name of God. He then becomes the charismatic leader who answers the call of God and takes up the task of leading the community in the moment of danger—and only for this time. Buber adopts Max Weber's concept of anarchic rule, charisma, and stresses its religious origin from the term *charis*, a gift. This appointment and gift of God for the community is given only for this specific situation to secure the anarchist community, and it is to be returned the moment danger passes. So, Gideon's leadership as temporal appointment differs clearly from the political concept of a ruler, which Weber identifies as the legitimacy of monarchy. Buber, however, is critical of Gideon's and Samuel's theopolitics, and unlike them refused to countenance David's and Salomon's kingship even on a temporary basis. In fact, Buber's anarchist dialogical theopolitics, although applying the idea of a (temporal) leader, is meant as a critique of all political theology of sovereign power in monarchy or dictatorship.

Buber's theopolitics is the direct expression of dialogical action in the spirit of the name of God as *Geist,* or rather *Geistern.* Charisma is constituted by *charis* and by nothing else: charisma can never be institutionalized; it forever resists earthly appropriation, just as spirit is only a *Geistern,* offering no security of power, only the flux of the dialogical imperative to meet the other as Thou. As addressed to political life, charisma depends on the *charis* of the God who revealed himself to Moses as "I am there as who I am there"—if we are attentive to his eternal, dialogical presence.

In this passage we discern the climax and focus of Buber's dialogical politics, initiated by the Single-One, transferring the idea of the spirit into the heart of the Mosaic revelation with God's name of names. This dramatic scene is and remains the ultimate possibility in all historical time, as it is so often betrayed by the self-empowering self, who aims at a transfer of the temporal appointment into a permanent rule of power, relying on a religious cult and the priests as servants of power—or, in modern times, the cult of the ruler himself. The biblical conflict between anarchistic theopolitics and monarchic political theology thus serves as a paradigm for similar conflictual situations in the course of history and especially in the central political decisions of Buber's own time. When he adopts the modern eschatological project of Lessing, Hölderlin, and Landauer in his *Paths in Utopia,*[29] he understands this modern tradition as a continuation and realization of the biblical theopolitics of Gideon. Similarly, he joins the religious socialism of the Protestant theologians Leonard Ragaz and Paul Tillich in opposing Friedrich Gogarten's and Carl Schmitt's authoritarian nationalist political theology in the very moment of ultimate danger for German Jewry in 1933. No doubt Buber's biblical theopolitics was meant as well as a radical critique of David Ben Gurion's political theology of Zionism, based on the sovereign kingdom of the Bible. Buber's vision of the binational Jewish-Arab state was intended to challenge the Zionist idea of an exclusive Jewish state.[30]

*

Buber's unalphabetic thinking is always aimed at the situation and concrete practice. Unlike the various efforts to reconstruct his thinking in a systematic philosophy,[31] Buber understood dialogue as an ongoing, open practice, whether vis-à-vis other philosophers or theologians or vis-à-vis a concrete political situation. This becomes obvious in his later writings such as *Eclipse of God*[32] and "What Is Man?"[33]—which present dialogical encounters with contemporary thinkers like Martin Heidegger, Jean-Paul Sartre, Karl Jaspers, Carl Gustav Jung, and others, but especially in his engagement for political justice both in the German context and then in that of the Zionist state. One can define Buber's ultimate objective in these dialogical essays as the fundamental reform of the modern project of enlightenment and its specific eschatology of the realm of freedom as the realization of the kingdom of God here and now—which is always based on the modern canon of the three realms of Judaism, Christianity, and modernity.[34] Against its monological contraction and violent distortions in totalitarian forms, Buber's theopolitics seeks to realize a sustained dialogical relation between freedom and justice, the Single-One and society, meant as a dialogical relation between secular utopia and the religious hope for the messianic age.

When Buber adopts the idea of modern political eschatology in the tradition of Friedrich Hölderlin and Ludwig Feuerbach in a dialogical key, he seeks to avoid the classical effects of this eschatology in a modern supersession as well as the effects of a modern orthodoxy and gnosticism as the sources of modern monological violence. On the one hand, modern eschatology, in its Hegelian and especially post-Hegelian configuration (Marx, Engels, Bakunin), interprets the modern utopia with its specific canon, based on Judaism-Christianity-modernity as a full eschatological sublation (*Aufhebung*) of both Judaism and Christianity to be realized in the construction of the realm of freedom in a secular society or state and thus abolishes religion on the whole. On the other hand, modern orthodox and gnostic tendencies detach themselves from the other canonic elements as a reaction against this sublation (*Aufhebung*). Judaism wishes to save itself from both the Christian and the modern eschatological sublation by either an orthodox resistance or an exclusive national retreat from general history, while Protestant Christianity, culminating in Adolph von Harnack's liberal theology,[35] tends to create a pure ethical realm of modernity against its historical sources in Judaism, thus paving the way for a radical anti-Judaism. Secular modernity itself, by radicalizing its tendency toward a radical eschatological suspension, is itself in permanent danger of utterly eradicating religion writ large.[36]

Buber's dialogical politics aims then at a radical *tikkun* of the enlightened vision of the original realm of freedom. He wants to reconcile the modern secular utopia and the religious messianic hope, on the one hand, and the three monotheistic religions based on freedom by a new form of dialogical theopolitics, on the other hand. Buber adopted the modern canonic constitution created by enlightenment without its effects of exclusive eschatology, orthodoxy, or gnosis, sublation, or detachment—in an open, ongoing dialogical relation and communication. His post-traditional theology culminates then in a "post-canonic" eschatology, which remains open to an interreligious dialogue as the condition for the creation of political justice.[37]

Notes

1. Martin Buber, *Between Man and Man* (New York: Macmillan, 1967), 16, 15.

2. See Martin Buber, "Zur Geschichte des dialogischen Prinzips," in Buber, *Das dialogische Prinzip* (Heidelberg: Lambert Schneider, 1984), 299–320.

3. Cf. Martin Buber, *Eclipse of God: Studies in the Relation between Religion and Philosophy* (Atlantic Heights, NJ: Humanities Press, 1988).

4. Gotthold Ephraim Lessing, *The Education of the Human Race* (London: Oxford University Press, 2022).

5. Friedrich Hölderlin, *Hyperion, or The Hermit in Greece*, trans. Howard Gaskill (Cambridge: Open Book, 2019). Hölderlin exercised a direct influence on Buber, especially his *Celebration of Peace*: "Man has learned much since morning / For we are a conversation, and we can listen to one another. Soon we'll be song."

6. Gustav Landauer, *Revolution and Other Writings: A Political Reader*, ed. and trans. G. Kuhn (Oakland, CA: PM Press, 2010).

7. Martin Buber, *Königtum Gottes* (Berlin: Schocken Verlag, 1932).

8. Martin Buber, *I and Thou*, centennial ed., trans. Ronald Gregor Smith (New York: Scribner Classics, 2023), 9.

9. Buber, *I and Thou*, 16.

10. Buber, *I and Thou*, 39.

11. Buber, *I and Thou*, 13.

12. Buber, *I and Thou*, 54, 53.

13. Buber, *I and Thou*, 65.

14. Buber, *I and Thou*, 69–70.

15. Max Stirner, *The Ego and Its Own*, trans. Steven T. Byington (New York: Benj. R. Tucker, 1907).

16. Søren Kierkegaard, *Fear and Trembling*, trans. Walter Lowrie (Princeton, NJ: Princeton University Press, 1954); Søren Kierkegaard, *Philosophical Fragments and Concluding Unscientific Postscript*, in *Writings of Søren Kierkegaard* (Princeton, NJ: Princeton University Press), 12:1, 2; Kierkegaard, *Practice in Christianity*, in *Writings*, vol. 20.

17. Buber, *Between Man and Man*, 41.

18. Buber, *Between Man and Man*, 43.

19. Buber, *Between Man and Man*, 51.

20. Buber, *Between Man and Man*, 54.

21. *Fear and Trembling* was originally published in 1843 under the pseudonym of Johannes di Silentio. Pseudonyms were used often in the early nineteenth century as a means of representing and criticizing viewpoints other than the author's own. Kierkegaard's pseudonyms serve as "therapeutic" preparation of the reader for a return to authentic Christian belief. In *The Point of View of My Work as an Author* (Oxford: Oxford University Press, 1950), he explained this strategy of ironic masks as an effort to liberate the Danish public from the prevailing conception of Christianity as merely a pleasing aesthetic mode of worship. In this sense all earlier texts of Kierkegaard published under pseudonyms, from Victor Eremita and Johannes di Silentio to Johannes Climacus and Anticlimacus, should be read as a dialogical strategy born of the felt need to address the fundamental problem of how to convey religious truths. Like the biblical prophets, Kierkegaard retreated into a tactical loneliness to ponder a new form of dialogical speech to quicken among

his forlorn brethren a reaffirmation of genuine Christian faith. In *Practice of Christianity* (Princeton, NJ: Princeton University Press, 1991), Anticlimacus introduces Kierkegaard as the author of the central sermon, as in the *Works of Love* (Princeton, NJ: Princeton University Press, 1949) written by Kierkegaard under his own name.

22. For a systematic explanation of the meaning, origin, and development of the concept of *parrhesia* in politics, philosophy, and therapy, see Michel Foucault, *Fearless Speech* (Los Angeles: Semiotext(e), 2001). Buber's concept of dialogue can be reconstructed as a unique form of *parrhesia* in politics, philosophy, and therapy.

23. Martin Buber, "Das Wort, das gesprochen wird," in Buber, *Logos—Zwei Reden* (Heidelberg: Lambert Schneider, 1962), 27–29.

24. Buber, *I and Thou*, 95.

25. Buber, *Between Man and Man*, 7.

26. Buber, *Between Man and Man*, 7.

27. Buber, *I and Thou*, 103.

28. Buber, *Königtum Gottes*, 3.

29. Martin Buber, *Paths in Utopia* (Boston: Beacon Press, 1958).

30. See Martin Buber, "Ein tragischer Konflikt?," in Buber, *Ein Land und zwei Völker. Zur jüdisch-arabischen Frage*, ed. Paul Mendes-Flohr (Frankfurt am Main: Jüdischer Verlag, 1983).

31. The first effort was created by Buber's close friend Franz Rosenzweig with his 1921 *The Star of Redemption*, trans. Barbara E. Galli (Madison: University of Wisconsin Press, 2005). Still the best systematization has been formulated by M. Thuenissen, *Der Andere. Studien zur Sozialontologie der Gegenwart* (Berlin: De Gruyter, 1965), 243–373, dealing with Martin Buber's *I and Thou*. See also Jürgen Habermas, *Theory of Communicative Action*, trans. Thomas McCarthy (Boston: Beacon Press, 1985).

32. Buber, *Eclipse of God*.

33. Martin Buber, "What Is Man?," in *Between Man and Man*.

34. Karl Löwith, *Meaning in History: The Theological Implications of the Philosophy of History* (Chicago: University of Chicago Press, 1949); Eric Voegelin, *New Science of Politics* (Chicago, 1952); Henri de Lubac, *La Postérité spirituelle de Joachim de Flore* (Paris: Lethielleux, 1984). All authors deal with the impact of the Trinitarian dogma on the mystical historiography of Joachim de Fiori and its influence on the modern philosophy of history from Lessing to Hegel and beyond.

35. Adolf von Harnack, *Marcion. Das Evangelium des fremden Gotts. Eine Monographie zur Geschichte der Grundlegung der katholischen Kirche* (Leipzig: Hinrichs, 2021).

36. The most impressive effort to detach modernity entirely from its theological prehistory has been initiated by Hans Blumenberg, *The Legitimacy of the Modern Age* (Cambridge, MA: MIT Press, 1985).

37. See my essay "Rethinking the Modern Canon of Judaism—Christianity—Modernity in Light of the Post-Secular Relation," in *Is There a Judeo-Christian Tradition?*, ed. Emmanuel Nathan and Anya Topolski (Berlin: De Gruyter, 2016).

Annotated Bibliography

The theses presented in this essay are further developed in my "Martin Buber—the Theopolitical Hour," in *Jewish Modernity*, ed. J. Picard et al. (Princeton, NJ: Princeton University Press,

2016), and in my "Rethinking the Modern Canon of Judaism—Christianity—Modernity in Light of the Post-Secular Relation," in *Is There a Judeo-Christian Tradition?*, ed. E. Nathan and A. Topolski (Berlin: De Gruyter, 2011). The relevant Buber texts are indicated in the notes here. I would nonetheless highlight Martin Buber, *Königtum Gottes* (Berlin: Schocken Verlag, 1932; Heidelberg: Lambert Schneider, 1956); and Buber, *Kingship of God*, trans. Richard Scheimann (New York: Harper & Row, 1996).

2

Martin Buber and Philosophical Anthropology

ASHER BIEMANN

Toward the end of his life, when asked about his scholarly discipline, Martin Buber famously described himself an "atypical man."[1] Refusing any conventional label and rejecting all "excessive typologies," Buber insisted that his philosophy was a discipline sui generis: it was "dialogical philosophy" and as such not merely another school of thought, but a new form of thinking altogether.[2] This thinking was tethered to the "basic experience of man" without, however, being subsumable under the then fashionable label of existentialism, which Buber consistently struggled to avoid: "I have never included myself in such," he insisted in 1964, "but feel myself as standing perhaps between an existential thinking in Kierkegaard's sense and something entirely different, something which is still out of sight."[3] Buber notoriously dodged any definition of that "something." But he did, in the late period of his oeuvre, embrace a discipline that seemed broad enough to reflect upon our basic human experience while lending credibility to an otherwise "atypical" approach: the discipline of anthropology or, more specifically, philosophical anthropology.[4]

Indeed, philosophical anthropology was the only academic label Buber did not categorically reject. In his "Replies to My Critics," first published in 1961, Buber summarized his life work as an attempt to "explain the fact of man" (*das Faktum Mensch*), invoking an anthropology that must be philosophical rather than naturalist, and sociological rather than individualist.[5] And he insisted, perhaps unexpectedly, that this anthropology not be theological. To be sure, the fact that man "lives over against God" could not be ignored and always required, as Buber put it, a certain *theologoumenon*. But this did not lead him to accept what Karl Barth, who developed his own version of dialogical philosophy in the 1940s, had proposed as "theological anthropology" in his *Church Dogmatics*.[6] In fact, philosophical anthropology, as Buber wrote in his most distinctly anthropological work, *The Problem of Man*, "must renounce its theological presuppositions." But it must not forsake the "metaphysical presupposition of the concrete man's bond with the absolute."[7]

What Buber had in mind was an integrative anthropology of human "wholeness" (*Ganzheit*), a science of the human being in its most intimate humanity that left open the horizon of the absolute, but which had to be developed from everyday experience. "[W]hen we recognize man's finitude," writes Buber, "we must *at the same time* recognize his participation in infinity, not as two juxtaposed qualities but as the twofold nature of the processes in which alone man's existence becomes recognizable." In order to understand the "essence of man," the philosopher had to be at once immersed in the ordinary world and to participate in their own humanity, while remaining attentive to what could be called the religious. Thus, philosophical anthropology, if taken as a science, could be neither fully objective nor fully descriptive. Objectification, to Buber, was tantamount to "dehumanization" (*Entmenschlichung*). True anthropology, by contrast, or true knowledge of humanity, had to rely on the "reality of being-part," on *Dabeisein* as existential and simultaneous participation in the immanent and transcendent, which Buber distinguished from what he perceived to be the solitude of Heidegger's purely immanent and "monological" *Dasein* (Being-There).[8] "The I is actual through its participation in actuality," Buber had written already in *I and Thou* (1923). "Whoever stands in relation participates in actuality."[9]

The anthropological question, then, could not be resolved in the individual alone or addressed to a distant and anonymous collective. It was a question of fundamental relationality. "The man who knows a world is man *with* man," writes Buber.[10] "The genuine essence of man can be directly known only in a living relation."[11] In this sense, all genuine anthropology must be sociology, or as Buber put it, a "sociology of human thinking-together."[12] It must, in a word, be social philosophy, which Buber set apart from the empirical sciences. "Modern sociology," he argued in the inaugural lecture for his chair at the Hebrew University, "originates [. . .] in the meeting of the spirit with the crisis of human society, which the spirit accepts as its own crisis and which it undertakes to overcome through a spiritual turning and transformation." The "new" sociologist, Buber continues, must acquire not only knowledge, but also "a new life relationship in which he is bound with reality without being submerged in it."[13]

Philosophical anthropology, for Buber, required the same degree of relationality and strove toward the same goal of spiritual turning and transformation. Like social philosophy, and unlike ethnographic anthropology in our day, it was an inherently normative endeavor. And, like all philosophy, it had to reflect, ultimately, upon itself. The beginning and end of philosophical anthropology, therefore, was self-knowledge, or what Buber called the anthropological *Besinnung*: "Philosophical knowledge of man is essentially man's self-reflection [*Selbstbesinnung*], and man can reflect upon himself only when the cognizing person, that is, the philosopher pursuing anthropology, first of all reflects upon himself as a person." This reflection, however, can never offer certainty, nor can it ever claim completion. The German word *Besinnung* means less than knowledge, yet more than contemplation. It connotes introspective awareness, a coming-to-oneself that implies not only inward recognition but also the potential for transformation and self-transcendence. For Buber who, as we shall see, was deeply indebted to the humanist tradition, the human self was not a given but a task. Being human remained inseparable from becoming human, and becoming human remained inseparable from spiritual turning and transformation. When Buber, in *The Problem of Man*, spoke of the "anthropological hour" as being Immanuel Kant's legacy for our time, he understood anthropology not only as the task of self-reflection (*Selbstbesinnung*) but also as the task of humility and self-restraint (*Selbstbescheidung*).[14]

Based on a lecture course at the Hebrew University in the summer of 1938, *The Problem of Man* appeared first in Hebrew (1942), then in German and English (1947), and finally, in 1948, as Buber's first stand-alone book to be published in postwar Germany. It must be remembered that, in the spring of 1938, Buber and his family had been forced to leave their home in the bucolic town of Heppenheim to settle in Jerusalem, where Buber accepted a professorship in the subject titled "Philosophy of Society."[15] This appointment and the profound personal impact of his flight from Nazi Germany played an important role in Buber's philosophical reorientation. While his earlier scholarship, including his work on mysticism, Hasidism, biblical exegesis, Eastern traditions, and, of course, his signature book *I and Thou*, primarily wrestled with a phenomenology of religion and religiosity, the lectures in *The Problem of Man* emphasized the methods of social philosophy, consciously and critically engaging with the Western canon of thought from Plato to the present.[16] For Buber, this involuntary transition did not come without challenge. Holding a chair in a discipline he did not fully consider his own and preparing a series of lectures in a language that, while his own in an intimately emotional sense, he had not yet fully mastered were daunting tasks. But they also allowed him to explore his early philosophical intuitions, which often resorted to poetic language, with new scholarly methods and to express the central theses of his dialogical philosophy with greater systematic rigor. Indeed, both social philosophy and the emerging and still experimental field of philosophical anthropology were disciplines with which Buber, who had earlier created and edited a famed series of forty "social-psychological" monographs titled *Die Gesellschaft* (1906–12), could find intellectual kinship. Both had philosophical roots that touched upon some of his own teachers and formative interlocutors, including Wilhelm Dilthey, Georg Simmel, and Max Scheler. And both appeared to be capacious enough to accommodate Buber's multidisciplinary approach while offering thematic continuities with his earlier work. Thus, in November 1937, Buber confided in Ernst Simon, who had emigrated to Palestine a decade before, that preparing his lectures for *The Problem of Man* had given him a new direction: "My course *took* me to the fundamentals of an anthropological system (the I-Thou anthropology, as it were) that I had evaded for such a long time."[17]

But Buber's turn to philosophical anthropology was prompted not only by the formal nature and expectations of his new academic post. It also coincided with a broader anthropological turn and growing sense of human crisis that had festered since the catastrophe of World War I and which scholars have described as a distinctly "German" phenomenon.[18] Edmund Husserl, in a lecture of 1931, noted with some dismay the "rapidly growing attention to a philosophical anthropology" among German *Modephilosophen*, who claimed to recognize only the "concrete worldly Dasein of man" as the foundation of their knowledge.[19] By that time, Max Scheler had already published *The Human Place in the Cosmos* (1928) and Helmuth Plessner his *Levels of Organic Life and the Human* (1928), both of which explicitly presented themselves as contributions to a philosophical anthropology.[20] Yet despite his reservations, Husserl himself would later publish an essay entitled "The Crisis of European Man," in which he raised urgent anthropological questions calling for introspection and envisioning, in the end, a "radically new humanity" arising from the "ashes of great weariness."[21]

The "anthropological hour" of the late 1920s was, in truth, an ongoing moment elliptically centered around the two deepest crises of humanity yet. It belonged to a profound questioning of human nature and human destiny at a time when all common ground and all faith in humanity's oneness seemed to have been irreparably shattered. "In the first world war, and on both sides," Buber would later write, "man learned with ever greater horror how he was in the grip of incomprehensible powers, [. . .] which, once unleashed, trampled again and again on all human purposes, until they finally brought everything, on this side and on the other, to complete destruction." In 1933, Buber spoke of the "crisis of man that we experience at this hour" as a question of human personhood and truth.[22] A decade later, Buber wrote that "man calls himself into question, because his self-knowledge no longer enables him to affirm and confirm himself."²³ Still, in 1963, speaking at the award ceremony of the Erasmus Prize in Amsterdam, Buber addressed the "crisis of the human race which threatens it with extinction." But this time it was not the tragedy of war and the question of society that concerned Buber but the "voluntary enslavement of man in the service of the split atom."²⁴

In *The Problem of Man*, Buber identified two factors contributing to the crisis of humanity: The "increasing decay of the old organic forms of the direct life of man with man," on the one hand, and the crisis of modern "man's lagging behind his works," on the other.²⁵ While the first was a sociological crisis that echoed Ferdinand Tönnies's seminal critique of community and society from 1887, as well as Max Weber's well-known distinction of *Vergemeinschaftung* and *Vergesellschaftung*, the latter referred to the crisis of technology, economy, and politics which Buber considered the "paralysis and failure of the human soul."²⁶ Both were distinctly modern crises that, for Buber, indicated a certain "homelessness" of man in the world. The old organic forms of community had been shattered since the French Revolution, the "original contract" between universe and man had dissolved in the modern world, and the individual, albeit liberated and emancipated, was now confronted with an unprecedented "depth of solitude." It was from this experience of estrangement and solitude, which Kierkegaard had most clearly articulated in opposition to the isolated "I" in Fichte's and Hegel's idealism, that the "problem of the human being" arose. And it was this anthropological hour, Buber believed, that obliged us to ask anew the fundamental question Immanuel Kant had posed in the introduction to his *Logic* of 1800: "What is man?"

That the question concerning the essence of man should appear in Kant's handbook to his lectures on logic may be puzzling at first. After all, Kant did compose several anthropological studies, some of them rightly controversial today, including his 1775 essay *On the Different Races of Human Beings* and his extensive *Anthropology from a Pragmatic Point of View* of 1798. But since logic, for Kant, was the very organon of rules that gave philosophy its form, the study of logic offered an occasion to also probe the meaning of philosophy itself. And here, Kant distinguished between academic philosophy (*Schulphilosophie*) and philosophy *in sensu cosmico* (*weltbürgerliche Bedeutung*). While the former was concerned with mastery of rational knowledge, the latter signified the pursuit of reason's "ultimate end." That pursuit, to Kant, constituted the "elevated concept" and ultimate "dignity" of philosophy, which was reflected in its four fundamental questions—what we can know, what we should do, what we may hope for, and, finally, as if set apart from the first three, the anthropological question "What is man?" It was this last question that, for Kant, summarized the task of philosophy in its cosmopolitan sense:

metaphysics, ethics, and religion all belong to anthropology, argues Kant, for the first three questions inevitably refer to the last.[27] Thus, philosophy beyond the boundaries of its academic discipline was, indeed, anthropology, whereas anthropology became nothing less than *Weltkenntnis*: Knowing man "as an earthly being endowed with reason," Kant writes in the *Anthropology*, "deserves to be called knowledge of the world, even if man represents only a small portion of earthly creatures." But in order to truly know the human being, anthropology cannot remain "physiological," the mere study of human nature; it must become "pragmatic," the study not only of what man "is" but of "what he, as a freely acting being, makes of himself, or what he can and should become."[28] With this unapologetically normative question, which was deeply rooted in the spirit of the European Enlightenment, Kant's anthropology turned philosophical, opening the path to a school of anthropology that would define German thought during the Weimar period and then again through the first two decades after 1945, rendering its enduring significance, perhaps, a particular postwar phenomenon.

Buber followed Kant in considering philosophical anthropology the "fundamental philosophical science." But he also chastised Kant for having abandoned his own ultimate philosophical question. The "wholeness of man," man's "special place in the cosmos" and relation to the world of things and fellow men, the fullness of his "ordinary and extraordinary encounters with the mystery," eluded Kant.[29] Nevertheless, it was Kant who set philosophical anthropology in motion. But it was not until the First World War that Kant's anthropological question would be revived in earnest.

Max Scheler's 1914 essay *The Idea of Man* set the tone of twentieth-century philosophical anthropology and was followed by his 1928 treatise *The Human Place in the Cosmos*, which Buber discussed at great length in *The Problem of Man*, along with Heidegger's *Being and Time* (1927). If Heidegger had turned man into a "metaphysical homunculus," then Scheler, at least in his late, post-Catholic phase, had amplified man to suspend metaphysics altogether.[30] Scheler's late concept of human *Gottwerdung*—the "becoming of God," or self-deification—had pushed Scheler's anthropology to its limits, Buber argued, though it was but the logical conclusion of his earlier definition of man as a searcher for God (*Gottsucher*). In his *Idea of Man*, Scheler linked the "essence" of humanity to its self-transcendence, which was the defining interruption in the natural continuity between the human being and the animal: "'Man' in this completely new sense," writes Scheler, "is the intention and gesture of 'transcendence' itself, the being that prays and searches for God." In fact, continues Scheler, man does not pray but "*is* the prayer of life extending beyond itself." As such, there can be no definition of the human being except that of a "between," a "limit," or a "transition." "A definable human being would have no meaning," writes Scheler. And likewise, there can be no natural unity of mankind, no *homo naturalis*, but only a "God-oriented," "historical" man, whose unity is given only "by what he can and should become."[31]

That the human being "shall be and become" (*sei und werde*) was Johann Gottfried von Herder's motto in his *Letters for the Advancement of Humanity* and remained a ubiquitous theme throughout the German Enlightenment and its epigones.[32] But human self-fashioning and self-formation was not an arbitrary process. It was understood to be the self-realization of the individual and of humanity altogether toward its inherent destiny and vocation. The *Bestimmung* of man, as the Romantic idealist Johann Gottlieb Fichte would still believe, was his "self-making" (*Sichselbstmachen*).[33] In that sense, Scheler's early anthropology echoed the German ideal of *Humanität*, to which Buber, like many German Jews at the time, felt much beholden.[34] And it anticipated perhaps Husserl's reflections on "authentic humanity" of 1924, where Husserl identified the idea of God as the "absolute limit pointing beyond human finitude, towards which all human striving is directed."[35] In his later anthropological writings, however, Scheler, at least in Buber's account, lapsed into a gnostic dualism of spirit (*Geist*) and urge (*Drang*) that deprived the idea of the human of its spiritual foundation and sense of vocation. Scheler's man thus became divided, like a sick man, between spirit and urge and, therefore, separated from his own body and the world around him: "Hitherto man thought with his whole body to the very finger-tips; from now on he thinks only with his brain."[36] Scheler was unable to resolve this dualism, for he assumed an original powerlessness of the spirit. "The spirit is lame and powerless unless it draws its energies from the *natura naturans*," Scheler noted in 1927.[37] But the spirit, argues Buber, became powerless only as a result of the disintegration of community and the inability to "receive the word." Like Wilhelm von Humboldt, who drew on the biblical notion of *Ruah*, Buber understood "spirit" as humanity's primal force. "The concept of humanity," Humboldt wrote in 1797, "is nothing but the living force of the spirit animating it, speaking from its midst, and actively working inside it."[38] Likewise, Husserl understood human beings as "spiritual unities" endowing humanity with a common "spiritual telos" that allowed it to strive forward. "From the point of view of the soul," he wrote in *The Crisis of European Man*, "humanity has never been a finished product, nor will it be, nor can it ever repeat itself." It was this spirit that allowed for the "progressive transformation of collective humanity" by giving it its greatest strength: anticipation. "Anticipation is the emotional guide to all discoveries."[39] The dualism, then, that haunted Scheler's man, denied the "spirit" its generative power, was no dualism at all,

Buber argued, but the symptom of a spiritual crisis that manifested itself in the crisis of community.

The crisis of community and "spirit" was a central theme already in Buber's *I and Thou*. But the search for "true" community appeared long before. In a youthful speech of 1900 written for the *Neue Gemeinschaft* circle of the brothers Heinrich and Julius Hart, Buber celebrated community as the "overflowing desire for the wholeness of life," a desire that would ultimately supersede the rigid forms of society: "Our community should be called postsocial," Buber mused, "for it transcends society and its norms. [. . .] It does not seek to reform, it aspires transformation."[40] The "concrete transformation [*Umgestaltung*] of our lives" would later become Buber's programmatic imperative of a Jewish Renaissance and, as we shall see in due course, of what he called "Hebrew humanism." The life of community, in this respect, mirrored the life of the individual, just as the crisis of man, for Buber, mirrored the crisis of community.

In *Paths in Utopia*, first published in Hebrew in 1947 but written around 1945, Buber attributed the crisis of his time to the gradual loss of true community that had already beset the generation of World War I.[41] The magnitude of the Second World War and the destruction of European Jewry, for which Margarete Susman, in her 1946 essay "*Hiob*," found no other words than the "complete collapse of all human and humane in the Western world," had given the crisis of humanity an unprecedented urgency.[42] Buber, in 1945, spoke of the "greatest crisis humanity has ever lived through" and in 1949 described his time as "so evidently remote from a mankind-humanity."[43] But he did not consider it a fundamentally *new* crisis that required radically new answers. In fact, Buber's response to the predicament of 1945 echoed the same hope for a "new community" he had articulated in 1900: "The primary aspiration of all history is a genuine community of human beings—genuine because it is *community all through*."[44] This aspiration and desire was, for Buber, an anthropological fact, the destiny and *Bestimmung* of man. "World and humanity are destined by creation to become community," Buber wrote in 1930, at a time when ideas of "community" (*Gemeinschaft*), "covenant" (*Bund*), and "circle" (*Kreis*) were, for better or worse, common currency in German culture.[45]

Here it should be noted that the concept of community, which inevitably gained political traction in nationalist circles, was subject to scathing criticism already in the 1920s. Helmuth Plessner, in 1924, called community the "idol of our time," whereas Thomas Mann, in 1928, detected in the new predilection for *Gemeinschaft* a "romantic sound of aristocratic simplemindedness."[46] The young Plessner, who would soon become a major figure in philosophical anthropology, was particularly disturbed by the radical, antidemocratic, antiurban, and antimodern connotations of *Gemeinschaft* that frequently produced the notion of a "beloved center" (*Liebesmitte*) and, consequently, the desire for a model leader.[47]

Buber's quest for "authentic" community undoubtedly had a share in the romantic idiom of the time. But it also differed starkly from the ethnonationalist vision of communities of blood and soil. If Buber singled out the communities of destiny (*Schicksalsgemeinschaft*) and the communities of faith (*Glaubensgemeinschaft*) as two forms of "authentic" community, he did so because they were guided not by "feeling" or a certain political *Stimmung*, much less by authoritarian leadership, but by a sense and reality of "true living together" that required individual autonomy and resisted any kind of collectivism, whether communist or fascist. It was not "blood relations" that formed authentic communities, Buber wrote in 1900, but "elective affinity" (*Wahlverwandtschaft*): "We are concerned not with whence we come but whither we go."[48] It was the purposeful "interrelation" (*Wechselbeziehung*) and "correlation" (*Wechselwirkung*) among community members, not its natural ground, that made community alive. In *I and Thou*, Buber used the religiously colored term *Gemeinde* (congregation), introducing yet another concept to describe authentic communities: the "living center." "A community [*Gemeinde*] is built upon a living, reciprocal relationship," he writes, "but the builder is the living, active center."[49] Yet, this center was precisely *not* to be filled by a model leader or by unbridled authority, as Plessner would later fear. It was neither a physical place nor a hierarchical order. The "builder" was the intangible, unpredictable, yet actual space emerging from community itself, the ontological "middle" manifesting itself as an event between and among the members in relation to each other: "[E]verywhere a turning to, a dynamic facing of, the other, a flowing from I to Thou. Community is where community happens."[50] This elusive event and fragile "middle" Buber called the *Zwischenmenschliche*, the interhuman, in his earlier writings, whereas in his later, anthropological texts, he often used "the between"—*das Zwischen*. And it was this category that proved to be pivotal for Buber's philosophical anthropology.

In 1954 Buber published *Elements of the Interhuman*. This short text can be seen as a bridge between his dialogical and his anthropological thought and, at the same time, as an attempt to refine the meaning of social philosophy reaching back to his 1906 introduction to the *Gesellschaft* monographs. After all, Buber contends, what happens "between" people and in society are "essentially different areas of human life." As in his other writings from the time, the sense of crisis—the "crisis of the Between"—looms large, and the Kantian question concerning the "fact of man" forms the essay's thrust. But all "anthropological facts," writes Buber, that establish the realm of interhuman relations point to an ontology, and this ontology, like Kant's kingdom of ends, cannot be thought other than under the aegis of an "ought" which is sustained by the idea of human dignity. Thus, man "anthropologically exists" only by virtue of the interhuman which "discloses to us what otherwise remains undisclosed."[51] Anthropology must become dialogical. Human dignity (*Würde*) must become worthiness (*Würdigkeit*).[52] And the "ought" toward which our existence points must seek humanity's "self-realization" through participatory action.

Buber chose not to include *Elements of the Interhuman* in a small collection of texts intended to be the prolegomena for a systematic philosophical anthropology, which he never managed to write.[53] But already the first chapter of this unfinished anthropology—*Distance and Relation* (1950)—left little doubt that Buber had in mind an anthropology that was fundamentally dialogical and founded upon human relationality. Such an anthropology, as Buber readily acknowledged, had its most noteworthy precursor in Ludwig Feuerbach's *Philosophy of the Future* (1846), which explicitly stated that the "essence of man consists only in community," in the "unity of man and man," and in the "reality of I and Thou."[54] And it coincided, as Buber explained in a late postscript to the *Dialogical Principle*, with a veritable flurry of I-Thou publications during the Weimar period.[55] Among those, Karl Löwith's 1928 dissertation, "The Individual in the Role of the Fellow Human Being," written under the supervision of Martin Heidegger, was perhaps the most explicitly "anthropological" text. Declaring himself committed to Heidegger's concept of philosophical anthropology as the "foundation of ethical questions," Löwith developed a profoundly dialogical anthropology of *Miteinandersein* (being with each other) that engaged figures such as Feuerbach, Humboldt, Scheler, and Ferdinand Ebner, but curiously ignored Buber's by then highly visible book *I and Thou*.[56] Conversely, Buber maintained that Löwith's work had little impact on his own intellectual formation.[57] But another book published at around the same time seems to have been more formative for Buber's turn to anthropology: Bernhard Groethuysen's *Philosophische Anthropologie*, which was deeply indebted to Buber's dialogical thought while drawing its main inspiration from Christian humanism.

Groethuysen was a German-French philosopher and historian best known for his works on Diderot, Rousseau, and his *Philosophie de la Révolution française*. A student—like Buber—of Dilthey, Simmel, and Friedrich Jodl, Groethuysen was one of the first to interrogate the concepts of compassion and empathy (*Das Mitgefühl*, 1904), subsequently developing a cultural sociology of *Verstehen* which, during World War I, unfolded into an ambitious humanism of cultural exchange and dialogue that has lost little of its relevance today.⁵⁸ In 1931 he published his somewhat idiosyncratic (even "mystical," as Margarete Susman once put it) yet influential *Philosophische Anthropologie*, which offered a sweeping intellectual history from Plato to Montaigne while introducing the concept of philosophical anthropology as a refined form of *Lebensphilosophie*: "Every philosopher is, in a certain sense, a philosopher of life." And every philosophy of life is a "becoming aware of life through life itself."⁵⁹ Thus, philosophical anthropology is self-knowledge and *Selbstbesinnung*, "the ever-renewed attempt of man at grasping himself."⁶⁰ Becoming conscious of yourself, Groethuysen wrote in a later essay dedicated to Ernst Cassirer, means to "live in the consciousness of yourself, understand yourself, come to experience yourself, be present to yourself, live in the awareness of your present, come to yourself." But this act of self-knowing requires an inner dialogue: "Man finds himself as a thou. . . . Self-reflection, in this sense, denotes a dialogue in which man engages with himself."⁶¹ The origins of this inner dialogue, however, are not philosophical but religious. "Religious man knows himself as an I over against God. I and God. I and Thou." And Groethuysen continues in an even more strikingly Buberian vein: "In this *Zwiesprache* [dialogue], man becomes an I, is formed to be a new human being."⁶² The anthropological task of self-knowledge, then, required the encounter with an other. But Groethuysen did not credit Buber with this insight, nor, one could add, any other dialogical thinker at the time. Rather, he related it back to Augustine and to Luther's "believing I," which he considered to be the "demythologization" of the anthropocentric "I" found in myth and the "pagan" Renaissance.⁶³ Paradoxically, anthropology in the philosophical sense began with the decentering of *anthropos* and with the "transcendence of life in itself." Religion, to Groethuysen, gave here the decisive impulse, for it placed the I not merely in opposition to a non-I, but in relation to a Thou. Thus, religion offered not only the basis for cultural dialogue but also for what had to complement every introspective act of *Selbstbesinnung*: "It announces to man his destiny [*Bestimmung*]. . . . It gives meaning to live, formation, and desire for life."⁶⁴

It is not difficult to find solid traces of Groethuysen's philosophical anthropology in Buber's *The Problem of Man*, which began, as we recall, from a similar premise of *Selbstbesinnung* and maintained a similar commitment to a non-theological religious interrelationality. But the influence was clearly mutual, which should come as no surprise since both thinkers had been part of the Pontigny circle around the French philosopher Paul Desjardins and shared a similar intellectual pedigree.⁶⁵ In that sense, Groethuysen's considerable influence on philosophical anthropology was, implicitly, also Buber's. When Ernst Cassirer, in his *Essay on Man* (1944), cited Groethuysen as the main inspiration for his own "anthropological philosophy," and when in his *Logic of the Humanities* (1942) he found the "separation between 'I' and 'You,' and likewise that between 'I' and 'world,'" constitutive of "spiritual life," he may well have drawn, if only indirectly, on Buber's dialogical framework.[66] More directly, Victor Turner would later develop a cultural anthropology that invoked Buber's concept of community (*communitas* in Turner) and I-Thou encounter, while Kuno Lorenz drew on Buber for both his "dialogical logic" and his philosophical anthropology.[67] But there was another common thread in Groethuysen's and Buber's writings on philosophical anthropology that deserves mention and with which we shall conclude: their shared plea for a humble humanism that accepted the concreteness and weakness of humanity. As Groethuysen put it in reference to Erasmus of Rotterdam: "Know yourself as a human being, know of your humanity, consider yourself a fellow man, a member of the human world."[68]

That Buber's philosophical anthropology remained inseparable from his Hebrew humanism was noted already by Grete Schaeder in her classic work of 1966: "Buber's 'Hebrew humanism' is not a worldview; it is a conception of man."[69] Buber established his phrase "Hebrew humanism" in an essay of 1941. But he had already coined the term in 1913 and then referred to it in a speech at the Sixteenth Zionist Congress in 1929, advocating a "Hebrew humanism in the most real sense," the preparation, as he put it then, "to fulfill with unperturbed humanity the historical human task of a new Judaism at the gate of the nations."[70] In an essay written during the rise to power of the Nazi regime, Buber used the terms "biblical" and "Hebrew humanism" side by side to urge an alternative to the humanism of the West that had now begun to align itself with the new political reality.[71] Calling for a "rebirth of normative primal forces," Buber understood biblical humanism to be the "concrete transformation of our total—and not alone our inner—lives."[72] Whereas Western humanism was indeed human*ism*, an image "hammered into shape" by a "solitary, sculpting spirit," Hebrew humanism, for Buber, echoed Herder's vision of *Humanität*, for it was, as he called it in Hebrew, *humaniyut* in the most aspirational sense: the "faith in man" and the incessant "struggle against the imminent downfall of humanity."[73] And whereas Western, universal humanism existed with an aura of permanence, Hebrew humanism had to be affirmed and verified time and again, at every moment anew. Thus, classical humanism saw its highest realization in the polis, whereas biblical humanism, according to Buber, viewed its political realization as noted by the Hebrew term *edah*, the "present inter-community of all this people" and the "true immediacy between man and man."[74]

Biblical humanism, then, established a community in the sense of community-congregation (*Gemeinde*), a community of faith and faithfulness which, in turn, established the idea of biblical humanity. This ideal, Buber insisted, was rooted in the national experience of the Jewish people and could not be realized in a purely universal conception of humanity. True *Humanität*, Hermann Cohen had already noted in his *Aesthetics*, "cannot be abstract love of man."[75] Like divine love, it must, as Cohen's student Franz Rosenzweig wrote, "mysteriously encompass people, nations, ages, and things."[76] Writing from a perspective of sober realism after the 1948 *Universal Declaration of Human Rights*, Hannah Arendt would later remark that "the world found nothing sacred in the abstract nakedness of man."[77] Buber, too, believed that human rights were ultimately coextensive with national rights and that every humanism had to become concrete through a self-knowledge that did not exclude the reality of belonging. In that sense, every humanism needed a *Schicksalsgemeinschaft*. But like Cohen, who, as one should recall, was deeply influenced by Herder, Buber also believed that there existed a unity of mankind beyond nationalities, a unity vouchsafed by a Thou to which all human beings could relate, by a God to whom all human beings were equally accountable. "His concept of Dasein," Cohen wrote in his *Ethics*, "means nothing else than the fact that it is no illusion to believe, to think, and to know the unity of man."[78] This unity, like the idea of man itself, was not a given and nothing that could be derived from empirical nature. It belonged to the realm of the not-yet, to the Kantian kingdom of the "ought." And here anthropology had to become truly philosophical, perhaps even prophetic. For the prophets, as Cohen noted, were the first to hold a concept of humanity as one, the first to be rightfully called cosmopolitans.[79]

This prophetic ideal, however, has yet to be realized. In a speech given in 1953 in Germany, Buber acknowledged, possibly for the first time, the fact of human individuals so radically removed from the "human sphere" and so transposed into the "sphere of monstrous inhumanity" that they shared a common humanity only in a formal sense. With this and the untold number of ordinary bystanders and unmolested perpetrators in mind, he encouraged the "preparation for the final battle of the *homo humanus* against the *homo contrahumanus*" that would require a "solidarity of all separate groups in the flaming battle for the rise of a true humanity."[80] To hear the *vox humana* had now become a global duty. It required introspection, *Selbstbesinnung*, and an "existential turning," a *Wesensumkehr*. It required a new sense of trust. And it required, most importantly, a humanity willing to *become* humanity. The imperative of *Menschwerdung*—of becoming human—rendered Buber's philosophical anthropology not only deeply humanistic but also profoundly vocational. Like his philosophy of dialogue, philosophical anthropology, for Buber, was no science of knowing but an act of doing, an existential risk and a task. Or as he put it in a 1949 speech on Goethe's concept of humanity: "Human truth is not conformity between a thing thought and a thing being; it is participation in Being."[81]

Notes

1. Martin Buber, "Replies to My Critics," in *The Philosophy of Martin Buber*, ed. Paul Arthur Schilpp and Maurice Friedman (LaSalle, IL: Open Court, 1967), 690.

2. Buber spoke of a "neue Denkweise" initiated by Ludwig Feuerbach. Cf. Martin Buber, "Afterword: The History of the Dialogical Principle," in Buber, *Between Man and Man* (New York: Macmillan, 1965), 210.

3. Sidney Rome and Beatrice Rome, eds., *Philosophical Interrogations* (New York: Holt, Rinehart & Winston, 1964), 23.

4. Grete Schaeder, *The Hebrew Humanism of Martin Buber* (Detroit: Wayne State University Press, 1973), 411–70. See also the excellent introduction by Ashraf Noor to *Martin Buber Werkausgabe* (Gütersloh: Gütersloher Verlagshaus, 2017), 12:13–86.

5. Buber, "Replies to My Critics," 690. For stylistic reasons, the outdated term "man" (*Mensch*) will be kept throughout this essay to connote a gender-inclusive, nonbinary "human being."

6. Barth, *Mensch und Mitmensch* (Göttingen: Vandenhoeck & Ruprecht, 1967), 5. Also, Buber, "Afterword," 222. Max Scheler had already distinguished among theological, philosophical, and scientific (*naturwissenschaftlich*) anthropology. Cf. Scheler, *Philosophische Anthropologie*, in *Gesammelte Werke*, vol. 12, *Schriften aus dem Nachlaß III* (Bern: Francke Verlag, 1976), 6.

7. Buber, *Between Man and Man*, 163. Translation altered.

8. Buber, *Between Man and Man*, 121, 122, 125–26.

9. Martin Buber, *I and Thou*, trans. Walter Kaufmann (New York: Simon & Schuster, 1996), 113.

10. Buber, *Between Man and Man*, 155.

11. Buber, *Between Man and Man*, 205. Translation altered.

12. Buber, *Between Man and Man*, 155.

13. Martin Buber, "The Demand of the Spirit and Historical Reality," in Buber, *Pointing the Way: Collected Essays* (New York: Harper & Brothers, 1957), 178, 179.

14. Buber, *Between Man and Man*, 124, 137.

15. See also Paul Mendes-Flohr, *Martin Buber: A Life of Faith and Dissent* (New Haven, CT: Yale University Press, 2019), 202–11. "Philosophy of Society" corresponded to the German *Sozialphilosophie*.

16. Buber referred to *Ich und Du* as his *Religionswerk*. Cf. Martin Buber, *Briefwechsel aus sieben Jahrzehnten* (Heidelberg: Lambert Schneider, 1973), 2:99. However, in a later (1957) afterword to *I and Thou*, he acknowledged its "anthropological foundations" and "sociological implications." Cf. Buber, afterword to *I and Thou*, 171.

17. Nahum Glatzer and Paul Mendes-Flohr, eds., *The Letters of Martin Buber* (New York: Schocken Books, 1991), 462.

18. Cf. Joachim Fischer, "Philosophische Anthropologie," in *Soziologische Denkschulen in der Bundesrepublik Deutschland* (Berlin: Springer, 2019), 181–248.

19. Edmund Husserl, "Phänomenologie und Anthropologie," in *Aufsätze und Vorträge 1922–1937*, ed. Thomas Nenon and Hans Rainer Sepp (Dordrecht: Kluwer, 1989), 164–81.
20. Max Scheler, *Die Stellung des Menschen im Kosmos*, in *Gesammelte Werke*, vol. 9, *Späte Schriften* (Bern: Francke Verlag, 1976), 9. Also Helmuth Plessner, *Die Stufen des Organischen und der Mensch* (Berlin: De Gruyter, 1928).
21. Cf. Husserl, "The Crisis of European Man," in *Phenomenology and the Crisis of Philosophy*, trans. Quentin Lauer (New York: Harper & Row, 1965), 169, 192.
22. Buber, *Between Man and Man*, 158, 79.
23. Martin Buber, *Good and Evil* (New York: Charles Scribner's Sons, 1952), 135.
24. Martin Buber, "Believing Humanism," in *A Believing Humanism: My Testament, 1902–1965*, ed. Ruth Nanda Anshen (New York: Simon & Schuster, 1967), 121.
25. Buber, *Between Man and Man*, 157–58.
26. Cf. Buber, *Between Man and Man*, 157.
27. Cf. Immanuel Kant, *Logik: Ein Handbuch zu Vorlesungen*, in *Werke in sechs Bänden*, ed. Wilhelm Weischedel (Darmstadt: Wissenschaftliche Buchgesellschaft, 1963), 3:446–48.
28. Kant, *Anthropologie in pragmatischer Hinsicht*, in *Werke in sechs Bänden*, 4:399.
29. Cf. Buber, *Between Man and Man*, 119.
30. Cf. Buber, *Between Man and Man*, 182.
31. Max Scheler, "Die Idee des Menschen," in Scheler, *Abhandlungen und Aufsätze* (Leipzig: Verlag der Weissen Bücher, 1915), 1:346, 348, 363.
32. Cf. Herder, "Briefe zur Beförderung der Humanität," in *Herders Werke*, ed. Heinrich Kurz (Leipzig: Verlag des Bibliographischen Instituts, n.d.), 4:91.
33. Johann Gottlieb Fichte, *Reden an die deutsche Nation* (Leipzig: Kröner, 1924), 47 (Rede 3).
34. Similarly, Michael Landmann would later emphasize "Schöpferbegabung" as the anthropological foundation of human culture; Landmann, *Philosophische Anthropologie* (Berlin: De Gruyter, 1955), 259.
35. Husserl, "Erneuerung als individualethisches Problem," in *Aufsätze und Vorträge 1922–1937*, 33–34.
36. Buber, *Between and Man*, 198.
37. Scheler, *Philosophische Anthropologie*, 114.
38. Wilhelm von Humboldt, "Über den Geist der Menschheit," in *Werke in fünf Bänden*, ed. Andreas Flitner and Klaus Giel (Darmstadt: Wissenschaftlich Buchgesellschaft, 1960), 1:515.
39. Husserl, "The Crisis of European Man," 158–60.
40. Paul Mendes-Flohr and Bernhard Susser, "Alte und neue Gemeinschaft: An Unpublished Buber Manuscript," *AJS Review* 1 (1976): 51, 54; also Paul Mendes-Flohr, "Prophetic Politics and Meta-Sociology: Martin Buber and German Social Thought," *Archives de sciences sociales des religions* 60, no. 1 (1985): 67–82.
41. Cf. Martin Buber, *Paths in Utopia*, trans. R. F. C. Hull (Boston: Beacon Press, 1950), 129–38.
42. Margarete Susman, *Das Buch Hiob und das Schicksal des jüdischen Volkes* (Frankfurt am Main: Jüdischer Verlag, 2018), 23.
43. Cf. Martin Buber, "Über die Große Krise," in *Martin Buber Werkausgabe* (Gütersloh: Gütersloher Verlagshaus, 2019), 11.2, 79; Martin Buber, "Remarks on Goethe's Concept of Humanity," in *Goethe and the Modern Age*, ed. Arnold Bergstraesser (Chicago: Henry Regnery, 1950), 233.
44. Buber, *Paths in Utopia*, 133.
45. Martin Buber, "How Can Community Happen?," in *The Martin Buber Reader: Essential Writings*, ed. Asher D. Biemann (New York: Palgrave, 2002), 252. Translation altered. On the darker

popularity of the community theme, see Stefan Breuer, "Gemeinschaft in der 'deutschen Soziologie' (1933–1945)," *Zeitschrift für Soziologie* 31, no. 5 (October 2002): 354–72.

46. Helmuth Plessner, *Grenzen der Gemeinschaft* (Frankfurt am Main: Suhrkamp, 2002), 28. Thomas Mann, "Kultur und Sozialismus," *Gesammelte Werke in zwölf Bänden* (Oldenburg: S. Fischer, 1960), 12:645.

47. Plessner, *Grenzen der Gemeinschaft*, 48.

48. Mendes-Flohr and Susser, "Alte und neue Gemeinschaft," 56, 52.

49. Buber, *I and Thou*, 94; also Bernhard Susser, *Existence and Utopia: The Social and Political Thought of Martin Buber* (Rutherford, NJ: Fairleigh Dickinson University Press, 1981), 50–53; and more recently, Dan Avnon, "The 'Living Center' of Martin Buber's Political Theory," *Political Theory* 21, no. 1 (February 1993): 55–77.

50. Cf. Martin Buber, "Dialogue," in *Between Man and Man*, 31.

51. Martin Buber, "Elements of the Interhuman," in *The Knowledge of Man*, ed. Maurice Friedman (London: George Allen & Unwin, 1965), 72, 84, 86.

52. Buber speaks of "jüdische Würdigkeit" but insists that the intrinsic dignity of man cannot be conceived without relational and aspirational worthiness. Cf. Martin Buber, "Biblical Humanism," in Buber, *On the Bible: Eighteen Studies*, ed. Nahum N. Glatzer (New York: Schocken Books, 1982), 211–12.

53. These texts included, in this order, "Distance and Relation" (1950), "Man and His Image-Work" (1955), "The Word That Is Spoken" (1960), "What Is Common to All?" (1956), and "Guilt and Guilt Feelings" (1957).

54. Ludwig Feuerbach, *Grundsätze der Philosophie die Zukunft* (Frankfurt am Main: Klostermann, 1983), 110.

55. Buber, "Afterword," 209–24.

56. Karl Löwith, *Das Individuum in der Rolle des Mitmenschen*, in *Sämtliche Schriften*, vol. 1, ed. Klaus Stichweh (Stuttgart: Metzler, 1981), 11. Cf. also Martin Heidegger, *Sein und Zeit* (Tübingen: Max Niemeyer, 2001), 17.

57. Cf. Martin Buber, letter to Maurice Friedman, August 11, 1951 (*Briefwechsel* [Heidelberg: Verlag Lamber Schneider, 1975], 3:290): "Als ich Löwith's Buch las, war alles bereits voll ausgereift, und ich konnte nichts von seiner Methode übernehmen."

58. See Michael Ermarth, "Intellectual History as Philosophical Anthropology: Bernard Groethuysen's Transformation of Traditional Geistesgeschichte," *Journal of Modern History* 64, no. 4 (December 1993): esp. 678–80.

59. Bernhard Groethuysen, *Philosophische Anthropologie* (Munich: Oldenbourg, 1931), 3–4. Also Margarete Susman, "In Memoriam Bernhard Groethuysen," *Zeitschrift für Religions- und Geistesgeschichte* 1, no. 1 (1948): 81: "[E]ine mystische Anthropologie: die Seele hat in ihr durchweg den Primat vor Welt und Mensch." On the actual publication date of *Philosophische Anthropologie* (1928 or 1931), see Fischer, "'Philosophische Anthropologie' versus 'philosophische Anthropologie'—Paradigma und Disziplin: Groethuysen als Gründer der Disziplin," in *Bernhard Groethuysen: Deutsch-französischer Intellektueller, Philosoph und Religionssoziologe*, ed. Richard Faber and Claude Conter (Würzburg: Königshausen & Neumann, 2021), esp. 22–23.

60. Groethuysen, *Philosophische Anthropologie*, 3.

61. Bernhard Groethuysen, "Toward a Philosophical Anthropology," in *Philosophy and History: The Ernst Cassirer Festschrift*, ed. Raymond Klibansky and H. J. Paton (New York: Harper & Row, 1963), 77, 82.

62. Groethuysen, *Philosophische Anthropologie*, 97.

63. Cf. Groethuysen, *Philosophische Anthropologie*, 191–92.

64. Groethuysen, *Philosophische Anthropologie*, 5.

65. See Klaus Große Kracht, "Europa im kleinen: Die Sommergespräche von Pontigny und die deutsch-französische Intellektuellenverständigung in der Zwischenkriegszeit," *Internationales Archiv für Sozialgeschichte der deutschen Literatur* 27, no. 1 (2007): 144–69. On Buber's role in the circle, see the commentary in *Martin Buber Werkausgabe* (Gütersloh: Gütersloher Verlagshaus, 2017), 12:696–99.

66. Ernst Cassirer, *An Essay on Man* (New Haven, CT: Yale University Press, 1944), 6; Cassirer, *The Logic of the Humanities*, trans. Clarence Smith Howe (New Haven, CT: Yale University Press, 1961), 188.

67. Cf. Victor Turner, *Dramas, Fields, and Metaphors* (Ithaca, NY: Cornell University Press, 1974), 274; Kuno Lorenz, *Einführung in die philosophische Anthropologie* (Darmstadt: Wissenschaftlich Buchgesellschaft, 1990), 7–9. On Turner and Buber, see also Yoram Bilu, "Dialogic Anthropology," in *Dialogue as a Trans-Disciplinary Concept: Martin Buber and Its Contemporary Reception*, ed. Paul Mendes-Flohr (Berlin: De Gruyter, 2015), 141–56.

68. Groethuysen, *Philosophische Anthropologie*, 190.

69. Schaeder, *The Hebrew Humanism of Martin Buber*, 11. Translation altered.

70. Martin Buber, "Rede auf dem XVI. Zionistenkongress in Zürich," in *Martin Buber Werkausgabe* 21:124.

71. See Barbara Stiewe, *Der "Dritte Humanismus": Aspekte deutscher Griechen-Rezeption vom George-Kreis bis zum Nationalsozialismus* (Berlin: De Gruyter, 2011).

72. Martin Buber, "Biblical Humanism," in *On the Bible: Eighteen Studies*, ed. Nahum N. Glatzer (New York: Schocken Books, 1982), 213.

73. Martin Buber, "Hebrew Humanism," in *Israel and the World: Essays in a Time of Crisis* (New York: Schocken Books, 1948), 242. Translation modified.

74. Buber, "Biblical Humanism," 216.

75. Hermann Cohen, *Ästhetik des reinen Gefühls* (Berlin: Bruno Cassirer, 1912), 2:52.

76. Franz Rosenzweig, *The Star of Redemption*, trans. William Hallo (New York: Holt, Rinehart & Winston, 1970), 164.

77. Hannah Arendt, *The Origins of Totalitarianism* (New York: Harcourt, Brace & World, 1966), 299.

78. Hermann Cohen, *Ethik des reinen Willens* (Berlin: Bruno Cassirer, 1904), 53. On this point also Michael Landmann, "Universalismus und Partikularismus im Judentum," in *Jüdische Miniaturen* (Bonn: Bouvier, 1982), 1:13–49.

79. Cf. Cohen, *Ästhetik*, 2:358, where Cohen speaks of the "Weltbürgertum der Propheten."

80. Martin Buber, "Genuine Dialogue and the Possibilities of Peace," in *A Believing Humanism*, 196–97.

81. Buber, "Remarks on Goethe's Concept of Humanity," 233.

Annotated Bibliography

PRIMARY SOURCES

Most of Martin Buber's writings related to philosophical anthropology are collected in Martin Buber, *Between Man and Man*, trans. Ronald Gregor Smith (New York: Macmillan, 1965), and Martin Buber, *The Knowledge of Man*, ed. Maurice Friedman (London: George Allen & Unwin, 1965).

SECONDARY LITERATURE

For excellent discussions of Buber's philosophical anthropology, see Grete Schaeder, *The Hebrew Humanism of Martin Buber*, trans. Noah J. Jacobs (Detroit: Wayne State University Press, 1973), and the introduction by Ashraf Noor in *Martin Buber Werkausgabe* (Gütersloh: Gütersloher Verlagshaus, 2017), vol. 12. The most extensive intellectual history of philosophical anthropology as an academic discipline remains Joachim Fischer, *Philosophische Anthropologie: Eine Denkrichtung des 20. Jahrhunderts* (Freiburg: Alber, 2022). A recent analysis of Buber's humanistic thought in a philosophical context is Hanoch Ben Pazi, "A Call to Ethical Judaism: 'Hebrew Humanism' in Martin Buber's Thought," *Australian Journal of Jewish Studies* 30 (2017): 28–73.

For an interesting discussion of Buber's philosophical anthropology in relation to Karl Löwith, see Agostino Cera, "Mitanthropologie, Zwischenontologie. L'antropologia löwithiana a confronto con il dialogismo di Martin Buber," *La Cultura* 51, no. 2 (August 2013): 251–81; this work is revised and translated as "The Other's Place in the Space of the Relation: Karl Löwith and Martin Buber as Theorists of *Duheit*," in *The Changing Faces of Space*, ed. Maria Teresa Catena and Felice Masi (Berlin: Springer, 2017), 57–74.

On Buber's reception in postwar Germany, see Abigail Gillman, "'Seit ein Gespräch wir sind und hören von einander': Martin Buber's Message to Postwar Germany," *Nexus: Essays in German Jewish Studies* 2 (2013): 121–52.

WORKS CITED

Arendt, Hannah. *The Origins of Totalitarianism*. New York: Harcourt, Brace & World, 1966.
Avnon, Dan. "The 'Living Center' of Martin Buber's Political Theory." *Political Theory* 21, no. 1 (February 1993): 55–77.
Barth, Karl. *Mensch und Mitmensch: Die Grundform der Menschlichkeit*. Göttingen: Vandenhoeck & Ruprecht, 1967.
Bergstraesser, Arnold, ed. *Goethe and the Modern Age*. Chicago: Henry Regnery, 1950.
Bilu, Yoram. "Dialogic Anthropology." In *Dialogue as a Trans-Disciplinary Concept: Martin Buber and Its Contemporary Reception*, edited by Paul Mendes-Flohr. Berlin: De Gruyter, 2015.
Breuer, Stefan. "Gemeinschaft in der 'deutschen Soziologie' (1933–1945)." *Zeitschrift für Soziologie* 31, no. 5 (October 2002): 354–72.
Buber, Martin. *A Believing Humanism: My Testament 1902–1965*. Edited by Ruth Nanda Anshen. New York: Simon & Schuster, 1967.
———. *Between Man and Man*. Translated by Ronald Gregor Smith. New York: Macmillan, 1965.
———. *Briefwechsel aus Sieben Jahrzehnten*. Vol. 2, *1918–1938*. Edited by Grete Schaeder. Heidelberg: Lambert Schneider, 1973.
———. *Good and Evil*. New York: Charles Scribner's Sons, 1952.
———. *I and Thou*. Translated by Walter Kaufmann. New York: Simon & Schuster, 1996.
———. *Israel and the World: Essays in a Time of Crisis*. New York: Schocken Books, 1948.
———. *The Knowledge of Man*. Edited by Maurice Friedman. London: George Allen & Unwin, 1965.
———. *The Martin Buber Reader: Essential Writings*. Edited by Asher D. Biemann. New York: Palgrave, 2002.
———. *On the Bible: Eighteen Studies*. Edited by Nahum N. Glatzer. New York: Schocken Books, 1982.
———. *Paths in Utopia*. Translated by R. F. C. Hull. Boston: Beacon Press, 1950.

———. *Pointing the Way: Collected Essays*. Translated by Maurice Friedman. New York: Harper & Brothers, 1957.

Cassirer, Ernst, *An Essay on Man*. New Haven, CT: Yale University Press, 1944.

———. *The Logic of the Humanities*. Translated by Clarence Smith Howe. New Haven, CT: Yale University Press, 1961.

Cohen, Hermann. *Ästhetik des reinen Gefühls*. Berlin: Bruno Cassirer, 1912.

———. *Ethik des reinen Willens*. Berlin: Bruno Cassirer, 1904.

Ermarth, Michael. "Intellectual History as Philosophical Anthropology: Bernard Groethuysen's Transformation of Traditional Geistesgeschichte." *Journal of Modern History* 64, no. 4 (December 1993): 673–705.

Faber, Richard, and Claude Conter, eds. *Bernhard Groethuysen: Deutsch-französischer Intellektueller, Philosoph und Religionssoziologe*. Würzburg: Königshausen & Neumann, 2021.

Feuerbach, Ludwig. *Grundsätze der Philosophie die Zukunft*. Frankfurt am Main: Klostermann, 1983.

Fichte, Johann Gottlieb. *Reden an die deutsche Nation*. Leipzig: Kröner, 1924.

Fischer, Joachim. "Philosophische Anthropologie: Ein Theorie- und Forschungsprogramm in der deutschen Soziologie nach 1945 bis in die Gegenwart." In *Soziologische Denkschulen in der Bundesrepublik Deutschland*, ed. Joachim Fischer and S. Moebius. Berlin: Springer, 2019.

———. "'Philosophische Anthropologie' versus 'philosophische Anthropologie'—Paradigma und Disziplin: Groethuysen als Gründer der Disziplin." In Faber and Conter, *Bernhard Groethuysen*, 21–41.

Glatzer, Nahum, and Paul Mendes-Flohr, eds. *The Letters of Martin Buber: A Life of Dialogue*. New York: Schocken Books, 1991.

Groethuysen, Bernhard. *Philosophische Anthropologie*. Munich: Oldenbourg, 1931.

———. "Toward a Philosophical Anthropology" (1936). In *Philosophy and History: The Ernst Cassirer Festschrift*, edited by Raymond Klibansky and H. J. Paton, 77–90. New York: Harper & Row, 1963.

Große Kracht, Klaus, "Europa im kleinen: Die Sommergespräche von Pontigny und die deutschfranzösische Intellektuellenverständigung in der Zwischenkriegszeit." *Internationales Archiv für Sozialgeschichte der deutschen Literatur* 27, no. 1 (2007): 144–69.

———. *Zwischen Berlin und Paris: Bernhard Groethuysen (1880–1946): Eine intellektuelle Biographie*. Berlin: De Gruyter, 2002.

Heidegger, Martin. *Sein und Zeit*. Tübingen: Max Niemeyer, 2001.

Herder, Johann Gottfried. *Herders Werke*. Edited by Heinrich Kurz. Leipzig: Verlag des Bibliographischen Instituts, n.d.

Humboldt, Wilhelm von. *Werke in fünf Bänden*. Edited by Andreas Flitner and Klaus Giel. Darmstadt: Wissenschaftliche Buchgesellschaft, 1960.

Husserl, Edmund. *Aufsätze und Vorträge 1922–1937*. Husserliana 27. Edited by Thomas Nenon and Hans Rainer Sepp. Dordrecht: Kluwer, 1989.

———. *Phenomenology and the Crisis of Philosophy*. Translated by Quentin Lauer. New York: Harper & Row, 1965.

Kant, Immanuel. *Werke in sechs Bänden*. Edited by Wilhelm Weischedel. Darmstadt: Wissenschaftliche Buchgesellschaft, 1963.

Landmann, Michael. *Jüdische Miniaturen*. Bonn: Bouvier, 1982.

———. *Philosophische Anthropologie: Menschliche Selbstdeutung in Geschichte und Gegenwart*. Berlin: De Gruyter, 1955.

Lorenz, Kuno. *Einführung in die philosophische Anthropologie*. Darmstadt: Wissenschaftliche Buchgesellschaft, 1990.

Löwith, Karl. *Das Individuum in der Rolle des Mitmenschen*. In *Sämtliche Schriften*, vol. 1, *Mensch und Menschenwelt*, edited by Klaus Stichweh. Stuttgart: Metzler, 1981.

Mann, Thomas. *Gesammelte Werke in zwölf Bänden*. Oldenburg: S. Fischer, 1960.

Mendes-Flohr, Paul. *Martin Buber: A Life of Faith and Dissent*. New Haven, CT: Yale University Press, 2019.

———. "Prophetic Politics and Meta-Sociology: Martin Buber and German Social Thought." *Archives de sciences sociales des religions* 60, no. 1 (1985): 67–82.

Mendes Flohr, Paul, and Bernhard Susser. "Alte und neue Gemeinschaft: An Unpublished Buber Manuscript." *AJS Review* 1 (1976): 41–56.

Plessner, Helmuth. *Die Stufen des Organischen und der Mensch: Einleitung in die philosophische Anthropologie*. Berlin: De Gruyter, 1928.

———. *Grenzen der Gemeinschaft: Eine Kritik des sozialen Radikalismus*. Frankfurt am Main: Suhrkamp, 2002.

Rome, Sidney, and Beatrice Rome, eds. *Philosophical Interrogations*. New York: Holt, Rinehart & Winston, 1964.

Rosenzweig, Franz. *The Star of Redemption*. Translated by William Hallo. New York: Holt, Rinehart & Winston, 1970.

Schaeder, Grete. *The Hebrew Humanism of Martin Buber*. Translated by Noah J. Jacobs. Detroit: Wayne State University Press, 1973.

Scheler, Max. *Abhandlungen und Aufsätze*. Leipzig: Verlag der Weissen Bücher, 1915.

———. *Gesammelte Werke*. Edited by Maria Scheler and Manfred Frings. Bern: Francke Verlag, 1976.

Schilpp, Paul Arthur, and Maurice Friedman, eds. *The Philosophy of Martin Buber*. LaSalle, IL: Open Court, 1967.

Stiewe, Barbara. *Der "Dritte Humanismus": Aspekte deutscher Griechen-Rezeption vom George-Kreis bis zum Nationalsozialismus*. Berlin: De Gruyter, 2011.

Susman, Margarete. *Das Buch Hiob und das Schicksal des jüdischen Volkes*. Frankfurt am Main: Jüdischer Verlag, 2018.

———. "In Memoriam Bernhard Groethuysen." *Zeitschrift für Religions- und Geistesgeschichte* 1, no. 1 (1948): 79–85.

Susser, Bernhard. *Existence and Utopia: The Social and Political Thought of Martin Buber*. Rutherford, NJ: Fairleigh Dickinson University Press, 1981.

Turner, Victor. *Dramas, Fields, and Metaphors*. Ithaca, NY: Cornell University Press, 1974.

3

"The Between": Martin Buber's Transformation of Consciousness

MICHAEL FISHBANE

When we open our eyes to the day, the world is already there as a presence, and I and you, separately and together, are amidst what comes to sight and mind. I am not the color or the tree or you, and yet we are related in this moment of feeling and experience: in this event of awareness. Our sense of these relations—sensing the color and the tree and the person nearby—only increases the mysteries of such relatedness and difference. What is between one thing and another as we perceive this relation and separation? Is the space between them a mere neutrality, as in some formal and abstract accounting; or does this intermediation change or vary as my personal distance changes? Is this "in-between" space just some construct, like correlations plotted on a grid, or does my lived relationship to this other have some ontological reality which varies in the course of my actualization or experience of it? As I move across the street to greet you, or take up an item that I am focused on, how might I understand what is between us and also modified by my physical approach toward it—including my emotional anticipation of the encounter? And what about the factor of temporality, which is modified in my human movement and mindfulness at different moments? Certainly, time and space are correlated as I move about in the world; and I sense the focus of consciousness in different ways as the gap between myself and another recedes or becomes tangible in a variety of ways. Here too we again wonder: What is between us, having both experiential and ethical valences? So much of our lives depends on these relations, and being alive to their various qualities.

The relations between friends and acquaintances also differ, and are affected by proximity and attention. What is between us on such occasions? And what is between me and some book or art object as I enter into a dynamic relationship with it—at one moment, or intermittently, over some duration?

And if, in a manner of speaking, a person uses a simile or metaphor, and I now imagine that this is like that in some way, what is between them in such constructed correlations? Do such acts of bridging and conjunction have ethical implications, or are they mere acts of the imagination—creative constructs with no further bearing on the world or how I live in it? We balk to think that nothing "more" is involved; but "what" is between these differences in unity? What kind of world do we inhabit as we live and think across these distinctions?

Something occurs between oneself and some other at such times; something conceptually ontological becomes concrete and actual in this here and now—and we want to know what it is. In our quandary, we may hope to learn from others—particularly those who have wrestled with these perplexities, and who regard this activity as an essential task of human wisdom. Martin Buber was such a person. In the following, we shall trace several stages in his thinking about "the between," most notably the transformation from thinking of this term as the terrifying abyss of Being that must be overcome through creative acts, to a special sphere marking the mystery of interpersonal human relations.

1

In the midst of the third of five "Dialogues on Realization," entitled *Daniel: Gespräche von der Verwirklichung* (published in 1913), Buber diagnosed a crisis of the contemporary European spirit and offered a solution rooted in the notion of authentic self-realization.[1] He was not unique in this quest, and his work repeatedly betrays the influence of Nietzsche, whose brooding meditations in *Thus Spoke Zarathustra* had an early impact. A similar temperament recurs in Rainer Maria Rilke's writing, at this same period and for years later.[2] No wonder that when their joint publisher, Insel Verlag, sent Rilke a copy of Buber's *Daniel*, Rilke responded with notable enthusiasm.[3]

How did Buber diagnose this crisis? He speaks of a shattering upheaval of consciousness, wherein every semblance of the coherence of things was ruptured: "I felt [says 'Daniel'] no connection [*Zusammenhang*]: but rather shriek, shriek, and in between [*dazwischen*] the abyss [*Abgrund*]." And again, in a more intense specification, the speaker adds: "The abyss was between piece and piece of the world, between thing and thing [*zwischen Ding und Ding*], between image and being, between the world and me." Indeed, this devastating rupture was also experienced in the depths of the self—splitting one "not into spirit and body [. . .] but in the thousandfold Protean doubleness of the bright One and the dark Other, with the eternal abyss in between [*mit dem ewigen Abgrund dazwischen*]." This sense of fracture signals the end of "security," the onset of a "discordant, disjointed life."[4]

In conjunction with this confession of radical alienation, the speaker refers to the ruptured *Zusammenhang des Seelenlebens* (interconnection of the spiritual life). Significantly, Buber's philosophical mentor, Wilhelm Dilthey, had promoted the term *Zusammenhang* to specify the primary "interconnection" that an individual experiences in relation to themselves and the world.[5] Buber's "Daniel" upends this harmony. With striking pathos, the speaker feels caught on the horns of multiple antinomies, without hope of resolution and bereft of any metaphysical ground. Here and everywhere is the primal *Abgrund*, the abyss that surges up and sunders any semblance of relations among the elements. It roils between "thing and thing"—the term "between" marking the gaps and emptiness of all disconnection. In this protean abyss, what promethean acts might counter total despair or nihilism, and create something out of chaos? Buber's dire answer: there is nothing that can eradicate this primal *Abgrund*; hence, one must resolve to repeatedly transform the elements through creative acts, since only in this way can one achieve any personal integration and self-realization (*Verwirklichung*). With courage and determination, one must descend into the "nameless polarity of all being, between piece and piece of the world, between thing and thing [*zwischen Ding und Ding*]"—a cleavage that even splits one's "inmost self." The supreme task: "to create unity out of your and all duality"; a "fulfilled unity out of tension and stream, such as will serve the polar earth—the realized countenance of God illuminated out of tension and stream." In an even more poignant challenge: one must acknowledge the terrifying *Abgrund*[6] and resolve to live with "holy insecurity" (*den heiligen Unsicherheit*).[7]

A variety of factors challenged Buber's commitment to this strong personal position, avowedly disconnected from the stream of ongoing social life. Among his companions, it was Gustav Landauer who had the greatest impact in urging Buber to turn from self-creativity and its enthusiasms toward social communities and issues of political justice—a veritable transvaluation of values.[8] This revision of orientation came to full expression in 1918, in the essay *Der heilige Weg* (The Holy Way), a work dedicated to his slain friend's memory. Herein, Buber came out decisively against the path of private intuition and intensity, and on behalf of the interpersonal realm as the sphere of truest realization. He stresses that although the Divine may come to life in an individual person, "it attains its earthly fullness only where individual beings open themselves to one another, [. . .] help one another; where immediacy is established between one human being and another [*zwischen den Wesen*]. [. . .] Where this takes place, where the eternal rises in the Between [*Dazwischen*], [. . .] that true place of realization [*Verwirklichung*] is community [*Gemeinschaft*], and true community is that relationship in which the

Divine comes to its realization between man and man [*zwischen den Menschen verwirklicht*]." Or, as he had just stated: God "must be realized between [all] the things [*zwischen den Dingen zu verwirklischen*]" of existence.⁹ The striking conceptual and verbal counterpoints to *Daniel* can hardly be missed. It is now *between* the multiple things or realities of existence where true realization occurs; and it is effectuated in the depth of life, with all its antinomies and contradictions. These are not to be overcome through some creative individuation or integration, but "lived through" in all their complexity. For it is precisely in the thickness of life, Buber stresses, that Judaism builds its home on earth; just here does it strive for the "realization of true community" and the "realization of the (religious) spirit" on earth.

Five years later, in 1923, following continuous thought and revision, Buber published his momentous *Ich und Du* (I and Thou), in which the notion of a "lived actuality" (*Wirklischem Leben*) becomes a repeated theme to specify the realization of personal relations. Significantly, these latter do not have their interconnection (*Zusammenhang*) in the realm of things or objects, but rather in the center (*Mitte*) where the lines of all true relations intersect: in the eternal Thou of God. Buber returns to this locution at the conclusion of his work, and he marks this sphere as one "between beings" (*zwischen den Wesen*) and "hidden in our midst [*Mitte*]—there between us [*im Dazwischen*]."¹⁰ What is conveyed or is meant by this realm, and what is its nature? A lifetime of reformulations and explications followed. Before we consider these ruminations, two phrases found in Buber's lectures entitled "Presence" (which precede *I and Thou* by two years) deserve some note.¹¹ Their like is unique among Buber's writings, and bear (I suggest) on the foregoing (puzzling) idioms in a suggestive manner.

2

In the course of various reflections on "the mystery of presence," Buber makes it clear that this is a primary experience of pure or absolute relation. It confronts the individual as an undifferentiated immediacy—not cognizable as such, and thus not known through the particulars of worldly awareness. Something happens—something is given—and the self may receive it in a total, undifferentiated way. This something cannot be named but is revealed to awareness as a total presence. Suddenly, reality addresses the self in the most immediate way. To characterize this presence, Buber now speaks of an "Absolute Thou." This term points to the absolute actuality of existence that confronts the self and lifts one beyond the facticity of subject-object differences. What surges from eternity, and sustains or conjoins these moments, is a feature of this "Thou" between them. Turning to a teaching from tradition that might mark this Absolute, Buber proposes that "this is no doubt what is meant by the saying that the *Shekhinah* is between the beings" (*zwischen den Wesen*).[12] Quoting from an ancient rabbinic logion, Buber glosses this experience by saying that when we face one another, and sense that something is held in common, we are gifted with the eternal all-present revelation of God in the here and now. In the language of ancient rabbinic tradition, this is the reality of the "Divine presence *beineihem*"[13]—"between" these conjoined realities. One may feel that perhaps Buber's use of this figure goes too far, and that by invoking a *theologoumenon* that names the phenomenon of presence, he veers a bit toward an objectification of the mystery. And yet, remarkable to say, in a draft of the lectures from 1918, Buber himself nominated "The Between as an Hypostatization of the *Relation*."[14]

A second passage offers another consideration of the mystery of Thou that may surge into consciousness. Each such moment is a revelatory breakthrough, in human terms, and each one varies by what it helps bring to conscious expression in art and religion. No form or formulation is fixed, and each breakthrough differs in terms of appearance and shape—not to mention the human experience itself. What abides or sustains the multiple moments of presence? Trying to give expression to this issue, while avoiding any hint of a substantive reality, Buber remarks that each gap between moments of manifestation is like a "holding of breath: [like] the silence between [*zwischen*] word and word, between revelation [and revelation], between forceful revelation and forceful revelation." In this context the "between" is the eternal mystery, an ineffable manifestation of the eternal Thou. "We stand and remain in the mystery. [...] We stand to it in community. We stand to it in its reciprocity [*Gegenseitigkeit*]. We stand in its presence [*Gegenwart*]."[15] This *Zwischen* is therefore not the *Abgrund*, but something like the pulse of presence—binding the moments of manifestation: like a covenant between the parts, in which the ultimate mystery (*Geheimnis*) hides in plain sight. The eternal Thou (in these lectures) is thus deemed both manifest and concealed: one simultaneous truth. The seeker strives to live this reality—to be a participant in its ever-new actuality. By contrast, the philosopher seeks words of specification, so that the lived event can be thought and somehow held in mind.

3

Buber's transformation of consciousness is thus a shift from a conception of the world "as idea and representation," to be engaged by the super creative ego for its self-centered individuation, to the interpersonal realm of our lived reality. How can we understand this move? It is, I suggest, not so much marked by the hyphen that conjoins "I-Thou," or by the conjunction that bridges "I and Thou," as by the interactive preposition "with" (*mit*). The "between" is the interactive dynamism of "with" (as in "being with," "living with," or "speaking with")—across the difference of persons. Language is such an expressive medium, and so is an engaged silence or the meeting of eyes. These moments are the activation of presence: a dialogical confirmation of shared sociality. Persons evoke this ontic realm. It only exists, as such, amidst the concrete particularities of human relations—when one person turns to another, with the requisite focus and intention of the soul. "Only the being whose otherness, accepted by my being, lives and faces me in the whole compression of existence, brings the radiance of eternity to me. Only when two say to one another with all that they are, 'It is *Thou*' [*Du bist es!*], is the indwelling of the Present Being between [*zwischen*] them."[16] The phrases used are evocative; for in this influential 1929 essay *Zwiesprache* (Dialogue), Buber underscores his discussion with a near-literal reference to his earlier, pivotal work *Der heilige Weg*—composed a decade earlier in memory of Gustav Landauer. Not for nothing does this paragraph precede the section entitled "Gemeinschaft" and its discussion of a true community—where people are "no longer side by side but *with* one another of a multitude of persons." Significantly, the key terms in this confusing formulation are *Beieinandersein* and *mitsammen sich*—both of which express the relationality of being "with" another in community. The stylistic redundancy has a striking rhetorical effect upon the reader.

It would take another decade for Buber to return to the phenomenon of "the between" and the meaning of dialogue in interhuman relations. Many topics only adumbrated earlier, and others needing philosophical clarity, were explicated and set upon a firmer foundation. If the melodic language of *I and Thou* was replaced with a more prosaic (and sometimes ponderous) syntax, the urgency and directness of Buber's voice remains. The leitmotiv of authentic personhood and the centrality of communication reverberate, calling upon the reader to attend and respond.

Pondering the nature of the person, through a series of possibilities discussed by thinkers over the millennia, Buber turns directly, near the end of the book *Das Problem des Menschen* (*Was ist der Mensch?*, published in 1948, and based on his Jerusalem lectures from 1938), to his major concern: not to the essence of man, but "to the reality of the relation *between* man and man."[17] Making his key point even more decisively, Buber stresses that the individual is "a fact of existence" insofar as he steps into a "living relation" with others, just there where "something takes place between one being and another [*zwischen Wesen und Wesen*]" which never occurs in nature. It is something established through the existence of individuals, this being "the sphere of the between [*die Sphäre des Zwischen*]," and he goes on to assert that this sphere is a "primary category [*Urkategorie*]" of human reality (*Wirklichkeit*). This bold formulation is a *novum* for Buber. Now we are clearly told that "the between" is something unique: a distinct category whose grounding is repeatedly constituted as a "fact between [*faktisch zwischen*]" people. Hence, it is a "real place" between them, and not to be found either in one person or in another. This reality is ontological and not reducible to the ontic facticity of any one person in a relationship—precisely because this reality is "between" the partners joined in dialogue (accordingly, the various modes of interpersonal communication, whether it be language or a silent gesture, are only signs of this happening). The between is therefore a realm that comes to pass in its own unique dimension: "[o]n the far side of the subjective, on this side of the objective, on the narrow ridge, where *I* and *Thou* meet."

Or do they? How can we comprehend this formulation? If the "dialogical situation can only be grasped in an ontological way"—and not on the basis of the "ontic of personal existence"—in what sense do the partners meet and cognize one another? If the truth is between persons, isn't its authenticity somehow in the lived differences or mutuality of communication? Indeed, if the Thou (as Buber himself stresses) is only a noumenal presence (and not a reality in the phenomenal world), does authentic dialogue falter as an unbridgeable *aporia*? Or must we nevertheless admit that we do experience such connections as a real presence? Indeed, serious philosophers have argued that such a sensed, interactive presence among persons gives good reason to say that "the between" is something more than a hypothetical construct one must posit in order to ground authentic communication.[18] Somehow, "the between" is a reality that constitutes our lifeworld[19]—and we stand within this ontological mystery. Considering this complexity led Buber to assert that the "eternal Thou" is the ever-present, ungraspable foundation of presence; and that the upsurge of "the between" becomes an ontic human experience of the reality of God. Or perhaps, better put, such moments are but a fleeting "glimpse" (a *Durchblick*) *to* God.[20]

4

Admittedly, Buber does not directly tackle these problems; but his ongoing writing reveals his great desire to expand his formulations and so move into new philosophical territory. The essay "Elements of the Interhuman" ("Elemente des Zwischenmenschlichen"), published in 1954, is exemplary of a new phenomenology of the dialogical situation and the topic of "the between."[21]

The first term (*Elemente*) marks some distinctive features that characterize the ontological dimension of the second (*Zwischenmenschlichen*). This raises a complexity similar to the one noted above; namely, that the concrete actualities (or persons) of an authentic dialogue can neither be thought nor objectified—for if I do so, and somehow concretize or conceptualize my dialogical intention, the other would not be a "Thou" but an "It," and there would also be no pure event or presence. What then is the actuality of "the between"? It would be paradoxically (and ontologically) absurd to say that "it" was "something" and that it joins two distinct "thous," neither of whom could be even abstractly substantivized. These considerations presumably galvanized Buber to some notable formulations.

The first expression to be noted is that the interhuman realm is now called a "special dimension" (*Sonderdimension*) of human existence, an actual "happening" (*Ereignisse*) whose "mystery of contact" (*Geheimnis des Kontakts*) is the true core of interpersonal relations (*Wirklichkeit des Zwischenmenschlichen*)—and that what unfolds in the "living interplay" of the participants in a dialogue is the "between [*zwischen*] which they live together." All modalities of objectification sunder the potential bond between persons. For Buber, it is only in "partnership" that one can become an "existing whole"; it is only in a nonobjectifying relationship (whereby one can paradoxically intend to engage in a specific relationship without thinking the other as an "other") that an authentic interpersonal reality may be activated and unfold. True dialogue is where one person enters into an "elementary connection with" another. This mode of turning toward other creatures is what Buber calls a "personal making present" (*Vergegenwärtigung*)—which he means as the intention to help realize the other person in all their creaturely uniqueness. I would further suggest that such a "turning toward" the other is a modality of the dative. The lived syntax of the dative is thus a wholehearted intention "toward" a relationship. For Buber, this is a primordial feature of our human nature. It also suggests that this "turning toward" another (the dative element) is also a primary element for an authentic meeting with others. Indeed, this intentional movement is the onset of the ontological sphere that is unique to human beings. In Buber's terms, this is called an *Einschwingen ins Andere*—a "bold swinging" into the life of the "other"; an "imagining" the particular "real" of the other person, a bold readiness to "expose" oneself fully to the "common situation" between them. If and when "mutuality" (*Gegenseitigkeit*) stirs, genuine dialogue may also blossom.

Making oneself wholly present to another person, through the requisite trait or attitude, constitutes a fundamental spiritual disposition of the soul, so necessary for authentic dialogue (Buber calls these *Seelungverfassungen*). They are similar to Kant's ethical prescription that one must never treat another as a means but as an "independent end [*selbständiger Zweck*]" only. This includes the requirement that one "means [*meine*] and makes present" the other in their personal being, precisely in the way that is peculiar and possible for them. Herewith we return to the basic intentionality of the other's possibility, mentioned earlier—an intentionality bent on a confirmation of the other's independent being, not on any specific content. By his use of the term *Meinung* Buber differs appreciably from the conceptual notion of intention as used by Husserl.[22] Here, it seems, "to mean" has the sense of "intending" the reality of a person and their situation. This is not the perception or representation of some object in consciousness, but the making another person an "actual real"—both to themselves and to oneself. It is "to exercise that degree of making [oneself] present" to another person at a shared "moment." The result is an "elemental togetherness [*elementaren Mitsammenseins*]"—and, insofar as the other person is confirmed in their being, this mode of relationship has an ethical accent, if not character. It must be stressed that this confirmation of another person does not mean any "approval" of the other person or the given event. Integrity requires that nothing be held back between the partners. In this context, intention changes into the positivity of the particular. One must "be intent [*bedacht sein*]" to "raise into an inner word" that which will only later be spoken. Such an intention is a true bending of one's mind toward the other in the specificity and demands of an authentic dialogue. It is an expression of "the ontology of the interpersonal" (*die Ontologie des Zwischenmenschlichen*) in all its mystery.

5

It must be emphasized that the sphere of "Dialogue" (*Gespräch*) is not the factual occurrence of this word or another, drawn from the historical thesaurus that may be available to a historical speaker at a given time and place. It is rather the more elementary reality of *Gesprochenheit* or "spokenness." *Gesprochenheit* is that which occurs in the lived "between," where one person turns toward another from a primary "will to communicate." This point is made in Buber's late but significant 1960 essay "The Word That Is Spoken" (*Das Wort, was gesprochen wird*).[23] The German formulation makes the primary point: there are many words that occur in language, but it is only a word that expresses the will toward relationship that is of ontological import. When such a vital word emerges, "communalizing" our verbal formulations, that human being becomes a person. Indeed, it is the very "striving toward language [*Sprachstrebigkeit*]" whereby one may reach beyond monologue and one's own private inwardness toward the world to confirm the shared reality of their creaturely being. For Buber, it is the will to communicate that generates the ontological sphere of "the between" and points to a concern to build a common lifeworld and resolve the ambiguities and multiple meanings (*Mehrdeutigkeit*) that complicate relationships. Deeper than the specific meanings of words, then, is the address *to* (the dative again) another person, "whom the speaker *means* as such." "[T]o mean a man [*einen Menschen meinen*] means nothing less than to stand by him and his insight with the element of the soul [*Seelenelement*] that can be sent forth." When this occurs, we may stand in the "between" of genuine interrelations. To repeat: whatever individuals are in their private inwardness, it is precisely here, in the profundity of their mutual *Gesprochenheit*, that they can be fundamentally confirmed as persons. Let it then be said: the narrow ridge stirs toward actuality when one person swings *toward* another, *intending* their lived reality to the extent possible. The two are no longer separated as subject here and object there, but are connected by the Divine dwelling in their midst. When a person intends another as a "thou," the "eternal Thou" dwells between them.

A Concluding Postscript

Over his long lifetime, Buber narrated the "Tales of the Hasidim," seeking to exemplify modes of sacramental existence in both word and deed. Indeed, Buber's interest was sustained for over thirty years, beginning with narratives and teachings of individual figures, such as the *Tales of Rabbi Nachman* (*Die Geschichten des Rabbi Nachman*) in 1906,[24] and culminating in the massive collection of narratives of eighteenth- and nineteenth-century holy teachers.[25] There is no reason to suppose that Buber's modern temperament identified with all this material; but there is ample evidence to assert that his editing and stylization of the texts were often in accord with his aesthetic taste and dialogical philosophy. A striking instance of the latter serves as a final postscript to the preceding discussion.

In 1922, Buber published a book on the great disciple of the Ba'al Shem Tov known as the Maggid of Mezritch—a charismatic preacher whose teachings cover a range of theosophical topics set within a radical spiritualized panentheism.[26] The original edition offered only selected teachings of this master, along with those of several of his followers.[27] This selection was considerably expanded in the magnum opus of the legends. It is here that a particular term stands out. That term is *Dazwischen*. What does it mean in this context? Basing himself quite literally on an oral report of one of the Maggid's sermons,[28] we are informed of a certain theosophical issue; namely, that "[n]othing [(k)ein Ding] in the world can change from one reality [Wirklichkeit] to another, unless it first come to the state of Nothing [Nichts]"—which is the supernal reality that preceded the creation, utterly beyond all human comprehension.[29] Thus this reality has a transcendental ontological character, one that is often designated (as in the Hebrew original) as ayin. To further characterize this transitional state, the Hasidic report utilizes the Talmudic term beinei beinei to designate an intermediate stage "betwixt" or "between."[30] But Buber imports his own philosophic conception here, and he translates this unique intervening sphere as Dazwischen—clearly suggesting something far more ontologically recognizable and, if not entirely beyond human grasp, something that can at least be referred to as "there" (Da)—this being a marker that only makes sense for a reality in the human (not theosophical) realm. With one stroke, a supernal domain is domesticated and brought down to earth. Admittedly, we are not dealing with some interpersonal or relational reality but with something that marks an organic shift in existence (the purported difference between a seed and its fruit being one of the Maggid's several examples). All this notwithstanding, Buber's choice of terminology is significant. The long path from the abysmal Dazwischen in Daniel to its more positive usage in the Tales reverberates to the attentive ear.

Notes

1. M. Buber, Daniel: Gespräche von der Verwirklichung (Leipzig: Insel-Verlag, 1913). Translated as Daniel: Dialogues on Realization, by M. Friedman (New York: McGraw-Hill, 1965). In the references below, the German text is cited first.

2. See E. Heller, The Disinherited Mind (Harmondsworth: Penguin Books, 1961), 109–55, the chapter "Rilke and Nietzsche, with a Discourse of Thought, Belief, and Poetry."

3. Cf. R. M. Rilke, Briefe auf seine Verleger (Leipzig: Insel, 1934), 180, 182.

4. Buber, Daniel, 64, 65 (English, 86).

5. See W. Dilthey, Gesammelte Schriften, vol. 6, Die Geistige Welt: Einleitung in die Philosophie des Lebens, ed. G. Misch, 3rd ed. (Stuttgart: B. Tuebner, 1958), 144; and the discussion in R. Makkreel, Dilthey: Philosopher of the Human Studies (Princeton, NJ: Princeton University Press, 1975), 98–100.

6. Remarkable to say, this notion first appears in Buber's early (1908) work on the Baal Shem, where he also says that "all things" were "in the Abyss" and that "the Abyss [Abgrund] was between one thing and another [zwischen jedem Ding und dem andern]," and only by virtue of the holy helper (the Baal Shem) were things joined and healed. See Die Legende des Baalschem (Frankfurt am Main: Rütten & Loening, 1920), 67–68.

7. See Buber, Daniel, 83–84 (English, 98–99).

8. For a nuanced examination of both Landauer's early intimacy with Buber's Daniel, and his later repulsion at the moral blindness that mystic enthusiasms (like Buber's) could lead to,

see P. Mendes-Flohr, *Martin Buber: A Life of Faith and Dissent* (New Haven, CT: Yale University Press, 2019), 73–74, 100–108.

9. See M. Buber, *Der heilige Weg* (Frankfurt am Main: Rütten & Loening, 1920), 15–16.

10. M. Buber, *Ich und Du* (Leipzig: Insel-Verlag, 1923). English renditions are adapted from the R. G. Smith (London: Kegan Paul, 1937) and W. Kaufman (New York: Charles Scribner's Sons, 1970) translations; 116, 137–38.

11. See R. Horowitz, *Buber's Way to "I and Thou": The Development of Martin Buber's Thought and His "Religion as Presence" Lectures* (Philadelphia: Jewish Publication Society, 1988). This book was originally published as *Religion als Gegenwart* (Heidelberg: Lambert Schneider, 1978). German citations are from the latter publication.

12. Buber, *Ich und Du*, 144.

13. *Mishnah Avot* 3.2.

14. Horowitz, *Buber's Way*, 135. German: *Das Dazwischen als Hypostasierung der Beziehung* (in facsimile).

15. Cf. German edition, 152.

16. See the rendition in Buber's *Between Man and Man* (London: Routledge & Kegan Paul, 1947), 30.

17. *Das Problem des Menschen* (Heidelberg: Lambert Schneider, 1948) was translated as the unit "What Is Man?" a year earlier in *Between Man and Man*, 118–205. The quotation appears in the English-language foreword. The concluding *Ausblick* (Prospect) appears in the German edition on 164–69.

18. See J. Habermas, *A Philosophy of Dialogue, Proceedings of the Israel Academy of Sciences and the Humanities* 8, no. 6 (2013): 114.

19. Cf. M. Theunissen, *The Other: Studies in the Social Ontology of Husserl, Heidegger, Sartre, and Buber* (Cambridge, MA: MIT Press, 1984), 291.

20. See J. Bloch, *Die Apriori des Du: Probleme der Dialogik Martin Bubers* (Heidelberg: Lambert Schneider, 1977), 80–86.

21. Originally in *Merkur* 7, no. 2 (1954): 112–27, and in *Neue Schweizer Rundschau* 21, no. 10 (1954): 593–608; then in *Das dialogische Prinzip* (Heidelberg: Lambert Schneider, 1962), 269–98 and *The Knowledge of Man* (London: George Allen & Unwin, 1965), chap. 3, 72–88.

22. Cf. K. Shurtz, "Husserl and Meaning," *Aporia* 1, no. 1 (1991), 43–51.

23. This essay was first printed in *Worte und Wirklichkeit*, Sechste des Jahrbuch Gestalt und Gedanke, edited by the Bayerischen Akademie der Schönen Künste (Munich: R. Oldenberg, 1960), 15–31; and later in *Logos. Zwei Reden* (Heidelberg: Lambert Schneider, 1962), 7–29, and in *The Knowledge of Man*, 109–20. A close associate of Buber suggested that he wrote this essay in response to Heidegger's lecture "Der Weg zur Sprache" and its central motif that *die Sprache zur Sprache bringen*. For Buber, it is not language itself that speaks but human beings. On this point, see W. Kraft, "Martin Buber über Sprache und deutsche Sprache," *Hochland. Zeitschrift für alle Gebiete des Wissens und den Schönen Künste* 60, no. 6 (1968): 525.

24. See the revised German edition of *Die Geschichten des Rabbi Nachman* (Heidelberg: Lambert Schneider, 1988).

25. These narratives were based on earlier sources, with others added during the war years of 1938 and 1946.

26. The Maggid (or Preacher) of Mezritch was the cognomen of R. Dov Ber Friedman (1704–71), a Hasidic master of great influence.

27. It was entitled *Der grosse Maggid und seine Nachfolge* (Frankfurt am Main: Rütten & Loening, 1922).

28. See the tract *Yosher Divrei Emet* in the collection *Liqqutim Yeqarim* (Jerusalem: Ma'arekhet Divrei Emunah, 2004), 116b–117a (no. 13).

29. See *Der Erzählung der Chassidim, Martin Buber Werkausgabe, Chassidismus* 3, 18, no. 1 (Gütersloh: Gütersloher Verlagshaus, 2015), 254–55. The original edition appeared in 1949.

30. This is also the terminology found in the earlier Hebrew edition. Cf. *Or Ha-Ganuz: Sippurei Ḥasidim* (Tel Aviv: Schocken Books, 1946), 110–11.

Annotated Bibliography

PRIMARY SOURCES

Buber's focus and emphasis on the between (*das Zwischen*) varied over time. Nowhere does he purport to provide a systematic exposition of the concept. His various considerations are embedded within long and short elaborations of his philosophy of dialogue, as these pertain to the notion of what is the "reality" that comes to "realization" between persons engaged in a "real" or "authentic meeting." The following are the most accessible compositions in English.

In his major address of 1918, entitled "The Holy Way: A Word to the Jews and to the Nations," translated and published in *On Judaism*, edited by N. Glatzer (New York: Schocken Books, 1967), Buber shows a shift in his hitherto highly subjectivist and personal thought toward the importance of interpersonal relations and community. He stresses that "immediacy is established between one human being and another," and that "the eternal rises in the Between" (see 109–10). Buber continued this concern in *I and Thou* and concluded his classical work with an emphasis on "the sphere that lies *between beings*" (2nd edition, translated by Ronald Gregor Smith [New York: Charles Scribner's Sons, 1958]), 120.

Similarly, in his essay "Dialogue" (originally a lecture delivered in 1929), Buber stressed the following point just prior to his discussion "Community": "Only when two say to one another with all that they are, 'It is Thou,' is the indwelling of the Present Being between them" (*Between Man and Man* [New York: Macmillan, 1948], 30). And finally, in his seminal essay "Elements of the Interhuman," Buber further deepens his discussion of dialogue and stresses that when "the word arises in a substantial way between men who have been seized in their depths," there is opened up between them "an essential togetherness" (*The Knowledge of Man*, edited by M. Friedman [London: George Allen & Unwin, 1965], chapter 3, and especially 72–88).

SECONDARY LITERATURE

The major analytic discussion (originally published in German in 1977) is that of M. Theunissen, *The Other: Studies in the Social Ontology of Husserl, Heidegger, Sartre, and Buber* (Cambridge, MA: MIT Press, 1986). In part 3, chapter 7, he discusses "The Ontology of the 'Between.'" This is a philosophical presentation much indebted to the transcendental method of German philosophy. The major emphasis is to present Buber's thinking in the context of social philosophy and the "ontological structure of interpersonal life." It is claimed that Buber's discussion erred by introducing the Transcendent as embodied in the Thou. This analysis has been criticized by J. Bloch in *Die Aporie des Du: Probleme der Dialogik Martin Bubers* (Heidelberg: Lambert Schneider, 1977), 15–34, who rightly and profoundly emphasizes that for Buber the "Thou" is neither an embodiment of God nor is in any way transcendent to the world—but a mystery deeply entwined in our this-worldly existence.

My discussion continues Bloch's line of thinking but in an independent manner. It is vital to bear in mind that Buber was loathe to substantialize the mystery of the Divine Reality or its earthly manifestations. His discussion of "the between" walks a narrow ridge of presentation and formulation and can easily be misconstrued by any attempt to conceptualize the dynamic mystery of its occurrence. To sharpen the point: the between is real but it is not experienced as such; rather, it is lived.

4

Imaging the Imageless, Making Present, and Coming to Light of the Other: Imagination and Buber's Dialogical Thinking

ELLIOT R. WOLFSON

Many scholars and thinkers have explored the conceptual nuances and historical repercussions of Martin Buber's philosophy of dialogue. In this chapter, I will focus on the role of imagination as it pertains to the fundamental claim of Buber's dialogical principle (*dialogische Prinzip*) that the relationship (*Beziehung*) characteristic of the I-Thou encounter (*Begegnung*) must be predicated on upholding the irreducible otherness of the other, or, as he put it in the essay "Distance and Relation" (1950), human life is constructed on the basis of a twofold movement, the "primal setting as a distance" and the "entering into relation." The first movement is the presupposition of the second movement inasmuch as "one can enter into relation only with being which has been set at a distance, more precisely, has become an independent opposite."[1] The only purpose of the relationship is the relationship through which the person—as opposed to the Ego (*Eigenwesen*)[2] of the I-It experience—appears by entering into relation with other persons, touching the Thou (*die Berührung des Du*), who is neither merely a part of oneself nor merely outside of oneself. The tactile sense is invoked to serve as the criterion of standing in a relation that facilitates participating in an actuality (*Wirklichkeit*), an activity in which the I participates but cannot appropriate.[3]

Notably, an assault on this sense of alterity can be elicited from Buber's early work *Ecstatic Confessions* (1905), where the ecstatic experience is described as a unitive consciousness that is not relative or limited by the other; it is a state of absolute and limitless solitude, the unsayable abyss that cannot be fathomed, the unity of the I and the world. Influenced in particular by the mystical piety of Meister Eckhart, Buber maintained that by stripping itself of all images, concepts, and words, the soul becomes one with the Godhead beyond its capacity to imagine, know, or describe. To be incorporated into the naked divinity, one must be naked, which is to say, one must abandon the kataphatic images engendered by the analogical imagination.[4] Prima facie, it would seem that Buber's understanding of mystical ecstasy is one in which the imagination is categorically rejected as a barrier to the direct experience, the discarding of the mask to behold the face, the seeing of the denuded truth.[5] I would contend, however, that even for Eckhart the uncovering of the mystery is brought to fruition by discerning that the mystical-pietistic recommendation to perceive the Godhead without images by becoming imageless is still configured imagistically as something, the "isness" (*isticheit/istikeit*),[6] or "beingness" (*weselicheit*),[7] both terms rendered in the modern German translation as *Seinsheit*,[8] which binds together the "I" of the subject and the "He" of the object.[9] In the manner that Eckhart appropriated Aquinas's expression "negation of negation" (*negatio negationis*) to name the fullest affirmation of God's all-encompassing oneness, outside of which there is nothing and in virtue of which we can speak of the abundance of the Godhead wherein all creatures are contained,[10] a similar gesticulation of a twofold negation is necessary to fortify the experiential possibility of the soul being assimilated into the pure and transcendent being of the nameless nothingness (*vngenanten nitheit*),[11] the nothing that is not (*nihtes niht*),[12] the mode of beyond being (*über wesene*) that is nonbeing (*unwesene*) before there was being.[13] And yet, just as darkness is not the privation of light but rather a deeper inflection of its resplendence, so the intermingling of the apophatic and the kataphatic discloses the paradoxical truism that nothing is not nothing but decidedly something.[14] As Eckhart expressed the matter in one sermon, in his uncreatedness (*ungeschaffenheit*), God upholds the nothingness (*nihtes niht*) of the soul and preserves it in his somethingness (*ihtes ihte*).[15] After the soul negates itself by plunging into utter nothingness, God sustains it in his utter somethingness. The radical repudiation of self is succeeded, therefore, by the reaffirmation of the soul restored to the superessential nothingness (*vberwesende nitheit*),[16] the abyss of his Godhead and the plenitude of his being and his nature (*den abgrunt sîner gotheit und die vüllede sînes wesens und sîner natûre*).[17]

The polysemous and dissembling nature of truth is such that when one lifts the veil on the inessential essence that is the nonmanifest vacuity of all things manifest, one does not uncover truth unveiled but rather another veil reveiling the imperceptible reality, or perhaps more accurately, what is reveiled is that there is no such reality but only the veil of the veil. The face that is covered and simultaneously exposed by the mask is itself nothing but a mask of the face that covers and exposes the face of the mask. The same dialetheic paradox can be ascribed to Buber's understanding of the role of the imagination as vacillating between speaking-not and not speaking. Imagining the unimaginable, therefore, is on a par with the apprehension of ecstatic speech as a form of silence, the apophatic gesture of saying the unsayable.[18] Tellingly, in *I and Thou* (1923), Buber retained the epistemological critique of the imaginative faculty but then turns the argument on its head by insisting that forsaking the imagination is the way to access the alterity of another human or of the eternal Thou. Near the beginning of the book, Buber stipulates that the realm of It, as opposed to the realm of Thou, is characterized by the I perceiving, feeling, imagining, wanting, sensing, and thinking something. The original German translated as "I imagine something" is *Ich stelle etwas vor*, which can be rendered as "I present something." It is reasonable to surmise that Buber deployed this expression to accentuate that in the domain of the It-World (*Es-Welt*) the imagination is prone to "thingify" the data of experience. This is exactly what must be denied with respect to the unmediated relation that is proper to the Thou-World (*Duwelt*), wherein no conceptuality (*Begrifflichkeit*), no foreknowledge (*Vorwissen*), and no imagination (*Phantasie*) can intervene between I and Thou. The experience of presenting something as object (*Gegenstand*) gives way to the disclosure of presence (*Gegenwart*) both in the intersubjective sphere and in relation to the primal ground identified as God, a process that Buber called "making present" (*Vergegenwärtigung*).[19]

In "Distance and Relation," Buber expanded on the ontological significance of the expression *Vergegenwärtigung* by linking it more overtly to the event of imagining the real (*Realphantasie*), which he glosses as "the capacity to hold before one's soul a reality arising at this moment but not able to be directly experienced."[20] The aesthetic underpinning of the capacity to imagine the real can be culled from the essay "From Religion as Presence" (1922), where Buber had already characterized the work of the artist as addressing the Thou in an exclusivity that is comparable to the relationship one has to a beloved person, an inimitability that eliminates everything experienceable. From the perspective of the It-World, the artist's inspiration is classified under the rubric of mediated experience, and thus it is categorized as a work of fiction confabulated in the imagination, but from the perspective of the Thou-World, the artistic moment as the immediate and unconditional uncovering of presence thoroughly defies the taxonomic parameters of experience.[21] Although in *I and Thou* Buber used different terminology, he alludes to this phenomenon when he remarked that the "eternal origin of art" is that "a human being confronts a form [*Gestalt*] that wants to become a work through him. [...] The form that confronts me I cannot experience [*erfahren*] nor describe [*beschreiben*]; I can only actualize it. [...] Not as a thing among the 'internal' things, not as a figment [*Gebild*] of the 'imagination' [*Einbildung*], but what is present [*Gegenwärtige*]."[22] The aesthetic imagination is not tethered to an object or to a fabrication of the soul; it is rather the demand on the soul's creative power to bring the work into being so that the form appears. What cannot be directly experienced is what is brought to light in the epiphanic moment of the encounter, that is, the present in which presence comes to presentness without the possibility of reification or representation. In this moment, which is unbound to the temporal flux and thus can serve as the prismatic portal wherein the invisible and the eternal are manifest,[23] all means have been disintegrated so that the particularity (*Einzelung*) that demarcates the contours of our experience, even of memory, gives way to a sense of wholeness (*Ganzheit*).[24] To be aware of the other person is to perceive the wholeness determined by the spirit, that is, to perceive the dynamic center that stamps the uniqueness of that person in terms of utterance, action, and attitude. This awareness is what Buber designated as "personal making present."[25]

The nexus between the present, presence, and relation to the other undergirds Buber's account of the temporal comportment of the moment of encounter:

> The present [*Gegenwart*]—not that which is like a point and merely designates whatever our thoughts may posit as the end of "elapsed" time, the fiction of the fixed lapse, but the actual and fulfilled present—exists only insofar as presentness [*Gegenwärtigkeit*], encounter [*Begegnung*], and relation [*Beziehung*] exist. Only as the You becomes present does presence come into being. [. . .] Presence is not what is evanescent and passes but what confronts us, waiting and enduring. [. . .] What is essential is lived in the present, objects in the past.[26]

Making present, or imaging the real, consists of this ability to dwell in the present moment wherein the presentness of the presence shows itself, albeit as that which resists presentification as an object, or, to translate Buber's insight into a more contemporary phenomenological idiom, we could say that the givenness of the present presupposes that the given is given as the ungiven barred from being given. Consider Buber's depiction of the artist's perception of nature in "Man and His Image-Work" (1955): "Vision is figurating faithfulness to the unknown and does its work in co-operation with it. It is faithfulness not to the appearance, but to being—to the inaccessible with which we associate." This act of figuration, as Buber explains in an accompanying note, means to make "the figure fully manifest," but as he readily admits, faithfulness to the being as opposed to the appearance or that figure must safeguard its unknowability, the "unfathomable darkness" of being that has intercourse with the being of the artist. Insofar as Buber avers that all visibility is directed toward figuration, it is reasonable to conclude that human perception more generally, in emulation of the work of the artist who forms an image of what stands over and against him in the world rather than objectifying it or trying to penetrate its underlying mystery or spirit,[27] is inescapably ensnared in the paradox of the showing of what cannot show itself except by not showing.[28]

When applied to the intercourse between humans, imaging the real means "that I imagine to myself what another man is at this very moment wishing, feeling, perceiving, thinking, and not as a detached content but in his very reality, that is, as a living process in this man."[29] The dialogical potential underscores Buber's prescient and crucial remark in "Zionism and Nationalism," an address to the Sixteenth Zionist Congress held in Zurich delivered on August 1, 1929, that "while self-assertion is a natural precondition of all our actions, it is not enough. It also requires imagination, the ability to imagine the soul of the other—of the stranger—from within the realities of our own."[30] This idea is already well attested in *I and Thou*. Thus, in his celebrated account in that treatise of an encounter with the tree as a Thou, Buber wrote that "there is no impression [*Eindruck*], no play of my imagination [*kein Spiel meiner Vorstellung*], no aspect of a mood [*Stimmungswert*]."[31] Concerning the tree—emblematic of every potential Thou—Buber wrote "it confronts me bodily" (*Er leibt mir gegenüber*), a turn of phrase that conveys the act of facing the other as a lived revelatory presence. The imagination is a hindrance to the encounter to the extent that it pulls one into the It experience.

With respect to the eternal Thou, the objectification of presence runs the risk of theistic belief lapsing into idolatry. As I have argued elsewhere,[32] the danger of the role of imagination in religious faith and the need to picture God anthropomorphically and anthropopathically appears to underlie the admonition in *I and Thou* that revelation as the encounter with God (*Gottesbegegnung*) is a calling that demands actualization (*Verwirklichung*) in the world, but most people tend to turn their attention and bend back to the revealer (*Rückbiegung auf den Offenbarenden*). This leads Buber to the astoundingly keen and still pertinent observation: "Even as the egomaniac [*ichsüchtige Mensch*] does not live anything directly, whether it be a perception or an affection, but reflects on his perceiving or affectionate I and thus misses the truth of the process, thus the theomaniac [*gottsüchtige Mensch*] [. . .] will not let the gift take full effect but reflects instead on that which gives, and misses both."[33] Just as the egomaniac's infatuation with ego prompts him or her to misconstrue the truth of the process of perception or affection, so the theomaniac is so obsessed with the deity that he or she fails to grasp the nature of either the giver or the gift.

To imagine the real would require that one divest oneself of egoity on the psychological plane and of divinity on the theological plane. Although Buber readily acknowledged that the absorption of self, which is essential to the religious act, involves imagining God, he was also mindful that there is a kind of lonesomeness (*Einsamkeit*) that entails the "real fall of the spirit into spirituality" (*der eigentliche Abfall des Geistes zur Geistigkeit*), an abysmal state "when self-deception reaches the point where one thinks that one has God within and speaks to him." This is a remarkably bold statement that challenges a fundamental tenet of scriptural monotheism and many of its subsequent iterations and embellishments. Our nature might force us to draw the absolute presence of the eternal and nonspatial Thou into modes of discourse befitting the It-World, which coheres in space and time. The "sublime melancholy of our lot" is such that every Thou invariably is covered by "the crust of thinghood" and thus disappears "into the chrysalis of the It."[34] However, the eternal Thou embodies the unconditional exclusiveness and unconditional inclusiveness that defy the imagination's anthropocentric proclivity to personify transcendence. To be sure, Buber did transpose the traditional idea of the divine presence in the world by valorizing the ethical mandate of the human to make God present, an idea that resonates with his conception of the realization (*Verwirklichung*) of the unity of God either through the experience (*Erlebnis*) of the individual (in the postmystical phase of his thinking) or through the community (*Gemeinschaft*) between human beings (in the dialogical phase).[35] Notwithstanding the primacy accorded this task in Buber's thinking, it did not blind him to the dangers of the theopoetic imagination and its tendency to specularize the divine through an anthropomorphic-anthropopathic lens.

In a section near the conclusion of the afterword added to *I and Thou* in 1957, Buber acknowledged that the "actuality of faith" (*Glaubenwirklichkeit*) requires that we apply to transcendence characteristics that we take from the realm of immanence:

> The designation of God as a person is indispensable for all who, like myself, do not mean a principle when they say "God," although mystics like Eckhart occasionally equate "Being" [*das Sein*] with him, and who, like myself, do not mean an idea when they say "God," although philosophers like Plato could at times take him for one—all who, like myself, mean by "God" him that, whatever else he may be in addition, enters into a direct relationship [*unmittelbare Beziehung*] to us human beings through creative, revelatory, and redemptive acts, and thus makes it possible for us to enter into a direct relationship to him. [. . .] The concept of personhood [*Personhaftigkeit*] is, of course, utterly incapable of describing the nature of God; but it is permitted and necessary to say that God is *also* a person.[36]

Buber confirmed—reminiscent of the inextricable link between the personhood and the invisibility of God in Herman Cohen[37] and Emmanuel Levinas[38]—

the need to apply the notion of *Personhaftigkeit* to God even though he surely discerned that God is not a person. It is precisely because God is not a person that we can attribute the "paradoxical designation" of absolute person to God to mark the "one that cannot be relativized. It is as the absolute person that God enters into direct relationship to us."[39] Buber accepted the inevitability of this paradox—he even goes so far as to call it a "contradiction" (*Widerspruch*)—but he nevertheless emphasized that the charge to imagine the real is compromised to the extent that the real that one imagines is reduced to an object.[40] The taking hold of the personhood of God—and by extension the personhood of the human—is predicated on making present a presence that cannot be presentified as something representable. The person, in other words, is what cannot be personified in the imagination.

Returning to this theme in *Eclipse of God* (1952), Buber went even further in challenging the theolatrous repercussions of a theistic understanding of transcendence:

> Thus the personal manifestation of the divine is not decisive for the genuineness of religion. What is decisive is that I relate myself to the divine as to Being which is over against me, though *not* over against me *alone*. Complete inclusion of the divine in the sphere of the human self abolishes its divinity. [. . .] He who refuses to limit God to the transcendent has a fuller conception of Him than he who does so limit Him. But he who confines God within the immanent means something other than Him.[41]

The reality of faith means "living in relationship" to the "absolute Being," the "unlimited" and "nameless" existential reality that cannot be conceived in personal form but that one believes in unconditionally.[42] To immanentize the transcendent presence to the point that it is confined within the constraints of human imagination is effectively to eradicate that transcendence and to obliterate the relationship that one might have to the divine being. In ontologizing the giver, one loses purchase on the gift.

In *Two Types of Faith* (1950), Buber noted a basic contrast between Judaism and Christianity with respect to the anthropomorphic manifestation of the divine. In Christianity, there is one permanent image by which the invisible is seen, the person of Jesus, who represents the human countenance of the Father; in Judaism, God appears in a plethora of visions, but, since none of these persist, the divine "remained unseen in all His appearances."[43] Buber's proclamation that the dialectic of concealment and disclosure is preserved more judiciously in Judaism than in Christianity is questionable, but for the purposes of this chapter this matter can be bracketed. What is more important is Buber's insight concerning the dangers of the imagination and the inexorable lapse of monotheism into idolatry even without the threat of deification. His words are worth citing in full:

> "Israel," from the point of view of the history of faith, implies in its very heart immediacy towards the imperceptible Being. God ever gives Himself to be seen in the phenomena of nature and history, and remains invisible. That He reveals Himself and that He "hides Himself" (Is. xlv. 15) belong indivisibly together; but for His concealment His revelation would not be real and temporal. Therefore He is imageless; an image means fixing to one manifestation, its aim is to prevent God from hiding Himself, He may not be allowed any longer to be present as the One Who is there as He is there (Exod. iii. 14), no longer appear as He will; because an image is this and intends this, "thou shalt not make to thyself any image." And to Him, the ever only personally Present One, the One who never becomes a figure, even to Him the man in Israel has an exclusively immediate relationship [...] not as an object among objects, but as the exclusive Thou of prayer and devotion.[44]

Monotheism, according to Buber, is not essentially a stance about the world, as is customarily believed, but rather the faith and piety that ensue from the "primal reality of a life-relationship." Insofar as God remains hidden in the "exclusive immediacy" of this relationship, the divine being is manifest in innumerable forms in space and time. To turn any of these manifestations into a fixed image is to subvert the prophetic truism that God is imageless. In Buber's dialogical language, God is the eternal Thou, the "personally Present One" that can never become a figure. This is the meaning of the name of God revealed to Moses on behalf of the Israelites, *ehyeh asher ehyeh*, that is, God is the supreme subjectivity that cannot be objectified, "the One who cannot be represented," "the One who cannot be confined to any outward form."[45]

Buber is here abbreviating the exegesis on this name that he offered more elaborately in *Moses: The Revelation and the Covenant* (1946):

> As reply to his question about the name Moses is told: *Ehyeh asher ehyeh*. This is usually understood to mean 'I am that I am' in the sense that YHVH describes himself as the Being One or even the Everlasting One, the one unalterably persisting in his being. [...] It means: happening, coming into being, being there, being present, being thus and thus; but not being in an abstract sense. [...] YHVH indeed states that he will always be present, but at any given moment as the one as whom he then, in that given moment, will be present. He who promises his steady presence, his steady assistance, refuses to restrict himself to definite forms of manifestation; how could the people even venture to conjure and limit him! [...] That Ehyeh is not a name; the God can never be named so; only on this one occasion, in this sole moment of transmitting

his work, is Moses allowed and ordered to take the God's self-comprehension in his mouth as a name.[46]

The name that is not a name is at the core of what Buber calls the "reality of faith" of Judaism, which is opposed by the Christian belief that "assigns to God a definite human countenance" through the historical person of Jesus. "The God of the Christian is both imageless and imaged, but imageless rather in the religious idea and imaged in actual experience. The image conceals the imageless One."[47] While the persistent defense of the alterity of God, which is essential to Buber's *dialogische Prinzip*, can be deemed a response to Franz Rosenzweig's critique of the mystical monism of the earlier phase of his thinking as an example of atheistic theology,[48] it is important to emphasize that Buber maintained that from the Jewish perspective, the paradox of the image and the imageless is kept intact. God hides and appears concomitantly; that is, the God that is manifest is the God that is withheld. As Buber put it in the *Eclipse of God*, "The religious reality of the meeting with the Meeter, who shines through all forms and is Himself formless, knows no image of Him, nothing comprehensible as object. It knows only the presence of the Present One." For this reason Buber suggests that the "critical atheism" of the philosopher, which proffers the "negation of all metaphysical ideas about God," is "well suited to arouse religious men and to impel them to a new meeting. On their way they destroy the images which manifestly no longer do justice to God."[49]

Buber professes nonetheless that in order not to succumb to the voice of nihilism we need to have recourse to the "images of the Absolute, partly pallid, partly crude, altogether false and yet true, fleeting as an image in a dream yet verified in eternity."[50] Commenting on this passage, Leo Strauss wrote:

> The experience of God is surely not specifically Jewish. Besides, can one say that one experiences God as the creator of heaven and earth, i.e. that one knows from the experience of God, taken by itself, that He is the creator of heaven and earth, or that men who are not prophets experience God as a thinking, willing and speaking being? Is the absolute experience necessarily the experience of a Thou? Every assertion about the absolute experience which says more than that what is experienced is the Presence or the Call, is not the experiencer, is not flesh and blood, is the wholly other, is death or nothingness, is an "image" or an interpretation; that any one interpretation is the simply true interpretation is not known but "merely believed." One cannot establish that any particular interpretation of the absolute experience is the most adequate interpretation on the ground that it alone agrees with all other experiences, for instance with the experienced mystery of the Jewish fate, for the Jewish fate is a mystery only on the basis of one particular interpretation

of the absolute experience. The very emphasis on the absolute experience as experience compels one to demand [. . .] that it be carefully distinguished from every interpretation of the experience, for the interpretations may be suspected of being attempts to render bearable and harmless the experienced which admittedly comes from without down upon man and is undesired; or of being attempts to cover over man's radical unprotectedness, loneliness and exposedness.[51]

Strauss offers a hypothetical rejoinder on the part of Buber that the atheistic suspicion about belief in the experience of the absolute is as much a belief as the theistic position.[52] What is crucial for this analysis is that Strauss offered an incisive critique of Buber's paradoxical avowal that the images of God are, at once, fictitious and true, ephemeral and enduring. In fairness to Buber, Strauss did not pay close enough attention to the point raised above concerning what Buber imagined to be the distinctive contribution of Judaism in realizing that every image is as much a concealment as it is a disclosure. From this standpoint, Buber would have assuredly consented to Strauss's admonition that no one interpretation of the experience is sufficient to account for all the other interpretations, a view that points hermeneutically toward the postmodern sensibility.[53] Without ignoring this caveat, the criticism of Strauss nonetheless has merit. It does seem that to some degree Buber remained faithful to a central facet of his understanding the constructive role of the religious imagination, an idea epitomized in the word *Spiegelung*, "mirrored illusion," which he used to translate the expression *aḥizat einayim* in the parable (*mashal*) transmitted in the name of Israel ben Eli'ezer, the Ba'al Shem Tov.[54] In the original text,[55] the trope of *aḥizat einayim*, which refers to the magical act of conjuring an optical delusion[56] (literally, "taking hold of the eyes," a locution equivalent to "sleight of hand"), is applied to the action of the king who has made various walls, towers, and gates in his palace, and has dispersed his treasures in each of the gates, and then commanded his subjects to approach him through these obstacles. Only the prince discerned that there was no barrier separating him from his father, for what appeared to be an obstruction was only a mirage. The parable is a means to elucidate the mystical truth of the scriptural idiom "his glory fills all the earth,"[57] corroborated by the zoharic formulation "there is no place devoid of him."[58] What appears to be a hindrance separating divinity and humanity is only an illusion. The mystical gnosis of God's omnipresence unveils the veil. By using the word *Spiegelung*, Buber meant to convey that the image of the divine concocted by the human imagination is a chimera, a false projection that distorts the nature of that reality just as an image is unfailingly defaced in the reflection of the mirror.[59] Thus, Buber glosses the parable by noting that the "mystery of grace cannot be interpreted." Moreover, he elicits from it that human life is marked by the tension between seeking and finding. God may wish to be sought, but the soul must wander anxiously, deferring the fulfillment of the "flight of the moment." In the end, what is possible is to unveil the veil; this is the import of the prince's perceiving that there was no barrier, that "all the labyrinth was a mirrored illusion."[60] I surmise that this sense of the chimerical is carried over to Buber's dialogical thought, attested, for instance, in the claim mentioned above that every Thou is destined to be disfigured in the shroud of an It.

It is apposite at this juncture to mention Buber's explication in *Good and Evil* (1952) of the biblical allegation (placed in the voice of the serpent) that by eating of the fruit of the Tree of Knowledge, the first couple became like God, knowing the opposites of good and evil (Gen. 3:5): "In the swirling space of images, through which he strays, each and every thing entices him to be made incarnate by him; he grasps at them like a wanton burglar, not with decision, but only in order to overcome the tension of omnipossibility; it all becomes reality, though no longer divine but his, his capriciously constructed, indestinate reality, his violence, which overcomes him, his handiwork and fate."[61] Circumscribed within the precinct of the Garden of Eden, the divine reality allotted to humanity is good, but once driven out of this state, the actuality gives way to the boundless possible, which is evil to the degree that it is fictitious. Within the transcendence of the divine—and, as Buber reminds the reader, "there is no other transcendence than that of the Creator"—the opposites are transcended; but in the human domain good and evil are torn asunder, reflected psychologically in the dual aspect of the imagination, rendered in rabbinic parlance as the good inclination (*yeṣer ṭov*) and the evil inclination (*yeṣer ra*), the division that brings about the "chaotic of the possible, which is continuously, capriciously incarnating itself, over the created world."[62] Reflecting the kabbalistic and Hasidic interpretation of one of the rudimentary maxims of rabbinic anthropology, Buber accentuates that the spiritual duty is to unite the two impulses by recognizing their underlying unity. What is crucial to our analysis is that this insight about the human predilection to incarnate the two inclinations can be cast as two aspects of the imagination, to imagine the other as an extension of the self or to imagine the other in his or her otherness. The former can be applied to the theistic propensity to imagine the transcendent in forms that are no more than a projection of our will to instantiate in form that which is formless.

In the essay "Myth in Judaism" (1916), Buber opined, "It is fundamental to Jewish religiosity, and central to Jewish monotheism [...] to view all things as utterances of God and all events as manifestations of the absolute. Whereas to the other great monotheist of the Orient, the Indian sage as he is represented in the Upanishads, corporeal reality is an illusion, which one must shed if he is to enter the world of truth, to the Jew corporeal reality is a revelation of the divine spirit and will."[63] Even the panentheistic tendency in Hasidism—often misconstrued as pantheism—mitigates against the view that the world is a veil of Maya, but if it is the revelation of the infinite, it must be a concealment, since the infinite cannot be revealed in the finite unless it is concealed. This is the crux of Buber's interpretation of the kabbalistic doctrine of *ṣimṣum*, the self-limitation by which the absolute person of the limitless Godhead dons the garment of creation and speaks the I of revelation. However, the paradox of the delimiting of the limitless renders erroneous the conjecture that the presence of God is made available to human beings in a "sensible completeness." Hasidism, therefore, can be viewed as a response to Spinoza insofar as it upheld the older rabbinic insight that God is the place of the world but the world is not the place of God, an insight that yields the paradox of transcendence and immanence; that is, God dwells in the very world from which God has withdrawn. The indwelling of the presence is what transfigures the physical world into a sacrament. If panentheism was affirmed and the world was envisioned as the place of God, or if pantheism was postulated and the world and God were identified, then the sacramentalization of the material could not be achieved; this is possible only because God transcends the world and yet dwells within it.[64] In the final analysis, Buber did not resolve the tension between the exteriority of form and the interiority of formlessness, a tension that shaped his aesthetics, understanding of mystical experience, and the dialogical relation.[65] The presence of God is made present through what we could call a process of imaging the real. The imagination is thus tagged with the mission to bring the abstract into the sensual, but to achieve that end, the appearance of the real must perforce persist as inapparent, and hence the presence of the absolute person will be most fully encountered as present in its being absent.

Notes

1. Martin Buber, *The Knowledge of Man: Selected Essays*, ed. Maurice Friedman, trans. Maurice Friedman and Ronald Gregor Smith (New York: Humanity Books, 1988), 50.

2. On the term *Eigenwesen* and the rationale for rendering it as "ego," see Martin Buber, *I and Thou*, trans. Walter Kaufmann (New York: Charles Scribner's Sons, 1970), 111–12n7.

3. Buber, *I and Thou*, 112–13; Martin Buber, *Ich und Du* (Heidelberg: Lambert Schneider, 1974), 76.

4. Martin Buber, *Ecstatic Confessions*, ed. Paul Mendes-Flohr, trans. Esther Cameron (San Francisco: Harper & Row, 1985), 156.

5. This position is encapsulated in the comment of Israel Koren, *The Mystery of the Earth:*

Mysticism and Hasidism in the Thought of Martin Buber (Leiden: Brill, 2020), 66: "On the whole, Buber did not grant an important place to the imagination in his early mystical view, just as he did not give it an important role in his later perception of prophecy and in his dialogical approach generally. For him, it would seem that imagination is a barrier against direct experience, of the order of face to face. This being the case, in his attitude toward the imagination and to the intellect, Buber is a nominalist—that is to say, there is no real relation between the thing itself and that which man's consciousness and imagination impose upon it." I have argued that the imagination plays a critical role in both the mystical and dialogical phases of Buber's thought.

6. The terms *isticheit* and *istikeit* are translated as "self-identity" in *The Complete Mystical Works of Meister Eckhart*, trans. and ed. Maurice O'C. Walshe (New York: Herder & Herder, 2009), 70, 263, 296, 330, 358, 463, 464. For the original German, see Meister Eckhart, *Werke*, vol. 1, texts and translation by Josef Quint, edited and commentary by Niklaus Largier (Frankfurt am Main: Deutscher Klassiker Verlag, 1993), 20, 80, 146; Meister Eckhart, *Werke*, vol. 2, texts and translation by Ernst Benz, Karl Christ, Bruno Decker, Josef Koch, Josef Quint, Konrad Weiß, and Albert Zimmerman, edited and commentary by Niklaus Largier (Frankfurt am Main: Deutscher Klassiker Verlag, 1993), 26, 140, 192, 194. The alternative spelling *istikait* in Eckhart, *Werke*, 2:572, is translated in *Complete Mystical Works*, 393, as "being." On the Eckhartian term *isticheit* and the Avicennean *anitas*, see the comments of Largier in Eckhart, *Werke*, 1:811–12, 852–53; and compare the additional remarks in Eckhart, *Werke*, 2:656, 878, 881–82.

7. *Complete Mystical Works*, 287; Eckhart, *Werke*, 1:270.

8. Eckhart, *Werke*, 1:147, 271, 673; Eckhart, *Werke*, 2:141, 193, 195, 673.

9. *Complete Mystical Works*, 463–64; Eckhart, *Werke*, 2:192–94.

10. *Complete Mystical Works*, 467–68; Eckhart, *Werke*, 1:248. The phrase *negatio negationis* is linked exegetically by Eckhart to the divine name *ego sum qui sum* (Exod. 3:14). Compare *Expositio libri Exodi* in Meister Eckhart, *Die lateinischen Werke*, edited by Albert Zimmermann and Loris Sturlese (Stuttgart: W. Kohlhammer, 1992), 2:77n74: "Nulla ergo negatio, nihil negativum deo competit, nisi negatio negationis, quam significat unum negative dictum: 'deus unus est,' Deut. 6; Gal. 3. Negatio vero negationis purissima et plenissima est affirmatio: 'ego sum qui sum.'" English translation in *Meister Eckhart: Teacher and Preacher*, ed. Bernard McGinn with Frank Tobin and Elvira Borgstadt (New York: Paulist Press, 1986), 68: "Therefore, no negation, nothing negative, belongs to God, except for the negation of negation which is what the One signifies when expressed negatively. 'God is one' (Dt. 6:4; Ga. 3:20). The negation of negation is the purest and fullest affirmation—'I am who am.'" On the use of the expression *negatio negationis*, and its German equivalent *versagen des versagennes*, in Eckhart and citation of other relevant sources, see Elliot R. Wolfson, "Patriarchy and the Motherhood of God in Zoharic Kabbalah and Meister Eckhart," in *Envisioning Judaism: Studies in Honor of Peter Schäfer on the Occasion of His Seventieth Birthday*, edited by Ra'anan S. Boustan, Klaus Hermann, Reimund Leicht, Annette Yoshiko Reed, and Giuseppe Veltri, with the collaboration of Alex Ramos (Tübingen: Mohr Siebeck, 2013), 1069n78.

11. *Complete Mystical Works*, 463; Eckhart, *Werke*, 2:192.

12. *Complete Mystical Works*, 69, 287; Eckhart, *Werke*, 1:18, 270. For a more extended discussion of this expression, see Wolfson, "Patriarchy," 1068, 1084–86.

13. *Complete Mystical Works*, 342; Eckhart, *Werke*, 1:106.

14. On the interplay of kataphasis and apophasis in Eckhart, see Wolfson, "Patriarchy," 1066–67, and references cited in n. 68 there.

15. *Complete Mystical Works*, 69; Eckhart, *Werke*, 1:18.

16. *Complete Mystical Works*, 463; Eckhart, *Werke*, 2:190.

17. *Complete Mystical Works*, 296; Eckhart, *Werke*, 1:144.

18. Martina Urban, *Aesthetics of Renewal: Martin Buber's Early Representation of Hasidism as Kulturkritik* (Chicago: University of Chicago Press, 2008), 79, 86, 93.

19. Buber, *I and Thou*, 54, 62, 63, 117, 152, 179; Buber, *Ich und Du*, 10, 18, 19, 81, 100, 127.

20. Buber, *Knowledge of Man*, 60.

21. *The Martin Buber Reader: Essential Writings*, ed. Asher D. Biemann (New York: Palgrave Macmillan, 2002), 173–74. See the analysis of *Realphantasie* and the disinterested reflective judgment that facilitates the capability of imaging the other in Sarah Scott, "From Genius to Taste: Martin Buber's Aestheticism," in *Martin Buber: His Intellectual and Scholarly Legacy*, ed. Sam Berrin Shonkoff (Leiden: Brill, 2018), 162–69. Buber returned to the question of artistic creativity and the relationship to the world in the essay "Man and His Image-Work," translated in *Knowledge of Man*, 139–55. The axis around which the argument of that study turns is summarized on 141: "The artist is not a slave to nature, but free as he may hold himself of it and far as he may remove himself from it, he may establish his work only by means of what happens to him in the sphere of the bound life of his senses—in the fundamental events of perception, which is a meeting with the world and ever again a meeting with the world.... The whole body-soul person is the human in man; it is this wholeness which is involved in his meeting with the world."

22. Buber, *I and Thou*, 60–61; Buber, *Ich und Du*, 16–17. On the human aptitude for figuration through artistic images in Buber, see Zachary Braiterman, *The Shape of Revelation: Aesthetics and Modern Jewish Thought* (Stanford, CA: Stanford University Press, 2007), 42–44; Urban, *Aesthetics*, 102–3.

23. Braiterman, *Shape of Revelation*, 137–44, set this dimension of Buber's thinking in the broader context of the antihistoricist trend of German expressionism. See also Asher D. Biemann, "Aesthetic Education in Martin Buber: Jewish Renaissance and the Artist," in *New Perspectives on Martin Buber*, ed. Michael Zank (Tübingen: Mohr Siebeck, 2006), 85–110. On the centrality of the notion of presence in Buber's construction of the religious sensibility, see Guy G. Stroumsa, "Presence, Not Gnosis: Buber as a Historian of Religion," in *Martin Buber: A Contemporary Perspective*, ed. Paul Mendes-Flohr (Syracuse, NY: Syracuse University Press, 2002), 25–47.

24. Buber, *I and Thou*, 62; Buber, *Ich und Du*, 18.

25. Buber, *Knowledge of Man*, 70.

26. Buber, *I and Thou*, 63–64; Buber, *Ich und Du*, 19–20.

27. Buber, *Knowledge of Man*, 149, 149n1, 148, 149, 150, 155.

28. Framing the matter in this way would raise the question for a reexamination of the possible affinity between Buber's idea of making present and Heidegger's delineation in section 7 of *Sein und Zeit* of appearance (*Erscheinung*) as the self-showing of the nonmanifest (*Nichtoffenbare*), which evolved in his later thought into the phenomenology of the unparent (*Unscheinbaren*), but this is a matter that is beyond the scope of this chapter. For discussion of this dimension of Heidegger's thought, see Elliot R. Wolfson, *Giving Beyond the Gift: Apophasis and Overcoming Theomania* (New York: Fordham University Press, 2014), 94–102, esp. 95–98. Many have written on Buber and Heidegger, and here I mention a few of the more salient studies: David Novak, "Buber's Critique of Heidegger," *Modern Judaism* 5 (1985): 125–40; Haim Gordon, *The Heidegger-Buber Controversy: The Status of the I-Thou* (Westport, CT: Greenwood, 2001); Paul Mendes-Flohr, "Martin Buber and Martin Heidegger in Dialogue," *Journal of Religion* 94 (2014): 2–25; Yemima Hadad, "Fruits of Forgetfulness: Politics and Nationalism in the Philosophies of Martin Buber and Martin Heidegger," in *Heidegger and Jewish Thought: Difficult Others*,

ed. Elad Lapidot and Micha Brumlik (London: Rowman & Littlefield, 2018), 201–20; Daniel M. Herskowitz, *Heidegger and His Jewish Reception* (Cambridge: Cambridge University Press, 2021), 128–74.

29. Buber, *Knowledge of Man*, 60.

30. *Martin Buber Reader*, 278. I take issue with the criticism leveled against Buber's remark that the "notion of imagining the other is not quite the same as a dialogue" offered by Judith Butler, "Versions of Binationalism in Said and Buber," in *Martin Buber: His Intellectual and Scholarly Legacy*, 126. The imputation of an implicit orientalism fails to take into account that the imaging of the other upheld by Buber resists reification of the other in both the anthropological and theological domains. The imagination that construes the other in such reductive terms is one that Buber steadfastly rejected as inappropriate to the I-Thou encounter.

31. Buber, *I and Thou*, 58; Buber, *Ich und Du*, 14.

32. Elliot R. Wolfson, "Theolatry and the Making Present of the Nonrepresentable: Undoing (A)Theism in Eckhart and Buber," in *Martin Buber: His Intellectual and Scholarly Legacy*, 26–27. See also the section "Theomania and the Eclipse of the Giving" in Wolfson, *Giving*, 25–29.

33. Buber, *I and Thou*, 164; Buber, *Ich und Du*, 136–37.

34. Buber, *I and Thou*, 152, 69, 147–48, 68, 146, 148; Buber, *Ich und Du*, 124, 25, 117–119, 24, 117, 119.

35. Paul Mendes-Flohr, *From Mysticism to Dialogue: Martin Buber's Transformation of German Social Thought* (Detroit: Wayne State University Press, 1989), 72–73, 95–96, 106–7, 113–19; Paul Mendes-Flohr, *Martin Buber: A Life of Faith and Dissent* (New Haven, CT: Yale University Press, 2019), 80–109. On the concept of *Verwirklichung*, see also Elliot R. Wolfson, "The Problem of Unity in the Thought of Martin Buber," *Journal of the History of Ideas* 27 (1989): 419–39, esp. 429–35; Phil Huston, *Martin Buber's Journey to Presence* (New York: Fordham University Press, 2007), 106–84; Martina Urban, "The Paradox of Realization: Buber on the Transcendental Boundary of Spatial Images," *Journal of Religion* 95 (2015): 72–93, reprinted in *Martin Buber: His Intellectual and Scholarly Legacy*, 171–93.

36. Buber, *I and Thou*, 180–81 (emphasis in original); Buber, *Ich und Du*, 158.

37. Hermann Cohen, *Religion of Reason Out of the Sources of Judaism*, trans. Simon Kaplan (Atlanta: Scholars' Press, 1995), 41. See discussion in Wolfson, *Giving*, 19–21, 25.

38. Emmanuel Levinas, *Totality and Infinity: An Essay on Exteriority*, trans. Alphonso Lingis (Dordrecht: Kluwer Academic Publishers, 1969), 78. See the fuller analysis of this passage in Wolfson, *Giving*, 140–41.

39. Buber, *I and Thou*, 181–82; Buber, *Ich und Du*, 159.

40. My argument has some resonance with the analysis of Emil L. Fackenheim, "Martin Buber's Concept of Revelation," in *The Philosophy of Martin Buber*, ed. Paul Arthur Schilpp and Maurice Friedman (LaSalle: Open Court, 1967), 273–96. In particular, Fackenheim emphasizes the antimony to which the dialogical nature of revelation unavoidably leads: one must respond to the divine call, but one is never in the position to measure or to determine the content of the revelatory moment of encounter. Going beyond Fackenheim, I would assert that the Buberian idea of revelation entails the unraveling of the knot of theism.

41. Martin Buber, *Eclipse of God: Studies in the Relation between Religion and Philosophy* (New York: Harper & Row, 1952), 28 (emphasis in original).

42. Buber, *Eclipse of God*, 31.

43. Martin Buber, *Two Types of Faith: A Study of the Interpretation of Judaism and Christianity*, trans. Norman P. Goldhawk (New York: Macmillan Company, 1951), 129.

44. Buber, *Two Types of Faith*, 130.//
45. Buber, *Two Types of Faith*, 130–31.//
46. Martin Buber, *Moses: The Revelation and the Covenant* (Amherst, NY: Humanity Books, 1998), 51–53. See also 117–18: "The sage of the Fathers [. . .] has something to tell of human figures, in which YHVH lets himself be seen. But there is nothing supernatural about them, and they are not present otherwise than any other section of Nature in which the God manifests himself. What is actually meant by this letting-Himself-be-seen on the part of YHVH has been shown in the story of the Burning Bush; in the fiery flame, not as a form to be separated from it, but in it and through it. [. . .] And it is in precisely such a fashion [. . .] that the representatives of Israel come to see Him on the heights of Sinai. [. . .] He allows them to see Him in the glory of His light, becoming manifest yet remaining invisible." See also Martin Buber, *Kingship of God*, 3rd ed., trans. Richard Scheimann (Amherst, NY: Humanity Books, 1990), 105–6.//
47. Buber, *Two Types of Faith*, 131–32.//
48. See Franz Rosenzweig, *Philosophical and Theological Writings*, trans. and ed. Paul W. Franks and Michael L. Morgan (Indianapolis: Hackett Publishing, 2000), 5–6; Urban, *Aesthetics*, 93.//
49. Buber, *Eclipse of God*, 45, 46.//
50. Buber, *Eclipse of God*, 119.//
51. Leo Strauss, *Spinoza's Critique of Religion* (New York: Schocken Books, 1965), 11–12. On Strauss's criticism of Buber's privileging the "immediate experience of God," see David Janssens, *Between Athens and Jerusalem: Philosophy, Prophecy, and Politics in Leo Strauss's Early Thought* (Albany: State University of New York Press, 2008), 23–24.//
52. Strauss, *Spinoza's Critique of Religion*, 12.//
53. On the attempt to read Strauss as a postmodern political thinker, see Catherine H. Zuckert, *The Truth about Leo Strauss: Political Philosophy and American Democracy* (Chicago: University of Chicago Press, 2006), 80–114.//
54. Martin Buber, *The Legend of the Baal-Shem*, trans. Maurice Friedman (New York: Harper & Row, 1955), 25.//
55. The parable is transmitted in the name of the Besht by Jacob Joseph of Polonnoye, *Ben Porat Yosef* (Korzec: Avraham Dov of Melnyk, 1781), 55a, 88a. It was copied as well in the anthology *Keter Shem Ṭov ha-Shalem* (Brooklyn: Kehot, 2004), 31.//
56. See Philip S. Alexander, "The Talmudic Concept of Conjuring ('Aḥizat 'Einayim) and the Problem of the Definition of Magic (*Kishuf*)," in *Creation and Re-Creation in Jewish Thought: Festschrift in Honor of Joseph Dan*, ed. Rachel Elior and Peter Schäfer (Tübingen: Mohr Siebeck, 2005), 7–26.//
57. Isaiah 6:2.//
58. *Tiqqunei Zohar*, ed. Reuven Margaliot (Jerusalem: Mosad ha-Rav Kook, 1976), sec. 69, 122b.//
59. My analysis of Buber's use of *Spiegelung* has benefited from the discussion of this term in Urban, *Aesthetics*, 83–84, 90–93. On 197–98n36, Urban suggests that the understating of *Spiegelung* as "mirroring self-deception" was known to Buber from Gustav Landauer's *Skepsis und Mystik*.//
60. Buber, *Legend*, 24.//
61. Martin Buber, *Good and Evil: Two Interpretations* (New York: Charles Scribner's Sons, 1952), 92. For an analysis that builds on the Buberian typology, see Richard Kearney, *The Wake of Imagination: Toward a Postmodern Culture* (Minneapolis: University of Minnesota Press, 1988), 37–61.//
62. Buber, *Good and Evil*, 92.//
63. Martin Buber, *On Judaism*, ed. Nahum N. Glatzer (New York: Schocken Books, 1967),

105. See Urban, *Aesthetics*, 89. On the contrast between Indian redemption as "a divesting of all appearance" and Jewish redemption as "a grasping of truth," see Buber's "Judaism and Mankind," in *On Judaism*, 27–28.

64. Martin Buber, *The Origin and Meaning of Hasidism*, ed. and trans. Maurice Friedman (New York: Horizon Press, 1960), 196, 147, 96.

65. Urban, *Aesthetics*, 80, 106. I have extended Urban's insight to the dialogical phase of Buber's thinking.

Annotated Bibliography

PRIMARY SOURCES

The role of the imagination was vital to all the stages on the path of Buber's thinking. I here refer to the main works where the topic is engaged:

Martin Buber. "Distance and Relation." In *The Knowledge of Man: Selected Essays*, edited with an introductory essay by Maurice Friedman, translated by Maurice Friedman and Ronald Gregor Smith, new introduction by Alan Udoff, 49–61. New York: Humanity Books, 1988.

———. *Ecstatic Confessions*. Edited by Paul Mendes-Flohr, translated by Esther Cameron. San Francisco: Harper & Row, 1985.

———. *Good and Evil: Two Interpretations*. New York: Charles Scribner's Sons, 1952.

———. *I and Thou: A New Translation with a Prologue "I and You" and Notes*. Translated and with a prologue by Walter Kaufmann. New York: Charles Scribner's Sons, 1970.

———. "Man and His Image-Work." In *The Knowledge of Man: Selected Essays*, edited with an introductory essay by Maurice Friedman, translated by Maurice Friedman and Ronald Gregor Smith, new introduction by Alan Udoff, 139–55. New York: Humanity Books, 1988.

SECONDARY LITERATURE

The major monographs that deal with Buber's aesthetics include Asher D. Biemann, "Aesthetic Education in Martin Buber: Jewish Renaissance and the Artist," in *New Perspectives on Martin Buber*, edited by Michael Zank (Tübingen: Mohr Siebeck, 2006), 85–110; Zachary Braiterman, *The Shape of Revelation: Aesthetics and Modern Jewish Thought* (Stanford, CA: Stanford University Press, 2007); and Martina Urban, *Aesthetics of Renewal: Martin Buber's Early Representation of Hasidism as Kulturkritik* (Chicago: University of Chicago Press, 2008).

On the trajectory of Buber's intellectual development, see Paul Mendes-Flohr, *From Mysticism to Dialogue: Martin Buber's Transformation of German Social Thought* (Detroit: Wayne State University Press, 1989); and Paul Mendes-Flohr, *Martin Buber: A Life of Faith and Dissent* (New Haven, CT: Yale University Press, 2019).

Noteworthy discussions of the imagination in Buber include Sarah Scott, "From Genius to Taste: Martin Buber's Aestheticism," in *Martin Buber: His Intellectual and Scholarly Legacy*, edited by Sam Berrin Shonkoff (Leiden: Brill, 2018), 151–70; Martina Urban, "The Paradox of Realization: Buber on the Transcendental Boundary of Spatial Images," *Journal of Religion* 95 (2015): 72–93, reprinted in *Martin Buber: His Intellectual and Scholarly Legacy*, edited by Sam Berrin Shonkoff (Leiden: Brill, 2018), 171–93; and Elliot R. Wolfson. "Theolatry and the Making-Present of the Nonrepresentable: Undoing (A)Theism in Eckhart and Buber," in *Martin Buber: His Intellectual and Scholarly Legacy*, edited by Sam Berrin Shonkoff (Leiden: Brill, 2018), 3–32.

5

To Hallow the Everyday

PAUL MENDES-FLOHR

Martin Buber was wont to distinguish between his earlier mystical writings and his "mature thought," which developed starting with the publication of *Ich und Du* in 1923. Yet one may detect the crystallization of the *Fragestellung* that he addressed in his philosophy of dialogue while still in his youth, especially as nurtured by his principal university teachers, and even his life's partner, Paula née Winkler (1877–1958). In a letter dated August 1899, she tells her beloved Martin:

> . . . Our attitudes to each other ought above all to be "person to person" [*Mensch zu Mensch*]—not "Frenchman to German," not "Jew to Christian," and perhaps less of "man to woman." So, as one says in Sanskrit *tat tvam asi*. Simply: That you are! But what does that mean? Are we to blur distinctions, obliterate all contradictions for that reason? For what? To be able to deal more easily with our humanity? Would we then be able to deal more easily with it? Do we love what is least different from us? Do we love what is most polished, flattest? Are not the contradictions the highest and ultimate and finest stimulants in life? Do we not love fullness in color, form, and sound—fullness in individualities?[1]

The twenty-two-year-old Paula's insistence that *Mensch zu Mensch* relations need not, indeed, should not deny individual difference would later be elaborated by Buber as the *Urdistanz*—the primal distance—between individuals that allows for the differentiation between I *and* Thou, and hence, the ontological ground of the dialogical relation.[2]

Shortly after receiving Paula's cri de coeur, Buber went to Berlin to study with Wilhelm Dilthey (1833–1911) and Georg Simmel (1858–1918). They taught him to focus philosophical attention on the imponderables of everyday life and relations. In a seminal lecture, "Die Kultur der Gegenwart und die Philosophie," which Dilthey frequently delivered before his students, he noted that he wanted to offer them more than *bloße Kathederphilosophie* (mere academic philosophy):

> One can convey an appropriate philosophy only on the basis of an understanding of the present age. Let us attempt then to grasp the basic features of the present that shape this generation and determine its philosophic character. The most general characteristic of our age is its sense of reality and the worldliness of its interests.³

This world-immanent realism, Dilthey contends, was heralded by Goethe, who proclaimed in *Faust*:

> The earthly sphere I know sufficiently,
> But into the beyond we cannot see.
> A fool, that squints and tries to piece those shrouds,
> And would invent his like above the clouds!
> Let him survey this life, be resolute,
> For the able this world is not mute.⁴

Dilthey urged his students to heed Goethe's counsel: "Steep ourselves fully in this actuality, in this-worldly nature of our interests, and the mastery of science over life." Yet, Dilthey acknowledged that this worldliness of interests could not satisfy the human desire to understand existence and its purpose (*Ziel*). Alas, he told his students, we are no wiser in this respect than the denizens of ancient Ionia or an Arab at the time of Averroës. Despite the rapid progress of the sciences, we are even more at a loss regarding the ultimate meaning and goal of life. The foundations of religious faith and philosophical convictions of former times have been ever increasingly undermined by the sciences. Further, "historical consciousness demonstrates with ever greater clarity the relativity of all metaphysical and religious doctrines, which in the course of time are superseded. It appears to us that the human quest for knowledge is tragic, beset by a contradiction between will and capability." A grim pessimism has taken hold of us. "This pain of emptiness, the consciousness of anarchy at the heart of all our convictions, the uncertainty of values and life," Dilthey held, "call forth diverse attempts in poetry and literature to address the questions of the value and goal [*Ziel*] of our existence."⁵

Significantly, Dilthey's epistemology differs from those of the empiricists and Kant. "In the veins of the knowing subject as constructed by Locke, Hume, and Kant runs no real blood, but the diluted fluid of reason in the sense of mere thought-activity."⁶ Accordingly, he insisted that knowledge of the world and of oneself is not limited to the experience (*Erfahrung*) of the world that *appears* to us as refracted by sense perceptions, preeminently that attained by sight. But we also have knowledge of the subjective, dynamic events of the human spirit. Such knowledge is mediated not by *Erfahrung* but by *Erlebnis*, lived, affective experience, which facilitates knowledge of the subjective, inner reality of ourselves and a fortiori of others.

Whereas *Erfahrung* is the basis for explaining (*Erklärung*) the objective conditions of the world, *Erlebnis* allows for the understanding (*Verstehen*) of others as well as oneself. For human beings share common, fundamental epistemic features, which Dilthey calls "the categories of life," the formation of worldviews (*Weltanschauungen*) in response to the enigma of human existence.[7] Hence, "Understanding is a rediscovery of the I in the Thou [*das Ich im Du*]; mind [*Geist*] rediscovers itself on higher levels of systematic connection; this identity of minds [*Selbigkeit des Geistes*] in the I, in the Thou, in every subject in a community, in every system of culture, and finally in the totality of the mind and world history, makes possible the joint results of the various operations performed in the human studies [*Geisteswissenschaften*]."[8]

Nevertheless, Dilthey acknowledges the limits of his epistemology. Ultimately, he concedes, subjectivity—as manifest in the "will"—and the objective, rational ground of the world remain irreconcilable. "Will and thought cannot be reduced to one another. Logical thinking about the ground of existence ends here, and only the reflection of its vitality in and through mysticism remains."[9]

While still enrolled in Dilthey's classes, Buber published in 1901 the essay "Über Jakob Boehme," in which he reformulated his teacher's epistemological impasse: "The world remains an enigma that affects one, and yet is forever distant and alien. The individual is consumed in mute, hopeless loneliness."[10] The recovery of a *locus standi* from which to affirm the meaning of existence would determine both Buber's earliest interest in mysticism and the later turn in his thought, which he would characterize as an *Ontologie des Zwischenmenschlichen*, the ontology of the interhuman. An I-Thou meeting *between* two autonomous subjects is sustained by the Eternal Thou (God), a presence that is always present in genuine dialogue.

Although Buber would until the very end of his life reverentially refer to Dilthey as "my teacher," he also acknowledged his early indebtedness to Georg Simmel, with whom he also studied in Berlin. One of the founders of the discipline of sociology, Simmel focused Buber's attention on the transient nature of interpersonal relationships, especially within the context of modern, urban life. His seminal influence on Buber is evidenced by the series of sociological monographs *Die Gesellschaft*, edited by Buber from 1905 to

1912. In the foreword to the first of the forty volumes of *Die Gesellschaft*, Buber coined the term *das Zwischenmenschliche* (the interhuman) to designate the social space between individuals in mutual interaction. At the University of Vienna, he later studied with Friedrich Jodl (1849–1924), who reinforced Dilthey's rejection of metaphysical speculation and, like Simmel, advanced a critical realism, which posits the factual existence of a trans-subjective reality confirmed by the Thou-experience and thus the existence of one's fellow human beings. As the editor of Ludwig Feuerbach's *Sämmtliche Werke*, Jodl also introduced Buber to the latter's anthropological critique of religion. In his essay "Über Jakob Boehme," Buber cites Feuerbach as amending the German mystic's teaching that everyone creates a path to a unity with the upper world:

> According to Boehme, however, this is the right way to the new God that we create, to the new unity of powers. This view is confirmed and supplemented in a word by Ludwig Feuerbach: "Man for himself is man (in the ordinary sense); man with man—the unity of I and you [*Ich und Du*]—is God." Feuerbach wants the unity he is talking about to be based on the "reality of the difference between I and you." Today, however, we are closer to Boehme than to the teachings of Feuerbach, to the feelings of Saint Francis of Assisi, who called trees, birds and stars his siblings, and even closer to Vedanta [i.e., the Hindu doctrine that the seemingly individualized, divisive reality of the world is but "a veil of maya," a terrible illusion fraught with pain].[11]

Although the youthful Buber took Feuerbach's anthropology in a mystical direction, he would later note that Feuerbach's "discovery of the Thou, which has been called 'the Copernican revolution' of modern thought," provided him with the "decisive impetus" that, after its mystical gestation of some fifteen years, yielded the philosophy of dialogue.[12] The impetus would prove to be twofold. In explicit opposition to Kant and Hegel, who focused upon human cognition, Feuerbach sought to understand man anthropologically.[13] Accordingly, he held, man is not to be considered purely as a cognizing subject; not as an individual *an sich*, but as constituted by interpersonal relations. At the earlier, mystical stage of Buber's thought, however, the influence of Feuerbach's philosophical anthropology remained dormant.

A confluence of influences contributed to Buber's conception of mysticism, the most seminal of which was Dilthey's concept of *Erlebnis*. As employed by Buber, *Erlebnis* transcends the cognitive limitations of *Erfahrung*, which, grounded in the *principium individuationis*, perceives reality as a confounding whirl of multiple, individuated entities, by virtue of which the cognizing self (*Erkennede*) finds itself in opposition not only to objects (*Dinge*) but also other human beings. In contrast, *Erlebnis* overcomes the scourge of individuation and facilitates the realization of unity and the meaning of life beyond the isolation of the self inherent in the *Erfahrungswelt*—the "It-World" in the lexicon of *I and Thou*—the "chaos, the swarming of darkness that knows no unity."

The mystical experience (*Erlebnismystik*) frees one from the experience (*Erfahrung*) of the It-World and the *principium individuationis*; and, most significantly, it liberates one from a consciousness of the self as particular and limited by others, human and otherwise. From the perspective of this conception of the mystical experience, Buber would write extensively on mysticism in diverse cultural traditions and the universal quest for the experience (*Erlebnis*) of a unity above the confounding multiplicity of the *Erfahrungswelt*. In his early writings on Hasidism, he highlighted the spiritual journey of the solitary ecstatic who is "above nature and above time and above thought," who experiences (*erlebt*) all individual things of the world as one, before whom the All is nothing and the Soul is all, and whose truest life is not among his fellow men.[14] Yet, Buber acknowledges that Hasidism is characterized by a dialectic of worldly withdrawal and return to one's community, a process that distinguishes it from other mystical traditions:

> Hasidism is Kabbalah become ethos. But the life that it teaches is not asceticism but joy in God. [. . .] It brings the transcendent over into the immanent and lets the transcendent rule in and from it, as the soul forms the body. Its core is a highly realistic guidance to ecstasy as to the summit of existence. But ecstasy is not here, as, say, in German mysticism, the soul's "*Entwerden*," but its unfolding; it is not self-restraining and self-renouncing, but the self-fulfilling soul which flows into the Absolute.[15]

It was, however, not this dialectic that captured the imagination of the young Buber. In a seemingly autobiographical passage in *Daniel* (1913)—a work that anticipates his break with *Erlebnismystik*—he acknowledged that he—in the person of the "faithful one" as cast in *Daniel*—had been tempted by a mystical retreat from the fractured, individuated everyday reality. But the "faithful one" ultimately resists this temptation and resolves to find "unity" as a human being who "lives through the whole oscillation of duality, who receives and endures a terrible blessing. [. . .] Henceforth he will not retreat before the fluctuating, raging, whirling world of division and contradiction; he will stand standfast therein, in the midst of it stand steadfast and dare just out of it to derive and create unity."[16]

This declaration is voiced at the conclusion of *Daniel*, and thus it heralds a seminal shift in Buber's quest to overcome the *principium individuationis* by a revised conception of the duality that torments the soul. From time immemorial "the longing for unity is the glowing ground of the soul." *The overcoming of duality is the philosophia perennis; variously named and differently understood (spirit and matter, being and becoming, reason and will, soul and world),* but, at bottom, *"the duality remains in tension."* The "faithful one" concluded that "none of the ways that the wisdom of the ages takes could satisfy him." Duality is not to be overcome by trying to eliminate the tension "but [instead] to embrace it." The I is not to be detached from the world; indeed, "There is in reality no I except the I of the tension." Although human life cannot escape the fact that it is conditioned by the imperious laws of the *Erfahrungswelt*, the It-World, one also has the power to act upon and shape reality. The "faithful one" is attuned to the tension inherent in universal human experience. One is to affirm this twofold "mystery of his life-experience" and thereby create its unity. "He creates it by bringing together in himself the tension that he has taken upon him: by *awakening the I of this tension.*" Indeed, "the unity must be able to be lived, to be *realized*. [...] True unity cannot be found; it can only be created."[17]

This tension perforce also yields a contrasting response to one's experience (*Erlebnis*): realization and orientation. Either one lives and realizes within oneself the unity of the contending claims of reality, or one surrenders to the laws governing experience of the It-World (*Erfahrungsgrundgesätze*) and seeks to rationally orient one's life accordingly. While remaining on the temporal and spatial "surface of things," this attitude provides the chimera of security, albeit a "false security," for it condemns the self to isolation amidst the multiple and inherently instable pull of *Erfahrung*. To be sure, a rational orientation to the world governed by the *principium individuationis* is necessary, but "a purely orienting man degenerates into nothingness." "Orientation, which acts as the all-embracing, is thoroughly godless." On the other hand, "a purely realizing man would disappear in God," and thus fail, as Buber emphasized especially in his presentation of Hasidic lore, to *hallow the everyday*. Orientation and realization are as dialectically complementary as they are necessary. "Human life cannot escape the conditioned [reality of life, the everyday reality of the It-World]. But the unconditioned stands ineffaceably in the heart of the world."[18]

As Buber would later note, *Daniel* gave expression to "the great duality of human life"—realization and orientation corresponding embryonically to what Buber presents in *I and Thou* as man's twofold attitude to the world, the I-Thou and the I-It manner of relating to the world. But in *Daniel*, Buber underscored, the duality is expressed "only in its cognitive and not yet in its communicative and existential character."[19] It was still in the individual and not *between* being and being. "But I had already prepared the way for this distinction presented in my book *Daniel* between an 'orienting,' objectifying basic attitude and a 'realizing,' making-present one [that is, affirming the presence of the other]. This is a distinction that coincides in its core with that carried through in *I and Thou* between I-It and I-Thou relations, except the latter is no longer grounded in subjectivity but the sphere between the beings."[20]

The crucial moment in the transition to "a new kind of thinking," grounded in the concept of the interhuman encounter, as Buber attested, "arose, on the road of my thinking, out of the criticism of the concept of *Erlebnis*, to which I adhered in my youth, out of a radical self-correction." In the process, he reached the realization that "what really matters is not the 'experiencing of life' (*Erleben*)—detached subjectivity—but life itself; it is not religious experience, which is part of the psychic realm, but religious life itself, that is, the *total* life of an individual or of a people in their relationship to God and the world. To make the human element absolute means to tear it out of life's totality, out of reality."[21]

In contradistinction to the mystic, Buber now declared, "I am enormously concerned with just this world, this painful and precious fulfillment of all that I see, hear and taste," that is, the world of *Erfahrung*, the It-World. Therefore, "I cannot wish away any part of its reality. [. . .] Reality is no fixed condition, but a quantity, which can be heightened." For, "how can I give this reality to my world except by seeing the seen with all the strength of my life, hearing the heard with all the strength of my life, tasting the tasted with all the strength of my life?"[22] The concept of dialogue—and the hallowing of the world, the It-World—would slowly percolate.

In a short book proposal, dated February 5, 1918, Buber referred to *das Gegenüber*, "he who stands over against one."[23] In that proposal, *das Gegenüber* is God, but, as Buber developed his concept of dialogue, *das Gegenüber* came to designate every dialogical partner, whose radical otherness is constituted by an *Urdistanz*, a primal distance, "the anthropological basis"[24] of every dialogical relation. By virtue of the *Urdistanz* between all being, "every real relation in the world rests on individuation, this is its joy—for only in this way is mutual knowledge of different beings won."[25]

At the behest of Franz Rosenzweig, Buber delivered in January and February 1922 a series of lectures at the Freies Jüdisches Lehrhaus in Frankfurt am Main, which Rosenzweig had founded and directed. These lectures, under the general title "Religion as Presence" ("Religion als Gegenwart"),[26] served to clarify further Buber's *Gedankengang* (train of thought).[27] Rosenzweig sought to attend the lectures as much as his failing body, stricken with the onset of Lou

Gehrig's disease (ALS) and the loss of muscle control, would allow; when it was no longer possible, he would review the transcript of the eight lectures. He shared with Buber his critical reflections, as he later did when he read the printer's proofs of *Ich und Du*. Buber would gratefully respond to Rosenzweig's critique and duly attend to the clarification and revisions his friend suggested.

Their subsequent epistolary exchange was interspersed with reflections on the nature of religion—a term Rosenzweig vehemently rejected as constricting and distorting the genuine life of faith. Buber shared Rosenzweig's fear that "religion" often deflects one from God and from heeding the call to what in his Hasidic writings he celebrated as the "hallowing of the everyday," not beyond and thus not limited to the precincts of the synagogue, the church, the mosque. In an essay he wrote shortly after the publication of *I and Thou*, he observed that:

> It is far more comfortable to have to do with religion than have to do with God, who sends one out of home and fatherland into restless wandering. In addition, religion has all sorts of aesthetic refreshments to offer cultivated adherents. [. . .] For this reason, at all times awake spirits have been vigilant and have warned of the diverting forces hidden in religion.[28]

In a similar vein, Rosenzweig described religion—marked by formal, institutional affiliation, and relegated to the private sphere of personal disposition, whereby it is innocuously sequestered from the secular, public realm—as thus opposed to the life of faith manifested as a determined affirmation of divine creation. He thus cautioned Buber not to privilege I-Thou relations at the expense of the world of It (which constitutes God's created order). "What is to become of I and Thou," he mused, "if they have to swallow up the entire world and the Creator as well? Religion? I am afraid so—and shudder whenever I hear it [religion]. For *my* sake and *your* sake, there must be something else in this world besides—me and you!"[29] Portraying himself as "a very unselfish knight of the It," he unflinchingly accused Buber in his lectures of depicting the I-It as a "cripple" and thus easy game for "an antagonist":

> The fact that his cripple governs the modern world does not make it less a cripple. Of course, it's easy for you to dispose of *this* It. But it's a false It, you know, the product of the great deception [the faith in reason, and material, scientific, technological progress], not even three hundred years old in Europe.[30]

To be sure, Rosenzweig continues, Buber is correct that the "basic word I-It" cannot be spoken "with one's whole being," but it is "not a basic *word*, it is at most a basic idea," a questionable, philosophical proposition at that. If the It-World is nevertheless "entirely real," and is to be spoken with one's whole being, it is in dialogical response to he—God—who has spoken to us with his whole being in creating the world, the It-Word. "Spoken by Him," the basic world *is* I-It; "spoken by us, He-It." Thus, in reciting the Jewish liturgical benediction, "*He who causes death and life,*" you "will have said this basic word and said it in its deepest essence." Although death belongs to the It-World: "*It* is not dead. [. . .] It is created."[31]

In reply to Rosenzweig's critique, Buber acknowledged that one might gain the impression from the conclusion of part 1 of the galleys of *I and Thou* that he treated the It-World in an unwarranted cavalier manner, but he assures Rosenzweig that once he receives the next set of the page proofs, he would readily note that in the second and especially the third part of *I and Thou* "justice has been done to It." We thus read in the second part:

> The basic word I-It does not come from evil—any more than matter comes from evil. It comes from evil—like matter that presumes to be that which has being. When man lets it have its way, the relentlessly growing It-world grows over him like weeds, his own It loses its actuality, until the incubus over him and the phantom inside him exchange the whispered confession of their need for redemption.[32]

In asserting that the material world per se is not evil, Buber rejects the gnostic view that what the Hebrew Bible celebrates as divine creation is, in fact, the source of human agony, indeed, the embodiment of evil from which one must liberate one's soul. For Buber, it is only when the I-It World is presumed to have a reality of its own that one can speak of absolute evil.

For both Buber and Rosenzweig, the affirmation and the redemption of the It-World took on an urgency consequent to a "neo-gnostic spirit"[33] that swept through the intellectual landscape of the fledgling Weimar Republic, threatening to undermine its commitment to liberal democracy. This ominous development was signaled by the publication in 1921 of Adolf von Harnack's magisterial study of Marcion, the second-century Christian heretic, *Marcion: Das Evangelium von dem fremdem Gott.* They read Harnack's monograph not simply as a scholarly treatise but as indicative of a profound crisis in Christianity. Although they shared Harnack's and other liberal Protestants' disaffection with the worldly optimism of nineteenth-century moral theology, they were wary of Harnack's endorsement of Marcion's rejection of the Hebrew Bible and the God of creation. While Harnack held that it would have been mistaken for the early church to follow Marcion, they concluded, in the words of Rosenzweig, that the "conservation of the Old Testament as a canonical book in modern Protestantism is a result of a paralysis of religion and the Church."[34] But Rosenzweig feared that Harnack's call for the church to jettison the Old Testament and what he deemed to be its delusory belief in creation and earthly life as a divine gift would encourage, intentionally or otherwise, a hatred of the people who had propagated this foundational message of biblical faith. In a letter of July 1925 to Buber, with whom he was then working on their translation of the Hebrew scriptures into German, Rosenzweig wrote:

> It should be quite clear to you that the situation for which the neo-Marcionites [e.g., Harnack] have striven to achieve on the theoretical plane in actuality has already been obtained [in practice]. [. . .] When the Christian speaks of the Bible, he means only the New Testament, perhaps together with the Psalms, which then he mostly believes already belongs to the New Testament. Thus, in our new translation of the Hebrew Bible we are becoming missionaries.[35]

The Buber-Rosenzweig translation of the Hebrew Bible—which Christian supersessionists call the Old Testament—was not simply another translation but rather an attempt to capture in German the perduring voice of God as resonant in the Hebrew, and thus his ever-renewed relation with the world of his creation. For Buber and Rosenzweig, the God of the Hebrew Bible is indeed the God of creation—the It-World—and thus marks the shared destiny of *all* the world. In retaining the "Old Testament" despite Marcion's gnostic exhortations to jettison it, Rosenzweig and Buber observed, Christianity in effect acknowledged that salvation as a universal promise must be grounded in creation.

Redemption is thus not to be sought beyond the created order but in the given historical hour and its political and ethical imperatives; it cannot be realized in a flash, in one frenzied dash to the *eschaton*. Buber elaborated this thesis with scholarly detail in his 1932 *Kingship of God*,[36] which is an extended critique of both the concept of political theology[37] and ideologies that enjoin apocalyptic leaps into an imagined future beyond the prevailing political realities. To Buber's mind, the apocalyptic ideologies that flourished in the Weimar Republic—and which ultimately paved the way for Hitler—were manifestations of a gnostic despair. In abandoning the world to the diabolic, these gnostic-inflected ideologies marked a flight from a genuinely responsible politics, which cannot take place apart from the world as it is given, even when political actions are by *force majeure* limited to simple acts of human decency. As he admonished Kierkegaard for sequestering himself far from the "crowd," the Single One "must put his arms round the vexatious world, whose true name is creation."[38]

This message was encapsulated in an *obiter dictum* of Buber's wife, Paula, which he cited as the epigraph introducing his essay on the "Single One": "Responsibility is the umbilical cord of creation"—*Verantwortung ist der Nebelsrang der Schöpfung*.[39]

Notes

1. *The Letters of Martin Buber: A Life of Dialogue*, ed. Nahum N. Glatzer and Paul Mendes-Flohr, trans. Richard Winston, Clara Winston, and Harry Zohn (New York: Schocken Books, 1991), 67.
2. Martin Buber, "Distance and Relation," in Buber, *The Knowledge of Man: Selected Essays*, trans. Maurice Friedman and R. G. Smith (New York: Harper & Row, 1965), 59–71.
3. Wilhelm Dilthey, "Die Kultur der Gegenwart und Philosophie," in Dilthey, *Gesammelte Schriften* (Leipzig: B. G. Teubner, 1933), 8:190.
4. Johann Wolfgang von Goethe, *Faustus*, pt. 2, Mitternacht.
5. Dilthey, "Die Kultur der Gegenwart und Philosophie," 146, 194.
6. Wilhelm Dilthey, "Introduction to the Human Studies," trans. H. A. Hodges, in *Wilhelm Dilthey: An Introduction*, by H. A. Hodges (London: Routledge & Kegan Paul, 1944), 109.
7. Wilhelm Dilthey, *Weltanschauungslehre*, trans. William Kluback and Martin Weinbaum, *Dilthey's Philosophy of Existence* (New York: Bookman Associates, 1957).
8. Wilhelm Dilthey, "The Task of a Critique of Historical Reason," in Hodges, *Wilhelm Dilthey*, 114; Dilthey, "Entwürfe zur Kritik der historischen Vernunft," in *Gesammelte Schriften* (Leipzig: B. G. Teubner, 1927), 7:192.
9. Wilhelm Dilthey, "Die Typen der Weltanschauung und ihre Ausbildung in den metaphysischen Systemen," in *Gesammelten Schriften*, 8:17–18.
10. Martin Buber, "Über Jakob Boehme," *Wiener Rundschau*, May 15, 1901, in *Martin Buber Werkausgabe* (Gütersloh: Gütersloher Verlagshaus, 2017), vol. 2, pt. 1, 70.
11. Buber, "Über Jakob Boehme," 71–72.
12. Martin Buber, "What Is Man?," in Buber, *Between Man and Man*, trans. R. G. Smith (Boston: Beacon Press, 1955), 148.
13. Ludwig Feuerbach, *Grundsätze der Philosophie der Zukunft* (Leipzig, 1847), #1:1; #37:62–63; ##61–65:83–84.148.
14. Martin Buber, *The Legend of the Baal-Shem*, trans. Maurice Friedman (1908; New York: Schocken Books, 1955), 19.
15. Martin Buber, "Jewish Mysticism," in Buber, *The Tales of Rabbi Nachman*, trans. Maurice Friedman (1906; Bloomington: Indiana University Press, 1956), 10.
16. Martin Buber, *Daniel: Dialogues on Realization*, trans. Maurice Friedman (Syracuse, NY: Syracuse University Press, 2018), 91.
17. Buber, *Daniel*, 94–95.
18. Buber, *Daniel*, 32, 23, 44, 23, 98.
19. Letter to Friedman, quoted in translator's preface to Buber, *Daniel*, n.p.
20. Buber, "The History of the Dialogical Principle," afterword to Buber, *Between Man and Man*, 216.
21. Buber, "Replies to My Critics," in *The Philosophy of Martin Buber*, ed. Paul Arthur Schilpp and Maurice Friedman (LaSalle, IL: Open Court, 1967), 711–12.
22. Martin Buber, foreword to *Pointing the Way*, ed. and trans. Maurice S. Friedman (New York: Harper, 1963), ix.
23. Rivka Horwitz, *Buber's Way to "I and Thou"* (Heidelberg: Verlag Lambert Schneider, 1978), 156–65.
24. Martin Buber, *Ich und Du*, Nachwort vom Oktober 1957; Buber, *I and Thou*, trans. Smith, 124.
25. Buber, *I and Thou*, trans. Smith, 99.

26. Martin Buber, "Religion als Gegenwart," in *Martin Buber Werkausgabe*, 12:87–160.
27. Martin Buber, Nachwort, *Die Schriften des dialogischen Prinzips*, 233.
28. Martin Buber, "Religion und Gottesherrschaft," *Frankfurter Zeitung*, April 27, 1923; Buber, "Religion and God's Rule," in Buber, *A Believing Humanism: My Testament, 1902–1965*, trans. Maurice Friedman (New York: Simon & Schuster, 1967), 110.
29. Letter, Franz Rosenzweig to Buber, undated, *Letters of Martin Buber*, 280.
30. Letter, Rosenzweig to Buber, 278.
31. Letter, Rosenzweig to Buber, 278, 279.
32. Buber, *I and Thou*, trans. Smith, 95–96.
33. Benjamin Lazier, *God Interrupted: Heresy and the European Imagination between the World Wars* (Princeton, NJ: Princeton University Press, 2008), 30.
34. Adolf von Harnack, *Marcion: Das Evengelium vom fremden Gott*, 2nd ed. (Leipzig, 1924), 127.
35. Letter, Rosenzweig to Buber, July 25, 1925, in *Briefe und Tagebücher*, ed. Rachel Rosenzweig-Scheidmann (The Hague: Martinus Nijhoff, 1979), 2:1055–56.
36. See Martin Buber, *Kingship of God*, trans. Richard Scheimann (New York: Harper & Row, 1996).
37. The reference in *Königtum Gottes* to Schmitt is but indirect. Although he excoriates the politics of friend-foe dictum, Buber does not mention Schmitt by name.
38. Martin Buber, "The Question to the Single One," in *Between Man and Man*, trans. Ronald Gregor-Smith (New York: Routledge, 2002), xx.
39. Buber, "The Question to the Single One."

Annotated Bibliography

PRIMARY SOURCES

On Buber's spiritual journey and ultimate realization that one cannot, indeed, should not flee everyday reality as vexatious as it may be, see my *Martin Buber: A Life of Faith and Dissent* (New Haven, CT: Yale University Press, 2019), chapter 8, "The Tragic Grace of Everyday Reality." With reference to the series of lectures that Buber delivered at the Freies Jüdisches Lehrhaus, founded by Franz Rosenzweig, Rivka Horwitz traces the gestation and crystallization of Buber's philosophy of dialogue: *Buber's Way to "I and Thou": An Historical Analysis and the First Publication of Martin Buber's Lectures "Religion als Gegenwart"* (Heidelberg: Verlag Lambert Schneider, 1978). The Irish scholar Phil Huston provides a finely tuned exegesis of Buber's early predialogical writings and his evolving concept of God as the divine presence manifest in I-Thou relations: *Martin Buber's Journey to Presence* (New York: Fordham University Press, 2007).

Buber himself attests to this journey as one of conceptual clarification. See the 1923 preface to his collected essays on Judaism (Vorrede, *Reden über das Judentum. Gesamtausgabe* [Frankfurt am Main: Rütten & Loening, 1923]); also Buber, *On Judaism*, ed. Nahum N. Glatzer (New York: Schocken Books, 1967), 3–19, and in particular: "This preface is intended as an explanation rather than correction, for I describe what has happened to me as a process of clarification [in which] my words became clearer to myself. Many inexact, or indeed inaccurate, expressions in the early addresses [are] clarified in the later ones, in correspondence with my progress toward clarity. [. . .] What really matters is not the 'experience of life' [*Erleben*]—the detached subjectivity—but life itself" (3, 8).

SECONDARY LITERATURE

In Rosenzweig's early struggle to overcome a Marconian pessimism about worldly existence, see Benjamin Pollock, *Franz Rosenzweig's Conversions: World Denial and World Redemption* (Bloomington: Indiana University Press, 2014). On the *Sitz im Leben* in which his and Buber's resolute opposition to the philosophic and theological denigration of what Buber called the It-World (*Es-Welt*), see my "Gnostic Anxieties: Jewish Intellectuals and Weimar Neo-Marcionism," *Modern Theology* 34, no. 4 (October 2018): 71–80.

6

Martin Buber's Ethics of Perception

SARAH SCOTT

A press photo marking his 1957 visit to the United States showed Buber beckoning the viewer. Entitled "The Prophet," affixed to it was this statement: "Dr. Martin Buber—shown here lecturing at the Washington, DC School of Psychiatry—looks like a biblical prophet. And some think the 80-year-old Israeli writer and religious philosopher is just that. Unfortunately, even expert attempts to explain Dr. Buber's 'I-Thou' theory of human relationships is likely to end in bewilderment for the listener not well schooled in psychology." In this chapter I aim to reconstruct Buber's ethics as neither that of a prophet nor as necessarily bewildering. Buber was enormously influential for the development of twentieth-century popular moral philosophy, which focused on his distinction between I-Thou, or dialogical, and I-It, or monological, modes of existence, as laid out in his 1923 *I and Thou*. I first present this main theme and how it was received and then show how Buber's moral philosophy developed from his early engagement with Neoplatonism and aesthetics to create what may be called his "ethics of perception." Throughout I indicate comparisons to other movements in ethics, not to categorize or systematize, but to identify further potential avenues of study.

1. The Popular Moral Philosophy of *I and Thou*

In one of the most well-known applications of Buber's ethics, Martin Luther King Jr. used Buber's distinction between I-Thou and I-It relations in his 1963 "Letter from Birmingham Jail": "Segregation, to use the terminology of the Jewish philosopher Martin Buber, substitutes an 'I-It' relationship for the 'I-Thou' relationship, and ends up relegating persons to the status of things.

Hence segregation is not only politically, economically and sociologically unsound, it is morally wrong and sinful."[1] King's application provides two insights into Buber's moral philosophy and its reception. First, Buber is often taken to complement broadly Kantian twentieth-century movements, such as the personalism of King and the critique of the objectification of "the other" by existentialists such as Simone de Beauvoir, Frantz Fanon, and Jean-Paul Sartre. Buber's notions of I-Thou and I-It identify two modes of relationship: in the former, self and other are whole, unique beings in a dynamic, responsive relationship, and in the latter, self and other are mere objects of experience to be categorized and used. To many, this seemed a helpful reiteration of the Kantian insight that persons are ends in themselves and that an instrumental relationship toward them such that they are reduced to mere objects is the fundamental ethical error.

Second, when King criticizes the isolationism not just of segregation but also of political disengagement, he indicates a main way Buber differs from much of the philosophic tradition. While segregation demeans personhood, disengagement assumes we can extract ourselves from relationship and live as if others did not exist. This calls our attention to I-Thou and I-It as word pairs: there are four elements, and none exist alone, but always as part of a pair. For the other to manifest as a Thou, we must be in the mode of the I of the I-Thou relation; in seeing the other as a Thou, the I of the I-Thou relation is called forth. Indeed, since Buber takes beings to be interdependent and constituted by relationships, there are two different "I"s: the I of an I-It relation is an "ego" that does not just instrumentalize the other but also itself, while the I of an I-Thou relation appears as a "person."[2] As Buber explains his relational ontology, "the individual is a fact insofar as he steps into a living relation with other individuals. The aggregate is a fact of existence insofar as it is built up of living units of relation."[3] Thus King's famous lines, "Injustice anywhere is a threat to justice everywhere. We are caught in an inescapable network of mutuality, tied in a single garment of destiny. Whatever affects one directly, affects all indirectly,"[4] are the ethical-political offspring of Buber's central refrain in *I and Thou*, the ontological claim that "in the beginning is the relation."[5]

Buber hence clarified that, while he shares a lot with Kant, he has another source and goal, namely the "presuppositions of the interhuman."[6] Buber's notion of the "interhuman" (which he sometimes referred to as the "between") challenges the tradition, running from Descartes through Kant and existentialism, that grounds all phenomena in the experiencing I, which already is what it is without the other. Buber criticized this philosophy that begins from the "situation of the radically solitary man, and wants to derive the essence of existence from the experience of a nightmare."[7] While some existentialists did posit intersubjectivity, Buber rejected common attempts to label him an existentialist by stating no existentialist opened the door to otherness far enough, further cementing his role as the forerunner of the mid- to late twentieth-century preoccupation with "the other."[8] Indeed, his emphasis on the primacy of relationship and the moral obligation to respond to the other would cause Buber to occasionally be seen as a forerunner of the feminist care ethics of the late twentieth century.

Buber mapped I-Thou and I-It relationships onto what he called dialogical and monological modes of existence. While dialogue presupposes openness and engagement with the other, monologue is characterized by inward-turning reflection. For post–World War I readers grappling with the problem of evil, Buber's analysis of monologue was illuminating. Banal monological preoccupation with our own experience, efforts to manufacture an image of ourselves, projection of prejudices, inattentiveness to the uniqueness and call of the other, and desire to impose one's view on others can strengthen into the radical evil that seeks to make universal the aforementioned nightmare of the radically solitary man and eradicate otherness through totalitarianism and genocide. For example, in his 1936 "Question to the Single One," a diagnosis of the political climate of Germany, Buber maintained that flight from personal sociopolitical responsibility into solitary mysticism, suppression of difference by merging into a sociopolitical collectivity, and tyrannical megalomania all stem from the same monological impulse. However, Buber qualified popular attempts to characterize monologue in general as evil. Instead he recognized a limited, appropriate use of I-It forms of knowing, such as technical analysis, when balanced by I-Thou relations.

The corollary to monologue being seen as the manifestation of evil is that dialogue becomes seen as the manifestation of good. In an indication of the widespread embrace of Buber's ethics, calls for dialogue became ubiquitous. For example, besides King's appropriation, Catholicism also absorbed Buber's language.[9] In Pope Paul VI's inaugural encyclical he wrote, "[Dialogue] is a way of making spiritual contact. [. . .] We can think of it as a kind of thought transfusion. It is an invitation to the exercise and development of the highest spiritual and mental powers a man possesses."[10] Pope Francis continued the Buberian legacy, stating "Dialogue is our method."[11] As an example of his uptake beyond religious leaders, United Nations Secretary-General Dag Hammarskjöld met with Buber to discuss the possibilities for dialogue across political conflicts and was working on a translation of *I and Thou* at the time of his death, inspiring the *New York Times* to publish an article entitled "Sage

Who Inspired Hammarskjöld: He Is Martin Buber—Scholar, Philosopher, a Voice of Conscience for Modern Man."[12]

2. Challenges with Dialogue as a Method

So much for the widespread attractiveness of Buber's moral philosophy. Why, as indicated by the text affixed to "The Prophet" photo, do many then throw up their hands in bewilderment? Perhaps because, inspired by the notion that, as Pope Francis put it, "dialogue is our method," we want to know how exactly to create and live in dialogue, as if it was like following a kind of Kantian moral proceduralism. But when we take a step back from the popular reception of *I and Thou* and consider Buber's bigger picture—the "presuppositions of the interhuman"—we find ourselves grappling with some of the most intransient problems in philosophy. For instance, when considering barriers to dialogue, Buber identifies the problem of lives dominated by appearance and the need to live through an event in common with others while simultaneously retaining one's own view. This poses not just ethical and psychological but also epistemological and ontological questions: How can we distinguish between appearance and reality? How can two beings live through an event in common if we are each unique and "other"? For Buber, the answers to these questions are not found through the application of a method or the following of principles. Insofar as it presupposes static procedures, stable categories of things, and a subject that is separate from what it knows and acts upon, this approach is of limited applicability—to merely I-It relations. When dealing with dialogical relations, attention must be directed instead to cultivating the unique unfolding of each being and witnessing and learning from exemplars.

In recognition of the millennia-long efforts to understand the presuppositions of the interhuman, in his 1957 "What Is Common to All" Buber goes back to the pre-Socratic philosopher Heraclitus. He appeals to Heraclitus to combat two points of view: "the first of which values collectivity above all else, whereas the second believes the meaning of existence to be disclosed in the relation of the individual to his self."[13] A similar false dichotomy is depicted in *I and Thou* as a vision of the world embracing the soul versus a vision of the soul encompassing the world.[14] In each case relationship is undermined, on the one hand by submerging the self in another and on the other hand by subsuming the other within one's self. Buber identifies a third alternative in fragments from Heraclitus such as "the waking have a single cosmos in common," "one must follow what is common," and "do not listen to me but to the logos." In Buber's explanation, Heraclitus is not distinguishing between two types of persons, for example, self and other, or good and evil, but two spheres of human existence that each of us traverse: the "waking" one, in which we share a single cosmos, intelligible through a common logos, and the "dreaming" one, in which we flee from the demands of the "we" or common world into a private sphere of illusion. To live in dialogue—as the etymology of the word suggests, to live in and through the logos—is to be "flowing ever again into a great stream of reciprocal sharing of knowledge," awake to, knowledgeable of, and cocreating our cosmos.[15] To live in monologue is to be turned away from the logos, alienated from the cosmos, walking through life as if in a dream state.

The greatest depiction of the ethical injunction to "wake up and see" in Western philosophy is Plato's allegory of the cave, in which chained prisoners, imbibing images as if they were reality, break free and learn to see things as they actually are. Like Plato, Buber's ethical writings promote liberation from illusion, exile, alienation, and sophistry. In Buber's analysis, one of the greatest illusions is the belief that liberation from the "cave" comes from falling deeper into monologue, through the mistaken belief that enlightenment is achieved through isolation and withdrawal. For Buber, liberation is not *from* but *in and for* relationship. Imagine therefore not the solitary quest of the individual out of the populated cave of illusion but a cave enclosed around each person, a suit of armor, so to speak, grown so thick and heavy it counterproductively blinds and paralyzes each from entering the interhuman logos. Buber writes, "Each of us is encased in an armor whose task is to ward off signs. Signs happen to us without respite, we would only need to present ourselves and to perceive." These calls from the other elicit a response; when we do take heed and respond, and wonder if something unusual happened, our conscience tells us, "it is like this every day, only we are not there every day."[16]

Buber worked in a psychiatric clinic as a student; he was well aware of tragic mental illnesses that thrust patients into private worlds of illusion and the suffering that accompanies such isolation. More perplexing was the widespread phenomenon of unafflicted persons, who have the capacity to live in a common world but who nonetheless shut themselves off, as if they are willfully "not there." Liberation is a psychosocial problem for Buber; some "armor" or respite is necessary, but, taken to excess, protection becomes entrapping. On the one hand, Buber's ethics is simple: a method for dialogue or moral principles for I-Thou relationships would not say much more than "we would only need to present ourselves and to perceive." On the other hand, Buber recognized this ethics of perception to be among the most difficult and yet necessary tasks of a human life, requiring both the development of ourselves as individuals and the dismantling of excess "armor" so that we can be fully present and perceptive in the realm of the interhuman.

3. Individuation and Confirmation

Present ourselves and perceive not self *or* other, but self *and* other. How is this possible? In tune with fin de siècle German thought, the early Buber drew on Neoplatonic and aesthetic philosophy to develop his ethics of perception. In 1903 he completed his short thesis on the German Neoplatonic philosophers Nicholas of Cusa (1401–64) and Jakob Böhme (1575–1624) and planned to go on to advanced work in art history, which he never pursued. At the same time he began his lifelong project of Jewish cultural renewal and wrote enthusiastically about Jewish art. He coined the phrase "Jewish Renaissance," with the unity of his interests coming to the fore in proclamations such as that Hasidism is "an absolutely original, popular, and living renewal of Neoplatonism."[17] Although he seldom explicitly referenced these interests later, his central insights remained steady enough that he could quote his thesis in "What Is Man?" (1938), suggesting a greater significance for these early influences than has been typically recognized.[18]

Throughout his life, Buber called dialogue a "coincidence of opposites." The term is from Cusa, who used it to describe God as the ultimate being in whom all polarized categorizations (e.g., one-many, self-other, etc.) coincide. Cusa called this type of knowledge "learned ignorance," an act of humility that sets aside category-reliant discursive reason to open oneself to knowledge of the uncircumscribed other. Cusa's model of how one may know *God* as other through "learned ignorance" can be seen as a forerunner of Buber's model of how one can know and adequately respond to *beings* as others in his distinction between I-Thou and I-It relations. In Buber's modification of Neoplatonism, we cultivate perception not to make a vertical ascent out of this world in order to glimpse transcendent logos, but to extend our understanding horizontally, as it were, and build a common logos with others. Entering into dialogue we actualize the "coincidence of opposites," or, as Buber put it, "we expect a theophany of which we know nothing but the place, and the place is called community."[19]

Dialogue is a co-including of self and other, not a merging into unity that suppresses difference. Since relationship requires distinct participants, individuation is a key component of dialogue. One of the insights into individuation Buber takes from Cusa is his modification of the Platonic theory that each particular being is an instantiation of a transcendent, universal idea. I-It relations grasp the similarities between beings such that they are seen to participate in universal categories, so that sameness is essential, as in the Platonic model, while I-Thou relations grasp the way each being uniquely participates in the infinite God, so that difference is essential, as in Cusa's model. Alluding to both the Neoplatonic unity of truth, beauty, and goodness with being and the principle of plenitude, which maintains that perfected creation entails maximal diversity, Buber writes, "Each being must then also manifest infinite worth in its objective individuality. Just because it is at all, since being is good and noble and delightful. Mainly, however, because it is particular and unique."[20]

Moral conduct is hence guided by the development of the uniqueness of each being: "Uniqueness is thus the essential good of man that is given to him to unfold. [. . .] For the more unique a man really is, so much more can he give to the other and so much more will he give to the other."[21] Unlike Kantian or Aristotelian ethics that accords moral status to rational beings, or utilitarianism that accords moral status to beings who can feel pain and pleasure, Buber extends moral status to include the whole chain of being by virtue of the uniqueness of each being. This would often prove perplexing to readers struggling with Buber's examples of I-Thou or dialogical relationships not just with fellow persons or God, but also with trees, cats, and horses.[22] Buber clarified that the varying use of language and reason does render each relationship unique and characterized by differing degrees of mutuality; nonetheless he maintained a radically expansive moral sphere, which opened him up for use by later philosophers working in animal and environmental ethics.

From Böhme, Buber explores the notion of an innate self-persistence that manifests as the will to individuate and actualize an exemplary version of oneself. This is a microcosmic manifestation of the "birthing power" of the infinite creator within each creature. Buber, citing Böhme, writes: "As in God himself, so is there also in each its [own] power of the will to [its] shape; in its potentiality each power is a 'shape in the spirit' and each shape in the spirit 'is an imagination, a desiring will, and it desires to reveal itself.'"[23] The German word for "shape" used here is *Gestalt*, a term that also had significance from Buber's interest in art and aesthetics. Foreshadowing his later distinction between I-It and I-Thou relations, an alternative German term, *Form*, connotes a rigid and lifeless image, while *Gestalt* connotes dynamic, organic, patterned activity.[24] I-It relations do not just objectify the other but also the self; the ethical task is not just to individuate but to do so as *Gestalt*, not according to an alienated ideal, or *Form*. On this, throughout his life Buber would offer Rabbi Zusya's saying: "In the coming world, they will not ask me 'Why were you not Moses'; they will ask me: 'Why were you not Zusya?'"[25] Thus Buber bases moral motivation on creative, birthing power, each the artist of themselves, manifesting God as the ultimate artist.

An emphasis on individuation can be associated with isolationism and seem problematic for ethics. Buber, however, maintains that individuation happens through interaction, so that the good of the self is realized through moral relationships with others. The seeds of Buber's relational ontology, which would influence figures such as King, are found in his study of Böhme. Böhme used the Neoplatonic language of Renaissance alchemy to describe each creature as having a "signature" or unique personal trace that is drawn out in the presence of others. An analogy is that of a musical instrument that lies dormant until its unique tone is elicited by another. Even as the instrument retains its singularity and uniqueness, its expression varies in response to elicitation by different beings. Buber would refer to this dynamic decades later, writing in *I and Thou*, "No thing is a component of experience or reveals itself except through the reciprocal force of confrontation."[26] Hence, one cannot follow a monological method for individuation but instead must be open and responsive to being surprised by the other and one's own self as various qualities are drawn forth.

Buber identifies two intertwined challenges to individuation: "negative experiences with our environment, which denies us the confirmation of our being that we desire, underlie the one; negative experiences with oneself, in that the human person cannot say Yes to himself, underlie the other." Since genuine individuation does not follow an alienated ideal but rather is an actualization of our uniqueness, for which no universal rules or methods can direct us, it is necessarily fraught with anxiety. Consequently, the interhuman does not just need us to present ourselves but also for each to be perceived and confirmed as intrinsically valid by the other: "Again and again the Yes must be spoken to him, from the look of the confidant and from the stirrings of his own heart, to liberate him from the dread of abandonment, which is a foretaste of death."[27] Without this confirmation we may be moved to wrap ourselves in "armor," avoiding abandonment, anxiety, and responsibility by putting ourselves to sleep, to use the Heraclitean image, and withdrawing from the common world into monologue. Individuation makes us who we are, but because this is always relational, "a society may be termed human in the measure to which its members confirm one another."[28]

4. Aesthetic Vision and Imagining the Real

In 1952, the *New York Times* reported on Buber's talk "Hope for This Hour" at Carnegie Hall to an audience of 2,500, stating that Buber called for "the establishment of new standards of perception and understanding to begin genuine conversation" across divides.[29] From a philosophic perspective, this was a question of social epistemology: How can we build on individuation and confirmation to not just perceive and affirm uniqueness but also have a single cosmos and a common logos? Normative ethics tended to answer this by using reason to develop universal principles. However, Buber criticized principle-based ethics as the absurdity of attempting to use an It-mode to grasp a Thou: "I say that where a situation accosts one, then that is not the time to consult a dictionary. [. . .] I do not have to consider what general concept to subsume this situation and what principle thereby to apply to it. Rather, it is incumbent upon me to take my stand before this 'new' situation, it goes without saying to take my stand before it with all that I am and all that I know."[30] In emphasizing nuanced perception of novel particulars and relational context, Buber foreshadowed later twentieth-century moral particularism. But whereas particularists often revived Aristotelian virtue ethics to explain how one could just "see" appropriate moral response without the use of principles, Buber instead drew on his background in aesthetics to develop standards of perception.[31]

Buber's early engagement with art and aesthetics helped him to develop both the obscure Neoplatonic references of Cusa into a type of knowing beyond discursive reason that can grasp otherness and those of Böhme into imagination and *Gestalt*. In Kant's main work on aesthetics, the *Critique of Judgment*, he distinguishes between determinate and reflective judgment. In the former, reason uses preestablished categories to make sense of the particulars it encounters. In the latter, when faced with a novel particular for which no prior concept is sufficient, its unique, purposive, holistic *Gestalt* is grasped through an interplay between imagination and reason. Although reflective judgments are not *universally* valid like reason-based determinate judgments, they may be *generally* valid as judgments of taste exercising the capacity of the imagination to grasp novel entities. Determinate and reflective judgment may be mapped onto I-It and I-Thou forms of knowing. Thus, while Buber's early work on individuation and confirmation is in keeping with the aesthetic notion of developing genius and celebrating uniqueness, his later work on moral response may be seen as developing the aesthetic notion of taste—the capacity to make a generally valid judgment of a novel particular and navigate the interhuman without using preestablished concepts or principles.

Following his aesthetic orientation, Buber focuses on the role of memory and imagination in guiding moral response. Buber explains that, as it encounters beings, memory "educates itself" and constructs concepts of its self and others in order to gain a sense of predictability and control.[32] This is necessary and inescapable, but an overgrowth of memory undermines our capacity to relate, as we may fail to see uniqueness and instead form a relationship with a preconceived concept of the other, that is, with an It instead of a Thou. In contrast, in an I-Thou relation the other is known without being subsumed under a universal, through the use of imagination to grasp novel particulars, as occurs in aesthetic perception. To mark off the difference between the use of imagination to enter the interhuman and mere monological illusion, Buber coined the term *Realphantasie*, or "imagining the real." Imagining the real is "the capacity to hold before one's soul a reality arising at this moment but not able to be directly experienced."[33] When we imagine the real we practice "inclusion." Inclusion entails three components: "[1] a relation between two persons, [2] an event experienced by them in common, in which at least one of them actively participates, [3] the fact that this one person, without forfeiting anything of the felt reality of his activity, at the same time lives through the common event from the standpoint of the other."[34] To readers who thought perhaps Buber referred to empathy, he insisted that he was not talking about a feeling but a "living with others" through the imagination.[35] Empathy, he worried, could easily slip into monologue disguised as dialogue, as one might become enamored by the way the other is the source of feelings.[36]

Buber criticized the tendency in moral philosophy to forget that reason and empathy are not the only ways we relate: "The technical is only what can be easily surveyed, easily explained, it is the coordinated. But besides and in the midst of this, there is a manifold relation to things in their wholeness, their independence, and their *purposelessness*. The man who gazes without purpose on a tree is no less 'everyday' than the one who looks at a tree to learn which branch would make the best stick."[37] "Gazing without purpose" paraphrases Kantian aesthetics in which he describes a precondition for taste as the ability to disinterestedly perceive an entity as purposive but without external purpose, that is, as having its own organized qualities and reasons for being that are independent of its usefulness for any onlooker. Like Kant, Buber maintains that seeing the standpoint of the other requires us to be disinterested. He calls this "distancing," which is the imagination's depiction of what we encounter as a unity that exists for itself, independent of our emotional and practical investment in it. Buber declares, "only [aesthetic] vision and, in its wake, art transcend need and make the superfluous into the necessary."[38] Hence, to the extent he may be situated in the broadly Kantian movements of his era, Buber is best seen as following Kantian aesthetics rather than ethics. As in the work of Hannah Arendt, Buber's use of aesthetics is ethical-political, an exploration of the conditions for a single cosmos and common logos.

Besides his account of individuation and confirmation, Buber's description of moral imagination comes closest to offering the method for dialogue often searched for by readers. Yet even here there are no procedures to be followed, only learning from exemplary figures and examples of common pitfalls. We leave *Realphantasie* for mere fantasy when, for instance, we become aesthetically absorbed in the other as a source of feelings, when we slip into the aforementioned fantasies of the self-absorbed in the other or the other absorbed in the self, and when we forget that dialogue has "as its minimum constitution one thing, the mutuality of the inner action," and instead imagine a relation where none exists.[39] Sometimes the barrier to dialogue is not that we are not present but that the other does not turn to us. Distancing and reflective judgment help us to recognize when there is actual mutuality and the varying degrees of dialogue possible with each being that confronts us. Aesthetic vision corrects the failures of I-It perception to see what is new about the other, to see the other as a dynamic entity capable of change and spontaneity, and to see the other as a distinct subject that enters into relation with us, and not merely as an object whose existence is relative to our own experience. In drawing from now unusual sources such as Neoplatonism and philosophy of aesthetics, Buber showed himself a man of taste, foreshadowing many of the main developments in later twentieth-century moral philosophy, yet producing a unique vision of ethics based on creative and relational life.

Notes

1. Martin Luther King Jr., "Letter from Birmingham Jail," in *Why We Can't Wait* (New York: Penguin Signet Classic, 2000), 71.
2. Martin Buber, *I and Thou*, trans. Walter Kaufmann (New York: Touchstone, 1996), 112.
3. Martin Buber, "What Is Man?," in *Between Man and Man*, trans. Ronald Gregor-Smith (New York: Routledge, 2002), 240.
4. King, "Letter from Birmingham Jail," 65.
5. Buber, *I and Thou*, 69.
6. Martin Buber, "Elements of the Interhuman," in *The Knowledge of Man: Selected Essays*, trans. Maurice Friedman and Ronald Gregor Smith (Amherst, NY: Prometheus Books, 1998), 74.
7. Buber, "What Is Man?," 200.
8. Martin Buber, "Interrogation of Martin Buber," in *Philosophic Interrogations*, ed. Sydney Chester Rome and Beatrice K. Rome (New York: Holt, Rinehart & Winston, 1964), 23.
9. On Buber's influence on Vatican II, see Peter Huff, "Martin Buber and Catholic-Atheist Dialogue," in *Martin Buber: Creaturely Life and Social Form*, ed. Sarah Scott (Bloomington: Indiana University Press, 2022).
10. Paul VI, *Ecclesiam Suam*, August 6, 1964; see https://www.vatican.va/content/paul-vi/en/encyclicals/documents/hf_p-vi_enc_06081964_ecclesiam.html.
11. Pope Francis, "Meeting with the Bishops of the United States of America," September 23, 2015; see https://www.vatican.va/content/francesco/en/speeches/2015/september/documents/papa-francesco_20150923_usa-vescovi.html.
12. "Sage Who Inspired Hammarskjöld," *New York Times*, December 3, 1961, 43.
13. Martin Buber, "What Is Common to All," in *Knowledge of Man*, 87.
14. Buber, *I and Thou*, 122.
15. Buber, "What Is Common to All," 96.
16. Martin Buber, "Dialogue," in *Between Man and Man*, 12.

17. Martin Buber, "The Jewish Cultural Problem and Zionism," in *The First Buber: Youthful Zionist Writings of Martin Buber*, trans. Gilya G. Schmidt (Syracuse, NY: Syracuse University Press, 1999), 178.

18. For an elaboration of claims made in this section, see Sarah Scott, "Knowing Otherness: Martin Buber's Appropriation of Nicholas of Cusa," *International Philosophical Quarterly* 55, no. 4 (2015): 399–416.

19. Buber, "Dialogue," 9.

20. Buber, "On the History of the Problem of Individuation," trans. Sarah Scott, *Graduate Faculty Philosophy Journal* 33, no. 2 (2012): 377.

21. Martin Buber, *The Legend of the Baal-Shem*, trans. Maurice Friedman (Princeton, NJ: Princeton University Press, 1955), 41–42.

22. On Buber's notion of dialogue with animals, see Dustin Atlas, "The Eloquent Muteness of Creatures," in *Martin Buber: Creaturely Life and Social Form*, ed. Scott.

23. Buber, "On the History of the Problem of Individuation," 338–89.

24. On *Form* and *Gestalt*, see Zachary Braiterman, *The Shape of Revelation: Aesthetics and Modern Jewish Thought* (Stanford, CA: Stanford University Press, 2007), 33–36.

25. Martin Buber, *Tales of the Hasidim (The Early Masters and the Later Masters)*, trans. Olga Marx (New York: Schocken Books, 1991), 251.

26. Buber, *I and Thou*, 77.

27. Martin Buber, "Images of Good and Evil," in *Good and Evil: Two Interpretations* (Upper Saddle River, NJ: Prentice Hall, 1997), 134, 136.

28. Martin Buber, "Distance and Relation," in *Knowledge of Man*, 57.

29. "Israeli Scholar Honored," *New York Times*, April 7, 1952, 23.

30. Martin Buber, "Replies to My Critics," in *The Philosophy of Martin Buber*, ed. Paul A. Schilpp and Maurice Friedman, Library of Living Philosophers 12 (LaSalle, IL: Open Court, 1967), 696.

31. For an elaboration of claims made in this section, see Sarah Scott, "From Genius to Taste," *Journal of Jewish Thought and Philosophy* 25, no. 1 (2017): 110–30; and Scott, "Monologue Disguised as Dialogue," in *Martin Buber: Creaturely Life and Social Form*, ed. Scott.

32. Buber, *I and Thou*, 72.

33. Buber, "Distance and Relation," 60.

34. Martin Buber, "Education," in *Between Man and Man*, 115.

35. Martin Buber, *The Martin Buber–Carl Rogers Dialogue: A New Transcript with Commentary*, ed. Rob Anderson and Kenneth N. Cissna (Albany: State University of New York Press, 1997), 25.

36. Buber, "Education," 115.

37. Buber, "What Is Man?," 211.

38. Buber, "Man and His Image-Work," in *Knowledge of Man*, 150.

39. Buber, "Dialogue," 9.

Annotated Bibliography

PRIMARY LITERATURE

The classic starting point for understanding Buber's ethics is the basic distinction between I-Thou and I-It relations: Martin Buber, *I and Thou*, trans. Walter Kaufmann (New York: Free Press, 2023). However, readers looking for a more straightforward writing style, with clearer definitions and examples, should read the essays "Dialogue" and "What Is Man?," both in Martin Buber, *Between Man and Man*, trans. Ronald Gregor Smith (New York: Routledge, 2002).

Buber explicates his relational ontology in another good collection of later philosophic writing, including the essays "Distance and Relation," "Elements of the Interhuman," and "What Is Common to All," in Martin Buber, *The Knowledge of Man: Selected Essays*, trans. Maurice Friedman and Ronald Gregor Smith (Amherst, NY: Prometheus Books, 1998).

For Buber's exploration of ethics through an existential and religious orientation (e.g., the meaning of the psalms for the human condition) see Martin Buber, *Good and Evil: Two Interpretations*, pt. 1, "Right and Wrong," trans. R. G. Smith, and pt. 2, "Images of Good and Evil," trans. M. Bullock (Upper Saddle River, NJ: Prentice Hall, 1997).

SECONDARY LITERATURE

In my analysis, an important source for Buber's unique approach to ethics is his early study of Neoplatonic philosophy. For his early study of Nicholas of Cusa and Jakob Böhme, see Martin Buber, "On the History of the Problem of Individuation: Nicholas of Cusa and Jakob Böhme," trans. Sarah Scott, *Graduate Faculty Philosophy Journal* 33, no. 2 (2012): 371–401.

The relation between Buber's use of Cusa and the ethical dimensions of his later philosophy of dialogue are explored in Sarah Scott, "Knowing Otherness: Martin Buber's Appropriation of Nicholas of Cusa," *International Philosophical Quarterly* 55, no. 4 (2015): 399–416.

Buber's engagement with art and aesthetics is also foundational to his unique approach to ethics. For his youthful text placing artistic development at the foundation of existential and political development, see Martin Buber, "The Jewish Cultural Problem and Zionism," in *The First Buber: Youthful Zionist Writings of Martin Buber*, trans. Gilya G. Schmidt (Syracuse, NY: Syracuse University Press, 1999). For a mature analysis of human nature as essentially artistic in its orientation, see Martin Buber, "Man and His Image-Work," in *The Knowledge of Man: Selected Essays*, trans. Maurice Friedman and Ronald Gregor Smith (Amherst, NY: Prometheus Books, 1998). For analyses of the philosophic significance of Buber's engagement with art and aesthetics, see Zachary Braiterman, *The Shape of Revelation: Aesthetics and Modern Jewish Thought* (Stanford, CA: Stanford University Press, 2007), and Sarah Scott, "From Genius to Taste: Martin Buber's Aestheticism," *Journal of Jewish Thought and Philosophy* 25, no. 1 (2017): 110–30.

For a famous example of the influence of Buber's ethics, see Martin Luther King Jr.'s use of Buber's I-Thou distinction: Martin Luther King Jr., "Letter from Birmingham Jail," in *Why We Can't Wait* (New York: Penguin Signet Classic, 2000). For essays on Buber's relevance for contemporary philosophic anthropology, politics, and ethics, see *Martin Buber: Creaturely Life and Social Form*, ed. Sarah Scott (Bloomington: Indiana University Press, 2022).

WORKS CITED

Primary Sources

Buber, Martin. "Dialogue." In *Between Man and Man*, trans. Ronald Gregor-Smith. New York: Routledge, 2002.

———. "Distance and Relation." In *The Knowledge of Man: Selected Essays*, trans. Maurice Friedman and Ronald Gregor Smith. Amherst, NY: Prometheus Books, 1998.

———. "Education." In *Between Man and Man*, trans. Ronald Gregor-Smith. New York: Routledge, 2002.

———. "Elements of the Interhuman." In *The Knowledge of Man: Selected Essays*, trans. Maurice Friedman and Ronald Gregor Smith. Amherst, NY: Prometheus Books, 1998.

———. *I and Thou*. Translated by Walter Kaufmann. New York: Touchstone, 1996.

———. "Images of Good and Evil." In *Good and Evil: Two Interpretations*. Pt. 1: "Right and Wrong," trans. R. G. Smith. Pt. 2: "Images of Good and Evil," trans. M. Bullock. Upper Saddle River, NJ: Prentice Hall, 1997.

———. "Interrogation of Martin Buber." Conducted by M. S. Friedman. In *Philosophic Interrogations*, ed. S. Rome and B. Rome. New York: Holt, Rinehart & Winston, 1964.

———. "The Jewish Cultural Problem and Zionism." In *The First Buber: Youthful Zionist Writings of Martin Buber*, trans. Gilya G. Schmidt. Syracuse, NY: Syracuse University Press, 1999.

———. *The Legend of the Baal-Shem*. Translated by Maurice Friedman. Princeton, NJ: Princeton University Press, 1955.

———. "Man and His Image-Work." In *The Knowledge of Man: Selected Essays*, trans. Maurice Friedman and Ronald Gregor Smith. Amherst, NY: Prometheus Books, 1998.

———. *The Martin Buber–Carl Rogers Dialogue: A New Transcript with Commentary*. Edited by Rob Anderson and Kenneth N. Cissna. Albany: State University of New York Press, 1997.

———. "On the History of the Problem of Individuation: Nicholas of Cusa and Jakob Böhme." Translated by Sarah Scott. *Graduate Faculty Philosophy Journal* 33, no. 2 (2012): 371–401.

———. "The Question to the Single One." In *Between Man and Man*, trans. Ronald Gregor-Smith. New York: Routledge, 2002.

———. "Replies to My Critics." *In The Philosophy of Martin Buber*, ed. Paul A. Schilpp and Maurice Friedman, Library of Living Philosophers, 12. LaSalle, IL: Open Court, 1967.

———. *Tales of the Hasidim (The Early Masters and the Later Masters)*. Translated by Olga Marx. New York: Schocken Books, 1991.

———. "What Is Common to All." In *The Knowledge of Man: Selected Essays*, trans. Maurice Friedman and Ronald Gregor Smith. Amherst, NY: Prometheus Books, 1998.

———. "What Is Man?" In *Between Man and Man*, trans. Ronald Gregor-Smith. New York: Routledge, 2002.

Secondary Sources

Atlas, Dustin. "The Eloquent Muteness of Creatures: Affect and Animals in Martin Buber's Dialogical Writings." In *Martin Buber: Creaturely Life and Social Form*, ed. Sarah Scott. Bloomington: Indiana University Press, 2022.

Braiterman, Zachary. *The Shape of Revelation: Aesthetics and Modern Jewish Thought*. Stanford, CA: Stanford University Press, 2007.

Francis, Pope. "Meeting with the Bishops of the United States of America." September 23, 2015. Vatican website. https://www.vatican.va/content/francesco/en/speeches/2015/september/documents/papa-francesco_20150923_usa-vescovi.html.

Huff, Peter A. "Martin Buber and Catholic-Atheist Dialogue." In *Martin Buber: Creaturely Life and Social Form*, ed. Sarah Scott. Bloomington: Indiana University Press, 2022.

King, Martin Luther, Jr. "Letter from Birmingham Jail." In *Why We Can't Wait*. New York: Penguin Signet Classic, 2000.

Paul VI, Pope. *Ecclesiam Suam*. August 6, 1964. Vatican website. https://www.vatican.va/content/paul-vi/en/encyclicals/documents/hf_p-vi_enc_06081964_ecclesiam.html.

Scott, Sarah. "From Genius to Taste: Martin Buber's Aestheticism." *Journal of Jewish Thought and Philosophy* 25, no. 1 (2017): 110–30.

———. "Knowing Otherness: Martin Buber's Appropriation of Nicholas of Cusa." *International Philosophical Quarterly* 55, no. 4 (2015): 399–416.

———. "Monologue Disguised as Dialogue: Almodóvar's *Talk to Her* and Buber on the 'Lovers' Talk.'" In *Martin Buber: Creaturely Life and Social Form*, ed. Sarah Scott. Bloomington: Indiana University Press, 2022.

PART TWO

Language and Hermeneutics

Introduction

PAUL MENDES-FLOHR

"In the beginning is the relation"—the I-Thou relation. With this oblique commentary on the Gospel of John 1:1 (King James)—"In the beginning was the Word, and the Word was with God, and the Word was God"—Buber posits dialogical speech as the primordial, ontological ground of human being, of being human. In an I-Thou dialogue (which may be silent) we are addressed by the Eternal Thou and, in turn, even one who "fancies" oneself to be godless, "when he addresses with his whole devoted being" another person as a Thou, "he addresses God."[1]

Raised in the multicultural Austrian-Hungarian Empire, Buber not only mastered numerous languages—Slavic and Latin as well those of the Jewish tradition—he also developed a keen interest in language as a distinctive intersubjective mode of being, what Joachim Oberst calls the "religious-ontological force of language" as the spoken word. Qua speech, language instantiates the possibility of human beings meeting one another in the between, where—Oberst cites Buber—they "give each other the heavenly bread [John 6:33] of being-oneself."

Buber's understanding of dialogue as an intersubjective relationship is thus, as Johan Siebers underscores, to be distinguished from rhetorical conceptions of dialogue that reach back to Socrates and thenceforth to contemporary theories of communication. Dialogue as a reciprocal existential "I-Thou" confirmation does not seek to elucidate propositional and logical truth, nor does it serve to convey information. As a radical break with regnant theories of communication, particularly those that focus on cybernetic and cognate technologies facilitating the flow of information and social interaction, Siebers concludes, Buber's notion of dialogue as "the living word" between two existentially independent individuals calls for a fundamental revision of cognitive and sociological theories of communication.

Siebers observes that "the living, spoken word" and response are central to the Hebrew Bible: "*The Lord God called to Adam and said to him, 'Where are you?'* (Gen. 3:9). Creation itself is an act of speech (Gen. 1:3, "*Then God said, 'Let there be light'; and there was light*"). For Buber, the Hebrew Bible documents—and when read aloud, resonates—the spoken word of God and the response of the children of Israel, albeit often haltingly. In his German translation of the Bible, Buber sought to convey its dialogical "spokenness" (*Gesprochenheit*). In detailing the linguistic and semantic practices that Buber deployed to sound anew God's spoken word, Steven Kepnes illuminates not only that the per-during, ever renewing aurality of God's address informs Buber's scriptural hermeneutics but is also seminal for his understanding of the divine-human relationship.

Imagining the lived reality of the other, as Claudia Welz notes, requires listening to—not merely hearing—the voices of others, resonating their life experience. Dialogical listening is at the heart of Buber's relational ontology.

Note

1. Martin Buber, *I and Thou*, trans. Walter Kaufmann, 100th anniversary reissue (New York: Free Press, 2023), 16–23, 64.

7

Buber and Language

JOACHIM OBERST

> Speech is the twin of my vision, it is unequal to measure itself,
> It provokes me forever . . .
> WALT WHITMAN, "Song of Myself"

1. Introduction: The Existential Ontology of Language

Martin Buber, poet, philosopher, religious leader and theologian, thinker, activist, visionary and prophet, husband, humanist, and psychologist, would be none of these without his special affinity to language. To understand the importance of language for Buber, from his earliest years in Vienna, Austria, and Lemberg, Poland, to the end of his life in Jerusalem, a deeper look at the intrinsic connection between (human) being and speech is essential. This critical examination will help us come to terms with the lifelong, intense relationship Buber entertains with the phenomenon of language, a relationship that grows as much out of him as it grows to and in him. In, through, and with language Buber could become one with himself, evidenced in the self-reflection of his being in *his* language. He could *become what and who he is* in a mysterious way that merits special attention. There is a reason why this is so, and this reason is borne in the mystery of language itself as Buber understands it. That Buber could maintain his creativity in multiple languages—German, Yiddish, Polish, Hebrew, French, and English—both out of necessity and by choice—is indicative of the intimacy he nurtured with language as his *modus operandi*. Language is Buber's *way and means* of *being,* of *being himself,* which means of *being himself with others.*

Pindar, the ancient Greek poet, advises the ambitious to "become who you are" by striving for excellence, for it is the striving that bears the greatness of their ambition before stunning excellence is prone to happen. His poetry proves his point as it *words* the witnessed greatness into a language that is reflective of the celebrated deed. Thus, too, Buber's distinctive diction turns the object of language as a tool of communication into the subject of *its* religious-ontological force and mission to enter what he calls "the sphere" of "the between" where "the word that is spoken" originates, belongs, abides, to return home, to "its actual occurrence" of "dialogue" (*Gespräch*), and thus create an inclusive community of interhumanity. In the distinctive way Buber works and lives (with/in) (his) language, he remains stubbornly faithful to what he considers to be the essence of language, whose prime mode of being is not the definite result (*Ergebnis*) of communication as expedient-efficient information-transportation, but the actual event of its occurrence (*Begebnis*).[1] Buber becomes who he is, revealed in the lived and living word as he touches on the essence and origin of the word, the ontological fact of its being spoken as and in(to) acts of speech, and this non-monolithically in its manifold forms of silence, physical performance, and acoustic resonance. Hence, his speech is not just a mirror of himself but truly himself reaching out to those ready to listen and meet him. We have evidence of this linguistic-ontological force in his writing as a witness that language is as much the personal endeavor to speak (to) the mysteries of reality as it is a (re)collective enterprise Buber is content and eager to join and propel. Like the iconic American poet Walt Whitman, Buber knows language is the element of his being, "the twin of [his] vision, unequal to measure itself." Outmatched by itself, its likeness "provokes" Buber to continuous compositions that are borne by the air of personal address. Thus, even the written word reveals itself as speech to the other as the newfound You.[2] To understand how, a brief look at Pindar's paradox can help illuminate the mystery.

2. Solving Pindar's Paradox of Being One's Own Self-Becoming

1. LINGUISTIC SELF-BECOMING VIA THE OTHER

The paradox of Pindar's imperative to "become such as [you know] you (already) are" is a topos in the existential-phenomenological tradition.[3] Søren Kierkegaard is famously keen in advancing Pindar's principle of self-overcoming when he admonishes his reader "to strive to become what one already is" but wonders "who would take the pains to waste his time on such a task?" Its seeming triviality is deemed too futile to deserve particular attention, while, as Kierkegaard is quick to point out, this *is* precisely what is needed, namely, the highest degree of subjectivity. For Buber, however, the intensified passion of such attention is not a question of "the greatest imaginable degree of resignation" but the opposite. Egocentric self-authentication in the Christian service for God, as Kierkegaard envisions it,[4] is detrimental to the self.[5] In a similar move, Buber spurns secularized versions of personal salvation such as the authenticated self in its ontological opposition to the collective of society, the They, *das Man*, or Everyone, as Martin Heidegger depicts it in *Being and Time*. Heidegger's promotion of Pindar's paradox culminates in his existential-ontological reading of the imperative: "Become what you are!"[6] Human being consists in *its* (!) calling to self-becoming.[7] For Heidegger, possibility is the essence of humanity which, in contrast to Aristotle, stands higher than actuality.[8] Humans can and ought to become ontically what they are already existentially, that is, authentic. In the transition from existentiality (as the reality of possibility) to onticality (as the "existentiellness" of concrete reality) this process of self-becoming happens. One is oneself only in one's own(most) self-becoming.[9]

Buber sees in both Kierkegaard's existential pietism and Heidegger's existential ontology forms of a philosophical nihilism he categorically rejects. Kierkegaard's pietism shuns the collective embeddedness of the self. Heidegger's "monologism [...] is [too] well acquainted with the *existentiale* (*Existentialem*) but not with the *existentiell* (*Existentiellem*)" (ontological and the ontic being, respectively), where real living actually and only happens.[10] For Buber, the task of self-actualization is neither a question of resignation nor the feat of a self-creative self-relation, but the mutuality of a twofold self-assertion he calls "the personal making present" (*personale Vergegenwärtigung*) of each other to each other, that is, the affirmation of oneself assisted and promoted by a fundamental acceptance, namely, that of the confirmation by another.[11] Within the mystery and ministry of this interhuman space, language has its real and genuine place. Not to recognize "the dialogical character of language" contributes to the "radical destruction of the mystery between man and man"[12] in the modern age. The modern age of *de-Socratization*, Buber says, is no longer inspired by dialogical exchange but driven by "monologizing hubris." It deems itself, its "thinking" and "speaking to itself," ontologically prior and superior, thus, the essence and origin of language. Against this misconception Buber points out that all *soliloquy* is the subsequent "internalization" of *communication*, of "the basic fact" that "humans speak *to* each other" *before* they can speak to themselves.[13] The ontic-ontological priority of dialogue grounds all solipsistic soliloquy. The modern-philosophical prejudice of onto-solipsism is trapped in its onto-idolatry of the absolute self as the cradle of language and thought. One can never speak to oneself as if to another, because one can never be another to oneself. One always knows already what one is about to say to oneself. Pure "otherness," however, constitutes a higher dimension of human reality, that of unpredictability. Otherness is the place of total *un*anticipation, where "the moment of surprise" prompts one to "heed the call of the spirit," respond in the most originary ways (*ursprunghaft*) with the thorough novelty of oneself to join the genuine dialogue. Buber warns that to disregard the primacy of the dialogical nature of human being will, and already does, lead to catastrophic implosions of the human collective.[14]

Buber learned his lesson the hard way, as he confesses in his remorseful report of his painful "conversion" away from the *un-* and *other*worldly "religious experience" to the mundane reality of *this* life. We must *understand* that we *stand under* the relentless claim of response-*ability* (*im Anspruch angesprochen*) to respond *in* responsibility (*in der Verantwortung antworten*) with the fullest meaning (*Sinn*) of human being—our mutual "personal presencing" (*personale Vergegenwärtigung*)—to the human need of a real presence (*Gegenwärtigkeit*) in a world that is quick to disregard the delicate intricacies of our interhuman connectedness (*Verbundenheit*).[15] Thus, we are bound neither to reject nor to disregard but to embrace our boundedness, "for in such boundedness [*Gebundenheit*] lies the bonding of commitment to each other [*Verbundenheit*]."[16] The meaning of being human is not to be found in one single person, nor in more than one, "but only in the embodiment of their concerted play together [*leibhaften Zusammenspiel*], in this, their in-between."[17] Language is the bond of this between, as both evidence of distance and execution of relation to bridge that distance. In language distance (*Entfernung*) instantiates relation to *dis-stance* (*ent-fernen*) itself to *re-lation* (*Be-ziehung*).[18] Thus, it is language that enacts what Buber calls "the twofold principle of human being" which consists in the "double movement" of "primal distancing" (*Urdistanzierung*) and "relating" (*In-Beziehungtreten*).[19]

Notwithstanding his bibliomania, Buber understood the human need of the between. He knows it as the most "sincere truth." He knows, "without [the] It [of books] he cannot live but were [he] to live with [books] only, [he] would no longer be human."[20] Although he loves to seclude himself with his beloved books, he understands, he can do so only because the world of *human* beings whom he loves is ready to receive him as soon as he opens the door to meet them. Thus, he resists the idolatry of the written word. It is the word that is spoken from one to another, the living word, that grants earthly salvation. For only as speech (*Rede*) does language (*Sprache*) *happen between* humans as their connective bond of responsive, community-grounding communication.[21] In the ontology of Buber's mystic philosophy all linguistic insight motivates—because it is motivated by—ethical sensibilities. Words can be spoken not because they are awaiting their retrieval from a linguistic realm in ontological space but only because their being consists in their being spoken. Their realm of being (*Ort des Bestandes*) is the togetherness (*Miteinander*) of speakers whose (re-)creative speech-enactments (*Sprachgewirk*) keep the otherwise deadened dictionary alive. The mode of being of words consists in performance first, not inheritance. Their standing reserve (*präsenter Bestand*) is grounded on their potential possession by speakers who keep them alive in continued re-actualization. Thus, it is "spokenness [*Gesprochenheit*], or rather [the event of the actual occurrence (*aktuelles Begebnis*)] of their being spoken," that brings words into (their) being, first as gesture (*Gebärde*), then as voiced sign (*Lautgebärde*) to become the word that is spoken. This can only happen from the basic standpoint of a comportmental stance (*Grundhaltung*), that of *being turned to* one another (*Sich-einander-Zuwenden*), something that is increasingly lost to our hypermodern, digital age of de-Socratization.[22] This onto-mystic insight into the mystery of language explains Buber's special knack of speaking and working in the many languages he acquired. His conceptual sensation of words let them do their work in him—and thus let him do his work in them.

2. THE DIVINITY OF INTERACTIVE SELF-(TRANS)FORMATION

Nietzsche offers another important insight into Pindar's paradox as he adopts Pindar's words to subtitle his autobiography *Ecce Homo*. Pilate's words form the title as they are spoken in stunned recognition of the brutal irony in plain sight[23]—an innocent man tortured to death. Nietzsche's self-reference to the torments of Jesus is his answer to the interrogative couched in the tone of the indicative: *How One Becomes What One Is*. Unconditional love of life, *amor fati*, leads to the best version of oneself.[24] When "what does not kill [. . .], makes [one] stronger,"[25] the best avenue to oneself is life itself. Adversity is good, perhaps even the best teacher of life. Nietzsche is well aware of the Greek *dictum* on education (*Bildung*) embraced and advanced, both to the benefit and detriment of generations of Germans, which the most accomplished German poet Johann Wolfgang von Goethe adopted as his foreword to his autobiography *Poetry and Truth*.

> Ὁ μὴ δαρεὶς ἄνθρωπος οὐ παιδεύεται.
> Undisciplined the human being will not be educated.[26]

Education is a lifelong pursuit assisted by the benevolent educator. Ideally, it never ends, for humans are beings not of perfection but, as Rousseau put it, *perfectibility*. We face the task of *overcoming* imperfection through an ongoing process of *transformation* toward higher *forms* of human being. The sky is the limit of *education* understood in its literal sense of *elevation*. The vertical movement aims at the *formation* of its *image* in its likeness with the divine. Divinity is the telos of humanity. In the heavenly countenance, the human I (eye) faces and is faced by the omnipresence of the divine, the eternal

You that stands as the creator behind every earthly You. Buber's iconic event of the I-You encounter finds its fulfillment in all domains of life where the vertical I-Thou unfolds into horizontal instantiations. All rearing and upbringing (παιδαγωγία) aim at the "unique, single person" (*einmalige, einzige Person*) the individual is destined to be as "the bearer of a special task of life [*Seins-Auftrags*] which can be fulfilled [. . .] through him alone."[27] Education (*Erziehung*) understood in this existential sense of "unfolding disclosure" (*Erschließung*)[28] is what the German tradition calls *Bildung*, the *iconic (trans-)formation* of the essence of human being[29] into the divine mission of being human, the shining resemblance to the divine.[30] The biblical description bears the calling of a prescription. Being created in the image of God entails the commandment to live up to it. Godlikeness entails work and care, the "creative preservation"[31] of the earth, which *names* life into existence, into the existence of the human being. Once words are spoken that call beings by their names, divine creation is met with recognition by word-creative human beings to assert and confirm their godlikeness.[32] This is how Buber sees the world. This is how he experiences it. World-creation happens in divine calling. The calling is persistent and, in its persistence, constitutive of the world. Its divine voice seeks a resonance in the human response.[33] *How* the response is given, whether in contemplative silence or voiced explication, is secondary. *That* it is given, in continual renewal of the human world (communion), is decisive. Correspondence with the world is the way of being in the world. Humans *are asked to respond to the calling* of creation. For Buber this is an *ontological fait accompli*, a state and status of human being that is imperative since it seeks its constant refulfillment in continuous repetition.[34] Buber is adamant in joining the cosmic event in word and deed, in speech and the written word.

Goethe, one of Buber's deepest German inspirations, speaks to the cosmic human-divine relation in a similar vein:

> Wär nicht das Auge sonnenhaft,
> Die Sonne könnt es nie erblicken;
> Läg nicht in uns des Gottes eigne Kraft,
> Wie könnt uns Göttliches entzücken?[35]
>
> Were the eye not like the sun,
> The sun it could never see;
> Were God's own might in us undone,
> How could we be in godly ecstasy?[36]

To Buber, as to Goethe, divine delight grounds human recognition. Recognition, of oneself in the other, happens in the ecstatic moment of the encounter between an I and a You, which is always a reminiscent foreboding of the divine omnipresence in its permanent address[37] that conditions the earthly event within its concrete world reality (*Weltkonkretum*). To a human being there is no truth, no reality outside this mundane world of creation. The plain uniqueness of every moment is truth, the truth of the "kairological Gods" (*Augenblicksgötter*) that speak the language (*Rede*) of everyday events in their appeal (*Anrede*) to our response-ability to elicit the responsible response given in a language (*Sprache*), not necessarily of acoustic sound, but of sounds that make up *lived* speech (*Sprache*), that of initiating *deed* (*Tun*) and (de)liberating *release* (*Lassen*). This is the onset of language. The encounter, in its mystic divinity *within* its earthly domain, is the cradle of language. Just as there is no self-recognition without speech, there is no speech outside mutual recognition. Speech is the bridge *within* the meeting of two, *between* an I and a You. This bridge is a continuous bridging and as such the rise of language as the wording of the event of mutual recognition. The event is as much a spiritual as a physical happening and could not be spiritual were it not of a physical nature. Speech happens as the embodiment of human being in the embodied togetherness of human beings in the word. As the cosmic address is heeded, it is met with the personal reception of "all the pores of my body." The physical dimension of apprehension prepares the *corresponding* response. It is found in the inception of articulation at the onset of "an honest stammering," where "sense and throat unite in their fundamental agreement about what is to be said." Even though, at this earliest stage of language emergence, the frightened throat lacks the confidence of pure resonance with the already comprehended sense, the physical tools of the activated body are actuated for the possibility of shedding the pure light of sound on the already comprehended sense (*den schon geschlichtenen Sinn rein auszutönen*).[38] Language is made ready to speak and speech is about to happen as a human being finds and founds itself in human being to (cor)respond to the divine address.

3. Conclusion: Language—the Gift of the Self

Language (emergence) is a twofold event since humans are beings of relation to the world and through the world to each other. They mold their stance *at* a distance *to* an embrace *of* that distance to dissolve it into a word. Thus, language bridges distance *into* relation: via the bridged distance to things, it bridges the distance between humans. When the distance to a thing is shaped into the form of a picture, distance gets transformed into "the sediment of relation" (*Niederschlag der Beziehung*) as which human being embodies the thing, words it (in)to existence, and, born from human being, speaks the word *to* human being. Thus, the spoken word is born with a measure of independence. By virtue of the double nature of this ambivalence, words can be used as mere tools of communication (*Wortsprache*), but they never lose the original power of their personal address (*Anrede*) that gave rise to them to meet the other in that one's otherness through the reality of speech (*Sprachwirklichkeit*) in lived genuine conversation.[39] Here the other finds presence in "self-becoming-with-me," *as* I my presence in my self-becoming with the other. The mutuality of this self-becoming (*Selbstwerdung*) completes the ontological movement of human evolution (*Menschwerdung*). The process is sacred. The reminiscence of lived salvation wants repetition. Language is not just witness and evidence (*Ergebnis*) but *its* occurrence (*Begebnis*).[40] Thus, Buber's religious-ontological elevation of Pindar turns into a rejection of Heidegger's seemingly solipsistic conception of language as an existential-ontological monologue of being.[41] To put it bluntly, Heidegger's mineness of existence becomes the togetherness of Buber's (each-)otherness which opens up the between of language where and how the meeting of one another, of one *and* the other, takes place. Consequently, Buber states, seemingly apodictically, in a simple culmination of his thinking of language:

> [E]inander reichen die Menschen das Himmelsbrot des Selbstseins.
>
> [T]to each other human beings give each other the heavenly bread of being-oneself.[42]

The heavenly bread of words and language nourishes human being. The self is a gift from the other to the other, given in the mode of speech as only language can speak human being to existence.

Deeply aware of this gift of the self,[43] Buber pours his gratitude into a poem. "To Paula" is dedicated to his wife, midway through their life together of almost sixty years:

> Steep abyss and light of cosmic hue,
> Need of time and urged eternity,
> Vision, event and poetry:
> Dialogue it was and is with you.[44]

Notes

1. Martin Buber, "The Word That Is Spoken," in *The Knowledge of Man*, ed. Maurice Friedman and trans. Maurice Friedman and Ronald Gregor Smith (Amherst, NY: Humanity Books, 1998), 100–102.

2. Recall Whitman's two brief addresses "To You" . . . "Thou Reader"; *Leaves of Grass*, 1892 edition (Toronto: Bantam Books, 1983), 10, 11.

3. Pindar, Pythian Ode 2, line 72: γένοι' οἷος ἐσσὶ μαθών.

4. Søren Kierkegaard, *Concluding Unscientific Postscript*, trans. David F. Swenson and Walter Lowrie (Princeton, NJ: Princeton University Press, 1974), 116–17.

5. How so Buber explains with impressive elaboration in his 1933 address "The Question to the Single One" (published 1936), and included in the first English edition of *Between Man and Man*, trans. R. G. Smith (London: Kegan Paul, 1947). Buber rejects the conception of "the single one" (*der Einzelne*) that Kierkegaard had advanced as the only religious-human category (*hiin Enkelte*) that, in its diametrical opposition to the crowd, can relate to God. Cf. "The Question to the Single One," 40–82, and Smith's n. 9, p. 207.

6. Martin Heidegger, *Sein und Zeit* (Tübingen: Max Niemeyer Verlag, 1986), 145: "werde, was du bist!"

7. Heidegger, *Sein und Zeit*, 274: The call is the call *of* conscience which calls *upon* the deauthenticized They-self everyone becomes as a member of the collective in order *to* become its *own* self that stands in distinction to the They-self. This call has the force of an imperative. Hence, Heidegger says: "In conscience *Dasein* calls itself." Cf. Heidegger, *Sein und Zeit*, 275. See also *Sein und Zeit*, 273: "And to what is [the They-self (*Man-selbst*)] called? To one's *own Self*.... To the Self the They-self gets called."

8. Heidegger, *Sein und Zeit*, 38.

9. As Heidegger explains in his marginal note to the existential imperative in *Being and Time*. See Heidegger, *Sein und Zeit*, 443: "Who are 'you'? The one, as ... who you *become*."

10. Martin Buber, "Das Wort, Das Gesprochen Wird," in *Werke. Erster Band. Schriften zur Philosophie* (Munich: Kösel-Verlag, 1962), 445. Translator Maurice Friedman misses Buber's reference to Heidegger's two neologisms, the categorical distinction (first made in *Being and Time*) between the (ontological) "existentiale" (*Existenzial*) and the (ontic) "existentiell" (*Existenzielle*). Friedman translates the first with "existentialist" and the second with "existential." Cf. Buber, *Knowledge of Man*, 103.

11. Martin Buber, "Distance and Relation," *Knowledge of Man*, 61; "Elements of the Interhuman," *Knowledge of Man*, 65, 70, 73, 75.

12. Buber's word is *Entgeheimnissung*, a neologism. Buber, "Elemente des Zwischenmenschlichen," *Werke. Erster Band. Schriften zur Philosophie*, 279. Cf. Buber, *Knowledge of Man*, 71.

13. Martin Buber, "The Word That Is Spoken," *Knowledge of Man*, 102–3.

14. Buber, "The Word That Is Spoken," 103; Buber, "Elements of the Interhuman," *Knowledge of Man*, 77.

15. Martin Buber, "Dialogue," *Between Man and Man*, 13–14; Buber, "Zwiesprache," in *Das dialogische Prinzip* (Heidelberg: Verlag Lambert Schneider, 1979), 157–59; Buber, "Elements of the Interhuman," in *Knowledge of Man*, 70; Buber, "Elemente des Zwischenmenschlichen," in *Das dialogische Prinzip*, 284; Buber, "Distance and Relation," *Knowledge of Man*, 61; Buber, *Urdistanz und Beziehung* (Heidelberg: Verlag Lambert Schneider, 1978), 35–36.

16. Buber, "The Question to the Single One," in *Between Man and Man*, 80; Buber, *Das dialogische Prinzip*, 264: "... denn diese Gebundenheit ist Verbundenheit." I have altered Smith's translation.

17. My translation of Buber's German: Buber, "Elemente des Zwischenmenschlichen," *Das dialogische Prinzip*, 276. Cf. Smith's translation in Buber, *Knowledge of Man*, 65.

18. As far as I know Buber does not *explicitly* play with the *etymological* ambivalence of the word "Ent(-)fernung," as Sartre and Heidegger do, understood as "distance" and the removal of distance, indicated by the hyphen, but in spirit he does invoke it, for example, with his

notion of "primal distancing" (*Urdistanzierung*) and the immediate bridging of that distance (*entfernen*) that comes with it and is conditioned by it, in and as the movement of relating (*In-Beziehungtreten*). Cf. Buber, "Distance and Relation," in *Knowledge of Man*, 50. Buber, *Urdistanz und Beziehung*, 11. Cf. Jean-Paul Sartre, *Being and Nothingness* (New York: Washington Square Press, 1992), 54–55, where Sartre points out that the space between two points is in its recognition instantly covered and thus removed by the segment between them, since in its essence "Dasein is 'ent-fernend'" (dis-tancing distancing). Cf. "Nous admettrons volontiers avec Heidegger que la réalité-humaine est 'déséloignante,' . . . elle surgit dans le monde comme ce qui crée, et, à la fois, fait s'évanouir les distances (*ent-fernend*)." Jean-Paul Sartre, *L'être et le néant* (Paris: Éditions Gallimard, 1943), 55. Cf. Heidegger, *Sein und Zeit*, 104ff.

19. Buber, "Distance and Relation," in *Knowledge of Man*, 49–50, 52–53, 61; Buber, *Urdistanz und Beziehung*, 11, 14–15, 17–18, 34–37.

20. My adaptation of Buber's German in *I and Thou*. Cf. Martin Buber, *Ich und Du*, trans. R. G. Smith, centenary ed. (New York: Simon & Schuster, 2023), 44, and Buber, *I and Thou*, trans. Walter Kaufmann (New York: Simon & Schuster, 1996), 85.

21. Martin Buber, *Pointing the Way* (New York: Harper & Brothers, 1957), 3–4; Buber, "Dialogue," in *Between Man and Man*, 16–17; Buber, "Zwiesprache," in *Das dialogische Prinzip*, 161–63.

22. Buber, "The Word That Is Spoken," in *Knowledge of Man*, 100–101, 103; Buber, *Schriften zur Philosophie*, 442–43, 445.

23. John 19:15: ἰδοὺ ὁ ἄνθρωπος. "Behold the man!"

24. Friedrich Nietzsche, *Ecce Homo*, in *Basic Writings of Nietzsche*, ed. Walter Kaufmann (New York: Modern Library, 1992), 714: "My formula for greatness in a human being [*am Menschen*] is *amor fati*: that one wants nothing to be different, . . . , not in all eternity. Not merely bear what is necessary [*Notwendige*], . . . , but *love* it." Also, 780: "what is *necessary* [*das Notwendige*] does not hurt [*verletzt*] me; *amor fati* is my inmost nature." Nietzsche, *Werke*, ed. Karl Schlechta (Darmstadt: Wissenschaftliche Buchgesellschaft, 1997), 2:1098, 1151.

25. Friedrich Nietzsche, "Maxims and Arrows," aphorism 8, *Twilight of the Idols*, in *The Portable Nietzsche*, ed. and trans. Walter Kaufmann (New York: Penguin Books, 1982), 467. I altered Kaufmann's translation. Cf. Nietzsche, *Werke* 2:943: "Was mich nicht umbringt, macht mich stärker."

26. Johann Wolfgang von Goethe, *Dichtung und Wahrheit*. The first volume (of four) was published in 1811.

27. Buber, "Elements of the Interhuman," in *Knowledge of Man*, 73; Buber, "Elemente des Zwischenmenschlichen," in *Werke. Erster Band. Schriften zur Philosophie*, 282.

28. Buber, "Elements of the Interhuman," in *Knowledge of Man*, 72. Buber, "Elemente des Zwischenmenschlichen," in *Werke. Erster Band. Schriften zur Philosophie*, 281.

29. For a brief discussion of the significance the word *Bildung* has played in the German philosophical tradition, see Hans-Georg Gadamer, *Wahrheit und Methode. Gesammelte Werke* (Tübingen: J. C. B. Mohr, 1990), 1:15–24.

30. Genesis 1:26–28.

31. Genesis 2:15. The *Septuagint* translates "ἐργάζεσθαι αὐτὸν καὶ φυλάσσειν" as "to work and preserve (guard) [the land]."

32. Genesis 2:19–20.

33. Recall Buber's account of his recurring "dream of the double cry" (*Traum vom Doppel-*

ruf). What starts as a cry turns out to be both question and response, namely to the divine cosmic reply from both nowhere and nearby "from the air round about me" only to reveal the *a priori perfect* "that it has already been there" (*eben daß sie schon da war*). That the answer "in fact did not come," but "was there," is its "unknown perfection" (*ungekannten . . . Vollkommenheit*) and as such the divine world-reality of humanity, i.e., dialogicality. Buber, "Dialogue," *Between Man and Man*, 1–3; Buber, "Zwiesprache," *Das dialogische Prinzip*, 141. That the dialogical principle *is* the fundamental situation of human reality is confirmed later in the text. For the "factual actuality [*Tatsächlichkeit*] of lived life" *is* the "situation of creation" (*Schöpfungssituation*), "which is mightier and truer than all ecstasies." This is the situation of "dialogue" (*Zwiesprache*), which consists in "God's attentive directedness toward [humanity]" (*Zugewandtheit Gottes*). Here God "gives himself as the I to a Thou and as the Thou to an I." Human reality is this "position of confrontation" (*Gegenüberstande*), namely, the [unity] of the gapless and raptureless remaining in concreteness, wherein one apprehends the word and dares to utter a reply." I altered R. G. Smith's translation. Cf. Buber, "Dialogue," *Between Man and Man*, 25. Buber, "Zwiesprache," in *Das dialogische Prinzip*, 175–76.

34. Buber's 1929 essay "Dialogue" (*Zwiesprache*) is filled with examples of the mystic-cosmic dialogue human beings find themselves embedded in. Thus, we are all "willed for communion [*Verbundenheit*]." Cf. Buber, "Dialogue," *Between Man and Man*, 14. Buber, "Zwiesprache," in *Das dialogische Prinzip*, 159. Even within the context of our social-political relations, which Buber calls "our entanglement in a manifold We," we are enabled to recognize in this "creaturely narrowness" (*geschöpfliche Enge*) our "genuine width [*echte Weite*]: for this [our] being bound [*to* each other] [*Gebundenheit*] is [our] relation *with* one another [*Verbundenheit*]." (The last rendition in English is mine.) Cf. Buber, *Between Man and Man*, 80; Buber, *Das dialogische Prinzip*, 264. The facticity of our social-political and physical historical connectedness entails ethical *response-ability*, or, as Buber says, "die verantwortende Antwort" (the responsible response). Cf. Buber, *Between Man and Man*, 80; Buber, *Das dialogische Prinzip*, 263.

35. Johann Wolfgang von Goethe, *Gedichte. Ausgabe letzter Hand 1827*, "Zahme Xenien," chap. 3.

36. My translation.

37. Buber calls the speaker of the language of the address with respect to each instant of apprehension "the God of a moment of vision" (*der Gott eines Augenblicks*), a "kairological God" (*Augenblicksgott*) who, with time, reveals himself in the organic entirety of his panoramic whole, out of the manifold instances of his polyphone presence, i.e., he reveals himself through his fragmentations in "kairological Gods" (*Augenblicksgötter*) in human life as "the Lord of the voice, the One." Buber, "Dialogue," *Between Man and Man*, 15. Buber, "Zwiesprache," in *Das dialogische Prinzip*, 160.

38. Buber, "Dialogue," in *Between Man and Man*, 12, 13, 15, 16–17, 2, 17; Buber, "Zwiesprache," in *Das dialogische Prinzip*, 156, 157, 160, 162–63, 141, 163.

39. Buber, "Distance and Relation," in *Knowledge of Man*, 56, 58–59. Buber, *Urdistanz und Beziehung*, 24, 29–30.

40. Buber, "The Word That Is Spoken," *Knowledge of Man*, 101–3.

41. In reminiscence of Parmenides, Heidegger says in his *Letter on Humanism*, "language speaks," namely, (as) being itself, i.e., in and as the "House of Being." More than ten years later, Heidegger says, "Language is monologue. Language alone [*allein*] . . . speaks . . . lonesomely [*einsam*] . . . *not* being alone [*nicht allein*] . . . in reminiscence [*Fehl*] of a fundamental togetherness

[*Gemeinsamen*] as the most binding relation *to* this [togetherness]." Despite (t)his turn toward a new (less metaphysical) kind of thinking, this language conception still resonates with *Sein und Zeit*. As "dispositional understanding of (its) being-in-the-world" Dasein "speaks itself into speech" (*spricht sich als Rede aus*), i.e., its own being in pursuit of its authenticity (*eigenstes Seinkönnen*). Cf. Heidegger, *Sein und Zeit*, 161–63; Heidegger, *Über den Humanismus*, 5, 10, 24; Heidegger, "Der Weg zur Sprache," in *Unterwegs zur Sprache*, 265. Despite their fundamental (ontological) differences, the two have more in common than either thinks, as is evidenced (a) by the way the two let their German speak, which (b) is manifest also in their contributions to a conference on language organized by the Bayrische Akademie der Schönen Künste (Bavarian Academy of the Fine Arts), which Buber had to miss due to the sudden death of his wife, Paula, in August 1958. "The Word That Is Spoken" is Buber's response (delivered in Munich in 1960) to Heidegger's 1959 conference contribution "The Way to Language" (Der Weg zur Sprache).

42. Buber, "Distance and Relation," in *Knowledge of Man*, 61; Buber, *Urdistanz und Beziehung*, 37. The translation is mine and only in seeming violation of the German original which uses word order for special emphasis captured in English with the repetition of the first word, *einander* (each other).

43. The genitive is to be understood subjectively and objectively, which completes the hermeneutic circle of selfhood.

44. My translation. The dedication appeared first as the foreword to Buber's 1929 piece "Dialogue" (*Zwiesprache*), published as a separate book in 1932, and now included in *Das dialogische Prinzip*, first published under this title in 1962. Cf. *Das dialogische Prinzip*, 138. The poem is not included in *Between Man and Man*, which contains the text of "Dialogue."

Annotated Bibliography

PRIMARY SOURCES

Buber's panoramic conception of language is dispersed throughout his writings and must be pieced together with complementary glimpses (in)to his onto-linguistic worldview. Further, one must read Buber in German to understand him in English. It is the iconic diction of his German that reveals and confirms, namely, in the *way* he speaks, *what* he says about language. Thus, the first volume of the 1962 three-volume anthology is still a treasure trove: Martin Buber, *Werke. Erster Band. Schriften zur Philosophie* (Munich: Kösel-Verlag; Heidelberg: Verlag Lambert Schneider, 1962). Another compilation of his writings concerning language as speech is Martin Buber, *Das dialogische Prinzip* (Heidelberg: Verlag Lambert Schneider, 1997). English renditions that contain some of these compositions are Martin Buber, *The Knowledge of Man*, edited by Maurice Friedman and translated by Maurice Friedman and Ronald Gregor Smith (Amherst, NY: Humanity Books, 1998), and Martin Buber, *Between Man and Man*, translated by Ronald Gregor Smith (Mansfield Center, CT: Martino Publishing, 2014).

SECONDARY LITERATURE

For a concise comparative look at Buber's and Heidegger's (dis)agreement on language, Paul Mendes-Flohr's contributions are extremely helpful: Paul Mendes-Flohr, "Martin Buber and Martin Heidegger in Dialogue," *Journal of Religion* 24 (2014): 2–25; and Paul Mendes-Flohr, *Martin Buber: A Life of Faith and Dissent* (New Haven, CT: Yale University Press, 2019), 278–91.

8

Martin Buber and the Philosophy of Communication

JOHAN SIEBERS

Philosophers generally place the emergence of the contemporary concept of communication in the nineteenth century and link it to advances in technology.[1] We might speculate that the demise of rhetoric as a leading discipline in education and humanistic scholarship around the same time can be seen as part of a single intellectual development. The split in European thought between philosophy and rhetoric, between the search for truth and the art of persuasion, between mind and body[2] haunted consciousness until, on one hand, unquestioned appeals to transcendence became problematic or were at least no longer self-evident (Feuerbach, Marx, Nietzsche) and, on the other hand, the diversification of media as a result of technological developments began to inflect our understanding of the influence the media of relatedness have on the lived world and the constitution of the human sensorium. Beyond orality and literacy, the nineteenth century invented telecommunications, the recording of sound, the global distribution of printed matter, and the fast transportation of bodies through space, with all the accompanying changes in the perception of place, space, and time.[3] God died, and a kind of communicative innocence, or perhaps we should rather say "oblivion," was lost.

Buber's discovery of the centrality and irreducibility of the dialogical relationship needs to be seen against this backdrop. The living, spoken word and voice, which create relatedness in addressing and being responded to, had been central to Hebrew thought (Gen. 3:9, "*Then the Lord God called to Adam and said to him, 'Where are you?'*"). Indeed, the act of creation itself was a speech act (Gen. 1:3, "*Then God said, 'Let there be light'; and there was light*"). For Greek thought, on the other hand, the apprehension of truth (*eidos*) had been a matter of vision, of the eye and the look, itself grounded in form (*morphè*), shape, or appearance;[4] the articulation in speech was secondary, open to distortion, manipulation, and abuse in all directions and only safeguarded in the context of a communicative exchange (dialogue) that let itself be guided by the eidetic, ocular apprehension of what is truly real (*to ontos on*). While Socratic thought elevated dialogue as the privileged vehicle of truth (as opposed to the holding of speeches), this dialogue itself was not so much a matter of recognition and relatedness between the participants in the dialogue as a joint process of coming to an apperception of truth (or of our ignorance or limited grasp of it).[5] If, for Platonic thought, the voice was privileged because it renders present, then this was only the case because presence as direct apprehension of reality was the criterion of truth. I recall an arresting remark by Iris Murdoch about the unmistakable yet implicit "open, happy, sunny" atmosphere that pervades Plato's dialogues: the Mediterranean at noon on a summer's day, when all things lay languidly and neatly packed within their own boundaries, even the sounds that travel from shade to shade in the distance.[6] This atmosphere of *eidos* as lived experience will not escape anyone who has spent any time with Socrates and Plato, but after a while we also become aware of a much more uncanny element in that same atmosphere: a kind of deafening silence, an exclusive orientation on what the relation with, even love for, the other can do for *me*, rather than what the relation itself might mean for both of us, quite apart from our own virtuousness, either as philosophers or as social animals.[7] Plato begins the *Phaedrus* with a chance encounter between Socrates and Phaedrus, when Socrates asks, "Where do you come from, dear Phaedrus, and where are you going?" (227a; my translation). The question has an everyday meaning, but it also immediately puts the encounter on a moral and philosophical plane. Socrates asks Phaedrus to become aware of his life as a whole, with a direction and a purpose. We are right away in the midst of philosophy. Contrast this with the question God puts to Adam: "Where are you?" Both speak, but God is looking for a person he wants to find and meet, whereas Socrates seeks answers during an open, happy, sunny noon in the shadow of a tree outside the city walls, and thus the significance of the encounter itself recedes irretrievably into the background.

Between classical rhetoric and the Socratic understanding of dialogue, the significance of the "word that is spoken" is lost.[8] German idealists postulated an irreducible, processual form of relatedness per negation at the basis of the constitution of reality, which they called "dialectic," and which led an early exponent, Friedrich Heinrich Jacobi, to the formulation of the insight that "the I is impossible without the Thou."[9] Yet also there the particular, reciprocal nature of the dialogical situation still remained out of view.[10] Buber's thought, I claim, contains a radical break with the entire edifice of philosophical thought and its unhappy, codependent relation to its other, rhetoric, a break in which communication is theorized in a way it had not been theorized before and that offers a decisive, radically new starting point for a philosophy and theory of communication.

It is surprising that Buber's thought has received relatively little attention in communication theory, because with it we can come to understand that what communication requires of those who want to achieve a coherent understanding of it implies a fundamental shift in basic ontological and epistemological parameters.[11] I think that the relative neglect is partly due to Buber himself, who often and quite pragmatically used conceptualization and ideas from philosophical approaches that did not really have room for his revolutionary insight, such as phenomenology and hermeneutics—schools of thought to which, for example, Emmanuel Levinas sought to return Buber's ideas, in the process divesting them of much of their radical nature. A contemporary reading of Buber as a philosopher of communication will therefore first be concerned to identify the moment of radical rupture. It shows the way to an understanding of both the radical innovation in our theoretical understanding of communication as well as to the unwavering dialogical practice Buber engaged in, in so many personal, spiritual, cultural, artistic, educational, social, political, and religious contexts.

There is a telling story about Buber's life.[12] In the two years prior to writing *I and Thou*, Buber undertook what he referred to himself as an "intellectual fast." He stopped reading books, except for the Hebrew Bible and Descartes's *Discours de la méthode*, one of the founding texts of modern philosophy. I imagine that this quickly purified his thinking to such an extent that soon he became aware of the—implicit and silenced—dialogical, relational subtext in Descartes's philosophy. While Descartes erected his "certain" method of philosophy on a radical egological basis, on the subjective awareness of my own being as a mental substance not needing anything else besides this subjective awareness to exist, it must have started to dawn on Buber that Descartes was expounding this philosophy in a text, directed at a really existing reading public, whom he addresses, gives advice and instruction to, and talks about. Moreover, Descartes explicitly mentions he wrote the *Discours* in French rather than Latin so that people who did not have a traditional education (especially women) could read it. Perhaps there are few texts up to this point in the history of philosophy that were so self-consciously dialogical and relational as this one, addressing a really existing public audience, and yet the content of the philosophy we find in it is almost completely uncommunicative.[13] If we want to be more Cartesian than Descartes, more modern than modernity, we have to give due acknowledgment to the fact that we are already in a concrete, relational dialogue at the moment we start to think. We can see *I and Thou*, in this way and with a pinch of salt, as a radicalized version of the *Discourse on the Method*, made possible by the Hebrew emphasis on address and response in human interaction, a version that puts at the center of self-evidence what remains an implicit, unacknowledged, but ever-present periphery for Descartes. Just as people recognize the sunniness of Plato's Mediterranean thought-world, so people have often felt the everyday modernity of Descartes's world. In both cases, the unassuming reality of dialogue makes the philosophy possible and at the same time is masked by them. It was left to Buber to draw our attention to that reality.

I and Thou begins with the relatedness of the world and of the human beings within it. That relatedness is a result of words: *Grundworte*, "basic words" or "primary words." These words, or rather word-complexes (*I-Thou* and *I-It*), when spoken, place us in relation rather than signifying things. They open up the space in between those who are in dialogue by relating to each other across what lies between them:

> Grundworte sagen nicht etwas aus, was außer ihnen bestünde, sondern gesprochen stiften sie einen Bestand. Grundworte werden mit dem Wesen gesprochen.[14]
>
> Primary words do not describe something that might exist independently of them, but being spoken they bring about an existence. Primary words are spoken from the being.[15]

It is easy to overlook the radical nature of what happens here. Primary words exist only as spoken, that is as relating, as directed, as incomplete from each side and seeking completion in the relatedness that is created in the going-together of address and response. As such, in other words *as communication*, they create the world that can then become the place in which to live, encounter, and relate to others. This communication is not an exchange of signified content but rather the nature of reality itself, the act of being as the act in which relationality occurs. If we think about this in a concrete context, in which words are spoken at will by already existing complete beings (persons) and in which what it means to be is seen as involving determinateness, definiteness, and independence, we would never be able to grasp what Buber is pointing to here. At the beginning of *I and Thou*, we find an ontological understanding that sees relatedness as a primary constituent of the nature of reality. Moreover, Buber contends here that relatedness is not a general, structural, given characteristic of what there is, but the result of "speech," of concrete occurrences of speaking the primary words (either the fully relating primary word *I-Thou* or the partially relating word *I-It*). These words are spoken with one's *Wesen*, one's essential being. We are very far removed here from, let us say, cognitive or psycholinguistic accounts of what occurs when we utter words, when we speak.[16] Those accounts objectify the act of speaking in order to study its component parts and conditions of possibility. But prior to that, there is the irreducible reality of our existence-in-speech, which precedes all other forms of relatedness and which clothes and envelops even the life of the infant and, for Buber's religious sensibility, the nonhuman world as well, which is held in the creating and sustaining word of God.

The reality of dialogue is thus more than an anthropological phenomenon; it is the very fabric of reality, that which escapes us because it is all around us all the time. The history of philosophy, like so much of the history of humanity, is a history of the forgetting of dialogue while it never leaves us. Becoming aware of it carries the features of an experience of conversion or an "aha" experience, one we need to remind ourselves of constantly. Insofar as we live dialogue in its full reality, as the I-Thou relation, in concrete dialogical practice, to that extent we are fully alive. This remains forever a task, as the full reality is shot through with its fragmentation into partial relationships, which on one hand carry, for Buber, the mark of evil, precisely because they are limited, while on the other hand they seem necessary for human life. Yet, life would probably come to a standstill if we were always in every way inhabiting the I-Thou relationship, although this is by no means certain. Perhaps we can say that other living things always, within their sphere of activity, fully inhabit their being with others, while it is only the human being that is open to the fallenness of the partial, instrumental relationship. The reality of dialogue is, then, not a neutral reality but is essentially morally qualified: it has a value orientation.

We may begin to see why Buber's philosophy, which assigns such a central place to communication and understands communication in such a radical and new way, has not had the influence that we might have expected on the study of communication, its foundations and implications. Communication theories and philosophies of all persuasions, from post-structuralism, critical theory, and systems theory to cybernetics and rhetoric, all work with partial, I-It relations, seen as constitutive of communication. From a Buberian point of view these theories think of communication the wrong way around: first comes the holistic, I-Thou, enactment of relatedness through concrete acts of communication; only then can partial modes of relating play a role. We cannot overestimate Buber's insistence on dialogue as a concrete happening of living, embodied, mutual relatedness through spoken words (even if silence is an ever-present factor in dialogue and the first "Thou" is the silent relating of the child, the "inborn Thou").[17] The most pressing formulation of this insistence that I have found in his writings occurs in the essay "Elements of the Interhuman," where dialogue is called "the *phonetic event* [*phonetisches Ereignis*] fraught with meaning," which is to be found "neither in one of the two partners nor in both together, but only in their dialogue itself, in this 'between' which they live together."[18] Buber writes these words in the context of arguing that, in the psychological process, the participants in dialogue do not constitute the heart of it. In fact, psychology (including cognitive science) does not even begin to address the nature of dialogue. What goes for psychology also goes for sociology: much of "Elements of the Interhuman" is concerned with making a distinction between social relations and interhuman relations. Social relations are partial and collective—they belong to the world of I-It—whereas interhuman relations are individual and whole and belong to the world of I-Thou. Besides information theory, sociology and psychology have been the most important influences on communication theory. While communication philosophers and theorists have emphasized that the perspective of communication has its own explanatory role to play and is not merely consequent upon psychological, sociological, informational, and other modes of explanation, they have not grasped the radical innovation Buber's thought brings.[19]

We may further clarify the problematic place of Buber's far-reaching insights into the nature of communication in communication theory by considering the so-called phenomenological strand of communication theory. In one of the most influential, classical texts in communication theory, Robert T. Craig's "Communication Theory as a Field," we find an analysis of communication theory as a field that is committed, on one hand, to what Craig calls "the constitutive meta-model of communication," and, on the other, to what he calls the "dialogical-dialectical coherence" of the field. The constitutive metamodel is broadly shared among different strands of theorizing communication. For it, communication is "a constitutive process that produces and reproduces shared meaning," not only or fundamentally a process in which already constituted messages and meanings are transmitted and circulated via channels of exchange such as media and linguistic or other codes (although there is a place for that view as well). By "dialogical-dialectical coherence," Craig understands the irreducibility of the diversity of communication theories: all stem from pretheoretical, reflective ideas about communication that occur spontaneously in human life that are systematized for particular purposes, such as critique, orientation, transformation of communicative behavior. For example, rhetoric starts from everyday experiences of the power of words, and is then systematized in rhetorical scholarship which can in turn be used to influence practically relevant interventions in public or interpersonal discourse. Other strands of communication theory can do the same:

for example, semiotics, with respect to the function of sign structures in our lives, or psychoanalysis, with respect to the unconscious dimensions of communication. The goal of communication theory is not to achieve a unified theory but to develop practices that allow these different perspectives to challenge and illuminate each other in a dialogical-dialectical tension, in order "to assist in the cultivation of communication as a social practice, and so for communication to develop as a practical discipline."[20]

One of the strands of communication theory that Craig discusses is the phenomenological tradition. Here Buber is mentioned, but only once. In the phenomenological tradition, "communication is theorized as *dialogue* or *experience of otherness*. Communication theorized in this way explains the interplay of identity and difference in authentic human relationships and cultivates communication practices that enable and sustain authentic relationships."[21] Linked to the constitutive metamodel, the phenomenological tradition will help us to produce and reproduce shared meaning by putting at our disposal insights, arguments, and tropes that remind us of the difference between authentic and inauthentic relationships.

To be sure, Buber did not help himself by often reaching for concepts and ideas of a broadly phenomenological provenance. They invariably are tainted with the solipsistic and idealist origin of the phenomenological reduction. Yet, it is clear from the above how far Buber's notion of dialogue is removed from what communication theory understands by phenomenology and dialogue: "As experience, the world belongs to the primary word *I-It*. The primary word *I-Thou* establishes the world of relation."[22] If we try to understand the relatedness established by communication as rooted in an experience of the other or of the world, we are missing Buber's fundamental point about the spoken word. "I do not experience the man to whom I say *Thou*. But I take my stand in relation to him, in the sanctity of the primary word. Only when I step out of it do I experience him once more. In the act of experience *Thou* is far away."[23]

The very act of speaking the primary word *I-Thou* is an embodied, phonetic event. It is not a far-off, imaginary, or contemplative dimension of awareness but as concrete as a speech act was to ordinary language philosophy. What "speaking," or even "phonetic," means here, what it means for someone to open their mouth and speak, not as a lived experience but as a relational reality, this is what the philosophy of communication seeks to understand and articulate. It is, indeed, a philosophical undertaking in that it requires us to develop a fundamental reflective awareness that cannot be outsourced to any kind of methodological procedure the sciences, arts, or other activities can offer us, including mystical spirituality, which Buber entertained in his early years and from which only his own fright at his descent into the spirit of militarism during the Great War freed him.

Part of the conversion in our thinking that Buber's philosophy issues in lies in the fact that we reclaim the words "speaking" and "listening" for a nonderivative philosophical analysis.[24] We have two coordinating principles: (1) dialogue is established in "speaking the primary word I-Thou" (and we need to clarify further what that means, but we have to do so on its own terms), and (2) dialogue is concrete relatedness (and again, what this means has to be clarified further). What we call "communication," also in its derived I-It manifestations, does not exist outside of the dialogical constitution of the world.

Buber uses spatial metaphors to express this constitution: the partners in dialogue inhabit a "between," in which they are "over against" (*gegenüber*) each other, in other words, facing each other across the space that is open between them.[25] The preposition "over against" occurs in many places throughout Buber's writings to express the particular nature of dialogue, of the I-Thou relationship. It is not a relationship that necessarily seeks shared meaning. It is a relationship in which acknowledgment and encounter are possible. The partners in dialogue do not stand next to each other, moving in the same direction, as we do when we follow shared social conventions and shared meanings, but they rather stand opposite each other (*gegenüber*), directed, as it were, to each other. The dialogical situation is, quite literally, an encounter, in which we can meet someone because they are "countered" against us so we can see them and they can see us, as we speak and listen. It is perhaps a coincidence that the Hebrew word for "over against," *negdo* (נגדו), is used in Genesis 2:18, where the sphere of interhuman relations is created with the creation of Eve, the second human being, who is said to be "over against" Adam (a meaning that is preserved, for example, in the Dutch Staten translation [1637] as *tegenover*, "over against," but misconstrued as "matching" in the King James Version [1611], where it is translated as "meet"); Adam and Eve meet one another. Of course, "meeting" carries the semantic component of "encountering," and "matching" connotes not just "fitting" but also a match, as in a contest, between two parties (which can still be a match made in heaven).

It seems that the relational "existence" (*Bestand*) which the spoken primary word brings about is that of the over against.[26] This existence is paradoxical: *in one and the same movement, which we call communication in the emphatic sense of I-Thou dialogue, we are together and separate, in the same respect*. This is the heart of Buber's revolutionary insight. No prior mode of philosophical rationality, from Greek logos to the great chain of being, to the dialectic and the schools of phenomenology, hermeneutics, and even logical analysis, has been able to capture this, as it turns out pervasive, feature of our world. For

Buber, his philosophy was less a theory that sought to explain than a mere pointing toward this ubiquitous, life-giving, incomprehensible fact so that we might become aware of it as something we always already knew and with which we are more intimately familiar than with our own souls. In the essay "Urdistanz und Beziehung," from 1950, translated as "Distance and Relation," he finally comes close to formulating his key insight in a few words:

> In this way we reach the insight that the principle of human life is not simple but twofold, being built up in a twofold movement which is of such a kind that the one movement is the presupposition of the other. I propose to call the first movement the "primal setting at a distance" and the second "entering into relation." That the first movement is the presupposition of the other is plain from the fact that one can enter into relation only with being which has been set at a distance, more precisely, has become an independent opposite. And it is only for man that an independent opposite exists.[27]

We notice the shackles of phenomenological thinking in the final consideration, which relies on a Husserlian-Heideggerian notion of world as something only the human being occupies because, according to this notion, only human beings can be aware of a totality that they know and can never totalize by themselves (e.g., the totality of a perceived object, or of the world as a whole), which sets free a world of independent existents. We, today, do not have to commit ourselves to any form of human exceptionalism, precisely because hidden in this paragraph lies the awareness that it is not only the "setting at a distance" that is the presupposition of the "entering into relation," but also, in equal measure, and, again, in the same movement, the "setting at a distance" that presupposes the "entering into relation." Only when taken together as concretely real sides of a single shared act do they make sense, for how could you set something at a distance you were not already in relation with (even if you think of yourself, to make the point, as a transcendental subject)? But when we take them together as concretely real sides of a single act, we see that we are simply talking about communication, the free encounter of dialogue as the giving and receiving of, and responding to, the word that is spoken.

As we become more and more aware of the vast diversity of communication media and their affordances, we develop a heightened sensitivity for the independence of media from one another and from any overarching notion of a unitary subject that could avail itself of these media without compromising its undividedness.[28] This has become a familiar trope in the philosophy of media and communication. Craig's metamodel can, in part, be seen as a way to make pragmatic sense of this circumstance,[29] without inordinately relying on what were then perceived to be essentialist, metaphysical notions of personhood, recourse to which could only lead to regressive and potentially dangerous exclusionary discourses, or postmodern reprisals of romantic celebrations of difference. A close reading of Buber's philosophy of communication, however, liberates us from all three: from a metaphysical, substantialist notion of personhood connected with repressive universalism, from the postmodern fragmentation into incommunicative difference, and from the pragmatic reduction of communication to rational deliberation, which has its uses but fails to motivate.[30] I have tried to show that here we have the beginnings of a different way of thinking about human beings, and nonhuman nature, in communication. I have also tried to be to some extent precise in identifying where the real innovation in Buber's thinking lies, an innovation that can play a significant role in contemporary philosophy of communication.[31]

Three themes suggest themselves immediately for elaboration: embodiment, materiality, and futurity. The strong conception of communication that I have indicated here is concrete, embodied, in the here and now. This generates the possibility to bring together an understanding of dialogue as encounter with attention for the physical dimensions of such an encounter. We may gain a deeper understanding of the importance of embodiment, space, place, and time for genuine dialogue, and we may study the ramifications of changes in the way we live in space, place, and time for the dialogues we have with each other. Again, with Buber's notion of dialogue we can explore in a nonreductive way what dialogue looks like with nature, with the nonhuman, and with more-than-human actors. We can extend our notions of language, of speaking and listening, to include the voice of many beings in a way that is not simply metaphorical, not simply a generous extending of the word to mutes and brutes, but the discovery that what we know as speech exists in other forms and summons us to the same kind of dialogical relations with the natural world of which we are a part as it does to the interhuman. An interspecies conception of I-Thou dialogue could make significant contributions to peace, sustainability, and well-being in our world. Finally, we can come to understand that communication is inextricably linked to anticipation, to a response from another, who is more than a presence in my consciousness that I might interpret, but a real person who can listen to what I have to say and to whom I can listen. The burden of mental health, under which so many people, young and old, worldwide, labor today, can be relieved a bit by promoting the insight that listening to what the other has to say constitutes us as persons as well as the sense that we are not alone but oriented toward community. And this is not "community" that exists only by the grace of shared essential identity, but community that thrives in the acknowledgment and

MARTIN BUBER AND THE PHILOSOPHY OF COMMUNICATION

recognition of each other's open "over-againstness" (*Gegenüber*) of the going-together of distance and relation. To accord dialogical speech this central place in communication is not a return to the primacy of orality that the critique of metaphysics sought to dispel. We have a very different notion of the spoken word, namely as concrete relation rather than as Aristotle's outward "symbols of affections in the soul."[32] Once we grasp the point of distance and relation, we see that there is no communication without hope and no hope without dialogical communication. Walter Ong once wrote, "I speak because I have hope in others."[33] With Buber we can be more precise and thus intensify this insight for future good use: I speak because I have hope in you, my Thou.

Notes

1. Dirk Baecker, *Kommunikation* (Leipzig: Reclam Verlag, 2008); and John Durham Peters, *Speaking into the Air: A History of the Idea of Communication* (Chicago: University of Chicago Press, 2001).

2. Theodor W. Adorno, *Negative Dialectics*, trans. E. B. Ashton (1966; New York: Seabury Press, 1973).

3. Thomas De Quincey, *The English Mail Coach: And Other Essays*, ed. John E. Jordan (1849; reprint, London: Dent, 1970).

4. Martin Heidegger, *The Question concerning Technology, and Other Essays*, trans. William Lovitt (1954; New York: Garland, 1977).

5. Plato, *Phaedrus*.

6. Iris Murdoch, *Metaphysics as a Guide to Morals* (New York: Penguin, 1993).

7. Johan Siebers and Maaike Engelen, "Het Gesprek van de Ziel: Plato's Vriendschapsfilosofie," *Wijsgerig Perspectief Op Maatschappij En Wetenschap* 34, no. 4 (1993): 117–22.

8. Martin Buber, *Knowledge of Man*, trans. Ronald Gregor Smith and Maurice Friedman (New York: Harper & Row, 1965), 9. Cicero appears to have been one of the few authors in antiquity who expressed an awareness *avant la lettre* of the ideological nature of the split between philosophy and rhetoric as cultural institutions (*De Oratore* 3:56–61), while Christian homiletics from Augustine onward, standing in the light of the word that became flesh, can be seen as an attempt to overcome both philosophy and rhetoric and establish a new mode of discourse beyond them, that of faith. Yet this attempt was ultimately unable to destabilize the philosophy-rhetoric complex. Rhetoric "became the carrier of the lie in philosophy. [. . .] [T]he persecutors of the rhetorical element that saved expression for thought contributed as much to the technification of thought, to its potential abolition, as did those who cultivated rhetoric and ignored the object" (Adorno, *Negative Dialectics*, 56).

9. Martin Buber, *Between Man and Man*, trans. Ronald Gregor Smith (London: Routledge, 2002), xx.

10. Michael Theunissen, "The Repressed Intersubjectivity in Hegel's Philosophy of Right," in *Hegel and Legal Theory*, ed. Drucilla Cornell et al. (London: Routledge, 1991); https://doi.org/10.4324/97813158319.

11. Eli Dresner and Johan Siebers, "I Interpret You: Davidson and Buber," *Review of Metaphysics* 73, no. 1 (2019): 109–26. For example, in the *International Encyclopedia of Communication*

Theory and Philosophy (ed. Jensen et al. [London: John Wiley & Sons], 2016), discussion of Buber is limited to a subsection of the entry on dialogue, a situation reflected in the dislike of dialogue in many strands of communication theory; see John Durham Peters, *Speaking into the Air: A History of the Idea of Communication* (Chicago: University of Chicago Press, 1999); Per Linell, *The Written Language Bias in Linguistics: Its Nature, Origin and Transformations* (Oxford: Routledge, 2005).

12. Maurice Friedman, *Martin Buber: The Life of Dialogue*, 4th ed. (New York: Routledge, 2003), xx, https://doi.org/10.4324/9780203398197.

13. Even Kierkegaard seems to relate mostly to imagined fantasy audiences or a depersonalized public and to be concerned mostly with the "what" of communication rather than with communication as relational dialogue. Andrew F. Herrmann, "Kierkegaard and Dialogue: The Communication of Capability: Kierkegaard and Dialogue," *Communication Theory* 18, no. 1 (January 2008): 71–92; https://doi.org/10.1111/j.1468-2885.2007.00314.x.

14. Martin Buber, *Ich und Du* (Leipzig: Insel Verlag, 1923), 3.

15. Martin Buber, *I and Thou*, trans. Ronald Gregor Smith (London: Bloomsbury Academic, 2018), 3 (translation modified).

16. W. J. M. Levelt, *Speaking: From Intention to Articulation* (Cambridge, MA: MIT Press, 1989).

17. Buber, *I and Thou*, 27.

18. Martin Buber, "Elements of the Interhuman," in *Knowledge of Man*, 72–88, 75 (my emphasis).

19. Stanley Deetz, *Communication Yearbook 17: International Communication* (London: Routledge, 2021); Eli Dressner, "Davidson's Philosophy of Communication," *Communication Theory* 16, no. 2 (May 2006): 155–72; https://doi.org/10.1111/j.1468-2885.2006.00266.x.

20. Robert T. Craig, "Communication Theory as a Field," *Communication Theory* 9, no. 2 (May 1999): 119–61, quotes at 125, 130; https://doi.org/10.1111/j.1468-2885.1999.tb00355.x.

21. Craig, "Communication Theory as a Field," 138.

22. Buber, *I and Thou*, 6.

23. Buber, *I and Thou*, 9. The final sentence reads in German "Erfahrung ist Du-Ferne," experience is Thou-distance. The English translation renders "Thou" into an it, saying Thou "is far away," rather than "in the act of experience, Thou art far away." Since objectifying "Thou" in experience is the theme of discussion here, the translation survives.

24. Lisabeth Lipari, *Listening, Thinking, Being: Toward an Ethics of Attunement* (University Park: Pennsylvania State University Press, 2014).

25. Buber, "Man and His Image Work," in *Knowledge of Man*, 149–65.

26. Buber, *I and Thou*, 3.

27. Buber, "Distance and Relation," in *Knowledge of Man*, 59–71, quote at 60. The title "Urdistanz und Beziehung" might be better translated as "Primal Distance and Relation."

28. See Friedrich Kittler, *Optical Media* (Cambridge: Polity, 2010), and Marshall McLuhan, *Understanding Media: The Extensions of Man* (New York: McGraw-Hill, 1964).

29. Perhaps, in a somewhat related way, Habermas's theory of communicative action tried to do the same many years ago, in response to the depersonalizing systems theory perspective on social interaction that was prevalent then; see Jürgen Habermas, *The Theory of Communicative Action*, vol. 1, *Reason and the Rationalization of Society*, trans. Thomas McCarthy (Boston: Beacon Press, 1984), and Niklas Luhmann, *Social Systems*, trans. John Bednarz Jr., with Dirk Baecker (Stanford, CA: Stanford University Press, 1995).

30. Jürgen Habermas, *The Divided West*, ed. and trans. Ciaran Cronin (Cambridge: Polity, 2006).

31. Buber is quite explicit in *I and Thou* about dialogue with nonhuman beings, including trees, animals, works of art, and God. What "speech" in this context, that of the language of nature, means was a question that occupied Buber even in *I and Thou*. Heurich and Hauck argue for diverse ontologies of language and associate metaphorical extensions of Western or European notions of language with colonizing gestures; see the special issue *Language in the Amerindian Imagination*, ed. G. Heurich and J. Hauck, *Language and Communication* 63 (2018).

32. Aristotle, *De Interpretatione* 16a:3-8. I should like to add that there is a profound parallel between Buber's notions of relatedness and dialogue and the notions of prehension and actual occasion in Whitehead's process philosophy, Buber and Whitehead being two thinkers who otherwise inhabit very different universes. Charles Hartshorne, however, with characteristic acumen, picked this up in his very appreciative article "Martin Buber's Metaphysics," in *The Philosophy of Martin Buber*, ed. Paul Arthur Schilpp and Maurice Friedman (LaSalle, IL: Open Court, 1967), 49-68.

33. Walter J. Ong, *The Presence of the Word: Some Prolegomena for Cultural and Religious History*, 2nd ed. (1967; Albany: State University of New York Press, 2000), xx.

Annotated Bibliography

An overview of Buber's influence on the philosophy of communication can be found in the entry "Dialogue" of K. B. Jensen et al., eds., *The International Encyclopaedia of Communication Theory and Philosophy* (London: John Wiley & Sons, 2016). Buber's unique conception of the spoken word of dialogue in the history of European philosophy includes a recognition of the embodied nature of dialogue, through which we exist for each other as we give and receive the *I* and the *Thou*. For a comprehensive overview of Buber's (implicit) philosophy of language, see the essay by Joachim Oberst in this volume. Even the most basic observation regarding the primary words *I-Thou* and *I-It* points in the direction of an ontology of language that distances itself incommensurably from many views on the nature of language that we find in linguistics and philosophy of language today: "The existence of *I* and the speaking of *I* are one and the same thing. When a primary word is spoken the speaker enters the word and takes his stand in it"; see Buber, *I and Thou*, trans. Ronald Gregor Smith (London: Bloomsbury Academic, 2018), 4. Buber used what was known at the time about the grammar of some Amerindian languages to sensitize his readers to his understanding of language as "the word that is spoken," which was as far removed from the traditional European view of language as *vehiculum mentis* as it was from the Heideggerian speculations, popular in his day, of language as the house of being, "language speaks," or the Gadamerian view of interpretation as the fusion of horizons; see Buber, *The Knowledge of Man: A Philosophy of the Interhuman* (New York: Harper & Row, 1965). In this light I have found that contemporary work on the ontological turn in linguistic anthropology, inspired partly by Viveiros de Castro, may have the potential to further develop an ontology of language suitable for dialogue. A starting point is the special issue *Language in the Amerindian Imagination*, edited by G. Heurich and J. Hauck, *Language and Communication* 63 (2018).

9

Buber and Expressionism

BERNHARD LANG

Life in Germany and Austria during the first three decades of the twentieth century was dominated by a prosperous bourgeois culture, materialistic in spirit and appreciative of two new developments: the concentration of life in big metropolitan centers and the unprecedented technological innovation arising within capitalist industry. But this dominant culture was challenged by numerous artists and poets who developed a counterculture that came to be called "expressionism."[1] Painters such as Oskar Kokoschka and Ernst Barlach and poets like Georg Trakl, Franz Werfel, Paula Ludwig, and Ernst Toller represented a subculture that was ambivalent about or critical of urban and technological civilization. In their often intensely personal paintings, poems, and essays, they experimented with new styles, forms, colors, and words. In their critical writing, they lamented the deficient forms of social life which led to the loneliness of the modern individual and to the spiritual failure of organized religion. But they also celebrated what they held was the emergence of the "new man" (*der neue Mensch*), constituting the revolutionary avant-garde of a new way of life.

To speak of expressionism as a subculture is not the whole story, however. After the First World War, the winds changed. Expressionism would emerge from obscurity and enter the public sphere. German cultural life in the major cities, especially Berlin, suddenly metamorphosed into an expressionist spectacle. Films such as Fritz Lang's *Metropolis* (1927) and novels like Hermann Hesse's *Demian* (1919) or Alfred Döblin's *Berlin Alexanderplatz* (1929), which breathed with the expressionist spirit, were widely discussed. Earlier, in 1913, Martin Buber had published a book in the expressionist mode—*Daniel: Gespräche von der Verwirklichung* (*Daniel: Dialogues on Realization*). In 1923, he published *Ich und Du* (*I and Thou*), written "in the magical, visionary style of German literary expressionism."[2] But it is not only Buber's highly stylized and sometimes oracular language that reflects the spirit of expressionism; it is also characteristic of the book's subject matter.

The following essay is divided into two parts: the first deals with expressionist elements in Buber's critique of modern life; the second highlights aspects of the "new man" as viewed by Buber and the expressionists.

Critique of Modern life: Loneliness and Religion

"Expressionist literature begins with the complaint about cultural decline, about the brokenness and poverty of the time, with the protest against the enslavement to mammon, matter and machine," writes Wilhelm Knevels, a contemporary observer of the expressionist movement.[3] Major themes common to Buber's *I and Thou* and expressionist poetry are the loneliness of the modern individual and the spiritual drought of organized religion, two subjects that Knevels subsumed under the category of "complaint about cultural decline." While not exhausting expressionism's critique of modern society, a review of its overarching themes will indicate how deeply Buber shared its lament about the cultural and spiritual degeneration of modern society.

In villages and small-town communities, people are bonded by shared traditions, kinship, and integration into an organic network that offers not only a *home* but also, when needed, mutual help and support. In contrast, modern metropolitan life is said to be utterly devoid of these interpersonal virtues, rendering its denizens "homeless." *I and Thou* is based on an analysis of this social situation, which Buber highlights by noting "the palpable manifestation of modern man's lack of relation" and "the amassing of human units that have no relation to one another" in the big cities.[4] Buber accounts for this situation in his theory of the inverse correlation between sociability and materialism: the decline of human sociability through the centuries is a result of people's ever-increasing enmeshment in what he calls the It-World, the Realm of Things. At the present time, materialism has reached its zenith, while sociability has declined to its lowest level.

Social isolation, one of expressionism's central themes, found its most graphic representation in George Grosz's lithograph "Friedrichstrasse" (1918). It shows more than forty people against an urban panorama of buildings, neon signs, and a metropolitan railroad bridge. In the confusion of Berlin's Friedrich Street, couples are absent or barely recognizable, prostitutes loiter. People hurry past each other without encounter or interaction.

What Buber describes and Grosz visualizes frequently received lyrical expression. A good example, by Franz Werfel, is "An den Leser" ("To the Reader," 1910), used as the preface to a book of his poems:

> Mein einziger Wunsch ist es, Dir, o Mensch, verwandt zu sein. / . . . / Oh, könnte es einmal geschehen, / Dass wir uns, Bruder, in die Arme fallen.[5]

> My only wish is to be related to you, O man. / . . . / Oh, that it could it happen one day / that we, brother, fall into each other's arms.

Even closer to Buber's emotive language of mutuality are lines in a poem entitled "Freundschaft" ("Friendship," 1920) by Kurt Heynicke:

> Oh, dass wir DU sind einander, [. . .]
> wir schenken einander das Ich und das Du.[6]

> Oh, that we are each other's YOU! . . .
> We give each other the I and the you.

A literal English rendering of the first line does not make much sense, because "Du" is the form of address Germans use only for family members and close friends, and never for strangers or superiors in the social hierarchy. But the second line could serve as an apt epigraph for *I and Thou*.

In her "Psalm" (1919), Paula Ludwig expresses a similar sentiment, using the plural "we":

> Wir Menschen. / Wir. / Dass unsere Hände doch behutsamer / Ineinandergriffen, sich zum Troste! / Aber der Tag ist laut von den schreienden Stimmen.[7]

> We people. / We. / That our hands would intertwine / more gently, to comfort each other! / But the day is loud with shrieking voices.

Finally, mention must be made of a poem by Jakob Levy, published in the Vienna periodical *Daimon* in 1918. Like Buber, the poet identifies "encounter" (*Begegnung*) as the means of healing:

> Es gibt kein Mittel zwischen mir und andern. / Ich bin unmittelbar: in der Begegnung. / Ich bin nicht einzig: bloß in der Begegnung. / Ob ich ein Gott, ein Narr oder ein Dummer. / Ich bin geweiht, geheilt, erlöst in der Begegnung. / Ob ich das Gras oder die Gottheit treffe.[8]

> There is no medium between me and others. I am immediate, in the encounter. Alone, I am not, only in the encounter—whether I am a god, a fool or a dimwit. I am consecrated, healed, redeemed in the encounter—whether I meet grass or God.

Buber was well aware of these voices (and may have known the poetry of Levy[9]) and concurs in a 1919 essay, published in the short-lived expressionist journal *Neue Erde*: "A great desire for fellowship [*Gemeinschaft*] passes through all souls of soulful people at this hour in the life of occidental culture."[10] Expressionists are "soulful people" (*seelenhafte Menschen*). One might immediately ask whether the soulful are also religious people, and whether religious communities would be able to quench the thirst for fellowship. As we shall see, the expressionists did not believe in such a solution. For them, religion was "dead."

Since the Enlightenment, religion has been regarded by many intellectuals as the embodiment of the conservative, fossilized, and therefore problematic side of Western culture. The expressionists shared this view and often stated it in stark terms. In 1909, the young Austrian pharmacist Georg Trakl wrote a poem he titled "Die tote Kirche" ("The Dead Church"). The following lines convey its depressing message:

> Auf dunklen Bänken sitzen sie gedrängt
> Und heben die erloschnen Blicke auf
> Zum Kreuz. [. . .] Der Priester schreitet
> Vor den Altar; doch übt mit müdem Geist er
> Die frommen Bräuche—ein jämmerlicher Spieler,
> Vor schlechten Betern mit erstarrten Herzen,
> In seelenlosem Spiel mit Brot und Wein.[11]

> Packed onto dark benches, they lift their dim eyes to the cross. [. . .] The priest strides before the altar. Dispiritedly he performs the pious rites—a wretched player before bad worshippers with frozen hearts acts out a soulless play with bread and wine.

Trakl is disillusioned with the Catholic Church in which he was raised. According to Trakl, the Catholic congregation, its priest, and the ritual have all lost their power to the point of being "dead"—a characteristic expressionist exaggeration. His sentiment was shared by many expressionist writers. In a 1919 essay, Kurt Heynicke extends this critique to all traditional religion, be it Christian or Buddhist: "All religions have become dead idols. Thanks to dogmatization by empty priests, Christianity today is only a mannequin. The pure face of the Buddha has been painted over with all kinds of colors by deaf and blind monks. Once God stood amid us, but priests expelled his white figure, and now he hangs in empty churches—and cries."[12] Heynicke adds an aphorism on how spiritual movements, including religions, develop dogmas, and to what that leads: "The clear water of idealism is becoming cloudy, dogma is rising. Dogma, however, kills" (*Das klare Wasser des Idealismus trübt sich, das Dogma steht auf. Dogma aber tötet*). Heynicke no doubt echoes Saint Paul: "the letter kills, but the spirit gives life" (2 Cor. 3:6).

Buber concurs. In a 1910 essay, he describes religion as "a product of decay, contamination and decomposition" of an experience that once was real, vital, and pure.[13] In *Daniel* (1913), he states even more emphatically that "all religiousness"—or authentic religious sentiment—"degenerates into religion and church when it begins to orient itself: when instead of the one thing needful [Luke] it provides a survey of what one must believe in this life and the beyond, and promises having instead of becoming, security instead of risk."[14] Later, in *I and Thou*, Buber explains that existing religions can at best be appreciated as emerging from (*verpuppt*) the chrysalis of religiosity—which, however, does not happen in the present. Buber characterizes the religious community as having fallen into the It-World, the realm of impersonal things—and he resorts to a shocking image: "the countenance of the form [of God] is extinguished, its lips are dead, its hands hang down, God does not know it anymore."[15] Buber apparently is thinking here of an instance of Christian iconography in medieval and Renaissance art: the bust image of the dead Christ as the Man of Sorrows. In Christianity, the Man of Sorrows serves as a focus for pious meditation on the redemptive suffering of Christ; Buber, by contrast, uses the image boldly and iconoclastically to personify a religion which, having lost its vitality and its contact with God, offers the viewer a sorrowful picture. Buber's words come close to those of Heynicke, who also described God as a weeping outlaw.

Buber contributes to the expressionist description of "dead religion" the notion that God is still there, and still willing to approach human beings—"he always comes toward them and touches them"[16]—but they have become unresponsive. At the end of the relevant passage of *I and Thou*, Buber suddenly switches from prose to poetry:

> O einsames Angesicht sternhaft im Dunkel, / o lebendiger Finger auf einer unempfindlichen Stirn, / o verhallender Schritt![17]

> O lonely face, starry in the dark, / O living finger on an unfeeling brow, / O footstep fading away![18]

Contextually, this represents what literary critics call an apostrophe, a switch to a different audience—perhaps the writer speaking to himself or to God (and, of course, to the reader of *I and Thou*). Considered by itself, this is a perfect example of an expressionist poem. Like many such poems, it is not immediately understandable but requires close reading and interpretation.

In Buber's *I and Thou*, "face" (*Angesicht*) is one of the names given to God; accordingly, the poem's subject is God. He is invoked as a light in the darkness, as one who approaches the human individual, touches him with his finger in a gesture of blessing, and then retreats, because there was no response. The gesture of touching someone's forehead is known as a traditional gesture: someone would greet a child by touching the child's forehead—and this is exactly how Buber used to welcome his grandchildren.[19] A lovely gesture— but one performed by God in vain, for human beings remain unresponsive. They may not even notice that he touches them. So God withdraws in silence.

Aspects of the "New Man": Conversion and How to See Things

Expressionist literature, Knevels explains, moves beyond the complaint about cultural decline in its "call to let the spirit come to the fore again. The expressionist pamphlets, poems and plays aim to promote the rebirth of the spirit. Here 'spirit' is taken to be transcendent, standing beyond all calculable processes and facts. [...] At the center of all expressionist literature is the human being [*der Mensch*]. [...] All expressionist works want to lead to humanity, to true humanity [*zum wahren Menschsein*]."[20] Accordingly, the expressionists saw themselves as the avant-garde of a new type of person with a new ethos that would bring human society to its ultimate fruition. "Der neue Mensch" became its watchword and slogan. In this section we will deal with the question of how the "new man" emerges, and how the new person feels about the world around him. Again, these two subjects do not exhaust the message the expressionists and Buber wished to send to their contemporaries, but they give us a general idea of it.

Expressionists knew that they were a small minority within the larger society. The majority was still bound up with the traditional social, economic, political, and religious fabric that they, the expressionists, strongly rejected. Fortunately, some came to change sides and joined the new movement. The changeover occurred either gradually or abruptly and was experienced as a drama of conversion—a sequence of doubt and crisis, followed by a moment of enlightenment and the adoption of a new worldview. But we must not exaggerate the presence of a pattern, because as soon as we consider biographical and literary accounts, we find that each case is unique.

A first example is Friedrich's conversion in Ernst Toller's stage play *Die Wandlung* (*The Transformation*) of 1919.[21] It tells the story of Friedrich, a young Jewish man who works as a sculptor. Eager to prove that he is a valuable, well-integrated, and patriotic member of German society, he joins the army to fight in Africa where colonial rule is to be imposed. Wounded in battle, he survives the experience and is decorated. But back at home, while working on the statue of a huge human figure designed to represent the "victory of the nation," he begins to be troubled by doubts about the matter. His doubt is compounded by the appearance of a former fellow-soldier whose face is disfigured by syphilis, one of the prices to be paid for the victory. Friedrich's patriotism crumbles. In an act of self-liberation, he takes final leave from patriotism by destroying the statue. He also contemplates suicide to end a life built on false ideals. At the moment when he reaches for the gun to end his life, his sister enters the studio. She persuades him not to commit suicide. She encourages him to redirect his life "toward God who is spirit, love, and strength, to God who lives in humankind."[22] Friedrich plucks up courage, decides to follow his sister's advice, and, as the stage direction explains, walks out full of energy, overflowing with enthusiasm. His new life is that of a socialist activist. In short: the conversion of a conservative patriot who, after a brief crisis, becomes a socialist.

Another example is Emil's biography in Hermann Hesse's novel *Demian: The Story of Emil Sinclair's Youth* (1919). In his school and college days, Emil is increasingly influenced by Demian, a precocious boy who befriends him and eventually acts as his mentor. He guides Emil away from the pietistic Christianity of his parents. Eventually, he helps Emil interpret a peculiar scene that appeared to Emil in a dream: a bird struggling to free itself from a giant egg. The bird, none other than a metaphor for Emil, is fighting its way out of the past. The egg, Demian explains, is the world, and in order to be reborn to adulthood, the world of childhood must be destroyed. "The bird flies to God. This God's name is Abraxas," Demian adds.[23] Those who believe in this deity—a God above the Christian God—form a distinct, avant-garde group that seeks to develop a new philosophical culture: a culture, in fact, reminiscent of that envisaged by the expressionists. In brief: in Hesse's novel, we learn of a young man's initiation into a new, post-Christian group of intellectuals.

Conversion also forms the center of Buber's *I and Thou*—in a scene that no doubt echoes Buber's life-changing discovery of the I-Thou philosophy and this philosophy's religious dimension. The scene is as follows.

A young man, most likely a student of philosophy, tosses and turns in bed, half asleep, half spun into a waking dream. He has lost belief in God, but this loss bothers him. He somehow feels that a return to believing in God might be the solution to his problems. Strange images torment him. First a scene with a woman: she lies there and stares at the dreamer with cruel eyes. He used to play with her; her eyes used to smile at him. Then a scene with two film projectors, each directed at one wall of the bedroom; both of the films present a particular pantheistic worldview in the form of a rapidly running stream of flickering images—the world as God and the human ego as God.[24] At the end of the scene a shudder seizes and overwhelms the young man.

Buber does not make it easy for his readers. It is clear enough that he distances himself from the pantheistic philosophies that he had come to believe in. It is also clear that he regains belief in God. But what about the woman? The scene with the woman echoes an earlier work of Buber, understandable only to those who know the 1913 book *Daniel: Dialogues on Realization*. There Reinold reveals his deep spiritual crisis to his friend and mentor Daniel. Reinold feels like a stranger in the world, cut off from everything; he no longer finds any meaning. He is alienated from the world, poetically called his sister.[25] Daniel shows Reinold the way to reconciliation with his sister: "You must win [her] anew, and as an awakened one. [She] had light feet and a flowerlike glance, and [she] knew nothing of [risks]. Now you are dragged out with [her] and visited by [risks]. And from every path [she] will return with stronger longing and steadier eyes. But be comforted: [her] feet will not unlearn the dance and [her] glance the caress."[26] *I and Thou* mentions only the estrangement from the "sister," not the reconciliation.

Of the three conversions, that of Toller's Friedrich is the simplest, because the protagonist's new identity is clearly defined. The new identity of Hesse's Emil Sinclair is more complex because it is woven into a gnostic mythology in which Demian's revelation leads to higher knowledge. The most complex account is that of Buber's student, reflecting as it does Buber's own lonely, mentor-free philosophical struggles. Psychologically, one might call it a regression experience, a return to an earlier identity, that of a believer in God. What makes Buber's account more complex than the others is his evasion of describing exactly the outcome of the nighttime experience. Buber's account remains mysterious and strikingly incomplete, no doubt due to the author's understanding that an extraordinary event cannot be spoken of in ordinary language, and perhaps cannot be spoken of at all. In the poetic description of his nocturnal conversion experience, Buber takes his cue from the literary motif of the existential night—from Plato's dark cave with its artificial light and shadow images, as well as from Blaise Pascal's "half hour after midnight" in 1656, a night of tears and return to the God of Abraham.[27] Buber took up the motif of the night of transition, of initiation, of redemptive enlightenment, and at the same time provided it with new features. But despite this novelty, it complies with expressionism's quest for a second birth.

Expressionists not only seek new individual identities gained through conversion and rebirth; they also wish to establish a new way of seeing the world. In an essay published in 1919, Kasimir Edschmid explains that expressionists seek to create "a new view of the world [*ein neues Weltbild*]," one "that no longer has a part in the world of the naturalists which could only be grasped experientially, and no longer has a part in that fragmented space occupied by the impression. Instead, it"—the new vision—"has to be simple, authentic, and therefore beautiful."[28] While Edschmid's essay is to be commended for its elegant language, its argument about the new way of seeing the world requires elucidation, at least for the twenty-first-century reader—who can find the best commentary in Buber's aphorism about what may be considered the most human-like plant: the tree.[29]

According to Buber, there are three ways of looking at a tree—the aesthetic, the scientific, and the new way. Each has its own protocol. As an impressionist artist, you look at the tree to find beauty, to form in your mind a picture that could be put on canvas, perceiving it for instance as "a rigid pillar in a flood of light," or perhaps as "splashes of green traversed by the gentleness of blue silver ground." Or you may be struck by a detail such as "with a streak of sunshine on a maple twig."[30] Not concerned with mere momentary impressions, the scientist focuses on the tree's botanical properties, measures its size, studies the form of the leaves, locates everything in a classificatory system, and, not to forget, assesses the tree's economic value. All of this is fine, but those committed to a third, new way—the expressionists—want to dig deeper. In contemplating the tree, Buber explains, they seek to experience a moment in which the tree no longer appears as an object, but as another being, so that a meaningful encounter can occur which forms a connection, a togetherness, thus creating a relationship. While this togetherness does not have the full character of an interpersonal human relationship characterized by mutuality, it is nevertheless a real one—and vastly different from the mere impressionistic or scientific subject-object relations.

The difference between the impressionistic and the expressionistic modes of perception merits a brief aside. In an essay he wrote before *I and Thou*, Buber distinguishes between two epistemologies, two ways or styles of encountering the world, and attributes the one to Western and the other to Eastern culture—the East understood as the region which "embraced the territory from eastern Vienna to the Bering Straits."[31] In the West, perception of the world is detached and passive—"an impression falls into one's soul and becomes an image."[32] This image is perceived as reflecting a solid, static, ultimately abstract and lifeless essence of things. In the East, by contrast, people go out to meet the world actively. They themselves have active souls, perceive life in everything and relate to everything. They are aware not so much of the static quality of things as of their dynamic nature, their being in process and their being part of a web of relationships within a community. One can observe the Western epistemology when studying how the ancient Greeks and present-day Germans see the world; by contrast, the Eastern perception of the world can be found among Jews and Taoists. Is it too bold to suggest that Buber would classify the Western way as that of impressionism, and the Eastern way as that of expressionism? And that Buber, by promoting oriental truth, sought to challenge the arrogant hegemonial position of Western thought?[33]

Back to the tree: Does Buber's expressionist approach award the tree mythological status, as if it had a soul or were inhabited by a dryad, an ancient Greek arboreal spirit? Although he does come close to doing so, Buber explicitly rejects this notion. Nevertheless, one can understand that some orthodox Jews felt that Buber here was courting pagan tree-worship, which is forbidden in the Bible. As a warning, Cynthia Ozick, in her short story "The Pagan Rabbi" (1966), tells of a scholar of religious history who fell in love with a tree (in one of the parks of New York) and its female spirit.[34] One day, he was found dead under this very tree. An investigation determines what has happened: in order to join the invisible resident and spiritual owner of the tree, the scholar, who was a rabbi, had committed suicide. Readers of both Buber's discussion of the tree and the short story can hardly miss the novelist's implied critique of Buber.

Although Buber himself does not use the adjectives "impressionistic," "scientific," or "expressionistic," these labels help us understand how expressionists think. Buber describes the range of possible perceptions of reality and states his preference for one specific kind—the expressionist one. Buber's brief aphorism about the tree can be read as a complete explanation of the expressionist approach to reality. It does not come as a surprise that this chapter has become a favorite passage of many readers.

We must beware, however, of overstating the romantic side of the matter, Buber's re-enchantment of nature. Those who immerse themselves in the text of *I and Thou* will soon realize that Buber does not leave the tree (and the rest of the world) in the *Duwelt*, the Realm of Thou. Like everything else, the tree remains firmly rooted in the *Es-Welt*, the Realm of Things, and inevitably must be treated as such—it will be felled and transformed into lumber for building, making wooden objects such as chairs and tables, and producing cardboard and paper. For all his emphasis on not reducing things to being mere objects to be used for human purposes, Buber never forgets the pragmatic aspect of things. According to Buber, everything, including trees, animals, and human beings, exists in two worlds at the same time: in a higher world of persons and in a lower world of things. In the higher world, Buber asserts, there is no history, and there are no causal relationships, a thought that he somewhat cryptically, but very expressionistically, sums up in this brief poem:

> Solang der Himmel des Du über mir ausgespannt ist, / kauern die Winde der Ursächlichkeit an meinen Fersen, / und der Wirbel des Verhängnisses gerinnt.[35]
>
> As long as the firmament of the You [Du] is spread over me, the tempests of causality cower at my heels, and the whirl of doom congeals.[36]

The poem is meant to conjure up the image of someone whose head is up in the Realm of the Thou, while at his feet is the ground of facts, in Buber's terminology: the Realm of the It. As long as you have your head in the higher realm, the realm of God, the It-World has no power over you. This powerlessness, as the poem indicates, is only temporary, however, because humans cannot spend much time outside the normal, pragmatic world, the prosaic everyday world of getting and spending, of producing and consuming goods, the world in which we have to put things to use (including trees), and have little time—tragically, too little time—for contemplating nature. But Buber would insist on the necessity of returning to the realm of the Thou and of mobilizing this higher realm's superior powers so that the It-World does not gain the upper hand (as it tends to do in the modern world).

Conclusion

Putting *I and Thou* back into its original historical context, that of the German expressionist subculture of the early twentieth century, we arrive at a better understanding of the work. Some passages that initially seem cryptic and difficult to understand can be elucidated in this way. The four subjects of social isolation, religion, the life-changing event, and the perception of things were selected to show how deeply Buber is rooted in expressionism or, more precisely, in this movement's rich repertoire of idioms and ideologies. This essay, whose very genre allows it to be tentative and incomplete, is certainly not exhaustive. Buber wrote expressionist poetry;[37] and he wrote extensively on three eminent authors whose works are regarded as seminal for the flowering of expressionism: Kierkegaard, Nietzsche, and Bergson.

Embedded in German expressionist subculture, Buber was not only indebted to it but also significantly contributed to it. *I and Thou* can be read as a work that sums up expressionism and seeks to give it a coherent theoretical basis. Admittedly, Buber never consciously intended to rethink and theorize expressionism; but considered in retrospect, this is exactly what he did in *I and Thou*.[38]

Notes

1. See Thomas Anz, "Soziologie einer Subkultur," in Anz, *Literatur des Expressionismus*, 2nd ed. (Stuttgart: Metzler, 2010), 24–44.

2. Asher Biemann in the introduction to *The Martin Buber Reader: Essential Writings*, ed. Asher D. Biemann (New York: Palgrave Macmillan, 2002), 10. See also Biemann in the introduction to volume 6 of the *Martin Buber Werkausgabe* (Gütersloh: Gütersloher Verlagshaus, 2003), 12.

3. Wilhelm Knevels, "Expressionismus: II. In der neuesten Literatur," in *Die Religion in Geschichte und Gegenwart*, 2nd ed., 5 vols. (Tübingen: Mohr, 1927–31), 2:480–82, at 481. My translation.

4. Martin Buber, *I and Thou*, trans. Walter Kaufmann (New York: Charles Scribner's Sons, 1970), 155.

5. Franz Werfel, *Gesänge aus den drei Reichen: Ausgewählte Gedichte* (Leipzig: Kurt Wolff Verlag, 1917), 4; following translation by the author.

6. Kurt Heynicke, "Freundschaft," in *Menschheitsdämmerung: Symphonie jüngster Dichtung*, ed. Kurt Pinthus (Berlin: Rowohlt, 1920), 267; following translation by the author.

7. Paula Ludwig, *Gedichte: Gesamtausgabe*, ed. Kristian Wachinger and Christiane Peter (Ebenhausen: Langewiesche-Brandt, 1986), 28; following translation by the author.

8. Jakob Moreno Levy, "Einladung zu einer Begegnung" [Invitation to an Encounter], *Daimon* 1, no. 4 (1918): 206; following translation by the author. The poet was to become a famous American psychologist under the name Jacob L. Moreno.

9. Robert Waldl, "J. L. Morenos Einfluß auf Bubers *Ich und Du*," *Zeitschrift für Psychodrama und Soziometrie* 4, no. 1 (2005): 169–73, suggests that Buber was directly influenced by Moreno, then a very prolific author whose texts centered on the notion of "encounter." See also Christoph Hutter, "Morenos Begriff der Begegnung," *Zeitschrift für Psychodramatik und Soziometrie* 9, no. 2 (2010): 211–24.

10. Martin Buber, "Worte und die Zeit: Gemeinschaft," in *Martin Buber Werkausgabe*, 11.1:166. This essay is quoted in a detailed study of expressionism's ideas of community: Christoph Eykman, "Zur Sozialphilosophie des Expressionismus," in Eykman, *Denk- und Stilformen des Expressionismus* (Munich: Francke Verlag, 1974), 28–43.

11. Georg Trakl, "Die tote Kirche," in Trakl, *Aus goldenem Kelch. Die Jugenddichtungen*, ed. Wolfgang Schnedlitz, 2nd ed. (Salzburg: Otto Müller, 1951), 81; following translation by the author.

12. Kurt Heynicke, "Aufbruch," *Der Weg*, no. 3 (March 1919): 4. This expressionist periodical, edited by Walther Blume in Munich, was discontinued after its first year.

13. Martin Buber, afterword to *Reden und Gleichnisse des Tschuang-Tse*, *Martin Buber Werkausgabe*, 2.3:103.

14. Martin Buber, *Daniel: Dialogues on Realization*, trans. Maurice Friedman (Syracuse, NY: Syracuse University Press, 2018), 44.

15. Buber, *I and Thou*, 165, 167–68.

16. Buber, *I and Thou*, 92. For the tactile metaphor, see "Religion als Gegenwart," where

Buber speaks of God's "touching" the human being's "surface," i.e., as he explains, his "skin" and "ear." *Martin Buber Werkausgabe*, 12:158.

17. Buber, *I and Thou*, 92.

18. Compare the two English translations: "O lonely Face like a star in the night, o living Finger laid on an unbending brow, o fainter echoing footsteps," *I and Thou*, trans. R. G. Smith (New York: Charles Scribner's Sons, 1958), 42–43; "O lonely countenance, starlike in the dark; O living finger upon an insensitive forehead; O steps whose echo is fading away!" *I and Thou*, trans. Walter Kaufmann (New York: Charles Scribner's Sons, 1970), 92.

19. "When we [grandchildren and Buber] would meet after a long time or part for an extended period, he would kiss our head or pat it and say 'A Jewish head.'" Buber's granddaughter Judith Buber Agassi (1924–2018), quoted in Haim Gordon, *The Other Martin Buber: Recollections of His Contemporaries* (Athens: Ohio University Press, 1988), 20. A similar gesture is mentioned in the New Testament (Mark 10:16).

20. Knevels, "Expressionismus," 481. My translation.

21. Ernst Toller, *Gesammelte Werke*, ed. John M. Spalek and Wolfgang Frühwald, 5 vols. (Munich: Hanser, 1978), 2:7–61.

22. Toller, *Gesammelte Werke*, 2:40.

23. Hermann Hesse, *Demian: The Story of Emil Sinclair's Youth*, trans. Michael Roloff and Michael Lebeck (New York: Harper Perennial, 1999), 78.

24. For a fuller commentary on the "films" (as well as the entire life-changing nighttime experience), see my commentary in Buber, *Ich und Du*, 143–44 and 223–24.

25. Buber, *Daniel*, 36. In German, the word for "world" (*die Welt*) is feminine.

26. Buber, *Daniel*, 51.

27. Pascal's *mémorial*, the secret note of his conversion, is often included in editions of Pascal's *Pensées*; see Blaise Pascal, *Pensées*, trans. A. J. Krailsheimer (Harmondsworth: Penguin Books, 1966), 309–10.

28. Kasimir Edschmid, "Über den dichterischen Expressionismus," in Edschmid, *Über den Expressionismus in der Literatur und die neue Dichtung*, 4th ed. (Berlin: Erich Reiß Verlag, 1919), 39–78, quote at 53.

29. Buber, *I and Thou*, 57–58.

30. Buber, *I and Thou*, 57, 135–36. Buber echoes Georg Simmel, *Die Religion*, 2nd ed. (Frankfurt am Main: Rütten & Loening, 1912), 19: we may be deeply touched by insignificant things such as "a ray of sunlight passing through foliage, or the bend of a branch in the breeze" (my translation). Simmel is considered a philosopher of impressionism.

31. Martin Buber, "Der Geist des Orients und das Judentum," in Buber, *Vom Geist des Judentums* (Munich: Kurt Wolff, 1916), 9–48. See I. A. Ben-Yosef, "'The East' in the Thought of Martin Buber," *Religion in Southern Africa* 61, no. 1 (1985): 47–58. A recent study of the subject is Richard E. Nisbett, *The Geography of Thought: How Asians and Westerners Think Differently . . . and Why* (New York: Free Press, 2003). Geographic description from Suzanne Marchand, "German Orientalism and the Decline of the West," *Proceedings of the American Philosophical Society* 145 (2001): 465–73, at 465.

32. Buber, *Vom Geist des Judentums*, 12. My translation.

33. Buber was one of the promotors of the "Eastern wisdom" that fascinated Germans in the early decades of the twentieth century. For a view similar to that of Buber, see Theodor Lessing, *Europa und Asien* (Berlin: Verlag der Wochenschrift die Aktion, 1918); interestingly, Lessing explains that Eastern art is close to the art of Western expressionism (95). For an instructive

survey that mentions Buber only briefly, see Suzanne Marchand, "Eastern Wisdom in an Era of Western Despair: Orientalism in 1920s Central Europe," in *Weimar Thought: A Contested Legacy*, ed. Peter E. Gordon and John P. McCormick (Princeton, NJ: Princeton University Press, 2013), 341–60.

34. Cynthia Ozick, *The Pagan Rabbi and Other Stories* (New York: Penguin Books, 1991), 3–37. The short story was published in 1966, a year after Buber's death in 1965, which had prompted innumerable essays and obituaries that celebrated Buber as the greatest Jewish philosopher of his time, and regularly mentioned *I and Thou*.

35. Buber, *Ich und Du*, in *Martin-Buber-Werkausgabe*, 4:43.

36. Buber, *I and Thou*, 59.

37. "Der Abgrund und das Weltenlicht, / Zeitnot und Ewigkeitsbegier, / Vision, Ereignis und Gedicht: / Zwiesprache wars und ists mit Dir" (*Martin Buber Werkausgabe*, 7:135). In approximate translation: "Dark abyss and cosmic light, / time constraints and longing for eternity, / vision, event and verse: / dialogue with you, which was and is." The accumulation of nouns, typical of expressionist poetry, marks Buber's unpublished handwritten poem, inscribed into the dedicatory copy of *Zwiesprache* (1932) that he gave his wife, Paula.

38. I wish to thank Marie Robinson, Johannes Waßmer, and Samuel Zinner for their comments on this article.

Annotated Bibliography

Two titles on German expressionism provide good introductions to the subject: Peter Gay, *Weimar Culture: The Outsider as Insider* (New York: Harper & Row, 1968), specifically the chapter "The Revolt of the Son: Expressionist Years" (102–18); and Neil H. Donahue, ed., *A Companion to the Literature of German Expressionism* (Rochester, NY: Camden House, 2005), a book of essays.

The remarkable Jewish presence in German expressionism is dealt with in the following books, the first of which is a collection of German source texts: Armin A. Wallas, ed., *Texte des Expressionismus. Der Beitrag jüdischer Autoren zur österreichischen Avantgarde* (Linz: Edition Neue Texte, 1988). See also Lisa Marie Anderson, *German Expressionism and the Messianism of a Generation* (Amsterdam: Rodopi, 2011). Finally, mention must be made of an article that surveys Buber's literary (rather than academic) language: Paul Mendes-Flohr, "Martin Buber's Rhetoric," in *Martin Buber: A Contemporary Perspective*, edited by Paul Mendes-Flohr (Syracuse, NY: Syracuse University Press, 2002), 1–24.

10

Buber's Hermeneutical Biblical Theology

STEVEN KEPNES

Although Buber was wary of traditional theological discourse and thus did not regard himself as a theologian, his ramified writings on the Hebrew Bible may be understood as exegetical or "hermeneutical" theology. Hermeneutical theology, unlike philosophical theology, begins with the text and with neither doctrinal affirmations nor metaphysical presuppositions. Hermeneutical theology is grounded in scripture, that is, the word of God, and seeks to discern its abiding meaning for contemporary readers.[1] We may delineate six principles guiding Buber's hermeneutical biblical theology.

First, the Bible provides a record of I-Thou encounters between God and Israel. The Bible then is witness to what Buber calls a "dialogue between heaven and earth."[2] Second, Buber believes with Franz Rosenzweig, and we may say, with the Rabbis as well, that God's message is to be found in the *pshat* or the literal and literary words (what Rosenzweig calls "the unaesthetic-superaesthetic aesthetic"[3]) of the Bible. Third, Buber asserts that exegesis of the literary text of the Bible requires the use of technical or "scientific" modes such as historical study, philology, and analysis of literary genres of the Bible like the *Leitwort*, or leading word, principle. Thus, what can be considered technical, I-It analyses are used along with an I-Thou approach to interpreting the Bible. Fourth, Buber insists that the Bible's message, although originally addressed to the needs of ancient Israel, has what Paul Ricoeur called a "surplus of meaning" that makes it a living text, indeed, *Schrift* or scripture.[4] And this means, fifth, that the Bible's message can be relevant to the life of today's readers and to the contemporary world. And finally, as scripture, the Bible does not only relate a message about and for the world today, but it also transmits a theology, a portrait or, rather, a series of portraits of God. This implies that despite Buber's misgivings about theology as conceptual discourse about God's attributes, he nonetheless had a theology, indeed a "hermeneutical theology."[5] In his biblical writings, he not only presents a personal God who has a name, "I will be there as I will be there," but this God possesses attributes of power, compassion, and judgment. To be sure, Buber's hermeneutical theology, following the narratives and images of the Hebrew Bible, is neither a systematic nor a philosophical theology. It is rather a multilayered theology filled with dynamic tensions and oppositions, marked often by questions and even a deep hiddenness; but it is precisely the dynamism, tensions, and hiddenness of Buber's biblical theology that makes it a compelling model for a Jewish theology to this day.

In his essay of 1938, Buber reflects on "how and why" he and Franz Rosenzweig undertook to translate the Hebrew Bible into German.[6] He relates that, unlike Rosenzweig, who came to the Bible later in his life, he grew up with the Bible. Still in 1925, some two years after the publication of *I and Thou*, when he was presented with the opportunity to do a new translation of the Bible into German with Rosenzweig, it seems to have opened a new chapter in his intellectual and religious journey. Buber devoted significant time from 1925 almost until his death to biblical translation as well as the writing of several books and essays on select biblical figures and topics.

Indeed, Buber seems to have come to see that most of the elements of the life of dialogical relations that he outlines in his book *I and Thou* can be found in the Bible. In part 1 of *I and Thou*, Buber speaks of three spheres in which I-Thou relations occur: nature, the human sphere, and art.[7] What I believe we see in his biblical writings is that the Bible provides a fourth sphere in which one can have I-Thou relationships. This means that the biblical text is not only a record of I-Thou encounters between God and the people Israel in the past, but that the Bible becomes a "Thou" that can bear on I-Thou relations in the present. One readily hears echoes of Buber's philosophy in his essay on how to read the Bible, as rendered in his translation of the sacred text:

> People today have little sure access to sure belief, and cannot be given such access. [. . .] But an openness to belief is not denied them. They too can, precisely when they are in earnest, open themselves up to this book [the Bible], and let themselves be struck by its rays wherever they may strike. They can without anticipation and without reservation yield themselves and let themselves come to the text, receive it with all their strength, and await what may happen to them. [. . .] They must place themselves anew, before the renewed book, hold back nothing of themselves [. . .]. They do not know what speech, what image in the book will take hold of them and recast them, from what place the spirit will surge up and pass into them so as to embody itself anew in their lives, but they are open.[8]

When Buber speaks of the proper attitude to take toward a work of art in *I and Thou*, he uses the phrase "receptive beholding" (*empfangend Schauender*). This is precisely what he is asking of his readers of the Bible when he asks them to "open themselves up to this book." He is asking them to assume an I-Thou attitude of "receptive beholding." Furthermore, just as the I-Thou encounter cannot be determined or forced but must occur spontaneously "through grace,"[9] similarly he instructs his readers of the Bible to simply remain open and let the Bible "strike them" where it will. And finally, just as he tells us that those who enter into an I-Thou encounter emerge as different from before they entered, an encounter with the biblical text as Thou "will take hold of them and recast them."

Another way of referring to the biblical text as Thou is to say that Buber takes the Bible seriously as scripture, as a repository of the word of God. Therefore, when the Bible is regarded with the proper attitude, the I-Thou attitude, it may still be a vessel for the divine word, even in today's secular world, rife with disbelief and suspicion about the relevance of the scripture. Furthermore, as a record of I-Thou encounters, the Bible becomes what Edmund Husserl, Martin Heidegger, and the phenomenologists call a *Lebenswelt* or "lifeworld," the lived experience of the world as self-evident or given, which individuals share and experience together. Accordingly, for Buber the *Lebenswelt* of the Bible is constituted by an I-Thou ontology, ergo a perduring experiential reality. This means that the Bible presents a world in which the dynamics of I-Thou—wholeness, presence in the moment, relationality, personality, and a deep sense of responsibility and destiny—rule, and in which the presence of God hovers over all relations, events, and encounters. Thus, what Buber says about Hasidism as "the hallowing of the everyday" also applies to the Bible.[10]

This means that, in Buber's view, the life of ancient Israel is marked by a continuous possibility of beholding the presence of God, be the graced encounter shepherds grazing their sheep in the desert, farmers attending to the fields, city dwellers, prophets, or in an individual's inner voice, "the still small voice" (Kings 19:12). Buber stresses that biblical law is intended to render holy the natural processes of procuring food, eating, and sex. "Law [...] concerns the natural life of human beings. Eating meat and sacrificing animals are linked; marital purity is consecrated monthly in the sanctuary; people in their drives and passions are accepted as they are and included in holiness."[11]

The second feature of Buber's hermeneutics is his exacting attention to the language of scripture. Together with Rosenzweig, he developed a theory about the primal oral nature of biblical scripture as the spoken word, *Gespro-*

chenheit of God. Buber argues that the oral nature of the Bible leads to the use of "colometric" breath-units—"units corresponding to the breathings of the human speaker"—to allow for ease in uttering biblical verses.[12] A good example of this is seen in the very opening of the Bible in Genesis.

> God said: Let there be light! And there was light.
> God saw the light: that it was good.
> God separated the light from darkness.
> God called the light: Day! And darkness He called: Night![13]

In addition to the theory of the Bible as a spoken work, Buber and Rosenzweig developed the principle of *Leitworte* or "leading words." These are words based on Hebrew roots that are repeated in both the small and large linguistic units of scripture.[14] Buber argued that if one follows the *Leitwort* one has a key to the message that the biblical text is trying to convey. One particularly illuminating example of the leading word interpretative principle is found in Buber's essay "Abraham the Seer," where he shows how the Hebrew *Leitwort*, based on the root for "to see," *resh, aleph, heh*, is used throughout the Abrahamic narrative. This use culminates in the Akedah, where Abraham not only sees *Moriah*, literally "God will see," but also sees God seeing him:

> God sees man, and man sees God. [. . .] God sees the innermost reality of the human soul, the reality He has brought out by testing the soul: and man sees the way of God, so that he may walk in his footsteps. The man sees, and sees also that he is being seen.[15]

It is important to say that, as attuned to literary techniques of biblical prose as Buber is, his interpretive method differs from purely literary approaches to the Bible in that he is clear that the Bible is more than a work of literature. As in his interpretation of Abraham, Buber shows how the *Leitwort* "to see" serves the divine message given to Abraham, the first prophet of the Jewish people. For the Bible is, above all, to be read as a sacred text; its literary genius is inflected with the sacred function of conveying religious instruction and God's supernal message (*Botschaft*). Hence, the Bible as literature and as the transmission of God's message are intertwined. "It would be a fundamental misunderstanding of the nature of the Bible that it tacks on *Botschaft* here and there as morals are tacked on to bad parables. There is no 'content' to be smelted from Biblical ore; each biblical content exists in its unitary and indissoluble *Gestalt*."[16]

One of the important theological uses of the *Leitwort* principle for Buber and Rosenzweig is its application to the issue of whether the Pentateuch is a multiauthored anthology of literary strands or a literary whole. Buber and Rosenzweig deploy their theory of the supernal inflections determining the literary structure and semantics of the Torah to argue against the documentary hypothesis and other attempts to slice the Bible up into different strands. For example, they point to the repetition of *Leitworte* throughout the Pentateuch as a sign that the text that we have must be considered a literary whole. And with somewhat of an ironic pun, they refer to the final redactor of the Torah as "R" for *Rabbenu*, our divinely appointed Rabbi.[17] This seriously measured pun marks a middle position between Orthodox and liberal views on the nature of the Torah as the revealed word of God, since it insists on the literary wholeness of the text while allowing that a human hand was involved in its final production as a theologically unified text.

In addition to the discernment of the animating literary principles of the Bible, Buber was very well versed in the historical, anthropological, and sociological scholarship on the Bible in the Germany of his day. Thus, a third dimension of his biblical hermeneutic is found in his use of social scientific methods in interpreting the Bible. In opposition to his writings on Hasidism where he took poetic license to alter certain of its aspects, his biblical writings resulted from careful consideration of philological, historical, and other "scholarly" methodologies.[18] Here, Buber sought to widen his hermeneutical approach by supplementing the neo-Romantic *Verstehen* hermeneutics of understanding (his "hermeneutics of I-Thou") with a "hermeneutics of *erklären*" or causal explanations. This latter method might even be called a method of I-It analysis. And in his overall approach to the Bible Buber uses both methods. Thus, Buber employs a two-pronged hermeneutical method akin to that which would receive extended theoretical articulation in the work of Paul Ricoeur.[19]

Buber turns to history, sociology, and anthropology not only to provide context and to identify where Israel differed from its neighbors in matters of religion and ethics, but also to argue that the God of Israel and the "holy life" of Israel were reflected in and through its history, society, culture, agriculture, and shepherding. One of many examples can be seen in Buber's analysis of the sabbatical seventh year of agricultural rest for all crops:

> Six years the land is to be cultivated, the seventh year it is to cease; seven times the law repeats the word "cease" and "cessation." And just as the commandment of the Sabbath took up all creatures—the servant, the settler, even the domestic animal—in one common rest (Ex 23:12), so the commandment of the sabbatical year takes up all creatures. [. . .] *This is a "societal" commandment, though "societal" and "religious" cannot be severed in the Torah. The "religious" is the direction; but the "societal is the way."*[20]

The fourth element of Buber's hermeneutic relates to the *lived experience attested in* the Bible as scripture. Though the Bible warrants philological, literary, historical, and anthropological contextualization, its meaning transcends these explanatory procedures, precisely because the Bible is Torah, that is, scripture. As scripture, the Bible resonates the word of God, the living word that has transhistorical meaning. Perhaps inspired by Buber, Hans-Georg Gadamer developed a full-blown philosophical hermeneutics to highlight the transhistorical significance of foundational texts. And this is perhaps the most important point in all hermeneutical approaches to any classic text, which speaks to the very reason why we read them—to discern their unique manifestations of a truth about life, death, the good, and their contribution to the development of a high moral culture, which Gadamer identifies as the very heart of the German ideal of *Bildung*.[21]

For Buber, reading the Bible is also *Bildung*, an exercise in the formation not just of cultural and existential sensibilities but of how to listen and heed God's ever rearticulated address in the protean matrix of life. He most forcefully illustrates this message in his reading of the biblical prophets, who came neither to predict the future nor to teach religious law, but rather to proclaim the imperative of ethical responsibility for the exigent political and social challenges of the hour. Buber goes as far as to say that seeing the present moment as a commanding call for ethical responsibility is equivalent to "revelation." And as he puts it, "people today resist scripture" precisely because they wish to avoid responsibility.

> People today resist Scripture because they cannot abide revelation. To abide revelation means to sustain the full decisiveness of the moment, to respond to the moment, to be responsible for it. [People today] claim to venture much; but the one true venture, the venture of responsibility they industriously avoid.[22]

Buber's notion of radical responsibility for the demands of the present moment as the central message of the Torah has a splendid vagueness about it that allows him to apply it equally to the prophets Amos and Isaiah and to living in a modern world driven by the ever-increasing salience of the I-It attitude promoting materialistic and individualistic values. In this "historic hour," the prophetic voice beseeches us to assume responsibility for the disinherited—the poor and powerless—made so by the ascendency of the I-It attitude.[23] In heeding the prophetic voice, reading scripture takes on existential and political urgency.

Yet there is more to Buber's biblical theology than his ethics of responsibility. For after all, the ethics of responsibility assumes that individuals are in a position of some power and freedom so that they can exercise their will to ameliorate the suffering of others in the present moment. Therefore, as well as being the God who exhorts his people to use their power to address the ills of the social and political world, the God of the Bible also addresses Israel when its people are powerless and themselves victim to the cruel power of others. In this case the God of Buber's biblical theology acts as the "God of sufferers."[24] He is a God who hears the cries of sufferers and gives them comfort and hope. He is the God who redeemed the Hebrew slaves in Egypt, the memory of which is continuously evoked in scripture and, later, in Judaism's liturgy.

The dynamic element in hermeneutical theology is to use the message of scripture as relevant today. Thus Buber finds, in the biblical God of sufferers, a message for his own German Jewish community that experienced the unspeakable tragedies of the Shoah. However, when Buber, as a German Jew in the time of the Shoah, speaks of the God of sufferers, he realizes that there are no easy answers.[25] Simply put, God did not redeem the Jews of Europe as he did the Israelite slaves. Therefore, the problem of a theodicy of the Shoah cannot be solved through easy reference to the Exodus story. At the same time, it also cannot be solved through a logical philosophical analysis. But precisely here is where hermeneutical theology helps. For hermeneutical theology works in and through scripture and its metaphors and narratives, not logic alone. And the Bible has additional metaphors and texts of hope that go beyond Exodus.

The metaphor Buber turns to for his theodicy of the Shoah is what the prophet called the *Hestar Panim*, the "hiddenness of God's face" (Isa. 45:15). In the dark hours of the Shoah, God was in a mysterious state of "eclipse" but is neither dead nor helpless.[26] As in times past, his absence is not permanent. Therefore, we can then hold on to faith in spite of suffering. With his notion of the eclipse of God, Buber is careful not to strike at the very heart of Judaism by declaring God dead or powerless in the face of evil, as many post-Holocaust theologians do.[27]

However, Buber's hermeneutical theodicy in its deepest form is found in his writings on Job. To begin with, Buber does not sugarcoat Job's experience.[28] Taking his cue from God himself, who sides with Job in protesting the theological platitudes of his friends who insist that Job must be guilty of sin, Buber declares that there is a tear, a "rent," in the moral fabric of the world. Thus, Buber offers us what may be called a "theology of rending," a theology that acknowledges that injustice is present in the world, so deeply interwoven that its threads cannot be cut by the simple insistence on God's salvific power. Job's is a "contradictory faith," so that while not loudly bemoaning the injustice he experiences, he affirms a faith in the God of justice.[29] The rent at the "heart of the world" is real, yet it is the existential paradox of faith to remain true to the God of the creation, *ki tov*, because he is good. Like Abraham, Job sees God seeing him:

> The true answer that Job receives is God's appearance only, only this, that distance turns to nearness, that his "eye sees Him" (Job 42:5), that he knows Him again. Nothing is explained, nothing adjusted; wrong has not become right nor cruelty kindness. Nothing happens but that man hears God's address.[30]

There is no theologically satisfactory answer to the question of theodicy for Job. But perhaps this very admission contains within it some redeeming truth. God responds to Job's anguished cry with his presence alone; his very presence is an affirmation of the relationship between God and Job. God allows Job to "see him," and thus Job is calmed and "repents in dust and ashes" (Job 42:6). As Buber reads Job, the problem of theodicy is not to be addressed theologically or conceptually but hermeneutically. In reading the biblical text, attuned to its existential throbbing, one shares in Job's anguish and his paradoxical affirmation of the God of creation, even in the manifest absence of justice.

The book of Job, as Buber teaches us to read it, ultimately eschews despair for the avenue of hope. It instructs us not to sever the delicate bond of our relationship with God. And Buber instructs us, despite—indeed, because—of a sober acknowledgment of prevailing evils, to maintain a "Hebrew humanism."[31] One is to read scripture precisely because it illustrates the depth of the struggle to retain an unyielding faith in God, and "not because of its literary, historical, and national values, important as these may be."[32]

True to his own philosophy of I and Thou and to the covenantal tradition in the Bible, Buber preserves the dialogical relationship between God and Israel despite the tear in that relationship which is also a tear in the heart of the world, and perhaps, even, a tear in God himself. This relationship is preserved because of the original and everlasting covenant—the *brit olam*—established "in the beginning" between the people of Israel and the eternal God of Israel.

Notes

1. See my *The Text as Thou: Martin Buber's Dialogical Hermeneutics and Narrative Theology* (Bloomington: Indiana University Press, 1992), chaps. 1–3.

2. Martin Buber, "The Dialogue between Heaven and Earth," in *On Judaism*, ed. N. Glatzer (New York: Schocken Books, 1967), 214–27.

3. Martin Buber and Franz Rosenzweig, "The How and Why of Our Translation," app. 2, in *Scripture and Translation*, trans. Lawrence Rosenwald and Everett Fox (Bloomington: Indiana University Press, 1994), 218.

4. Paul Ricoeur, *Interpretation Theory: Discourse and the Surplus of Meaning* (Fort Worth: Texas Christian University Press, 1976).

5. Buber's antipathy to theology stems from his insistence on addressing God in the second person as a "Thou" and "eternal You," and not in the third person as a "He" with attributes, powers, qualities. Buber's view of theology is summed up in *I and Thou*. God "may properly only be addressed, not expressed." Buber, *I and Thou*, trans. Ronald Gregor Smith (1958; New York: Scribner's Classics Edition, 2000), 81.

6. Buber and Rosenzweig, "How and Why of Our Translation."

7. Buber, *I and Thou*, 22. For discussion of Buber's use of the term "spiritual beings" (*geistige Wesenheiten*) as a designation for art, see my *The Text as Thou*, 23–26. I employ Buber's notion of *geistige Wesenheiten* as a bridge to show how the biblical text could be seen as a "Thou" on the model of a work of art.

8. Buber, "People Today and the Jewish Bible," in *Scripture and Translation*, 7.

9. Buber, *I and Thou*, 25, 26.

10. Martin Buber, *Hasidism and Modern Man* (New York: Harper & Row, 1958), 27.

11. Buber, "People Today and the Jewish Bible," 6.

12. Buber and Rosenzweig, "How and Why of Our Translation," 217.

13. I use the English translation of Edward Fox, which was styled in the spirit of the Buber-Rosenzweig German translation of the Hebrew Bible. Fox, *In the Beginning* (New York: Schocken Books, 1983), Gen. 1:3–5. Here is the German: "Da sprach Gott: Licht werde! Und Licht ward. / Und Gott sah das Licht, dass es gut war. / So schied Gott zwischen dem Licht und der Finsternis. / Dem Licht rief Gott: Tag! und der Finsternis rief er: Nacht!" Martin Buber with Franz Rosenzweig, *Die Schrift: Das Buch im Anfang* (Berlin: Verlag Lambert Schneider, 1926).

14. Martin Buber, "*Leitwort* Style in Pentateuch Narrative," in *Scripture and Translation*, 114–27. See also my *Text as Thou*, chap. 3, for further review of this principle.

15. Martin Buber, "Abraham the Seer," in Buber, *On the Bible: Eighteen Studies*, ed. Nahum N. Glatzer (New York: Schocken Books, 1968), 42.

16. Martin Buber, "The Language of *Botschaft*," in *Scripture and Translation*, 28.

17. Franz Rosenzweig, "The Unity of the Bible: A Position Paper vis-à-vis Orthodoxy and Liberalism," in *Scripture and Translation*, 23.

18. Buber altered his later approach to the translation of Hasidic texts to stay closer to the original materials. See my discussion of his changed method of Hasidic translation as well as my hermeneutical response to the Buber-Scholem debate on the historicity of Buber's translations in *The Text as Thou*, 32.

19. Paul Ricoeur, "Explanation and Understanding," in Ricoeur, *The Philosophy of Paul Ricoeur* (New York: Beacon Press, 1978). Ricoeur avers that explanation develops understanding but understanding "envelops" explanation. In this way scientific methods of explanation become one step in an overall interpretative process that aims at understanding a text as an entrance into its lifeworld.

20. Buber, "The Language of *Botschaft*," 32 (my italics).

21. Hans-Georg Gadamer, *Truth and Method* (Tübingen, 1960; New York: Crossroad, 1982), 445, 11.

22. Buber, "People Today and the Jewish Bible," 9.

23. Martin Buber, "Prophecy, Apocalyptic and the Historical Hour," in *On the Bible*, 172.

24. Martin Buber, *The Prophetic Faith*, trans. C. Witton-Davies (New York: Macmillan, 1949), chap. 8.

25. Buber, "Dialogue between Heaven and Earth," 224.

26. Martin Buber, *The Eclipse of God* (New York: Harper & Row, 1952).

27. See the classic statement of Elie Wiesel in *Night* (New York: Hill & Wang, 2006), 65, as well as Richard Rubenstein, *After Auschwitz* (Indianapolis: Bobbs-Merrill, 1966), 277.

28. For an extensive analysis of Buber's writings on Job, see my "Job and Post-Holocaust Theodicy," in *Strange Fire: Reading the Bible after the Holocaust*, ed. Tod Linafelt (Sheffield, UK: Sheffield Academic Press, 2000), 252–67.

29. Martin Buber, "Job," in *On the Bible*, 191, 192.

30. Buber, "Dialogue between Heaven and Earth," 224.

31. Buber, "Hebrew Humanism," in *The Martin Buber Reader*, ed. Asher D. Biemann (New York: Palgrave Macmillan, 2002), 161.

32. Quoted in editor's postscript to Buber, *On the Bible*, 235.

Annotated Bibliography

PRIMARY SOURCES

The best collection of Buber's writings on biblical figures and themes is Martin Buber, *On the Bible: Eighteen Studies*, edited by Nahum N. Glatzer (New York: Schocken Books, 1968). Buber and Rosenzweig's writings on the principles that guided their translation of the Hebrew were collected by Buber in *Die Schrift und ihre Verdeutschung* (Berlin: Schocken Verlag, 1936). That volume was translated as Martin Buber and Franz Rosenzweig, *Scripture and Translation*, translated by Lawrence Rosenwald and Everett Fox (Bloomington: Indiana University Press, 1994). Each of the translators wrote an introductory essay: Everett Fox, "The Book in Its Contexts," and Lawrence Rosenwald, "Challenge to Translation Theory."

SECONDARY LITERATURE

Steven Kepnes, *The Text as Thou: Martin Buber's Dialogical Hermeneutics and Narrative Theology* (Bloomington: Indiana University Press, 1992) places Buber's biblical translation and writings on the Bible in the context of the German hermeneutical tradition of *Verstehen* (understanding) from Hans-Georg Gadamer to Paul Ricoeur. On Buber's biblical hermeneutics, see also Michael A. Fishbane, "Martin Buber as an Interpreter of the Bible," *Judaism: A Quarterly Journal* 27, no. 2 (1978): 184–95. The following two essays provide a synoptic overview of Buber's manifold writings on biblical interpretation: Nahum Glatzer, "Buber as an Interpreter of the Bible," in *The Philosophy of Martin Buber*, edited by Paul Schilpp and Maurice Friedman (LaSalle, IL: Open Court, 1967), 361–81; and James Muhlenberg, "Buber as an Interpreter of the Bible," also in *The Philosophy of Martin Buber*, 381–403. Glatzer places Buber's biblical writings in the context of his work as a whole, whereas Muhlenberg reviews central theological themes in Buber's biblical books and places them in the context of Protestant biblical theology and scholarship of Buber's time. See also Daniel M. Heskowitz, "Martin Buber's *Two Types of Faith* in Its Protestant Context," *Journal of Religion* 104, no. 1 (January 2024): 79–100.

11

Buber's Relational Ontology and Dialogical Listening

CLAUDIA WELZ

Dialogue is a comprehensive hermeneutical method promoting "the art of unmediated listening."[1] In one's utter openness to another, all conceptual "mediations" are suspended, especially one's prejudices, so that the other's voice can reach one unencumbered. Correspondingly, Buber states in *I and Thou*:

> The relation to the You is unmediated. Nothing conceptual intervenes between I and You, no prior knowledge and no imagination. [...] No purpose intervenes between I and You, no greed and no anticipation. [...] Every means [*Mittel*] is an obstacle. Only where all means have disintegrated encounters occur.[2]

The dialogical I-Thou encounter with the other is unmediated by foreknowledge, whether as a given mental image, a goal-directed interest, or any certain expectations.

However, one may doubt whether "unmediated" understanding of the other is at all possible. Bearing Hans-Georg Gadamer's insight into the heuristic and epistemological value of provisional "pre-judgments" (*Vorurteile*) in mind, the latter are necessary "conditions of understanding" even though they must be revised again and again.[3] Nonetheless, Buber's thesis of immediacy of a dialogical encounter makes sense insofar as it denotes the attitude of unbiased listening. This is not to say that we forget our presuppositions when we listen empathically, but that we are to become aware of our biases and question them. This, in turn, allows us to understand something new not only about the other but also about ourselves, and thus to be transformed.

Listening to Creatures and Their Creator

In the first part of *I and Thou*, Buber divides the world of I-Thou relationships into three spheres: the first is "life with nature," which is sublinguistic since, for example, a tree cannot give a verbal answer; the second sphere concerns intersubjective "life with people," which is linguistic (*sprachgestaltig*) as we communicate with each other with the help of words; while the third sphere is speechless but language-producing as it includes cultural life with the products of the human spirit (*geistige Wesenheiten*) such as art, philosophy, and religion.[4]

Remarkably, in every sphere, through everything that becomes present to us as a You, we can "look toward the hem of the eternal Thou," and from each sphere "we hear a waft of it [*vernehmen wir ein Wehen von ihm*]," which is why "in every You we address the eternal You, in every sphere according to its manner."[5] In his dialogical optics, acoustics, and haptics, Buber couples our everyday encounters with people, animals, plants, and artifacts with the subtle presence of God, the "eternal Thou." In this way, God is not located in some metaphysical world "behind" or "beyond" the terrestrial world but rather in the middle of our earthly life. Hence, the encounter with God, the creator of the All, takes place in and through our dialogical relationships with other creatures. The separation between a "religious" and "secular" realm is removed in dialogue, so that even outside of the houses of worship, we can look at the "hem" of God's imagined garment and listen to its movements. Buber presumably takes up the vision of the prophet Isaiah who saw the Lord sitting on a high and lofty throne, "and the train of his robe filled the temple."[6] Hearing, seeing, and touching are combined in this theophany. Divine nearness and sublimity go together in a dynamic understanding of "transcendence": God is not statically "here" or "there" but is "near to all who call on him."[7]

Paul Mendes-Flohr has compellingly described Buber's intellectual path in his *From Mysticism to Dialogue*.[8] While Buber's doctoral thesis on Nicholas of Cusa and Jakob Böhme as well as his collection of mythical and mystical texts, for example, the narratives of the Hasidim,[9] represent the search for a union of the self with the All, the dialogic of *I and Thou* describes at most a kind of pan-en-theism, for everything is seen "in" a God who is always within call. Buber prefixed the first edition of *Ich und Du* (1923) with a motto from Johann Wolfgang von Goethe's *West-östlicher Divan* (1819), which Buber in a letter to Franz Rosenzweig called "a golden ornament [*eine goldne Zier*]" at the inner entrance door[10] of the "house" (i.e., his book) which belongs to its edifice "since the laying of the foundation stone": "Thus I have awaited and finally obtained from you / God's presence in all elements."[11]

As Walter Kaufmann points out in the prologue to his English translation of *Ich und Du*, Buber deleted the epigraph from the 1957 reprint because it had been misunderstood in a pantheistic sense (i.e., as an identification of God and the world). Buber rather wished to emphasize actual interhuman relationships through which we can encounter God. For Buber, "God is no object of discourse, knowledge, or even experience. He cannot be spoken of, but he can be spoken to; he cannot be seen, but he can be listened to. The only possible relationship with God is to address him and to be addressed by him."[12] In his introduction to the hundredth anniversary reprint of *I and Thou*, Mendes-Flohr extends Kaufmann's claim and clarifies that, according to Buber, one encounters God in *all* aspects of life—not only in interhuman relations but also in relations with nature and "the creative works by one's fellow human beings," and this belief is indeed "to be understood as the ground of Buber's existential ontology."[13]

Buber himself testifies to the importance of listening to music when remarking about the Bach concerts at the Saint-Thomas Church that he attended as a student at the University of Leipzig: "What had the strongest effect on me there was undoubtedly hearing Bach's music. [. . .] The groundtone of my life was obviously modified in some manner and through that my thinking as well."[14] As noted by Mendes-Flohr in his classic Buber biography, listening to Johann Sebastian Bach's polyphonic and contrapuntal music influenced Buber so much that he wrote: "Slowly, waveringly, grew the insight into the problematic reality of human existence and into the fragile possibility of doing justice to it. Bach helped me."[15] Bach helped Buber understand the complexities of the intertwined relations in human life. Bach felt that it was God who made the music through him. After completing a composition, he wrote the letters SDG at the bottom of the page, meaning "Soli Deo Gloria" ("For the glory of God alone"). In Bach's music, the human soul is in tune with the divine, despite all the struggles and agonies of this earthly life. Bach's music, which turns Bible verses into sound, makes audible precisely the divine "voice" that Buber listened to when reading the Hebrew Bible that he had been translating with Franz Rosenzweig since 1925.

In the third part of *I and Thou*, which is dedicated to our relationship with God, Buber asks how prayer is distinguished from magic. He answers that the latter wants to act without entering into relationship, whereas in prayer a mutual interaction occurs through listening and speaking. Those who pray "say You and listen [*vernehmen*]." Buber notes that one cannot truly pray to God and only make use of the world, because the one who knows the world only as something to be utilized also knows God in no other way. Then prayer is nothing but a procedure of exonerating oneself: "it falls into the ears of the void [*es fällt ins Ohr der Leere*]."[16] God as a listener and the one answering our prayers[17] eludes one where the approach to the world is nihilistic or instrumental. Whoever wants to lead a life permeated by the God-relationship must seek to ensure that all beings are met as a "Thou" (and not only as an "It") so that "the holy basic word sounds through all of them [*sich in allen austönt*]."[18] For Buber, genuine prayer is *Beziehungskraft*: relational power.[19]

On the last page of his epilogue to *I and Thou*, Buber affirms that the dialogue with God should not be understood as something "beside" or "above" everyday life, biographical and historical events: "Often we think that there is nothing to be heard [*nichts zu vernehmen*] as if we had not long ago plugged wax into our own ears."[20] Buber believed that everything that happens in this world contains an appeal to us, whether to stand firm or to resist. To be able to orient ourselves, we must *want to* hear the divine call, even if this means hearing not with our ears but with our hearts.[21] This is especially true in the face of ambiguous situations in which God's will is not obvious but hidden and must be sought.

Buber, who had been a lecturer in religious studies and Jewish ethics at Frankfurt University since 1923, was dismissed by the Nazis in 1933. In 1934, he founded a new institution for Jewish adult education, the Mittelstelle für jüdische Erwachsenenbildung, and in this context, he lectured at various places in Germany.[22] From July 1 to 8, 1934, a teacher training conference took place at the Jewish Retreat Home in Lehnitz near Oranienburg.[23] Buber had already held Bible courses there a few months earlier.[24] The third newsletter of the Mittelstelle contains "A Note for Bible Courses" (1936) where Buber underlines that the biblical word cannot be detached from the situation of its "spokenness" (*Gesprochenheit*), otherwise it loses its concreteness and corporeality: "A commandment is not an aphorism [*Sentenz*], but an address [*Anrede*]" which is heard "as spoken to this very generation, but never to be lifted into the timeless; if one turns it into an aphorism, one transfers it from the second to the third person, from the binding obligation of hearing [*Verbindlichkeit des Hörens*] to the non-binding nature of interested reading."[25]

It is not incidental that Michael Fishbane calls Buber's biblical hermeneutics a "training for human listening" that is attentive to the choice of words.[26] Dan Avnon points out that Buber, when translating the Hebrew Bible into German, developed a "guiding-word principle" which postulates that the biblical text uses certain words (*Leitworte*) arousing the reader's attention to interpretative connections between disparate passages of the Bible. Its text is listened to rather than merely read.[27] According to Mendes-Flohr, Buber and Rosenzweig conceived of their Bible translation as "revalorizing the reading of scripture as a performative act [...] in which the reader is prompted to listen to the voice resonating in the text." Without doubt, for Buber, the commanding word of the Bible is a personal address calling for a personal response.²⁸

Listening and Belonging: Buber's Relational Ontology of the Interhuman

Similarly, in his 1957 afterword to *I and Thou*, Buber refers to traditional sayings of a sage who died thousands of years ago. We may try to "listen" to the sayings, receiving them now as the speaker had spoken these words in the presence of their original recipients. This requires an attitude of "Thou-saying" with which the recipient "will hear a voice [*eine Stimme*]," which is identical with the voice that sounds toward the recipients (*entgegentönen*) from other genuine sayings of the same sage.²⁹ The text as a readable object is thus subordinated to the voice of the person speaking out of it.

There is a special linguistic link between the German words for "listening" (*zuhören*) and "belonging" (*zugehören*). Community-building presupposes listening to each other. In the second part of *I and Thou*, where Buber unfolds a critical social theory, aural and sonic metaphors are seminal.³⁰ Here Buber contrasts the I-It relationship between alienated people, whose fragmented society (*Gesellschaft*) is characterized by lust for domination and control, with the genuine community (*Gemeinschaft*) grounded in mutual recognition and solidarity between I and Thou.

Compared to desperate people who have already given up hope, who know no attachment and no sacrifice but always want to intervene in the tenor of events, Buber describes the truly free human being as someone who "listens [*lauscht*]" to that which grows in order to actualize it. Without heeding the rationality of purpose, the truly free human being is freed from the belief in bondage, from "the belief in unfreedom [*vom Glauben an die Unfreiheit*]," and believes that it is possible to contribute to the realization of their own destiny (*Bestimmung*).³¹ This objective is not attained by hyperactive intervention in the way of the world, but rather by a patient attitude of waiting and "listening" for something that unfolds slowly because it cannot be forced.

Buber speaks of "two kinds of human beings":³² While the individual ego (*Eigenwesen*) of the "doer" sets that person apart from others, the personality (*Person*) of the human subject enters into a (not only functional) relationship with fellow human beings and participates in our shared reality by "resonating" with others: "Genuine subjectivity can be understood only dynamically, as the vibration [*Schwingen*] of the I in its lonely truth. This is also the place where the desire for ever higher and more unconditional relation and for perfect participation in being arises and keeps rising."³³

It is not without reason that sociologist Hartmut Rosa's theory of resonance is based on Buber's philosophy of dialogue. The contrast of a "mute" versus a "resonant" world-relation can be understood as a continuation of Buber's dichotomy of the basic word pairs "I-It" versus "I-Thou."³⁴ Yet "resonance," a metaphor taken from a mechanical context, is not the same as "responsivity," which presupposes freedom.³⁵ That is why Rosa has to take recourse to concepts from phenomenology and the philosophy of dialogue in order to distinguish "resonance" from a purely repetitive "echo," to give "resonance" its own voice, as it were, and to define "hearing and responding" as the gold standard of a better world.³⁶

Importantly, Buber's philosophy relies not only on affective and intellectual "resonance," where people are "on the same wavelength" with each other, but also on the phenomenon of call and response, which allows for resistance. In his view, the human person leads a hidden existence until he or she "is summoned" or called upon (*aufgerufen*).³⁷ The way in which someone says "I" is revealing: "The word 'I' is the true shibboleth of humanity," Buber writes in *I and Thou*:

> Listen to it [*Hört nur darauf*]! How dissonant [*miβtönig*] the I of the ego sounds! [. . .] But how beautiful and legitimate the vivid and emphatic I of Socrates sounds [*klingt*]! It is the I of infinite conversation [*des unendlichen Gesprächs*]. [. . .] Even solitude cannot spell forsakenness, and when the human world falls silent [*schweigt*] for him, he hears [*hört*] his *daimonion* say You.³⁸

The voice of one's conscience (or its ancient Socratic "predecessor") "speaks" in one's self-relation and determines how harmonious or discordant it is. Buber presents Goethe's "I," which was in constant conversation with nature, and Jesus's "I," which was closely connected with his Father in heaven, as exemplarily melodious. By contrast, Napoleon's "I" spoke "without the power to relate" and thus merely betrayed "the hopelessness [*Heillosigkeit*]" of his own self-contradiction.³⁹

Bernhard Lang's anniversary article for a Swiss newspaper bears the telling title: "In Search of the You That Is Lost: One Hundred Years Ago, Martin Buber's Major Work *I and Thou* Was Published—a Basic Text for Understanding Human Relationlessness."⁴⁰ Only in the encounter with another can a human being recognize themselves, and in this recognition lies the lasting significance of Buber's book for Lang. Following Søren Kierkegaard, whose existential philosophy was one of Buber's sources of inspiration, I would prefer not to speak of a lack of relations (in German: *Beziehungslosigkeit*) but rather of "mis-relations" (Danish: *Misforhold*). For even when we break off our relationship with another person, or when others no longer want to stay in touch with us, we are still in some relationship with each other, albeit a damaged relation without mutuality.

Similarly, in his 1938 preface to the French translation of *Ich und Du*, Gaston Bachelard argues that the individual is ontologically complete only in relation to another person and, even more radically, that we were "nothing" before "being united" in an I-Thou relation: "The encounter creates us."[41] Here the question can be asked whether a conscious person can be equated to a thing, and whether being created must not chronologically and ontologically precede being dialogically united. Bachelard compares "I and Thou" to two inseparable magnetic poles that attract each other and destroy themselves when they separate: "I am a person if I am linked to a person. Detaching myself from my brother, I destroy myself. Losing concern for my brother, I abandon God."[42] Bachelard regards the human being as a composite of I and Thou existing "in the linking of the I-Thou" where these two are not centers but "vectors" turning to each other. In his description of dialogue, Bachelard emphasizes the activity of listening: "The ear then becomes *active*, since lending an ear is wanting to respond." The person who listens to another is *doing* something, and in turning to the other [. . .], there is already self-expression and the wish to respond: "How can we hear without expressing! How can we express without hearing! Once again, our spiritual substance is within us only if it reaches out from within us."[43] The movement is thus simultaneously inward and outward in impression and expression, from self to other, and vice versa.

Likewise, Mordechai Gordon emphasizes that speaking and listening are reciprocal and interdependent because it is listening that first of all creates conversational space. Therefore, in his eyes, dialogue can only be grasped "as an ontological phenomenon—a meeting of one whole being with another whole being" in which each of the interlocutors "gives his or her whole being to the other" without reserve. Buber's attitudes of "I-Thou" and "I-It" are "not only psychological outlooks"; they also designate "two distinct ontological modes of existence."[44] Whoever listens well is present and engaged, attentive to *what* is being said and *how* this is done.

On this basis, the process of listening to each other can open spaces of belonging in the realm "in-between" self and other, people and peoples. Buber himself called his theory an "ontology of the interhuman [*Ontologie des Zwischenmenschlichen*]."[45] Accordingly, the "I-Thou" is not only a speech act but also the bedrock of ontology: "the cradle of actual life."[46] It is vital for us to live "opposite" to someone else, vis-à-vis a listening and speaking *Gegenüber* to interact with.[47]

According to Bernhard Casper, Buber does not understand reality as "a substance at hand [*vorliegende Substanz*]" but rather as an opening in actual relationships.[48] This thesis is confirmed by a programmatic statement in the first of part of *I and Thou*: "In the beginning is the relation."[49] This statement is opposed to the first verse of the Gospel of John, which claims that the *logos*, that is, Jesus Christ as God's incarnated Word, was in the beginning, even before the world was created.[50] Buber also suggests an alternative to Goethe's Faust, who translates *logos* as "the deed."[51] For Buber, individual agency cannot be the starting point of everything that is and takes place in the world. Neither does he presuppose some foundational entity from which everything else would emanate. Unlike Aristotle, Buber does not consider the category of "relation" to be accidental or dependent on an underlying, sustaining "substance." Rather, he defines the "relation" as an "a priori" that discloses and constitutes reality insofar as the "I" cannot exist at all without a "Thou" and develops only in interaction with it.[52]

This is also revealed by Buber's use of language, for instance, the symmetrically constructed participial construction *Ich-wirkend-Du und Du-wirkend-Ich*[53] (I-effecting-Thou and Thou-effecting-I) or the generalizing proposition *Der Mensch wird am Du zum Ich*[54] (meaning that the human being becomes an "I" through the "Thou"). The priority of relationality applies to all human beings, for none of us could grow as a sole, disembodied *ego cogito* that only secondarily enters relations with others. The "I" and the "Thou" are equiprimordial, co-emerging entities arising out of their reciprocal relations.

However, since these relations unfold in our empirical lifeworld, it seems slightly misleading to speak of "the *a priori* of relation" that is supposed to antecede experience as a "category of being, as readiness, as a form that reaches out to be filled, as a model of the soul" including "*the innate You.*"[55] In a psychoanalytic context, Buber's idea of the innate You has been interpreted as the mental representation of the external other and as part of an intrapsychic matrix of two people.[56] But if the Thou is an internalized Thou, it becomes reified as an "inner object," and an object cannot achieve the same as a subject. No response can be expected from an inner object. Moreover, the real-life and real-time relationship to someone who can be met in the outside world is not the same as a transcendental, pre-empirical structure or inner dyad of "I and Thou." Even though Buber's choice of the Kantian term "a priori" has given birth to a fruitful history of reception in post-Holocaust trauma theory, philosophically speaking, it is inaccurate and confusing, for if the "I-Thou" indeed is a transcendental structure, it cannot be lost, not even in a person's utter desolation. For this very reason, Buber's transcendental terminology loses its explanatory power when coupled to an alleged loss of "the innate Thou."

Nonetheless, Buber's ontology is relational in the sense that the relations between entities are regarded as ontologically more fundamental than these entities themselves. Relations are primary as they form and transform the *relata*, whereas in a substance ontology, the category of "relation" is regarded as derivative.[57] The space in which relations take place, the realm "in-between" self and other, is for Buber a force field nourished not only by ontology but also by a relation to God, the Eternal Thou.

Ontology, Betweenness, and the Eternal Thou

In Buber's work, the interhuman is interlaced with something more-than-human. In his epilogue to *I and Thou*, Buber states that his most essential concern is "the close association of the relation to God with the relation to one's fellow-men."[58] This implies that Buber is not exclusively advocating an ontology of the interhuman, since the God-relationship weaves through our interhuman relations. Buber's holistic approach connects the human and the divine. As such, it contrasts starkly with Martin Heidegger's nonreligious ontology in *Being and Time* (1927) and with the latter's understanding of language and truth.[59]

Dorothy Emmet has criticized Buber for using the term "ontology" and rejecting the term "metaphysics" because "'ontology' in the past has generally stood for a much more rigorously impersonal kind of discussion than has 'metaphysics.' [. . .] Buber's ontology comes from his belief that reality appears in the 'I-Thou' relation as something welcomed and welcoming, to be reverenced, not manipulated. This is the special 'Betweenness'[:] a presence, perhaps a Shekinah, which comes about when man meets his neighbor, including non-human nature, in this particular attitude of loving contemplation."[60] I would like to add that saying "Thou" to God in prayer may provide us with the experience that everything stands in relation to the divine force of life. Dialogical relationality may even provide a home that is not bound to national territories but to a "betweenness" determined by spirit, love, and language.[61] This "betweenness" designates the intensity of "presentness" to each other.[62]

As Robert E. Wood points out in *Martin Buber's Ontology: An Analysis of "I and Thou"* (1969), Buber's emphasis on the I-Thou relationship "undercuts the subject-object dichotomy" in order to bind together subject and object, spirit and life in "an ontologically prior relation of *Presence*." Accordingly, the space "between" subject and object is neither subjective nor objective: "the Between for Buber would still exist as a surplus, for it is the place where the Transcendent is present in the world." The "Between" is a space of immediate encounter in which self-constitution co-occurs with the appearance of the other person: "The Between is the place where the I—which is the *conscious* self—and the *manifest* Other arise simultaneously." Moreover, self and other "are held together by reference to the Transcendent" that resembles the keystone holding the arches of two bridge columns.⁶³

Buber presupposes that the self and the other remain distinguishable, which is why he is not interested in merging the human being with God. Conversely, he also sees the danger that the divine is reduced to the human when human beings conflate the idea of God, their object of thought, with God himself. Buber tries to prevent the disappearance of God's alterity by defining the presence of God transcendent as indefinable in the realm "between" human beings. Wood further states:

> God Himself is total Presence without absence, the Source of all light, i.e., the Source of all being. Man as the *imago Dei* is the ability to be more deeply present. This ability is itself grounded upon man's own a priori reference to the Transcendent, so that he who learns to dwell in the presence of beings is the one who actualizes his own personal reference to God.⁶⁴

The capitalization of "Presence" and "Source" indicates that they are regarded as divine, while the human likeness to God is seen in the capacity to establish copresence with other beings. The comparative "more deeply present" suggests a deficiency in everyday life, since we are often unaware of the fact that we are always "before God" wherever we are, regardless of whether our "counterpart" is a stone, a tree, or a human being. The implicit, pre-experiential reference to God that is quasi "built into" our being is "materialized" and "put into practice" when we ourselves become present to our respective counterpart.

Buber's critique of metaphysics might be due to the assumption that metaphysics is about something nonexperiential, abstract, whereas ontology is "basically *description* of what is deepest in our experience." For Buber, the "in-between" is "the place of Being" and ontology "a description of encounter with Being."⁶⁵ Importantly, an interpersonal encounter cannot be reduced to a private mental experience in an inner imaginative space accessible only to one person. A real encounter in the world happens "between" us in such a way that two or more people contribute to it, thus creating togetherness. For Buber, "betweenness" is the human "mode of existence" *par excellence* "between persons communicating with one another" in "the human cosmos" that is guarded by "the common logos" of dia-logue.⁶⁶

At the same time, the realm "in-between" human beings is the space of a potential encounter with God. In all three spheres defined by Buber, we can enter into "I-Thou" relationships, and from all three spheres (i.e., life with nature, with people, and with culture), we can come into contact with the Most

High. Buber begins the third part of *I and Thou* by maintaining: "Extended, the lines of relationships intersect in the eternal You. Every single You is a glimpse of that."[67] Consequently, the God-relationship is mediated through other relations. God's "voice" is perceptible only indirectly: in encounters with people and things, with nature and art.

This presents us with a problem of interpretation: How is the voice of God identifiable? In Buber's booklet *Zwiesprache* (1932), dedicated to his wife, Paula, there is a chapter on religious disputations (*Religionsgespräche*). Buber objects to Martin Luther and John Calvin, who believe that the word of God has descended among human beings in such a way that it can be clearly known and defended; instead, Buber compares the word of God to a falling star. I can only bear witness to the light, Buber claims, but not bring out the star and say: This is it. Of God's theophany we know nothing but its place: community. Buber concludes that there is no clearly knowable word of God in the singular; rather, the words that have been handed down in the plural are interpreted in and through our facing each other, acknowledging each other's humanity.[68] True community does not build on a shared content of faith but rather on the willingness to listen to each other and the divine Word. The latter is "wrapped" in human words and therefore not available in a purely divine form.

Accordingly, in *I and Thou*, we read: "That before which we live, that in which we live, that out of which and into which we live, the mystery—has remained what it was." The origin and source of life is unfathomable. "We have come close to God, but no closer to an unriddling, unveiling of being."[69] Therein lies a rejection of any onto-theology that conceptualizes God either as the top of the "pyramid of being" or its foundation.

> The meaning we receive can be put to proof in action only by each person [*Wir können nur gehen und bewähren*]. [...] This is the eternal revelation. [...] I do not believe in God's naming himself or in God's defining himself before man. [...] The eternal source of strength flows, the eternal touch is waiting, the eternal voice sounds [*die ewige Stimme tönt*], nothing more.[70]

God is here circumscribed as a resounding presence and ever-flowing source of energy. But let us ask again: How exactly is Buber's dialogical acoustics bound up with his relational ontology? He does not explain this to us in *I and Thou*; he only hints at it.

Yet, in his remarks on a verse by Friedrich Hölderlin from the hymn "Friedensfeier [Peace Celebration]," Buber accentuates in the 1950s that Hölderlin does not write "Seit im Gespräch wir sind [Since *in* conversation we are]," but rather "Seit ein Gespräch wir sind / Und hören voneinander" (Since a conversation *we are* / And hear from each other), which means for Buber "Wir selber sind das Gespräch" (We ourselves *are* the dialogue).[71] We ourselves *are* the dialogue. In this way, Buber dismisses Heidegger's explanation that the gods bring us into conversation.[72] Does this mean that our human condition is dialogical existence? Note Buber's *passive* formulation: "Unser Gesprochen-werden ist unser Dasein," that is, our being-spoken is our being-there, while, on the other hand, he also speaks of "Hörenkönnen des Daseins in der Gegenseitigkeit,"[73] that is, our being-able-to-hear in reciprocity, which is formulated in an *active* voice. By whom are we spoken? Is our life traced back to God's creative word, without this being made explicit by Buber?

Buber also mentions the "saying [*Spruch*]" that the human being "is"[74]—an expression that recalls Bible verses with the phrase *Spruch Gottes* in the Buber-Rosenzweig translation.[75] Once humans are called into being, they can hear and speak and be heard. Listening to each other in dialogue is essential for the genuinely human mode of existence, including the creation of new words. Man is "not a mouthpiece [*Sprachrohr*]," it is aptly said in *I and Thou*, but "an autonomous, sounding organ [*lautendes Organ*]; and to sound means to modify sound [*lauten heißt umlauten*]."[76] We do not merely repeat or pronounce what God tells us. Even a theophany is not merely "God passing through" but "a mixture of the divine and the human."[77] The revealed, "living word" of God is at work when the bond between human beings is renewed, and then the theophany "comes ever *closer* [...] to the sphere *between beings*," the realm that "hides in our midst, in the between [*im Dazwischen*]."[78]

Cornelia Muth illuminates the "between" both dialogically as an existential practice of being-with-others and phenomenologically in terms of a bodily conscious mode of perception in which the world and fellow human beings appear to us.[79] As ground of being, however, it remains withdrawn from us: "Neither I nor You have any influence on the between."[80] The life-sustaining love in the "between" remains just as unavailable as God.[81]

In a felicitous turn of phrase, Lang labels Buber's approach a "metaphysical minimalism [*metaphysischer Minimalismus*]" that is reminiscent of Kant insofar as God's existence must be postulated, but nothing can be learned about God himself. Therefore, our God-relationship is not a direct relation to God but runs through the *Duwelt*, the world of other creatures who become a Thou for us. Perhaps it is thanks to this circumstance that Buber's religiously grounded social philosophy has enjoyed such high esteem, not only among philosophers and theologians, but also among educators and therapists, civil rights activists and sociologists.[82]

As Jochanan Bloch has demonstrated, Buber points to something that cannot be represented symbolically in any adequate manner. The concrete presence of real life, in its richness and superabundance, eludes any concept. Reality happens to us but can neither be understood nor experienced as a whole. Despite Buber's contrasting assertion, divine presence cannot be regarded as a part of this world, even though the relation to "the eternal Thou" may arise in and through one's relation to a finite Thou.[83] Consequently, Buber's ontology of the interhuman cannot but point beyond itself.

Coda: Listening for Peace in the Borderland

The "between" is, so to say, the borderland between I and Thou, here and there, then and now. We are not always able to cross the borders, even less so in times of war. However, listening to each other in a genuine dialogue is the key that can open the door to a more peaceful future.[84]

In his address on the occasion of being awarded the Peace Prize of the German Book Trade in Frankfurt am Main on September 27, 1953, which was entitled "Das echte Gespräch und die Möglichkeiten des Friedens [Genuine Dialogue and the Possibilities of Peace],"[85] Buber portrayed "fulfilled speech, the speech of genuine conversation in which men understand one another and come to a mutual understanding" as the adversary of war, of "the speechlessness of slaughter."[86] Buber was fully aware of the prevailing inability to speak directly and unreservedly with each other, which is due to the lack of trust in one another.

Could one respond to this crisis of trust between human beings by suggesting that there is still the possibility of a dialogue with the "eternal Thou" where interhuman dialogue has become impossible—at the very least the possibility of a call *de profundis*? I want to hold on to the possibility of addressing God in a relationship of prayer that is not necessarily mediated by human beings, even against the Buber of *I and Thou*, since this might be the only hope for those abandoned by humankind. However, the late Buber calls our attention to the fact that the interhuman crisis of speech is not unrelated to the religious crisis of our age, "the fact that it is so difficult" for present-day people "to pray." Still, the entanglement of multiple crises is no reason to give up: "And yet this must be said again and again, it is just the depth of the crisis that empowers us to hope."[87]

One of Buber's main messages is this: "Hearkening to the human voice, where it speaks forth unfalsified, and replying to it, this above all is needed today. [. . .] This voice must not only be listened to, it must be answered and led out of the lonely monologue into the awakening dialogue of the peoples."[88] This message is still urgently relevant. We may conclude that the invaluable meaning of dialogue lies, above all, in its bridge-building potential.

Even so, the strength of dialogue is also its weakness: it depends on people who are willing to listen. That's why we should not want to leave the borderland but remain where we are: "in-between" self and other, here and there, then and now, listening for the sake of peace.

Notes

1. Paul Mendes-Flohr, "Introduction: Dialogue as a Trans-Disciplinary Concept," in *Dialogue as a Trans-Disciplinary Concept: Martin Buber's Philosophy of Dialogue and Its Contemporary Reception*, ed. Paul Mendes-Flohr (Berlin: Walter de Gruyter, 2015), 3.

2. Martin Buber, *I and Thou*, trans. Walter Kaufmann, 100th anniversary reissue (New York: Free Press, 2023), 10.

3. Hans-Georg Gadamer, *Wahrheit und Methode. Grundzüge einer philosophischen Hermeneutik*, 6th rev. ed. (Tübingen: J. C. B. Mohr [Paul Siebeck], 1990), 281.

4. Martin Buber, *Ich und Du* (Stuttgart: Philipp Reclam, 1995), 6.

5. Buber, *Ich und Du*, 7; Buber, *I and Thou*, 5.

6. Isaiah 6:1 (New International Version; hereafter NIV).

7. Psalm 145:18 (NIV).

8. Paul Mendes-Flohr, *Von der Mystik zum Dialog: Martin Bubers geistige Entwicklung bis hin zu "Ich und Du"*, trans. Dafna A. von Kries (Königstein/Ts.: Jüdischer Verlag im Athenäum Verlag, 1978).

9. Cf. *Die Geschichten des Rabbi Nahman: Nacherzählt von Martin Buber* (Frankfurt: Rütten & Loening, 1906).

10. See *The Letters of Martin Buber: A Life of Dialogue*, ed. Nahum N. Glatzer and Paul Mendes-Flohr, trans. Richard Winston, Clara Winston, and Harry Zohn (Syracuse, NY: Syracuse University Press, 1996), letter no. 105, 282, mistranslates "ornament" as "cornerstone."

11. My translation. See Goethe: "So hab ich endlich von dir erharrt: / In allen Elementen Gottes Gegenwart" (*West-östlicher Divan* [Stuttgart, 1819]).

12. Walter Kaufmann, "*I and Thou*: A Prologue," in Martin Buber, *I and Thou*, trans. Walter Kaufmann (New York: Touchstone / Simon & Schuster, 1970), 26–27, 28, 26.

13. Paul Mendes-Flohr, explanatory note to Buber, *I and Thou*, 124.

14. Martin Buber, *Meetings: Autobiographical Fragments*, ed. Maurice Friedman (London: Routledge, 2002), 38.

15. Paul Mendes-Flohr, *Martin Buber: A Life of Faith and Dissent* (New Haven, CT: Yale University Press, 2019), xvi, with reference to Buber, *Meetings*, 40.

16. Buber, *Ich und Du*, 79, 103; Buber, *I and Thou*, 70, 90.

17. See Claudia Welz, "Gott als Gesprächspartner oder Horizont des Hörens? Zur philosophischen Kritik des Bittgebets," in *Interesse am Anderen: Internationale Beiträge zum Verhältnis von Religion und Rationalität*, ed. Gerhard Schreiber (Berlin: De Gruyter, 2019), 97–121.

18. Buber, *Ich und Du*, 110; Buber, *I and Thou*, 96.

19. Buber, *Ich und Du*, 114.

20. Buber, *Ich und Du*, 130; Buber, *I and Thou*, 182.

21. As Mendes-Flohr formulates felicitously: "Both Buber and Rosenzweig [. . .] raised for a post-traditional Jewry a vision of a homeward journey forged by listening with the heart." Paul Mendes-Flohr, *Cultural Disjunctions: Post-Traditional Jewish Identities* (Chicago: University of Chicago Press, 2021), 65.

22. See Sabine Hock, "Buber, Martin," in *Frankfurter Personenlexikon* (Onlineausgabe), from *Frankfurter Biographie* 1 (1994), 116; https://frankfurter-personenlexikon.de/node/1898.

23. Martin Buber, *Briefwechsel aus sieben Jahrzehnten*, vol. 2, *1918–1938* (Heidelberg: Verlag Lambert Schneider, 1973), 541n1.

24. See https://frauenorte-brandenburg.de/wp-content/uploads/2022/12/Bodo-Becker-Das -,Juedische-Erholungsheim-Lehnitz.pdf.

25. Martin Buber, "Ein Hinweis für Bibelkurse" (1936), in Buber, *Martin Buber Werkausgabe*, vol. 14, *Schriften zur Bibelübersetzung*, ed. Ran HaCohen (Gütersloh: Gütersloher Verlagshaus, 2012), 140.

26. Michael A. Fishbane, *The Garments of Torah: Essays in Biblical Hermeneutics* (Bloomington: Indiana University Press, 1989), 88.

27. Dan Avnon, "*Limmud* and *Limmudim*: Guiding Words of Buber's Prophetic Teaching," in *Martin Buber: A Contemporary Perspective*, ed. Paul Mendes-Flohr (Syracuse, NY: Syracuse University Press, 2002), 102, 101–3.

28. Mendes-Flohr, *Cultural Disjunctions*, 63.

29. Buber, *Ich und Du*, 122; Buber, *I and Thou*, 108, 109.

30. Judith Winther, *Martin Buber* (Copenhagen: Anis, 2003), 119–22, 125–27.

31. Buber, *Ich und Du*, 58, 56, 57; Buber, *I and Thou*, 50, 49, 50.

32. Buber, *I and Thou*, 55.

33. Buber, *Ich und Du*, 61–62; Buber, *I and Thou*, 54.

34. Bernhard Lang, "Anhang," in Martin Buber, *Ich und Du* (Stuttgart: Philipp Reclam, 2021), 230–23, with reference to Hartmut Rosa, *Resonanz: Eine Soziologie der Weltbeziehung*, 5th ed. (Berlin: Suhrkamp, 2017).

35. This critique is elaborated by Dieter Thomä, "Hartmut Rosa: Soziologie mit der Stimmgabel," *Die Zeit*, June 30, 2016; Bernard Waldenfels, *Erfahrung, die zur Sprache drängt: Studien zur Psychoanalyse und Psychotherapie aus phänomenologischer Sicht* (Frankfurt am Main: Suhrkamp, 2019), 261–65; 280; Günter Bader, *Abyssus abyssum vocat. Zur Kritik der Resonanz* (Gomadingen: cmz-Verlag, 2020), and Claudia Welz, "At høre det uhørte: Teologisk epistemologi som dialogisk livsorientering," *Dansk Teologisk Tidsskrift* 86 (2023): 56–62.

36. See Rosa, *Resonanz*, 762 (italics per original): "*Eine bessere Welt ist möglich*, und sie lässt sich daran erkennen, dass ihr zentraler Maßstab nicht mehr das Beherrschen und Verfügen ist, sondern das Hören und das Antworten."

37. Buber, *Ich und Du*, 63; Buber, *I and Thou*, 55.

38. Buber, *Ich und Du*, 64; Buber, *I and Thou*, 55f.

39. Buber, *Ich und Du*, 68; Buber, *I and Thou*, 57.

40. Bernhard Lang, "Auf der Suche nach dem verlorenen Du: Vor hundert Jahren ist Martin Bubers Hauptwerk 'Ich und Du' erschienen—ein Grundtext zum Verständnis menschlicher Beziehungslosigkeit," *Neue Zürcher Zeitung*, October 17, 2022.

41. Gaston Bachelard, preface to Martin Buber's *I and Thou*, trans. Edward K. Kaplan, in *Adventures in Phenomenology: Gaston Bachelard*, ed. Eileen Rizo-Patron, Edward S. Casey, and Jason M. Wirth (Albany: State University of New York Press, 2017), 272.

42. Bachelard, preface to Martin Buber's *I and Thou*: "The *I* and *thou* are not separable poles" (272).

43. Bachelard, preface to Martin Buber's *I and Thou*, 272, 274.

44. Mordechai Gordon, "Listening as Embracing the Other: Martin Buber's Philosophy of Dialogue," *Educational Theory* 61, no. 2 (2011): 207, 208, 209.

45. Martin Buber, *Das dialogische Prinzip* (Heidelberg: Verlag Lambert Schneider, 1979), 290.
46. Buber, *Ich und Du*, 10; Buber, *I and Thou*, 8.
47. Cf. Buber, *Ich und Du*, 19, 22.
48. Bernhard Casper, afterword to *Ich und Du* (Leipzig: Reclam Verlag, 1995), 157.
49. Buber, *Ich und Du*, 18; Buber, *I and Thou*, 16.
50. John 1:1 (NIV): "In the beginning was the Word."
51. See Goethe, *Faust. Der Tragödie, erster Teil* (1808), "Im Studierzimmer," line 58: "Im Anfang war die Tat!"
52. Buber, *Ich und Du*, 28; Buber, *I and Thou*, 24.
53. Buber, *Ich und Du*, 22 (my translation). Kaufmann translates "I-acting-You and You-acting-I"; Buber, *I and Thou*, 73.
54. Buber, *Ich und Du*, 28.
55. Buber, *Ich und Du*, 24.
56. See Dori Laub, "Reestablishing the Internal 'Thou' in Testimony of Trauma," *Psychoanalysis, Culture and Society* 18, no. 2 (2013): 186, in which she refers inter alia to Sigmund Freud, Donald Winnicott, and Heinz Kohut; and Claudia Welz, "Trauma, Memory, Testimony: Phenomenological, Psychological, and Ethical Perspectives," *Scripta Instituti Donneriani Aboensis* 7:108–9.
57. Andrew Benjamin argues that relationality is always primary in his *Towards a Relational Ontology: Philosophy's Other Possibility* (Albany: State University of New York Press, 2015). Wilfried Joest explains why God is to be regarded as *Seinsträger* of the human being: the One who bears our being; see Wilfried Joest, *Ontologie der Person bei Luther* (Göttingen: Vandenhoeck & Ruprecht, 1967), 25.
58. Buber, *Ich und Du*, 117; Buber, *I and Thou*, 104.
59. See Meike Siegfried, *Abkehr vom Subjekt. Zum Sprachdenken bei Heidegger und Buber* (Freiburg im Breisgau: Alber, 2010); Paul Mendes-Flohr, "Martin Buber and Martin Heidegger in Dialogue," *Journal of Religion* 94 (2014): 2–25; Asher Biemann, "Kommentar," in *Martin Buber Werkausgabe*, ed. P. Mendes-Flohr and P. Schäfer, vol. 6, *Sprachphilosophische Schriften*, ed. Asher Biemann (Gütersloh: Gütersloher Verlagshaus, 2002), 149–86; Claudia Welz, "Wahrhaftigkeit zwischen *aletheia* und *emet*: Kierkegaards Existenzdenken, Heideggers Ontologie und Bubers Dialogphilosophie," *Hermeneutische Blätter* 24, no. 1 (2018): 200–215; and Niels Wilde, "Buoyant Ontologies: The Roots and Ramifications of Dialogue in Buber and Heidegger," *Religions* 12 (2021): 778.
60. Dorothy Emmet, "Review of: *Martin Buber's Ontology* by Robert E. Wood," *Journal of the British Society for Phenomenology* 1, no. 3 (1970): 91.
61. Cf. Claudia Welz, "In-Between Subjectivity and Alterity: Philosophy of Dialogue and Theology of Love," in *Dynamics of Difference: Christianity and Alterity—a Festschrift for Werner G. Jeanrond*, ed. Ulrich Schmiedel and James M. Matarazzo (London: Bloomsbury T&T Clark, 2015), 125–34.
62. Buber, *I and Thou*, 11.
63. Robert Wood, *Martin Buber's Ontology: An Analysis of "I and Thou"* (Evanston, IL: Northwestern University Press, 1969), xi–xii, 111.
64. Wood, *Martin Buber's Ontology*, 119.
65. Wood, *Martin Buber's Ontology*, 120, 121, 122.
66. Martin Buber, *The Knowledge of Man: A Philosophy of the Interhuman*, ed. Maurice Friedman, trans. Maurice Friedman and Ronald Gregor Smith (New York: Harper Torchbooks, 1965), 107.

67. Buber, *Ich und Du*, 7; Buber, *I and Thou*, 63.
68. Martin Buber, *Zwiesprache*, in *Martin Buber Werkausgabe*, vol. 4, *Schriften über das dialogische Prinzip*, ed. Paul Mendes-Flohr; commentary by Andreas Losch and Bernd Witte (Gütersloh: Gütersloher Verlagshaus, 2019), 119, 120.
69. Buber, *Ich und Du*, 107; Buber, *I and Thou*, 93.
70. Buber, *Ich und Du*, 107; Buber, *I and Thou*, 93.
71. Martin Buber, "Seit ein Gespräch wir sind," in *Martin Buber Werkausgabe*, vol. 6, *Sprachphilosophische Schriften*, ed. Asher Biemann (Gütersloh: Gütersloher Verlagshaus, 2003), 83 (emphasis added).
72. Buber, "Seit ein Gespräch wir sind," n. 2, with reference to Heidegger: "Seit die Götter uns in das Gespräch bringen"; Martin Heidegger, *Erläuterungen zu Hölderlins Dichtung*, complete ed., sect. 1, vol. 4 (Frankfurt am Main: Klostermann, 1944), 40.
73. Buber, "Seit ein Gespräch wir sind," 83, 84.
74. Buber, "Seit ein Gespräch wir sind," 84.
75. See Amos 8:11 and Ezek. 47:23 in the Buber-Rosenzweig translation.
76. Buber, *Ich und Du*, 113; Buber, *I and Thou*, 97.
77. Buber, *I and Thou*, 98.
78. Buber, *Ich und Du*, 115; Buber, *I and Thou*, 99.
79. Cornelia Muth, *Das Zwischen!? Eine dialog-phänomenologische Perspektive* (Cologne: GikPress, 2015), 13.
80. "Weder Ich noch Du haben Einfluss auf das Zwischen"; Muth, *Das Zwischen!?*, 65.
81. Muth, *Das Zwischen!?*, 66.
82. Bernhard Lang, "Anhang" in Martin Buber, *Ich und Du* (Stuttgart: Philipp Reclam, 2021), 175–76, 219; and also 229–31, with reference to Hans Joas, *Martin Buber: His Intellectual and Scholarly Legacy*, ed. Sam B. Shonkoff (Leiden: Brill, 2018), 212–15.
83. Jochanan Bloch, *Die Aporie des Du: Probleme der Dialogik Martin Bubers* (Heidelberg: Verlag Lambert Schneider, 1977), 19, 24, 314.
84. For Buber's vision for a dialogical concord between Jews and Arabs in Palestine/Israel, see his *A Land of Two Peoples: Martin Buber on Jews and Arabs*, ed. Paul Mendes-Flohr (Chicago: University of Chicago Press, 2005).
85. Martin Buber, *Nachlese* (Heidelberg: Verlag Lambert Scheidner, 1965), 219–30; Martin Buber, *A Believing Humanism: Gleanings*, trans. and ed. Maurice Friedman (New York: Simon & Schuster, 1969), 195–202.
86. Buber, *A Believing Humanism*, 199.
87. Buber, *A Believing Humanism*, 201, 200.
88. Buber, *A Believing Humanism*, 198.

Annotated Bibliography

Buber's relational ontology of the interhuman, his *Ontologie des Zwischenmenschlichen*, is mentioned in his book *Das dialogische Prinzip* (Heidelberg: Verlag Lambert Schneider, 1979). Other important dialogical writings such as *Zwiesprache* are included in *Martin Buber Werkausgabe*, vol. 4, *Schriften über das dialogische Prinzip*, edited by Paul Mendes-Flohr, commentary by Andreas Losch and Bernd Witte (Gütersloh: Gütersloher Verlagshaus, 2019). Buber's *Ich und Du* (Stuttgart: Philipp Reclam, 2021), edited with commentary by Bernhard Lang, is warmly recommended, not least because of Lang's "Nachwort" appendices.

Buber's ontology is discussed extensively and thoroughly by Robert E. Wood in *Martin Buber's Ontology: An Analysis of "I and Thou"* (Evanston, IL: Northwestern University Press, 1969), which is the standard work on the theme. However, Gaston Bachelard, in his 1938 preface to the French translation of *Ich und Du*, had already touched upon the theme, though in a more controversial way, as discussed in my chapter here.

A comparison of Buber's and Heidegger's approaches to ontology and their differing understanding of language is appropriate. See, for instance, Asher Biemann's brilliant "Kommentar" in *Martin Buber Werkausgabe*, vol. 6, *Sprachphilosophische Schriften* (Gütersloh: Gütersloher Verlagshaus, 2003), 149–86; Meike Siegfried's solid monograph *Abkehr vom Subjekt: Zum Sprachdenken bei Heidegger und Buber* (Freiburg im Breisgau: Alber, 2010); Paul Mendes-Flohr's very helpful article "Martin Buber and Martin Heidegger in Dialogue," *Journal of Religion* 94 (2014): 2–25; and Niels Wilde's experimenting, original approach in "Buoyant Ontologies: The Roots and Ramifications of Dialogue in Buber and Heidegger," *Religions* 12, no. 778 (2021): 281–94.

The notion of "relational ontology" was coined by Wilfried Joest, in his by now classic monograph entitled *Ontologie der Person bei Luther* (Göttingen: Vandenhoeck & Ruprecht, 1967). Here, Luther's ontology is compared to Aristotelian and scholastic substance ontology. In his "Nachwort" to the German Reclam edition of *Ich und Du* (1995), Bernhard Casper provides a useful comparison of Buber and Aristotle. For a more recent comparison of Luther and Buber, see Sasja E. Mathiasen Stopa, "'Ich werdend spreche ich Du': Creative Dialogue in the Relational Anthropologies of Martin Luther and Martin Buber," *Religions* 14 , no. 5 (2023): 564. Together with Stopa, I am currently editing a special issue of *New Journal of Systematic Theology and Philosophy of Religion* on the topic "Dialogue and Relational Ontology: Rethinking the Significance of the Second-Person Perspective" that will appear in 2024–25.

My essays "In-Between Subjectivity and Alterity: Philosophy of Dialogue and Theology of Love," in *Dynamics of Difference: Christianity and Alterity—a Festschrift for Werner G. Jeanrond*, edited by Ulrich Schmiedel and James M. Matarazzo (London: Bloomsbury T&T Clark, 2015), 125–34, and "Wahrhaftigkeit zwischen *aletheia* und *emet*: Kierkegaards Existenzdenken, Heideggers Ontologie und Bubers Dialogphilosophie," *Hermeneutische Blätter* 24, no. 1 (2018): 200–215, compare Kierkegaard, Buber, and Heidegger.

A practice-based approach to the realm "between" self and other is provided by Cornelia Muth, who explores it on the backdrop of *gestalt* therapy and the phenomenology of the body, yet often without providing concrete references to Buber but rather paraphrasing his thoughts: *Das Zwischen!? Eine dialog-phänomenologische Perspektive* (Köln: GikPress, 2015).

Buber's understanding of "listening" is investigated by Mordechai Gordon in his article "Listening as Embracing the Other: Martin Buber's Philosophy of Dialogue," *Educational Theory* 61, no. 2 (2011): 207–19. The relevance of "listening" in relation to Bible reading is made explicit by Buber himself in his 1936 "Hinweis für Bibelkurse" (reprinted in *Martin Buber Werkausgabe*, vol. 14, *Schriften zur Bibelübersetzung*, edited by Ran HaCohen [Gütersloh: Gütersloher Verlagshaus, 2012], 139–41) and explored further in a chapter by Michael A. Fishbane in *The Garments of Torah: Essays in Biblical Hermeneutics* (Bloomington: Indiana University Press, 1989) and Dan Avnon in "*Limmud* and *Limmudim*: Guiding Words of Buber's Prophetic Teaching," in *Martin Buber: A Contemporary Perspective*, edited by Paul Mendes-Flohr (Syracuse, NY: Syracuse University Press, 2002), 101–19.

In his *Cultural Disjunctions: Post-Traditional Jewish Identities* (Chicago: University of Chicago Press, 2021), Paul Mendes-Flohr judiciously juxtaposes Buber's and Franz Rosenzweig's ways of reading scripture and listening with the heart. See also my section on Buber and Rosenzweig in Claudia Welz, Essi Ikonen, and Aslaug Kristiansen, "Learning through Listening and Responding: Probing the Potential and the Limits of Dialogue in Online Environments," *Religions* 14, no. 2 (2023): 241, and the forthcoming topical issue of the online journal *Open Philosophy* titled "Dialogical Approaches to the Sphere 'In-Between' Self and Other: The Methodological Meaning of Listening" (2024) that will contain contributions on Buber.

PART THREE

Psychology and Education

Introduction

PAUL MENDES-FLOHR

When applied to educational and psychotherapeutic practice, Buber's philosophy of dialogue is befuddled by an aporia. Whereas a dialogical meeting is unmediated, transcending categories and concepts by which one perceives the other, teachers and therapists by the nature of their professional calling relate to socially defined others and thus perforce assume a hierarchical "I-It" attitude toward the other. Nonetheless, Buber held that pedagogues and therapists are beckoned to engage their students and patients dialogically. He addressed this aporia as an asymmetrical relation.

By challenging the Platonic conception of the soul as spiritually detached from the body, Buber argued that one can—should—honor the soul of the other (the Thou) while attending to the torments of the embodied soul or nurturing the soul of one's pupils and students so that the soul may flourish in the It-World. The overarching task of the pedagogue and therapist is to engender trust between themselves and their students and patients, and thereby trust in themselves, in their integrity and inalienable, unique souls.

12

Buber's Concept of the Soul

CORNELIA MUTH

> By means of spiritual dialogue, the I-It relationship becomes an I-Thou relationship.
> God comes and goes in man's soul. And men come and go in each other's souls.
> SAUL BELLOW, *Herzog*

Buber was wont to elaborate his philosophy of dialogue with reference to an individual's *soul* (*Seele*). Hence, he speaks of the "inborn Thou" as animating "the development of the child's soul" as "indissolubly" bound up with a longing for the Thou.[1] When Buber speaks of the "soul," it is no mere poetic flourish, however. Yet it is principally in his writings on Jewish themes that he delineates his conception of the soul. Therein he enjoins the denotation of the soul—which abounds in the Hasidic texts he collected—as *Yichud*, the singularity of every individual (*Einzigkeit*). Thus we read in an essay on the sages of the Talmud and their teaching of *imago dei*:

> We perfect our souls "toward" God. "Being like" to God is then not something which is unconnected with our earthly life; it is the goal of our life, provided that our life is really a perfection of our soul "toward" God. And this, we may add, the perfection of a soul is being so, we may well add that the perfection of the soul is called its being like God, which yet does not mean any equality, but means that this soul has translated into reality that likeness to God, which was granted it. We perfect our souls toward God; this means that each of us who does this makes perfect *his* likeness to God, his *yechida*, his soul, his "only one," his uniqueness *as* God's image.[2]

In a draft of the essay, Buber depicts *yechida* as "a singular and irreplicable."[3]

The soul, Buber underscores, is not to be understood as some spiritually inner essence or disembodied physical or libidinal life-force. As the defining uniqueness of an individual, the soul is not independent of one's body, of one's distinct existential being (*Dasein*). Detached from one's embodied *Dasein*, the soul is "amputated" and rendered a mere abstraction, torn "from its basic character of relationship [to a Thou]. [...] The place of the soul [...] is [on] the plane of relationship between man and the world."⁴ Hence, "the body and soul cannot at all be distinguished from each other."⁵ The life of dialogue is realized in the "embodied soul."

Read from this perspective, Buber's references to the soul in his philosophical writings denote a primordial expression of authentic being, which is suppressed by the epistemological and social constructs of the self. Hence, he distinguishes between the self-centered "individual" (*Eigenwesen*), whose life is determined by the calculated aims (*Zwecke*) guiding one in the It-World, and a "person" who emerges in an I-Thou relation. In this relation one's soul is manifest.

In the I-Thou relation one beholds the presence (*Gegenwart*) of the other, the existential reality over against one (*Gegenüber*), be the other a fellow human being, a phenomenon of nature, or an artistic or literary work, or God, the Eternal Thou. In meeting the other as a Thou, one finds oneself in an "immediate connection of I and the world [. . .] , a connection, however, which signifies no fusion, but a connection of relation. It is founded upon the I and the world as entities clearly separate from each other. The arch of relationship rises, as it were, on these two clearly individual pillars."⁶

The I-Thou meeting with one's fellow human beings has the promise that the other will respond in kind and confirm one's own presence. Should that come to pass, one may say an I-Thou dialogue is a meeting between two souls, a mutual confirmation of two "singular, irreplicable" souls. Indeed, the I-Thou encounter touches the very ground of one's being, and if one says, as in the nineteenth-century German fraternal greeting, "soul of my soul" (*Seele meiner Seele*),⁷ one has not "said too much"—for one in effect affirms their relation as sustaining the meaning of life: "without you I cannot live."⁸

The soulful meeting is primed by an "inborn Thou." Nurtured in the maternal womb, this primal experience of I-Thou continually "drives" one to reach out beyond its isolated existence to seek the Great Mother, symbolizing primordial maternity and the fertility of earthly life. "In the beginning is relation—as category of being, readiness, as form that reaches out to be filled, as *a mold for the soul* [*Seelenmodel*]: the *a priori* of relation, the innate You."⁹ *Das eingeborene Du* is a Platonic form that gains concrete, existential expression in *soulful* dialogical relations.

Alas, the imperious rule of the It-World all too often prevents one from taking the "holy risk" of reaching out to the other as a Thou. Buber thus speaks of the existential challenge to break the hold of the I-It attitude and to discard its protective garments before the imponderable challenge of the life of dialogue. Though suppressed by the tenacious grip of the It-World, the inborn Thou relentlessly throbs within one. There are situations in which one musters the courage to take the "risk" and heed the call "to make the decision, from our person, and from our person as we feel it is 'meant' for us, [and answer] the situation confronting us. Such decisions can only be taken by the whole soul that has become one [with one's embodied, existential reality]. [...] It is a cruelly hazardous [endeavor], this becoming a whole, becoming a form, of crystallization of the soul."[10]

The body alone perforce dwells in this world of It, bound by the calculus and constraints of time and space, whereas when manifest as embodied soul one overcomes the chaos of the It-World, governed by the laws of causality, which ineluctably "grows into an oppressive crushing [sense of] doom."[11] "Yet it could happen that we venture to respond [to the call], stammering perhaps—the soul is but rarely able to attain surer articulation—but it is an honest stammering."[12]

Already in "Religion as Presence," the series of eight lectures he delivered in 1922 at Franz Rosenzweig's Freies Jüdisches Lehrhaus, Buber speaks of the soul and the decisions that take place in "elementary depths of the soul." The lectures effectively constituted a draft of *I and Thou* and, as such, record the development and clarification of concepts that were initially inchoate, one being that of the soul, which seems to embrace that of the inborn-Thou, first introduced with the publication a year later of *I and Thou*. In the first lecture, the soul is said to experience the absolute presence of God, but not just as that of spiritual "inwardness"; in response to a question from the audience, Buber was quick to distinguish religious experience from that of musical appreciation, and as he noted in reply to yet another question, neither is the soul's experience of divinity's absolute presence to be construed as prompting an ethical act.[13]

In the third lecture, Buber distinguishes his conception of the soul from psychological definitions, which regard the soul as separate from the phenomenal world. For Buber, the soul, like the religious, is not a feeling in the human being but a true happening in the human being, with another human being—a process which he elaborates in the fifth lecture. In deciding to reach out to a Thou, the soul undergoes a process whereby the polarity of the I and the world is annulled.

In the eighth and final lecture, Buber speaks of the soul's "future [as] reaching beyond death," and asks how the world can be completed.[14] At this point, his indebtedness to Jewish mysticism is apparent when he not only describes the soul as unique in every individual but also as integrated into the eternal world structure. In comparison to German mysticism, which according to Buber is about an "emerging" of the soul, according to the Kabbalah "the completing soul" flows into the "unconditioned," namely God. The souls themselves come into wo/man either at birth or during life. "In all these ways the purification of the souls from the primordial turbidity and the redemption of the world from the first confusion takes place."[15] For this, he concludes in the eighth and last lecture, it is necessary to keep the soul pure or to "purify" it, which one can achieve through real decisions and thus be able to receive the divine Thou with the "innermost strength of the soul." But this does not mean that one should revile evil or impurity. On the contrary, one should and can come to terms with them; moreover, one only becomes a whole person when one feels the "evil urge" and harnesses it as primordial power to sanctify the world.[16] Here again, Buber's long-standing involvement and identification with Hasidism become clear.

According to Hasidic teachings, to perceive the divine Thou in one's life, one is to be true to one's soul, to one's unique, irreparable being. Thus, Buber relates that "Before his death, Rabbi Zusya said, 'In the world to come, they will not ask me: "Why were you not Moses?" They will ask me, "Why were you not Zusya?"'"[17] Although one must honor one's *Yichud*, it is but the *condictio sine que non* to gather the "strength and direction" to serve the divine Thou in the world. Ultimately, the sole, quintessential divine commandment is to love the world. Whoever loves the world—also loves God.

In the afterword to *I and Thou*, Buber avers that, as an act of love, those who are beckoned to heal a "diffuse soul that is poor in structure" must "grasp with the profound eye of a physician the buried, latent in the suffering soul, which can be done only if one enters into a person-to-person relationship."[18]

Indeed, this is true of each of us. We are all in need of healing. "Each individual who you meet needs help, needs *your* help." Attuned to the cry of others, "in need of help and the capacity to help make way for one another so that each not only does not know about the other but does not even know about himself." Indeed, "it is the nature of man to leave equally unnoticed the innermost need and the *innermost gift of his own soul*, although at times, too, a deep hour reminds him of them [both]." At such a juncture in one's existential journey, "you shall awaken in the other the need of help," by virtue of which you will quicken "in yourself the capacity to help. Even when [you] yourself are needy—and you are—you can help others and, in doing so, help yourself."[19]

Buber intoned this injunction in an essay he penned in 1919, in which he addressed a question initially formulated two decades earlier by Lenin: "What is be done?" Buber shifted the question's focus from the revolutionary proletariat to the suffering soul that constitutes the human condition. Hence, one who has the resolve to pose the question, "with the earnest of his soul on his lips," means, "What am I to do?" The answer is echoed in Saint Paul's imploration: "You shall not withhold yourself" (1 Cor. 7:5).

Notes

1. Martin Buber, *I and Thou*, trans. Walter Kaufmann (New York: Charles Scribner's Sons, 1970), 79.
2. Martin Buber, "*Imitatio Dei*," in Buber, *Israel and the World: Essays in a Time of Crisis* (New York: Schocken Books), 72.
3. Martin Buber, *Martin Buber Werkausgabe*, ed. Paul Mendes-Flohr and Peter Schäfer (2001–10), Bernd Witte (2010–19) (Gütersloh: Gütersloher Verlagshaus, 2001–19), 20:405.
4. Martin Buber, "On the Psychologizing of the World," in Buber, *A Believing Humanism: My Testament, 1902–1965*, trans. Maurice Friedman (New York: Simon & Schuster, 1967), 147–48.
5. Martin Buber, "The Unconscious," in Buber, *A Believing Humanism*, 155–56.
6. Buber, *I and Thou*, 144–45.
7. Buber, *I and Thou*, 84.
8. See Bernhard Lang, commentary to Martin Buber, *Ich und Du* (Ditzingen: Reclam, 2021), 128.
9. Buber, *I and Thou*, 78.
10. Martin Buber, *Good and Evil*, trans. Ronald Gregor Smith (Upper Saddle River, NJ: Prentice Hall, 1952), 128–29.
11. Buber, *I and Thou*, 102–3.
12. Martin Buber, "Dialogue," in Buber, *Between Man and Man*, 17.
13. Rivka Horwitz, *Buber's Way to "I and Thou": An Historical Analysis and the First Publication of Martin Buber's Lectures "Religion als Gegenwart"* (Heidelberg: Verlag Lambert Schneider, 1978), 63, 48–49.
14. Horwitz, *Buber's Way to "I and Thou"*, 141.
15. Martin Buber, "Die jüdische Mystik," in Buber, *Schriften zum Chassidismus* (Munich: Kösel Verlag, 1963), 13.
16. Martin Buber, *Religion als Gegenwart*, 263.
17. Martin Buber, *Tales of the Hasidism*.
18. Buber, *I and Thou*, 176.
19. Martin Buber, "What Is to Be Done?," in Buber, *Pointing the Way: Collected Essays*, trans. Maurice Friedman (London: Routledge & Kegan Paul, 1957), 110.

Annotated Bibliography

Crucial for an understanding of Buber's concept of the soul is his distinction between the "individual" (*Eigenwesen*), defined by the objectifying categories of the It-World, and the "person," the unique being confirmed and affirmed in the dialogical relation. See Robert E. Wood, *Martin Buber's Ontology: An Analysis of "I and Thou"* (Evanston, IL: Northwestern University Press, 1969), 81–84; and Bernhard Lang' s commentary to Martin Buber, *Ich und Du* (Ditzingen: Reclams Universal-Bibliothek, 2021), 182–83. Without reference to Buber, the English philosopher John Cottingham regards the soul as a conceptual placeholder to denote that by virtue of which we are each a self, a unique subject," rather than merely an object, an It. John Cottingham, *In the Search of the Soul: A Philosophical Essay* (Princeton, NJ: Princeton University Press, 2020).

13

Buber on Solitude

MICHAL BIZOŇ

Introduction

The philosopher Martin Buber is well known for his emphasis on the singularity of intersubjective relations, preeminently the dialogical relationship between individuals and their partners. In the introduction to his "programmatic" work *I and Thou* (1923), he writes: "There is no *I* taken in itself, but only the *I* of the primary word *I-Thou* and the *I* of the primary word *I-It*."[1] One might thus think it paradoxical, at the very least, to write about solitude in his thought. Yet, solitude is not just a minor digression in Buber's writing on the philosophy of dialogue but integral to its very development.

Typology of Solitude

Buber's reflections on solitude are scattered throughout his writings. He reflects on solitude in different contexts and in different ways.[2] One can glean a basic understanding of Buber's ideas on solitude from two short passages categorizing the forms of solitude. One is solitude as noted in his short article "What Is to Be Done?" from 1919, in which he discusses the two forms of solitude.[3] On the one hand, there is the solitude in which an individual seeks to be alone and withdraws from social life. Such solitary individuals find themselves incapable of participating in the life of the community (*Gemeinschaft*). On the other hand, there is the ever-again-becoming-solitary individual, who withdraws temporarily as a preparatory exercise to enter a community with a renewed sense of communal commitment and responsibility.

A community qua *Gemeinschaft* is not just any group of individuals, but one in which its members form essential relationships of mutual regard and trust. Accordingly, Buber later says that collectivism as a possible response to a person's solitude, when born of a sense of existential isolation, does not overcome it but merely, as it were, overpowers it—*nicht überwunden sondern übertäubt*;[4] individuals escape from existential loneliness by immersing themselves in the anonymity of the masses and letting their individual selves and responsibility dissolve in the general will of the collective. It is in this context that Buber speaks of "mass or collective loneliness."[5] Buber thus speaks of two fundamental forms of solitude: positive and negative solitude[6] or good and bad solitude.[7] Solitude is negative when it occludes community; positive solitude, on the other hand, prepares one existentially and emotionally to engage in the relationships constituting genuine community.

Characterizations of solitude can be found in Buber's other writings as well. Addressing a meeting of Jewish youth in 1919, he bemoaned the increasing intellectualization of European culture that has brought in its wake "a depressing loneliness to [contemporary] youth." The hypertrophy of the intellect tends to remove one from the matrix of the "organic" life of the spirit connecting individuals—be it the bonds of "love, friendship, companionship, or fellowship"—the life of spirit to spirit, because it can only connect "thinking apparatus with thinking apparatus and thus leads to loneliness."[8] We read about the evils of loneliness in one of the Hasidic tales related by Buber:

> [T]here are those who always sit in their rooms behind closed doors and study, and never leave the house to talk with others. For this they are called wicked. If they talk to others, they would bring to perfection something they are destined to make perfect. That is what the words mean: "be not wicked by facing yourself only" [Ethics of the Fathers, 1:14, 2:4]. Since you face yourself only, and do not go among people, do not become wicked through solitude.[9]

Solitude is negative or bad when the individual does not seek to enter dialogical relationships and chooses to remain alone.[10]

In the third part of *I and Thou*, which considers one's relationship to God, Buber postulates the central idea of the book: Every dialogical relationship between individuals is a portal to God. He then asks *en passant* whether solitude can also be a gateway to God.[11] The answer lies in distinguishing several forms of solitude, based on two criteria: (A) what one turns away from, and (B) what one turns toward.[12]

Based on the first criterion, (A) what we turn away from, Buber distinguishes the following forms of solitude. A1: Solitude as turning away from I-It relations of using and experiencing our fellow human beings as objects. That does not mean a failure to enter an I-Thou relationship with them, but rather not clinging to them, not being dependent on them, and in that sense finding solitude from them. The solitude of "not clinging" is key to realizing all essential relationships with the world and God.

A2: Solitude as the absence of a dialogical relationship. It is possible to not have a relationship, either (A2.1) because the Thou has forsaken the individual or (A2.2) because the individual has forsaken their peers. In the first case (A2.1), the individual's solitude comes about because others turn away from them;[13] in the second case (A2.2), it occurs because the individual turns away from others. In the first case (A2.1), the person's relationship with God is not restricted because the solitude is not the result of avoiding essential relationships with other people and the world. In this respect, one may speak of loneliness. In the second case (A2.2), it occurs because the person refuses to enter a dialogical relationship with the world, making it impossible to have a relationship with God.

Based on the second criterion (B), what one turns toward, Buber distinguishes two forms of solitude. B1: Solitude as a place of purification and rest whereby one seeks to regain the inner power to re-establish a dialogical relationship with the world and with God.

B2.1: Solitude as a place of isolation where one conducts a dialogue (more accurately a monologue) with oneself. It is turning to oneself, not to prepare oneself for a relationship with another but to enjoy the self-formation of the self. B2.2: A specific variant of this type of solitude is a situation in which a person begins to believe that "he has God in himself and is speaking with Him."[14]

Thus, there are two classifications of the forms of solitude that are not mutually exclusive but complementary. The later classification from *I and Thou* is a more subtle variation on the earlier classification. In the first classification, Buber viewed solitude through the individual's relationship with the community. In the second classification, this view of solitude is extended to include the individual's relationship with God, which is conditioned but not limited by the essential relationship with other individuals. That is, Buber's attitude to solitude is based on whether the path from it leads to essential relationships with other people, with the community. Buber does not deny that the relationship with God may take place separately from the relationship between one individual and another, in the realm of the relation with nature and the forms of the spirit (*die geistige Wesenheiten*),[15] but he rejects the idea that the way to God may lead through the rejection of relations with others: "Often we hear of animals who have been loved by holy hermits, but I would not be able to regard anyone as holy who in the desert ceased to love the man whom he had left."[16]

If we apply the criterion from the first classification (the ability or inability to enter relationships with other people) to the second, we get the following synthesis of the forms of solitude. On the one hand, there are (A1), the solitude of "not clinging," and (B1), the solitude of turning to oneself for the purpose of unifying the soul, which can be considered positive or good forms of solitude. On the other hand, (A2.2), the solitude of turning away from others, and (B2), the solitude of isolation, can be considered negative or bad solitudes.

✷

Buber reflects most extensively on the problem of solitude in his systematic historical exploration of the essence of man in "What Is Man?"[17] He regards the feeling of solitude as prerequisite to man's existential inquiry into his own essence;[18] it is also true that the more solitary a person is, the deeper their self-reflection, anthropological inquiry, and quest for an answer. From this perspective, Buber distinguishes two basic alternating epochs in the Western tradition of thought that set the direction of thinking about what constitutes the human being. These are the epochs of habitation (*Behaustheit*), in which humans inhabit the world as if it were a home, and the epochs of homelessness (*Hauslosigkeit*),[19] which are characterized by a strong feeling of solitariness in the world and can therefore be called epochs of solitude (qua aloneness). Each subsequent episode of solitude is more complete and harder to overcome, "colder and stricter than the preceding, and redemption therefrom ever more difficult,"[20] because the old image of the world cannot be used to overcome it, and a new one must be sought. On the one hand, "the fundamental meaning of each new solitude" is "that it must be overcome on a more comprehensive level than any earlier one";[21] on the other hand, its questioning power must be preserved if we are to answer the question about the essence of man.[22]

Buber further highlighted his conception of the dialectic of solitude with reference to the thought of Søren Kierkegaard (1813–55) and Martin Heidegger (1889–1976), who represent the two types of solitude according to Buber's typology.

Kierkegaard's Religious Doctrine of Loneliness

The negative solitude (A2.2) of turning away from other people to form a relationship with God is best represented in Kierkegaard and his category of the single one. In "The Question to the Single One" (1936), Buber begins his most extensive polemic with Kierkegaard with the assertion that his category of the "'single one' cannot be understood without his solitariness," which is radical in nature.[23] He places Kierkegaard, along with Augustine and Pascal, among the thinkers of the age of solitude who sought "a form of being which is not included in the world," that is, a God whom they could encounter in solitude.[24] His solitariness, however, differs substantially from that of Augustine and Pascal. Augustine's mother, Monica, stood alongside him, and Pascal's sister Jacquelin "maintained the organic connection with the world as only a woman as the envoy of elemental life can." Kierkegaard consequently renounced his connection with the world by breaking his engagement to his fiancée, Regina Olsen. According to Buber, it was "the central event in Kierkegaard's life and the crystallizing point of his thought." From a historical and anthropological perspective, Buber admires the fact that in Kierkegaard's category of the single one, man as a person enters an essential relationship with the other person for the first time, namely, with God. He is critical of the idea that "everyone should be chary about having to do with 'the others,' and should essentially speak only with God and with himself."[25] It is from this claim, argues Buber, that the acosmic nature of man's relationship with God follows. For Kierkegaard, every essential relationship between the individual and a person other than God is an obstacle to the essential relationship with God. The essential relationship with God is both exclusive (*ausschließliche*) and excluding (*ausschließende*); that is, it "in virtue of its unique, essential life expels all other relations into the realm of the unessential." Man is faced with a choice between God and the world,[26] but, for Buber, the choice runs contrary to the understanding of God the creator in Judeo-Christian tradition because it places God's creation in irreconcilable opposition to its creator. Any relationship with God that excludes a relationship with other creatures would no longer be a relationship with the God of all creation.[27] Such a God is more akin to the "God of the philosophers" than to the "God of Abraham and Isaac and Jacob."[28] He is either a demiurge fighting against his creation or a savior who is nonetheless alien to that creation.[29] For Buber, "creation is not a hurdle on the road to God, it is the road itself"; moreover, God wants us to come to him through our relationships with the "Reginas" whom he created, not by renouncing them.[30] God and the world are not rivals. The essential relationship with God may be exclusive, but it does not exclude. On the contrary, the relationship between man and God is the only relationship that is "unconditioned exclusiveness and unconditioned inclusiveness."[31]

On the one hand, Buber's critique of religious acosmism points to a deformed image of God. The individual turns away from the world and toward solitude in order to reach God, who cannot ultimately be reached in this way. On the other hand, Buber points out the consequences that follow from the fact that the "religious" man here stands alone before God. The exclusivist relationship with God is *per naturam* acosmic, asocial, and apolitical,[32] and therefore it prevents the individual from establishing a community with other people through essential relationships.

Contra Heidegger's Glorification of Solitude

Many of the motifs in Kierkegaard's philosophy appear in modified form in Heidegger, who represents the negative solitude (B2.1) of turning to oneself for the purpose of self-formation. Both emphasize that the task is to liberate oneself from an impersonal and inauthentic mode of existence from the "crowd" or the "one" (*das Man*) and become a "single one" or "a self." In Kierkegaard, "to become a single one" is merely prerequisite to something else; in Heidegger, "to become a self" is an end in itself. Kierkegaard's man becomes a single one to enable the formation of an essential relationship with God. For Heidegger, in the age after the "death of God," this relationship is unknown, and so he secularizes his single one.[33]

Buber does not consider the solicitude (*Fürsorge*) relationship, which Heidegger discusses in *Being and Time* (1927), to be an essential relationship because it does not involve immediate contact between two persons, just the solicitude of one person lacking another person who needs help. Buber makes two arguments. The first concerns the essentiality of the relationship: solicitude is a derived relationship. That is, it becomes essential only because of another essential relationship, such as the one between mother and child, or in friendship or love. Second, solicitude is not an essential relationship because there is no mutuality. Although the individual turns to the other to help, the individual does not open up to the other. The individual is concerned with the other but does not want the other to concern themselves with him.[34] From the point of view of the person doing the caring, it is a one-sided and therefore nonessential relationship.

In the realm of interpersonal relations, we can distinguish between a man's relationship with an individual and with multiple people. For Heidegger, just as for Kierkegaard, both relationships are nonessential. Kierkegaard states: "Everyone should be chary about having to do with 'the others,' and should essentially speak only with God and with himself." Heidegger accepts only the first and last part and, according to Buber, changes it thus: "Everyone can essentially speak only with himself." However, one's relation with oneself cannot be regarded as essential because of the absence of the prerequisite to any relationship—the presence of a counterpart. This criticism is true of both Heidegger and Kierkegaard in equal measure, although in the latter the relationship with oneself takes on meaning and consecration from God.[35] However, that does not change the fact that joining "with God" and "with himself" is contradictory in Kierkegaard's case, because "speaking with God is something *toto genere* different from 'speaking with oneself'; whereas, remarkably, it is not something *toto genere* different from speaking with another human being." Ontically, one human being can never become two, just as two can never become one.³⁶ All genuine relationships are conditioned by the true ontic difference between the counterparts. The conclusion that follows is that Heidegger's man knows no essential relationship. He cannot overcome his solitariness by addressing the "dead" known God or by addressing the living unknown God in the living and known man whom he meets on his journey through life. For Heidegger, then, as for other scholars of modern individualism, all one can do is glorify the solitude they shut themselves up in, away from God and the world.³⁷

The Absolute Solitude of the Mystic

An example of the negative solitude (B2.2) of turning within oneself so as to establish a union with God and the world is the solitude of the mystic. Buber describes it best in the introduction to his 1909 anthology *Ecstatic Confessions*. The soul of the mystic is submerged entirely in itself, has reached the very ground of itself, and experiences an ecstasy that is the most inward experience that grows out of itself, "free of the other, inaccessible to the other." The mystic experiences in ecstasy the unity of the I but interprets it as experiencing God; the unity of the ecstatic means that the subject and the object of that experience, the I and the world, have flowed into one, and therefore his unity is absolute and limitless.³⁸

> One's unity is solitude, absolute solitude: the solitude of that which is without limits. One contains the other, the others in oneself, in one's unity: as world; but one no longer has others outside oneself, no longer has any communion with them or anything in common with them. [. . .] It is unity, solitude, uniqueness: which cannot be transferred. It is the abyss that cannot be fathomed: the unsayable.³⁹

Having elaborated on the dialogical principle, Buber criticizes mystical experiences where the essential element is the experience (*Erlebnis*) of the union between man and himself, and God, and the world, because it removes the duality of I and Thou that makes the dialogical relationship possible. In the Western mystical tradition, the abolition of the relationship occurs dynamically through the absorption of the human self into the divine Thou at the moment of its consummation—union—and, in the Eastern tradition, the abolition of the relationship occurs statically through glimpsing the reality of the identity of the *atman* with the *brahma*, of the human self with God (cosmic self), which implies that there is no duality, nor has there ever been. The existence of the relation is a great illusion to be overcome through the elimination of ignorance.⁴⁰

The experience of the union can be explained in two ways. First, it is the unification of the soul in which all the person's forces, including the instinctive, the sensual, and the emotional, are concentrated at the core; however, this unification of the self does not take place between the individual and God, but within that individual, and whether it constitutes an end in itself or is merely a prerequisite to exiting solitude to meet another person and God is up to that person. Second, it can be explained as a relational act, in which the individual believes that they and their counterpart have become one. They may experience a feeling of union in the encounter with the other, but it is a "union that was no union." While the feeling of unity may exist, actual unity does not. The union of which the mystic speaks is in fact, according to Buber, "the enrapturing dynamic of relation." The problem with the Eastern doctrine is, in his view, that it has nothing in common with lived reality.[41]

The Religious Solitude of the Prophet

The opposite of the previous examples of solitude is positive solitude, which Buber called "the religious solitude of the prophet."[42] The figure of the prophet combines (A1) the solitude of turning away from using and experiencing things with (B1) the solitude of turning to oneself in order to unify one's soul so the person is able to enter into a relationship with others with his whole being. The solitude of the prophet is characteristically anchored in openness to society and the community of fellow human beings.[43] Communion with others lies at the very core of what it means to "be a prophet," for the prophet's task is to proclaim God's will to God's people. To do this, the prophet must retreat into solitude from time to time.

Here, one cannot overlook Moses, one of the great figures of the Hebrew Bible and ancestor of all the prophets of Israel.[44] First of all, God appears to him in a burning bush in the solitude of the wilderness on Mount Horeb. God reveals his name and sends Moses to lead the people of Israel out of Egypt's captivity and into the Promised Land.[45] Later, as the people of Israel wander through the wilderness of Sinai, Moses "withdraws to the loneliness of God's mountain, far from the people and overshadowed by God's cloud, in order to write God's law for the people."[46] Another great figure is the prophet Elijah, who, after having all the prophets of Baal killed, flees from the wrath of Queen Jezebel, wanders alone in the wilderness for forty days, finally taking refuge, as Moses did, in the solitude of Mount Horeb. Here Yahweh speaks to him in the sound of sheer silence and sends him to anoint Hazael as King of Aram, Jehu as King of Israel, and Elisha as a prophet in his place.[47] In *Elijah and the Mystery Play* (1963), Buber has Elijah say, "Only he who has borne loneliness ripens into a prophet."[48] Elijah also engages in a form of asceticism. For a time, he was fed by the ravens at Wadi Cherith,[49] and later he stayed with a widow from Zarephath who cared for his livelihood.[50] In the scriptures he is described as "a hairy man, with a leather belt around his waist."[51]

In several places in the *New Testament*, John the Baptist, whom Buber regarded as a prophet, is likened to Elijah,[52] or indeed thought to be him.[53] John the Baptist lived modestly, walking around dressed in camel hair, a leather belt around his waist, and subsisting on locusts and wild honey.[54] Though he retreats into the solitude of the wilderness, he emerges from it to proclaim to God's people his repentance and the coming of God's kingdom.

Conclusion

Buber's critique of the exclusion of the world from a relationship with God concerns man's *life*, not *a* discrete *hour* of spiritual exaltation. He considers it legitimate for an individual, in the hour of religious fervor, to repeatedly enter a relationship with God that is not bound to the world as in, for example, personal prayer when speaking with God, "Alone to the Alone."[55] He does not question the direct relationship with God but states that "the essential relation to God must find its complement in the essential relation to man."[56] What he was criticizing was a "life with God" built on rejecting the world.[57] The individual longs for a continuous relationship with God, but that cannot happen by remaining in solitude, for the relationship has to be embodied throughout life. The relationship with God can only endure because one can encounter others as Thou. Yet Buber recognized the need for solitude in human life. He recognized that man "must let himself be helped from time to time by an inner-worldly monastery," "staying" there to engage in a dialogical way of life—to attest to his relationship with God in his relationship with the world. This form of solitude, and relationship, is the systole and diastole of the human soul, and the real task and meaning of solitude is not to shut but "to keep open the gates of finitude."[58]

Notes

1. Martin Buber, *I and Thou*, trans. R. G. Smith (London: Bloomsbury, 2013), 3.

2. In tracing Buber's understanding of solitude, it is important to note that the German term *Einsamkeit* denotes both solitude and loneliness (as well as aloneness and seclusion), which are differentiated semantically by context.

3. Martin Buber, "What Is to Be Done?," in *Pointing the Way: Collected Essays*, trans. and ed. Maurice Friedman (New York: Harper & Brothers, 1957), 110.

4. Martin Buber, "What Is Man?," in Buber, *Between Man and Man*, trans. R. G. Smith (London: Routledge & Kegan Paul, 2004), 239.

5. Martin Buber, *Paths in Utopia*, trans. R. F. C. Hull (Boston: Beacon Press, 1958), 14.

6. Ivan Stuppner, *Die Metamorphose der Einsamkeit zum Dialog. Ein möglicher Denkweg zwischen Martin Buber und Emmanuel Lévinas* (Marburg: Tectum Verlag, 2013), 56.

7. See the Czech translation of *I and Thou*, *Já a Ty*, trans. Jiri Navrátil, commentary by Jan Heller (Prague: Kalich, 2005), 163.

8. Martin Buber, "Herut: On Youth and Religion," in *On Judaism*, ed. Nahum N. Glatzer (New York: Schocken Books, 1973), 158–59.

9. Buber, *Tales of the Hasidim*, trans. Olga Marx (1949; New York: Schocken Books, 1991), 89–90.

10. Stuppner, *Die Metamorphose der Einsamkeit zum Dialog*, 58.

11. Buber, *I and Thou*, 72.

12. On this distinction, see Buber, *I and Thou*, 72–73.

13. This form of solitude is also likely to occur following the death of a dialogical partner.

14. Buber, *I and Thou*, 72.

15. Buber, *I and Thou*, 5, 70.

16. Buber, *Philosophical Interrogations*, ed. Sydney Rome and Beatrice Rome (New York: Holt, Rinehart & Winston, 1964), 86.

17. The book is based on the inaugural lectures he delivered as professor of social philosophy at the Hebrew University in 1938, which first appeared in book form in 1943 under the title *The Problem of Man* (German and English, 1947). Martin Buber, "Foreword," in Buber, *Between Man and Man*, trans. R. G. Smith (London: Routledge & Kegan Paul, 2004), x.

18. Buber, "What Is Man?," 150.

19. Buber, "What Is Man?," 150; German original in *Martin Buber Werkausgabe*, ed. Paul Mendes-Flohr and Peter Schäfer (2001–10), Bernd Witte (2010–19), vol. 12 (Gütersloh: Gütersloher Verlagshaus, 2001–19), 231.

20. Buber, "What Is Man?," 158, 198.

21. Martin Buber, "Prophecy, Apocalyptic, and the Historical Hour" (1954), in Buber, *Pointing the Way*, 205.

22. Buber, "What Is Man?," 236.

23. Martin Buber, "The Question to the Single One," in *Between Man and Man*, 46.

24. Buber, "What Is Man?," 198.

25. Buber, "The Question to the Single One," 46–47, 58. Cf. Buber, "What Is Man?," 203. See also Søren Kierkegaard, "'The Single Individual': Two 'Notes' concerning My Work as an Author," in Kierkegaard, *The Point of View*, ed. and trans. Howard V. Hong and Edna H. Hong (Princeton, NJ: Princeton University Press, 1998), 106.

26. Buber, "The Question to the Single One," 58, 63.

27. Buber, "The Question to the Single One," 60. Cf. "What Is Man?," 212.

28. Buber, "The Question to the Single One," 60.

29. Buber, "What Is Man?," 212.

30. Buber, "The Question to the Single One," 60. In "What Is Man?," Buber admits that a single one can have an essential relationship with God in addition to an essential relationship with another person. Ironically, this is a situation in which the single one communicates to his counterpart the reasons for renouncing the essential relationship. Buber, "What Is Man?," 204.

31. Buber, *I and Thou*, 55, 69.

32. Peter Šajda, "Kierkegaard's Contribution to Buber's Philosophy of Judaism and His Theories of Patriotism and Political Groups" (in Slovak), *Filozofia* 68, no. 1 (2013): 13.

33. Buber, "What Is Man?," 203, 207, 212. The relationship between Heidegger's thought and religion is discussed in more detail later in Buber's *Eclipse of God: Studies in the Relation between Religion and Philosophy*, trans. Maurice Friedman, Eugene Kamenka, Norbert Guterman, and I. M. Lask (Princeton, NJ: Princeton University Press, 2016).

34. Buber, "What Is Man?," 201.

35. Buber, "What Is Man?," 204, 213–14.

36. Buber, "The Question to the Single One," 58, 59.

37. Buber, "What Is Man?"

38. Martin Buber, "Ecstasy and Confession," in Buber, *Ecstatic Confessions*, trans. Esther Cameron, ed. Paul Mendes-Flohr (San Francisco: Harper & Row, 1985), 2, 5, 3, 5, 6.

39. Buber, "Ecstasy and Confession," 6.

40. Buber, *I and Thou*, 59.

41. Buber, *I and Thou*, 62, 60, 61, 62.

42. Buber, *The Prophetic Faith*, trans. Carlyle Witton-Davies (New York: Harper & Row, 1960). Besides the figure of the prophet, this solitude is embodied in, e.g., the figure of the Hasidic *zaddik*.

43. Stuppner, *Die Metamorphose der Einsamkeit zum Dialog*, 61.

44. Deuteronomy 34:10 describes Moses as the greatest of Israel's prophets.

45. Exodus 3:1–14.

46. Buber, *Moses: The Revelation and the Covenant* (New York: Harper & Brothers, 1958), 139.

47. 1 Kings 19:1–16.

48. Buber, "Elijah a Mystery Play," in *Martin Buber and the Theater*, ed. and trans. Maurice Friedman (New York: Funk & Wagnalls, 1969), 162.

49. 1 Kings 17:4–6.

50. 1 Kings 17:9.

51. 2 Kings 1:8.

52. Cf. Buber, "Prophecy, Apocalyptic, and the Historical Hour," 206–7.

53. Matthew 11:13–14, 17:11–13; Luke 1:16–17.

54. Matthew 3:4; Mark 1:6.

55. Buber, "Philosophical Interrogations," 86.

56. Buber, "Replies to My Critics," in *The Philosophy of Martin Buber*, ed. Paul Arthur Schilpp and Maurice Friedman (LaSalle, IL: Open Court, 1967), 710.

57. Buber, "Philosophical Interrogations," 86.

58. Buber, "The Question to the Single One," 63, 64.

Annotated Bibliography

PRIMARY SOURCES

The *loci classici* of Buber's consideration of solitude are his essays on the Danish philosopher Søren Kierkegaard: "The Question to the Single One," in Buber, *Between Man and Man*, translated by Ronald Gregor Smith with an introduction by Maurice Friedman (London: Routledge & Kegan Paul, 2004), 40–97; "What Is Man?," also in Buber, *Between Man and Man*, 140–244; and "'The Single Individual': Two 'Notes' concerning My Work as an Author," in Buber, *The Point of View*, edited and translated by Howard V. Hong and Edna H. Hong (Princeton, NJ: Princeton University Press, 1998), 101–26.

SECONDARY LITERATURE

The Italian scholar Ivan Stuppner places Buber and Emmanuel Levinas in a dialogue on solitude: *Die Metamorphose der Einsamkeit zum Dialog. Ein möglicher Denkweg zwischen Martin Buber und Emmanuel Lévinas* (Marburg: Tectum Verlag, 2013). Buber's concept of solitude has also engaged Slovakian scholars: Jan Heller, Commentary to Buber, *Já a Ty*, translated by Jiří Navrátil, introduction and commentary by Jan Heller (Prague: Kalich, 2005), 151–64; and Peter Šajda, "Kierkegaard's Contribution to Buber's Philosophy of Judaism and His Theories of Patriotism and Political Groups," *Filozofia* 68, no. 1 (2013): 5–16.

14

Buber on Psychotherapy and Psychoanalysis

HENRY ABRAMOVITCH

Martin Buber had a lifelong concern with mental health, and healing has had an abiding influence on psychotherapy.[1] He received psychiatric training under some of the foremost figures of his time, including Eugen Bleuler, who was C. G. Jung's mentor. He maintained an active correspondence with other leading figures in psychotherapy, including Freud, from whom he sought unsuccessfully to solicit a volume on psychoanalysis for a series of monographs on modern urban culture which he had edited in the first decade of the twentieth century. When two decades later Buber developed his philosophy of dialogue, he intended to write a critique of classical psychoanalysis, which he deemed to be perversely I-It. For in traditional psychoanalysis, the analyst sits out of sight of the patient and endeavors to be a blank screen for projections; the analyst's studied emotional distance and "intellectualized" interventions, Buber held, failed to understand the existential depth of the patient's anguish. The recent turn to a relational psychoanalysis—which regards the establishment of a mutual relationship of trust—may be viewed as a response to Buber's philosophy of dialogue, at least sharing in its basic premises. One of Buber's most powerful lines is, "A soul is never sick alone, but there is always a *betweenness* also, a situation between it and another existing human being."[2] Likewise, in this view genuine healing can never come from self-help books. Just as one cannot mourn alone, so one cannot heal psychic wounds by oneself.

One of Buber's most fruitful connections was with Carl Rogers, the founder of client-centered psychotherapy. Buber and Rogers had a public encounter in 1957 that was transcribed with commentary. This unique night of dialogue directly influenced both their work. In his postscript to *I and Thou*, written only months after his dialogue with Rogers, Buber wrote: "But again the specific 'healing' relation would come to an end the moment the patient thought of, and succeeded in, practicing 'inclusion' and experiencing the events from the doctor's pole as well."[3] The Buber-Rogers dialogue also had a seminal impact on Rogers's thinking, as he himself attested seventeen years later: "This recognition of the significance of what Buber terms the I-thou relationship is the reason why, in client-centered therapy, there has come to be a greater use of the self of the therapist, of the therapist's feeling, greater stress on genuineness, but all of this without imposing the views, values, or interpretations of the therapist on the client."[4]

Buber also maintained a long correspondence and friendship with existential psychiatrist Ludwig Binswanger, considered a founding figure in the development of existential, humanistic, and transpersonal psychotherapy. And Buber had a profound influence on the Jungian psychoanalyst Hans Trueb. Trueb's last work, *Healing through Meeting*, published posthumously in 1952, included a preface by Buber.[5] Buber's approach to psychotherapy is most succinctly summed up in the phrase "healing through meeting." In his preface, Buber writes:

> [T]he psychotherapist, whose task is to be the watcher and healer of sick souls, again and again confronts the naked abyss of man, man's abysmal liability. [. . .] The psychotherapist meets the situation [. . .] as a mere person equipped only with the tradition of science and the theory of his school. It is understandable enough that he strives to objectivize the abyss that approaches him and to convert the raging "nothing-else-than-process" into a thing that can, in some degree, be handled. [. . .] The psychotherapist [. . .] will return from the crisis [. . .] as a changed person in a changed situation. He returns to it as one to whom the necessity of genuine personal meetings in the abyss of human existence between the one in need of help and the helper has been revealed.[6]

Buber's notion of *healing through meeting* has been discovered and rediscovered by subsequent generations of therapists. Buber anticipates the groundbreaking work of Harold F. Searles, "The Patient as Therapist to His Analyst";[7] the "now" moment described by Daniel Stern;[8] and the work of Owen Renik.[9] Renik's idea dovetails with Jung's idea of the uniqueness of every genuine therapeutic encounter, when *this* patient has come to *this* therapist, to *this wounded healer*, to heal first the analyst, who can then heal the "between" and allow a deeper healing to take place for both. Michael Balint, the Hungarian psychoanalyst who fled to England during the Holocaust and taught general practitioners to do psychotherapy in ten minutes, crystallized his approach with the maxim, "The doctor is his best pill": it is the relationship rather than the medications which provides the most crucial healing. He also developed a method known today as "Balint groups" in which physicians discuss their most difficult cases in an atmosphere of dialogical and I-Thou relations. All of these and more are spiritual disciples of Martin Buber.

In 1957, Buber delivered the annual William Allison White Lectures at the Washington School of Psychiatry. These talks were published in the journal *Psychiatry* and collected into the volume *The Knowledge of Man: A Philosophy of the Interhuman*.[10] The essays are entitled "Distance and Relation"; "Elements of the Interhuman"; "What Is Common to All"; "The Word That Is Spoken"; "Guilt and Guilt Feelings"; "Man and His Image-Work." The most influential pieces are "Distance and Relation" and "Guilt and Guilt Feelings," to be discussed below. Maurice Friedman argues that Buber's influence can be seen in virtually every school of psychotherapy: Freudian, Jungian, interpersonal, object-relations, self-psychology, existential therapy, gestalt, and especially family therapy.[11] One school of family therapy, contextual family therapy, is explicitly based on Buber's ideas. The founders of contextual therapy, Ivan Boszormenyani-Nagy and Barbara Krasner, expressly credited their theory to Buber.[12]

Even more recent and exciting developments within contemporary psychoanalysis—such as relational psychoanalysis, intersubjective psychoanalysis, and dialogical psychotherapy—are likewise indebted to Buber, even if it seems at times that the recognition of Buber remains in their collective unconscious. Buber's ideas have been applied to work in diverse settings and populations,[13] such as therapists in prisons,[14] social work and pastoral counseling,[15] therapeutic communities,[16] dream work,[17] ecological psychotherapy,[18] and more. His clear influence can also be seen in the works of Alfred Adler,[19] Donald W. Winnicott,[20] R. D. Laing,[21] and Leslie Farber.[22] It was Buber's insight that dialogue and authentic encounter are at the heart of psychotherapy rather than insight and interpretation.

The main texts touching on psychotherapy are first and foremost Buber's outstanding collection of autobiographical fragments, *Meetings*. In the opening fragment, he tells how he understood from a playmate that his mother, who abandoned him at age three for a career in the theater, would never return. Based on that formative experience, he coined a new word, *Vergegnung*, a mis-meeting or a mis-encounter, "to designate the failure of a real meeting between people." When he saw his mother again for the first time after thirty years, he looked into her beautiful blue eyes and saw once more the word, *Vergegnung*. He ends the story with a confession that is both simple and true, "I suspect that all that I have learned about genuine meeting in the course of my life had its origin in that hour on the balcony" at the age of three. In another story, "Languages," he writes how via private, imaginative play (he was a precocious only child), he anticipated the key issue in cross-cultural encounter: "I devised for myself two-language conversations between a German and a Frenchman, later between a Hebrew and an ancient Roman and came ever again, half in play and yet at times with beating heart to feel the tension between what was heard by the one and what was heard by the other, from his thinking in another language."[23] The necessity of understanding the "language" of the other, and the even more specific contemporary initiative to train "culture brokers" for work in transcultural psychiatry, derives from this insight.

One of the defining aspects of psychotherapy is that it involves intense personal interaction, followed by long periods of reflection by both the patient and the analyst on what has taken place. In the model of medical dialogue developed by the Israeli physician Eliezer Schwartz and myself, the physician must move from an initial I-Thou to a subsequent I-It relation and back to a renewed I-Thou, containing the "fruit and pit" of the I-It wisdom.[24] Personal encounters go wrong when the self-reflection occurs at the expense of real meeting. In the autobiographical fragment "The Horse," Buber describes just such a mistimed moment:

> When I was eleven years of age, spending the summer on my grandparent's estate, I used, as often as I could do it unobserved, to steal into the stable and gently stroke the neck of my darling, a broad dapple-gray horse. It was not a casual delight but a great, certainly friendly, but also deeply stirring happening. If I am to explain it now [. . .] I must say that what I experienced was the Other, the immense otherness of the Other. [. . .] But once—I did not know what came over the child, at any rate it was childlike enough—it struck me about the stroking, what fun it gave me, and suddenly I became conscious of my hand. The game went on as before, but something had changed, it was no longer the same thing. And the next day, after giving him a rich feed, when I stroked my friend's head he did not raise his head. A few years later, when I thought back to the incident, I no longer supposed that the animal had noticed my defection. But at the time I considered myself judged.[25]

Buber's well-known collection of Hasidic stories also touches on many therapeutic issues. Buber implicitly showed how stories were vehicles for healing, and this approach is itself the basis of narrative therapy. Even Freud confessed to using Hasidic stories in his treatments.

Buber also received young people in his home at set times, for something akin to therapy sessions. In "A Conversion," he wrote of the essence of the psychotherapeutic enterprise, whose task is to hear the question which is not asked:

> What happened was no more than that one forenoon, after a morning of "religious" enthusiasm, I had a visit from an unknown young man, without being there in spirit. I certainly did not fail to let the meeting be friendly, I did not

treat him any more remissibly than all his contemporaries who were in the habit of seeking me out about this time of day as an oracle that is ready to listen to reason. I conversed attentively and openly with him—only I omitted to guess the questions which he did not put. Later, not long after, I learned from one of his friends—he himself was no longer alive—the essential content of these questions; I learned that he had come to me not casually, but borne by destiny, not for a chat but for a decision. He had come to me; he had come in this hour.[26]

Buber seems to indicate that the young man had come to him concerning a decision to commit suicide. Research has shown that this is indeed a common situation in which individuals who are about to commit suicide see doctors, teachers, friends, and family who fail to hear the unasked question. (In one dramatic suicide prevention commercial shown on Israeli television, a young man goes through his entire day ringing a large bell no one hears.) Nevertheless, Buber's biographers have revealed that the man's question was not about suicide but whether to return to the front in World War I. In the end, the man did rejoin his unit and was killed shortly thereafter. In Buber's own mind, the encounter became a *Vergegnung*, "the failure of a real meeting between individuals."

This story illuminates the heart of psychotherapy as essentially an I-Thou process, in which a unique individual comes to a unique therapist "not casually but borne by destiny." Buber understood that encounters such as he had with young men seeking him out at a fixed time of day were therapeutic. Buber did not exactly treat this particular man as an "It" but not fully as a "Thou." In *I and Thou*, Buber dichotomizes, "To man the world is twofold, in accordance with his twofold attitude [...] the *I* of man is also twofold. For the *I* of the primary word *I-Thou* is a different I from that of the primary word *I-It*."[27] In practice, there are probably gradations in the degree of I-Thou-ness (or indeed I-It-ness), just as psychotherapists learn from their failures, not from their successes. Buber then goes on to ask a most daring paradoxical question: "What do we expect when we are in despair and yet go to a [fellow] human being?" To this he gives an even more profound answer: "Surely a presence by means of which we are told that nevertheless there is meaning." Note Buber does *not* say words by which we are told that nevertheless there is meaning. Words will not work and certainly not be believed. Rather it is the existential "presence" of the one to whom one turns which is healing.

In his essay, "Distance and Relation," Buber thus argues, "Man wishes to be confirmed in his being by man and wishes to have a presence in the being of the other. The human person needs confirmation because man as man needs it." He concludes the essay, "It is from one man to another that the heavenly bread of self-being is passed."[28]

Buber also raises the issue of guilt. In one of his lectures at the Washington School of Psychiatry, he made a fundamental distinction between actual guilt as opposed to guilty feelings. Reacting against the psychoanalytic tendency to absolve patients of all feelings of guilt, Buber felt that such healers were making a serious moral error. Neurotic guilt truly needed cleansing, but actual guilt required illumination. In one Jewish tradition, Cain, the first murderer, calls out not "My punishment is too great" but "My sin is too great to be borne!"[29] (The ambiguity in the original Hebrew revolves around the double meaning of *avoni*, which means both punishment for sin and sin itself.) In the latter version, Cain's cry is one of deep and painful insight. Only now, under God's questioning and punishing, does he come to realize the enormity of his deed. This moment of realization is what Buber called the "illumination of guilt," the necessary first stage in coming to terms with real guilt. Cain's punishment—never being able to rest in peace—impels him to continue delving into his guilt. This second of Buber's stages is persevering in the knowledge of the guilt, leading to sincere regret: it is reflected in a Midrash describing how Cain wandered the world everywhere rejected, until finally he slapped himself on the head and returned to the presence of the Lord. For Buber, however, "returning," as repentance is called in the Hebrew tradition, is not enough. Buber emphasized a third stage in which the guilty party must enact a *tikkun* or "repair" of the guilt, at the place in which the human order was injured. Robert Jay Lifton developed Buber's ideas into a more clinical idiom. He distinguished "static guilt" (a deadening immobilization of the self), which can be either self-lacerating ("self-condemnation in which unchanging imagery of unmitigated evil prevents actual 'knowledge' of guilt and results instead in what resembles a continuous killing of self") or "numbed guilt," in which guilt is avoided by "freezing" of the self and a numbing of experience in general. He contrasted these with "animating" guilt, which is energizing and transformative toward a goal of renewal and change.[30]

Can a killer, like Cain, ever achieve such a *tikkun*? Is not a dead brother "like water spilled on the ground that can never be gathered up again"? A thief can restore his loot; a slanderer may make a tearful, public apology. What can a murderer do? Buber, nevertheless, suggested that "the wounds of the order-of-being can be healed in infinitely many other places than those at which they were inflicted."[31] *Tikkun* as a prime goal of therapy has been one of Buber's most poignant contributions to the fundamental project of psychotherapy and the human condition of healing.

The strength of Buber's emphasis on the eternal present of genuine dialogue is also its weakness. The lack of technique may allow therapy to flounder. At the extreme, the overemphasis on confirming the existential presence of the patient within an I-Thou relation may work against the necessary discipline of I-It that psychotherapy demands. The encounter, the very healing through meeting, is susceptible to misuse and exploitation by narcissistic therapists who justify their abuse in terms of *one's own truth*, which is imposed on the patient in a form of what might be called psychic rape. In a similar manner, Buber was naively unaware of the impact of a psychotherapist's own projections onto the patient and lacked any idea of how to deal with such a situation of countertransference. Nevertheless, Buber was a wounded healer who explored the depths of his own wound and helped solve for us all what he could not solve for himself alone.

Buber once said that he had no new doctrine to teach; instead he compared his efforts to taking someone to the window and pointing outside or pointing to what was forgotten. In an era of cognitive behavioral therapy, evidence-based medicine, time-limited psychotherapy, and managed care, Buber's message is all the more timely. We must all follow him again and again to the window, look outside, and see what we once knew but have forgotten.

Notes

1. For an overview of Buber's contribution to psychotherapy, see Judith Buber Agassi, ed., *Martin Buber on Psychology and Psychotherapy: Essays, Letters and Dialogues* (Syracuse, NY: Syracuse University Press, 1999).

2. Martin Buber, *Pointing the Way* (New York: Harper, 1958), 142.

3. Rob Anderson and Kenneth N. Cissna, *The Martin Buber–Carl Rogers Dialogue: A New Transcript with Commentary* (Albany: State University of New York Press, 1997), 39; Martin Buber, trans. Ronald Gregor Smith, *I and Thou* (New York: Charles Scribner's Sons, 1958), 133.

4. Carl Rogers, "Remarks on the Future of Client-Centered Therapy," in *Innovations in Client-Centered Therapy*, ed. David A. Wexler and Laura North Rice (New York: John Wiley & Sons, 1974), 11.

5. Martin Buber, "Heilung aus der Begegnung," *Neue Schweizer Rundschau* 19, no. 6 (October 1951): 382–86; reprinted as the preface to Hans Trüb, *Heilung aus der Begegnung. Eine Auseinandersetzang mit der Psychologie C. G. Jungs*, ed. Ernst Michel and Arie Sborowitz (Stuttgart: Ernst Klett Verlag, 1952).

6. Buber Agassi, *Martin Buber on Psychology and Psychotherapy*, 17–19.

7. H. F. Searles, "The Patient as Therapist to His Analyst," in *Tactics and Techniques in Psychoanalytic Therapy*, ed. Peter L. Giovacchini (New York: Jason Aronson, 1975), 95–151.

8. Daniel N. Stern, *The Present Moment in Psychotherapy and Everyday Life* (New York: W. W. Norton, 2004).

9. Owen Renik, "Subjectivity and Unconsciousness," *Journal of Analytical Psychology* 45 (2000): 3–2.

10. Martin Buber, *The Knowledge of Man*, ed. Maurice Friedman (New York: Harper & Row, 1965), 121–48.

11. Maurice Friedman, *The Healing Dialogue in Psychotherapy* (London: Jason Aronson, 1985).

12. Ivan Boszormenyi and Barbara Krasner, *Between Give and Take: A Clinical Guide to Contextual Therapy* (New York: Brunner/Mazel, 1986).

13. E. T. Barker and M. H. Mason, "Buber behind Bars," *Journal of the Canadian Psychiatric Association* 13 (1996): 67–74.

14. Henry Abramovitch and Eliezer Schwartz, "The Three Stages of Medical Dialogue," *Theoretical Medicine* 17 (1996): 175–87.

15. Robert L. Katz, "Martin Buber and Psychotherapy," *Hebrew Union College Annual* 46: 413–31.

16. Tamar Kron, "The 'We' in Martin Buber's Dialogical Philosophy and Its Implications for Group Therapy and the Therapeutic Community," *International Journal of Therapeutic Communities* 11, no. 1 (1990): 13–20; Tamar Kron and Rafi Yungman, "Intimacy and Distance in Staff Group Relationship," *International Journal of Therapeutic Communities* 5 (1984): 99–109.

17. Tamar Kron, "The Dialogical Dimension in Therapists' Dreams about Their Patients," *Israel Journal of Psychiatry and Related Subjects* 28 (1991): 1–12.

18. Jürg Willi, *Ecological Psychotherapy* (Seattle: Hogrefe & Huber, 1999).

19. M. J. Skellin, "A Comparative Study of Adler and Buber: From Cooperation to Contact," *Journal of Individual Psychology* 56 (2000): 2–19.

20. E. A. Ticho, "Donald W. Winnicott, Martin Buber and the Theory of Personal Relationships," *Psychiatry* 37, no. 3 (1974): 240–53; Charles Brice, "Pathological Models of Interhuman Relating and Therapeutic Dialogue between Buber's Existential Relation Theory and Object Relations Theory," *Psychiatry: Journal for the Study of Interpersonal Processes* 47, no. 2 (1984): 109–23.

21. R. D. Laing, *The Divided Self: An Existential Study in Sanity and Madness* (1960; New York: Penguin, 2010); Laing, *The Politics of Experience* (New York: Penguin, 1983); Laing, *The Self and Others* (New York: Penguin, 1969).

22. L. H. Farber, *The Ways of the Will* (New York: Basic Books, 2000).

23. Buber, *Meetings: Autobiographical Fragments*, ed. Maurice Friedman (London: Routledge, 2002), 19, 21.

24. Abramovitch and Schwartz, "Three Stages of Medical Dialogue."

25. Buber, *Meetings*, 26–27.

26. Buber, *Meetings*, 45–46.

27. Buber, *I and Thou*, 3.

28. Buber, *Knowledge of Man*, 16.

29. Genesis 4:13.

30. Robert Jay Lifton, *The Broken Connection* (New York: Simon & Schuster, 1979), 139.

31. 2 Samuel 14:14, Jerusalem Bible.

Annotated Bibliography

PRIMARY SOURCES

The most important collection of Buber's writings on psychotherapy is Martin Buber, *The Knowledge of Man: A Philosophy of the Interhuman*, edited and with an introduction by Maurice Friedman (New York: Harper Torchbooks, 1965). It includes some of his most influential essays, particularly "Guilt and Guilty Feeling" and "Distance and Relation."

His pioneering essay, "Healing through Meeting," was originally written as a preface to Hans Trueb, *Heilung aus der Begegnung: Eine Auseinandersetzung mit der Psychologie C. G. Jungs*, edited by Ernst Michel and Arie Sborowitz with a preface by Martin Buber (Stuttgart: Ernst Klett Verlag,

1952). It is available in English translation in another important collection of essays, Martin Buber, "Healing through Meeting," in *Pointing the Way* (New York: Harper Torchbooks, 1975), 93–97.

In some ways, Buber's most masterful and poignant book is about his own personal meetings and mismeetings, and remains an enduring, seminal contribution: Martin Buber, *Meetings: Autobiographical Fragments*, edited and with an introduction and bibliography by Maurice Friedman (LaSalle, IL: Open Court Publishing, 1973). Another valuable source book is the collection by Buber's granddaughter: Judith Buber Agassi, *Martin Buber on Psychology and Psychotherapy: Essays, Letters, and Dialogue* (Albany, NY: Syracuse University Press, 1999).

For the most accurate and informative version of the famous encounter between Buber and Rogers, see *The Martin Buber–Carl Rogers Dialogue: A New Transcript with Commentary*, edited by Rob Anderson and Kenneth Cissna (Albany: State University of New York Press, 1997).

SECONDARY LITERATURE

A solid, if now dated, overview of Buber's influence on psychotherapy is Maurice Friedman, *The Healing Dialogue in Psychotherapy* (London: Jason Aronson, 1985). For an intelligent discussion of the centrality of the Buber–Jung dispute by a Jungian analyst, see Barbara Stephens, "The Martin Buber–Carl Jung Disputations: Protecting the Sacred in the Battle for the Boundaries of Analytical Psychology," *Journal of Analytical Psychology* 46, no. 3 (2001): 455–91.

A leading psychoanalyst argues that Buber's (and Gabriel Marcel's) theory can revitalize an aging psychoanalysis: see Paul Marcus, *Psychoanalysis as a Spiritual Discipline: In Dialogue with Martin Buber and Gabriel Marcel* (London: Routledge, 2021). Buber's enduring influence on counseling psychology may be seen in Matthew Martin and Eric W. Cowan, "Remembering Martin Buber and the I–Thou in Counseling," *Counseling Psychology*, May 8, 2019, https://ct.counseling.org/. Alan Flashman incorporates Buber's concept of dialogue in his *Family Therapies for the 21st Century: Mutuality-Based Theory and Practice* (Chisinau, Moldova: Lap Lambert Academic Publishing, 2022).

15

Martin Buber: Education toward Humanism

ASLAUG KRISTIANSEN

> The teacher must show the pupil the direction. He must point the way. But the pupil must make the journey himself.
>
> MARTIN BUBER

Since the turn of the millennium, European higher education has been under the sway of the so-called Bologna Process of 1999, adopted by no fewer than forty-nine countries from across the planet. The objective of the document is to restructure university education in order to accommodate a competitive economy and global labor market by facilitating students' mobility and employability across borders.[1] Acknowledging the imperious dictates of the regnant market economic, the educational reforms envisioned by the Bologna Process have had a profound effect not only on higher education but also on all levels of public education.[2] The overarching objective was to render education more efficient, transparent, and standardized to meet the challenges of the global market economy.[3]

The Bologna reforms advocate quality control mechanisms such as standardized tests to evaluate students' achievements as well as to assess teachers' pedagogical effectiveness. A marked consequence of these tests is to direct both teachers' and students' attention and educational horizon toward achieving the highest possible scores. As a consequence, there is an ever-increasing concern among educators that this focus weakens education as a humanizing process. For when education is ruled by a strictly rational and competitive calculus, the uniqueness of individual students and their distinctive intellectual resources may be overlooked and neglected,[4] if not utterly suppressed. But the supreme pedagogical task should be to create a safe, nonthreatening educational environment and support for individual students. Indeed, it has been observed that "when students fear failure, seeing themselves as competing against one another, and lacking the support necessary for additional growth, they often hesitate to voice questions and admit being confused."[5]

Buber's writings on education might be read as addressing this quandary. In his two central articles on pedagogy and education of character, he emphasized the importance of inclusion and trust as fundamental to teaching.[6] The most "inward achievement" of the relation between the teacher and pupil, he writes, is for the teacher to be able to win "the child's trust" and to gain the child's "confidence."[7]

Buber understands interpersonal trust as the primordial existential reality of a child embraced by a mother's "dialogical" love:

> A child lying with half-closed eyes waiting for his mother to speak to him. But many children do not need to wait, for they know that they are unceasingly addressed in a dialogue which never breaks off. In face of the lonely night which threatens to invade, they lie preserved and guarded, invulnerable, clad in the silver mail of trust.[8]

The maternal relationship of trust has an "effect" beyond the relationship itself and will influence the child's encounter with the world. Findings from child psychology show that a basic trust is established in relation to caregivers at an early age and is crucial for a child's further development of identity. *Failure* in this early stage entails serious consequences for the child's psychological well-being, identity, and views on life.[9] Trust equips the child with a safety mechanism that enables life in a world of uncertainty and potential threats.[10]

In consonance with these presuppositions, Buber continues and emphasizes the role of the teacher:

> Trust, trust in the world, because this human being exists—that is the most inward achievement of the relation in education. Because this human being exists, meaninglessness, however hard pressed you are by it, cannot be the real truth. Because this human being exists, in the darkness the light lies hidden, in fear salvation, and in the callousness of one's fellow men the great Love.[11]

Some children arrive on the first day of school with a basic trust. Other children lack this experience, and for some a teacher can become a very significant person in their lives. However, regardless of the child's previous experiences, a trusting relationship can provide insights characterized by optimism and hope and, as such, prevent an existential darkness from taking over. For the adolescent who is frightened and disappointed by an unreliable world, Buber observes, "confidence means the liberating insight that there is a human truth, the truth of human existence."[12] This "liberating insight" reveals that I am not alone in the world. It's a truth based in participation, and it cannot be proven or measured. Like faith, it can be lived and shared, and it contributes to certainty toward the future.[13] Trust provides the strength to reach out to others without protective emotional armor, and yet it perforce entails risk—a risk of being rebuffed, of what Buber calls "mismeeting." Existential trust thus requires the faith to bear the risk of mismeetings.

To be sure, a teacher is required to provide knowledge, which is often by its very nature transmitted with the conceptual categories drawn in what Buber calls the "world of It." In transmitting knowledge, the teacher perforce describes and analyzes critically the content based on objective, universal propositions of truth. But the teacher is beholden, Buber insisted, to be alert to the limits of propositional knowledge and "the relentlessly growing It-world [that] grows over him like weeds" whereby he is liable to lose his attunement to his and his student's existential "actuality."[14] The formulation suggests that in performing their responsibility to transmit knowledge of the It-World, teachers court the danger of boxing themselves into a particular perception of their students in accord with their "objective" expectations and the students' academic record, blinding them, as it were, to the existential reality and distinctive intellectual rhythm of their students. Jean-Jacques Suurmond writes: "[T]he ego imprisons the other in a picture which it has formed from earlier experiences. So, the others are not really encountered in the here and now since the pictures from the past stand as a screen between the two of them."[15] A dynamic relation is hindered by "the pictures from the past."

From this dialogical perspective, Buber gave particular attention to the education of character. In the teaching of mathematics, Buber writes, there are right and wrong answers, but the education of character demands of the teacher a process of self-reflection. It is a subjective process that must consider the pupil's "whole" being and freedom. The pupil must voluntarily take part in the process and at his own cadence. It thus presupposes a relationship of trust. The pupil believes that the teacher wishes him well and is "not making a business out of him, but is taking part in his life, accepting him before desiring to influence him."[16]

In nurturing the pupil's trust, Buber writes, the teacher does not need to be a moral paragon but must act wholeheartedly and be wholly attentive to the existential reality of others, "affecting them most strongly and purely when he has no thought of affecting them." What is most crucial is not the teacher's objective pedagogical goals, competence in the subject, or teaching methods, but rather the teacher's human, dialogical trustworthiness. In this regard, Buber emphasizes the importance of being truthful and existentially present in the encounter with students, writing that "it is not the educational intention, but it is the meeting which is educationally fruitful."[17] The teacher can be a "forceful presence" in pupils' lives sometimes even without knowing it. In a conversation with a group of teachers at his home in Jerusalem, Buber attested: "I consider the profession of teaching the most important [responsibility] in human society. [. . .] The teacher can have an influence. And the most effective way to influence a pupil is through example. Not an overt example but unconsciously, without any didactic intention."[18] The teacher can also be a "forceful presence" when expressing a welcoming gesture, a friendly smile, or by listening in empathetic silence.

Trust in their teacher grants the students the "strength" to ask questions that matter to them.[19] Responding entails responsibility to listen to—and not just hear—their questions, and so doing, the teacher does not determine the correct answer or dictate what is right or wrong. In this regard Buber differs radically from what Paulo Freire characterizes as a "banking pedagogy" inspired by "the banking system," an approach to learning, according to bell hooks (1994), that is rooted in the notion that what all students need to do is to consume information fed to them by a professor, memorize and store it.[20] For Buber, the pedagogical responsibility beckons the teacher to share with the students self-reflection, mutual curiosity, and open inquiry. Teaching is thus a *dialogical responsibility*.

In a 1934 lecture, Buber dilated on the difference between dialogue as understood in the Hebrew and Greek traditions. The Socratic dialogue works more like a game that reveals ignorance and does not ask "real questions" of an existential nature. In the Hebrew tradition, according to Buber, teaching is conceived of as personality-forming, thus weaving together learning and life experience. Hence the "real questions" do not primarily concern subjects and facts. The "real questions" aim to bring the student to greater clarity about existence.[21] The decisive shaping of the student's character occurs in these dialogical processes of mutual trust. The mutuality of the relationship also renders the teacher a learner. Teachers who listen might not only learn about their students but also about themselves as teachers and their own existential "trustworthiness."[22]

Even if the dialogical mutuality of the teacher and pupil relationship is crucial for the nurturing of character, the teacher's part in their dialogue is informed by what Buber calls "inclusion" (*Umfassung*). The German term denotes enclosing by a hedge or fence.[23] The idea "enclosed with a hedge" is metaphorically demonstrated by Buber's story about a teacher that enters the classroom for the first time and "the class before him is like the mirror of mankind."[24] The educator finds himself in front of a diversity of faces and individual stories. Some voices are louder than others. Some voices are hardly audible. But the attentive teacher looks across the group of pupils, and "the glance of the educator accepts and receives them all."[25] The teacher accepts them as they are in their otherness. However, the acceptance also includes a trust of a becoming.[26] The teacher meets each of the students with a confirmative "yes" to their respective histories and realities: "a Yes which allows him to be, and which can come to him only from one human person to another."[27] Wayne Veck and Michael Hall describe the teacher's confirmation in the encounter with the pupils as a choice "to turn to them, to welcome and to confirm them in the distinctiveness of their becoming."[28] The teacher has "enclosed them with a hedge," secured in trust and acceptance in all their otherness.

Inclusion in the student encounter involves for the teacher "a twofold gesture," a swinging over to the side of the other and living through "a common event from the standpoint of the other" without losing their own ground. The experience is not a fusion of horizons. Buber describes the actions as both "being bound to the other side" and "limited of otherness."[29] In "imagining the real"—the felt reality of the students—the teacher is engaged in an act of "self-education." According to Maurice Friedman, "imagining the real means to imagine and to some extent experience what another is at this very moment, wishing, feeling, perceiving, thinking, not as a detached content but in his very reality."[30] To be sure, it is often easier to resort to a fantasy than to try to make present the reality of the distinct other. But imagining the real demands an existential, primal distance, acknowledging "the otherness" of the person, as "something that refuses to be owned and cannot be given up," as Veck puts it.[31]

The inherent asymmetry attendant to the primal distance of dialogical relationships is bridged by trust. In this respect, the pupil and the teacher are not equals; the asymmetry of their relationship is all the greater, for the pupil is unable—certainly not called upon—to "imagine" the existential reality of the teacher.[32] There is also a difference in terms of trust. While the student's trust in the teacher is implicit to the classroom situation, the teacher's trust in the student is "the trust that he—the student—will become what he will become."[33] The former may be said to be sociological, at least initially; the latter emphatically existential.

In sum, Buber's philosophy of education may be deemed a crucial correction to the prevailing ethos of the Bologna Process, wedded to the utility ethos of the market economy. In stark contrast, Buber's pedagogical point of departure is the quotidian existential reality that teachers share with their students. They stand in front of the classroom, see all the faces before them, and are thus mandated to garner and nurture their trust—their trust in the teacher and ultimately in themselves, as noted in the epigraph to this essay: "The teacher must show the pupil the direction. He must point the way. But the pupil must make the journey himself." In conjunction with providing students with knowledge and the technical and analytical skills necessary for the journey, teachers point not only to "the way" to be taken, but must also embody and exemplify "the I-Thou attitude," a dialogical orientation ensuring one's own existential integrity as well as that of others along the uncharted path of life's destiny. One cannot avoid nor should one ignore the pragmatic exigencies of the It-World, but one must be ever alert to the peril of allowing instrumental reason to define the value and meaning of life. By personifying a dialogical attentiveness and respect for the existential dignity of each student placed in their care, teachers bequeath to them an attitudinal compass to ensure that the path taken enhances their personal flourishing and, pari passu, ennobles their humanity.

Notes

1. On the European Higher Education Area and Bologna Process, see http://www.ehea.info/page-ministerial-conference-bologna-1999.

2. Stefan Thomas Hopmann, "No Child, No School, No State Left Behind: Schooling in the Age of Accountability," *Curriculum Studies* 40, no. 3 (2008): 417–56.

3. Jelmer Evers and René Kneyber, eds., *Flip the System: Changing Education from the Ground Up* (London: Routledge, 2011).

4. See Zygmunt Bauman, *Modernity and the Holocaust* (Cambridge: Polity Press, 1989), 102–4.

5. Sara L. Shady and Marion Larson, "Insights from Martin Buber," *Educational Theory* 60, no. 1 (February 2010): 89.

6. Martin Buber, "Education," in Buber, *Between Man and Man* (London: Macmillan, 1947), 83–103; Buber, "The Education of Character," in Buber, *Between Man and Man*, 104–17.

7. Buber, "Education," 98; Buber, "Education of Character," 106.

8. Buber, "Education," 98.

9. Erik H. Erikson, *Childhood and Society* (New York: W. W. Norton, 1993), 218; Jean Liedloff, *The Continuum Concept: In Search of Happiness Lost* (1981; London: Penguin, 1986), 33–35; Donald Winnicott, here from M. Davis and D. Wallbridge, *Frihed og grænser: En introudktion til D. W. Winnicott* (English, 1969; Copenhagen: Hans Reitzel, 1988), 56.

10. Anthony Giddens, *The Consequences of Modernity* (Stanford, CA: Stanford University Press, 1990), 94.

11. Buber, "Education," 98.

12. Buber, "Education of Character," 106.

13. Buber, "What Is Man?," in *Between Man and Man*, 142.

14. Martin Buber, *I and Thou*, trans. Walter Kaufmann (New York: Free Press, 2024), 95–96.

15. Jean-Jacques Suurmond, "Beyond Buber: Gestalt Therapy in the Light of Levinas," 69.

16. Buber, "Education of Character," 104–5, 106.

17. Buber, "Education of Character," 104–5, 107.

18. Aubrey Hodes, *Martin Buber: An Intimate Portrait* (New York: Viking, 1971), 124.

19. Buber, "Education of Character," 107.

20. bell hooks, *Teaching to Transgress: Education as the Practice of Freedom* (London: Routledge, 1994), 14.

21. Martin Buber, "Interrogations by Martin Buber: Conducted by Maurice Friedman," in

Philosophical Interrogations, ed. Beatrice and Sydney Rome (New York: Holt, Reinhart & Winston, 1964), 53, 68, 53, 68.

22. Wayne Veck and Michael Hall, "Inclusive Research in Education: Dialogue, Relations and Methods," *International Journal of Inclusive Education* 24, no. 10 (2018): 1081–96, doi:10.10 80/13603116.2018.1512659.

23. John Brynhildsen, *Tysk-norsk ordbok* (Oslo: Aschehough, 1926), 958.

24. Buber, "Education of Character," 112.

25. Buber, "Education," 94.

26. Buber, "Education of Character," 112.

27. Buber, "Distance and Relations," 61.

28. Veck and Hall, "Inclusive Research," 1090.

29. Buber, "Education," 97, 101.

30. Maurice Friedman, "Becoming Aware: A Dialogical Approach to Consciousness," *Humanistic Psychologist* 24, no. 2 (1996): 215.

31. Wayne Veck, "Martin Buber's Concept of Inclusion as a Critique of Special Education," *International Journal of Inclusive Education* 17 (2013): 621.

32. Buber, "Education," 100–101.

33. Buber, "Interrogations," 67.

Annotated Bibliography

Some foundational articles that provide a theoretical and philosophical introduction to Buber's views on education are Ernst Simon, "Martin Buber, the Educator," in *The Philosophy of Martin Buber*, edited by P. A. Schilpp and M. Friedman (London: Cambridge University Press: Open Court, 1967), 543–76, and Adir Cohen, "Martin Buber and Changes in Modern Education," *Oxford Review of Education* 5, no. 1 (1979): 81–103.

See also Robert Assagoli, Heinz-Joachim Heydorn, and Richard M. Hutchins, "Interrogations of Martin Buber [on Education]," in *Philosophical Interrogations*, edited by Sidney Chester Rome and Beatrice Rome (New York: Holt, Rinehart & Winston, 1964), 61–68. For an exchange on fundamental questions of education, in which Buber notes that "true education is never in vain, even if the hour makes it appear so" and that "the first task of the educator" is to acknowledge "the pain" of students, to keep it alive, and to "awaken the longing" to be addressed, and hence, "our most pressing task is to educate educators," see F. H. Hillard, "A Re-Examination of Buber's Address on Education," *British Journal of Educational Studies* 21, no. 1 (1973): 40–49. See also Juliane Jacobi, introduction to *Martin Buber Werkausgabe*, vol. 8, *Schriften zu Jugend, Erziehung und Bildung* (Gütersloh: Gütersloher Verlagshaus, 2005), 11–76. Joshua Weinstein provides an overview of Buber's concept of dialogue as it applies to adult education in his "The Philosophy of Martin Buber: A Keystone of Adult Education in Israel," *Lifelong Learning: The Adult Years* (April 1970): 8–9, 32–35.

Wayne Veck presents a succinct appraisal of the significance of Buber's concept of "inclusion" for education: "Martin Buber's Concept of Inclusion as a Critique of Special Education," *International Journal of Inclusive Education* 17, no. 6 (2013): 614–28.

On the pedagogical challenge of establishing trust between a teacher and students, see Aslaug Kristiansen, "How to Develop a Culture of Trust in Schools? Insights from Martin Buber's Philosophy of Dialogue," *Critique and Humanism: Journal for Human and Social Studies*

26 (2008): 95–108. On the ethical dimension of teacher-student "dialogical" relation, see Aslaug Kristiansen, "The Interhuman Dimension of Teaching: Some Ethical Aspects," in *Martin Buber and the Human Sciences*, edited by M. Friedman (Albany: State University of New York Press, 1996), 215–23. Buber's concept of dialogue plays a seminal role in peace education: W. J. Alexandre Guilherme Morgan, "I and Thou: The Educational Lessons of Martin Buber's Dialogue with the Conflicts of His Time," *Educational Philosophy and Theory* 44, no. 9 (2012): 979–96. In an exchange with Aubrey Hodes, Buber ruminates on what constitutes a good education and pedagogy: see *Martin Buber: An Intimate Portrait* (New York: Viking Press, 1971), 117–29.

PART FOUR

Interfaith Dialogue

Introduction

PAUL MENDES-FLOHR

Religious faith, Buber taught, has its foundation in "the bond of being with being," the bond of I and Thou. Bereft of this bond, all religious concepts and practices are vacuous. The bond of being is not properly called faith but is established by virtue of a relationship to God, a relationship that does not remove one to the transcendent, otherworldly heights of the spirit; on the contrary, it preeminently unfolds in the matrix of everyday life. So conceived, religious faith does not begin in one's inner life but is constituted by a mode of being in the world whereby one enters into a relation with the presence (*Gegenwart*) of the other and in consonance with the presence of God. In the I-Thou relationship, one does not *experience* but *meets* the other.

Judaism, then, exists to give witness to this religious reality—a reality that is "not the prerogative of any particular religion."[1] Divine revelation is not the privileged knowledge of any religion; "it does not flash from the clouds, but [...] whispers to us in the course of every ordinary day, and it is alive quite near us, quite close"[2]

In interfaith dialogue, Buber thus sought to lead the exchange beyond supersessionist theology and claims to privileged, divinely revealed knowledge. While respecting the distinctive language of the various faith communities—in particular Christian and Asian—he rather understood the I-Thou encounter as a sharing of the witness to the universal ground of religious faith.

Though he extended his ecumenical gaze to the Far East, even to the extent of learning basic Chinese, Buber's consideration of the Islamic witness to faith was at best exiguous. As Khaled Furani gently and respectfully notes, this neglect was not only inconsistent with Buber's irenic, interfaith commitment, but rather surprising given his resolve to foster Jewish-Arab understanding.

Moreover, as Furani observes, Buber would have found in Islamic teachings eloquent testimonies in support of his philosophy of dialogue.

Notes

1. Martin Buber, "Religion as Presence," in Rivka Horwitz, *Buber's Way to "I and Thou": The Development of Buber's Thought and His "Religion as Presence" Lectures* (Philadelphia: Jewish Publication Society, 1988), 112.

2. Buber, "Preface of 1923," in Buber, *On Judaism*, ed. Nahum N. Glatzer (New York: Schocken Books, 1976), 6.

16

Buber and Christianity

KARL-JOSEF KUSCHEL

Many Christians like to quote the following words from Buber's *Two Types of Faith*:

> From my youth onwards I have found in Jesus my great brother. That Christianity has regarded and does regard him as God and Savior has always appeared to me a fact of highest importance which, for his sake and my own, I endeavor to understand. [. . .] I am more than ever certain that a great place belongs to him in Israel's history of faith and that this place cannot be described by any of the usual categories. Under history of faith, I understand the history of the human part, as far as known to us, in that which has taken place between God and man. Under Israel's history of faith, I understand accordingly the history of Israel's part as far as known to us, in that which has taken place between God and Israel. There is a something in Israel's history of faith which could only be understood from Israel, just there is a something in the history of Christian faith which is only to be understood from Christianity. The latter I have touched only with the unbiased respect of one who hears the Word.[1]

A remarkable statement indeed by a Jewish thinker, published in 1950, five years after the horror of the Shoah. Christian interpreters understood it as confirmation of their faith in Jesus Christ and appropriated it accordingly. Caution is advised, however. Buber was more interested in the origins of Christianity than almost any other Jewish scholar. This is by no means a matter of course in view of the monstrous history of Christian contempt for Judaism and antisemitic hatred of Jews. But at the same time, Buber maintained a critical distance from this sad legacy. From the very beginning of his publications on Judaism, Buber portrayed Jesus of Nazareth as a representative figure in the history of the Jewish faith, as can be read in the three Prague

"Addresses on Judaism" published in 1911.[2] He starts from the elementary fact that Christians embrace in their faith Jesus of Nazareth, who was a Jew in Palestine in the first century CE. Hence, a seasoned Jewish scholar like Buber has something to say about this foundational historical moment of Christianity.

For decades, Buber held up a mirror to Christians in his statements and writings, alerting them to appreciate the historical and cultural origins of Jesus. Christian scholars have, in turn, learned to ask new and more radical questions about what is originally "Christian," if not the figure of Jesus himself, who called upon his disciples to heed the proclamation of the "kingdom of God." If you meet the historical Jesus, you meet Judaism. But can everything that Christians believe in "in Jesus" as the Son of God and Redeemer be reconciled with the proclamation of the Jew Jesus?

Buber's questions about the Christian belief in Jesus as Christ are exactingly formulated and pursued in *Two Types of Faith* regarding salvation "in" Christ. Did not this belief, which commenced with Paul and John, remove Jesus from the historical context of his message of the imminent approach of the messianic "Kingdom of God"? Wasn't the man from Nazareth separated from his Jewish origins over the centuries under the influence of a Gentile culture? And what price has "Christianity" paid for dehistoricizing Jesus and, under the influence of Hellenistic culture, developing the doctrine of the divinity of Christ? Would Jesus himself have countenanced and understood his deification? What's more, hasn't the image of Jesus Christ disfigured the imageless, transcendent God? Is not the consequence of the doctrine of *extra Ecclesiam nulla salus* a profoundly questionable division of humanity into believers and unbelievers, redeemed and damned, saved and lost? Anyone who, as a Christian, meets Buber as a Christian is challenged by such questions.

And any Christian who is cognizant of the historical origins of the Jew Jesus inexorably asks such questions and thus must confront the dark legacy of the church's supersessionist theology of Israel and contempt of postbiblical Judaism and Jewry. After the horror of the Shoah, a revision of the church's relation to the people of Israel has become a theological imperative. Not the least under the influence of Jewish thinkers like Buber, the church has increasingly acknowledged that faith in Christ has engendered a ruthless theological contempt of Judaism: a fatal theology of disinheritance and replacement. How "naturally" the church declared Israel, "God's people," as "disinherited"; it rejected and even killed the Messiah from Nazareth; and, after the destruction of the temple in Jerusalem in AD 70, it declared the Jews allegedly "punished" by God with "scattering" among the peoples of the world and therefore "damned" to a shadowy existence, wandering uneasily across the earth. And how naturally the church assumed that it had replaced

Israel as the people of God, *verus Israel*. Accordingly, conversion and baptism of Jews were expected, and offensive missions to the Jews were initiated. What does Buber have to say about this?

Buber Offers a Dialogue with Christians

On January 14, 1933, the eve of Hitler's ascension to power, Buber engaged in a dialogue in Stuttgart with the theologian Karl Ludwig Schmidt. Since 1929 Schmidt had served as a professor of New Testament studies at the Protestant Theological Faculty of the University of Bonn. A member of the Social Democratic Party since 1924, he was politically an opponent of the National Socialists and theologically an opponent of the "German Christians," that is, the German Protestants who aligned Christian spirituality with Nazi ideology. Hence, in engaging Schmidt in debate about Judaism and its relation to the church, Buber was not confronted by an inveterate Nazi or a fanatical German nationalist. Schmidt's Christian theology of Israel was, however, deeply rooted in the tradition of Protestant theology since Martin Luther.

Though beholden to the teachings of Luther, Schmidt did not lack respect for Buber as a thinker and person, nor did he lack appreciation for Israel as "God's chosen people."[3] But Schmidt makes it clear from the outset: The "kingdom of God" that Jews and Christians await together is "in the history of God with his people as his church is once and for all realized in the Jew Jesus of Nazareth as the Messiah of the Jews and Redeemer of the world." Schmidt therefore affirmed in all candor the Christian "mission" to the Jews. The mission is not to be construed as "propaganda and agitation" but rather as the "self-representation and self-determination of the church, which as [the true] Israel seeks for Jews and Gentiles alike."[4]

Schmidt thus made it clear that he engaged in the dialogue with Buber as a representative of *verus Israel*. This and only this is decisive for him when it comes to an exchange with a Jewish partner. Schmidt, however, has not ignored the fact that the "fight against Judaism" in Germany in 1933 has long since been waged on a different level—on the basis of "a national and state ideology" whereby "Judaism was separated from the Israel of the Old and New Covenants" and had become a fight against Jewry—a fight that was pari passu also "a fight against the substance of the church." Schmidt had long recognized that the confrontation with Judaism in Germany was no longer conducted on the basis of the Bible but lamentably on the basis of a Germanic-Aryan national ideology, which he held filled the ideological vacuum created by the extensive secularization and ergo de-Christianization of the German public. And by defaming "Israel," the church's claim to be the true Israel was also affected. The Protestant theologian nonetheless also assumed, as a matter of course, that Jews differ not only "from the Christian church as a Mosaic synagogue," but also as "a nationality and race [*volkshaft-rassisch*] from citizens of other ethnic origins. [. . .] It would be an ostrich policy to attempt to deny the racial biological [*rassenbiologische*] and racial hygienic [*rassenbiologische*] problems with existence of Jews among other people."[5] Yet, he only complains vehemently that "the Jewish question" is now exclusively "treated as a question of race."

For Schmidt, reducing the Jewish question to a "racial dispute" means minimizing it. Why? Because Judaism "in the eyes of the Christian church carries a claim" that is "related to its character as Israel, as the people of God." And "only the church of Jesus Christ, which for its part claims" to be "the true Israel," is capable of "responding to the claim of Judaism" to continue to be God's chosen, "not to trivialize the claim but to take it so seriously that it honors [Buber] with a discussion that corresponds to the dignity of Judaism, which sees itself as Israel."[6]

Schmidt thus sought to focus the dialogue on the theological issue that divides the Christian church and Judaism. Christian confession, he underscores, is born of Israel's rejection of the Messiah Jesus of Nazareth. World history as God's history, as salvation history, can only be understood from this caesura. Yet the church of Jesus Christ, which is sure of itself as the true Israel, does not see Judaism as a danger, as do the votaries of German racial nationalism, because Judaism as Israel is inevitably on its way to the church.[7]

Why Jesus Cannot Be the Messiah

In his response to Schmidt, Buber acknowledges the theological divide between the church and Judaism. He is well acquainted with the Christian supersessionist doctrine, which has been handed down for centuries and is anchored in Christology. His partner in Stuttgart had merely reiterated it. The church sees Israel "as a being rejected by God," Buber notes, and this depravity necessarily results from the "church's claim to be the true Israel." Those "of Israel then lost their claim because they did not recognize Jesus as the Messiah."[8] And indeed, Buber affirms unequivocally:

> If we wish to formulate the division between Jews and Christians, between Israel and the Church, we can say: "The Church stands on the belief that with the advent of Christ salvation is bestowed upon all mankind. We Israel cannot believe that." [. . .] As we know that there is air that we breathe into our

lungs, that there is space in which we move, deeper, more genuinely do we know [. . .] that the world has not yet been redeemed. We feel [spüren] the unredeemed world.[9]

It is precisely "this feeling of ours," Buber continues, that the church is beckoned to understand. To be sure, the church sees our refusal to believe in Jesus's messiahship "either as a refusal to believe, as a stubbornness in a very dubious sense, or as a ban, as a fundamental limitation of the ability to recognize reality, as Israel's blindness, preventing it from seeing the light." But as a Jew, Buber attests to the belief that "the redemption of the world is inviolably one for us with the completion of creation—in which there will no longer be the disabled, no longer the suffering of the contradictions [of earthly existence], [and instead] the realization of the unity in all the diversity of the world." Furthermore, "we are not able to grasp an anticipation of realized redemption of the world in any part, such as a salvation of the soul, although in our mortal hours redemption and being redeemed make themselves known to us."[10]

Nor was Buber under any illusion about the upshot of the dialogue with the Christian theologian: "The knowledge of the church about Israel and Israel's self-knowledge are opposed to one another in a way that is stricter in their opposition than a mere logical contradiction."[11]

A Theology of Alterity

But at this juncture, Buber radically shifted the direction of the dialogue. Instead of sharply confronting Christian claims with Jewish counterclaims, he now brought another category into play: the category of "otherness." He no longer responded to Christian exclusivism with a Jewish one. He well realized the church's view of Judaism was beyond argument. "Verbal duels" cannot gainsay religious convictions and, indeed, can only yield what the poet Heinrich Heine in his brilliant satire of interfaith "Disputations" (in his volume of poetry *Romanzero* of 1852) bitingly characterized as a vacuous rehearsal by know-it-alls of irreconcilable dogmatic proclamations, what Buber would call mismeetings.

As a believing Jew, Buber could only attest to an inner knowledge of Israel's spiritual patrimony of God's covenantal election:

> We Israel know about Israel from within, in the darkness of knowledge from within, in the light of knowledge from within. We know Israel differently [than those who stand outside our inner reality]. We know (here I can no longer even say "see," because we know Judaism from within, and not with

the "eye of the spirit," but in terms of life) that we have sinned a *thousandfold*, we who have sinned a thousandfold, we who fallen from God a thousand times, we who have experienced God's providence [*Schickung*] over the millennia—the punishment is too light to call it such, it is something greater than punishment—we know that we have not yet been rejected. We know that what we have experienced is not conditioned by the worldly reality, but rather by the space between God and us. And we know that in this reality we are not rejected by God, that God's hand holds us in this discipline and chastisement and does not let go, holds us into this fire and does not let us fall.[12]

Buber took a first step in a Jewish-Christian religious dialogue that had been unusual up to then: he clearly distanced himself from an exclusive Christian point of view, and yet he did not replace the Christian with a Jewish exclusivism. He knew there was a "fundamentally different, incompatible, fundamentally different knowledge" of "Israel" that separated Judaism and the church once and for all. For this fundamental difference cannot be eliminated by man. One can "wait for" this reversal, of course, but it must come from God, if it comes at all. Until then, Buber advocated a theology of alterity, whereby one affirmed one's otherness in the face of those who would challenge and question it.

Mutual Recognition of the Mystery of God

With all the enduring basic differences between Judaism and the church, "down to the most fundamental roots of faith," there would seem to be no more to be said. What follows in Buber's statement during the Stuttgart dialogue is a theologically innovative advance that will have major consequences. Buber proceeds accordingly cautiously. It's as if he's slowly, step by step, approaching his core message. We want to follow him.

So where do we go from here? Buber asks. Something "difficult," he concedes, something that must be exceedingly difficult for a religiously committed person, because it "seems to go against his relation to God," the personal religious self-understanding and deepest theological convictions. To meet the challenge, he proposed that we "accept what others believe against our existence, as opposed to their religious reality, as a mystery. We cannot judge its meaning because we do not know it from within as we know ourselves from within." Just as "no one who is not of Israel understands the mystery of Israel, no one who is not of Christianity understands the mystery of Christianity; but unknowingly they may acknowledge each other in mystery."[13] In other words: for Buber there is an irresolvable coexistence of the church and Israel in relation to God. And this coexistence is not a coincidental product of history but an expression of God's providence. From which follows the second step that Buber is now taking. The first step was the acknowledgment of the enduring otherness of each other (everyone knows about "Israel" differently); now it is the mutual acknowledgment of each one's own "mystery of God." Buber's core theological statement on the relationship between the church and Judaism has now been finally named:

> What connects Jews and Christians in all this is their shared knowledge of one thing, and from there we can also confront what is deeply separating; each true sanctuary can acknowledge the mystery of another true sanctuary. The mystery of the other is within him and cannot be perceived from the outside. No one outside of Israel knows the mystery of Israel. And nobody outside of Christianity knows the mystery of Christianity. Mutually "ignorant" of one another, they can acknowledge one another in the mystery.[14]

But why do these mysteries of God exist side by side at all? "How it is possible for the mysteries to coexist is God's mystery." We, Jews and Christians, are thus not "to shirk the reality of our faith by seeking to insinuate a togetherness despite our differences." In acknowledging our fundamental difference, "we are to share with unreserved trust what we know about the unity of God's house, by which we hope that we will someday feel surrounded without dividing walls by His unity, serving separately and yet together, until someday we will be united in the one common service, until we all become, as the Jewish New Year prayer says, 'one covenant to do His will.'"[15]

The Unbroken Covenant

For Buber, however, this mutual recognition of the different divine mysteries of Israel and the church is based on the one and only basic conviction: God's calling of Israel as his people is irrevocable. The covenant of God with "Israel" is not terminated. This brings us to the theologically most dense part of the Stuttgart dialogue of 1933. Buber presents a text of a completely different character. Now he no longer addresses the theological issues that had thus far determined the trajectory and tone of his and Schmidt's exchange. Buber now surprisingly changes the *genus litterarium*. He switches from theological reasoning to a kind of meditation. The result is a dramatic, autobiographically stylized text that has no parallel in Buber's writings:

> I live not far from the city of Worms, to which I am bound by a tradition of my ancestors; and from time to time, I go there. When I go, across, I first go to the city's cathedral. It is a visible harmony of its parts, a totality in which no part deviates from perfection. I walk around the cathedral with consummate joy, gazing at it. Then I go over to the Jewish cemetery, consisting of crooked,

> shattered, shapeless, random stones. I stand there, gaze upward from this jumble of cemetery to that glorious harmony and seem to be looking up from Israel to the church. Below, there is no semblance of form; there are only the stones and the dust beneath the stones. The dust is there no matter how thinly scattered. There lies the corporeality of man, which has turned to dust. There it is. There it is for me. There it is for me, not as corporeality within the space of this planet, but as corporeality within my memory, far into the depths of history, as far back as Sinai.
>
> I stood there, having been united with the dust, and through it with the Patriarchs. That is a memory of the transaction with God, which is given to all Jews. From this the perfection of the Christian house of God cannot separate me, nothing can separate me from the sacred history of Israel.[16]

Buber, then pausing, pensively reflects aloud.

> I stood there, experiencing everything myself; with all that this death has confronted me, all the dust, all the ruin, all the wordless misery that is mine; but the covenant has not been withdrawn from me. I lie on the ground, fallen like these stones. But it has not been withdrawn from me.[17]

Both in its narrative dramaturgy and in its substance, the text is not only a key text of Buber's narrative and eloquence, but also a key text of Buber's theology and spirituality. And with it is a challenge to both Jews and Christians.

Why Worms? It is no coincidence that Buber "meditates" on the cathedral and the Jewish cemetery of this very city. It doesn't have anything to do with the coincidental proximity of Buber's residence, Heppenheim an der Bergstrasse, because Worms is for Judaism not just any city. The oldest synagogue on German soil is in Worms, completed in 1034. The Jewish cemetery is considered to be the oldest preserved in Europe. The city had already become a center of Jewish learning in the Middle Ages. Its great reputation had to do with a young man who studied there around 1060 and who was later to achieve world fame as one of the most important rabbinic scholars: Rabbi Salomon Ben Isaak (1040–1105), from French Troyes in Champagne, known as "Rashi." His interpretations of the Hebrew Bible are studied to this very day, and his commentary on the Babylonian Talmud has enduring normative significance. The *Heiliger Sand*—the holy earth—of the cemetery also bears a legendary reputation, with around two thousand gravestones in a history spanning almost a thousand years. The oldest surviving tombstone refers to the year 1058/59!

And the cathedral? Its long building history also dates to the beginning of the eleventh century, when Burchard was named bishop of the imperial city of Worms in the Holy Roman Empire. He had a cross-shaped basilica built, with two semicircular east and west choirs, that was inaugurated in 1018 in the presence of the then emperor, Heinrich II (1014—24). A hundred years later, under Bishop Burchard II, a new structure was built, which largely corresponds to today's cathedral and even then had the enormous spatial dimensions that make the cathedral to this day (reinforced by extensions) a powerful building. It represents the unity of the Holy Roman Empire, and the only comparable imperial cathedrals are those of Speyer and Mainz. It is thus no coincidence that Buber speaks of a "visible harmony of its parts, a totality in which no part deviates from perfection."

Worms Cathedral and cemetery. What Buber has sketched here is an original *Ecclesia-Synagoga* diptych of his own. At first glance, the text seems slightly kitschy, which undoubtedly has to do with the dominance of the autobiographical "I": "I live," "I transform," "I stood there," "I am lying on the ground." But both stylistically and in terms of content and symbolism, the whole text is extremely well crafted. On the one hand, this is due to the visual axis drawn by Buber and the resulting contrasting juxtaposition of "dome" on the one hand and "cemetery" on the other: harmony here, tangle there. What is meant, however, is not a confirmation of Christian triumph over defeated Judaism. That would be a grotesque misunderstanding. Buber's point is more subtle and subversive at the same time, because the Jewish cemetery with the "crooked, shattered, shapeless, random stones" undermines every possible Christian triumph of salvation simply by its sheer existence. No place could make more visible than this, with the dust and the stones, how unredeemed the world is. As a counterpart to the Christian "claim," it is at the same time its denial. Certainly, from an aesthetic perspective the speaker can delight in beholding the wholeness and perfection of the Christian edifice without reservation, but as soon as he changes perspective, from a historical perspective the cemetery proves to be a disruptive dialectical contrast to the image of perfection, a rupture in harmony, a fragment in its "wholeness." In short: With this cemetery, "Israel" holds up the mirror of an unredeemed world to the church.

A second dimension of meaning is added. The cemetery is not only a "scene" of Jewish destiny, but also a time shaft into the "depths of history." The speaker of this text is able to descend from today into primeval times, into the time of the "primeval fathers," Noah, Abraham, Isaac, Jacob, Joseph, "up to Sinai." A connection is created, a breathtaking timeline: Worms–Sinai. Why is this axis possible? Because one belongs to a people and has entrusted oneself to a God who has spoken to one's primeval fathers and primeval mothers. This is what is meant when the speaker speaks of the "God-time" of Israel. For those who participate in this time, the temporal barriers disappear, the spaces merge. One has a personal relationship with Abraham then, as one has today. As a Jew, one has a personal connection to everything that happened in the history of Israel. One experienced oneself everything that happened to this people, all the death, all the dust, all the silent misery. Recalling the past happens. The forefathers? They are one's fathers and mothers, because the God of Israel spoke to them, he continues to speak to Israel. Their stories are part of the lore of a people who are my people.

But this evocation of the "depth of history" must be read again in the opposite direction toward the cathedral. In its own way, it undermines the Christian claim that so powerfully confronts the viewer in a building like Worms Cathedral. The invoked dimension of depth subverts the Christian historical witness. God spoke to "Israel" long before Christian cathedrals were even to be thought of. What is the time of Christianity compared to the time of God in Israel? "This is a remembrance of what happened with God that is given to all Jews. The perfection of the Christian realm of God cannot take me away from that, nothing can take me away from the God-time of Israel."[18]

From this follows: With this diptych of his *Ecclesia-Synagoga*, Buber has done no more or less than dialectically undermine the centuries-old pair "church-synagogue," the classic pair as it is publicly exhibited, for example, at the cathedrals in Bamberg, Freiburg, or Strasbourg, or at the cathedrals of Paris or Metz. With this couple, carved in stone sculpture, stands the victorious, triumphant *Frau Kirche*, cross-staff in hand and a reflective smile on her face, facing *Frau Synagoge*, blindfold over her eyes, clutching a broken spear, head lowered by grief, Buber dialectically shows the reversal through his perspective and meaning axis "church-cemetery": what looks small, insignificant, as mere "dust" from a human perspective, is seen from God's as unique and emblematic of the everlasting loved. And what looks so perfect on the outside must be humble before God. Why? Because there is a reason that gives Israel its unique status as God's people, which after all has not been abolished.

None of this has anything to do with the peaceful coexistence of Jews and Christians. So Buber could be thoroughly misunderstood: he does not advocate the nonbinding nature of coexistence, does not mean a pat on the back: "I am okay, you are okay!" Rather, for Buber, encounter in dialogue includes the obligation of Jews and Christians to still struggle for the truth of God that they acknowledge and affirm. Buber expressly emphasizes that, as a Jew or Christian, one cannot "shirk" one's own "reality of faith," that is, one cannot "shirk" one's own testimony of faith, which is binding on one's conscience. Every individual's own testimony of faith is "to be communicated" to another in "unreserved trust." This is the opposite of a superficial acceptance of each other's otherness or a hasty acknowledgment of each other's divine mystery, which might only provide an excuse for passivity and indifference. Rather,

Buber's commitment to dialogue is combined with adherence to one's own theological axiomatics. And for Buber this becomes concrete again and again in the dialogue between man and God, whether Jew or Christian, and in the dialogue with the respective counterpart in moments of encounter. Buber's conception of interfaith dialogue calls upon Jews and Christians for mutual humility, to be humble before God. Here, too, Buber argues theocentrically and concludes by committing both Jews and Christians to peace and practical cooperation. Both know that they are shrouded in the mystery of God, which also divides them, but which nevertheless endows them with the knowledge of the unity of the house of God and with the hope that, one day, they will be united in the one "common ministry."

Notes

1. Martin Buber, *Two Types of Faith*, trans. Norman F. Goldhawk (New York: Macmillan, 1951), 12–13.
2. Martin Buber, *On Judaism*, ed. Nahum N. Glatzer, trans. Eva Jospe (New York: Schocken Books, 1967), 11–55, esp. 45–47.
3. See, e.g., Schmidt to Buber, January 11–12, 1933, in Buber, *Briefwechsel aus sieben Jahrzehnten* (Heidelberg: Verlag Lambert Schneider, 1973), 2:460–63.
4. Martin Buber, "Kirche, Staat, Volk, Judentum. Zwiegespräch im Jüdischen Lehrhaus in Stuttgart am 14. Januar 1933," in *Martin Buber Werkausgabe*, vol. 9, *Schriften zum Christentum*, 145, 156.
5. Buber, "Kirche, Staat, Volk, Judentum," 154–55, 146.
6. Buber, "Kirche, Staat, Volk, Judentum," 147.
7. Buber, "Kirche, Staat, Volk, Judentum," 153.
8. Buber, "Kirche, Staat, Volk, Judentum," 156.
9. Buber, "Kirche, Staat, Volk, Judentum," 158.
10. Buber, "Kirche, Staat, Volk, Judentum," 158.
11. Buber, "Kirche, Staat, Volk, Judentum," 156.
12. Buber, "Kirche, Staat, Volk, Judentum," 156.
13. Buber, "Kirche, Staat, Volk, Judentum," 158.
14. Buber, "Kirche, Staat, Volk, Judentum," 158.
15. Buber, "Kirche, Staat, Volk, Judentum," 159.
16. Buber, "Kirche, Staat, Volk, Judentum," 166–68.
17. Buber, "Kirche, Staat, Volk, Judentum," 175.
18. Buber, "Kirche, Staat, Volk, Judentum," 175.

Annotated Bibliography

PRIMARY SOURCES

Buber's extensive writings—lectures, correspondence, and books—on Christianity as Judaism's sister religion are gathered and published in *Martin Buber Werkausgabe*, vol. 9, *Schriften zum Christentum*, edited and introduced with commentary by Karl-Josef Kuschel (Gütersloh: Gütersloher Verlagshaus, 2011). In 1934 Buber delivered three lectures on Christianity at the

Jüdisches Lehrhaus in Frankfurt, "Jewish and Christian Faith," "Jewish and Christian Conceptions of Redemption," and "Jewish and Christian Conceptions of Messianism." These previously unpublished German lectures, with two versions of each, are introduced and edited with a commentary by Orr Scharf in *Martin Buber Werkausgabe*, vol. 5, *Vorlesungen über Judentum und Christentum* (Gütersloh: Gütersloher Verlagshaus, 2017).

SECONDARY LITERATURE

A veritable battery of scholars posed questions probing Buber's conception of religion, divine creation, revelation, and God as person, and his distinction between biblical Judaism's concept of faith as trust in contradistinction to Pauline faith as *pistis*. See "Interrogation of Martin Buber," conducted by M. S. Friedman, in *Philosophic Interrogations*, edited by S. Rome and B. Rome (New York: Holt, Rinehart & Winston, 1964), 80–95, 108–10. Two eminent theologians—Emil Brunner of the Swiss Reformed Church and the Roman Catholic priest Hans Urs von Balthasar—wrote critical reflections on Buber's writings on Christianity for a volume addressing salient themes in Buber's oeuvre; see Paul Arthur Schilpp and Maurice Friedman, eds., *The Philosophy of Martin Buber* (LaSalle, IL: Open Court, 1967).

Hans Urs von Balthasar published a book-length appreciation of Buber before Vatican II (1962–65) when Catholic-Jewish dialogue was virtually nonexistent; see his *Einsame Zwiesprache. Martin Buber und das Christentum* (Cologne: Hegner, 1958), translated as *Martin Buber and Christianity: Dialogue between Israel and the Church*, translated by Alexander Dru (New York: Macmillan, 1961). For a post–Vatican II theological perspective on Buber's "challenge to Christianity" by Karl-Josef Kuschel, see *Martin Buber: Seine Herausforderung an das Christentum* (Gütersloh: Gütersloher Verlagshaus, 2015). The Israeli scholar of early Christianity David Flusser offers a Jewish perspective on Buber's writings on Christianity in his afterword to Buber, *Two Types of Faith*, translated by Norman P. Goldhawk (Syracuse, NY: Syracuse University Press, 2003). In this volume Buber contrasts the faith of Abraham (*emunah*, existential faith in) with the faith of St. Paul (*pistis*, doctrinal faith that). He ponders the possibilities of reconciliation between the two.

17

Martin Buber and Eastern Wisdom

HUNE MARGULIES

Martin Buber had an abiding interest in Eastern religions, particularly Chinese Taoism. In *I and Thou*, the Taoist concept of *wu-wei*, the "action of no-action" is recurrently enjoined to characterize the I-Thou relationship as a nonintentional, noncontrolling, and nonmanipulative way of being in the world. Lao-Tzu wrote, "Life is a series of natural and spontaneous changes. Don't resist them; that only creates sorrow. Let reality be reality. Let things flow naturally forward in whatever way they like." It is however an error to understand *wu-wei* as mere passivity. Buber wrote: "The I-Thou relationship is election and electing, passive and active at once. An action of the whole being...."[1] The concept of whole-being indicates that there is no distinction between the inner and the outer, between the contemplation and the deed. In Buddhist terms this is known as "unity within differentiation and differentiation within unity." It is also true that some forms of intervention in nature are consistent with the ways by which nature reveals itself to us. Zen master Dogen explained the seeming tension between passivity and activity: "The actualization of the Buddha-dharma, the vital path of its correct transmission, is like this: If you say that you do not need to fan yourself because the nature of wind is permanent and you can have wind without fanning, you will understand neither permanence nor the nature of wind." That is to say: irrespective of the fact that Buddha, or Tao, or God is everywhere and everything, we will never actualize their presence in our lives unless and until we do the deeds of Buddha, Tao, or God. By adhering to the "path" of *wu-wei*, one is spontaneously and wholly open to the moment, to the here and now, and thus utterly mindful to the "presence" of the other. Buber found in *wu-wei* an intimation of the principle that "duality" is not the same as "dualism," and from this we can derive the essential distinction that "self" is not the same as "ego."

In a lecture he gave in October 1928 at a conference of the University of Frankfurt's China Institute, Buber occasioned his elaboration of the overarching significance of *wu-wei* for the future of Western civilization. Entitling his paper "China and Us," Buber presented *wu-wei* as denoting the personal and social transformation necessary for the healing of "Western man," particularly of his spiritually and ethically debilitating subjugation to the ethics of a material and social success primed by instrumental reason and deemed the "necessary means to succeed." But "the great wisdom of China," as quintessentially distilled in the Tao concept of *wu-wei*, teaches us that genuinely "powerful existence does not yield success that can be exploited." Buber's paper was a response to the conference's opening lecture by the China Institute's director Richard Wilhelm (1873–1930), celebrated as the "Marco Polo" of the inner world of China. Wilhelm, through his translations, introduced the West to the spiritual heritage of China. The fact that Wilhelm invited Buber to respond to his paper was due to the recognition of his earlier, acclaimed writings on Chinese literature and philosophy. In 1910 Buber published German translations of "Tales and Parables of Zhuangzi," and in 1911 "Tales of Liao-Chai." At the time he was translating the Taoist texts, under the rubric of "ex Oriente lux" (light comes from the Orient), Buber sought to affirm that Judaism was too an "Oriental faith," and as such it stands in contrast to the ongoing decadence of occidental religions.[2] In particular, Buber saw in the early Hasidic movement a manifestation of the latent oriental content in Jewish spirituality, and this is important because Buber presented Judaism as a spirituality that reflects principles of practice that not only differ from occidental religions but can also serve as a fertile alternative. Buber's presentation of the Hasidic movement as an oriental spirituality was essential for his entire understanding of the Jewish faith and its role in the spiritual renewal of the world.

Buber's project was the recovery of primordial spirituality, and he found in Taoism a kindred wisdom teaching. Buber argued for a spirituality that relies entirely on the practice of the deeds of dialogue while avoiding and bypassing formulaic theologies and proscribed ritual sacraments. For Buber, the encounter with God does not depend on at its inception, nor does it engender as a response, the founding of systems of creedal and institutional religion, for the entirety of the encounter with God is the standing in the between of I and Thou.[3] Common to both Buber's understanding of the Taoist concept of *wu-wei* and early Hasidism is the rejection of the self-other *dualism* prevalent in Western thought, which, generally speaking, predilects cognition over action, and the mind over the body; hence, both eschew the *via contemplativa* to focus the spiritual quest instead on existential deeds. From a Buberian perspective we can understand "dualism" as the engagement in the interactions of I-It, while "duality," in contrast, is the standing in the between of the relationship between I and Thou. Ego is what emerges from the dualistic interactions of I-It, while the *self* is what emerges in the between of I and Thou.

There is a clear distinction between knowledge and wisdom. Knowledge belongs to the realm of I-It. *Wu-wei* implies that *wisdom* cannot be found by searching, for, in contrast to knowledge, it cannot be conceptually conceived; it can only be lived. The Hasidic master Maggid of Mezhrech once said: "Certain opportunities and potentials are so lofty, that they cannot be accessed by the conscious self, they can only come about by mistake." This is an anarchic-Tao insight taught by a follower of strict Halacha. The Tao's *wu-wei* contemplates the attaining of spiritual insights as if by mistake or accident, that is, without specified intentionality. In similar terms Zen master Dogen held that one's spiritual life is of a "continuous mistake," filled with fortuitous, unanticipated moments of enlightenment. Zen likewise speaks of *subitism*, namely a sudden, unexpected, and unintended attainment of enlightenment. One does not engage in any particular activity with the intention of becoming enlightened, as intentionality is itself a hindrance in the path. When the Buddha silently held a lotus flower in his hand, one disciple smiled and attained enlightenment. This simple event is deemed the original moment of Zen. Likewise, for Buber the life of the spirit cannot be accessed through intentional cognitive practices—be it by mystical and esoteric exercises, or religious rituals—for the spiritual life is nothing other than our everyday life lived in dialogical mindfulness.

In *I and Thou*, Buber makes a distinction between Hinduism and Buddhism.[4] He identified Hinduism with forms of mysticism that deny the basic intersubject duality necessary for relationships, but in Buddhism Buber identified a nascent form of dialogical relationships in the manner of student-teacher encounters. Zen emphasizes the practices of personal meetings between teacher and student, where in some instances verbal discourses are not required and in others, such as the case with Zen koans, conversations are purposely nonrational and filled with perplexity and humor. Nondiscursive teachings appear in all spiritual traditions. In the *Tales of the Hasidim*, Buber reports that a student would seek the presence of his master simply to observe how he ties his shoes.[5]

The encounter between Buber's dialogical philosophy and Eastern thought results in a fruitful understanding concerning two fundamental issues: the genesis and structure of events of spiritual primordiality, and the manner whereby these "moments of inception" manifest in the realm of social life. A primordial practice is one that antecedes intentionality and that cannot be purposefully reenacted. Since dialogue and meditation are primordial practices, both reject the necessity to establish institutional religious frameworks. Buber rejected the need for theologies and religious institutions. The Indian poet Rabindranath Tagore, who met with Buber on three occasions, wrote: "Go not to the temple to put flowers upon the feet of God. [. . .] Go not to the temple to pray on bended knees. First bend down to lift someone who is down-trodden." Zen poet Basho wrote: "How I long to see among dawn flowers, the face of God. [. . .] There is nothing you can see that is not a flower, there is nothing you can think that is not the moon. [. . .] The temple bell stops but I still hear the sound coming out of the flowers."[6] Buber reflected in similar terms: "The demanding silence of forms, the loving speech of human beings, the eloquent muteness of creatures—all of these are gateways into the presence of the word."[7]

Buber made a distinction between religion and religiosity and between spirit and spirituality, arguing that the dialogical relationship of I and Thou is the genuine manifestation of primordial spirituality.[8] This conception of avoidance and bypassing mirrors Zen's self-definition as a system that dispenses with theologies and rituals and which, through its practices, attains directly to the essence of the human mind.[9] It bears indicating that Zen is a confluence of Indian Buddhism and Chinese Taoism. In this sense, Buber and Zen coincide in the positing of a spiritual practice in which the entirety of its significance is contained within its practices alone, with no need for any external referent, be that a theological concurrence or a philosophical premise. Primordial practices do not require a definition of the concept of *Being*. Whatever Being is, the question is not ontological but existential. The Buddhist Heart Sutra says: "Nothing is as it seems, neither is it otherwise." In other words, ontological claims abstracted from the lived life are rooted in the errors of ego-ego dualism, that is, the I-It interaction. With Buber we can say that whatever Being may be, it is our responsibility, our responding to the presence of the other we meet that constitutes the authentic approach to existence. With Zen we can say that Being *is*, but we refrain from giving it a name. Or Being *isn't*, and we won't give it a no-name. Nagarjuna, reflecting on the issue of dualism, put it succinctly: "Nirvana is *saṃsāra* [the painful karmic cycles of life], *saṃsāra* is nirvana." The Heart Sutra also says that "form is emptiness, emptiness is form."[10] In other words: The dualism that posits two opposites is wrong, and the nondualism that posits itself as an alternative to dualism is likewise wrong, and for the same reason. Once we say Thou to a Being we realize that there is no distinction between nirvana and *saṃsāra*; there is only the "narrow bridge" of dialogical encounter. As Zen master Thich Nhat Hanh explained: "Mindfulness is above all the capacity simply to recognize the presence of an object without taking sides, without judging, and without craving or despising that object."[11] In other words, from a dialogical perspective, meditation, as practiced by Zen, teaches to cease and to avoid the saying of "It" to people and to all Beings of nature. Master Dogen said: "Handle even a single leaf of green in such a way that it manifests the body of the Buddha. This in turn allows the Buddha to manifest through the leaf."[12]

From a wisdom perspective, it is not necessary to know what the true nature of things is; what is essential is to recognize our existential task to relate to all Beings in a dialogical manner. *Wu-wei* and Zen meditative consciousness imply the denial of the instrumentalizing of the other to serve the purposes and interests of our inner *saṃsāra*'s ego. I-It interactions give birth to the ego, not to the self, while the relationship of I-Thou discovers our inborn Buddha-nature. However, as Buber said, we cannot completely avoid the realm of It, but we must determinately orient ourselves toward the reality of Thou. In one formulation Lao-Tzu described *wu-wei* as follows: "To bear and not to own, to act and not lay claim, to do the work and let it go: for just letting it go is what makes it stay." In other words, *wu-wei* is engaging the flow of nature with a proper practice, a practice we can identify as the relationship of I and Thou.

Emmanuel Levinas said that ethics is first philosophy. Ethics is not a corollary of an antecedent conception of Being but the foundation from which all philosophies are derived. From a Buberian perspective, we can say that dialogue is first practice. In contrast to classic existentialist thought, for Buber dialogue precedes existence, and only then existence precedes essence. In Buber's words: "In the beginning is the relation."[13]

Buber found that legend and folklore, such as Hasidic tales, are repositories of truths in ways that formalized philosophy or theology cannot access. With the aid of some Zen stories, we can elucidate Buber's premises concerning the difference between the *duality* of I and Thou and the ego-other *dualism* of I-It. The Buddhist Prajnaparamita speaks of two shores: the shore of enlightenment and the shore of nonenlightenment. In other words: There is the realm of I-Thou and the realm of I-It. The Buddhadharma is likened to a vessel that can ferry us from this shore to the next. That is to say: there is a practice that can lead us from within the realm of I-It to the primordial spiritual realm of the between of I-Thou. Ultimately, however, there aren't two separate shores, there is no dualism, there is only our response to the shore we find ourselves on right here and right now. To illustrate the point that two shores do not imply dualism, consider this Zen tale: A traveler wishes to cross the river but finds no vessels to navigate. Upon seeing another person on the other shore, he loudly inquired of him how he could cross the river. The person on the other shore replied: Why do you need to cross the river? To which our traveler responded: because I need to reach the other shore. The person on the other shore retorted: But you already are on the other shore![14] One important conclusion of primordiality is that since there are no two shores, the vessel is an illusionary tool, and, as such, it must be discarded lest its weight and upkeep become a hindrance. In contrast to Buber and Zen, for orthodox Judaism, the *halacha* is the vessel, and the entirety of both shores is contained within it. To discard the vessel is tantamount to discarding the word of God. For Buber, however, the *halacha* is likened to the Zen vessel; namely, it is only a tool, and as such it is a manifestation of It-ness. Buber saw formalized *halacha* as a hindrance the way Zen sees formalized dharma. Whether it is a vessel or a narrow bridge, once we say Thou to the "ten thousand things," there is nowhere we need to go.[15] Zen master Dogen said it well: "If you can't find enlightenment here and now, where else do you expect to find it? [. . .] The color of the mountains is Buddha's body, the sound of running water is his great speech." Buber said likewise, "Not the way one seeks something: in truth, there is no God-seeking because there is nothing where one could not find him."[16] A Zen story offers this same not-seeking, permeating presence insight. Zen teacher Harada Sogaku (1870–1961) said: "For forty years I've been selling water by the shores of a river. Ho, ho! My labors have been wholly without merit."[17]

It is worth relating Buber's conception of a dialogical reconstruction of society to the Buddhist concept of *saṃsāra*. Indeed, Buber's social vision might well resolve Zen's issue, first raised by Zen master Hakuin, concerning the "post-satori" status of the practitioner, that is to say, the way enlightenment manifests in the realm of the social, whereas Zen, in turn, might help Buber regarding the cultivation of I-Thou consciousness. Buber's dialogical philosophy is a social spirituality. In other words, for Buber, engagement with society is not an ancillary choice but the essential corollary of the primordial relationship of I and Thou. In the Chinese Ch'an tradition of "Pure Land," the social embodiment of dharma is the test of enlightenment. The Ch'an Buddhist teachings of Master Sheng-Yen proclaim the principle that the Buddha's mind of enlightenment is actualized in the context of the creation and establishment of a Buddha's pure land on earth.[18] Sheng-Yen speaks of humanist Buddhism and the "necessity of building a pure land on earth." Notice Sheng-Yen's use of the term "humanist Buddhism" and Buber's use of the term "Hebrew humanism." The Ch'an Pure Land school is a form of engaged Buddhism that mirrors the principles of interhuman relationships in similar terms to those found in Christian liberation theology and in Buber's philosophy of dialogue. In this context it is noteworthy to reflect on how, shortly before his untimely passing, Thomas Merton, who studied and wrote about Zen while being a

Catholic monk, remarkably shifted toward Buber's I and Thou philosophy and viewed its principles as both a challenge to "the hollowness and falsity of my life" as well as a spiritual task in which "my business is to verify Buber's spirituality with my own." Pure Land also teaches that relationships are not ancillary behaviors but primordial practices of the enlightenment project. Like Buber's becoming an I through a Thou, Sheng-Yen said, "By helping others achieve enlightenment, you achieve it yourself." In other words, by going forth one attains the goal. The teachings of Zen's Pure Land of the Buddha are vast and elaborate, including the practices of "socially engaged Buddhism" and "dharmic socialism."[19] From the perspective of Buber's engagement with the Eastern religions, the fundamental point is to recognize that the confluence between dialogue and Zen's Pure Land occurs at the existential level, even if not necessarily on philosophical principles. I-Thou dialogue represents the practice of "mindful awareness" concerning the Thou status of the other, as well as the enactment of the awakened Thou consciousness in the realm of the social. Zen master Daido Roshi said it well: "strictly speaking there are no enlightened persons, there is only enlightened activity."[20] In his *Shobogenzo*, Dogen wrote: "Arousing the aspiration for enlightenment is making a vow to bring all sentient Beings to the shore of enlightenment before you bring yourself, and actualizing the vow. Even a humble person who arouses this aspiration is already a guiding teacher of all sentient Beings."[21] There is no I before You; there are only the deeds of dialogue.

Buddhism speaks of nonattachment as a crucial component of enlightenment. It is essential to understand that I-Thou relationships are not attachments in the Buddhist sense. Attachments are I-It interactions where the participants approach their exchange from the perspective of ego. In contrast, I-Thou relationships are manifestations of the true self, or Buddha nature, and therefore they constitute the realm of enlightenment.

The fundamental dialogical principle is that God is neither in heaven nor on earth, God is neither above nor below, not within and not without, neither in the soul nor in the flesh, God is not an entity anywhere: God is presence in the meeting between an I and a Thou. From this we learn that the dialogical social praxis is itself the realm of the spiritual, as there can be no spiritual life except within the life of community. As a result of doctrinal constraints, Taoism, Buddhism, and Zen in particular do not articulate a unified answer as to how the social and economic structures of society must be designed and organized once the state of awakened consciousness is attained, nor, on a more fundamental basis, whether this state of consciousness can possibly be attained outside of a relationship with the other and the community. In some interpretations of Buddhism, particularly in the Theravada tradition, the realm of political activity is seen as one of the manifestations of *saṃsāra*, thus as a hindrance to the attainment of enlightenment. *Saṃsāra* is precisely that which needs to be overcome, and the immersion in its demands and activities not only is not conducive to enlightenment, but it effectively prevents its attainment.[22] Buber distinguished the realm of the political from the realm of the social. The political realm can be likened to *saṃsāra*, but the realm of the social is the world of relationships.

In his discussions of dialogical relationships, Buber does not speak about how to attain a state of dialogical consciousness. We may ask whether I-Thou encounters are but acts of the pure will. Buber speaks of will and grace, which in a deeper sense are manifestations of *wu-wei*. Grace, by definition, is beyond individual will, but will should lead to a decision to respond to the presence of the other grace has placed before us. The question therefore remains, How does one nurture the will to say Thou? From a Zen perspective, our existential decision-making process requires the cultivation of a guiding consciousness, one that can only be attained through the meditative practices of *zazen*. When Buber speaks of solitude as a place of purification, we can pursue this line of thought to argue that the necessary purification can be attained through Zen meditation.[23] But for Buber, one purifies oneself only to be able to return to life in the community; otherwise the purification in and of itself remains devoid of meaning. Zen might learn from Buber the outlines of the community that needs to be built for it to be a full expression of the purified mind. The Mahayana concept of the Bodhisattva is in many respects an existential manifestation of the principle that I-Thou dialogue and enlightenment are actualized in a dialogical or dharmic society.[24] Buber's libertarian socialism offers a model of community in which Zen enlightenment can be fully actualized, and Zen's meditation practices offer the opportunity to attain consciousness of the Thou status of all Beings. In terms of Buber, we should say that dialogical philosophy can fruitfully utilize the practices of Zen, as the will to recognize the Thou in the other, and that the finding of quotidian ways to enact that recognition in relationships requires more than a philosophical and volitional decision-making process. The Zen practices of meditation and mindfulness can bring an individual to the conscious recognition of the Thou in all Beings and teach its actualization in "real life." I-Thou requires awareness of the Thouness of all that exists, and Zen requires the adoption of social practices through which it can fully manifest. In terms of Zen, we should say that Zen can fruitfully adopt Buber's project of the dialogical society, for enlightenment cannot be reduced to inner states of emotional equanimity or to the attainment of inner experiences: enlightenment is a social project, and I-Thou dialogue with one another and with nature is the actual practice of enlightenment. In other words, dialogue is enlightenment manifested as the practice of relationships. Enlightenment manifests itself, naturally and organically, in the realm of dialogical relationships throughout all realms of existence.

We can subsume Buber's project by affirming that the dialogical principle is primarily an existential task and an ethical responsibility. The spiritual task is neither to reform nor to convert, but to reawaken in us those primordial dialogical moments which are the inception of the deep poetic insights that alone engender our spiritual imagination. How do we reawaken moments of inception? By returning to meet the world in the I-Thou embrace of a being and allowing that meeting to be the entirety of the practice. Ultimately, how do we know it is God we are speaking to? We know when we stop speaking of God and start doing God. The Zen of God is precisely the between of I and Thou. As Martin Buber said: "The relationship of faith is certainly no book of rules which one can consult to find what is to be done in this hour. What God demands of me in this hour, I learn, in so far as I learn it, not before this hour, but in it."[25]

Notes

1. Martin Buber, *I and Thou*, trans. Walter Kaufmann (New York: Charles Scribner's Sons, 1970), 62.

2. Paul Mendes-Flohr, "Fin-de-siècle Orientalism, the Ostjuden, and the Aesthetics of Jewish Self-Affirmation," in *Studies in Contemporary Jewish History*, ed. Jonathan Frankel (Bloomington: Indiana University Press, 1984), 96–139; see also Mendes-Flohr, "Tagore, Buber and Einstein in Dialogue" (unpublished manuscript, University of Chicago Divinity School, 2011), quoted in Abhik Roy, *Rabindranath Tagore and Martin Buber: A Meeting of Two Great Souls* (Edinburgh: Scottish Center for Tagore Studies, 2012).

3. "The encounter with God does not come to man in order that he may henceforth attend to God but in order that he may prove its meaning in action in the world. All revelation is a calling and a mission" (Buber, *I and Thou*, 164).

4. Buber, *I and Thou*, 138–42.

5. "I did not go to the Maggid of Mezhrech to learn interpretations of the Torah from him, said Aryeh Leib Sarahs (1730–91) but to note his way of tying his shoes and taking off his shoes." Martin Buber, *Tales of the Hasidim: The Early Masters*, trans. Olga Marx (New York: Schocken Books, 1961).

6. Martin Buber, "A Conversation with Tagore," in Buber, *A Believing Humanism: My Testament*, trans. Maurice Friedman (New York: Simon & Schuster, 1967), 183–85. Rabindranath Tagore, *Gitanjanali*, translated from Bengali by the author (London: Macmillan, 1914); *Basho: The Complete Haiku*, trans. Jane Reuchold (Tokyo: Kodansha International, 2008).

7. Buber, *I and Thou*, 150.

8. "Those who pronounce the severed I, wallowing in the capital letter, uncover the shame of the world spirit that has been debased to mere spirituality" (Buber, *I and Thou*, 115). "But if it is the castle of separation where man conducts a dialogue with himself, not in order to test himself and master himself for what awaits him but in his enjoyment of the configuration of his

own soul—that is the spirit's lapse into mere spirituality. And this becomes truly abysmal when self-deception reaches the point where one thinks that one has God within and speaks to him" (Buber, *I and Thou*, 152).

9. Bodhidharma (fifth–sixth century), the recognized founder of Zen Buddhism, explained the Zen practice in these terms: "A special transmission outside the scriptures, not founded upon words and letters. By pointing directly to the mind, it lets one see into one's own true nature and thus attain Buddhahood." Guo Jun, "A Special Transmission: Teachings from the Heart of the Chan Buddhist Tradition," *Buddhist Review* (Spring 2013), https://tricycle.org/magazine/special-transmission/.

10. Nagarjuna, *A Reader's Guide to the Great Master of the Perfection of Wisdom and Madhyamaka* (Boulder, CO: Shambhala Publications, 2005); *A New Heart Sutra*, trans. Thich Nhat Hanh (Loubès-Bernac, France: Plum Village, 2011).

11. Thich Nhat Hanh, *Peace Is Every Step: The Path of Mindfulness in Everyday Life* (New York: Bantam, 2022).

12. Heijei Dogen, *Treasury of the True Dharma Eye: Zen Master Dogen's Shobo Genzo*, ed. Kazuaki Tanahashi (Boulder, CO: Shambhala Publications, 2013).

13. Buber, *I and Thou*, 69.

14. *Zen Flesh, Zen Bones*, classic ed., comp. Paul Reps and Nyogen Senzaki (North Clarendon, VT: Tuttle Publishing, 2008).

15. "That the self advances and confirms ten thousand things is called delusion. That the ten thousand things advance and confirm the self is called enlightenment." Dogen, *Treasury of the True Dharma Eye*.

16. Buber, *I and Thou*, 128.

17. Harada Sogaku, quoted in Philip Kapleau, *Three Pillars of Zen* (Boston: Beacon Press, 1967), 303–4.

18. "The meaning of the Pure Land in the Human Realm indicates that the present world in which we actually live is the Pure Land. . . . When we look in the ten directions it is only the Pure Land that we see." Sheng-Yen, *A Pure Land of Earth, Thoughts and Ideas* (Taipei: Dharma Drum Mountain Cultural Center, 2002).

19. A number of Buddhist teachers, such as Buddhadasa Bikkhu, a Thai monastic in the Theravada school, have spoken of the necessity to transform society in the model of a dharmic socialist system. For Bikkhu, socialism was not only a better social and economic system, but the only societal organizing principle in which dharma could be implemented and actualized. In 1904, Japanese Pure Land priest Takagi Kenmyo wrote an essay called "My Socialism." Kenmyo's argument was that in the land of bliss, that is, the Buddha's Pure Land, the community lives in accordance with principles and practices of humanist socialism. Consider the Dalai Lama's statement concerning being "half Buddhist and half Marxist": "I am humanitarian Marxist, I am Buddhist Marxist, I am not nationalistic Marxist, I am also a socialist. Marxism and Buddhism are working in a similar line" (hhdl.dharmakara.net). A Marxism based on moral principles is not the political Marxism Lenin implemented. The Dalai Lama's formulation of socialism is similar in both content and contours to Buber's "religious socialism." Paraphrasing Buber's "Moscow or Jerusalem" (in his *Paths in Utopia*), we may say that the Dalai Lama distinguishes between Beijing and Lhasa.

20. Daido Roshi, quoted in Shunryu Suzuki, *Zen Mind, Beginner's Mind: Informed Talks on Zen Meditation and Practice* (Boulder, CO: Shambhala Publications, 2011).

21. Dogen, *Treasury of the True Dharma Eye*.

22. The ambivalence concerning political activity in the context of the pursuit of enlighten-

ment can be illustrated by the Abbott U Kay Tha Ya, who led a monastery in Yangon, Myanmar, and decided to resign his clerical vows to become fully involved in the armed struggle against his country's dictatorship: "As a monk I couldn't kill them, so I decided to become a soldier. It's like going down from heaven to hell. But I think it was necessary." "Quotation of the Day. Monks Once Led Protests. Myanmar's Coup Changed That," *New York Times*, August 28, 2021.

23. "And again there are two kinds of lonesomeness, depending on what it turns to. If lonesomeness is the place of purification which even the associate needs before he enters the holy of holies, but which he also needs in the midst of his trials, between his unavoidable failures and his ascent to prove himself that is how we are constituted" (Buber, *I and Thou*, 87).

24. A Bodhisattva is described as a practitioner who defers entry to nirvana in order to stay behind and help all beings end suffering. However, nirvana is not to be regarded as a transcendent realm of existence, but as a mode of relational deeds enacted in the here and now, on this fragile and impermanent Buddha land. The Bodhisattva dedicates his life to helping others end their suffering, and it is this dedication itself that is the life of nirvana.

25. Martin Buber, *I and Thou*, 181.

Annotated Bibliography

PRIMARY SOURCES

Martin Buber, *Schriften zu chinesischer Philosophie und Literatur*, edited by Irene Eber, *Martin Buber Werkausgabe*, vol. 2.3 (Gütersloh: Gütersloher Verlagshaus, 2014). At a time when European sinology was still in an early stage of development, Martin Buber already showed a deep understanding of some basic ideas of Chinese thought. This includes, above all, his interpretation of the Tao as transcendent and immanent at the same time, by which one becomes aware of the all-encompassing order within which the world on this side and the world to come touch. The volume, edited by the late sinologist of the Hebrew University of Jerusalem, Irene Eber (1929–2019), brings together Buber's writings on Chinese philosophy and literature, some of which had hitherto not been published.

See also Martin Buber, *Chinese Tales: Zhuanzi, "Saying and Prophets," and Chinese Ghost and Love Stories*, with an introduction by Irene Eber (Atlantic Highlands, NJ: Humanities Press, 1991). Buber's most extensive treatment of the implications and applications of his philosophy of dialogue within the *realm of the social* (in contrast to the *realm of the political*) is found in his *Paths in Utopia* (London: Routledge & Kegan Paul 1949; Syracuse, NY: Syracuse University Press, 1966). Also see Martin Buber, *Schriften zur politischen Philosophie und Sozialphilosophie: 1906–1938*, in *Martin Buber Werkausgabe*, vol. 11, pt. 1, edited with commentary by Stefano Franchini; introduction by Francesco Ferrari (Gütersloh: Gütersloher Verlagshaus, 2019).

SECONDARY LITERATURE

The following is a selection of Zen and Buddhist works that inform my discussion of the affinities between Buber and Eastern wisdom: Master Dogen Zenji's magnum opus *Shobogenzo*. Ch'an master Sheng-Yen's "The Method of No-Method" and "The Poetry of Enlightenment." Master Thich Nhat Hanh's "Interbeing: Fourteen Guidelines for Engaged Buddhism." "The True Dharma Eye: Zen Master Dogen's Three Hundred Koans," by Roshi John Daido Loori (a study of the earlier versions of the *Shobogenzo*). Theravada master Buddhadasa Bikkhu's *Dhammic Socialism*.

On the philosophical and practical convergence between Buber's philosophy of dialogue and Zen Buddhism, Taoism, and Ch'an Buddhist "Pure Land" doctrines, see Hune Margulies, *Martin Buber and Eastern Wisdom Teachings: The Recovery of the Spiritual Imagination* (Newcastle upon Tyne: Cambridge Scholars Publisher, 2022). The most direct references to Buber's approach to Taoism are found in his own writings on the topic, in particular the works quoted in the body of this essay. Jonathan R. Herman, *I and Tao* (Albany: State University of New York Press, 1966), provides an English translation of Buber's German rendition of Chuang Tzu, along with references to Buber's other essays, some unpublished, on the topic of Chinese folk tales inspired by Taoist teachings.

A number of essays have been published reviewing Buber's representation of various aspects of Buddhist and Taoist doctrines. Particularly noteworthy are Keiji Nishitani and N. A. Waddell, "On the I-Thou Relation in Zen Buddhism," *Eastern Buddhist*, n.s., 2 (November 1969): 71–87; Edith Wyschogrod, "Martin Buber and the No-Self Perspective," in *Religion and Spiritual Democracy: Essays in Honor of Joseph L. Blau*, edited by Maurice Wohlgellernter (New York: Columbia University Press, 1980); and Irene Eber, "Martin Buber and Taoism," *Momumenta Serca* 42 (1994): 445–64. The Scottish Center of Tagore Studies published a blog essay by Abhor Roy titled "Rabindranath Tagore and Martin Buber: A Meeting of Two Great Souls." In this essay the author referred to Paul Mendes-Flohr's unpublished manuscript "Tagore, Buber and Einstein in Dialogue," in which Mendes-Flohr discusses Buber's deployment of the term "ex Oriente lux" in regard to Taoism.

18

Buber Meeting and Not-Meeting Islam

KHALED FURANI

Perhaps it is apt that I begin by explaining my title. Invoking "meeting" (and not "seeing"), I take a cue directly from Buber. Buber wrote that "all life is meeting" (*Alles wirkliche Leben ist Begegnung*). Here I wish to merely begin exploring the ways in which Buber in his pursuit of dialogue both met but largely did not meet Islam. Before I begin, I should address a rather rudimentary question: Why should Buber's relation to Islam matter?

Perhaps an obvious but not very profound answer is: Such an exploration contributes to a critical appraisal of Buber's promotion of dialogue. In his pursuit of intercultural and interfaith dialogue, Buber would encounter Islam but, curiously, not dialogically. One might have expected that after emigrating to Palestine in 1938 and settling in Jerusalem—where he would have heard the *adham*, the call for daily prayer—he would have sought a dialogue with Islam. A less obvious, but perhaps more compelling, answer to this preliminary question is that this relation between Islam and Buber may point beyond his project to articulate a grammar of dialogical intersubjectivity, communal vitality, and a world not beholden to the conceits and deleterious consequences of Europe's Enlightenment triumphal reason. It is from this perspective that I wish to consider the ways in which Buber both met and failed to meet Islam.

Buber had, indeed, a complex, uneasy, and conflictual relation with the particular other that is Islam (which is not to be conflated with Arabs per se). In Buber's writing, one can note at once recognition and misrecognition of Islam. More precisely, I find Buber vindicating many truths of Islam while also erasing Islam from his writing, that is, from the site of his "meeting."

In some sense this contradiction should not surprise us. It would be useful to recall the ways in which Buber had a troubled relation with his own "Jewish faith," marking him as a kind of heretical Jew, an *epikores*, or an "obstinate

Jew," as he actually called himself.[1] Yet this critical traditionalist's overlooking of Islam, even while fully living in its midst (he probably would say next door as a neighbor) should perhaps not surprise us for another reason. He may have shared the regnant European philosophical opinion, forcefully articulated by his friend and close associate Franz Rosenzweig in *Der Stern der Erlösung* (*The Star of Redemption*, 1920), that Islam is not an authentic religious faith. Jean Cahan tells us that, hard as Rosenzweig tried to overcome Hegel, he remained ensnared by speculative and resentful views of religions that were not in accord with his conception of *Offenbarungsglaube*, faith based in divine revelation.[2] I am, however, principally concerned with how Buber encountered Islam. On the one hand, he met or, rather, as he himself might have put it, "mismet" Islam through a locutionary act (refracted by words themselves) that, in effect, erased Islam; and, on the other hand, he met Islam through a perlocutionary act (impact of words) that vindicated its truths.

Buber's Acts of Locutionary Erasure

I want to illustrate two ways in which Buber conducted what I am calling his locutionary erasure of Islam. First, in his work comparing religions, Buber generally omits Islam when providing examples to support his claims. He refers to religious traditions much farther afield, including many times when Islam could have readily provided the same or an even more poignant example. I would like to review four instances by way of illustration.

As a first example, I wish to refer to Buber's writings on Sufis, probably the most prominent and direct work expatiating on things Islamic. He notes Muslim mystics, yet without naming them as such, instead rather and quite strikingly referring to them only with the ersatz title of "Sufi," and that applied to only one among them, in his book *Ecstatic Confessions* (1909). This covering of Islam joins, of course, an entrenched discursive practice in the West which, simply put, inhibits or dilutes a vision of Islam as the condition of possibility for Sufism. In keeping with this venerable procedure, Buber incorrectly (even misleadingly) titles a section "India" in which he places four well-known mystics of Islam, who hailed from what are today Turkey, Iran, and Iraq. They include Rumi of Konyeh, 'Attar of Kadkan, al-Hallaj of Fars province, and al-Bistami of Bistam. In a subsequent section of *Ecstatic Confessions*, titled "The Sufis and Their Followers," he seems to arbitrarily add another mystic of Islam, Rabi'aa, who came from Basra (although Buber doesn't say so). Islam is not allowed into the table of contents alongside nearly every other world religion, civilization, or tradition. As a result, in Buber's typology,

Muslims alone have no mysticism to their name, but Jews, Greeks, Christians, and Chinese all do.

A second example: Buber's locutionary erasure occurs in the way he conceives of religion in contrast to philosophy. In the *Eclipse of God*, he identifies a common perception whereby the investigation of essences is allocated traditionally to philosophy and the investigation of salvation to religion, but, in rejecting this view, Buber states that "the principal tendency of religion is rather to show the essential unity of the two": the unity of investigating essences and salvation.[3] His illustrations here come, as they typically do, from Hebrew scriptures and the New Testament, but also here from Taoism, and not from, shall I say, "next door," Islam, which could have most readily served his point, given Islam's understanding of God's unity and oneness, as in "the Sustainer of the Universes" ر ب العالمين.

In a third example, Islam appears to have been locutionarily locked out from Buber's statements in his "Teaching and Deed" (1934). Buber quotes only Hasidism and ancient church fathers who saw, according to him, that "the simple man who acts is given a preference over the scholar whose knowledge is not expressed in deeds." On the relation between knowing and doing, he adds: "What counts is [. . .] to know what one knows, and to believe what one believes so directly that it can be translated into the life one lives."[4] If Buber had allowed himself a view of Islam, I wonder to what extent he would have "met" the Hasids and the ancient fathers and found them alive and breathing in Muslim lives around him in Palestine. Recall that Buber acknowledged that "making [the other] present" occurs when "the other becomes a self for me."[5] Perhaps this is an apt place to posit a particularly relevant question: In what ways does Buber's defense of Hasidism (as he understood it), as posthieratic (priestless) and a lived relation to God, arguably constitute a defense of Islam or what Islam stands for?

For the fourth and final example, recall that when Buber imagined Palestine as justly to be shared one day, he pinned a great part of his hopes on Arab and Jewish intellectuals. Crucially they (as neither Muslims nor Christians) were to engage in a dialogue based on mutual sincerity and recognition. We must take note of the importance of this class of "spiritual representatives" as invoked by Buber because for him they stand for intellectuals, and intellectuals stand for custodians of "culture and spirit."[6] Yet if the "intellectual" class is entrusted with the "spirit," it remains doubtful that members of such a class can heed his call, without any reliance on, or reconciliation with, forces in their society that are manifestly concerned with "spirit," namely those of "religion."[7]

With regard to this mode of erasure, consider Buber's call for a binational state. It entails the discursive role allotted to "the Arab" (in contrast with the Muslim) in constituting a Palestine shared on an equal political basis with the Jews. This very call implicitly entails a dismissal of *ummatic* (Muslim communal) aspirations. While affirming the emergence of the Jews as a revitalized community in Palestine, in advocating a binational state it would sever the Arabs and Muslims of Palestine from wider communities of Arab and Muslim peoples. One would have expected this biblical humanist to love his neighbor as he would have others love him (Lev. 19:18), and, theoretically at least, allow in his thinking the Muslim what he allows the Jew. To the extent that the Land of Israel (*Eretz Yisrael*) remained the horizon of Buber's political imagination, and if one is to think along with the logic of a political entity shared between two communities, a more dialogical solution, consistent with Buber's own vision, rather than a binational state, would have been a bitraditional or bicommunal state—or still better, not a state but an intercommunal framework allowing for the spiritual vitality of all communities. But I truly wonder if Palestine was to host in Buber's eyes the collective "spiritual renewal" of only one community, "the Jewish people."

However, this erasure is not where the story of Buber and Islam can or should end. Therefore, in the remainder of this exploration, I want to focus on how, while Buber conducts, as we just saw, a locutionary erasure of Islam, he also and crucially conducts a perlocutionary vindication of it.

Buber's Perlocutionary Vindication of Islam

Buber's inability to "meet" Islam does not negate the fact that he also vindicated, perhaps unwittingly, its truths for thinking and acting in the world. This should not surprise anyone who recalls that Buber's project, offering an exit from the edifice that is the Cartesian subject, was to seek "a new way of being in the world."[8] Buber vindicated the truths of Islam as a form of life striving for excellence. Here I detect "a musical affinity" between Buber and Islam, such as in a testimony from his friend, the Muslim Qadi of Jerusalem (al-Quds) Farid Wajdi al-Tabari, who wrote, "I even felt [. . .] that you [Buber] are close to my soul."[9] I wish to identify seven truths or truthful features of Islam as vindicated by Buber, which suggest that Buber was close to Islam's "soul."

1. Revelation: In "The Nature of Man," Buber offers this vindication of the lasting epistemic emancipatory space that is Islam (and any other tradition—whether religious or not—that admits revelation): "Dogma, even when its claim of origin remains uncontested, has become the most exalted form of

BUBER MEETING AND NOT-MEETING ISLAM   255

invulnerability against revelation. Revelation will tolerate no perfect tense, but man with the arts of his craze for security props it up to perfectedness." In "The Social Dimension of Man," Buber further evokes revelation, though not by name, saying, "super-rational truth does not disown reason, but holds it in her lap."[10] The Qur'an continually reminds humans how revelation hosts reason, as in the verse: "He has made subject to you the night and the day; the sun and the moon; and the stars are in subjection by His Command: verily in this are signs for those who reason."[11]

وَسَخَّرَ لَكُمُ ٱلَّيْلَ وَٱلنَّهَارَ وَٱلشَّمْسَ وَٱلْقَمَرَ ۖ وَٱلنُّجُومُ مُسَخَّرَٰتٌۢ بِأَمْرِهِۦٓ ۗ إِنَّ فِى ذَٰلِكَ لَءَايَٰتٍ لِّقَوْمٍ يَعْقِلُونَ

2. The Conditions of Muhammad's Prophetic Mission and Islam's Founding: In searching for his community's renewal by visiting the foundational moments of a people's arrival and ascent in the historical scene, Buber's statements about the Israelites are resonant with the founding of the early Muslim communities in Mecca and Medina. The prophet Muhammad began by exhorting the Arabs, be they pagans, Jews, or Christians, to unite in rekindling their worship of the one and common God. This prophetic beckoning followed degrading tribal wars among the tribes of Arabia and a degraded Ka'abah, which the prophet Muhammad strove to revive, the Qur'an tells us, according to the plans of its original builders, Ibrahim and his son Ismael. It was to be a site for worshiping God alone, not idols. We hear this history musically in Buber's words about the Jewish people: "The people falls away [...] and Israel, from a historical point of view fallen apart and disunited, does not stand firm. But in its conquered state, it again makes itself subject to the will of God, resolves anew to accept God's dominion, and again, a divine mission occurs."[12] Consider also how Buber sets a relation and even affinity between the prophetic act and attempts at establishing justice on earth, all but naming Muhammad in his mission: "The prophets are calling a community to establish its task: the task of justice in the community and beyond."[13] He seems to paraphrase the Qur'an in this sura: "Indeed We sent our messengers with clear signs, and sent down with them the Book and the balance that people may uphold justice."[14]

3. Religion and Life: In describing Islam without naming it, along the way Buber describes what has been so challenging for liberal secular reason to understand about Islam's insistence on wholeness, a wholeness he aspired to witness in modern Jewish life. This difficulty, to be sure, does not face liberal reason only in regard to Islam, but in relation to any religious formation that refuses to be caged in the Protestant grammar of the modern category of "religion." Buber clearly has that plurality of religious formations in mind as they variously arrange their relation to life, including the life of "the political." Buber captures such religious traditions for whom living and living religiously are one and the same in saying, "The realer the religion is, so much the more it means its overcoming. It wills to cease to be the spiritual domain of 'Religion,' and wills to become life itself. [. . .] [I]t strives towards the pure Everyday."[15] I would add that in the case of Islam, and especially Islam in Palestine, close to where Buber lived and closer still to where he taught, this "everyday" has children playing football and hide-and-seek on the esplanade of the al-Haram al-Sharif, the noble sanctuary of al-Aqsa Mosque and the Dome of the Rock.

4. Religion's self-understanding in relation to philosophy: Buber effectively vindicates vast strands of Islam that have exhibited suspicion toward, distance from, unease about, or rejection of philosophy in its Greek or Western sense. Presenting philosophy through a Greek post-Socratic idiom, Buber writes, "When [religion] has to define itself philosophically [. . .] it means the covenant of the absolute with the particulars, with the concrete," or, to put it in schematic terms, this philosophical definition of religion according to Buber means Plato's forms entwined with Aristotle's practices. Such a self-definition of religion, Buber holds, would differ from that of philosophy in the West, which is "grounded on the presupposition that one sees the absolute in the universals."[16] Granted that we, for a moment, forgive Buber his excess in here identifying that undertaking known in the West as philosophy with Plato and his descendants.

Moreover, when Buber speaks of only a "totality" of life as available to the philosophical enterprise, yet both a "totality" and a "unity" of being as available in religious life, we have an occasion to hear the music of the ancient Muslim mistrust of philosophy reverberating in his words: "It is only as a unified being that a person is able to live religiously. [. . .] A totalization also takes place in genuine philosophizing, but no unification. [. . .] In a great act of philosophizing even the fingertips think—but they no longer feel."[17]

5. Wisdom: A particularly powerful place in which Buber vindicates, without meeting, the truths of Islam is evident in his contrasting the Greek concept of *Sophia* with the Hebrew חכמה, which is stunningly close (phonetically, semantically, and conceptually) to the Muslim locution evident in the Arabic word حكمة. In this great act of not identifying the neighbor or the kin, linguistically at least, Buber brashly claims, "Among all the peoples in the world, Israel is probably the only one in which wisdom that does not lead directly to unity of knowledge and deed is meaningless." Buber also adds that חכמה supremely unifies teaching and life, for only through such unity can we recognize and avow the all-embracing unity of God.[18] In response to Buber's claim, we could perhaps invoke the centrality of حكمة in the Qur'an, which occurs some twenty times. However, more compelling might be to reflect upon all the occasions in which the Qur'an weds faith/belief (إيمان) to work (عمل). A verse offering an example states: "Whoever works righteousness, whether male or female, while he [or she] is a true believer verily, to him We will give a good life and We shall pay them certainly a reward in proportion to the best of what they used to do."[19]

مَّنْ ذَكَرٍ أَوْ أُنثَىٰ وَهُوَ مُؤْمِنٌ فَلَنُحْيِيَنَّهُ حَيَاةً طَيِّبَةً ۖ وَلَنَجْزِيَنَّهُمْ أَجْرَهُم بِأَحْسَنِ مَا كَانُوا يَعْمَلُونَ مَنْ عَمِلَ صَالِحًا

Another especially pertinent Qur'anic verse states: "The likeness of those who were entrusted with bearing the Torah but who subsequently bore it not, is as the likeness of an ass who carries huge burdens of books."[20]

مَثَلُ الَّذِينَ حُمِّلُوا التَّوْرَىٰةَ ثُمَّ لَمْ يَحْمِلُوهَا كَمَثَلِ الْحِمَارِ يَحْمِلُ أَسْفَارًا

In other words, to bear books that one does not understand, does not implement, or simply does not live with, that is, does not allow them to give form to life, is to live like an ass.

6. God: In not wanting to allow Muslims to partake in the ultimate truth that Christians, and especially Jews, according to Buber have, the truth of God or the truth that is God, Buber appears to refuse to widen the circle of belonging to God, as when he says, "Our God." He implies the God of Judaism is not the God of Christianity, although what he says about the former very much applies to Allah—the God of all peoples and universes in the plural, as in the phrase رب العالمين "Sustainer of All Peoples /All Universes." Buber again echoes a cardinal Qur'anic principle in writing, "For our God makes only one demand upon us. He does not expect a humanly unattainable completeness and perfection, but only the willingness to do as much as we possibly can at every single instant."[21] Islam similarly comprehends God through mercy more frequently than through love, as evident in the Qur'an stating: "God does not burden any human self with more than it is well able to bear: in its favor shall be whatever good it does, and against it whatever evil it does."

[22]لَا يُكَلِّفُ اللَّهُ نَفْسًا إِلَّا وُسْعَهَا ۚ لَهَا مَا كَسَبَتْ وَعَلَيْهَا مَا اكْتَسَبَتْ

✷

To conclude: I started by stating that my primary concern is to describe the modes (not the motives) by which Buber both erases Islam in his writing and yet vindicates it. I am thus ultimately concerned with understanding "the case" for which this duality of erasure and vindication stands. This is part of the puzzle with which I want to conclude. To say it more specifically, What do we stand to learn from a Jew who, while erasing Islam from his writing, ends up affirming it in his overall project to exit the ensnaring, monological Cartesian subject?[23] For despite his apparent myopia in regard to Islam, could Buber's insights offer ways to cease to see Islam as a mere "religion," but as instead outside or without "religion"? He pushes us to see it (as he does for religion in general) as a paradigm for thinking *and* living at once, for asking and for searching, for fulfilling and overcoming, for striving for excellence or "wholeness" while living our finite and fixable lives on this earth.

Buber was not for foreclosure, but understood himself to be conducting a conversation, with its tensions and risks, evasions notwithstanding.[24] And so the puzzle remains: Could the type of conversation about emancipating how we all may prophetically live in Palestine, about how we prophetically think about what religion can and should stand for the world over, and about how the world itself may prophetically rebound and flourish out of the ruins of a deceived and deceiving conception of reason, inherited from the Enlightenment, with Islam's full and robust participation, all be part of Buber's legacy today?

Notes

1. Martin Buber, *Between Man and Man* (London: Routledge Classics, 2002), 6.

2. Jean Axelrad Cahan, "Rosenzweig's Dialectic of Defiance and Critique of Islam," *Journal of Jewish Thought and Philosophy* 9, no. 1 (2000): 1–20. Incidentally, as the cunning of history (or what is beyond it) would have it, Rosenzweig's library ended up in Tunisia, that is, in the land of Fatima al-Fihriyyah, arguably the founder of the first university in the world in the ninth century, al-Qarawyyin University in Fez.

3. Martin Buber, *Eclipse of God* (New York: Harper & Row, 1957), 33.

4. Martin Buber, "Teaching and Deed," in *The Writings of Martin Buber*, ed. Will Herberg (New York: Meridian Books), 320–21.

5. Martin Buber, "Distance and Relation," in Buber, *The Knowledge of Man* (Atlantic Highlands, NJ: Humanities Press International, 1988), 60–61.

6. Martin Buber, *Land of Two Peoples*, ed. P. Mendes-Flohr (Chicago: University of Chicago Press, 2005), 305.

7. I concede that I am doubtful only because I consider it warranted to assume that "the spirit," as Feuerbach has long sensed, can no longer be the telos of a reputable social theory in the modern research university—Buber's teacher George Simmel being the exception, and perhaps Foucault upon visiting Tehran on the eve of the 1979 revolution.

8. Rémi Brague, "How to Be in the World: Gnosis, Religion, Philosophy," in *Martin Buber: A Contemporary Perspective*, ed. Paul Mendes-Flohr (Syracuse, NY: Syracuse University Press, 2006), 144–46.

9. Buber, *Land of Two Peoples*, 260.

10. Buber, "The Nature of Man," in *On Intersubjectivity and Cultural Creativity*, ed. S. N. Eisenstadt (Chicago: University of Chicago Press, 1992), 56.

11. Qur'an, al-Nahl: 12.

12. Buber, "Biblical Leadership and the Community," in *On Intersubjectivity and Cultural Creativity*, 115.
13. Buber, *Land of Two Peoples*, 181.
14. Qur'an, al-Hadid: 25.
15. Buber, *Eclipse of God*, 34.
16. Buber, *Eclipse of God*, 41.
17. Buber, *Eclipse of God*, 44.
18. Martin Buber, "In the Midst of Crisis," in Buber, *Paths in Utopia* (Syracuse, NY: Syracuse University Press, 1996), 319, 320.
19. Qur'an, al-Nahl: 97.
20. Qur'an, al-Jumu'ah: 5.
21. Buber, "In the Midst of Crisis," 320.
22. Qur'an, al-Baqarah: 286.
23. In the introduction to this volume, Paul Mendes-Flohr notes that Buber himself acknowledges what he ontologically shared with Heidegger: a rejection of Cartesian dualism (e.g., mind-body, subject-object).
24. Here I am alluding to Buber's understanding of embarking on "dialogue" as " holy risk." See Martin Buber, "Drama und Theater," *Masken. Zeitschrift für deutsche Theaterkultur*, 18 Jg., Erstes Oktoberheft 1924, S. 3–5; translated in *Martin Buber and the Theater*, ed. and trans. Maurice Friedman (New York: Funk & Wagnalls, 1969), 83–84.

PART FIVE

Judaism

Introduction

PAUL MENDES-FLOHR

Initially drawing upon the concept of *religiosity* as a universal faith sensibility that is not limited to institutional religion, Buber sought to identify the spiritual core of Judaism as an expression of a faith not bound by traditional normative and particularistic structures. As a distinctive "attitude of the soul," religiosity is first and foremost manifest in the relationship of trust between individuals, on the basis of which the idea of God crystallizes as the "absolute object of human faith." Buber's concept of religiosity would resonate in his later conception of the I-Thou relationship as one of trust, sustained by the Eternal Thou.

The I-Thou relationship is the transcultural, universal "ontological" ground of the authentic life between human beings. Judaism is to give witness to the life of dialogue as "the cradle of the Real Life."[1] So Buber understood Israel's divine election. Yet, he had to acknowledge that in the history of Judaism election took on a pronounced particularistic hue, an ethnocentrism that was amplified by Zionism. He was thus faced with the challenge of stirring the movement from what he regarded as a parochial political and cultural nationalism that betrayed the divine election of Israel to be a "light onto the nations."

Buber presented Hasidism as an antidote both to rabbinic Judaism—which he saw as suffocating the pristine spiritual core of Israel's election with inordinate ritual injunctions and defensive postures to resist the allure of assimilation—and to political nationalism. The Shoah *particularized* the Jewish people with unprecedented brutality. Where was God when his elected servants were dispatched to the crematoria at Auschwitz? Buber was among the very first to pose this harrowing question. Was it God who hid his face and withdrew his providential care from his people, indeed, from all of humanity—or was it we, humanity at large, who turned from God to embolden the It-World and its divisive ethos of instrumental reason, unabetted personal ambition, narcissistic culture, and ethnic nationalism?

Note

1. Martin Buber, *I and Thou*, trans. R. G. Smith (New York: Charles Scribner's Sons, 1958), 24.

19

Martin Buber on Israel's Divine Election

MANUEL DUARTE DE OLIVEIRA

In March 1938, merely six months before the November pogroms (*Kristallnacht*) would shatter any remaining hope of a reprieve from the Third Reich's assault on the civil rights and dignity of Germany's Jews, Martin Buber published an essay on the election of Israel.[1] It would be one of Buber's last contributions to the "spiritual resistance" of German Jewry. Between the lines of this academic essay, one cannot but hear a defiant affirmation of Israel's divine destiny, a spiritual and ethical sensibility that Jewry had come to believe was shared by the German *Bildungskultur*. The essay's muffled message was in consonance with Buber's call to the leaders of the spiritual resistance to "learn how to live in the catacombs": "What is required of writers like us, is to write so subtlety [*sic*] that those currently in power won't immediately detect our resistance and grab us by the scruff of the neck, so subtlety [*sic*] that as many people will have read us before one can be held responsible."[2]

But why, at this particular moment, when National Socialism's grip on power was growing ever tighter, would Martin Buber focus on Israel's election and the command to affirm "God's reign" above any other concern? Shortly after having published his essay, Buber emigrated to Palestine, where he delivered a lecture, apparently penned while still in Germany, in which he offered an explanation for why at this critical hour it was incumbent on Israel to affirm divine election. He ascribed "the 'momentary' triumph of 'the reign of evil'" to despair, "a loss of confidence in humanity, and a corresponding loss of faith in a truth that transcends the opposition of sects and nations—a loss of faith in the possibility of a life of justice and righteousness, of a life of [human] unity and peace."[3]

Martin Buber opens his essay "The Election of Israel: A Biblical Inquiry (Exodus 3 and 19; Deuteronomy)" by confronting two texts of the prophet Amos (9:7; 3:2) which are seemingly contradictory. While the Exodus text attests to God's universal providence, the second refers to the specific particularity of God's relationship with Israel. In Buber's opinion, what differentiates God's relationship with Israel from the one he has with all the other nations is the personal and intimate "knowledge" he has with Israel. This "knowledge," Buber avers, corresponds with Israel's acknowledgment of his kingship, in anticipation of the crossing of the sea. Crucial to Buber's reasoning about the divine election is his understanding of God's revelation to Moses at Mount Sinai, and God's "meeting" with Israel where a unique covenant is established between the two. Buber's conception of "meeting" is the *locus par excellence* where divine revelation takes place. The structure of this "meeting" ultimately is at the basis of his philosophical and mystical thought, identified as a dialogical I-Thou encounter.

Martin Buber's exegesis of the expressions "my people" (*ammi*) and the revelation of God's name, *Ehyeh asher ehyeh*, which in his view is a reflection of God's unconditional freedom, are intimately related to Israel's election. In Buber's view, the concept of "imitation of God" is Israel's privileged way to fulfill God's will, expressed in the "charge" imposed by the covenant at Sinai. Through such fulfillment Israel is to become a "new people," elected and called upon to repair the effects of the sin of the Tower of Babel that fatefully led to the division of humanity into nations. The "new people" is thus to become a model community to the world's multitude of nations. Although, according to Buber, Israel has its origin in God's love, that does not negate the conditionality of its election. In fact, Buber declares, the election grants no such "security." Israel is elected only when it realizes its covenantal calling.

While probing the biblical roots of the view that human history is divided into the history of the nations and that of Israel, Martin Buber reveals two different, albeit complementary lines of thought. On the one hand stand Amos and Isaiah, according to whom the only advantage that Israel has over other nations "now" is that it alone knows God "already," while the other nations will know Him "in the end" of days. This "already" imposes on the people of Israel the specific task of preceding them "in the light of the Lord" (Isa. 2:5), so that his mountain may be ready as the goal of a universal pilgrimage. Buber then professes that "the two sides of world history" will be fused into one united world of God. A different view is found in the prophet Micah, who contends that even when the nations have gathered on the holy mountain, each will walk, as before, in the name of its god, while Israel alone will walk in the name of the Lord its God (Mic. 4:1–5). This means that, even in the end of days, "the two sides of world history" will remain separated, but not divided.

Martin Buber assumed an anomalous position in modern Jewish life. While vigorously rejecting most forms of institutional religion—including the heart of traditional Jewish piety, the adherence to the *mitzvot* (ritual commandments), *which he felt are liable* to deflect one from the life of dialogue and thus true service to God—he was a man of profound religious faith. In an elegant book published in Hebrew in 1945, *Bein 'Am le-Artzo: Iykarei Toledotav shel Raiyon* (Between the People and Its Land),[4] Buber gave testimony to the depth of his faith, as elaborated in his celebration of the election of the people of Israel in its relation to the land. In this work, Buber held that a proper conception of the divine election should guide and regulate the Zionist project and its divinely ordained role in human history. Yet he had a challenging problem in evoking Israel's divine election, for in traditional Jewish faith this concept was associated with another theological concept: the divine covenant binding the people to the Torah, to be fulfilled through the performance of revealed commandments.[5] To a certain extent, Buber's interpretation of the election allowed him to overcome this problem and to translate his understanding of Judaism into a language that could speak to his contemporaries. At the core of his message is what he describes as a demand that Israel establish a just society, serving the rest of humanity as a constructive and inspiring paradigm. While other nations might speak of their election in the process of their self-definition, in Buber's view, Israel's conception remains rather different. Unlike other nations, the election of Israel was not meant as a pretext for an exclusive type of nationalism; on the contrary, it obliges Israel to eschew self-centered nationalism and expand its horizons to embrace all of humanity.

Buber employed the concept of divine election to promote an understanding of Zionism that he characterized as Hebrew humanism.[6] In doing so, Buber hoped to enjoin the concept of election as a way to restrain the introduction into Zionism of what he considered to be a destructive form of nationalism, a chauvinist form of *sacro egoismo*, the sacrilege of regarding one's national interests as ethically self-evident and, even when it involves the blatant disregard and abuse of another group, sacred.[7] In his essay "Hebrew Humanism," published in 1941, Buber unambiguously contests a type of "Jewish nationalism" that regards Israel as a nation like all the other nations, recognizing no other task save that of preserving and asserting itself. By proposing Hebrew humanism as an alternative to a nationalism which is nothing but "empty self-assertion," Buber challenges the Zionist movement which, in his opinion, should decide either for "national egoism" or "national humanism." In the end, Buber contends, the point is not whether we feel or do not feel that we are chosen: "The point is that our role in history is actually unique."[8]

Buber asserts that the nature of the Jewish doctrine of election is entirely different from that of the theories of election of other nations, even though they frequently depend on it:

What they took over was never the essential part. Our doctrine is distinguished from their theories, in that our Election is completely a demand. This is not the mythical shapes of a people's wishful dreams. This is not an unconditional promise of magnitude and might to a people. This is a stern demand, and the entire future existence of the people is made dependent on whether or not this demand is met.[9]

Differently from other nations, Buber maintains, the God addressing Israel is not a God whom the people created in their own image, as their sublimation. In the case of Israel, "What He demands He calls 'truth' and 'righteousness' [...] not for certain isolated spheres of life, but for the whole life of man, for the whole life of the people." Buber avows that the "chosenness" of Israel is enacted upon the people in order to liberate and elevate its nature from "the biological law of power," which other nations glorify in their wishful thinking, to the sphere of "truth and righteousness." In this election are included every single individual and the whole of humankind, uniting the first six days of creation with the eschatological events of redemption: "God wishes man whom He has created to become man in the truest sense of the word and wishes this to happen [...] in the life of an entire people, thus providing an order of life for a future mankind, for all the peoples combined into one people. Israel was chosen to become a true people, and that means God's people."[10]

With respect to the relation of the Jewish people to the land, which God has entrusted to them as their spiritual patrimony, there are three "evils" that inexorably corrupt its election: bloodshed, idolatry, and pride. In relation to the third, Buber invokes the Passover Haggadah's statement: "Whoever is proud causes the pollution of the Land and the withdrawal of the *Shekhinah* [the divine hypostasis], which God humbly caused to dwell within the world."[11] Buber interprets this Haggadic maxim as referring to the election itself—that is, the election must be assumed and fulfilled with humility, otherwise it is voided:

> Whoever believes in the Election and fulfills its commission in all humility gives sustaining power to the Land and helps to keep the *Shekhinah* near to it; but whoever makes the Election a motive of haughtiness, whoever imagines himself protected and exalted by it, instead of being laid under an obligation and set to work by it, weakens the Land and sets the *Shekhinah* against it.[12]

As Buber expounded in his address at the Twelfth Zionist Congress in Karlsbad, Germany, in 1921, the idea of the election of Israel "does not indicate a feeling of superiority," but rather a sense of "destiny": "It does not spring from a comparison with others, but from the concentrated devotion to a task, to the task which molded the people into a nation when they attempted to accomplish it in their earlier history." Indeed, Buber concludes, the Hebrew prophets formulated that task and never ceased uttering their warning: "If Israel boasts of being chosen instead of living up to it, if it turns Election into a static object instead of obeying it as a command, it will forfeit it!"[13]

Notes

1. Martin Buber, "Die Erwählung Israels: Eine Befragung der Bibel," in *Almanach des Schocken Verlags auf das Jahr 5699* (Berlin: Schocken Verlag, 1938); Martin Buber, "The Election of Israel: A Biblical Inquiry (Exodus 3 and 19; Deuteronomy)," in Buber, *On the Bible: Eighteen Studies*, ed. Nahum N. Glatzer (New York: Schocken Books, 1982), 80–92.

2. Cited by Lambert Schneider, *Rechenchaft, 1925-1965: Ein Almanach* (Heidelberg: Verlag Lambert Schneider, 1965), 38; quoted in Paul Mendes-Flohr, "A Post-Modern Humanism: From the Sources of Judaism," *Revista Portuguesa de Filosofia* 62 (2006): 370n2.

3. Cited in Paul Mendes-Flohr, "Buber and the Metaphysicians of Contempt," *Living with Antisemitism: Modern Jewish Responses*, ed. Judah Reinharz (Hanover, NH: University Press of New England, 1987), 161.

4. Later published in the English version as Martin Buber, *On Zion: The History of an Idea* (Edinburgh: T. & T. Clark, 1985).

5. See Arnold Eisen, "Off Center: The Land of Israel in Modern Jewish Thought," in *Land of Israel: Jewish Perspectives*, ed. Lawrence Hoffman (Notre Dame, IN: Notre Dame University Press, 1986), 263–96, esp. 282–83.

6. See Paul Mendes-Flohr, *Martin Buber: A Life of Faith and Dissent* (New Haven, CT: Yale University Press, 2019), xv.

7. As Paul Mendes-Flohr illustrates: "a political ethic that assumes that the pursuit of national self-interest is sacred and thus morally justified spells not only spiritual desolation but also political disaster." Mendes-Flohr, "Buber's Provocation," in *Martin Buber: His Intellectual and Scholarly Legacy*, ed. Sam Berrin Shonkoff (Leiden: Brill, 2018), 144–45. Cf. Paul Mendes-Flohr, "The Politics of Covenantal Responsibility: Martin Buber and Hebrew Humanism," *Orim: A Jewish Journal at Yale* 3, no. 2 (Spring 1988): 7–21, esp. 9–10.

8. Martin Buber, "Hebrew Humanism," in Buber, *Israel and the World: Essays in a Time of Crisis* (New York: Schocken Books, 1976), 248, 250; first published in Hebrew as "Humaniut Ivrit," *Ha-Poel ha-tzair* 34, no. 18 (May 30, 1941): 4–7.

9. Buber, "Hebrew Humanism," 250.

10. Buber, "Hebrew Humanism," 250–51.

11. Martin Buber, *On Zion*, 51.

12. Buber, *On Zion*, 51.

13. Buber, *Israel and the World*, 223–24.

Annotated Bibliography

PRIMARY SOURCES

The following is a brief selection of Buber's writings particularly relevant to his conception of the election of Israel: Martin Buber, "The Election of Israel: A Biblical Inquiry (Exodus 3 and 19; Deuteronomy)," in *On the Bible: Eighteen Studies*, edited by Nahum N. Glatzer, introduction by Harold Bloom (New York: Schocken Books, 1982), 80–92. The essay had been first published as

"Die Erwählung Israels," in *Almanach des Schocken Verlags auf das Jahr 5699* (Berlin: Schocken Verlag, 1938), 12–31; it was later reprinted again as "Die Erwählung Israels" in *Werke: Zweiter Band: Schriften zur Bibel* (Heidelberg: Verlag Lambert Schneider/Munich: Kösel-Verlag, 1964), 1037–51. See also Martin Buber, *On Zion: The History of an Idea*, foreword by Nahum N. Glatzer (Edinburgh: T. & T. Clark, 1985).

SECONDARY LITERATURE

Crucial for an understanding of Buber's conception of Israel's election and its implications for Zionism and the Jewish state is Manuel Duarte de Oliveira, *Humanity Divided: Martin Buber and the Challenges of Being Chosen* (Berlin: De Gruyter, 2021). Other relevant contributions on the topic of Israel's divine election include:

Borowitz, Eugene. *Renewing the Covenant: A Theology for the Postmodern Jew*. Philadelphia: Jewish Publication Society, 1991.
Eisen, Arnold. *The Chosen People in America: A Study in Jewish Religious Ideology*. Bloomington: Indiana University Press, 1983.
Frank, Daniel. *A People Apart: Chosenness and Ritual in Jewish Philosophical Thought*. Albany: State University of New York Press, 1993.
Hollander, Dana. *Exemplarity and Chosenness: Rosenzweig and Derrida on the Nation of Philosophy*. Stanford, CA: Stanford University Press, 2008.
Krinis, Ehud. *God's Chosen People: Judah Halevi's Kuzari and the Shīʿī Imām Doctrine*. Translated by Ann Brener and Tamar Liza Cohen. Turnhout, Belgium: Brepolis Publishers, 2014.
Mendes-Flohr, Paul. "In Pursuit of Normalcy: Zionism's Ambivalence toward Israel's Election." In *Many Are Chosen: Divine Election and Western Nationalism*, edited by William Hutchison and Hartmut Lehmann, 203–29. Minneapolis: Fortress Press, 1994.
Novak, David. *The Election of Israel: The Idea of the Chosen People*. Cambridge: Cambridge University Press, 1995.
Walzer, Michael, Menachem Lorberbaum, Noam J. Zohar, and Ari Ackerman, eds. "Election." In *The Jewish Political Tradition*, 2:9–107. New Haven, CT: Yale University Press, 2003.
Wyschogrod, Michael. "Divine Election and the Commandments." In *Abraham's Promise: Judaism and Jewish-Christian Relations*, edited by R. Kendall Soulen, 25–28. Grand Rapids, MI: William B. Eerdmans Publishing, 2004.

20

Buber and Hasidism

SAM S. B. SHONKOFF

In a remote corner of southeast Poland in the mid-eighteenth century, an eclectic cluster of disciples coalesced around a Jewish shaman named Yisraʾel ben Eliezer (1700–1760). Known as the Baʿal Shem Tov ("master of the divine name"), or acronymically the Besht, he is remembered as having proclaimed that every individual, no matter their station in life, is capable of attaining ultimate communion with God. Indeed, the Besht regarded all seemingly mundane moments and fleeting feelings as potential pathways to holiness. In the later decades of the eighteenth century, a movement began to emerge as small groups of individuals who had known the Besht, including some of his principal disciples, preached an approach to spiritual life that captured the hearts of many Eastern European Jews. Their teachings flourished through the activities of charismatic sages called *tsaddikim* (lit. "righteous ones," sing. *tsaddik*) or *rebbes* (affectionate Yiddish pronunciation of "rabbis," sing. *rebbe*), each of whom shaped the contours of Hasidic thought and theology. To be a Hasid ("pious one," pl. Hasidim) was to follow such leaders and, moreover, to infuse traditional Jewish practices, texts, and ideas with new spiritual meaning and devotional power.

Martin Buber, born just over a century after the emergence of Hasidism as an identifiable movement, was never a Hasid. However, there is literally no one in history who has done more than he did to introduce the broader public, Jewish and non-Jewish alike, to Hasidism.

Following his parents' separation when he was three years old, Buber was sent to be raised with his paternal grandparents in Lemberg, Galicia. This city in the heartland of Polish Jewish life was the publishing center of Hasidic tales.[1] Buber's grandmother Adele grew up in Sasov, a small Galician town only a few miles from the city of Zlotchev, both of which housed significant Hasidic communities. His grandfather Salomon was a prodigious and prolific scholar of Midrash, and despite the fact that he was a "Westernized" intellectual of the Haskalah (Jewish Enlightenment), Buber recalls that "he used to take me with him into his *klaus* [Hasidic prayer room], where he, the *maskil* [enlightened Jew], prayed exclusively among Hasidim—from a prayerbook full of *kavanot* [mindful "intentions" on the mystical power of prayer]."[2] Although his grandparents' religiously observant household was not Hasidic, the young Buber's religious sensibilities were formed, as it were, on the outskirts of the Hasidic orbit.

However, it is evident from Buber's scattered autobiographical reflections and anecdotes that his spiritual life transformed quite radically when he was fourteen years old. The most concrete change was that he left his grandparents' home to be reunited with his father, Carl, now remarried and a very successful agronomist who drew close to Judaism. It was thus probably not merely coincidental that Martin ceased his traditional Jewish observance that very same year.[3] Given the adolescent's traumatic memories of abandonment in his first home, perhaps he was especially quick to jettison his Hasidic-inflected practices for fear of his father's disapproval. Buber recounted nearly thirty years later how he had caused "offense" at his father's bourgeois liberal "temple" when he prostrated himself during a penitential prayer in the Day of Atonement service in accord with the practice of his grandfather's *klaus*.[4]

After moving in with his father, Buber recalls, "I looked down on [Hasidism] from the heights of a rational man. I now saw nothing more of its life, even when I passed quite close to it—because I did not want to see anything." The precocious and bookish Buber plunged into philosophy, from Kant to Nietzsche, and developed a secularist disdain for what he regarded as "unenlightened" Jewish traditionalism. While this was a time of intellectual flowering, it also evidently involved a sense of groundlessness. When the fourteen-year-old Buber left his grandfather Salomon's care, the feeling of floating commenced: "So long as I lived with him, my roots were firm, although many questions and doubts also jogged about in me. Soon after I left his house, the whirl of the age took me in."[5]

In fact, as the nineteenth century turned into the twentieth, Buber was hardly alone in his sense of uprootedness. In the eyes of many Europeans, Enlightenment promises of progress appeared to be devastatingly misguided. From what they could see, modernist celebrations of scientific reason, liberal secularization, industrialization, and urbanization did not liberate humanity as much as alienate it. While these shifts may have facilitated material well-being, they left the modern individual in what Max Weber famously characterized as a "disenchanted world." In response, a nostalgic, neo-Romantic wave started to swell, guiding young Europeans to precisely those cultural and spiritual elements that their bourgeois parents and grandparents had so denigrated—mysticism, mythology, and folklore.

As a university student Buber plunged passionately into the study of mysticism,[6] and he went on to write his doctoral thesis in 1904 on the Christian mystics Nicholas of Cusa and Jacob Böhme. However, Buber's post-Enlightenment sentiments also rekindled his connection to Jewishness, in the spirit of many other young Europeans who were reconsidering liberal universalism that sought to dissolve cultural differences. For Buber, this entailed a turn toward the incipient movement of cultural Zionism and calls for a "Jewish Renaissance," a term which he himself coined and which galvanized quests among Jewish young adults to identify expressions of Judaism that could be adapted to contemporary post-traditional cultural horizons. But Buber was soon to realize that his affirmation of Jewishness remained ungrounded. "I professed Judaism before I really knew it," he confessed years later. With his grandfather's encouragement he resolved to read Hasidic texts. Buber recalls that reading these sources disclosed "a primally Jewish reality [which] was a primal human reality, the content of human religiosity. Judaism as religiosity, as 'piety,' as *Hasidut* opened to me there."[7] For Buber, the "primally Jewish" (*Urjüdisches*) was not the institutional, normative forms of Jewish "religion" but rather the personal and spontaneous, spiritual expressions of Jewish "religiosity."[8] Moreover, this Jewish religiosity that Buber saw in Hasidic sources was not some bourgeois adaptation of Judaism to fit new historical circumstances, like the nineteenth-century movements of "reform" that sought to perpetuate Judaism "in an easier, more elegant, Westernized, more socially acceptable form." Rather, Buber envisioned a radical outpouring from the very roots of the people's soul—not to make religious life lighter to bear, but to permeate it with even more weightiness.[9] To be sure, Buber did not want to become a Hasid; as far as he was concerned, the movement was already in steep decline, smothered by the static structures of religion that invariably follow great religious awakenings. But he wanted to fan the still glowing coals beneath the ashen edifice and kindle it anew. "No renewal of Judaism is possible that does not bear in itself the elements of Hasidism," he would soon declare.[10]

With such intention and direction, Buber retreated from all other work at the age of twenty-six to immerse himself in Hasidic texts for the next five years. He was drawn primarily to the legendary literature, as opposed to the movements' theoretical disquisitions, and during his early years of study he published his first two books, *The Tales of Rabbi Nachman* (1906) and *The Legend of the Baal-Shem* (1908). Buber would for the duration of his life be engaged in rendering Hasidic texts for Western-educated Jewish and non-Jewish readers, distilling what he considered to be their core spiritual teaching.

Perhaps Buber's single most enduring statement about Hasidism was that the movement was "Kabbalah become ethos." He declared these words in the introduction to his very first Hasidic anthology and reaffirmed the formulation in one of his last essays on Hasidism, nearly fifty years later.[11] This phrase "Kabbalah become ethos" gestured toward ways in which Hasidic religiosity was rooted more in experience and encounters than in traditional Jewish liturgical and ritual practice, or even kabbalistic theosophical meditation. As he put it in 1934, if medieval Kabbalah offered a "gnosis"—an esoteric "knowledge" about divine mysteries—then Hasidism protested precisely against that "schematizing of the mystery."[12] Indeed, Buber contended, "Hasidism is agnostic; it is not concerned with the objective knowledge [*Erkenntnis*] that can be formulated and schematized, but with the vital, Biblical 'knowing' [*Erkennen*] in the reciprocity of the essential relation to God."[13]

Crucially, for Buber, this does not necessarily imply an abandonment of theology but rather a revalorizing of it. In fact, he wrote to Gershom Scholem quite openly about his plans "to write a Hasidic theology [*Theologie*]."[14] What is essential to grasp is that the theological core of Hasidism attained expression, for Buber, not primarily through objective statements but through intersubjective meetings. Just as religious truth, according to Buber's dialogical writings, is manifested ultimately through *Bewährung*, or "putting to proof in action," Buber casts the Hasidic *tsaddikim* as *die Bewährten*, the ones in whom truth is put to proof in action.[15] In his estimation, these sages were not theologians in any formal sense, yet they did convey theological meaning, for they *were* the teaching. "The people in whom 'being a Torah' fulfills itself are called zaddikim, 'the righteous,' the rightful ones, the ones in whom truth is put to proof in action [*die Bewährten*]. They bear the Hasidic teaching, not only as its apostles, but its working reality. They are the teaching."[16] Thus, Buber counts the founder of Hasidism, the Ba'al Shem Tov, among those extraordinary religious figures who "did not proceed *from* a teaching, but moved *to* a teaching, in such a way that their life worked as a teaching, as a teaching not yet grasped in words."[17] Hence Buber's prioritization of tales over theosophical writings as the most vivid representation of Hasidic theology. Narrative is the optimum genre for conveying a theology of "Kabbalah become ethos" in textual form.

The phenomenological textures of this "ethos" changed for Buber over time, as his own spiritual sensibilities shifted from mysticism to dialogue. Inasmuch as Buber was engaged with Hasidic sources over nearly seven decades, they offer a lucid glimpse into how his own religious consciousness evolved, which is generally characterized as a transition from his early *Erlebnis*-mysticism

(*Erlebnis* connoting "inner experience") to dialogue that takes place in the concrete relations between human beings.[18]

To be sure, one's perspectives on the world and on texts are interrelated, and thus we might read Buber's early Hasidic tales in light of his emphases in that period on an individual's ecstatic transcendence. In this particular case, if physical events in life are seen as the outer crusts of an inner truth, then all the more so the plotlines of Hasidic narratives may trace the rumblings of a concealed core. And if the depths of self and world are one, as Buber believed that they were in his mystical years, then inner truth is fundamentally *inward* truth, and the meaning of texts is bound up with the contemplative reader-source encounter. For Buber in his mystical period, therefore, the art of retelling required personal plunges into the marrow of sources, especially in the case of tales that he considered poorly written or otherwise pale expressions of the experience (*Erlebnis*) they sought to convey. For instance, regarding one text that Buber sent his wife, Paula, to adapt for his *Legend of the Baal-Shem* anthology, he instructed her to "really *renew* it," to "illuminate, elevate, [and] pour your own nature out over the narrow-hearted material."[19] Thus, according to Buber's mystical hermeneutics of *Erlebnis*, the contemporary narrator must penetrate Hasidic texts to their spiritual core, which is perhaps only subtly manifest in the words of the sources. Indeed, Buber's early hermeneutical approach to Hasidic sources was certainly informed by his university teacher Wilhelm Dilthey.[20] Dilthey identified the hermeneutical task as one of "understanding" (*Verstehen*), whereby "an inside is conferred on a complex of external sensory signs" and through which "we recognize, behind signs given to our senses, that psychic reality of which they are the expression."[21] Thus, one can appreciate not only how Dilthey's hermeneutical method influenced Buber's early approach to Hasidic sources, but also how Dilthey's conception of the relation between language and meaning was bound up with his views on the relation between appearance and being, bodies and psyches.[22]

It is no surprise, then, that Buber's hermeneutical approach to Hasidic tales changed with his shift from mysticism to dialogue, which also involved a shift from physical-spiritual dualism to a sort of dialogical monism.[23] Buber was now committed to remaining attentive to corporeal concreteness and, thus, in relation to textual sources he would focus more firmly on the language itself. Indeed, Buber conceded eventually that in his early years of Hasidic text study he "did not listen attentively enough to the crude and ungainly but living folk-tone which could be heard from this material."[24] It is no coincidence, then, that Buber's book *The Great Maggid and His Successors* (1922), published just a year before *I and Thou*, exhibits a remarkably different form of Hasidic tale. Upon opening the book, one observes readily that the tales are much shorter and the language is less flowery than those in Buber's two earlier Hasidic anthologies, and, indeed, this simplicity of style bears greater resemblance to the original Hasidic texts. To be sure, Buber continues to alter and retell the narratives according to his own religious sensibilities, but he does so now with far greater subtlety and humility. He strives more to "listen attentively" to the voice of the texts. Indeed, intrinsic to Buber's turn from mysticism to dialogue was a turn away from materiality-spirituality dualism, so now the very concrete events and utterances described in the texts are significant in and of themselves. They do not simply gesture toward psycho-spiritual states or transcendent truths; they are narrations of sacred events in particular lives and communities. Like the majority of moments in life, frankly, these later tales may initially appear mundane, anticlimactic, even banal—but therein lies their profundity. They make readers lean in and listen. And they remind us that, actually, there is nothing more meaningful and mysterious than the everyday—if only we offer it due attention. Buber's Hasidic tales in his "dialogical" years—that is, the last four decades of his life—resemble the way he described his own father's storytelling style: "At times in conversation, just as its way led him, he told of people whom he had known. What he reported of them there was always the simple occurrence without any embroidery, nothing further than the existence of human creatures and what took place between them."[25]

Thus, whereas Buber's early work portrays Hasidism as a religious culture of mystical spiritualization, Buber's later writings depict the movement as one of down-to-earth hallowing and sanctification of everyday life. One discerns these differences through comparing his introductory essays to *The Legend of the Baal-Shem* (1908) and *The Great Maggid and His Succession* (1922). The former is structured around four different aspects of Hasidic spirituality that Buber deems central: *hitlahavut* (ecstasy), *avodah* (service), *kavanah* (intention), and *shiflut* (humility).[26] Unsurprisingly, the opening section on *hitlahavut* is the most striking representation of Buber's early mystical sensibilities. He defines *hitlahavut* unequivocally as the transcendence of materiality—"the shaking off of the last chains, the liberation which is lifted above everything earthly," and "embracing God beyond time and space." Thus, *hitlahavut* is a deeply personal, inward, and even antisocial state. "*Hitlahavut* is the individual way and goal," and "the truest life of the fervent one is not among people."[27] Those experiencing *hitlahavut* continue to inhabit sensory reality, of course, but their perceptions penetrate beyond the superficialities of physical reality and social relations. Such a person "raises everything corporeal to spirit" and "can sit in a community of people, yet walks with God: mixing with the creatures yet secluded from the world.'"²⁸ In a bold illustration of the ecstatic mystic's detachment from materiality, Buber cites here a tale in which Rabbi Zusya of Hanipoli chides himself for pulling his hand reflexively out of flames: "'How coarse Zusya's body has become that it is afraid of fire.' The fervent one rules life, and no external happening that penetrates into his realm can disturb his consecration."²⁹ In a similar vein, Buber relates how a deceased sage appears in a dream and describes how "from the hour of his death he went each day from world to world. And the world which yesterday was stretched out above his gaze as heaven is today the earth under his foot; and the heaven of today is the earth of tomorrow. And each world is purer and more beautiful and more profound than the one before."³⁰ According to this mystical mapping of the "worlds," the Hasidic mystic strives to ascend in consciousness as high as possible above the lowliness of crude materiality.

Buber's discussion of *kavanah* (mystical intentionality) in this essay is clearly rooted in the same worldview and conception of mystical life, according to which materiality is mere appearance and it is the mystic's task to access incorporeal transcendence. In the way of *kavanah*, as Buber portrays it here, Hasidim regard sensory reality as the dungeon of immaterial souls and sparks of divinity—"each form is their prison"—and every moment of life is an opportunity to liberate and uplift them. Just "this is the meaning of *kavanah*: that it is given to people to lift up the fallen and to free the imprisoned." Young Buber even goes so far as to quote a Hasidic dictum that "no setting free of [actual human] captives is greater" than the work of liberating holy sparks trapped within stones, plants, and other animals. To be sure, the rest of Buber's introduction to *Legend of the Baal-Shem* complicated the mystical path of Hasidism with the earthbound dimension of *avodah* (religious service) and the ethical stance of *shiflut* (humility). At this stage in Buber's thought, however, he maintained that *hitlahavut* is "the basic principle of Hasidic life," and all other streams of the movement flow ultimately into ecstasy.³¹

Buber's 1922 introduction to *The Great Maggid* depicts the life of the Hasidim in patently different terms.³² At its foundations, this later portrayal of Hasidism offers an alternate map of its spiritual universe. In stark contrast to his representation of Hasidic spirituality in 1908, Buber now insists that notions of a "divine soul imprisoned in the material world" are fundamentally foreign to the kabbalistic commitment to "the Jewish idea of unity, which rejects a [notion of] primal duality," and any such dualistic imagery in Jewish literature is merely a consequence of foreign influences from "Iranian religiosity."³³ Thus, Buber presents the kabbalistic doctrine of the "worlds" in a wholly different light than he did in 1908. The concepts of "upper" and "lower" worlds do not denote any literal or ontological distinctions, he insists now, but rather different levels of consciousness, so that "the [lowest] world of making is this one that appears to our material eye; however, if you fathom it deeper and disclose its materiality, then just this is the [higher] world of formation," and so on. Moreover, Buber clarifies: "By this is not meant that all world being is, in fact, mere appearance." Indeed, the language of "above" and "below" does not signal any hierarchy of importance: "'Above' and 'below'—the decisive importance is ascribed to the 'below.'"[34]

This alternate portrayal of the Hasidic worldview in Buber's later writings is bound up with a different vision of religious practice. It would not make sense any longer, for instance, to set liberation from corporeality at the heart of spiritual life. In direct contrast to his 1908 reference to Zusya and the fire, therefore, now Buber asserts that "he who does harm to his body, does harm to his soul." Moreover, solitary spirituality and inner experiences are no longer sufficient. Whereas he had written in 1908 that "the truest life of the fervent one is not among people," Buber now underscores Barukh of Mezhbizh's commentary on the ancient rabbinic exhortation "Do not be bad before yourself" (*Pirkei Avot* 2:13) as a call to "not be bad in that you stay before yourself and do not go to people; do not be bad through solitude."[35] In the same spirit, regarding Menahem Mendel of Kotsk, who "after the prayer was transformed as though he came from another world, and scarcely recognized his own family," Buber affirms that "he is not a true tsaddik who remains satisfied with this." Indeed, only when seekers pry themselves away from inner euphoria and open their eyes anew to fellow human beings do they approach religious illumination. A *tsaddik*, Buber now emphasizes, is "the person in whom transcendental responsibility has grown from an event of consciousness into organic existence."[36]

We might further illustrate the difference between Buber's mystical and dialogical representations of Hasidism through comparing two tales from his early and late anthologies, both entitled "The Language of the Birds." In Buber's earlier tale by that title, in *Legend of the Baal-Shem*, the Besht rode in a carriage with a young rabbi and told him to withdraw his senses "from all that exists," save the sound of his voice. The Besht then whispered into his ear metaphysical mysteries that caused him to perceive "individual words and sentences" from the sounds of the surrounding birds, and even "a great conversation" complete with "a gay, lovely meaning"—until the Besht plucked this newfound skill from the man with just a quick brush of his hand. Thus, according to this tale that Buber featured in his early Hasidic anthology, the language of the birds is an esoteric speech that lies beyond sensory manifestations, and the mystical master guides his disciple's attention to that transcendent dimension.[37]

Buber tellingly omitted this tale from his later Hasidic anthologies in his dialogical years, as its messages no longer rang true for him. Moreover, he presented an alternate "Language of the Birds" tale in his anthologies from 1922 until the end of his life, with a fundamentally different lesson. Now, the young Shneur Zalman of Liady declines an offer from the sage Rebbe Pinḥas to teach him a thorough lesson about the language of the birds, for "a person needs only to understand *one* thing"—and then, in his old age, Shneur Zalman leans his head out of a carriage to take in the sights and sounds of birds "hopping about and twittering everywhere," and marvels to his grandson, "One needs only to listen well and grasp well in order to understand their language."[38] In this latter tale, Shneur Zalman intimates that the mystical meaning of birdsongs is intuitively graspable to anyone who listens closely. In contrast to the earlier tale of the Besht, here there is no code to decipher, no esoteric knowledge to be given or extrapolated, no distinction between physical sounds and spiritual meaning—there is only a decision to listen, a leaning in toward what is present. In fact, Buber even goes out of his way to omit from the original source any allusions to kabbalistic training that might have equipped Shneur Zalman to decode the language of birds.[39] In short, whereas Buber's 1908 tale describes an inward experience, where one shuts out the world and absorbs a sage's magical assistance in order to hear, Buber's 1922 tale narrates a moment of attuned listening to this-worldly, sensory beings.

Clearly, for Buber, Hasidic theology is not necessarily verbal at all. Nowhere is this clearer than in his tales about Rebbe Mendel of Vurke (1819–68), the so-called Silent Tsaddik. Mendel presided during an era that Buber identified with the decline of Hasidism, which was not so much a degradation "in the sphere of the spirit and teachings" of the movement, "but in that of its inner structure."[40] That is, while *tsaddikim* continued to offer novel teachings and intriguing sermons, their interpersonal relationships and communal bonds lacked the immediacy of their predecessors' and tended to vitiate the earlier Hasidic emphasis on the unity of learning and life. In short, the "ethos" of Hasidic theology was crumbling. In truth, Buber's depiction of Hasidism's decline was strikingly similar to his critique of religion and intellectual life in his own time, which he saw as dangerously disembodied and asocial.[41] Buber concludes his entire, extensive introduction to *Tales of the Hasidim* (1947) with an insistence that Mendel of Vurke recognized the movement's decline: "By reading between the lines we discover that it is particularly Mendel of Vurke's reaction to the hour in which 'the present too is corrupted.' The time for words is past. It has become late." This rebbe, Buber writes, "gave an immediate and forceful expression to the crisis, not so much in one or the other of his sayings as through his silence." In an era when teachings floated vacuously above the grounds of life, practice, and relationships, Mendel was known to sit in silence with his Hasidim at their Third Meal gatherings, where it was customary for *tsaddikim* to "speak Torah." Indeed, these pregnant moments *were* Mendel's "words" of Torah. Buber emphasizes that his silence "was not based on a negative principle; nor was it merely the absence of speech. It was positive and had a positive effect. Mendel's silence was a shell filled with invisible essence, and those who were with him breathed it." Just as Buber claimed that in epochs of spiritual flourishing disciples actually live with their master and "'learn' by being within range of their breath,"[42] here Buber envisions the palpable atmosphere of Mendel's silence, wafting as if on the sound waves of words.

Of course, Buber's portrayal of the Silent Tsaddik reflected his own religious sensibilities. In the original Hasidic sources that Buber consulted, the authors intimated that Mendel communicated discrete content in his silence, as if telepathically.[43] However, as we should expect, Buber envisions the *tsaddik*'s wordless teachings in a different light. For example, Buber's vision of "speaking Torah" in the medium of embodied presence gains vivid clarity in his rendition of a tale that he drew from Yo'ets Kim Kadish Rakats's collection *Siaḥ Sarfei Qodesh*, which Buber entitles "Speech in Silence." The original source by Rakats is as follows:

> One time [the Hasidim] sat for hours at the table of the holy rabbi, Mendel of Vurke, and not even a whisper was heard due to the great fear and very great decorum. The silence was so great that even the hovering of a fly on the wall was heard. And following the grace after meals, the holy rebbe of Biała[44] said, "Now that was a *tish* [lit. 'table,' a festive Hasidic gathering that typically culminates in words of Torah from the rebbe]"! He studied me and my veins burst, but I didn't back down. I responded to all the matters about which he asked me. And it was wondrous because nothing was heard, as everything occurred through thought and hinting.[45]

Just as in the previous tale, this silence at the rebbe's *tish* is portrayed here as polite and reverential. But in his exclamation, the Bialer rebbe suggests that Mendel had been conducting intense interrogations telepathically with those at the table, penetrating their minds with his questions and reading their minds for their answers.

As we might expect, Buber presents the scene in a different light:

> Rabbi Mendel's hasidim once sat silently together at his *tish*. The silence was so great that one could hear the fly on the wall. After the *tish*-blessing, the rabbi of Biala said to his neighbor: "What a *tish* we had today! He probed me so [deeply] that my veins threatened to burst, but I stood firm and responded to all questions."[46]

Thus, as before, Buber emphasizes the active, reciprocal nature of the silence in the room. Whereas Rakats's Hasidim sustained the silence before their master out of "great fear and very great decorum," Buber's Hasidim simply "sat together silently," ready and receptive. Most significantly, however, Buber erases the elements of telepathic communication, in favor of more embodied modes of encounter. In the original text, Mendel "studied" the Bialer's thoughts like a mind-reader, but Buber says enigmatically that the *tsaddik* "probed" or "tested" him. And whereas Rakats's Bialer boasts that he "didn't back down," Buber's Bialer notes that he "stood firm" in the pressing presence of the *tsaddik*. This difference may appear only stylistic, but to "stand firm" (*standhalten*) is a key term in Buber's philosophical writings for capturing the awakened attitude of dialogue. For example, in his slim book *Dialogue* of 1932, Buber includes a section entitled "Responsibility" about what it means to respond to the unique "question" that issues forth from every moment of existence. He characterizes this response broadly as a dialogical "attentiveness" that involves "withstanding [*standhalte*] creation as it happens."[47]

In fact, Buber's reflections on responsiveness in this essay shed much light on his understanding of the Bialer rebbe's report. Rakats's formulation, "I responded to all the matters about which he asked me," suggests that Mendel posed literal questions about various issues. In contrast, Buber's Bialer says more cryptically, "I responded to all questions." From this context alone, it is unclear how, exactly, Buber understood that statement. Indeed, although the original source went on to note explicitly that the content of this conversation was conveyed psychically "through thought and hinting," Buber omits that sentence completely and just lets the enigmatic words "I responded to all questions" linger. Our previous intertextual analyses of Buber's tales do provide some assistance, but Buber's discursive reflections in *Dialogue* elucidate even more. For Buber, the dual imagery of response (*Antworten*) and responsibility (*Verantwortung*) is foundational in the dynamics of dialogue. However, this does not imply that one is literally answering a verbalizable question. Buber clarifies:

> Responding to what?
> To what happens to one, to what is to be seen and heard and felt. Each concrete hour allotted to the person, with its substance drawn from the world and from destiny, is speech for one who is attentive. One who is attentive; for no more than that is needed in order to begin to read the signs that are given to you.[48]

Now, then, how might Buber conceive of the Bialer's "responses" to Mendel? His reflections in *Dialogue* are again illuminating: "The words of our response are, like the address, spoken in the untranslatable speech of action and letting be—whereby the action may behave like a letting be, and the letting be, may behave like an action. What we say thus with the being is our entering upon the situation, into the situation."[49] And, for Buber, this ephemeral yet timeless *situation*—the renewed sense of being situated in life as a responsive, responsible subject—is immeasurably transformative.

In Buber's religious imagination, Mendel's Hasidim emerge from the silent *tish* with such a clarified air of dialogical responsibility. It is in this spirit that Buber's Bialer does not just blurt out to the crowd about his personal experience, as he seems to have done in the original source; rather, he turns "to his neighbor" to relate his gleanings. The call to respond, the heightened attention to responsibility—this is the "Torah" that Buber's Mendel speaks in silence at the table. And it is also the core of the Bialer rebbe's testimony, "I stood firm, and responded to all questions." For Buber, the renewal of beholding and responsibility is itself the kerygmatic core of this teaching. The message of the tale is one of embodied theology, irreducible to dogma or concept, yet as sensible as body and breath.

Martin Buber's childhood encounters with Hasidism and traditional Jewish practice equipped him for his later studies of Hasidic sources. However, he first had to abandon the cultural wellsprings of his youth and plumb the philosophical and social sensibilities of "enlightened" modernity. Ultimately, this intellectual interlude led Buber circuitously back to Hasidism. Yet this did not entail a return to the Polish heartland, let alone a return to his grandfather's Hasidic prayer practices. Rather, Buber's engagement with Hasidism was overwhelmingly textual. Moreover, his neo-Hasidic anthologies and essays that sprang from this engagement were always at the nexus of East and West, negotiating between traditional sources and his own post-traditional religiosity. As his own spiritual outlook shifted over the decades, so did his Hasidic tales. And yet, he remained consistently committed to the notion that Hasidic theology was no abstract teaching or esoteric secret but rather an "ethos," expressed and embodied in moments of life.

Notes

1. On the "Lemberg period," see Gedalyah Nigal, *The Hasidic Tale*, trans. Edward Levin (Oxford: Littman Library of Jewish Civilization, 2008), 18–31.

2. See Buber's comments to Franz Rosenzweig in *The Letters of Martin Buber: A Life of Dialogue*, ed. Nahum N. Glatzer and Paul Mendes-Flohr (Syracuse, NY: Syracuse University Press, 1991), 288, 290.

3. See Buber's letter to Rosenzweig in Buber, *Letters*, 290.

4. Buber, *Letters*, 288, 290.

5. Martin Buber, "My Way to Hasidism," in *Hasidism and Modern Man*, trans. Maurice Friedman (Princeton, NJ: Princeton University Press, 2016), 21, 22.

6. For further details, see Sam Berrin Shonkoff, "Martin Buber," in *A New Hasidism: Roots*, ed. Arthur Green and Ariel Evan Mayse (Philadelphia: Jewish Publication Society and University of Nebraska Press, 2019), 53–55.

7. Buber, "My Way to Hasidism," 23, 24. Here and elsewhere in this chapter, I have emended English translations slightly according to Buber's original German.

8. Martin Buber, "Jewish Religiosity," in *On Judaism*, ed. Nahum N. Glatzer (New York: Schocken Books, 1967), 88.

9. Martin Buber, "Renewal of Judaism," in *On Judaism*, 38.

10. Martin Buber, *Legend of the Baal-Shem*, trans. Maurice Friedman (New York: Harper & Brothers, 1955), 12–13.

11. Martin Buber, *Die Geschichten des Rabbi Nachman* (Frankfurt am Main: Rütten & Loening, 1906), 13; Martin Buber, "Christ, Hasidism, Gnosis" (1954), in *The Origin and Meaning of Hasidism*, trans. Maurice Friedman (New York: Harper Torchbooks, 1966), 252.

12. Martin Buber, "Symbolic and Sacramental Existence," in *Origin and Meaning of Hasidism*, 178–79.

13. Buber, "Symbolic and Sacramental Existence," 179; in German, "Sinnbildliche und sakramentale Existenz," in *Eranos-Jahrbuch 1934: Ostwestliche Symbolik und Seelenführung*, ed. Olga Fröbe Kapteyn (Zürich: Rhein Verlag, 1935), 363.

14. Buber, *Letters*, 385; in German, *Briefwechsel aus sieben Jahrzehnten*, ed. Grete Schaeder, 3 vols. (Heidelberg: Lambert Schneider, 1972–75), 2:435–36.

15. See, e.g., Martin Buber, *Chassidismus III: Die Erzählungen der Chassidim, Martin Buber Werkausgabe*, vol. 18, ed. Ran HaCohen (Gütersloh: Gütersloher Verlagshaus, 2015), 129; Buber, "Geist und Leib der Bewegung," in *Werke*, vol. 3, *Schriften zum Chassidismus* (Munich: Kösel Verlag, 1963), 813. This translation of *tsaddik* corresponds to Buber and Rosenzweig's rendering of terms derived from the root *ts-d-q* in their Bible translation. See Martin Buber, "Über die Wortwahl in einer Verdeutschung der Schrift," in Buber, *Schriften zur Bibelübersetzung, Martin Buber Werkausgabe*, vol. 14, ed. Ran HaCohen (Gütersloh: Gütersloher Verlagshaus, 2012), 79. Cf. Michael Fishbane, "Justification through Living: Martin Buber's Third Alternative," in *Martin Buber: A Contemporary Perspective*, ed. Paul Mendes-Flohr (Syracuse, NY: Syracuse University Press, 2002), 120–32. In Buber's Hasidic writings, he usually leaves the word *tsaddik* untranslated, unless it occurs in a biblical verse.

16. Buber, *Werke*, 3:813. Buber added the words "die Bewährten" here in a later version of this essay, so it does not appear in *Der große Maggid und seine Nachfolge* (Frankfurt am Main: Rütten & Loening, 1922), xxx, and it is not reflected in the English translation in *Origin and Meaning of Hasidism*, 129.

17. Buber, "The Beginnings," in *Origin and Meaning of Hasidism*, 25; in German, *Chassidismus II: Theoretische Schriften, Martin Buber Werkausgabe*, vol. 17, ed. Susanne Talabardon (Gütersloh: Gütersloher Verlagshaus, 2008), 254.

18. In addition to my analysis below, see Susanne Talabardon, "Einleitung," in Buber, *Chassidismus II*, 25–37.

19. Buber's December 1906 letter to Paula Winkler-Buber, in *Briefwechsel*, 1:250. On Winkler-Buber's unacknowledged contributions to some of her husband's early Hasidic tales, see Grete Schaeder, "Martin Buber: Ein biographischer Abriß," in Buber, *Briefwechsel*, 1:38–39.

20. Regarding Dilthey's influence on Buber's Hasidic writings, see Paul Mendes-Flohr and

Ze'ev Gries, introduction to Buber, *The Tales of Rabbi Nachman*, xvi–xviii. For Dilthey's influence on Buber's hermeneutics more generally, see Paul Mendes-Flohr, *From Mysticism to Dialogue* (Detroit: Wayne State University Press, 1989), chap. 1; and Steven Kepnes, *The Text as Thou* (Bloomington: Indiana University Press, 1992), 6–18.

21. Wilhelm Dilthey, "The Rise of Hermeneutics," in *Hermeneutics and the Study of History*, ed. Rudolf A. Makkreel and Rithjof Rodi (Princeton, NJ: Princeton University Press, 1996), 235–36.

22. For correlated reflections in the context of early rabbinic and Christian hermeneutics, see Daniel Boyarin, *Carnal Israel: Reading Sex in Talmudic Culture* (Berkeley: University of California Press, 1993), 8–9, 230–35.

23. On Buber's "dialogical monism," see Sam S. B. Shonkoff, "'The Bodily Fact of Otherness': Martin Buber's Post-Kantian Phenomenology of Dialogue," *Journal of Jewish Thought and Philosophy* 30, no. 2 (2022): 330–35.

24. Martin Buber, "Hasidism and Modern Man," in *Hasidism and Modern Man*, 2.

25. Martin Buber, *Meetings: Autobiographical Fragments*, ed. Maurice Friedman (London: Routledge, 2002), 22.

26. For a penetrating analysis of the religious phenomenology conveyed in this essay, see Martina Urban, *Aesthetics of Renewal* (Chicago: University of Chicago Press, 2008), chap. 9.

27. Buber, *Legend of the Baal-Shem*, 19, 23, 29, 21. It is significant to note here that Buber came to reject the notion that mysticism should even be treated as a sociological concept.

28. Buber, *Legend of the Baal-Shem*, 18.

29. Buber, *Legend of the Baal-Shem*, 20. Cf. Natan Neta Diener, *Menorat Zahav* (Warsaw, 1904), 107. Buber includes this tale in his later Hasidic anthologies as well, but combines it—in the very same paragraph—with a contradictory anecdote wherein Susya exclaims, "Earth, Earth, you are better than I, and yet I trample on you with my feet. But soon I shall lie under you and be subject to you." See "Zusya, and Fire and Earth," in Martin Buber, *Tales of the Hasidim: The Early Masters*, trans. Olga Marx (New York: Schocken Books, 1947), 1:249, based on Diener, *Menorat Zahsav*, 129.

30. Buber, *Legend of the Baal-Shem*, 19.

31. Buber, *Legend of the Baal-Shem*, 35, 37, 24, 40.

32. On this essay, see also Talabardon, "Einleitung," in Buber, *Chassidismus II*, 28–29, as well as her extensive commentary there, 351–83.

33. Buber, *Origin and Meaning of Hasidism*, 118; German: *Der große Maggid*, xviii.

34. Buber, *Origin and Meaning of Hasidism*, 119–120, 140.

35. Buber, *Origin and Meaning of Hasidism*, 126, 141. Cf. Barukh of Medzhibozh, *Butsina de-Nehora* (Piotrków, 1889), 12.

36. Buber, *Origin and Meaning of Hasidism*, 139, 131.

37. See Martin Buber, "The Language of the Birds," *Legend of the Baal-Shem*, 185–94; in German, *Die Legende des Baalschem* (Frankfurt am Main: Rütten & Loening, 1908), 227–39. According to his unpublished notebook, Buber adapted this tale from *Shivḥei ha-Besht* (Kraków, 1906), 103–4.

38. See Buber, "The Language of the Birds," *Tales of the Hasidim*, 1:266–67; in German, *Der große Maggid*, 88–89.

39. See Ḥayim Meir Heilman, *Beit Rabbi* (Berditschev, 1902), 4–5.

40. Buber, *Tales of the Hasidim*, 2:7.

41. See Sam Shonkoff, "'Corporeality, Not Spirituality': Martin Buber's Resistance at Eranos in 1934," *Journal of Religion* 101, no. 4 (October 2021): 505–23.

42. Buber, *Tales of the Hasidim*, 1:46, 18; in German, *Chassidismus III*, 188, 143.

43. On telephatic transmission in Hasidism, see Jonathan Garb, *Shamanic Trance in Modern Kabbalah* (Chicago: University of Chicago Press, 2011), 108–12.

44. Dov Berish of Biała (1820–76) was the spokesman and closest disciple of Mendel. After the latter's death, most Vurke Hasidim accepted Dov Berish as their new rebbe.

45. Yo'ets Kim Kadish Rakats, *Siaḥ Sarfei Qodesh*, vol. 4 (Lodz, 1927–28), 86.

46. Martin Buber, "Speech in Silence," in *Tales of the Hasidim*, 2:301; in German, *Chassidismus III*, §1231; in Hebrew, *Or ha-Ganuz*, 453.

47. Martin Buber, *Between Man and Man*, trans. Ronald Gregor Smith (New York: Macmillan, 1965), 16; in German, *Das dialogische Prinzip* (Gütersloh: Gütersloher Verlagshaus, 2002), 162.

48. Buber, *Between Man and Man*, 16; in German, *Das dialogische Prinzip*, 161.

49. Buber, *Between Man and Man*, 17; in German, *Das dialogische Prinzip*, 163.

Annotated Bibliography

PRIMARY SOURCES

Buber's two early anthologies of Hasidic tales, originally published in 1906 and 1908, reflected his so-called mystical phase. These are available in English translation as *The Legend of the Baal-Shem*, translated by Maurice Friedman (Princeton, NJ: Princeton University Press, 1995), and *The Tales of Rabbi Nachman*, translated by Maurice Friedman (Atlantic Highlands, NJ: Humanities Press International, 1988).

Buber's later anthologies of Hasidic tales, during his so-called dialogical years, began with his *Der Maggid und seine Nachfolge* (Frankfurt am Main: Rütten & Loening, 1922). It culminated ultimately with his momentous, two-volume *Die Erzählungen der Chassidim* (1949), in English as *Tales of the Hasidim*, translated by Olga Marx (New York: Schocken Books, 1991).

The most important English collections of Buber's essays on Hasidism are *The Origin and Meaning of Hasidism*, translated by Maurice Friedman (New York: Harper Torchbooks, 1966), and *Hasidism and Modern Man*, translated by Maurice Friedman (Princeton, NJ: Princeton University Press, 2016).

SECONDARY LITERATURE

Gershom Scholem published the first comprehensive scholarly profile of Buber's representation of Hasidism, judging it as idiosyncratic and tendentious. Although there has been a great deal of scholarship on the Buber-Scholem debate, far fewer scholars have looked beyond that controversy in order to elucidate the details of Buber's neo-Hasidism in its own context. The works below by Paul Mendes-Flohr and Martina Urban focus on Buber's early Hasidic writings, and the works by Sam Shonkoff focus on Buber's later Hasidic writings. The book by Israel Koren offers a broader perspective on the place of Hasidism in Buber's general philosophy.

Koren, Israel. *The Mystery of the Earth: Mysticism and Hasidism in the Thought of Martin Buber*. Leiden: Brill, 2010.

Mendes-Flohr, Paul. "Fin de Siècle Orientalism, the *Ostjuden*, and the Aesthetics of Jewish Self-Affirmation." In Paul Mendes-Flohr, *Divided Passions: Jewish Intellectuals and the Experience of Modernity*, 77–132. Detroit: Wayne State University Press, 1991.

———. "Martin Buber and Gershom Scholem on Hasidism: A Methodological Dispute." In *Sammelband: Mystik*, edited by Christoph Markschies, 68–76. Leipzig: Evangelische Verlagsanstalt, 2020.

Scholem, Gershom. "Martin Buber's Interpretation of Hasidism." In *The Messianic Idea in Judaism*, translated by Michael A. Meyer, 228–50. New York: Schocken Books, 1995.

Shonkoff, Sam Berrin. "Metanomianism and Religious Praxis in Martin Buber's Hasidic Tales." *Religions* 9, no. 12 (2018): 1–29.

Urban, Martina. *Aesthetics of Renewal: Martin Buber's Early Representation of Hasidism as Kulturkritik*. Chicago: University of Chicago Press, 2008.

21

Buber and the Holocaust

DAVID BARZILAI

The Holocaust challenged the very foundation of Martin Buber's dialogical thought that God—the Eternal Thou—continuously addresses us in the quotidian here and now and in response we are partners with God in a dialogue affirming the meaning and sacrality of life.[1] But where was God during the dark days of National Socialism, culminating with Auschwitz? How are we, then, to explain God's silence? When posed as a theological question, Buber would demur, for he insisted that he had no warrant to speak of God in the third person—to assume knowledge of God's will and thus make any theological claims. On the other hand, he would affirm God in "the second person": God addresses us (in the encounters with our fellow human beings). Thus, the haunting question of God's silence during the Holocaust should be posed as a theologoumenon whether his address was not heard, or rather ignored. In a lecture Buber delivered in December 1951 in New York City at Columbia University, he addressed the question.[2] His ruminations were apparently prompted by a letter he received from Ernsz Szilagyi (1898–1973), a Hungarian Jewish factory worker who survived the Bergen-Belsen concentration camp. In his letter, dated June 6, 1950, he asked Buber several questions: How is Jewish life at all possible after Auschwitz? How are we to understand "Job's cry"? Is it still possible to speak of the "renewal of Judaism," as Buber had some forty years earlier in Prague, in his *Three Addresses on Judaism*?[3] Clearly moved by these harrowing questions, Buber penned a lengthy reply, dated July 2, 1950.[4]

Together these two documents may be viewed as adumbrating what he would later call in a book of 1952 the *Eclipse of God*.[5] It is the account of a tormented believer struggling not merely to continue "to believe" but "to keep faith" in the living God: in Pascal's words, "the God of Abraham, Isaac and

Jacob, Him to whom one can say Thou," in a bond of mutual trust. In *I and Thou* (1923), Buber affirmed that "Only one You [the Eternal Thou] never ceases, in accordance with its nature to be You for us," and he added, "Only we are not always there."[6] In the concluding chapter of his *magnum opus*, Buber spelled out three necessary elements present in a genuine dialogical encounter with God: first, "actual reciprocity"; second, "the inexpressible confrontation of meaning"; and third, meaning as it touches our life in the here and now.[7] Needless to say, these three conditions were rendered problematic, if not utterly questionable, in the wake of the Holocaust.

Addressing the audience gathered at Columbia University, Buber observed that the imponderability of God's silence also weighed heavily on the author of Psalm 82, which opens with the plea, "Do not keep silent, O God! Do not hold Your peace. And do not be still, O God." "In our own time," Buber comments, the Psalmist's cry is also ours:

> How is a Jewish life with God still possible in a time in which there is an Oswiecim [Auschwitz]? The estrangement has become too cruel, the hiddenness [of God] too deep. One can still "believe" in Him who allowed these things to happen, but can one speak to Him? Can one still hear His words? Can one as an individual and as a people, enter at all in a dialogic relationship with Him? Dare we recommend to the survivors of Oswiecim, the Job of the gas chambers: "Call to Him, for He is kind, for His mercy endureth forever?"[8]

For the survivors of Auschwitz—indeed, presumably all Jews and humanity at large are survivors—the harrowing mystery of God's hiddenness remained inscrutable. But distinguishing the "surviving remnant" of Jewry from "the tragic hero of the Greeks before a faceless fate," Buber counseled his audience to continue the struggle to redeem the world, waiting for the renewed presence of God—a message he would he amplify upon his return to Jerusalem in his reply to Szilagyi.

In the Hebrew version of "The Dialogue between God and Man in the Bible," Buber expressly asks: "Can one still, as an individual and as a people, enter at all into a dialogical relationship with Him?"[9] In addition, Buber evoked for the first time the notions of the "eclipse of God" and "the hidden God" in connection with the Holocaust.[10] Buber's discussion of these two *theologoumena* represent his initial effort to address God's silence during the Holocaust.

Buber opens his address at Columbia University by evoking the biblical narrative of Job and by describing the relation between God and man as an ongoing dialogue, a dialogue between two independent subjects, in which the human being who, as God's creature, is graced with free will and thus the choice to heed or refuse to respond to the call of heaven. Yet Buber acknowledges that the nature of revelation had changed since biblical times, challenging the very heart of Israel's faith that God speaks to us. Direct revelation, the spoken words of the living God, has ceased. Both believers and nonbelievers concur, the former affirming that God's voice is now inscribed in scripture. There are others who bewail that "the holy spirit has been taken from us; heaven is silent to us." Consequently, some become atheists, and others adopt a deistic conception of God, denying that God speaks to us and can be spoken to. Buber, however, affirms that Divine address may still be heard:

> Everything, being and becoming, nature and history, is essentially a divine pronouncement [*Aussprache*], an infinite [chain] of signs meant to be perceived and understood by perceiving and understanding creatures.[11]

The presence of God in nature and history is continuous and open to all to behold. God now speaks to us in the infinite language of events and situations, eternally changing, but it is plain to the truly attentive that transcendence speaks to our hearts at the essential moments of personal life. And there is a language in which we can answer it; it is the language of our actions and attitudes, our reactions and abstentions; the totality of these answers is what we may call our answering for ourselves.[12] Both the individual and the community are addressed by God; both must respond.

Yet, Buber acknowledges, there are times when it would seem that God is silent. Indeed, God "hideth His face from the house of Jacob" (Isa. 28:21) on occasion, and we are unable to recognize God's presence in history and nature, "so uncanny and 'barbarous' do [his deeds] seem to us." These are the "mute times, when everything that occurs in the human world and pretends to historical significance appears to us as empty of God. [. . .] For one who believes in the living God, who knows about Him, and is fated to spend his life in a time of His hiddenness, it is [indeed] very difficult to live." Such a "mute time" is ours: our life is the life of Job, the forsaken of God. For that very reason, the only answer to our lament is the answer Job received: "the true answer that Job receives is God's appearance only, only this that distance turns into nearness, that 'his eye sees Him' (42:5), that he knows Him again." No explanation, no justification, no theodicy: "nothing [is] adjusted, wrong has not become right, nor cruelty kindness; nothing has happened but that man again hears God's address." Are we able, even in this "muteness," even in this dreadful time of "hiddenness," to maintain our side in the dialogue? "Do we stand overcome before the hidden face of God as the tragic hero of the Greeks before faceless fate? No; rather even now, we *contend*, we too, with God, even with Him, the Lord of Being, whom we once, we here, chose for our Lord. We do not put up with earthly being; we struggle for its redemption, and struggling we appeal to the help of our Lord, who is again and still a hiding one. In such a state, we await His voice...."[13]

The Holocaust, Buber suggests, is the consequence of a process that the Western world underwent with the onset of modernity, fanned by the Copernican revolution whereby the creator and created changed places. This process, the eclipse of the God of creation, reached its climax with Nietzsche's assertion that "God is dead": we killed Him. But, Buber observes, we killed but the god of *our* creation, a "human God." Alas, having slayed this god, we remain in darkness. God, the Eternal Thou, is eclipsed in silence.

A conversation Buber conducted with young kibbutz members in the late 1950s occasioned a candid elaboration on God's withdrawal into silence. In response to a question posed by a kibbutznik about faith after the Holocaust, Buber replied that a decade earlier a young person had already asked him that very question, to which he had replied that if a person believes in God, that person accepts him as he is, the way a person who falls in love accepts the person that he loves as that person is.[14] The young person to whom Buber referred was probably Ernsz Szilagyi (although he, in fact, was not as young as Buber assumed). The centrality and uniqueness of Buber's reply to Szilagyi commands special attention and analysis. Buber opened his response by spelling out for the first and only time how he candidly addressed the *existential* question of faith in God after Auschwitz. He did so metaphorically, but undeniably honestly and courageously. God is like the friend we trusted and loved that we come to realize by "all the signs" that he misleads us, and instead of being the angel we believe him to be, we find him to be, or rather he appears to be, "a demonic entity." In face of this realization, we are confronting an existential dilemma. What is the truth? What are we to believe: "the signs," or the heart? But first, Buber insists that any possible answer depends on accepting the apodictic view that God is a living entity and not our creation. He is not a man-made idea nor merely an ethical ideal. At the core of his address Buber refers to the experiences of Job and Abraham and suggests that it is indeed the way Abraham and Job accept God. If someone accepts him otherwise, he argues, he is accepting a statue, an idol crafted by his own hand, a "good" one that is easy to love. Buber reiterates in the letter to Szilagyi that Job despairs because God and the moral ideal seem divergent to him. Yet, Buber emphasizes, "He who answered Job out of the tempest is more exalted even than when He dwells in the ideal sphere. He is not the archetype of ideal but contains the archetype. [. . .] God desires that men should follow His revelation, yet at the same time He wishes to be accepted and loved in His deepest concealment."[15]

The uniqueness of God's demand of Abraham to sacrifice Isaac, Buber continues, is to believe in him beyond reason, and against what seems to be an unreasonable and unjust request. In short, we are to believe in "God's way" even when it seems "absurd and cruel." Although God stayed Abraham's hand at the last minute, Buber notes, "the killing of the son happened in the heart."

As for Job, continued Buber in the letter to his Hungarian interlocutor, Job does not doubt the existence of God, but asks for a justification of his ways. In his revelation to Job, God directly tells him that he cannot and should not know "the why." As Buber wrote, he does not say to Job that the world is just; he does not make a confession and does not reveal his secret of mercy. He is just there. Job "sees" Him as the One that is there. Without anything further happening, Job uttered "I am consoled." Buber continues to admit in the letter that he was well aware that no angel was sent to Auschwitz to stop the burning chimneys . . . that we can assume no one heard a comforting voice then, or since. No voice and no explanation, only a terrible surrendering silence.

This view was echoed in his "Reply to My Critics," composed two years before his death, where he expatiates on the notion of "a revelation" through the hidden face, a speaking through the silence. Indeed, Buber wrote, "He, the God of our fathers, probably will not stop being the 'hidden God,' even when he reveals Himself anew."[16] We may discern in such statements that Buber acknowledges, however hesitantly, that no trace of God's ways in human history is plausible or possible anymore, albeit not beyond our anticipation. Yet Buber resists a total "ontological break" with the very foundations of his philosophy of dialogue that God address us. As the Psalmist declares in the name of God, "I am always with you" (P. 73:23), a verse that Buber requested to be engraved on his tombstone.

We are to affirm faith "after Auschwitz" not for the "sake of heaven" but for our own sake.[17] The experience of faith beckons us to behold the Hidden God as the Eternal Thou.[18]

Notes

1. For Buber, God is the Eternal Thou who "whatever else he may be in addition, enters into direct relationship to us human beings through creative, revelatory, and redemptive acts, and thus makes it possible for us to enter into a direct relationship to him." Martin Buber, *I and Thou*, trans. Walter Kaufmann (New York, 1970), 180–82.

2. Martin Buber, "The Dialogue between Heaven and Earth," in Buber, *At the Turning: Three Addresses on Judaism* (New York: Farrar, Straus & Young, 1952); also in Buber, *On Judaism*, ed. Nahum N. Glatzer (New York: Schocken Books, 1967), 214–25.

3. Szilagy's letter was conveyed to Buber by the Hungarian rabbi Dr. György Klein in 1949; Martin Buber Archive, Mappe 370a. Buber subsequently exchanged six letters with Szilagy from 1950 through 1962.

4. See the draft of Buber's letter to Szilagy in Martin Buber, *Briefwechsel aus sieben Jahrzehnten*, vol. 3, *1938–1965* (Heidelberg: Verlag Lambert Schneider, 1975), 253–55.

5. Martin Buber, *The Eclipse of God: Studies in the Relation between Religion and Philosophy* (New York: Harper & Row, 1952).

6. Buber, *I and Thou*, 133. Particularly after the Holocaust this statement could be tragically and cynically reversed: "Only He is not always here."

7. Buber, *I and Thou*, 158–59.

8. In English this essay is entitled "The Dialogue between Heaven and Earth," in Buber, *On Judaism*, 214–25.

9. Martin Buber, "The Dialogue between Heaven and Earth in the Bible," *Teuda ve'Yeud* [in Hebrew], 214–25.

10. In the English edition, Buber dropped the phrase "in the Bible" from the title. More importantly, he also omitted two paragraphs dedicated to the distinction between "the eclipse" and "the hidden God."

11. Buber, "The Dialogue between Heaven and Earth," in *On Judaism*, 221.

12. Buber, "The Dialogue between Heaven and Earth," 216.

13. Buber, "The Dialogue between Heaven and Earth," 222, 225.

14. Avraham Shapira, "Hester-Panim ve'Dor ha-Soah," in *Hadoar* (New York, 1977), 408–9.

15. Buber's letter to Szilagy, 253–55.

16. Buber, "Replies to My Critics," in *The Philosophy of Martin Buber*, ed. P. Schilpp and M. Friedman (LaSalle, IL: Open Court, 1967), 716.

17. Emil Fackenheim later formulated a similar idea with his notion of the 614th command where the "authentic Jew of today is forbidden to hand Hitler yet another, posthumous, victory" (*Judaism* 16, no. 3 [Summer 1967]: 269–73). Yet, the focal point in Buber's address is categorically different. It is not the danger of giving the forces of *Contra-Humanus* (Hitler and his executioners) a final victory over us by distorting our "human face" and "killing God," and it is not only "for the sake of heaven," but mostly for our own sake, for the sake of *Homo-Humanus*. Symbolically, *For the Sake of Heaven* was the English title to Buber's only mystical novel, *Gog und Magog*. The Hebrew text was published in 1943 and the German version in 1949. Buber mentioned that the time of writing this book was very significant.

18. Buber, *Replies to My Critics*, 741–44.

Annotated Bibliography

PRIMARY SOURCES

Buber did not write extensively about the Holocaust per se. In addition to the two sources at the core of this article, we can consider the following as substantially related to Buber and the Holocaust: his collection of essays *Eclipse of God* (1958); his work of fiction from 1943, *Gog und Magog* (in English, *For the Sake of Heaven*), and his collected essays, *On Judaism*.

SECONDARY LITERATURE

The two comprehensive Buber biographies shed substantial light on his view of the Holocaust. See Maurice Friedman (who knew Buber personally and was responsible for introducing Buber to the American audience), *Martin Buber's Life and Work: The Later Years, 1945–1965* (New York: Dutton, 1984), 145–47; and Paul Mendes-Flohr, *Martin Buber: A Life of Faith and Dissent* (New Haven, CT: Yale University Press, 2019), 251–302, particularly 292–96.

Buber's writings bearing on the Holocaust were complemented by his historical leadership role during and after the Holocaust. See David Barzilai, *Homo Dialogicus: Martin Buber's Contributions to Philosophy* [in Hebrew] (Jerusalem: Magnes, 2000), 293–94; David Barzilai, "Three Mistakes and One More" [in Hebrew], *Haaretz* (June 1990); David Barzilai, "Agonism in Faith: Buber's Eternal Thou after the Holocaust," *Modern Judaism* 23, no. 2 (May 2003): 156–79; Michael Oppenheim, "Not Any Tom, Dick, and Harry: Abraham Heschel and Martin Buber on the Holocaust," *Studies in Religion/Sciences Religieuses* 44, no. 3 (2015): 334–55; and Dina Porat, "*Al-domi*: Palestinian Intellectuals and the Holocaust, 1943–1945," *Studies in Zionism* 5, no. 1 (1984): 97–124.

PART SIX

Politics

Introduction

As a spontaneous response to the presence of the other, dialogue is guided by no formula other than a readiness to respond. "The Thou meets me through grace—it is not found by seeking. [. . .] The Thou meets me. [In response] I step into direct [unmediated] relation with it. Hence the relation means being chosen and choosing, suffering and action in one."[1] The dialogical response to the other is guided by no normative grammar other than a decision to choose, fraught as it is with the "risk" of a "mismeeting." In this respect, dialogue is not only metaethical but also metapolitical.

The political positions that flowed from Buber's metapolitical ethos thus bear the stamp of a nonprescriptive, continuously revised orientation. Under the sway of his early mentor in matters political, Gustav Landauer (1870–1919), an anarchist intellectual, Buber was wary of all forms of heteronomous authority. As Landauer taught, "Anarchism's lone objective is to reach a point at which the belligerence of some humans against humanity, in whatever form, comes to a halt. And with this end point in mind, people must transcend themselves in the spirit of brother- and sisterhood, so that each individual, drawing on natural ability, can develop freely."[2]

And so Buber read the "theopolitics" of biblical Israel, as related by Sam H. Brody; and the modern quest to restore community (*Gemeinschaft*) and its fraternal, "organic" interpersonal relations, eclipsed by the onrush of urban society (*Gesellschaft*) governed by a divisive individualism and instrumental reason, explored by Inka Sauter.

Buber did have his blind spots, however. In advocating Arab-Jewish rapprochement in Palestine and later in the State of Israel, Amal Jamal argues, he imposed on the Arabs of Palestine implicit presuppositions which rendered the desired dialogical, binational relation paternalistic. And while sympathetic to women's struggle for gender equality and equity, Buber was nonetheless burdened with bourgeois conceptions of the social role of the second sex. Feminists, however, as Yemima Hadad details, have drawn inspiration from Buber's philosophy of dialogue.

Notes

1. Martin Buber, *I and Thou*, trans. Ronald Gregor Smith, 2nd ed. (New York: Charles Scribner's Sons, 1958), 26.

2. Gustav Landauer, "Anarchism in Germany" (1895), in Landauer, *Anarchism in Germany and Other Essays*, ed. Chris Dunlap, trans. Stephen Bender and Gabriel Kuhn (San Francisco: Barbary Coast Collective, 2011), 15.

22

Buber's Concept of Theopolitics

SAMUEL HAYIM BRODY

The concept of "theopolitics" undergirds Martin Buber's biblical writings, uniting disparate areas of his concern: the Hebrew Bible's conception of faith, the Zionist project, socialism, and the possibility of "realizing" Judaism in the modern world. The concept first emerges in his study of messianism in ancient Israel, but over the course of his career, he deploys the term *messianism* in varying and sometimes contradictory ways, and never clearly addresses its relationship to other elements of his thought. Sometimes he seems attracted to its explosive power to motivate dynamic action in the world; at other times he seems wary of its potential to inspire misguided, destructive politics.

In his earliest writings—from 1898 to 1916—the term *redemption* alternatively denotes the ransoming of captives (mundane, this-worldly liberation), and the consummation and completion of divine creation, culminating in the perfection of nature, including human nature. He tends to distinguish, albeit not consistently, *eschatology*—the vision of the last days—and *redemption* as the period immediately preceding the denouement of history. Within this context, he presents *apocalypse* as revelatory intimations of the eschatological trajectory of history; the *apocalyptic* imagination, accordingly, focuses on the "signs of the times." The correlative term *messianic* has manifold meanings and complex relationships to the foregoing terms. Buber's work focuses on separating the different senses of *messiah* (Heb. משיח): originally a living, present-day individual who is "anointed" (Heb. למשוח: "to anoint with oil") as the king of Israel according to God's will. The failures of the biblical kings gave rise to a new conception of the messiah as a future king who will faithfully fulfill God's commission. After the destruction of the kingdoms of Israel and Judah, this conception of the messiah gained new, powerful valences: first a future king who would restore Jewish sovereignty and independence, then a servant of YHVH who would bring knowledge of his sovereignty to all the nations, and finally a cosmic figure who would usher in transformative redemption leading to the eschaton.

The messianic idea is transformed yet again in the modern period with the birth of a hope that has been characterized as the "depersonalization" of redemption, focused not on an individual anointed as God's redemptive agent but rather on a period ushered in by "progressive" social and political action. In his Prague lectures of 1911 (the "Drei Reden"), Buber views Jewish teachings, including the idea of God, as products of the Jewish people's religious genius. Hence, he celebrates messianism as "Judaism's most profoundly original idea."[1] He presents socialism as a contemporary instantiation of the messianic ideal "reduced in scope, made finite."[2] This period concludes with Buber in the throes of a *Kriegserlebnis* (war-enthusiasm), imagining the fraternal solidarity forged in the trenches and on the home front during the Great War as heralding the overcoming of the decadent individualistic ethos of bourgeois civilization and the dawn of a new era.

Buber would eventually realize that the war was not to be viewed as a spiritual event but as a wholly unnecessary waste of human lives. Starting in 1916, he would develop what may be characterized as an anarchistic conception of messianism, adumbrating a vision of human community beyond the divisive boundaries of nation-states and the fury of nationalism. In an article he published in 1918, he observed with reference to the biblical book of Samuel that the moment when the people ask Samuel to give them a king—that they may "be like all the nations" (1 Sam. 8:20), rejecting God himself, who had previously been king over them—"*This* moment is the true turning point of Jewish history."[3]

The implications of this shift are not yet fully visible in his account of messianism. For Buber still equates the "wait for the Messiah" with "the wait for the true community."[4] Nonetheless, a new direction is proclaimed here, which will culminate in a logical extension of the principle of taking God's kingship seriously and rejecting as sinful the human king: the anointed one/messiah. Throughout the next decade, Buber immersed himself in the Bible to a deeper extent than before, through lecture courses at the Frankfurt Lehrhaus and through the translation of the Hebrew Bible into German he undertook with Franz Rosenzweig. As a result, a new "theopolitical" antimessianism crystallized. Throughout the 1920s he wrestled with this question of effective action either toward "redemption" in the world or as the test of the relation between religion and politics. In essays and lectures from the late 1920s and early 1930s, Buber reaches the conclusion:

BUBER'S CONCEPT OF THEOPOLITICS 301

One should, I believe, neither seek politics nor avoid it, one should be neither political nor non-political on principle. [. . .] There is no legitimately messianic, no legitimately messianically-intended, politics. But that does not imply that the political sphere may be excluded from the hallowing of all things. The political "serpent" is not essentially evil, it is itself only misled; it, too, ultimately wants to be redeemed.[5]

If we adopt the rhetoric of "maturity" from the discourse about Buber's dialogism, this is the "mature" theopolitical position. Theopolitics authorizes neither a politics nor an antipolitics, and it does not have an eschatological telos. It redeems, but in this world, which is to say it hallows. At the same time, theopolitics is torn by a powerful inner tension. On one hand, it opposes any attempt to legitimize politics theologically. On the other, it seems to engage in its own form of legitimation—not of any particular regime of state authority but rather of a radical politics, sometimes considered an antipolitics: anarchism. Buber's fullest exploration of this tension occurs not in any political essay but in a biblical study, *Kingship of God* (1932).

A tightly argued scholarly disquisition, *Kingship of God* was nonetheless heavily criticized by many of the scholars to whom it was directed. But this is unsurprising, since not only did *Kingship of God* advance a radical argument about biblical theopolitics, using unconventional methodology, it also criticized the same fields within which it tried to situate itself. Buber would later respond to his critics at length and in detail, but already in the preface to the first edition, he acknowledged his overarching objective, as it "matured in me," was to trace "the origin of 'messianism' in Israel."[6] Buber settled on a threefold division of the subject, which he would address in a trilogy entitled *Das Kommende. Untersuchungen zur Entstehungsgeschichte des messianischen Glaubens* (*The Coming One: Investigations into the Historical Origins of the Messianic Faith*). The first volume, *Kingship of God*, would treat the idea of God's direct kingship as "an actual-historical one for the early period of Israel." The second volume, *Der Gesalbte* (*The Anointed*), would show how the direct kingship of God turned into an indirect kingship, mediated by the "anointed one of God," the messiah/king of Israel. The final volume would address the transformation of the concept "from history to eschatology." From the publication of *Kingship of God* through the Nazi shutdown of the Schocken Press in 1938, just prior to Buber's flight to Palestine, he pursued this project, but upon arrival in Palestine he faced financial and other pressures to focus on other subjects. *Der Gesalbte* remained unfinished, the third volume never received a title, and *Das Kommende* never quite came into being.

Although no work by Buber entitled *Das Kommende* exists, an understanding of this plan is crucial for any attempt to understand *Kingship of God* and *Der Gesalbte*. Even Buber's other biblical writings, such as *Moses* and *The Prophetic Faith*, should be considered in light of the plan for *Das Kommende*. It is the key to Buber's theopolitical vision of Israelite history as a whole. It is also important to think of *Der Gesalbte* as a work of the mid-1930s, even though the individual pieces were only published decades later, as standalone essays about Samuel and Saul.

The central claim of *Kingship of God* is that the Sinai covenant is a theopolitical and not a "religious" covenant. YHVH does not want to give the Israelites a religion, but rather to establish a kingdom. Moses recognized this, which is why he did not claim rulership for himself, nor does he institute a dynasty and pass leadership onto his sons. YHVH, alone, is to be the king of Israel. Buber here is both close to and distant from a long tradition of thinking about Jewish theocracy, especially among the founders of early modern liberalism (Hobbes and Spinoza). Ancient Israel was indeed intended to be a theocracy, but Moses was not God's viceroy or governor; he was a speaker who attempted to educate the people, used to the visible gods and hierarchy of Egypt, what it would mean to have an invisible government. Nor is the Torah as we know it the "law" of God; Buber uses biblical criticism to separate priestly material, with its cultic concerns, from the originally Mosaic intention to found a pure theocracy. The book of Judges apparently records the failure of the direct theocracy and necessity of a human monarch. But Buber calls it a composite work combining pro- and antimonarchical elements; the final redactor placed the promonarchical piece at the end, giving the whole work its melancholy atmosphere.

In the contest within ancient Israel between the partisans of the theocracy and those of the human monarchy, Buber's loyalty is clear. In his hands, this contest becomes transhistorical, extending from the biblical authors, editors, and redactors down to the interpreters, including modern scholars. But as much as Buber sees the request for a human king as the product of fear, faithlessness, and weakness, there is no nostalgia here. Even in the period of the Judges, most or even many Israelites never fully understood or subscribed to their own system, beyond a few extraordinary figures like Gideon ("I will not rule over you, nor shall my son rule over you, but only YHVH shall rule over you" [Judges 8:23]). Buber recognizes that the direct theocracy faced the challenges of any attempt to create order purely through voluntary means: both the most and the least responsible may thrive, with the latter abusing their freedom for personal gain. This paradox, however, is elevated to existential status, since Buber argues that God chose not to force the world to become God's; God waits for the voluntary turning of the people toward God, and so do God's partisans. Therefore the common understanding of the word "theocracy" is incorrect: it is applied to authoritarian systems in which a self-declared caste of religious elites attempts to force the population into compliance with a narrowly conceived vision of the divine will. Such a system is what Buber, drawing on Max Weber, calls *hierocracy*, the rule of priests. A true theocracy must necessarily look more like anarchy, with only the occasional charismatic leader acting to preserve the people in an emergency, and then fading back into the people when the task is complete. In the case of ancient Israel, this meant going about ordinary life in the pre-existing organization of tribes, with their patriarchal clan structure and chiefs, only coming together as "Israel" in special emergencies when the life of the whole people was at stake. Nonetheless, YHVH remains the king of that nation, constituted at Sinai, even when the divine sovereign does not issue new orders.

How do the centralized monarchy and the idea of the "anointed one of YHVH" arise? Buber's answer shifts between *Kingship of God* and *Der Gesalbte*. The former deals primarily with Judges and with comparing the Israelite idea of divine kingship to other ancient Near Eastern societies. Only in *Der Gesalbte* does Buber turn to a detailed examination of 1 Samuel, in which the rise of the monarchy takes place. Thus, *Kingship of God* concludes with a discussion of the "Samuelic crisis," in which "the religio-political group for which the 'Elohistic' narrative knows only the person-like designation 'Samuel'" takes a stand for the theocracy against the partisans of monarchy. An external military threat from the Philistines imperils Israel and resists several attempts to beat it back:

> Then for the first time does the people rebel against the situation which the primitive-prophetic leaders tried, ever anew and ever alike in vain, to inflame with the theocratic will toward constitution. The idea of monarchic unification is born and rises against the representatives of the divine kingship. And the crisis between the two grows to one of the theocratic impulses itself, to the crisis out of which there emerges the human king of Israel, the follower of JHWH (12:14), as His "anointed," *meshiach* JHWH, χριστὸς κυριου.⁷

The sudden use of Greek here is purposeful. The emergence of the king is explicitly linked thereby to future developments of the messianic idea, as far forward as Christianity. The "idea of monarchic unification" is figured as rebellion against God, and the later developments are tainted with the same brush.

In *Der Gesalbte*, however, once Buber turns to in-depth study of 1 Samuel, he no longer implies that "Samuel" is shorthand, a "person-like designation" for a movement. Instead, while acknowledging that the early chapters of

1 Samuel are legendary, he takes the idea of Samuel's initial apprenticeship to the House of Eli seriously. He imagines the loss of the Ark as the failure of a priestly attempt to institute an antitheocratic human leadership by ending the Philistine crisis, thus paving the way for a prophetic attempt to seize national leadership. He also returns to a much earlier view, found in *The Holy Way* (1918), that Samuel bears partial blame for the introduction of the dynastic principle by attempting to pass power to his own sons. The external military crisis is thus tied more closely to the internal theopolitical conflict. This procedure reveals two things about Buber as a Bible scholar. First, he was unafraid to deploy critical scholarship in the service of his preferred theopolitical stance. But, second, he made bold statements based on preliminary studies, which he later revised upon deeper research. Thus, he allowed his study to correct his earlier statements.

That Buber's theopolitics is primarily presented in the genre of biblical criticism is significant: Buber tends to write sympathetically when he explicates the positions of other authors, and here he works under the assumption that the author of the text is always changing. Buber's analysis of 1 Samuel in *Der Gesalbte* is as relentless as any text by Alt or von Rad; when he is done with it, only a tiny core remains as the "authentic, original" text. This core tells what Buber believes to be the first account of the rise of the monarchy, as perceived by a tradition dating back to that period itself, and without the benefit of Deuteronomist hindsight: the tradition of the prophet Nathan and his school. Nathan, Buber hypothesizes, is the only prophet who could have ever really believed that the *in*direct monarchy might work, that it might possibly form a viable alternative to the direct theocracy. This is because he conceived—based on his own experience with David, and on Samuel's report that YHVH had granted permission for the monarchy to be created—of the prophet himself as being built into the system as a kind of check on the monarch, ensuring that YHVH still really ruled and that the human king was only his governor. However, by the time Solomon constructs the Temple this idea is already seen as naive; the monarchs claim "religion" for themselves under the auspices of the Temple cult, and thereby exclude YHVH from actual government. They trade heaven for earth. God can have sacrifices and prayers, while they will make the decisions about war, economy, and society. Thus, all the later prophets stand against the kings, even if they accept that YHVH at some point in the past did allow the monarchy to exist; only Nathan, however, could have really *believed* in it.[8]

The parallels to Buber's own situation are evident. His Zionism and socialism bear the stamp of his understanding of the theopolitical origin of messianism. Buber insisted that there could be no legitimate messianic politics. If we take him seriously, we must interpret his vision of an anarchosocialist, kibbutz-based Zionism, as expressed in *Paths in Utopia* and his writings on the conflict between the Zionists and the Palestinians, as nonmessianic. To Buber, a Zionism that would *not* attempt to establish a Jewish-majority nation-state under the sponsorship of the British Empire but would instead seek to negotiate terms of immigration and settlement with the indigenous Arab population of Palestine, was a worldly possibility. Of course, many criticized Buber harshly for supposed utopianism. But even if one agrees with such critics, it must be granted that, on his own terms, the vision is not messianic. Buber's theopolitical vision, which reserves sovereignty for God and enjoins humans to eliminate domination from human affairs as much as possible, is a kind of religious Zionism.

Buber thus directed his intra-Zionist polemics primarily against secular Zionism, which he accused of forgetting the divine nature of Judaism and the Zionist task. Had he lived to witness the rise of the Religious-Zionist movement Gush Emunim in the wake of the 1967 and 1973 wars as a settlement movement in the West Bank of Palestine—deemed to be the messianic redemption of biblical Samaria and Judah—he would surely have invoked once more his distinction between prophecy and apocalyptic, as laid out in "Prophecy, Apocalyptic, and the Historical Hour" (1954). "Prophecy," Buber writes, "has in its way declared that the unique being, man, is created to be a center of surprise in creation. Because and so long as man exists, factual change of direction can take place towards salvation as well as towards disaster, starting from the world in each hour, no matter how late." With apocalyptic, on the other hand, "Everything here is predetermined, all human decisions are only sham struggles. The future does not come to pass; the future is already present in heaven, as it were, present from the beginning. [. . .] The mature apocalyptic, moreover, no longer knows an historical future in the real sense. The end of all history is near."[9] The messianism of Gush Emunim is clearly apocalyptic. Moreover, it is enamored of sovereignty and domination, and in this sense it can rightfully claim to be heir to the ancient Israelite kingdom—but for Buber, this kingdom was from the very beginning an idolatrous rebellion against God.

The distinction between prophecy and apocalyptic does not seek to condemn eschatological hope, however. The prophets, too, look forward to a time when their hopes will be realized. They do not, however, script the movement from here to there, according to some kind of "revealed" plan. Moreover, they do not conceive the realization of the redemptive act of "turning" to God (*teshuvah*) as locked behind a wall to another world—*teshuvah* is possible here, it is possible now. If it were not, they could not demand it. Thus, prophetic eschatology distinguishes between the achievement in this world of the kind of society that YHVH always intended for his covenanted people, on the one hand, and the radical transformation of creation and human nature, on the other. Mundane redemption, the freeing of the captives, does not have to wait for transcendent redemption. The analogy, alluded to in the essay on prophecy and apocalyptic but developed more fully in *Paths in Utopia* (Hebrew, 1946), is to the advantages Buber sees in the utopian socialist/anarchist tradition as against Marxism. The former is prophetic, calling for the realization of socialism now, to the greatest extent possible, while the latter, according to Buber, suffers from apocalyptic tendencies, placing the achievement of the communist society only after the cataclysmic, final, global revolution.

In 1916, Buber argued against Hermann Cohen that the battle between the principle of creativity, embodied in the nation, and the principle of order, embodied in the state, will continue until "the *Malkhut Shamayim* [Kingdom of Heaven] arises on earth; until, in the messianic form of the human world, creation and order, people and state merge into a new unity, in the community of redemption."[10] In this still-early phase of his thinking, the messianic world is imagined as reconciling basic human contradictions. These are the same contradictions behind the collapse of the original Israelite political system, the divine anarchotheocracy, and the rise of the first messiah, the king of Israel. But the prophetic message is that things could be different next time: not because the contradictions disappear, but because the people learn to live with them in a different and better way. Thus, the prophetic hope for a good society, enacted in life through the dynamic practice of theopolitics, is firmly and finally separable from the apocalyptic wish for the end of the world and the transformation and perfection of creation. This is the underlying meaning of Buber's oft-spoken phrase, "the dialogue between heaven and earth."

Notes

1. Martin Buber, "Renewal of Judaism," in *On Judaism*, ed. Nahum N. Glatzer (New York: Schocken Books, 1967), 50.

2. Martin Buber, "Judaism and Mankind," in *On Judaism*, 28. The claim is repeated in the third lecture, where Buber says that "modern socialism is a diminution, a narrowing, a finitizing of the Messianic ideal" ("Renewal of Judaism," 52).

3. Martin Buber, "The Holy Way: A Word to the Jews and to the Nations," in *On Judaism*, 117; my emphasis.

4. Buber, "The Holy Way," 111.

5. Martin Buber, "Gandhi, Politics and Us," in Buber, *Pointing the Way: Collected Essays*, ed. Maurice Friedman (New York: Harper & Brothers, 1957), 136–37. See also Martin Buber, "Politics Born of Faith," in *A Believing Humanism: My Testament, 1902–1965*, ed. Maurice Friedman (New York: Simon & Schuster, 1967), 174–78.

6. Martin Buber, preface to the first edition of *Königtum Gottes* [*Kingship of God*] (Berlin: Schocken Verlag, 1932). Buber responded to his critics in the prefaces to the second and third editions of the volume in 1936 and 1954, respectively.

7. Martin Buber, *Königtum Gottes*, in *Werke* (Munich: Kösel Verlag, 1964), 2:718, 722–23.

8. Martin Buber, *Der Gesalbte*, *Werke*, 2:807.

9. Martin Buber, "Prophecy, Apocalyptic, and the Historical Hour" (1954), in Buber, *Pointing the Way*, 198, 201, 203.

10. Martin Buber, "Zion, der Staat, und die Menschheit," *Martin Buber Werkausgabe*, 3:311.

Annotated Bibliography

PRIMARY SOURCES

Buber's most sustained and focused political work is his *Paths in Utopia*, dealing with the contrast between utopian socialism and its "scientific," Marxist variety (translated by R. F. C. Hull [Syracuse, NY: Syracuse University Press, 1996]). The rest of his political thought is scattered in essays, most prominently in *Pointing the Way* (edited and translated by Maurice Friedman and Ronald Gregor Smith [Atlantic Highlands, NJ: Humanities Press, 1988]). His theopolitical work is concentrated in his biblical writings, most prominently *Kingship of God* (translated by Richard Scheimann [Atlantic Highlands, NJ: Humanities Press, 1990]), but it is the persistent theme of his other biblical writings as well, for example, *On Zion* (translated by Stanley Godman [Syracuse, NY: Syracuse University Press, 1997]). These in turn inform his binationalism in Palestine, on which see most prominently *A Land of Two Peoples* (edited by Paul Mendes-Flohr [Chicago: University of Chicago Press, 2005]).

SECONDARY LITERATURE

Several decades ago, Steven Schwarzschild complained about the relative dearth of secondary literature on Buber's political thought in "A Critique of Martin Buber's Political Philosophy: An Affectionate Reappraisal," in *The Pursuit of the Ideal: Jewish Writings of Steven Schwarzschild*, edited by Menachem Kellner, 185–207 (Albany: State University of New York Press, 1990). This has begun to be remedied in the past decade or two. Shalom Ratzabi deals with Buber as spiritual inspiration for the Brit Shalom movement in his comprehensive *Between Zionism and Judaism: The Radical Circle in Brith Shalom, 1925–1933* (Leiden: Brill, 2002).

A new focus on Buber and the problematic of "political theology," centered on the conservative German jurist Carl Schmitt, was initiated by Nitzan Lebovic in "The Jerusalem School: The Theopolitical Hour," *New German Critique* 35, no. 3 (Fall 2008): 97–120; as well as by Paul Mendes-Flohr in "The Kingdom of God: Martin Buber's Critique of Messianic Politics," *Behemoth* 1, no. 2 (2008): 26–38. This avenue was later taken up in turn by Gregory Kaplan in "Power and Israel in Martin Buber's Critique of Carl Schmitt's Political Theology," in *Judaism, Liberalism, and Political Theology*, edited by Randi Rashkover and Martin Kavka, 155–77 (Bloomington: Indiana University Press, 2013), and by Christoph Schmidt in "Martin Buber (1878–1965): The

Theopolitical Hour," in *Makers of Jewish Modernity: Thinkers, Artists, Leaders, and the World They Made*, edited by Jacques Picard, Jacques Revel, Michael P. Steinberg, and Idith Zertal, 187–203 (Princeton, NJ: Princeton University Press, 2016).

As of this writing, Samuel Hayim Brody, *Martin Buber's Theopolitics* (Bloomington: Indiana University Press, 2018) remains the only book-length monograph on the topic. However, the secondary literature is now far richer than in Schwarzschild's day and includes the work of numerous talented scholars. For a more comprehensive bibliography, updated every few years as new scholarship is published, see Samuel Brody, "Martin Buber," *Oxford Bibliographies* (oxfordbibliographies.com).

23

Buber's Concept of *Gemeinschaft* (Community)

INKA SAUTER

There is one term that runs like a red thread throughout the works of Martin Buber: *Gemeinschaft* (community). This term manifests an ongoing search that had a deep impact on various areas of his thought. In the way Buber reflected on the "Jewish Renaissance" and Judaism in general, in how he thought politically, or in how he wanted to see the essence of human coexistence, the question of *Gemeinschaft* surfaced continuously. In the wake of World War I, when Buber gave initial expression to his dialogical philosophy, a profound change in his considerations of *Gemeinschaft* became evident. If he had previously oscillated between images of substance such as shared "blood" (that is, ethnicity) in particular and the possibility of a community based on *Wahlverwandtschaft* (elective affinity) in general, between *uraltem Material* (ancient material) and hope for fundamental change in human coexistence, at the end of the war he found a new focus in the relation between I and Thou. In this new perspective he referred in a specific way to Ferdinand Tönnies's *Gemeinschaft und Gesellschaft* (*Community and Society*). Thus, in the preface to his study *From Mysticism to Dialogue*, Paul Mendes-Flohr emphasizes the affinity of Buber's dialogical thinking to Tönnies's romanticist tone.[1] This affinity, this approximation was reflected in particular in Buber's use of the German language; in his considerations of *Gemeinschaft* he exploited the possibilities this language had gained in the course of the nineteenth century.

Early Thoughts on Community

Buber first wrote about the concept of community in 1901 in his text *Alte und neue Gemeinschaft* (Old and New Community), which he presented in the Berlin circle Neue Gemeinschaft (New community), in which he participated with Gustav Landauer. In his text, Buber stated: "All old communities are subservient to the utilitarian objectives [*Nutzzwecke*]; all old communities want only to be a wave in the flow of humanity driven by the utilitarian objectives." And, as his title suggests, he postulated a new community, which he wanted to be understood as "post-social." He declared that the new community should be directed toward life, that it should no longer be oriented toward utility but toward freedom, and that it would be based not on blood but on "elective affinity." He explicitly distinguished this idea from a "well-known sociological work" that he quoted from and which, according to his account, states that community is "by its very nature [...] pre-social." Buber even polemically stated that, in this sense, his idea of community "could well be understood as anti-social."[2]

In the same year, Buber also published a text in *Der Kunstwart* entitled *Kultur und Zivilisation* (Culture and Civilization), in which he declared that the "preservation and facilitation of life [...] are the ultimate intentions of civilization; but culture [*Kultur*] is creating the elevation and ennoblement of life." And he continued, "Civilization is based on the principle of the useful and follows the law of the smallest expenditure of energy, that is, it wants to realize the broadest possible plans with the smallest possible means; however, the works of culture are not valued according to their usefulness but according to their beauty, and beauty is always the expression of surplus."[3] Thus, in this text, Buber assigned utility—which was ultimately a signature of the old community in *Alte und neue Gemeinschaft*—to civilization and declared beauty to be the standard of *Kultur*.

Also in 1901, in *Jüdische Renaissance* Buber was concerned with a "new creation from ancient material," and he pointed out: "[I]n time, I hope, a positive, cohesive program of action will emerge from the silent cooperation of fellow striving people. Not the program of a [political or ideological] party, but the unwritten program of a movement. This movement will, above all, restore to the throne the unified, unbroken feeling for life of the Jew." In this text, Buber also focused on the *schöpferischen Kräfte* (creative forces) that in his text *Kultur und Zivilisation* he attributed to *Kultur*, and hoped for a "community of life" that would be "the old ancestral and yet again a new one."[4] Thus, his early reflections on community were combined with the seeds of a prepolitical or suprapolitical agenda. He further developed this program nearly a decade later in his famous *Three Addresses on Judaism*. In these, too, he referred to *Gemeinschaft*, to a community based on shared "substance," as he explained in the first address, entitled "Judaism and the Jews": "[The] natural objective situation is present [...] when the community [*Gemeinschaft*] of those who share with him the same constant elements and the community of those who share the same substance are one and the same; when the homeland where he grew up is also the homeland of his blood; when the language and the ways in which he grew up are, at the same time, the language and the ways of his blood."[5] It was during this time that Buber also met Tönnies, the author of *Gemeinschaft und Gesellschaft*, personally. In 1909, he edited *Die Sitte* (custom) by Tönnies as the twenty-fifth volume of the series *Die Gesellschaft* (society); the following year, they met face to face at the first Deutscher Soziologentag (German sociologists' conference), along with Georg Simmel, Ernst Troeltsch, and Max Weber.[6]

At the beginning of the Great War, Landauer excoriated Buber, who viewed the patriotic enthusiasm engendered by the war as the seed of a renewal of *Gemeinschaft*, as a "Kriegsbuber" (war-Buber).[7] But during the year 1916, Buber changed his position on the war. This change became apparent in the context of the journal founded that spring and edited by Buber, *Der Jude*. In the first issue, inaugurated with his essay "Die Losung," Buber exclaimed that, "in the catastrophic process which the Jew now witnesses among the nations [at war against one another], he discovered the great life of the community [*Gemeinschaft*] in a startling and enlightening way. [. . .] The feeling of community has dawned in him, he felt something ignite in him, before which all utilitarian objectives [*Nutzzwecke*] have collapsed, he experienced coherence [*Zusammenhang*]."[8] Buber had initially seen the war as an opportunity for self-reflection, indeed, as a vehicle for community-building, and he took up this line of thought again in "Die Losung." After reading this essay, Landauer wrote to Buber: "'It is only community [*Gemeinschaft*]' that this war has brought, according to you, to people in general, to Jews in particular. [. . .] No living person feels this way and needs such detours."[9] By summer of 1916, however, the journal met with Landauer's approval, for in response to his critique, Buber began to reconsider his conception of community.[10]

At the end of the war a new form of thinking about *Gemeinschaft* fully crystallized, one intimately connected with his evolving philosophy of dialogue. In "The Holy Way: A Word to the Jews and to the Peoples," dedicated to Landauer and published in the Spring 1919 issue of *Der Jude*, Buber placed the *wahre Gemeinschaft* (true community) at the center of his reflections. He explained that the "divine" can "awake within the individual," but that it finds its true fulfillment when individuals open up to and help one another, "where immediacy is established between beings, where the dignified dungeon of the person is unlocked and human being to human being is freed, where in the in-between, in the seemingly empty space, the eternal substance [*ewige Substanz*] arises." Thus, Buber now reflected on the *ewige Substanz* related to the divine, and he summarized his perspective as follows: "[T]he true place of the realization is community [*Gemeinschaft*], and true community is that in which the divine is realized between people." And he added a fundamental observation: "These are the outlines of the teaching [*Lehre*] on which the vocation [*Berufung*] of Judaism is built." At the same time, Buber saw the realization of true community, grounded in the divine calling and the *Befreiung von Mensch zu Mensch* (human to human liberation), as occluded by specific factors, especially by the "cult of the so-called 'pure thought' that went hand in hand with the cult of so-called '*realen Politik*.'"[11] Buber insisted that the change, the becoming and formation of community, would not be brought about by political programs but only develop from within individuals. With this vision in mind, he revisited Tönnies's *Gemeinschaft und Gesellschaft*.

Language and *Wesen* (between Essence and Being)

In *Gemeinschaft und Gesellschaft*, first published in 1887, Tönnies employed a type of language that points far back to the beginning of the nineteenth century.[12] Apodictically, he stated, "community [*Gemeinschaft*] is old, society [*Gesellschaft*] is new, both as a fact and as a concept." He proceeded to elaborate a theory according to which traditional "community," marked by intimate, warm relations of human solidarity, was increasingly replaced by a "society" of deracinated impersonal relations, centered in urban civilization. While the *Gemeinschaft* is reflected in the family, the home, as well as in "concord, customs, [and] religion," *Gesellschaft* is represented in the metropolis, the state, international economic commerce, and in "[formal] conventions, politics, [and] public opinion."[13] Tönnies assigned to *Gemeinschaft* a *Wesenwille* (inherent will of the self), in which "thinking is contained" by considerations of supportive interpersonal relations, and to *Gesellschaft* a *Willkür* (arbitrary self-will), in which thinking determines individual behavior and values. Tönnies understood these as "two types of social relations—two types of individual configurations of will."[14] He differentiated them by their temporal references: "*Wesenwille* is based on the past [. . .]; *Willkür* can only be understood from a focus on the future."[15] Buber gradually referred to these two forms of will. In "Die Losung," he speaks derogatorily of a *Willkürtakt* (tact of the arbitrary self-will). Yet it was only three years later that he incorporated Tönnies's theoretical foundation of *Gemeinschaft* into his own reflections.

Tönnies traced the *Wesenwille* back to an *Urwillen* (original, primordial will); he also wrote about *Urerinnerung* (primordial memory), about *Ursprüngliches* (primordial origin of things) and the like. The semantic field of the prefix *Ur-*, with primordial reference, was connected in Tönnies's thought with terms formed with the suffix *-tum*. Although these appear only margin-

BUBER'S CONCEPT OF *GEMEINSCHAFT* (COMMUNITY)   313

ally, they show in the overall view the range of meanings of *Gemeinschaft* in Tönnies's work. Thus he wrote of *Geschwistertum* (siblinghood) and *Vatertum* (fatherhood); he also named a *frühe Epoche des Menschentums* (early epochs of humanhood) and claimed that *Wesenwille* would be *dem Menschentum natürlich* (naturally be humanity). At the end of his text he attributed *Volkstum* (folkhood) and *Kultur* to the *Gemeinschaft* and *Staatstum* (statehood) and *Zivilisation* to the *Gesellschaft*. While *Staatstum* may seem peculiar, *Volkstum* resonates with the overall tone of the text—the adjective *volkstümlich* is as much inscribed in the definition of *Gemeinschaft* as *Volks-Seele* (soul of the folk) and as *Volks-Gemeinschaft*.[16] With the exception of *Staatstum*, the few but significant terms formed with *-tum* in *Gemeinschaft und Gesellschaft* retrieved their meanings from the past. The subtitle of the first edition was *Abhandlung des Communismus und des Socialismus als empirischer Culturformen* (A Treatise on Communism and Socialism as Empirical Forms of Culture).[17] These *-ismen* (-isms) were pushed into the background over time: the second edition, published twenty-five years later in 1912, had the rather reserved subtitle of *Grundbegriffe der reinen Soziologie* (Basic Concepts of Pure Sociology). While Tönnies continued to include only a few *-tümer*, the peripheral inscription of *Volkstum* in the text is nevertheless significant. Buber also employed the suffix *-tum*: he used *Deutschtum* occasionally and *Volkstum* repeatedly. But most importantly, he referred to Tönnies's concept of *Gemeinschaft* and sought to envision it in his own unique way. For Tönnies as well as for Buber, the suffix *-tum* was self-evident in a specific way; it was, as it were, an expression of traditions, and so the linguistic coloring they sought to evoke gains its meaning through the history of the suffix.

At the end of the eighteenth century, the suffix was not yet endowed with the semantic depth that Tönnies implicitly evoked and Buber drew on in his own way. In 1780, Johann Christoph Adelung, who contributed to the standardization of the German language with his *Wörterbuch der hochdeutschen Mundart* (Dictionary of the High German Dialect), explained in the fourth volume quite clearly that the term *Thum* was obsolete and only in use as a suffix. As such it stood for "jurisdiction," "territory," "district," but also for "dignity" and "power" and was being used only to a limited extent.[18] Only twenty years later, in 1801, the linguist Joachim Heinrich Campe rediscovered or introduced various words with the suffix *-tum* in an effort to purify the German language of foreign expressions—to keep the German language comprehensible to all who spoke it. In particular, his suggestion for *Humanität* (humanity) is significant, for he first considered *Menschentum*, but this term was ultimately too static for him, not understood as an attitude, so he invented the neologism *Menschentümlichkeit*. In analogy to *Eigenthümlichkeit*, he added

-*lichkeit*, and *menschentümlich* was the term he coined for *human*.[19] Although these suggestions by Campe did not prevail, his view on *Menschentum* indicated an orientation toward the past in the semantics of the suffix -*tum* that was soon to be politicized. It developed into an imagined foundation on which a prospective community was to be built; it was envisioned to indicate something original, something that was supposed to have always existed.

Friedrich Ludwig Jahn, the founder of the *Turnbewegung* (gymnastics movement), created the words *Volksthum*, *volksthümlich*, and *Volksthümlichkeit* in his 1810 writing *Deutsches Volksthum*—in striking similarity to Campe's suggestions, but with an intermediate step to Johann Gottlieb Fichte's *Eigenthümlichkeit des deutschen Volkes* (distinctive individuality of the German Folk).[20] At first, Jahn did not use the term *Deutschthum*, which emerged at the time and gradually became the guiding concept for a connection of ethnic meaning and belonging. But in 1833, he wrote that the French words as "moral, legal and governmental terms would deface [and] distort *Deutschthum*." Jahn opposed the political overtones of French influences and related *Deutschthum* to the German language itself. Concerning *Thum* in general, he pointed out that it "remains an epitome, [of] what appears whole in connection [*Zusammenhang*] and in being together [*Zusammenseyn*], according to principal laws [*Grundgesetzten*] or principles [*Grundsätzen*], in an interrelation of all belongings [*Gehörigkeiten*]," where it stands above *Zeiten* (historical time).[21] In the semantic field of the suffix, this was an approximation on the topos of *Wesen* (oscillating between essence and being) in the German language, which was condensed in *Deutschtum* and effectively transcended the transient wiles of politics.

In the course of the nineteenth century, terms with the suffix -*tum*—also independent of political programs—were increasingly used to replace the horizon of expectations directed at humanity. This horizon of expectations was expressed in certain derivatives with the suffix -*ismus*, which tended to belong more to the ideas of modern society. *Deutschtum* and *Volkstum*, on the other hand, became expressions of *Gemeinschaft*; the suffix -*tum* itself was now used in the meaning of *Wesen*. Even though linguistic histories are rarely linear and this is only one example, it was possible for Karl Weigand to write in his dictionary in 1857 "*Deutschthum* (= *deutsches Wesen*)."[22] At the fin de siècle, -*tümer* began to be more frequently deployed and also reached beyond the limits of *völkisch* thought. The suffix -*tum* gave terms that were comparatively new the appearance of a supratemporal validity gained from the past, a validity of the *Wesen*, similar to how Buber used it. In 1918, for example, in a fictional, pedagogically oriented dialogue entitled *Jüdisch Leben* (Living Jewishly), he had the mentor say: "The people [*das Volk*] [. . .] is a multiplicity

[*Vielheit*] of human beings, but it is recognized as a unity [*Einheit*], namely as a unity of the idea. And this idea—which we do not wish to and are unable to formulate any further, but nevertheless [are] clearly aware of it—would be the *Volkstum*, here to be called *Deutschtum*."[23] The connection would exist in a unity that encompasses past, present, and future: it would transcend all times (*über den Zeiten*).

When Buber wrote these lines, the German language had gained a sphere of *Wesenhaftigkeit* (essentiality) that gave it depth and pathos and that was to have its effect from within. Nevertheless, this *Wesenhaftigkeit* remained mostly undefined and expressed itself rather in oppositions, as it also resonated in *Gemeinschaft* and *Gesellschaft*, *Kultur* and *Zivilisation*, *Wesenwille* and *Willkür*. And perhaps Buber still adhered to this indeterminacy when, on the occasion of his eightieth birthday, he recalled how he had grown up in a multilingual environment in which the "fact of different *Volkstümer* indelibly engraved itself on me," emphasizing the role of the German language: "[T]he German word had an inherent pathos. This came from the fact that my grandmother, Adele Buber, who raised me into my fourteenth year, guarded this language like a treasure. She had once [. . .] kept her beloved German books, forbidden as secular in her ghetto home, hidden in the attic; I still own her copy of Jean Paul's 'Levana.'"[24] This specific form of pathos echoed in Buber's dialogical philosophy—drawing on Tönnies's core concept of *Gemeinschaft*.

Emerging *Gemeinschaft*

Toward the end of the first edition (1887) of *Gemeinschaft und Gesellschaft*, Tönnies wrote: "And since the entire culture [*Kultur*] has been transformed into the social [*gesellschaftliche*] and governmental [*staatliche*] ambit of civilization, culture itself comes to an end in this transformed form."[25] Tönnies, however, did not completely abandon the hope for re-emergence of *Kultur* when he added to this sentence in the second edition: "unless its scattered seeds remain alive, [and] the essence [*Wesen*] and ideas of community [*Gemeinschaft*] are again nourished and secretly unfold new culture within the perishing one."[26] For Tönnies, therefore, there was the possibility, at least from 1912 onward, of *Gemeinschaft* and *Kultur* consolidating themselves anew. Buber placed this second, longer version of Tönnies's sentence, which was no longer merely directed to the past, before his text *Gemeinschaft*, published in 1919 in the series *Worte an die Zeit*, alongside a quotation from Landauer and one from Tolstoi.[27] Buber elaborated in his text, following Tönnies quite directly: "community [*Gemeinschaft*] is the expression and manifestation of the original (primordial), naturally homogeneous, relation-bearing will that represents the totality of humankind; society [*Gesellschaft*] is the expression and manifestation of differentiated, profit-seeking [will] that is generated by detached thought and removed from the totality of humankind." And Buber continued: "Community is grown relatedness [*Verbundenheit*], welded together by common possession (predominantly land), common work, common customs, common beliefs; society means regulated separateness, held together externally by coercion, contract, convention, or public opinion."[28]

This text was virtually on the way to *I and Thou*. Thus, in 1919, Buber took the perspective of the seeker of *Gemeinschaft*, called for "disengagement from all advantageous arbitrary self-will [*vorteilssüchtigen Willkür*]," and stated:

> It is a fact that we who have gone through the age of individualism, that is, the separation of the person from its natural social connex, can no longer find our way back to the original life of community. For [this original life] was not a union of separate individuals, but a whole that presented itself as binding together the manifoldness of individuals with strong and untouchable holy bonds. [. . .] To such elementary wholeness we cannot return. But we can advance to a different, creative unity that, though it is not *grown* like the first, can still be *created* from true soul material and is, therefore, no less authentic.[29]

The social was now also for Buber the generic term in which different ways of being and living together were described; his perspective was no longer antisocial or postsocial. He assumed that *Gemeinschaft* and *Gesellschaft* "were the expression and formation of types of wills [*Willensarten*]." He placed his hope in the new emergence of a *vital-bewußten Totalwillen* (vitally conscious will for totality). To explain this *Totalwillen*, he drew on Tönnies's concepts—with a slight variation: "The detached thinking once decomposed this '*Wesenswille*' [sic] to '*Willkür*'; from a won integrity of the spirit [*Geist*], to which also the thinking must fit in serving, it can resurrect on a later stage of transformed essence [*Wesen*]."[30]

He concluded his reflections in 1919 by outlining a path to this goal: People "who long for community [*Gemeinschaft*] long for God. All craving for real relationship points to God; and all craving for God points to community." However, "[C]raving God is not the same as willing God. Men search for God but cannot find Him, for He is 'not there.' Men want to possess God, but God does not give Himself to them, for He does not wish to be possessed but to be realized. Only when men want God to be will they practice community."[31]

Buber pursued this hope for the emergence of *Gemeinschaft*—as opposed to *Gesellschaft*—over the years on various levels. In doing so, he dynamized his conception of *Gemeinschaft*, but continued to let it emanate from the topoi discovered in Tönnies and, in particular, incorporated them into his expositions of *Beziehung* (relation). In *Ich und Du*, Buber writes in a way analogous to his earlier *Worte an die Zeit: Gemeinschaft*: "But in the idea of the social life two basically different things are combined—first, the community [*Gemeinschaft*] that is built up out of relation, and second, the collection of human units [*Mensch-Einheiten*] that do not know relation—the modern man's palpable condition of lack of relation." In this line of reasoning, *Gemeinschaft* was deeply related to "the basic word I-Thou," it was formed in I-Thou relations, while a collection of unrelated human beings was based in the "basic word I-It." In his specification of *Gemeinschaft* in *I and Thou*, Buber resorted to Tönnies's terms and emphasized an intrinsically related distinction, namely, that of "person" and "individuality [*Eigenwesen*]," "the free and the arbitrary self-willing human being [*willkürlichen Menschen*]" as the "two poles of humanity [*Menschentum*]." But in contrast to Tönnies, who understood his concepts in the scope of human history, Buber perceived them first and foremost as inherent in human interactions as such. In Buber's distinction between *Gemeinschaft* and an unrelated collection, the opening of *I and Thou*—the *zwiefältige Haltung* (twofold attitude) of the human being—was taken up again in the realm of the social, as Buber explained: "No human being is a pure person, no one is a pure individuality [*Eigenwesen*], no one is completely real, no one is completely unreal. Everyone lives in the twofold I."[32]

At the same time, Buber also connected the suffix *-tum*—at least in the periphery—with the core idea of his philosophy of dialogue when he elaborated: "Every particular Thou is a glimpse through to the eternal Thou; by means of every particular Thou the primary word addresses the eternal Thou. Through this mediation [*Mittlertum*] of the Thou of all beings fulfilment, and non-fulfilment, of relations comes to them."[33] Thus Buber inscribed quite inconspicuously the coloring of language connected to *Wesen* in the transition from the "[e]very particular Thou" to the eternal, as *Mittlertum*. Although the term *Gemeinschaft* itself was used only comparatively rarely in *I and Thou*— but *Gemeinde* (translatable also as community, but denoting specifically a religious community) and *Gemeinleben* (coexistence of human beings) were added—the questions related to the core of *Gemeinschaft* were inscribed in the philosophy of dialogue. After all, the duality still corresponded to Tönnies's distinction between *Wesenwille* and *Willkür*, and at the same time it became the argumentative key moment of the tracing back of social forms to the "basic words I-Thou" and "I-It." Buber did not use the term *Wesenwille* in this context, and when he used it in other texts, then only in a slight variation as *Wesen-s-wille* (with the letter *s* added in the middle), as for example in *Worte an die Zeit: Gemeinschaft*. Tönnies himself had explained the term in his text *Die Sitte*: "I invented the term (artificial expression) '*Wesenwille*' and keep it, although it has found almost no reception so far."[34] For Buber, who after all was the editor of *Die Sitte*, the artificial expression *Wesenwillen* was not suitable, but he quite clearly referred to the determinations that were assigned to it by Tönnies; indeed, for Buber they became the very medium of I-Thou relations.

In 1929, Buber again drew on Tönnies's notion of *Gemeinschaft* as a starting point for his reflections in *Erziehung zur Gemeinschaft* (Education toward Community). While writing again *Wesenswille*, he expanded the term *Gemeinschaft* from within. First, he set the basic condition: "Everything depends on whether there is a beyond in *Gemeinschaft* or not, i.e., whether there is not only a subsocietal [*untergesellschaftliche*] but also a supersocietal [*übergesellschaftliche*] community [*Gemeinschaft*] or not." Following this basic condition, he specified—and this is striking—the "new content of community [*Gemeinschaftsgehalt*] [. . .] is no longer based on commonality [*Gemeinsamkeit*], objective possessions such as custom and the like, [. . .] but this content of community can be founded on a community attitude [*Gemeinschaftlichkeit*], even more clearly: not on static but dynamic togetherness, [. . .] on a genuine relation between differently created, differently ordered human beings."[35] Thus, for Buber, the "grown connectedness" receded into the background in favor of relation; Buber described this inner dynamic as *Gemeinschaftlichkeit*—adding *-lichkeit* in order to refer to the attitude embedded in his concept of *Gemeinschaft*; its center is the fact that *Wesen* and *Wesen* turn to each other. In a typescript entitled *Individuum und Person—Masse und Gemeinschaft* (Individual and Person—Masses and Community), which can plausibly be dated to 1931, Buber described the isms as expressed in *Kollektivismus* (collectivism) as "ideological volatilities and inadequacies." On the other hand, he determined: "People [*Volk*] is community [*Gemeinschaft*], natural community i.e., a living together of human beings, which is more original than the human beings [*urtümlicher als die Menschen*]."[36]

In *Zwiesprache* (Dialogue), Buber further elucidated his thought of *Gemeinschaft* in terms of relation. This is the "not-anymore-next-to-each-other, but togetherness of a multiplicity [*Vielheit*] of persons, which [. . .] experiences everywhere a towards each other, a dynamic opposite, a flooding from I to Thou: community [*Gemeinschaft*] is where community happens." Now it was a *Kollektivität* (collectivity) illustrated with mass and marching that he took as a counterterm to *Gemeinschaft*, and he wrote: "[C]ollectivity is based on an organized dwindling of the personhood [*Personhaftigkeit*], the community on its increase and confirmation in being directed towards each other."[37] Buber's search directed at the emerging *Gemeinschaft*, which itself rested on passing notions of the collective, thus repeatedly came to the fore after *Worte an die Zeit: Gemeinschaft*. This, however, was also a search for suitable terms,

BUBER'S CONCEPT OF GEMEINSCHAFT (COMMUNITY) 319

in which he sought to dynamize the notion of *Gemeinschaft* through the word form itself—using the means of the German language. In parallel with these reflections, which, while increasingly addressing the interrelation of human beings, continued to refer to *Wesen*, Buber quite naturally used terms such as *Volkstum* and *Menschentum*. And still in *Pfade in Utopia. Über Gemeinschaft und deren Verwirklichung* (*Paths in Utopia: On Community and Its Realization*), written at the end of World War II, he stated: "The original hope [*Urhoffnung*] of all history goes to a genuine, thus quite *community-oriented* community [*gemeinschaftshaltige Gemeinschaft*] of humankind."[38]

In his later years Buber retrospectively explained that already in his childhood he had been concerned with the limits of languages: "I followed a single word or even a word structure from one language to another, found it there again, and yet always had to give up something in it which apparently existed only in one of the languages."[39] Accordingly, Buber reflected on the different logoi of languages, and so it is not accidental that he cast his philosophy of dialogue in words that were quite unique to the German language. In Buber's thinking, they referred to a conception of *Gemeinschaft* that—for all his hope of renewal—should transcend all times, which was ultimately directed against the distortions of modern society. Notwithstanding his intention of overcoming, without demanding a return to premodern manifestations of *Gemeinschaft*, and despite the dynamic character of I-Thou relations, an intimate connection of German language and *Wesen* was articulated in his choice of words. They referred to a semantics of belonging that emerged in the nineteenth century and found its paradigmatic expression in Buber's hope that *Wesen* and *Wesen* would turn to each other.

Notes

1. Cf. Paul Mendes-Flohr, *From Mysticism to Dialogue: Martin Buber's Transformation of German Social Thought* (Detroit: Wayne State University Press, 1989), 9.

2. Martin Buber, "Alte und neue Gemeinschaft," in *Martin Buber Werkausgabe*, vol. 2, pt. 1, *Mythos und Mystik. Frühe religionswissenschaftliche Schriften*, ed. David Groiser (Gütersloh: Gütersloher Verlagshaus, 2015), 62, 64–66.

3. Martin Buber, "Kultur und Zivilisation. Einige Gedanken zu diesem Thema" (1901), in *Martin Buber Werkausgabe*, vol. 1, *Frühe kulturkritische und philosophische Schriften 1891–1924*, ed. Martin Treml (Gütersloh: Gütersloher Verlagshaus, 2001), 157.

4. Martin Buber, "Jüdische Renaissance" (1901), in *Martin Buber Werkausgabe*, vol. 3, *Frühe jüdische Schriften*, ed. Barbara Schäfer (Gütersloh: Gütersloher Verlagshaus, 2007), 146, 147.

5. Martin Buber, "Judaism and the Jews," in Buber, *On Judaism*, ed. N. N. Glatzer (New York: Schocken Books, 1967), 16.

6. Ferdinand Tönnies, *Die Sitte*, ed. Martin Buber (Frankfurt am Main: Rütten & Loening, 1909); cf. Mendes-Flohr, *From Mysticism to Dialogue*, 80, 88–92.

7. Gustav Landauer to Martin Buber, May 12, 1916, in Martin Buber, *Briefwechsel aus sieben Jahrzehnten*, vol. 1, *1897–1918* (Heidelberg: Lambert Schneider, 1972), 433; cf. Mendes-Flohr, *From Mysticism to Dialogue*, 93–102.

8. Martin Buber, "Die Losung," in *Martin Buber Werkausgabe*, 3:287; see also Martin Buber, "Die Tempelweihe," in *Martin Buber Werkausgabe*, 3:284.

9. Landauer to Buber, May 12, 1916, 436.

10. Cf. Gustav Landauer to Martin Buber, August 22, 1916, in Buber, *Briefwechsel*, 1:451.

11. Martin Buber, *Der heilige Weg. Ein Wort an die Juden und an die Völker*, in *Martin Buber Werkausgabe*, vol. 11, pt. 1, *1906–1938*, ed. Stefano Franchini (Gütersloh: Gütersloher Verlagshaus, 2019), 130, 133.

12. Cf. Dieter Haselbach, "Vorwort," in Ferdinand Tönnies, *Gesamtausgabe*, vol. 2, *1880–1935. Gemeinschaft und Gesellschaft*, ed. Bettina Clausen and Diester Haselbach (Berlin: Walter De Gruyter, 2019), xiv.

13. Ferdinand Tönnies, *Gemeinschaft und Gesellschaft. Grundbegriffe der reinen Soziologie*, 2nd ed. (Berlin: Karl Curtius, 1912), 5, 303.

14. Tönnies, *Gemeinschaft und Gesellschaft*, xiv, 103. In the English translation, *Wesenwille* is translated as "'natural' will or 'organic' will or 'essential' will": Tönnies, *Community and Civil Society*, trans. Jose Harris and Margaret Hollis (Cambridge: Cambridge University Press, 2001), 95.

15. Tönnies, *Gemeinschaft und Gesellschaft* (1912), 104.

16. Tönnies, *Gemeinschaft und Gesellschaft* (1912), 106–7, 163, 259, 11–12, 105, 293–94, 191, 236, 238.

17. Ferdinand Tönnies, *Gemeinschaft und Gesellschaft. Abhandlung des Communismus und des Socialismus als empirischer Culturformen* (Leipzig: Fues's Verlag, 1887).

18. Johann Christoph Adelung, "Thum," in Adelung, *Grammatisch-kritisches Wörterbuch der hochdeutschen Mundart 4: Sche-V* (Leipzig: Breitkopf, 1780), 696–97.

19. Joachim Heinrich Campe, "Humanität," in Campe, *Wörterbuch zur Erklärung und Verdeutschung der unserer Sprache aufgedrungenen fremden Ausdrücke* (Braunschweig: Schulbuchhandlung, 1801), 404.

20. Friedrich Ludwig Jahn, *Deutsches Volksthum* (Lübeck: Niemann und Comp, 1810), 9; Johann Gottlieb Fichte, *Reden an die deutsche Nation* (Berlin: Realschulbuchhandlung, 1808), 186.

21. Friedrich Ludwig Jahn, *Merke zum Deutschen Volksthum* (Hildburghausen: Knopf, 1833), 206, 16–17.

22. Friedrich Ludwig Karl Weigand, *Deutsches Wörterbuch* (Gießen: Ricker'sche Buchhandlung, 1857), 243.

23. Martin Buber, "Jüdisch leben. Zwei Gespräche. Meinem Sohn Rafael gewidmet," in *Martin Buber Werkausgabe*, vol. 8, *Schriften zu Jugend, Erziehung und Bildung*, ed. Juliane Jacobi (Gütersloh: Gütersloher Verlagshaus, 2005), 96–97.

24. Martin Buber, "Erinnerung," in *Martin Buber Werkausgabe*, vol. 7, *Schriften zur Literatur, Theater und Kunst Lyrik, Autobiographie und Drama*, ed. Emily D. Bilski, Heike Breitenbach, Freddie Rokem, and Bernd Witte (Gütersloh: Gütersloher Verlagshaus, 2016), 272.

25. Tönnies, *Gemeinschaft und Gesellschaft* (1887), 288.

26. Tönnies, *Gemeinschaft und Gesellschaft* (1912), 303.

27. Martin Buber, "Worte an die Zeit: Gemeinschaft," in *Martin Buber Werkausgabe*, vol. 11, pt. 1, 162.

28. Martin Buber, "Community" (1919), trans. Asher D. Biemann, in *The Martin Buber Reader: Essential Writings*, ed. Asher D. Biemann (New York: Palgrave Macmillan, 2002), 245.

BUBER'S CONCEPT OF GEMEINSCHAFT (COMMUNITY)   321

29. Buber, "Community," 248 (emphasis in original).
30. Buber, "Community," 248; Buber, "Worte an die Zeit: Gemeinschaft," 164.
31. Buber, "Community," 251.
32. Martin Buber, *I and Thou*, trans. Ronald Gregor Smith, centennial ed. (New York: Scribner Classics, 2023), 103, 69; *Ich und Du*, in *Martin Buber Werkausgabe*, vol. 4, *Schriften über das dialogische Prinzip*, ed. Paul Mendes-Flohr, Kommentar, Andreas Losch (Gütersloh: Gütersloher Verlagshaus, 2019), 101, 76.
33. Buber, *I and Thou*, 77; Buber, *Ich und Du*, 82.
34. Tönnies, *Die Sitte*, 17.
35. Martin Buber, "Erziehung zur Gemeinschaft," in *Martin Buber Werkausgabe*, vol. 11, pt. 1, 304–5 (*Wesenswille*, 302; *Wesen zu Wesen*, 311).
36. Martin Buber, "Individuum und Person—Masse und Gemeinschaft," in *Martin Buber Werkausgabe*, vol. 11, pt. 1, 354–56.
37. Martin Buber, "Zwiesprache," in *Martin Buber Werkausgabe*, 4:141; "Dialogue," in Buber, *Between Man and Man*, trans. Ronald Gregor Smith (London: Routledge, 2020), 35–38.
38. Martin Buber, "Pfade in Utopia. Über Gemeinschaft und deren Verwirklichung," in *Martin Buber Werkausgabe*, vol. 11, pt. 2, *1938–1965*, ed. Massimiliano De Villa (Gütersloh: Gütersloher Verlagshaus, 2019), 255 (emphasis in original).
39. Martin Buber, "Begegnung. Autobiografische Fragmente," in *Martin Buber Werkausgabe*, 7:276 ("Logoi," 277).

Annotated Bibliography

For the development of Buber's conception of community, from its initial Romantic and ethnic inflections to its grounding in dialogical relations, see Paul Mendes-Flohr, *From Mysticism to Dialogue: Martin Buber's Transformation of German Social Thought* (Detroit: Wayne State University Press, 1989). Francesco Ferrari offers a synoptic account of Buber's thoughts on community: see his introduction to *Martin Buber Werkausgabe. Schriften zur politischen Philosophie und zur Sozialphilosophie*, vol. 11, pt. 1 (Gütersloh: Gütersloher Verlagshaus, 2019). Amir Engel provides insights into the connection between Jewish politics and Romantic mysticism: "From the *Neue Gemeinschaft* to Bar Kochba: The Jewish *Communitas* or the Idea of Jewish Politics as Mysticism," *Religions* 13, no. 12 (2022): 1143, https://doi.org/10.3390/rel13121143. Michael Löwy discusses the political underpinnings of Buber's dialogical conception of community: "Martin Buber's Socialism," *Journal of Jewish Thought and Philosophy* 25, no. 1 (2017): 95–104.

In an article from 1976, Paul Mendes-Flohr and Bernhard Susser noted Buber was likely indebted to Ferdinand Tönnies's *Gemeinschaft und Gesellschaft* (1887); see David Groiser, commentary to Buber, "'Alte und neue Gemeinschaft': An Unpublished Buber Manuscript," *AJS Review* 1 (1976): 41–56. Groiser, while emphasizing the importance of Tönnies, shows, however, that Buber quoted Tönnies's work as cited in Ludwig Stein's 1897 lectures, *Die sociale Frage im Lichte der Philosophie* (The Social Question in the Light of Philosophy); see Groiser, introduction and commentary to *Martin Buber Werkausgabe. Frühe religionswissenschaftliche Schriften*, vol. 2, pt. 1 (Gütersloh: Gütersloher Verlagshaus, 2013). Tönnies's influence on Buber was, indeed, only manifest two decades later.

For a discussion of Buber's relation to *Volkish* or Romantic ethnic conceptions of community and how he came decidedly to distinguish his dialogical understanding of what constitutes communal bonds, see Manuel Duarte de Oliveira, "A Passion for Land and Volk: Martin Buber and Neo-Romanticism," *Leo Baeck Year Book* 41 (1996): 239–60; and Yemima Hadad, "Hasidic Myth-Activism: Martin Buber's Theopolitical Revision of Volkish Nationalism," *Religions* 10, no. 2 (2019): 96, https://doi.org/10.3390/rel10020096.

On the far-reaching semantic change of the German suffix *-tum*, beyond its Volkish inflections, see Inka Sauter, "Sinn ohne Wort. Vom 'Volksthum' und anderen 'Thumheiten,'" *Geschichte der Gegenwart* (March 29, 2020), https://geschichtedergegenwart.ch/sinn-ohne-wort-vom-volksthum-und-anderen-thumheiten/; and Inka Sauter, "'Ein modernes Verdeutschungs-Unternehmen'. Über die historische Semantik der Buber-Rosenzweig-Bibel," *Naharaim* 15, no. 2 (2021): 243–67.

24

The Ethical View of the Palestinian Other

AMAL JAMAL

A critical examination of the relationship between Jews and Palestinians, in light of Martin Buber's views on their rights over the same land and the way he imagines their shared future, could assist in cautiously and modestly reflecting on the virtues, flaws, and tensions embedded in the ethical and ontological presuppositions of his thought.

Buber's political vision and discourse, based on his rejection of deontological ethics, draw our attention to his principle that "All actual life is an encounter."[1] Accordingly, how he conceived of the encounter between Jews and Palestinians could be a propitious avenue to engage in a critical evaluation of his philosophy of dialogue. When locating his ethical theory in the concrete context of Jewish-Palestinian relations, we cannot assume that Buber was not cognizant of the fact that the Jews and the Palestinians spoke different languages, came from different cultures, and each had a different relationship to the place they considered their homeland. Although it can be argued that he philosophically affirms cultural diversity and difference, nonetheless he does not discuss the question of the cognitive and cultural significance of their respective languages and cultures. I am referring not only to the linguistic differences between Jews and Palestinians, especially the Jewish community of which Buber was a member, coming from Europe and viewing the East through a tendentious orientalist lens, but also to differences of cultural and spiritual language. Buber's language assumed an egalitarian ontology between Jews and Palestinians. Therefore, from the perspective of this premise, we ought to pose questions regarding the Jewish-Palestinian encounter, its characteristics and implications. Exploring the ontological assumptions and their ethical ramifications as articulated in Buber's concept of a binational Jewish-Palestinian state could allow for a deeper understanding of the extent to which such a theory provides the right path for a genuine dialogue between Jews and Palestinians.

Nationalism, Binationalism, and the Politics of Nonrecognition

Buber advocated a binational state whereby Jews and Palestinians would share sovereignty on the land that both regarded as their ancient patrimony, thus intending to resolve the conflict between them. He deemed this framework to be not only just but also as promoting mutual understanding and fraternity.[2] He thus presented binationalism not just as a political framework but also and preeminently as an ethical relationship based on his more general philosophical conception of dialogical encounter. Binationalism was, therefore, conceived as a formula that would foster the overcoming of the conflict between Jews and Palestinians through a dialogue enabling mutual recognition of their respective existential and political reality. According to Buber, mutual respect based on mutual recognition emerges the moment that people are sympathetically attentive to the needs, the pain, and the distress of others.[3] The encounter leads to a sense of community based on a reciprocal confirmation of each other's existential and political reality.

The vision of such an encounter leads us to the question of whether the asymmetry of power relations allows for a genuine dialogical relation between the Jews and Palestinians. For their encounter is fraught with the challenge of establishing dialogical equality in a nonegalitarian political reality. Moreover, Buber assumed that the envisioned dialogue would lead to the Palestinians' affirmation of the Zionist settlement in Palestine, based as it was on the claim that the erstwhile proprietor of the land of Israel was returning to repossess this long-lost possession, and so implicitly assigning the Palestinians the responsibility of righting a wrong that been done by someone else in the distant past.

Thus, it is important to note from the Palestinian perspective the ethical and practical challenges that confound Buber's advocacy of the binational solution to the Zionist-Arab conflict. In this context, a basic argument is that the challenges of Buberian binationalism do not stem from external reality or political constraints over which Buber had no control, but are rooted in the Zionist project, which he himself endorsed, albeit he sought to free it from the sting of an aggressive, self-righteous nationalism. Ultimately, again from the Palestinian perspective, there is a fundamental contradiction between Buber's binationalism and the ethical I-Thou imperative. The attachment of the Jewish nation to its ancient homeland is an attachment to land where hundreds of thousands of Arabs have been living for centuries, a people with national aspirations identical to those of the Jews. In addition, the epistemology at the basis of binationalism is incompatible with the I-Thou imperative; indeed, it is burdened by an I-It attitude, considering Buber's implicit objectivization of the Palestinians.

Although Buber criticized Zionism for its alliance with British colonialism and its failure to acknowledge Palestinian national rights, when he emigrated to Palestine in 1938, he acted within the Zionist political framework in order to advance his own vision. To be sure, Buber cannot be held accountable for the development of the Zionist project and the establishment of the State of Israel. Nonetheless, as previously noted, one may question whether Buber's position with respect to the lived reality of the Palestinian Arabs was consistent with his philosophy of dialogue. Buber's concept of dialogue—the I-Thou relation—posits the fundamental humanity shared by both parties of the relation. When applied to the political reality of Palestine, it assumes that the *Jewish* "I" has an a priori, nonnegotiable right to Palestine. In other words, Buber talks about equality in an unequal political reality and thus blatantly contradicts the ontological presuppositions of a genuine dialogical encounter. Buber's call for partnership with the Palestinians was that of a small minority that had migrated to a place where the other was already living; his voice was, in effect, that of an entire nation demanding ownership, even when conceived as co-ownership, of the other's space without granting the Palestinians the freedom to respond in accordance with the ethical logic of an I-Thou relation, that is, as an I with a voice of its own. It is thus clear that Buber's call for a binational state was premised on the expectation that the Palestinians would consent, their presumed acceptance not questioned, and it ignores the inherent injustice of this expectation.

In a letter to Mahatma Gandhi of 1939, Buber echoes the Zionist narrative regarding the historical and religious connection of the Jewish nation to the land. He expected that the Palestinians would enable the Jews to carry out their task in establishing a just society because they "are not covetous [. . .] our one desire is that at last [they] may obey."[4] There is no doubt that Buber is expressing his deep-seated belief that the Jewish nation does not only want and need, but also must return to its homeland in order to fulfill the divine commandment and establish Jewish existence as the model, ethically just society that resonates throughout the Hebrew Bible. Although Buber opposed an independent Jewish state, his vision of a spiritually flourishing Jewish *national* community in Palestine blurs the gap between his vision and the guiding political vision of the Zionist movement.

Buber was aware that he spoke "only for those who feel themselves entrusted with the mission of fulfilling the command of justice delivered to Israel of the Bible. Were it but a handful, these individuals constitute the pith of the nation, and the future of the people depends on them." Despite the tension between fulfilling the commandment and the clash with Palestinian rights in their homeland, he explains, "We cannot renounce the Jewish claim; something even higher than the life of our people is bound up with the Land."[5] Here, his theological, metapolitical commitment becomes clear, affirming the ingathering of the Jews in their homeland—the homeland also of others—as a divine and ethical command. The fulfillment of the divine commandment that is incumbent on the Jews is not just for their security, nor does it entail rule over others. Yet as noble as this vision is, and which he held necessitated a binational state, it assumed the ultimate compliance of the Arab majority of the land.

We cannot avoid asking the question of on what basis Buber assumed that a Jewish national entity in Palestine, even if not under the umbrella of an independent sovereign Jewish state, would enable a genuine dialogue between Jews and Palestinians, especially given the political reality he himself acknowledged. Was it naïveté, conscious blindness, or some moral position that could have freed him from the burden of responsibility for what was happening? It is difficult to determine the answer to such a question, although it may be convincingly argued that Buber's religious-ethical posture leaves no room for doubt about its disconnection from the practical justifications adopted by the leaders of the Zionist movement, and later, of the State of Israel, which would condone the need to continue the Zionist project despite intensifying the conflict with the Palestinians and advancing at their expense. In addition, it is implicit in Buber's 1939 letter to Gandhi that because the nonbelieving Jews (the secular Zionists) who promoted the ingathering of Jews in their biblical homeland were doing so to rescue them from the ever-mounting horrors of life in the diaspora, they, despite their atheism, were advancing the divine mission. Thus, when he argues that he believes that it is important and even possible to change the opinions of the Arabs about Zionism, he is clearly referring to his own Zionism; he does not reflect on how Zionism is perceived by those same Arabs. The gap between his Zionism and political Zionism, of which he was aware, overshadowed not only his own theories but also willy-nilly underscored that Zionism could only be as it was in reality—a national project which ultimately disinherited the Palestinians from their country and their homeland, initially under the patronage of the British colonial empire and continuing under the protection of the Pax Americana with the founding of the State of Israel. But even if we acknowledge the consistency in Buber's position, his argument that "there is no real quarrel between the two neighbors, except for the strong feeling in the hearts of each of the neighbors that an injustice has been done to him,"[6] demonstrates that he recognizes that the Arabs he refers to (without characterizing them) have suffered an injustice. However, because Buber compares that to the injustice done by the Arabs to the Jews in Nazi Europe, he thus creates a kind of symmetry, ignoring that he himself admitted that the Jews had initiated the conflict in Palestine, albeit "in peaceful ways."

Buber did place a heavy responsibility on the Jewish side of the conflict, arguing to Gandhi that the path should have been "positive: the real development of common interests by including the other nation in the economic activities of the country. And negative: avoiding all one-sided political slogans and deeds. That means rejecting political decisions until the common interests have sufficiently found their practical expression. From these facts, and not from empty exhortations, everyone who knows what responsibility is, should check with the spirit of his conscience as to what we have done and what we have not done." Without a doubt, this is a courageous remark to have made during the 1948 war with the Arabs, but, at the same time, Buber does not consider that the Jewish "infiltration" into the country, from the outset, placed the Palestinians against their will in the position of being neighbors, seemingly equal to Jews, and regardless of the fact that an injustice had been committed against them with the establishment of the British Palestinian mandate and commitment to furthering a Jewish home in Palestine. We cannot ignore Buber's further words of 1948: "The facts are quite simple. Two thousand years ago, a nation inhabited the country and created greatness in it, and later, scattered across the world, they maintained their internal connection with it. In our times, [another] nation inhabited this land which did not create anything special but just lived here, worked the soil as if there were no modern techniques, cultivated ancient customs as if there was no literary language."[7] With these words, Buber expresses not only denial, alienation, and contempt for those "deserving" Arabs, but even reflects a lack of empathy with what was happening to the Palestinians during those days. Buber creates a clear orientalist distinction between those who use modern techniques and who have developed a literary language, as he himself has done, and those who have not, and he creates a clear link between the rights regime and cultural characteristics of the two sides, illustrating a lack of understanding of the Arab spiritual and cultural—not to speak of the political—reality consistent with his own ethical teaching. He clearly establishes a consequential relationship between being modern and having the right to impose a reality on the nonmodern population of Palestine, thereby echoing the "civilizing mission" discourse of Western colonialism.

When considering the gap between Buber's ethical-moral theories and the way they were expressed in practice, it is instructive to note his letter to Gandhi of 1939, in which he averred that there was no difference between Jews and Arabs in their rights to the country, as the two peoples achieved control over the land by conquest. If the two nations are both occupiers, the question of when the occupation took place becomes irrelevant, ergo the rights of the two sides are equal. Buber argues that his ethical doctrine depends on history and derives from it. He creates a historical equality where there is no actual equality, based on the principle that committing a crime against the perpetrator of a crime is not a crime, but he does not stop there. He adds that a historical right is acquired by virtue of a divine imperative, which not only does not expire but also has higher ethical and practical weight based on having once inhabited the land. With this, he anticipates liberal thinkers who claim that occupation confers a right over time because a historical right is acquired by the power of conquest,[8] and he supplies the foundation for a quasi-ethical justification which perforce appertains to the entire Zionist project. In order to soften the superciliousness of his argument, he asserts that the Jews are not taking away the Arab claim to realize their national rights but are only taking away what the Arabs "do not need." His position here is paternalistic; he determines what is needed not only for Jews but also for Palestinians, whose voice is not heard. For the purpose of making his point, he adds a request from Gandhi, "Ask the soil what the Arabs have done for her in thirteen hundred years and what we have done for her in fifty! Would her answer not be weighty testimony in a just discussion as to whom this land 'belongs'?" And in order to moderate his claim, he adds, "We have no desire to dispossess them; we want to live with them. We do not want to rule; we want to serve [the land] with them." Buber argues that "these claims are in fact reconcilable as long as they are restricted to the measure that life itself allots, and as long as they are limited by the desire for conciliation—that is, if they are translated into the language of the needs of living people for themselves and their children."[9]

This makes it clear that the Palestinians have no justification to express a position inconsistent with the principle of partnership, even if that "partnership" has been imposed on them and they did not independently choose to consider it. Furthermore, Buber assumes inequality between Jews and Palestinians; he judges Palestinians only in utilitarian terms and limits their rights in accord with their use of land, while he bases the rights of Jews on spiritual-religious grounds and a divine commandment. Moreover, those who must determine the ethical principles according to which the law of the land will be determined are those who have a priori knowledge of the needs of *both* peoples. Buber further asserts that the Zionist goal to establish a national homeland for the Jews has universal significance: "We want Palestine not for the Jews. We want it for humanity." And he adds that "the world cannot be redeemed except by the redemption of Israel, and the land of Israel cannot be redeemed except by [our] reunification in our land."[10] Considering that the Palestinians are part of humanity, the redemption of the Jews in their land is ipso facto also their redemption.

This is a position that reflects the precedence of the "Jewish I" over the "Palestinian Thou" and, thus, the necessity of granting a prerogative to the correctness of the endeavors of the "Jewish I." Buber ignores the dominant Jewish efforts in Zionist settlement prior to the establishment of the State of Israel, which led to the expulsion of many Palestinian farmers from their land, leading inexorably to a backlash by Palestinians, even before the consolidation of an anti-Zionist Palestinian national movement. Buber knew that the violent reaction by the Jews had been organized, especially after the establishment of the mandate. If it was really necessary in his opinion to protect family members, how was this not relevant to the Palestinians as well, who were facing a tangible and clear process of being pushed out of their homes, their lands, and their homeland? Buber was surely aware of the implications of his stance on a fundamental ethical level, especially considering that he himself had stated, "There are also many foolish hearts among us [Jews] that need to be changed, hearts that have fallen victim to the national selfishness that only recognizes its own claims."[11]

It is clear from Buber's statements that his mind and heart sided with the pursuit of justice and peace: "We have been taught that peace is the goal of the entire world and justice is the way to achieve it."[12] However, the lack of coherence in his reading of historical developments in Palestine with regard to his ethical principles reveals not only the failure to apply those principles consistently to the realities in Palestine in his day, but also fills the existing gap in his ethical theory, especially in view of his affirmation of the theological apriority of the "Jewish I," which both contains the other and subjects that other to the recognition of this I without a dialogical Thou. As such, Buber's words lead him to the kind of dichotomous division known to us since the mandate, between the good, as reflected in Zionism, which can never be realized except at the expense of the Palestinians, and the evil, as reflected in the Palestinian opposition to it. In all fairness, however, it should be noted that because Buber does not accept the dichotomous distinction between ethics and politics, he judges the leaders of the Zionist movement harshly for their actions against the Palestinians.

While Buber identifies Judaism and its values with universal ethics, it is to take into consideration circumstantial existential and political contingencies, and to act accordingly. Hence, as he argued in his letter to Gandhi, there are times when historical circumstances leave one with no choice but to take up the arms of violence against one's oppressors. It thus follows that both the Jews and Arabs are acting ethically when they fight each other because, in the view of each side of the conflict, the objective for which they are fighting is just, considering the circumstances in which they find themselves. This raises the question of whether, if both sides are justified, how it is possible to achieve a solution to the conflict. Here, Buber's ethical theories lead us to a dead end. In the absence of a moral standard according to which the judgment between different and conflicting positions in complex circumstances does not consider the circumstances of the process, its factors, the motives of actions and the power relations within it, we will find ourselves in a situation where total war prevails, ending in either surrender or mutual destruction. That is the dilemma raised by the ethics of Carl Schmitt, who not only required a decision but also defined the subject of sovereignty as "he who decides on the exception."[13] In the Jewish-Palestinian context, Buber, notwithstanding his rejection of political Zionism, recognizes the right of the Jews, and thus the State of Israel, not only to determine but also indirectly to establish a view of reality that justifies defining the political situation in which it finds itself as an "emergency" from which there is no alternative but to deploy the tools of violence in the face of existential danger. This viewpoint leads Buber to reconcile himself with the state and to grant it legitimacy even if he is critical of its policies. The fact that he struggled against government policies and tried to reduce their injustices as much as he could, including his opposition to the military administration over the Palestinian citizens between 1948 and 1966, does not alter the fact that he was part of the concrete and spiritual reality that had been created, and he thus assumed a measure of responsibility for it.

Buber continued to voice his criticism of the state's policies and bemoaned that Jewish existence, as it was reflected in the Jewish state, was not what he would have wished. That he consistently and unyieldingly voiced criticism until the very end of his life attests to his civil courage and abiding ethical commitment to a common, just existence with Palestinians. Nevertheless, his arguments for the right of Jews to the land, in light of the State of Israel's denial of the historical right of the Palestinians to their homeland, in effect provided an ethical and practical justification for Zionist policies he himself had been criticizing. These realities lead to the conclusion that, despite Buber's realism, he tended to aestheticize reality by using smooth poetic language that enabled him to present a moral position, on the one hand, but also to present justifications that allowed him to accept Zionist reality, on the other.

Epilogue

The relevance of Buber's thought for our times is conditioned by a number of factors. The most important of these is the way we must reinterpret his philosophy of dialogue and the significance of mutual recognition. One direction has been outlined by the philosopher Judith Butler, arguing that Buber's Zionism "is committed to international and ethnic cooperation and the universalization of rights,"[14] even though she is aware of his support for Jewish nationalism and colonization. Butler considers parts of Buber's thought as supplying the inspiration and conceptual tools to forge a path for Jews and Palestinians to live harmoniously side by side in their shared homeland. This is no doubt a worthy task, and the richness of Buber's conception of binationalism is a solid basis for thinking about how to solve the political entanglement in which Jews and Palestinians alike find themselves.

However, in order to succeed, it is impossible to contemplate binationalism in terms of Zionist settler colonialism, which still prevails in Israel/Palestine. It seems clear that it must be revisited without regard to Buber's unquestioned affirmation of Jewish ethnic nationalism, however softly he endorsed it, and his confirmation of the hegemonic Zionist narrative. It must also be considered in the light of the political and cultural reality of the Palestinians; indeed, the vision of a binational solution to the conflict needs to be based on a deep critique in accord with the ethical and dialogical principles of Buber's concept of an I-Thou encounter. This encounter bespeaks an intersubjective ontology of individuals, but, when applied to intercommunal encounters, it must consider the consequences of prevailing power relations between the respective communities. Is a Buberian dialogue at all possible when the national and political rights of Palestinians are ignored? Is a Buberian dialogue at all possible without regard for the consequences of the development of Zionism initially under the colonial tutelage of the British mandate? Is a Buberian dialogue at all possible given the continued and clearly inhumane impositions on the Palestinians within the State of Israel and the occupied territories?

The difficulty of achieving a political solution based on Buber's binational formula stems from the fact that it diverges from his own ethical I-Thou encounter, for it stipulates that Jewish existence in the land (the "Jewish I") as a priori to the dialogue with the Palestinians (the other, the Thou) and not as a possible result of a genuine dialogue between the Jews and the indigenous Arab community of Palestine. This stipulation undermines the existential grammar of dialogue as a process whereby the parties of the dialogue become aware of how they interact with one another, enabling them to gain mutual understanding, if not necessarily mutual recognition, because recognition requires open horizons and self-transformation implicit in the very objective of dialogue. *Respondeo etsi mutabor*—I respond *although* I will be changed (Eugen Rosenstock-Hussy). Therefore, conditioning Jewish-Palestinian dialogue on the theological premise of a divinely sanctioned right of Jewry to reclaim its biblical patrimony is not just an ontological contradiction, but it also forecloses the horizons of dialogue as a process of a fundamental self-understanding and transformation. Moreover, an intercommunal dialogue is a political process—which cannot deny that it is political. It thus cannot ignore the influence of power relations between the respective communities in the dialogical encounter.

Ignoring power relations actually serves to reinforce the power structure. The dialogical call for a like response from the other that does not involve recognition of the *political* other, and also occludes the possibility of the other's viewpoint, to challenge the cognitive and existential positions of the one calling for a response to one's call, constitutes a contradiction not only of dialogue theoretically, but also ethically and politically. At the heart of Buber's binationalism is the expectation that the Palestinians will acknowledge the narrative arc of Jewish religious and spiritual identity and thus the right to "return" to Palestine. Thus, in effect, Buber denied the integrity of the political identity of the Palestinians as the indigenous people of the land and their right to choose to be hospitable or not. The Buberian concept of the Jewish right to the land as a divine commandment could not but turn the Palestinians from prospective hosts to hostages, perforce entrapping them *nolens volens* in a position of noncompliance, turning hospitality into hostility, as Derrida put it.[15] In consonance with the Zionist narrative, Buber did not reach out to the Palestinians as a guest seeking their hospitality.

In spite of the promising vision of binationalism as the foundation upon which the relationship between Jews and Palestinians might live in harmony and mutual dignity, shared sovereignty also requires a dialogue that is not satisfied alone with ethics based on responding to the voice of the other but needs to be in tandem with a forthright acknowledgment of the political reality of the Palestinians. In reflecting on dialogue as an "act of self-reflection,"[16] Buber speaks of opening the I to the other, and that is in contrast to the monologue in which the I refers to others as the content of one's experience. Buber more than hints at the possibility of the merging of horizons, as expressed by Hans-Georg Gadamer, and discusses the agreement that is characterized by a mixture of agreements and disagreements, which reflect the constant tension between the partners in a relationship.[17] In this way, Buber anticipated Jürgen Habermas by several decades in establishing a rational communication theory that is necessary for dealing with the impasse of modern subjectivity, and provided a starting point for changing the reality that consists of antagonistic national identities.[18] But unlike Habermas, in Buber's thought there is a dichotomy in Jewish existence which, on the one hand, promotes dialogue, but on the other, occludes it. Buber refers to the realization of Judaism as a spiritual vocation, embracing all of humankind as created in the image of God. But this same Buber, who emphasized the universality of Judaism, silenced the *fullness* of the voice of the Palestinians, its political integrity and ethical sovereignty. It is not sufficient to assume the existence of the other on the ontological level; it is necessary to enable listening and responsiveness as an ethical and substantive horizon so that a genuine intercommunal dialogue can be realized. To promote a truly shared life of Jews and Palestinians, there must be mutual political recognition borne by a shared sovereignty with intercommunal and interpersonal space, on the one hand, and goodwill embedded in common ethical values, on the other.

Notes

1. Martin Buber, *I and Thou*, trans. Walter Kaufmann, 100th anniversary reissue (New York: Simon & Schuster 2023), 10.

2. Stefan Voigt, "The Postcolonial Buber: Orientalism, Subalternity, and Identity Politics in Martin Buber's Political Thought," *Jewish Social Studies: History, Culture, Society* 22, no. 1 (2016): 161–86.

3. Steven DeLue, "Martin Buber and Immanuel Kant: On Mutual Respect and the Liberal State," *Janus Head* 9, no. 1 (2006): 117–33.

4. Martin Buber, "A Letter to Gandhi, 24 February 1939," in Buber, *A Land of Two Peoples*, ed. Paul Mendes-Flohr (Chicago: University of Chicago Press, 2005), 118.

5. Buber, "A Letter to Gandhi," 118.

6. Buber, "A Letter to Gandhi," 191.

7. Buber, "A Letter to Gandhi," 191–92.

8. Jeremy Waldron, "Superseding Historic Injustice," *Ethics* 103, no. 1 (1992): 4–28.

9. Buber, "A Letter to Gandhi," 191; Buber, *A Land of Two Peoples*, 112.

10. Buber, *A Land of Two Peoples*, 120.

11. Martin Buber, *The Dialogue on Man and Being*, in Buber, *Philosophical Writings*, vol. 1 (Jerusalem: Bialik Institute, 1959), 112.

12. Buber, *The Dialogue on Man and Being*, 113.

13. Carl Schmitt, *Political Theology: Four Chapters on the Concept of Sovereignty*, trans. George Schwab (Chicago: University of Chicago Press, 1985), 5.

14. Judith Butler, "Jews and the Bi-National Vision," talk given at the 2nd International Conference on an End to Occupation, a Just Peace in Israel-Palestine: Towards an Active International Network in East Jerusalem, January 4–5, 2004.

15. Jacques Derrida and Anne Dufourmantelle, *Of Hospitality* (Princeton, NJ: Princeton University Press, 2000).

16. Martin Buber, *Between Man and Man* (New York: Routledge, 1947), 148.

17. Maurice Friedman, "Martin Buber and Emmanuel Levinas: An Ethical Query," *Philosophy Today* 45, no. 1 (2001): 3–11; Hans-Georg Gadamer, *Warheit und Methode* (Vienna: Akademie Verlag, 2001).

18. Jürgen Habermas, *Theorie des kommunikativen Handelns* (Frankfurt am Main: Suhrkamp, 1981); Jürgen Habermas, "A Philosophy of Dialogue," in *Dialogue as Trans-Disciplinary Concept: Martin Buber's Philosophy of Dialogue and Its Contemporary Reception*, ed. Paul Mendes-Flohr (Berlin: De Gruyter, 2015), 7–20.

Annotated Bibliography

PRIMARY SOURCES

On Buber's vision of binationalism, see:

Buber, Martin. *A Land of Two Peoples: Martin Buber on Jews and Arabs*. Edited and introduced with commentary by Paul Mendes-Flohr. Chicago: University of Chicago Press, 2005.

SECONDARY LITERATURE:

For critical examinations of the applicability of Buber's philosophy of dialogue to politics and intercommunal conflict, see:

Kegley, Charles. "Martin Buber's Ethics and the Problem of Norms." *Religious Studies* 5, no. 2 (1969): 181–94.
Vogel, Manfred. "The Concept of Responsibility in the Thought of Martin Buber." *Harvard Theological Review* 63, no. 2 (1970): 159–82.
Vogt, Stefan. "The Postcolonial Buber: Orientalism, Subalternity, and Identity Politics in Martin Buber's Political Thought." *Jewish Social Studies: History, Culture, Society* 22, no. 1 (2016): 161–86.

25

Feminism and Buber's Legacy: A Critical Reception

YEMIMA HADAD

1. Accepting Otherness

Martin Buber's philosophy of dialogue stressed otherness as radical subjectivity, a "thouness" irreducible to the world of "It." What matters in dialogue, Buber writes, is that "the other happens as the particular other, that each becomes aware of the other and is thus related to him in such a way that he does not regard and use him as his object, but as his partner in a living event."[1]

In "Distance and Relation" (1950), Buber demonstrates how the otherness of the thou secures the reality of dialogue: "Genuine conversation, and therefore every actual fulfillment and relation between men, means acceptance of otherness. [. . .] Everything depends, as far as human life is concerned, on whether each thinks of the other as the one he is, whether each, that is, with all his desire to influence the other, nevertheless unreservedly accepts and confirms him in his being this man and in his being made in this particular way."[2] In the historical context of Buber's life, the complete acceptance of the other's otherness was not only a philosophical construct. It could also be viewed as an appeal to Christian Europe to accept its Jewish citizens in all their difference, or be understood as an admonition to his fellow Zionists to build bridges between Jewish immigrants and native Arabs in Palestine and, later, the State of Israel.[3] But there was another context where the acceptance of otherness and difference should have mattered: The realm of women's rights and equity. Curiously, however, Buber—though married to a free-spirited feminist writer—rarely wrote about the women's cause and could hardly be considered a feminist by today's sensibilities. In fact, the few instances when Buber did specifically address the role of women, such as in his 1901 essay "The Zion of the Jewish Woman," reveal common clichés and stereotypes about motherhood, self-sacrifice, and domestic beauty rather than engaging with women as independent "others." To be sure, these early reflections of the twenty-five-year-old Buber were penned some twenty years before the crystallization of his philosophy of dialogue. Significantly in the same year, he also brought to the attention of the German reader the work of two of the earliest feminist writers, Ellen Key and Selma Lagerlöf.[4] Indeed, Buber's dialogical thought anticipated some of the concerns later feminists would express in their writings and occasionally served as a direct or indirect source of inspiration. The following essay will offer a few examples of Buber's remarkable afterlife in feminist thought, especially among Jewish feminists.

2. Retrieving Minor Voices

The American feminist activist Betty Friedan, who became a leading figure in second-wave feminism through her book *The Feminine Mystique* (1963), reflected on the connection between her own Jewishness and the feminism of her time: "After my book helped to revive the women's movement in the U.S., I sometimes thought, 'Why me?' Then it occurred to me that this passion against injustice, which made me address myself to the problems of women, probably had its roots in my own earliest experiences as a Jew growing up in Peoria, Illinois."[5] The injustice she experienced as a Jew made Friedan aware of the injustice she would later experience as a woman. But she also related to classical Jewish conceptions of social justice represented by the Hebrew prophets: "I have not been the only one of the social prophets through the ages who have been Jewish to have taken this fiery passion against injustice from our own experience and then applied it to the largest possible sphere of action in the community."[6]

It can be argued that Buber's notions of dialogical empathy emerged from similar experiences of exclusion and applied, therefore, to a universal human condition. Indeed, by the 1960s, when feminist thought reached broader audiences, Buber was considered a Jewish existentialist, whose philosophy of dialogue had become cultural commonplace among many young intellectuals, including feminist thinkers. For feminists, retrieval of their voices was an important step toward emancipation. From the early suffragettes, fighting for the right to vote, to postwar feminists pushing for equal pay and greater inclusion in all walks of life, having a voice meant being present and able to confront a male-dominated world. Today, minor voices are gradually being given respect in public discourse. For Buber, however, the presence of a voice made no distinction between "minor" and "major," outsider or insider. He understood dialogue as a confrontation requiring attentiveness to the presence of the other in order to *confirm* the other: "The sphere of the interhuman is one in which a person is confronted by the other. We call its unfolding the

FEMINISM AND BUBER'S LEGACY 337

dialogical."[7] Given the silencing of the female voices in different world traditions, including Judaism (*kol beisha erva*, or "the voice of a woman in public"), and depriving women of the privilege to study, read, and write throughout history,[8] Buber's conception of dialogue could be seen as a form of *protest* that would become an integral part of the feminist project.

Thus, in *Engendering Judaism*, the Jewish theologian Rachel Adler makes the power to speak an important aspect of her feminist view. Like other Jewish feminists, Adler connects the classical Jewish notions of *tikkun olam* and *teshuva* to the rehabilitation of the female voice in Judaism.[9] In an earlier work, Carol Gilligan, a trained psychologist who emerged as one of the leading feminist philosophers during the 1980s, published a book entitled *In a Different Voice*, arguing that "to have a voice is to be human. To have something to say is to be a person." And she continues in a strong Buberian vein: "But speaking depends on listening and being heard; it is an intensely relational act."[10] Silencing undercuts the possibility of dialogue and, therefore, refuses to acknowledge the other's presence. The ability to enter or refrain from entering dialogue, then, has to do with the power of the group to give voice to its members or to withhold voice from them. Deeply aware of this power differential, feminists could identify with Buber's principle of dialogue and adopt the assumption that "minored" voices should, if nothing else, then at least be *heard*. Accordingly, Gilligan writes: "As we have listened for centuries to the voices of men and the theories of development that their experience informs, so we have come more recently to notice not only the silence of women but the difficulty in hearing what they say when they speak."[11]

Neither Gilligan nor Adler make explicit references to Buber's work. But their language certainly suggests at the very least a conscious use of dialogical motifs. Likewise, their understanding of ethical repair is deeply rooted in a dialogical acknowledgment of unheard, or silenced, voices, a process Gilligan describes as "changing the voice of the world by bringing women's voices into the open, thus starting a new conversation."[12]

One might wonder, then, why Buber's philosophy of dialogue did not play a more *direct* role in feminist theory.[13] As mentioned, Martin Buber was not a feminist thinker or an active promoter of the feminist cause. To the contrary, his writings suggest a rather conservative view of the woman's "place." On the other hand, Buber, unlike many other philosophers at the time, did not view women as inherently inferior. Moreover, his life was interwoven with an ongoing dialogue with many female scholars, poets, and artists, such as Bertha Pappenheim, Margarete Susman, or Elsa Lasker-Schüler.[14] As the editor of the acclaimed series of monographs *Die Gesellschaft*, Buber also commissioned two volumes dedicated to feminist issues: *Die Frauenbewegung* (1909), by the

Swedish pedagogue and feminist Ellen Key, and *Die Erotik* (1910), authored by the Russian-German novelist and psychoanalyst Lou Andreas-Salomé.[15] Buber maintained a correspondence with both of them and was clearly willing to give voice to feminist intellectuals of his time, although he did not seem to have been actively engaged in their cause.

The most intimate source of inspiration for Buber came from his own wife, the writer and intellectual Paula Winkler.[16] Paula elicited his interest in mysticism, which, in turn, primed his study of Hasidism.[17] We see her influence in his book *Ekstatische Konfessionen*, published in 1909, in which Buber focuses on many female mystical figures in a tradition that was considered masculine.[18] Paul Mendes-Flohr also draws our attention to the fact that the love relationship presented in Buber's book *Daniel: Gespräche von der Verwirklichung* (1913), inflected with an autobiographical undercurrent, alludes to his love for his wife.[19]

It is well known that Paula edited and was actively engaged in Buber's work while also being a popular novelist in her own right.[20] Like other female authors during the nineteenth and early twentieth centuries, she published her work under a male pseudonym, Georg Munk. But her work was not only in literary fiction. Like Buber, she also published in leading Zionist and literary journals, including a series of essays entitled "The Jewish Woman" in *Die Welt*, which gave voice to what may be considered protofeminist sentiments.[21]

3. "Ladies' Philosopher" and "Woman-Thinking"

Perhaps Paula's pronounced feminist sensibilities may have influenced the literary reflexes of her husband's predialogical sensibility, which was occasionally labeled "feminine," an attribute sometimes meant to flatter while at other times used in opprobrium. Yeshayahu Leibowitz, for instance, called the dialogical Buber a "ladies' philosopher,"[22] insinuating a lack of rigor in Buber's philosophical thought that was at best suited to entertain the female bourgeoisie. But Leibowitz was not the first to attribute femininity to Buber's thought, nor did femininity always carry connotations of philosophical weakness. In response to Buber's book *Daniel* (1913), Gustav Landauer wrote that Buber "awakens and advocates a specific feminine form of thought without which our exhausted and collapsed culture cannot be renewed and replenished. Only [...] when abstract thought is conjoined and submerged in the depths of feeling, will our thought engender deeds, will a true life emerge from our logical desert. Towards that objective women will help us."[23] Landauer considered woman-thinking (*Frauendenken*), which he associated with peace and humanism, as a commandment that "has not yet taken its appropriate full share" in human thought.²⁴ "For the sake of human thinking," wonders Landauer, "should one expect the increasing of the specific woman-thinking within this human thinking? And I say: indeed yes, and I notice something like this with joy. I notice it in Goethe and his Iphigenia kingdom, which is embodied in our whole culture; [I notice it] in me, though I am quite masculine, in you; [and] I notice it in Rachel [Varnhagen], Bettina [Armin-Brentano], Margarete Susman etc. All these are the doers of humanity, the doers of oneness, whole, because in them dwells the woman-thinking [*Frauendenken*] vividly and because they are unique [*Einmalige*]."²⁵ If Buber, then, embodied what Landauer approvingly termed *Frauendenken*, should his philosophy not have been a significant source for feminist thought? And should it not be plausible that his ideas can be applied to current conversations about gender and feminist ethics? Is it possible to expand Buber's philosophy beyond what he imagined?²⁶

These questions were asked some twenty years ago in a book by James Walter, arguing that Buber's thought "plowed new ground in exploring the value of concrete relational experience, and thus significantly aided contemporary feminist theory."²⁷ Walter's book offers important insights into the affinities between dialogical and feminist ethics. It is the first systematic attempt to show how Buber's philosophy prepared, if only indirectly, the rise of a specific feminine ethic often focused on care, empathy, and an ethical concept of motherhood. The feminist reorientation of ethics from duty to care and from the subject to the other is frequently accompanied by a theological reorientation. As we shall see, Buber's impact on twentieth-century and more recent feminism has touched both the ethical and the theological.

4. Dialogue and Ethics of Care

We have seen that Carol Gilligan's unsilencing of minor voices was articulated in starkly dialogical terms. But she makes an even stronger claim: That speaking, listening, and being heard belong to an ethical disposition of care. She writes that "in the different voice of women lies the truth of an ethic of care, the tie between relationship and responsibility, and the origins of aggression in the failure of connection."²⁸ Some feminists, such as Judith Plaskow or Tamar Ross, would argue that women's voices are important not only in social and ethical but also in *theological* terms—for the unfolding of truth and even for revelation itself.²⁹ The ethics of care and correlation between relationality and responsibility, which were of great concern also to Buber, transpired into feminist notions of a caring God. For Gilligan, however, it was the concern for a relational ethics that defined her feminist project as a re-envisioning of the interpersonal. And while she did not explicitly build on Buber's dialogical thought, other scholars have noted the apparent intellectual affinities. Thus, Betty A. Sichel (1985) wrote of Gilligan's feminine moral language of care in strongly dialogical terms: "An individual acquires meaning only in relationships with others. In this sense, women's moral language can be compared with Martin Buber's I-Thou relationship."[30]

Indeed, like Buber, Gilligan spoke about relationality as a fundamental way to view the world. And echoing Buber's *I and Thou*, she claims that there are "two ways of speaking about human life and relationships, one grounded in connection and one in separation."[31] This not only recalls Buber's distinction between the I-You and I-It; it also reflects the distinction between authentic and inauthentic dialogue. Genuine dialogue, for Buber, "means that men communicate themselves to one another as what they are [...] letting no seeming creep in between himself and the other. [...] granting to the man to whom he communicates himself a share in his being. This is a question of the authenticity of the interhuman, and where this is not to be found, neither is the human element itself authentic."[32] The realm of the "between" (*das Zwischen*) returns also in Gilligan. However, unlike Buber, Gilligan speaks of a gender-based moral language that maintains a specificity Buber's I-Thou could not accommodate. In her view, women speak a language of caring, whereas men speak a language of rights and justice. Thus, dialogue could never be fully stripped of gendered presuppositions. It should be noted, however, that Gilligan's notion of gendered language would appear today as conservative and essentialist, reinforcing gender norms rather than liberating them.

Building on Gilligan's work, the philosopher Nel Noddings developed an ethics of care that was also informed by strong feminist and dialogical sensibilities.[33] But unlike Gilligan, Noddings directly engages Buber's philosophy of dialogue in her book *Caring: A Relational Approach to Ethics and Moral Education* (1984). In fact, Noddings explicitly uses Buber's terms in order to illuminate the distinction between *caring-for* and *caring-about*: "In the language of Martin Buber, the cared-for is encountered as 'Thou' a subject and not as 'It' an object of analysis. During the encounter, which may be singular and brief or recurrent and prolonged, the cared-for 'is Thou and fills the firmament.'" Expanding Buber's relational ethics, Noddings focuses on the actual *needs* of a Thou. If I-It relationships are focused on the needs of the I, then an I-Thou relationship is directed toward the needs of the Thou. Thus, contrary to Buber's understanding of the I-Thou, where the I "knows nothing and everything" of the Thou, the I in Noddings's philosophy of dialogue knows something *specific* about the Thou: It knows that a Thou has *needs*. Taking the selfless mother-child relationship as archetype of I-Thou, Noddings emphasizes an asymmetrical relationship between I and Thou, in which the I appears reduced compared to the Thou. Like Gilligan, Noddings uses gendered language. Thus, the language of caring is called "the language of the mother," guided by the specific needs of the other. By contrast, the language of the father is characterized by principles, rights, hierarchy, and justice.[34]

Contrary to Kantian ethics, Noddings argues, the understanding of ethics of care "may require monumental physical or emotional effort, but it does not require a moral effort; that is, we act out of inclination, not out of duty or concern for the status of our character." Moreover, ethics of care, according to Noddings, challenges "the Kantian emphasis on adherence to principle and duty." She asserts that: "Ethical caring, then, derives its strength from natural caring. This is clearly a reversal of Kantian priorities."[35] Whereas Noddings articulates her critique of the Kantian ethics in gendered terms, Buber, who anticipated the relational critique of Kantian ethics, formulated it without making such gender distinctions.[36] In fact, Noddings, like Gilligan before her, was criticized not only for her fixed dichotomies of gender but also for the indebtedness of her "feminine" philosophy to male authors—such as Martin Buber.[37]

A slightly different view on a feminist ethics of care has been articulated by Leora Batnitzky. She contends that feminist ethics of care shares, in fact, many of the presuppositions of femininity held by Buber and other Jewish philosophers. She argues that prominent twentieth-century Jewish philosophers used gender terms in noncritical traditional ways: "In my reading, Buber's, Rosenzweig's, and Levinas's use of 'the feminine' does much of the same moral work as it does in feminist philosophies of care. The broad, shared claim of these two sets of thinkers is that something characterized by 'the feminine' represents an ethic of caring in which responsibility is excessive, not contractual, and, at least at its most basic level, profoundly non-cognitive in nature." Batnitzky views this essentialism as problematic, for it is an attempt to "link biology to philosophical world views" and by doing so it confines women to the very traditional roles from which liberal feminism tried to release them: "Does a philosophy of care relegate women to the very roles from which the women's movement wants to provide potential freedom? [...] [I]n the end, these thinkers relegate women to the roles of mother and keeper of the home." Dependence and vulnerability, argues Batnitzky, are universal human attributes (not saved for women alone) and, as such, "Jewish philosophy and feminist philosophy would do better without the use of 'the feminine.'"[38] Hermann Cohen's nongendered concept of compassion (*Mitleid*) and loving-kindness, which is the source for Buber's, Franz Rosenzweig's, and Emmanuel Levinas's notions of care and intersubjectivity, would make a better concept in overcoming the gender-based language of the ethics of care.

5. Feminist Critiques of Buber's Dialogue

The ethics of care is one the most prominent themes emerging from dialogical thought. The Jewish feminist theologian Judith Plaskow, however, has warned against an uncritical repurposing of Buber's philosophy for feminist ethics. "The centrality of relation in Martin Buber's work has led feminists uncritically to adopt aspects of his thought without thinking to analyze it from the perspective of gender." Buber's I-You philosophy, argues Plaskow, "rests on the assumption that human beings spend most of their lives in the It-world, only occasionally experiencing moments of I-You connection." She suggests that "while relation is key both to Buber's philosophy and feminist theory, it seems that it enters their experience from opposite ends: Buber works toward relation, while feminists begin with relation."[39] What Plaskow argues is that whereas male relational philosophies typically start from an effort to overcome I-It relations in order to arrive at a genuine I-Thou relation, the feminist philosophy of care *begins* with the I-Thou relation in order to arrive at a deeper understanding of genuine relationality. Feminism, then, is primordially dialogical, a position Buber accorded only to the pre-objective child. But it is not the child Plaskow has in mind. Like Noddings, she faults Buber with overlooking the role of the mother in a parental relationship. This role, she claims, challenges Buber's reciprocity of I-Thou relations:

> The relevance of a gender analysis to Buber's work becomes especially clear in connection with his discussion of the emergence of the two modes of I-You and I-It relation. Here Buber focuses on the experience of the child and its gradual acquisition of self-consciousness without ever naming the mother as the one with whom the child is in relation or looking at the mother-child relationship from the mother's side. Were the child's development seen from the perspective of the mother, a third mode of relation might be required to capture her experience. The child is not characteristically an object to the mother—as in the I-It mode—but neither does she necessarily experience a perpetual reciprocity of relation. Her experience of care and connection even when mutuality is absent may constitute a third sort of relation insufficiently accounted for in Buber's theology.[40]

A similar critique emerges in Mara Benjamin's essay "Intersubjectivity Meets Maternity," which takes to task Buber's account of teacher-student and therapist-patient relationships as being essentially tone-deaf to parent-child relationships. For Benjamin, it is a lamentable symptom of modern Jewish thought and philosophy that it remains focused on intersubjective relationships modeled after male perceptions of dialogue while ignoring the parent-child relationship as a prototype of the interpersonal. Benjamin criticizes both Buber's and Levinas's concepts of intersubjectivity for what she considers to be their latent assumption that the "*normative* encounter between two humans is the encounter between two adult male subjects."[41]

It is, of course, little wonder that twentieth-century philosophy, written predominantly by male scholars, ignored parental relationships. For Benjamin, however, it is almost ironic that twentieth-century Jewish philosophers were most interested in "precisely those kinds of interpersonal relationships that characterize many post-industrial, bourgeois Western relationships that mothers have (and are enjoined to have) with their children—yet we find few traces of mothers or children, and certainly no satisfying traces of them in this body of literature." Thus she wonders, "What would happen if we made maternal caregiving, and parent/child relationships generally, central, rather than marginal, to an account of intersubjectivity and relationship?"[42]

Challenging the marginal place assigned to the parent-child relationship in twentieth-century Jewish thought and Western philosophy, Benjamin also elevates this particular relationship as the prototype for intersubjectivity and for relationships based on care. Moreover, Benjamin seeks to connect two discourses that were previously treated separately: Jewish theology and child-rearing. The parent-child relationship thus becomes itself "a site of religious meaning." "Moments of feeding, caring for, cleaning, and soothing children are *philosophically and existentially significant* moments, no less than are the moments of deep reciprocity or extreme obligation."[43]

Like Plaskow, Benjamin criticizes Buber for ignoring women's subjectivity even when addressing motherhood and women in *I and Thou*. The figure of the woman in Buber's writings "lacks subjectivity," and "her body quickly collapses into a mythical archetype." In fact, Benjamin concludes, "the single description of pregnancy in Buber's philosophy of dialogue underscores the complete absence of actual mothers (or, for that matter, fathers) and children engaged in ongoing, worldly relationships." Buber's description suggests that "the womb in which it [the fetus] dwells is not solely that of the human mother," but an image conceived in "cosmic" terms, "a womb of the great mother."[44] Buber seems to forget that the "womb" in which the child dwells is part of a particular subject, a woman, who is already in a relationship with the fetus growing inside her body.

6. Beyond Gender Dichotomy?

The criticisms of Judith Plaskow and Mara Benjamin offer powerful corrections of Buber's dialogical thought. But they leave unquestioned traditional gender divisions. For Buber, as well as for his wife, Paula, a strongly gendered world was still a given. In an 1898 letter to Buber, Paula articulated her feminism over against cosmopolitanism. Cosmopolitanism, she argued, not only ignores national diversity but also "seeks to minimize the differences between men and women and blur the contrasts between them in a way that, like bees, creates a sexless third sex. [...] Why not develop the man in the man and the woman in the woman to highest perfection to an extraordinary blossom?"[45]

About a century later, Judith Butler resisted the dichotomous model of gender in her writings starting with *Gender Trouble* (1990), which viewed strict genderization as downright oppressive. Interestingly, Butler once remarked that her theory of fluid and nonbinary gender was shaped by her earlier engagement with Buber's philosophy, which she started reading in her youth.[46] While Buber's mark on Butler's theories of gender may be less obvious, his writings on dialogue and binationalism are clearly present throughout her political work.[47] In a more recent interview, Butler restates Buber's concept of dialogue in relation to Hannah Arendt:

> I am struck by the way Arendt's position echoes that of Martin Buber, whose cultural Zionism interested her a great deal in the 1930s. For Buber, the I only knows its world because there is a you who has consciousness of that world. The world is given to me because you are also there as one to whom it is given. The world is never given to me alone but always in your company. Without you, the world does not give itself. We are worldless without one another.[48]

Butler's explicit reception of Buber is striking in this passage. And one can also discern Buberian traces. Her major work questions the determinist identification between gender and sex, arguing that "gender is received, but surely not simply inscribed on our bodies as if we were merely a passive slate obligated to bear a mark. But what we are at first obligated to do is enact the gender that we are assigned."[49] The enactment of gender is what she calls gender performativity. The category "sex," on the other hand, is but a biological category that Butler views as a linguistic construct. What allows Butler to ascribe nonbinary gender identities, without determinate fixity, is Buber's realm of the between. Freedom, as she argues, is tied to the sphere of the between, which bestows or deprives the legitimacy of gender performance: "Social freedom cannot be understood apart from what arises between people, what happens when they make something in common or when, in fact, they seek to make or remake the world in common."[50] By the same token, the between is the very space fluid gender can freely inhabit.

Butler's notion of performative gender emerged in response to French feminism, especially the work of Luce Irigaray. Both Butler and Irigaray developed their gender theories for the purpose of ensuring diversity. While Irigaray resists a "sameness" of the subject that conflates the category of women with that of men, Butler wishes to break with the rigid dichotomy of gender. For both, however, the structure of gender binary is inherently oppressive, a regime that dictates who is to be called a subject and who is to be objectified.[51]

Irigaray's feminism explicitly encourages us to view the female as "other" (unlike Simone de Beauvoir, whom she criticizes). The subjectivity of women should not, in her opinion, be considered by the very sameness that of men: "Instead of refusing to be the other gender, the other sex, what I ask is to be considered as actually an/other woman, irreducible to the masculine subject." Genders are two without being first and second. In traditional philosophy, argues Irigaray, the other was never considered as an "actual other," but as a lesser version of the normative male subject. The subject is not one, she claims, nor is it singular. The subject is a dual, and in order to allow for a female subject, one has to declare a philosophical scandal, which acknowledges precisely that "the subject is not one, nor is it singular."[52]

Here, Irigaray offers an explicit critique of Buber's *I and Thou*. She claims that "even in the privilege of the other over the subject, of the you over the I (I am thinking, for example, of certain works by Buber and a certain part of Levinas's work in which these privileges are perhaps more moral and theological than philosophical), we just end up with a stand-in for the model of the one and the many, of the one and the same, in which a singular subject inflects one meaning rather than another."[53] In *I Love to You* (1990), Irigaray contends that Buber's *I and Thou* remains "within the horizon of a single subject—more or less realized or fulfilled—in the horizon of the same, in the order of genealogy, of hierarchy."[54] What Irigaray seeks to establish in her critique is a female subjectivity that is completely different from the male, and which must not be reduced to that of the male subject. Today, such a dichotomous view of gender has become less popular, and might even be judged as essentialist and anachronistic. But Irigaray, in my view, would not have opposed the possibility and reality of nonbinary gender. Her goal was not to insist on a conservative binarism but to construct feminine subjectivity as a form of resistance to the normative order of gender and to liberate the female subject from the burdens of normative sameness. This was also meant to liberate femininity from its objectification. Like Arendt, Irigaray insisted that the liberation of femininity included feminine self-affirmation.[55]

The affirmation of femininity is a theme that returns in Martha Nussbaum's critique of Butler's gender theory and academic feminism at large. She accuses contemporary feminism of being a "complete turning from the material side of life, toward a type of verbal and symbolic politics that makes only the flimsiest of connections with the real situation of real women."[56] A similar critique can be found in Barbara Merrill's essay "Dialogical Feminism" (2005), which argues that "[s]econd wave feminism grew out of the voices and actions of both working class and middle class women, often with both groups working together, but such practice has largely now been lost in the theoretical world of academia." Merrill follows Nussbaum in claiming that gender studies "has little relevance to the grassroots work of feminist adult educators."[57] She proposes a *dialogical feminism* instead without, however, referring to Buber's thought. "Dialogical feminism," she argues, has to include working-class women, because "non-academics are also able to reflect upon and understand their life experiences and the oppression they have experienced." A more dialogical and egalitarian approach would allow "non-academic women to subjectively express their experiences as oppressed women."[58] This kind of dialogical feminism suggests that even inside feminist gender discourse there are silenced voices and minor voices that should be taken into account when we speak about gender. Being attentive to the unvoiced and silenced views will not only return us to the materialist conditions of women in different societies but also allow feminist and gender theory to develop as a polyphony of different worldviews.

7. Toward a Feminist Dialogical Thought

In "Disturbing Boundaries" (2005), the sociologist Deidre Butler asks: How can Buber's androcentrism in his dialogical thought "provide the methodological and theoretical tools to contribute to the development of feminist and Jewish feminist ethics?" A Jewish feminist ethic of relationship, she continues, "must critically question to what extent the I-Thou relation is genuinely egalitarian."[59]

When Buber spoke about genuine dialogue at the beginning of the twentieth century, he did not have feminism and women's rights in mind. Rather, he spoke as a Jew within a Christian majority and in an overall hostile political and theological climate. Perhaps this marginalized, "minor" position remains the common denominator of Buber's dialogue and feminist thought. The experience of discrimination and the hope for a truly egalitarian society where dialogue is conducted in a more genuine and equal way connect Buber's vision with the feminist liberation movement. I would argue that Buber's dialogical thought should not be read as an "existentialist" philosophy detached from historical context, but as a text written through the specifics of the Jewish social and political circumstances in the pre- and post-Weimar periods. As such, Buber's *I and Thou* and his later dialogical texts can be seen as a protest against social hierarchies, domination, and other unquestioned conventions that prevent genuine dialogue from being actualized.

Buber's perspective on dialogue from a minority point of view not only anticipated some of the social sensibilities of our time. It also allowed feminists and theorists of gender to draw on the dialogical principle and the realm of "the between" as realities pointing to the basic fact that in true dialogue one cannot dominate the other. Not to impose oneself on the other was one of the basic presuppositions of the interhuman for Buber. Dialogue is a reality that dwells between two people, "the conversation itself, the phonetic event fraught with meaning, whose meaning is to be found neither in one of the two partners nor in both together, but only in their dialogue itself, in this 'between' which they live together."[60]

Buber's reception among feminists changed, of course, with the development of feminism itself. While first-wave feminism concurred with Buber's earliest writings and was primarily concerned with women's voting rights, second-wave feminism of the 1960s coincided with Buber's popular reception in the United States and could draw on his fully developed dialogical philosophy. Its main objective was to bring women's voices to the forefront, to liberate women from being silenced, and to push for complete equality. But while second-wave feminists still used highly gendered language, third-wave feminists criticized the gendered language of care and saw it as limiting women to traditional roles and expectations. Moreover, it saw femininity as a form of coercion imposed on oppressed women. The current wave of feminism has sometimes questioned the term "feminism" itself and is committed to breaking gender dichotomies, allowing for more fluid and nonbinary gender identities. I suspect that Buber's notion of dialogue as a way of overcoming hierarchies and his concept of the interhuman "between" as transcending binaries will continue to function as important tools for shaping feminist ethics in the future.

Notes

1. Martin Buber, *Knowledge of Man: Selected Essays* (New York: Humanity Books, 1998), 74.
2. Buber, *Knowledge of Man*, 69.
3. Ekkehard W. Stegemann, "Martin Buber and Karl Ludwig Schmidt: A Jewish-Christian Dialogue on the Eve of the Shoah," *European Judaism: A Journal for the New Europe* 27, no. 1 (1994): 3–11. See also Martin Buber, *A Land of Two Peoples: Martin Buber on Jews and Arabs*, ed. Paul Mendes-Flohr (Chicago: University of Chicago Press, 2005).
4. Martin Buber, "Zwei Bücher nordischer Frauen," *Neue Freie Press* (Vienna), July 28, 1901, Literaturblatt.

5. Betty Friedan, "Women and Jews: The Quest for Selfhood," *Congress Monthly* 52, no. 2 (1995): 7–11.

6. Friedan, "Women and Jews," 7.

7. Buber, *Knowledge of Man*, 75.

8. Rachel Elior, *Grandmother Did Not Know How to Read and Write* (Jerusalem: Carmel, 2018).

9. Judith Plaskow, *The Coming of Lilith* (Boston: Beacon Press, 2005), 84.

10. Carol Gilligan, *In a Different Voice* (Cambridge, MA: Harvard University Press, 2013), xvi.

11. Gilligan, *In a Different Voice*, 173.

12. Gilligan, *In a Different Voice*, xxvii.

13. Judith Plaskow, "Jewish Theology in Feminist Perspective," in *Feminist Perspectives on Jewish Studies*, ed. Lynn Davidman and Shelly Tenenbaum (New Haven, CT: Yale University Press, 1994), 62–84. See also Hava Tirosh-Samuelson, *Women and Gender in Jewish Philosophy* (Bloomington: Indiana University Press, 2004), 1–25.

14. For more on Buber and Pappenheim, see Martin Buber, *Briefwechsel aus sieben Jahrzehnten*, vol. 1, *1897-1918*, ed. Grete Schaeder (Heidelberg: L. Schneider, 1972), 535. See also Abigail Gillman, *A History of German Jewish Bible Translation* (Chicago: University of Chicago Press, 2018), 200–207. On Buber and Susman, see Buber, *Briefwechsel*, 1:326. See also Margarete Susman, *Vom Geheimnis der Freiheit* (Berlin: Agora, 1994), 144–54. On Buber and Lasker-Schüler, see Buber, *Briefwechsel*, 1:353–54; and Grete Schaeder, "Geleitwort," in Buber, *Briefwechsel*, 1:59, as well as Else Lasker-Schüler, *Lieber gestreifter Tiger. Briefe von Else Lasker-Schüler*, vol. 1, ed. Margarete Küpper (Munich: Kösel, 1969), 116–29.

15. Ellen Key, *Die Frauenbewegung*, ed. Martin Buber, in *Die Gesellschaft. Sammlung sozialpsychologischer Monographien* (Frankfurt am Main, 1909), 28–29. Lou Andreas-Salomé, *Die Erotik*, ed. Martin Buber, in *Die Gesellschaft. Sammlung sozialpsychologischer Monographien* 33 (Frankfurt am Main, 1910). See also Buber, *Briefwechsel*, 1:265–67, 536, 337, 386.

16. Paul Mendes-Flohr, *Martin Buber: A Life of Faith and Dissent* (New Haven, CT: Yale University Press, 2019). See also Yemima Hadad, "Femininity, Motherhood, and Feminism: Reflections on Paul Mendes-Flohr's Biography *Martin Buber: A Life of Faith and Dissent*," *Religions* 13 no. 8 (2022): 1–12.

17. Mendes-Flohr, *Martin Buber*, 12.

18. Mark Verman, "Buber, Mysticism and Feminism," *CrossCurrents* 35 (1985): 470–72.

19. Mendes-Flohr, *Martin Buber*, 74.

20. Katharina Baur, "Die Schriftstellerin Paula Buber (1877–1958)," *Zeitschrift für christlich-jüdische Begegnung im Kontext*, no. 2/3 (2019): 195–203.

21. Rose Stair, "The Woman's Voice in Zionism: Disentangling Paula Winkler from Martin Buber," *Religions* 9, no. 401 (2018): 1–22.

22. Warren Zev Harvey, *Yeshayahu Leibowitz: Life and Thought*, ed. Avi Sagie (Jerusalem: Keter, 1995), 39–46.

23. Cited in Mendes-Flohr, *Martin Buber*, 78.

24. Martin Buber, *Briefwechsel aus sieben Jahrzehnten*, vol. 2, *1918-1938*, ed. Grete Schaeder (Heidelberg: L. Schneider, 1972), 326.

25. Buber, *Briefwechsel*, 2:326.

26. See, e.g., Jay Michaelson, "Queering Martin Buber: Harry Hay's Erotic Dialogical," *Shofar* 36, no. 3 (2018): 31–59.

27. James W. Walters, *Martin Buber and Feminist Ethics: The Priority of the Personal* (Syracuse, NY: Syracuse University Press, 2003), 84.

28. Gilligan, *In a Different Voice*, 173.

29. See, e.g., Judith Plaskow, *Standing Again at Sinai: Judaism from a Feminist Perspective* (San Francisco: Harper & Row, 1990); Tamar Ross, *Expanding the Palace of Torah* (Waltham, MA: Brandeis University Press, 2004).

30. Betty A. Sichel, "Women's Moral Development in Search of Philosophical Assumptions," *Journal of Moral Education* 14, no. 3 (1985): 149–61, 153.

31. Gilligan, *In a Different Voice*, xxvi.

32. Buber, *Knowledge of Man*, 74.

33. Richard L. Johannesen, "Nel Nodding's Uses of Martin Buber's Philosophy of Dialogue," *Southern Journal of Communication* 65, no. 3 (2000): 151–60.

34. Nel Noddings, *Caring: A Relational Approach to Ethics and Moral Education* (Berkeley: University of California Press, 1986), 176, xiii.

35. Noddings, *Caring*, xv, xvi.

36. Buber, *Knowledge of Man*, 84.

37. Johannesen, "Nel Noddings's Uses," 159.

38. Leora Batnitzky, "Dependency and Vulnerability: Jewish and Feminist Existentialist Constructions of the Human," in *Women and Gender in Jewish Philosophy*, ed. Hava Tirosh-Samuelson (Bloomington: Indiana University Press, 2004), 127–52, 142, 146, 145.

39. Plaskow, *The Coming of Lilith*, 67 (here Plaskow is quoting her student Lauren Granite).

40. Plaskow, *The Coming of Lilith*, 66.

41. Mara Benjamin, "Intersubjectivity Meets Maternity: Buber, Levinas and the Eclipsed Relation," in *Thinking Jewish Culture in America*, ed. Kenneth Koltun-Fromm (Lanham, MD: Rowman & Littlefield, 2013), 261–84, 267, 265.

42. Benjamin, "Intersubjectivity Meets Maternity, 262.

43. Benjamin, "Intersubjectivity Meets Maternity, 262, 272.

44. Benjamin, "Intersubjectivity Meets Maternity," 266. See also Martin Buber, *I and Thou*, trans. Ronald Gregor Smith (New York: Charles Scribner's Sons, 1958), 25.

45. Limor Sharir, *Martin Buber: Close Look—a Conversation with Prof. Judith Buber-Agassi* (Jerusalem: Carmel, 2011), 128 (my translation); Buber, *Briefwechsel*, 1:148–49.

46. Judith Butler, "Judith Butler: As a Jew, I Was Taught It Was Ethically Imperative to Speak Up," interview by Udi Aloni, *Haaretz*, February 24, 2010.

47. Judith Butler, "Versions of Binationalism in Said and Buber," in *Martin Buber: His Intellectual and Scholarly Legacy*, ed. Sam Berrin Shonkoff (Leiden: Brill, 2018), 103–30. See also Judith Butler, *Parting Ways: Jewishness and the Critique of Zionism* (New York: Colombia University Press, 2012).

48. Judith Butler, "We Are Worldless without One Another," interview by Stephanie Berbec, *The Other Journal*, no. 27 (2017), https://theotherjournal.com/2017/06/worldless-without-one-another-interview-judith-butler/. See also Judith Butler, *Notes Toward a Performative Theory of Assembly* (Cambridge, MA: Harvard University Press, 2015), 73.

49. Butler, *Notes Toward a Performative Theory*, 30–31.

50. Butler, "An Interview with Judith Butler."

51. Sarah Katharine Donovan, "Judith Butler and Luce Irigaray: Feminist Resources for Overcoming Oppressive Exclusions" (PhD diss., Villanova University, 2002), 7.

52. Luce Irigaray, "The Question of the Other," *Yale French Studies* 87 (1995): 9, 12.

53. Irigaray, "Question of the Other," 11.

54. Luce Irigaray, *I Love to You: Sketch for a Felicity within History*, trans. Alison Martin (New York: Routledge, 1996), 118.

55. Maria Markus, "The 'Anti-Feminism' of Hannah Arendt," *Thesis Eleven* 17, no. 1 (1987): 76–87.

56. Martha C. Nussbaum, "The Professor of Parody: The Hip Defeatism of Judith Butler," *New Republic*, February 22, 1999.

57. Barbara Merrill, "Dialogical Feminism: Other Women and the Challenge of Adult Education," *International Journal of Lifelong Education* 24, no. 1 (2005): 41, 43.

58. Merrill, "Dialogical Feminism," 43.

59. Deidre Butler, "Disturbing Boundaries: Developing Jewish Feminist Ethics with Buber, Levinas and Fackenheim," *Journal of Modern Jewish Studies* 10, no. 3 (2011): 327.

60. Buber, *Knowledge of Man*, 84, 75.

Annotated Bibliography

The most encompassing overview on Buber and the feminist ethics of care is James W. Walters, *Martin Buber and Feminist Ethics: The Priority of the Personal* (Syracuse, NY: Syracuse University Press, 2003). On the reception of Buber in feminist ethics, see Mara Benjamin, "Intersubjectivity Meets Maternity: Buber, Levinas and the Eclipsed Relation," in *Thinking Jewish Culture in America*, ed. Kenneth Koltun-Fromm (Lanham, MD: Rowman & Littlefield, 2013), 261–84. An exemplary anthology of essays on feminism and Jewish thought, including reflections on Buber's contribution to a feminist ethics, is Hava Tirosh-Samuelson, ed., *Women and Gender in Jewish Philosophy* (Bloomington: Indiana University Press, 2004).

PART SEVEN

Reception

Introduction

PAUL MENDES-FLOHR

As documented in this volume, Buber's philosophy of dialogue has resonated with scholars representing a wide spectrum of disciplines. In this section, two essays attest to how distinctive cultural climates have facilitated the reception of Buber's teachings. In his comprehensive review of the ramified interest in Buber's thought in Japan, Fumio Ono highlights that the semantic and syntactic structure of Japanese was particularly amenable to Buber's post-Cartesian philosophy, which allowed him to entertain existential and logical issues that also exercise Nipponese Buddhism.

France also provided Buber with a lively reception, with early premonitions of what, in the aftermath of World War II, would be celebrated as post-modernism. Like Buber, the postmodernist movement would question the epistemological and ontological presuppositions of the Enlightenment.

26

Buber in France: From Gaston Bachelard to Emmanuel Levinas

DOMINIQUE BOUREL

A polyglot, Martin Buber had a sovereign command of French. He gave lectures in French in Pontigny before the Second World War, then at the Sorbonne, and later at the Institut International d'Études Hébraïques, founded after the war in 1955 by Rabbi André Zaoui (1916–2009) in Paris. He learned French at an early age and, while still a schoolboy, was able to help his grandfather, a scholar of rabbinic Midrash, read Rashi's biblical commentary written in medieval Judeo-French.

Buber later corresponded in French with Swiss friends, the philosopher Henry Serouya (1895–1968), who was born in Jerusalem, and the Dominican monk Pater Roland de Vaux (1903–71), the head of the École Biblique et Archéologique de Jérusalem. Until the end of his life, he conversed and corresponded in French with United Nations Secretary General Dag Hammerskjöld (1905–61), who began before his death to translate *Ich und Du* into Swedish, as well as with the spiritus rectors of the Mediterranean Encounters in Florence, Giorgio La Pira (1904–77) and Joe Golan (1922–2003), although Buber's Italian was also excellent. His last secretary and the curator of the Buber archives in the Israel National Library was the French-born Margot Cohn (1922–2016), who deftly navigated all known *buberlogues* through the voluminous archive, including over fifty thousand letters. She was very active in the Resistance in France and was there when Max Brod (1881–1968) arrived on one of the last trains from Prague with the Kafka papers.[1]

Buber's first important encounter with the French intellectual milieu was in 1913 with the Catholic diplomat and poet Paul Claudel (1868–1955), at that time French general consul in Frankfurt. Buber was the dramaturge when Claudel's *Maria Verkündigung* was presented in the new and avant-garde experimental theater in Hellerau, near Dresden.[2] He defended his views with

Claudel, along with Alexander von Salzmann and Wolf Dohrn, both of whom were in charge of the production. The premiere on October 5, 1913, was a major cultural event, one of the last at the theater before World War I. (The manuscript of Jakob Hegner's translation was bought by Stefan Zweig!) At the premiere, alongside Buber, we find Lou Salomé, Rainer Maria Rilke, Max Reinhardt, Gerhardt Hauptmann, Ernst Robert Curtis, Julius Hart, Hélène von Nostiz, Franz Werfel, Kurt Pinthus, and Darius Milhaud. Following the performance, Buber wrote his essay "Das Raumproblem der Bühne" (1913).[3]

One of the first important letters in French came from Zionist leader Victor Jacobson (1869–1934), who in 1925 wrote to Buber that in France there was "fertile ground" for informing the French reading public about Zionism and asked his help for the short-lived *Revue juive*, published in Paris in 1925, under the direction of Albert Cohen (1895–1981), with prestigious contributors.[4] In that year the first translations of Buber's works into French were published. Among his most enthusiastic readers were the Catholic journalist, publisher, and poet Stanislas Fumet (1896–1983), who recommended to Jean de Menasce (1902–73), an Egyptian Jew who became a Catholic priest in the Dominican order and an expert in Zoroastrian studies, that he seek to publish Buber's essay "Quand Israel aime Dieu" (Paris, 1931; reprinted in 1992), one of the first discussions of Hasidism in French. Translations of Buber's work began to appear in the French Jewish and non-Jewish journals, among them *Europe* (1925), *Mesures* (1937), *Dieu vivant* (1945), *Les cahiers sioniens* (1949), *Revue de la pensée juive* (1950), *Évidences* (1952), *Evidences* (1953–57), *Cahiers de l'Alliance Israélite Universelle* (1954), *Mélanges de philosophie et de littérature juive* (1956/57), *L'Arche* (1957, 1960, 1968), *La table ronde* (1958), *La nouvelle revue française* (1960), and *Tempo présenté* (1960).

The important inaugural moment in the history of Buber's French reception was his lecture at the *Décades de Pontigny* series of philosophical conferences in Burgundy, to which he was invited by the organization's founder, Paul Desjardins (1859–1940). On July 17, 1928, Desjardins wrote to Buber: "Among all the German authors who continue to perpetuate the spirit of the *Aufklärung*, you are of deeper importance, one whose attendance at Pontigny would have the most positive impact."[5] At the *Décade*, Buber delivered lectures on asceticism (October 23–September 2, 1936), and again in 1936 the lecture "La volonté du mal," which occasioned his meeting with the French professor, philosopher, and historian of science Gaston Bachelard (1884–1962), who promoted the translation of *Je et Tu* (Paris, 1938). Bachelard wrote the introduction to the translation,[6] in preparation for which he wrote to Buber requesting that he highlight the major points of his book: "Don't forget that I am only a poor slave of reason, a man of figures, a being who is seized by anxiety in the *tomorrows* of reason, in the unknown that is to come, in the formation of thought. Through you, I know that there is a foundation in yesterday, an unknown from whence we come. Tell me, narrate this journey I have not made. And I will be the echo. Naturally, I will submit what I write to you just like a student to his teacher."[7]

After World War II, the Union des intellectuels juifs de France (in August 1945!) and the Union mondiale des étudiants juifs (1946) solicited Buber's assistance in the reconstruction of French Judaism. Jean Fischer of "La terre retrouvée" (1946), Renée Louys of the *Cahiers du Sud* (1950), and then the "Sinai" collection at the Presses universitaires de France took the first steps to introduce him to the French reader. Albert Memmi (1920–2020), still in Tunisia and head of the Charlot publishing house (Paris, Algiers), also sought to issue some of Buber's books in French. In France, at the invitation of the French government, Buber gave well-attended lectures (1946, 1956) and was awarded a doctorate *honoris causa* (1958). André Neher (1914–68) and André Chouraqui (1917–2007) played seminal roles in promoting his reputation in France, where he was defined as a "Jewish existentialist." In May 1947 he offered the lectures "L'amour de Dieu et l'idée de la divinité," and "L'amour de Dieu et l'amour du prochain dans le Hassidisme" at the Sorbonne.

The second key moment resulting from this visit to Paris was his exchange with the orientalist and Catholic philosopher Louis Massignon (1883–1962), an ardent supporter of the Arab refugees displaced with the establishment of the State of Israel. Massignon was a greater admirer of the advocate of the human and political rights of the Palestinian Arabs, Jehuda Magnes (1877–1948), whose grave he visited when he later traveled to the United States.[8] Buber came once again to Paris to teach at the Institut International d'Études Hébraïques, directed by Rabbi Zaoui.

In an undated French letter, presumably from early February 1952, Buber wrote to Albert Camus: "Dear Sir and Colleague, your book, *L'homme révolté* [The Rebel, 1951] seems to me to be of such importance for human life at this hour that I should like to recommend to Mossad Bialik, the national publishing house of Israel, of whose board of directors I am a member, that it be translated into Hebrew. Would you kindly tell me how you feel about this matter? There is only one phrase in your book that I find unjust, which especially disturbs me. It is on page 370 where you speak of the 'ciel implacable' [implacable heaven] of the Old Testament. That is absolutely incorrect. The divine words, 'I dwell on high, in holiness; yet with the contrite and the lowly in spirit' [Isa. 57:15] are not an exception; they are the very substance of this world [of the Hebrew Bible]."[9] Camus replied in a letter dated February 22, 1952: "I read your *I and Thou* with great admiration and profit, but I had not hoped, or expected, to receive a positive reaction from you [with respect to my own work]. It pleases and honors me that you have. I readily admit that the sentence that gave you pause deserves numerous nuances, and I would have no objection to its being modified. That is the drawback of projects that presume to sum up what cannot be summed up. But my main effort was directed at emphasizing the basic idea, even at the risk of obscurity and injustice. At any rate, I shall gratefully accept any critique that points these infelicities out to me and permits me to rectify them."[10]

Undoubtedly, Buber's intellectual relationship with Emmanuel Levinas (1905–95) is richly commented upon in the secondary literature on both.[11] Levinas, who was born in Kaunas, Lithuania, played a very important role in France, introducing select students and a more general audience not only to the Talmud but also to the German Jewish world (Hermann Cohen, Franz Rosenzweig, and Buber) at the École Normale Israélite Orientale, and also at the Sorbonne, where he was a professor of philosophy until his retirement. Buber last came to Paris in 1960 to participate in a conference on the condition of Soviet Jewry, where he delivered what was perhaps his last lecture in French (October 1–5, 1960) with more than sixty participants and 120 invited guests.[12]

Today many of Buber's books, on philosophy but also on politics and Hasidism, are regularly published, mostly in fine French paperback translations. He is widely discussed in contemporary French philosophical discourse about alterity, the asymmetry of relations, reciprocity, and more generally ethics and the overcoming of the bifurcated subject-predicate ontology that has dominated European thought since Socrates.

Notes

1. All letters cited here are in the Martin Buber Archives, at the Jewish National Library in Jerusalem. A list of the unpublished correspondence (and unpublished articles) is available at the Israel National Library, Archives: Buber, Martin (1878 Wien–1965 Jerusalem) ARC Ms. Var. 350.

2. Alain Beretta, *Claudel et la mise en scène: Autour de l'Annonce faite à Marie (1912–1955)* (Besançon: Université de France Comté, 2000), https://doi.org/10. For Buber, see also his "Claudel. L'Annonce faite à Marie (1913)," 524–530, and "Das Raumproblem der Bünde," 429–38, both in *Martin Buber Werkausgabe*, vol. 7, *Schriften zu Literatur, Theater und Kunst*, ed. Emily D. Bilsky, Freddie Rokem, and Bernd Witte (Gütersloh: Gütersloher Verlagshaus, 2016). The latter article was printed in *Das Claudel-Programmbuch* of the Festspielhaus, Hellerau, in October 1913.

3. Martin Buber, "Das Raumproblem der Bünde," *Martin Buber Werkausgabe*, 7:429–38.

4. Victor Jacobson to Martin Buber, March 31, 1925, Martin Buber Archive, Ms. Var. 350, Korrespondenz 325, 19.

5. Paul Desjardins to Martin Buber, July 17, 1928, Martin Buber Archive, Ms. Var. 350, Korrespondenz, Mappe 169, 1.

6. Translation in Edward K. Kaplan, "Imagination and Ethics: Gaston Bachelard and Martin Buber," *International Studies in Philosophy* 35, no. 1 (2003): 75–88.

7. Gaston Bachelard to Martin Buber, February 23, 1937. Also see Dominique Bourel, "The French Manuscript Collection at the Jewish National and University Library in Jerusalem," *Bulletin du Centre de Recherche Français de Jérusalem* 5 (1999): 71–81.

8. Dominique Bourel, "Six lettres de Louis Massignon à Martin Buber," *Pardès*, no. 2 (1985): 173–81.

9. Martin Buber to Albert Camus, February 1952, Martin Buber Archive, Korrespondenz, Mappe 151a.

10. Albert Camus to Martin Buber, February 22, 1952, in *The Letters of Martin Buber: A Life of Dialogue*, ed. N. N. Glatzer and P. Mendes-Flohr (New York: Schocken Books, 1995), 568–69.

11. *Lévinas and Buber: Dialogue and Difference*, ed. Peter Atterton, Matthiew Calarco, and Maurice Friedman (Pittsburgh: Duquesne University Press, 2004).

12. Dominique Bourel, "Martin Buber et la Méditerannée," *Perspectives: Revue de l'Université hébraïque de Jérusalem* 5 (1998): 145–57.

Annotated Bibliography

PRIMARY SOURCES

For the full text of Buber's seminal Pontigny lecture, "Le mal est-il une force indépendante," which paved the way for his French reception, see *Archives de Philosophie* (1988): 529–45. For an edition of Buber's lecture on Claudel's "Annonce faite à Marie" in Hellerau, with a commentary that also describes Buber's participation in other theater performances there, see Alain Beretta, *Claudel et la mise en scène: Autour de l'Annonce faite à Marie, 1912–1955* (Paris: Université de France Comté, 2000).

SECONDARY LITERATURE

On the politics of Pontigny's invitations to foreign intellectuals, see François Chaubet, *Paul Desjardins et les Décades de Pontigny* (Villeneuve d'Ascq: Presses Universitaires du Septentrion, 2000). For a more synoptic review of Buber's French reception, see Dominique Bourel, "Martin Buber et la culture française," *Bulletin du centre de recherche français de Jérusalem* 18 (2017): 122–39; and Dominique Bourel, "Martin Buber et la Méditerranéen," *Perspectives. Revue de l'Université hébraïque de Jérusalem* 5 (1998): 145–57.

On Levinas and Buber's often fraught intellectual relationship, see the anthology *Lévinas and Buber: Dialogue and Difference*, edited by Peter Atterton, Matthiew Calarco, and Maurice Friedman (Pittsburgh: Duquesne University Press, 2004). Also see Hilary Putnam, *Jewish Philosophy as a Guide to Life: Rosenzweig, Buber, Levinas, Wittgenstein* (Bloomington: Indiana University Press, 2008), 56–99.

27

Buber's Philosophy of Dialogue: A Japanese Perspective

FUMIO ONO

Buber's philosophy of dialogue resonated with a Japanese philosophical movement which sought an alternative philosophy. Buber's philosophy is characterized by the following triad that addressed key issues in the Japanese philosophical quest: (1) the between (the philosophy of relation), (2) the ontology of becoming (exploring the form of the formless), and (3) contradictory ideas in actuality (*coincidentia oppositorum* and the logic of lemma). These three elements help actualize Buber's philosophy of dialogue as regulative ideas crucial to the relentless pursuit of an elusive, yet indispensable, vision of a reconciliatory utopia comprising both harmonious coexistence and ample personal freedom.

The Encounter between Japanese Philosophy and Buber

Buber's ideas were disseminated in Japan in two broad periods. The early phase occurred in the 1930s, and the developmental phase spanned from the 1960s to the 1980s. The developmental phase saw the full-scale dissemination of Buber's thought in Japan. These two phases were suggested by Yoshimori Hiraishi in "Buber and Japanese Thought."[1] He identifies three broad areas of interest during the early Japanese reception of Buber's philosophy of dialogue: (1) its dissemination in Japan in the context of Germanic Protestant theology, especially the dialectical theology espoused by Karl Barth, Emil Brunner, and Friedrich Gogarten; (2) biblical hermeneutics; and (3) the relation between Buber's work and Japanese Buddhism.

Dialectical theology influenced the philosophical community in Japan, particularly the Kyoto school, during the 1930s and 1940s. Buber was rarely mentioned there because he only played an indirect role in shaping it. Nevertheless, it is worth noting that the Kyoto school extensively debated concepts and ideas such as "I and Thou," "encounter," and the "dialectics" of a lived life. For example, Kitaro Nishida (1870–1945), the founder of the Kyoto school, independently penned his own version of *I and Thou*, titled *Watakushi to Nanji*, in 1932, though he based his version on his concept of "absolute nothingness" (*zettai mu*). Buberian ideas commanded the attention of Nishida's students and those they influenced in turn. We could attribute Japanese philosophers' receptiveness to Buber to the simple fact that Buber discusses the Buddha and Mahayana Buddhism in the third part of *I and Thou*. To do so, however, would be to overlook other reasons; specifically, throughout the text, Buber repeatedly underscores the virtue of direct encounters with the Thou and the importance of what he called a "turning" (*Umkehr*)—ideas that would have resonated with Japanese people steeped in the ideas of Pure Land (*Jōdo*) Buddhism. Moreover, Japanese Zen Buddhism, aiming at the perfection of personhood, provided a spiritual and intellectual climate conducive to Buber's philosophy of religion.

Three Japanese translations of *I and Thou* were published: the Noguchi translation (Tokyo, 1958); the Ueda translation (Tokyo, 1964), which was republished by Iwanami-Shoten (Tokyo, 1979); and the Taguchi translation (Tokyo, 1967), which was included in the first volume of the ten-volume Japanese edition of Martin Buber's *Collected Works*. The very fact of these successive translations highlights the extensive Japanese interest in Buber's teachings. It was Yoshimori Hiraishi himself, who, having started out as a scholar of Philo of Alexandria, penned the first comprehensive Japanese monograph on Buber, *Būbā: Hito to shisō* (*Buber: The Person and His Ideas*; Tokyo, 1966). Hiraishi later played a central role in the publication of ten volumes of Buber's works in Japanese (Tokyo, 1967–70), further promoting an intensive engagement with Buber's thought in Japan. However, the dissemination of Buber's philosophy of dialogue in Japan decisively took place in Hiraishi's second "developmental" phase, in conjunction with an increasing existentialism. Hence, when the wave of existentialism ended, interest in Buber also waned.

Nevertheless, Buber continues to be read in Japan today and not just among those interested in German philosophy; Buber's works find readership across a wide spectrum of fields including theology, the Hebrew Bible, phenomenology, sociology, psychotherapy, pedagogy, psychology, and the arts. In fact, interest in Buber's thought has undergone something of a resurgence in Japan since the turn of the century, particularly in biblical scholarship and scholarly interest in Jewish thought.[2] With respect to biblical scholarship, the Old Testament scholar Hiroya Katsumura has contributed to the recent interest in Buber with Japanese translations of Buber's *Moses* (*Mōse*, 2002), *The Kingdom of God* (*Kami no Kuni*, 2003), and *The Anointed One* (*Abura Sosogareta Mono*,

2010). These translations have also had a seminal impact far beyond biblical scholarship. According to Katsumura, "The biblical hermeneutics of Buber is a key bridge between his anthropology and his social and political philosophy." Regarding the underlying reason, he avers that "the Hebrew Bible [...] is not a religious piece of literature in the sense we think of today. Indeed, in many respects it is highly political in nature." Katsumura's key point is that "Buber's biblical hermeneutics is a singular attempt to shed light on the ideological message contained in the Bible within a modern context."[3]

In consonance with this renewed interest in Buber was an interdisciplinary conference on his legacy in 2010 at the Center for the Interdisciplinary Study of the Monotheistic Religions, which was established in 2003 at Doshisha University in Kyoto. And in 2015, the Kyoto Association of Jewish Thought, established in 2008, held a symposium commemorating the fiftieth anniversary of Buber's passing. Additionally, in 2019, the association published a journal special issue, "Martin Buber: The Echo of His Dialogical Thought."

This modest "Buber revival" in Japan is not entirely unrelated to the trends of Buber studies in Europe, Israel, and the United States since 2000, including the publication of a new collection of Buber's works titled *Martin Buber Werkausgabe*. The revival may therefore be viewed as part of a broader global phenomenon.

The Philosophy of In-between: On Dialogical Relations

In *I and Thou*, Buber repeatedly refers to the "a priori relation," as evidenced by the following phrases: "In the beginning is the relation"; "the longing for relation is primary"; "the I and the Thou between whom [the relation] is established."[4] In his 1954 work *Elemente des Zwischenmenschlichen* (*Elements of the Interhuman*), Buber further develops his idea of a priori relation into a philosophy of "the between" (*Zwischen*), a concept that resonated powerfully with Japanese thought. First, the Japanese concept of *ningen*, or human beings, connotes "between humans," and this fact alone explains many Japanese people's intrigue with Buber's anthropology. Another factor concerns the idiosyncrasies of Japanese grammar. Japanese features a dazzling array of personal pronouns that can be used differently depending on the context or the referents' relationship to one another. Furthermore, Japanese sentences often do not require a subject. Given these features, the ontological status of the subject (agent) is contingent upon relation. Consequently, Japanese syntax is less likely to be predicated upon the independent existence of the individual "I" as examined in *I and Thou*. Despite this, or perhaps because of it, Buber's alternative idea that the individual "I" has no intrinsic existence but is rather contingent upon a priori "relation" was thus readily accepted in the climate of thought in Japan.

Illustrating this most strikingly is the case of Tetsuro Watsuji (1989–1960), a moral philosopher of the Kyoto school. Watsuji famously developed his own philosophy of the being in-between or interhumanity (*Aidagara-teki Sonzai*) in works such as *Ningen no Gaku toshite no Rinrigaku* (*Ethics as the Study of Inter-Humanity*; 1934). He was undoubtedly inspired by Buber's conception of the interhuman (*das Zwischenmenschliche*).[5] Admittedly, however, the direct influence never went beyond that. Nevertheless, Watsuji became the progenitor of *aida* (*the between*) thought in Japanese philosophy, and his work is still widely read.

Another thinker worth mentioning is the psychiatrist Bin Kimura (1931–2021). With a grounding in psychiatry and phenomenological anthropology, Kimura developed an independent philosophy of life, the self, the other, and time in works such as *Hito to Hito to no Aida* (*Between Person and Person*; 1972), *Jikan to Jiko* (*Time and the Self*; 1982), and *Aida* (*Between*; 1988).[6] As these titles illustrate, *aida* is a key word in Kimura's philosophy, and he certainly would have drawn inspiration from Buber's concepts of "between" and "I and Thou." That said, it was Victor von Weizsäcker (1886–1958) who exerted the strongest influence on Kimura, and the core component of Kimura's thought consisted of dialogues with the philosophies of Ludwig Binswanger, Martin Heidegger, and Kitaro Nishida.

As the two examples of Watsuji and Kimura attest, many thinkers in Japan were interested in Buber's key concept of "between," even if Buber's influence on them was not that extensive. This interest was not confined to philosophy either. Buber's "between" clearly inspired the Japanese architect Arata Isozaki (1931–2022), who won the 2019 Pritzker Architecture Prize and has earned international acclaim as a leader in postmodern architecture. In "Turning Point," Isozaki mentions Buber when describing his architectural vision, which features the elements "pitch-black" (*yami*) and "void" (*kyo*). In the same publication, he discloses his affinity with the Dutch structuralist architect Aldo van Eyck (1918–99). The son of a Jewish mother, Van Eyck was also influenced by Buber. Isozaki mentions that Van Eyck's architectural experience of space and time is incompatible with abstract Cartesian space and time:

> At one end of the shade spectrum is pitch-black. At the other is a void that goes beyond transparency. At the end of *Yami no Kūkan* [*Space of Darkness*], I summarized this as a confrontation between the polarities of pitch-black and void. I regarded pitch-black as more architectural and physical, and void as urban and media-like. This schema remains unchanged and valid today.

Perhaps a somewhat more fundamental interpretation is possible. Around that time, Aldo van Eyck was probably analyzing his findings on the villages of Pueblo Indians or the clustered dwellings of African tribes and was attempting to use them as a template for his designs of kindergartens. He also considered the ideas of Martin Buber. A Jew who engaged in Heideggerian Germanic philosophy, Buber is known for *I and Thou*. *I and Thou* adeptly dealt with an issue later described as "intersubjectivity" or, in Nishida philosophy, *aida* ("in-between"). I discussed this in the opening section to *Yami no Kūkan*. According to Buber's ideas about time and space, abstract Cartesian space and absolute time would be incompatible with our architectural experience of space and time, and they can never be meaningfully discussed insofar as they do not involve human beings in them. On this basis, he suggested substituting the word "time" with "occasion" and the word "space" with "place." In essence, *Yami no Kūkan* was a critique of the temporal and spatial ideas shared among European modernists like [Siegfried] Giedion [1888–1968]. By replacing time with occasion and space with place, Buber challenged the substratum of the West. I wrote *Yami no Kūkan* on the belief that we needed an anthropological and ontological approach to space.[7]

We can set aside the matter of the validity of Isozaki's interpretation of Buber as delineated in the passage above. The point is that this passage demonstrates that Japanese postmodernist architects were inspired, to some extent, by Buber's "between," his philosophy of dialogue, and his work *I and Thou*. It also evidences the interdisciplinary and transcontextual possibilities of Buber's concept of the "between" and the challenge that his anthropology and existential ontology posed to Western metaphysics. Accordingly, Buber found a uniquely receptive audience in the Far East, particularly in Japan.

The Ontology of Becoming: Exploration of the Form of the Formless

Buber describes the transition from the Thou-world to the It-World as an event in which the holistic form (*Gestalt*) of the dialogical present (*Gegenwart*) is untethered and transformed into an object (*Gegenstand*):

> Form is a mixture of Thou and It, too. In faith and cult, it can freeze into an object; but from the gist of the relation that survives in it, it turns ever again into presence.[8]

In regarding the dialogical encounter manifested as an amalgam of Thou and It, Buber argues that we are able to return (*Umkehr*) to the dynamic event of becoming (*Werden*) of I-Thou relations.

The ontology of becoming left an imprint on the scriptural hermeneutics of the Japanese Christian theologian Tetsutaro Ariga's Hayathology (*Hajathologia*). In *Kirisutokyō Shisō ni Okeru Sonzairon no Mondai* (*The Problem of Ontology in Christian Thought*; 1981), Ariga sets forth an ontological argument for God's existence based on the ancient Hebrew word for "to be," *hāyā* (הָיָה), rather than the ancient Greek word that is its counterpart, *ón* (ὤν), stable, resisting change, perduring. He also sought to demonstrate that Christian theology is correctly grounded not in Greek ontology but rather in the ontology of the Hebrew Bible, or hayathology. The Hebrew verb *hāyā* differs from the Greek verb *ón* in that, as well as meaning "to be," it can also mean "to act" (as in work, function, operate, take effect, etc.) and "to become." The verb appears in the famous response God utters to Moses in Exodus 3:14, which reads *'ehyeh 'ăšer 'ehyeh* (אֶהְיֶה אֲשֶׁר אֶהְיֶה) and is translated into Japanese as *Watashi wa Aru Mono de aru* (I am the Existing One) and commonly translated in English as "I Am that I Am." On this phrase, Ariga remarked as follows: "It is not that the subject must first exist in order to act. Rather, in its action, the subject declares its existence: *I am; therefore, I act. I act; therefore, I am*. However, this does not mean that God is immanent only within manifest phenomena. [. . .] For [*hāyā*] always remains in imperfect form, *'ehyeh*, suggesting future tense—the entity *will* perform a creative act."[9]

It is worth noting that Ariga's hayathology was also informed by the work of Thorleif Boman. In *Das Hebräische Denken im Vergleich mit dem Griechischen* (*Hebrew Thought Compared with Greek*; 1954), Boman emphasizes that the verb *'ehyeh* combines three meanings: "to be" (*Sein*), "to become" (*Werden*), and "to act" (*Wirken*).[10] Thus, Ariga's hayathology constitutes an alternative ontology, one that underscores the dynamic senses of "to become" and "to act."

Another Japanese theologian who showed interest in *'ehyeh*, the first person singular imperfective form of *hāyā*, was Hisao Miyamoto. Miyamoto focused on the same phrase in Exodus, which he described as "God's declaration of his first-person personhood [*'ehyeh*]" and on which he remarked that "God's ontology is imperfect. He *will* transcend from himself and become; and as regards the second person, he *will* liberate his enslaved people from the totalitarian tyranny of Egypt. His acts are characterized as enduring imperfect; he liberates the second person across the temporal flow of history."[11] To further underscore hayathology's ideological potential, Miyamoto suggested rebranding it as an emancipatory ontology to be called "ehyehlogy" (*Ehyehlogia*).

Grounded in Hebrew thought, Ariga's and Miyamoto's ontologies offer an alternative to Greek ontologies; they attempt to understand being as becoming.[12] Their ontologies emerged from a certain psycho-ideological lineage, which was certainly related to the fact that Buber's philosophy of dialogue was well established in Japan. The evidence for this is twofold. First, in *Zwei Glaubensweisen* (*Two Types of Faith*), Buber notes that the type of faith the Hebrew word *emunah* expresses differs from the type of faith the Greek word *pistis* expresses, and in underscoring the Hebrew Bible's unique qualities, he draws attention to elements that are distinctively Hebrew as well as to those that are distinctively Jewish. Second, in *I and Thou* and other writings, Buber criticizes objectification and advocates the ontology of becoming—he explores the form of the formless.[13]

The notion that the ontology of becoming is distinctly Hebrew or Jewish should not be taken at face value, and the matter of whether it is intrinsically Hebrew is not of interest here. Two things are of concern here. First, Buber, having based *I and Thou* on the ontology of becoming and having positioned himself "between" Western philosophy and Jewish thought, offered a perspective that was implicitly critical of Western philosophy. Second, the ontology of becoming has immense transcultural resonance.

The Logic of Lemma in *I and Thou*

In *I and Thou*, Buber writes: "In the It-world causality holds unlimited sway." By contrast, he also offers that, in the world of relation, "I and Thou confront each other freely in a reciprocity that is not involved in or tainted by any causality; here[,] man finds guaranteed the freedom of his being and of being."[14] From these words, one gains the impression that Buber needed an alternative type of reasoning to theoretically ground and explain the I–It categories. He thus took pains to find an alternative discourse that could communicate effectively his philosophy. What was this alternative type of reasoning? The answer lies in the logic of lemma.

Logical (logos-based) reasoning is a staple in Western philosophy. Logical reasoning operates according to three laws of thought: the law of identity, the law of noncontradiction, and the law of the excluded middle. By contrast, lemmatic (lemma-based) reasoning uses a tetralemma as set forth by the Indian philosopher Nagarjuna in *Mūlamadhyamakakārikā* (*Root Verses on the Middle Way*). For any proposition, there are four lemmata. The first lemma is affirmation signified by "A." The second lemma is "negation" or "not-A." The third lemma is "neither" or "neither A nor not-A." The fourth lemma is "both" or "A and also not-A." In traditional Western logical discourse, the third and fourth lemmas would be rejected as illogical or irrational in that they run afoul of the law of noncontradiction and the law of the excluded middle. However, the logic of lemma does not regard them as such, since it supposes that they have their own logical basis.

Tokuryu Yamauchi (1890–1982) discusses the logic of the lemma in depth in *Rogosu to Renma* (*Logos and Lemma*; 1974) and in *Zuimen no Tetsugaku* (*Philosophy of Anuśaya*; 1993). Most crucially, Yamauchi highlights the "neither A nor not-A" lemma, arguing that it forms the crux of Indian philosophy and of Mahayana Buddhism in particular. He also argues that the "neither A nor not-A" lemma and the "A and also not-A" lemma attest to the existence of a third or "middle" possibility between affirmation and negation.[15] Thus, in his exposition on the logic of lemma, Yamauchi contemplates the independent value of an included middle—or *aida* in Japanese—that can accommodate both the "neither" lemma and the "both" lemma.

Intriguingly, *I and Thou* features several instances involving something akin to the logic of lemma. Some examples are shown herewith. The first example features the "A and also not-A" lemma:

> Thus the relationship is election and electing, passive and active at once.[16]

> Yes, in the pure relationship you felt altogether dependent, as you could never possibly feel in any other—and yet also altogether free as never and nowhere else; created—and creative. You no longer felt the one; limited by the other; you felt both without bounds, both at once.[17]

Next is an example of the "neither A nor not-A" lemma. Here, we also see the reasoning that the "neither" lemma implies "both" lemmas: " 'Neither A nor not-A'; therefore, 'A and also not-A.' "

> Buddha, the "Perfected" and perfecter, asserts not. He refuses to claim that unity exists or does not exist; that he who has passed through all the trials of immersion will persist in unity after death or that he will not persist in it.[18]

> In the envisaged mystery, even as in lived actuality, neither "thus it is" nor "thus it is not" prevails, neither being nor not-being, but rather thus-and-otherwise, being and not-being, the indissoluble. To confront the undivided mystery undivided, that is the primal condition of salvation.[19]

Should we take such statements as evidence that Buber was being illogical? Surely, we ought rather see such reasoning, which is recurrent throughout *I and Thou*, as expressing a logic that must perforce depart from causal reasoning.

According to Paul Mendes-Flohr, Buber was under the sway of an atheistic mysticism in his younger years and had affirmed mystical experience as taking one beyond the inevitable torments of the world of phenomena, what he would later call the It-World, but he later departed from mysticism after experiencing his "(re)turning."[20] *I and Thou*, consequent to his (re)turning, retains the residue of the psychological sensibilities Buber imbibed from mystic traditions, and this residue is blended with a dialogical philosophy that seeks a critical distance from a secular understanding of mysticism. However, the rhetoric of *I and Thou* is too profound to be couched in such simplistic designations as the blend or residue of mysticism. If anything, Buber's rhetoric bears the trace of his painstaking contemplative enterprise, that is, his grappling for the words to express concepts—between, encounter, Thou, lived actuality—that could never adequately be expressed using the conventional rhetoric of Western formal logic.

The Significance of *Coincidentia Oppositorum*

None of the above observations would warrant regarding Buber simplistically as an Eastern thinker or even as a Jewish one. After all, Buber also bore all the psycho-ideological heritage of the *Western* philosophical tradition. We can see an illustration of this in the case of Nicholas of Cusa's *coincidentia oppositorum* (coincidence of opposites). That is, Buber's ontology of becoming and his concepts of (re)turning (*Umkehr*) and redemption (*Erlösung*) were primed by the dynamics of contradiction and antinomy expressed in *coincidentia oppositorum*. In *I and Thou*, Buber alludes to Nicholas of Cusa's *coincidentia oppositorum* when describing his conception of relationships as "bipolar":

> If one starts out from the soul, the perfect relationship can only be seen as bipolar, as coincidentia oppositorum, as the fusion of opposite feelings.[21]
>
> There are not two kinds of human beings, but there are two poles of humanity. [. . .] Each lives in a twofold I.[22]

Mysticism tends to be characterized as a pursuit of *unio mystica* (mystical union). To Buber, however, mysticism does not just gravitate toward unification (*Vereinigung*), for its orientation toward unification paradoxically entails a necessary orientation toward duality (*Zweiheit*), engendering change. This bipolarity is a critical element in Buber's thought. Insofar as it enables a dialectic without sublation (*Aufhebung*), Buber's bipolarity became a cornerstone in his philosophy of dialogue.[23]

To experience the dualities of I-Thou and I-It is to experience actualities teeming with contradiction and antinomy. In other words, it is to experience the "A and also not-A" lemma in actuality. At the end of the postscript of *I and Thou* (1957), Buber addresses "the most important [question] of all": "How can the eternal Thou be at the same time exclusive and inclusive?" Buber notes that answering this question requires reference to God, "For our relationship to him is as supra-contradictory as it is because he is as supra-contradictory as he is." He then adds, "[E]ven that [i.e., what God is in his relationship to a human being] can be said only in a paradox; [. . .] or still more precisely, by means of a paradoxical combination of a nominal concept with an adjective that contradicts the familiar content of the concept." Buber then invokes Spinoza to highlight the necessity of paradoxically describing God as a person: "The concept of personhood is, of course, utterly incapable of describing the nature of God; but it is permitted and necessary to say that God is *also* a person."[24]

The postscript was added to *I and Thou* in 1957. But previously Buber had already set forth the same argument in a 1928 work titled *Die chassidischen Bücher* (*Tales of the Hasidim*). The postscript therefore reveals that Buber maintained the same interpretation of Spinoza at the time he wrote *I and Thou*.

> Spinoza undertook to take from God His being open to man's address. [. . .] [H]e only wanted to purify Him from the stain of being open to address. A God who was capable of being addressed was not pure enough, not great enough, not divine enough for him. The fundamental error of Spinoza was that he imagined that in the teaching of Israel only the teaching that God is a person was to be found and he opposed it as a diminution of divinity. But the truth of the teaching is that God is *also* a person [*das auch personsein Gottes*], and this is, in contrast to all impersonal, nonaddressable "purity" of God, an augmentation of divinity.[25]

This statement should not be dismissed as a mere failure to understand Spinoza's philosophy. The matter of how we interpret Buber's use of the adverb "also" (*auch*) is certainly key to understanding Buber's dialogical philosophy in *I and Thou*. The statement instantiates the "A and also not-A" lemma, and Buber could only express this lemma by means of contradiction and paradox. The lemma retains the bipolarity and antinomy between the Divine's absolute transcendence and the Divine's personhood, and it could only ever be expressed using the *coincidentia oppositorum* formula. Though, in formal logical terms, *coincidentia oppositorum* would be dismissed as illogical, it is, in terms of lived actualities, indispensable rhetoric. In this sense, *coincidentia oppositorum* has some continuity with the logic of lemma. However, as noted already, we should avoid subjecting Buber's thought to any dichotomous schema by classifying it as *either* Greek *or* Hebrew or as *either* Western *or* Eastern. Instead, we should regard his reasoning as something he was inevitably required to undertake in order to explore an alternative structure thought. In that respect, Buber's contemplation has universal value.

Conclusion

In conclusion, the Japanese philosopher, poet, and civil activist Kohei Hanazaki (b. 1931) is worth mentioning. Hanazaki started out as a scholar of German idealism and Marxist philosophy and became known as an activist thinker. He has participated in protests against the Vietnam War as well as in antinuclear demonstrations. He also advocated global solidarity with indigenous peoples such as the Ainu of Japan and took a deep interest in Minamata neurological disease caused primarily by pollution. Given his vast expanse of writings and activities, his career is hard to summarize, but his thought can be characterized as follows: He studied minority and popular thought and developed the ideas of symbiosis and habitation through which an uncelebrated individual can create communal solidarity. Of interest here is that, although Buber did not directly influence Hanazaki to any great extent (though Hanazaki did read Buber), Hanazaki developed his own philosophy of personhood early in his career and focused on the logic of lemma to set forth his idea of symbiosis.[26]

Why would an advocate of coexistence believe that the logic of lemma and the idea of "emptiness" (*śūnyatā*) should be of exigent relevance? Perhaps the reason is that the "neither A nor not-A" lemma can be regarded as a principle that facilitates, through the medium of negation, cooperation among nonidentical individuals. Insofar as disparate individuals must cohabit in the same space and time, they must find ways to coexist harmoniously. Once that premise is accepted, the matter then becomes about finding the right social principles of coexistence in a given place and situation—the principles that will best reconcile individual diversity with social cohesion. If diversity and cohesion are established simultaneously—if people are nonidentical and also identical—then that would be an instantiation of the logic of lemma formulation " 'neither,' therefore, 'both' " ("neither A nor not-A"; therefore, "A and also not-A"). Hence, it seems that, in addressing the matter of coexistence, Hanazaki found that the logic of lemma could have a practical application in actuality.

It is also worth noting that Hanazaki, in his lemmatical reasoning and philosophy of "emptiness," expressed his belief in "fundamental contingency" (*kongenteki na gūzensei*) and "perennial negation" (*eieinteki na hiteisei*).[27] That is, he believed that the individual self always changes and unlearns. It seeks opportunities to be liberated from existing institutional and ideological constraints—the self seeks greater freedom. Coexistence, however, operates in accord with a different principle. It sometimes engenders cross-purposes instead of dialogue, and it can serve to facilitate group pressure, social constraints, and even renewed oppression and violence. In view of this possibility, the critical issue becomes how to reconcile the need for coexistence with the need to guarantee the freedom of individuals within the community.

The key concepts we explored in Buber's philosophy—the between, the ontology of becoming, the logic of lemma, and *coincidentia oppositorum*—are all indispensable to the relentless quest for harmonious coexistence combined with personal freedom. Just how much chaos this quest can involve is starkly illustrated by the case of Germanic society around the time *I and Thou* (1923) was published. At that time, Germanic society had experienced defeat in the First World War, the breakup of the Austro-Hungarian Empire, the short-lived Bavarian Soviet Republic (and the assassination of Buber's close friend and political mentor Gustav Landauer), economic destruction due to hyperinflation, and the Munich Putsch staged by Adolf Hitler and the nascent Nazi Party. Buber's own activities in the whirl of this troubled period were defined by intensive efforts to promote a Jewish spiritual and intellectual renaissance, interfaith understanding, and Jewish-Arab reconciliation. Never before had the concepts of German, Jew, Christian, Arab, and Palestinian been so emotionally and politically charged. It was therefore a time in which the ideas of dialogue, encounter, and coexistence commanded attention as an overarching practical issue. It was amid such a social climate that Buber's philosophy unfolded in the fullness of its philosophical, ethical, and political vision.

It is true that we should consider voices such as that of Judith Butler, who, while exploring in depth the potential for coexistence (which she has couched as "cohabitation"), warned that Buber's concept of a binational accommodation of Zionist aspirations and Palestinian political rights had inadequately questioned the settler colonialism of political Zionism.[28] However, we should also bear in mind something that Buber repeatedly stated: "I may not try to escape from the paradox I have to live." That is, as Buber consistently exemplified in his intellectual and political life as well as in the pages of *I and Thou*, he never sought to give us any definitive answers. Instead, *I and Thou* presents us with enduring problems of our life with others, and relentlessly urges us to be ever attentive to "lived actualities" we face, and to forge our own "way."[29]

Notes

1. Yoshimori Hiraishi, "Buber and Japanese Thought," in *Martin Buber: A Centenary Volume*, ed. Hayim Gordon and Jochanan Bloch (New York: Ktav Publishers for the Faculty of Humanities and Social Sciences, Ben Gurion University of the Negev, 1984), 351–62.

2. See Fumio Ono, "Martin Buber, the Whereabouts of Atypical Thinking: Commemorating the 50th Anniversary of His Death" [in Japanese], *Journal of Kyoto Association of Jewish Thought* 7 (2016): 86–125.

3. Hiroya Katsumura, "Past, Present, and Future Research on Martin Buber in Japan," *Journal of the Interdisciplinary Study of Monotheistic Religions* (CISMOR, Doshisha University) 6, nos. 1–7 (2010): 5.

4. Martin Buber, *Ich und Du*, 96, 90, 96, 137; *I and Thou*, 78, 69, 78, 135. All quotations from *I and Thou* are taken from Buber's German original (*Martin Buber Werkausgabe*, vol. 1) and Walter Kaufmann's English translation (New York: Charles Scribner's Sons, 1970), with the page numbers from the German original followed by the English translation. However, "You" in Kaufmann's translation has been changed to "Thou" in this essay.

5. Tetsuro Watsuji, *Ethik als Wissenschaft vom Menschen*, trans. Hans Martin Krämer (Darmstadt: Wissenschaftliche Buchgesellschaft, 2005), 8.

6. Giorgio Agamben discusses Kimura's theory of time and self in his *Remnants of Auschwitz: The Witness and the Archive*, trans. Daniel Heller-Roazen (Princeton, NJ: Zone Books, 2002), chap. 3.

7. Arata Isozaki and Naohiko Hino, "Turning Point, from Space to Environment" [in Japanese], Algorithmic Thinking and Architecture, *10+ 1*, no. 48 (September 30, 2007): 195.

8. Buber, *Ich und Du*, 167; I and Thou, 158.

9. Tetsutaro Ariga, *Kirisutokyō Shisō ni Okeru Sonzairon no Mondai* [The problem of ontology in Christian thought] (Tokyo: Sobun-sha, 1981), 189.

10. Thorlief Boman, *Das Hebräische Denken im Vergleich mit dem Griechischen*, vol. 2, *Durchgesehene Auflage* (Göttingen: Vandenhoeck & Ruprecht, 1954), 28. Oddly enough, in this book that discusses the uniqueness of the Hebrew Bible, Boman makes no reference to the Buber-Rosenzweig German translation of the Bible, and the only reference to Buber is in a footnote that mentions *I and Thou* as a source for the *Du* concept. Incidentally, the Japanese translator of Boman's book is Shigeo Ueda, who is also one of the translators of Buber's *I and Thou*.

11. Hisao Miyamoto, *Heburaiteki-Datsuzai-ron* [Birth of the ehyehlogy] (Tokyo: University of Tokyo Press, 2011), iv.

12. It is also noteworthy that Ariga translated into Japanese Leo Baeck's *Das Wesen des Judentums* in 1946.

13. As for Buber's "exploration of the form of the formless," see Fumio Ono, "Morphology of the Voice in the Hermeneutics of Martin Buber: An Inquiry into the Form of the Unformed," in *50 Jahre Martin Buber Bibel: Beiträge des internationalen Symposiums der Hochschule für jüdischen Studien Heidelberg und der Martin Buber Gesellschaft. Heidelberg 2012*, ed. Daniel Korchmalnik und Hans Joachim-Werner (Berlin: LIT Verlag, 2014), 317–49.

14. Buber, *Ich und Du*, 112; *I and Thou*, 100.

15. Tokuryu Yamauchi, *Rogosu to Renma* [Logos and lemma] (Tokyo: Iwanami-Shoten, 1974).

16. Buber, *Ich und Du*, 85; *I and Thou*, 62.

17. Buber, *Ich und Du*, 133; *I and Thou*, 130.

18. Buber, *Ich und Du*, 139; *I and Thou*, 138.

19. Buber, *Ich und Du*, 139; *I and Thou*, 138.

20. Paul Mendes-Flohr, *From Mysticism to Dialogue: Martin Buber's Transformation of German Social Thought* (Detroit: Wayne State University Press, 1989).

21. Buber, *Ich und Du*, 132–33; *I and Thou*, 130.

22. Buber, *Ich und Du*, 22; *I and Thou*, 114.

23. On Buber's dialectic without *Aufhebung*, see Fumio Ono, "The Tragedy of the Messianic Dialectic: Buber's Novel *Gog and Magog*," in *Martin Buber: His Intellectual and Scholarly Legacy*, ed. Sam Berrin Shonkoff (Leiden: Brill, 2018), 258–72.

24. Buber, *Ich und Du*, 168, 169; *I and Thou*, 180, 181.

25. Martin Buber, *Martin Buber Werkausgabe: Chassidismus II Theoretische Schriften*, vol. 17, ed. Susanne Talabardon (Gütersloh: Gütersloher Verlagshaus, 2016), 130; Martin Buber, *The Origin and Meaning of Hasidism*, ed. and trans. Maurice Friedman (New York: Harper & Row, 1966), 92.

26. Kohei Hanazaki, "Jutsugo-Ronri to Lemma no Ronri" [Predicate logic and the logic of lemma], in *Koza Seimei* [Lecture series life], vol. 5, ed. Yujiro Nakamura and Bin Kimura (Nagoya: Kawai Institute of Culture and Education, 2001), 91–111.

27. Hanazaki, "Jutsugo-Ronri to Lemma no Ronri," 111.

28. As for Butler's criticism of Buber, see Judith Butler, *Parting Ways: Jewishness and the Critique of Zionism* (New York: Columbia University Press, 2012), chap. 8. It should be noted, however, that Butler also states, "Since I began to be interested in philosophy when I was 14, I've never left Martin Buber" (Butler, "As a Jew, I Was Taught It Was Ethically Imperative to Speak Up," *Haaretz*, February 24, 2010). I would like to emphasize again the diverse aspects of Buber's thought that cannot be simply criticized.

29. Buber, *Ich und Du*, 143, 160; *I and Thou*, 144, 168. To forge our own "way": this reminds us of the literal and original meaning of Halakha, the Jewish law, which means "the way of walking."

Annotated Bibliography

PRIMARY SOURCES

On Buber's philosophy of the interhuman, see Buber, "Elements of the Interhuman," in *The Knowledge of Man: Selected Essays*, edited with an introduction by Maurice Friedman (Amherst, NY: Humanity Books, 1988). On Buber's own self-understanding of the relationship between Protestant theology and Buber's *I and Thou*, see Buber, "The History of the Dialogical Principle," in *Between Man and Man* (London: Routledge, 2002).

SECONDARY LITERATURE

As for Buber in the broader context of interreligious dialogue, see Christian Wiese, "Dialogical Turn?," in *Pluralitäts- und Dialogkonzepte in der Jüdischen Religionsphilosophie des 20. Jahrhunderts. Diversität, Differenz, Dialogizität: Religion in pluralen Kontexten*, edited by Christian Wiese, Stefan Alkier, and Michael Schneider (Berlin: De Gruyter, 2017). On Buber's religious and social thought, see Paul Mendes-Flohr, "The Desert within and Social Renewal: Martin Buber's Vision of Utopia," in *New Perspectives on Martin Buber*, edited by Michael Zank (Tübingen: Mohr Siebeck, 2006); and Laurence J. Silberstein, *Martin Buber's Social and Religious Thought: Alienation and the Quest for Meaning* (New York: New York University Press, 1989). With regard to the critical interpretation of Zionism and Jewish thought, Judith Butler, *Parting Ways: Jewishness and the Critique of Zionism* (New York: Columbia University Press, 2012) offers many points worthy of consideration.

On the relation between "Gestalt" and Buber's "Thought of Form," see my "Morphology of the Voice in the Hermeneutics of Martin Buber: An Inquiry into the Form of the Unformed," in *50 Jahre Martin Buber Bibel: Beiträge des Internationalen Symposiums der Hochschule für jüdische Studien Heidelberg und der Martin Buber-Gesellschaft Heidelberg 2012*, edited by Daniel Krochmalnik and Hans Joachim-Werner (Berlin: LIT-Verlag, 2014); and Zachary Braiterman, *The Shape of Revelation: Aesthetics and Modern Jewish Thought* (Stanford, CA: Stanford University Press, 2007).

For an overview of Buber's reception in Japan, see "Buber and Japanese Thought," in *Martin Buber: A Centenary Volume*, edited by Haim Gordon and Jochanan Bloch, 351–62 (New York: Ktav Publishing House, 1984); and Hiroya Katsumura, "Past, Present, and Future Research on Martin Buber in Japan: In Place of the Summary of the Symposium," *Journal of the Interdisciplinary Study of Monotheistic Religions* (CISMOR, Doshisha University) 6 (2010): 1–7. For a more comprehensive portrait of Buber's reception in Japan and global trends in Buber studies, see my article (in Japanese): Fumio Ono, "Martin Buber, the Whereabouts of Atypical Thinking: Commemorating the 50th Anniversary of His Death," *Journal of Kyoto Association of Jewish Thought* (Japanese edition) 7 (2016): 86–125.

For an introduction to Kyoto school philosophy, see Robert E. Carter, *The Kyoto School: An Introduction* (Albany: State University of New York Press), and *The Kyoto School of Philosophy*, edited by Masakatsu Fujita (Singapore: Springer, 2018). On the logics of lemma, see Yamauchi Tokuryu, *Logos et Lemme: Pensée occidentale, Pensée orientale*, translated by Augustin Berque (Paris: CNRS Éditions, 2020).

Glossary

"I have learned in the course of my life to appreciate terms. . . . When I find something that is essentially different from another thing, I want a new term. I want a new concept."[1]

Absolute Thou; the Eternal Thou (*das absolute Du, das ewige Du*): The Absolute is "a power which cannot be identified with any attribute accessible to human understanding."[2] It is thus not amenable to conceptual expression but only embodied in one's life of dialogue. Accordingly, belief in God—"the eternal Thou"—is not a theological construct. "If to believe in God means to be able to talk about him in the third person, then I do not believe in God. If to believe in him means to be able to talk to him, then I believe in God."[3] Abjuring theology as a third person discourse about God, Buber regarded the task of philosophical thinking to be that of *deixis*, pointing, rather than *apodeixis*, demonstration. Cognition, he held, is preeminently the act of recognition and knowledge as acknowledgment. He thus conceded he had no teaching to offer in a conceptually rigorous sense: "I only point to something . . . in reality that had not or had too little been seen. I take him who listens to me by the hand and lead him to the window. I open the window and point to what is outside. I have no teaching but carry on a conversation."[4]
Being (*Wesen, Sein*): The fullness or essence of human being is attained when one relates to another being as a Thou, an independent subject, whose otherness is impervious to the objectifications of the It-World. See "Confirmation," "Intentionality."
Between (*Zwischen, das Zwischenmenschliche*): Dialogical meeting or encounter takes place between an I and a Thou, in which the ultimate inaccessibility of the other, the Thou, is confirmed. Described as a "negative ontology,"[5] the between precludes a mystical absorption of the self into that of the other. "For Buber the Between is a realm which is neither objective nor subjective not the sum of the two."[6]
Collective, Collectivism (*Kollektiv, Kollectivismus*): As distinguished from "community," which is grounded in dialogical relations, collectives (e.g., labor and political movements) subordinate individuals (*Einzelne*) to an ideologically determined Will, in effect, relieving each of its members of personal responsibility, devouring "selfhood."[7] Moreover, by virtue of the bond of collective solidarity, one at the most relates to others as an object-of-feeling, not as a Thou.
Community (*Gemeinschaft, Gemeinde*): In contrast to ideological collectives, community promotes I-Thou relations, a genuine fraternity borne by a common, living center (*Mitte*) evoking unconditional response to each other. The living center is variously identified as God, and in the Hasidic community, the *zaddik*, who is graced to have an unfettered relation

to the Eternal Thou. By virtue of the relation to the center, utterly unconditioned by the It-World, the members of the community can genuinely say "we."[8] To underscore a community's single relation to the Absolute, Eternal Thou, Buber also spoke of it as a *Gemeinde*, a religious community: "True community [*Gemeinde*] does not come into being because people have feelings for each other (though this is required, too), but rather on two accounts: all of them have to stand in a living, reciprocal relationship to a single living center, and they have to stand in a living, reciprocal relationship to one another."[9]

Confirmation (*Bestätigung, Bewährung*): In the I-Thou relation one accepts the other in their otherness without seeking to subject them to instrumental ends or to dominate or change them. "Man wishes to be confirmed in his being man and wishes to have a presence [*Gegenwart*] in the being of the other. . . . Sent forth from the natural domain of species into the hazard of the solitary category surrounded by the air of chaos which came into being with him, secretly and bashfully he watches for a Yes which allows him to be, and which can come to him only from one human person to another."[10]

Creation (*Schöpfung*): When one meets the other as a Thou, one renews divine creation. "God's act of creation is speech; but the same is true of each lived moment."[11]

Decision, To decide (*Entscheidung, sich entscheiden*): To open oneself to the other is a "holy risk," for it entails more often than not the possibility of a "mismeeting" (*Vergegnung*), the failure when the other does not respond in kind. Having let down one's guard, one's "armor,"[12] one's vulnerabilities are exposed without a reciprocal act of confirmation. To respond dialogically to the other requires a conscious, existential decision to bear the risk of a mismeeting. See "Faith."

Destiny and Fate (*Schicksal, Verhängnis*): Destiny is in accord with one's "inborn Thou" and the quest for a dialogical relation and confirmation. It comes to expression when one "decides" (*sich entscheiden*) to respond to the address of the other. Hence, "destiny and freedom are vowed unto each other."[13] Fate, on the other hand, is a blind force that is said to determine one's life. The It-World governed by epistemologies of empirical cause-and-effect and social and cultural constructs that objectify others conspire, as it were, with biologistic and historiosophical theories that doom one to the imperious logic of *fate*: "the tempests of causality cower at my feet, and the whirl of doom (*Verhängnis*) congeals."[14]

Dialogue (*Dialog, Zwiesprache*): "Dialogue" is not a synonym for "conversation," for it could unfold in silence, beyond the spoken word. It is a reciprocal relationship between two individuals addressing each other as Thous, that is, in a confirming recognition of "the ontic and primal otherness of the Other."[15]

Distance, Distancing (*Distanz, Distanzierung*): In dialogue, one assumes a "primal distance" (*Urdistanz*) from the other—the Thou—in which one "distances" oneself from "experiencing" the other as an object—an "It"—defined by the epistemological "principle of individuation" and the prevailing social and cultural categories that violate the integrity of the dialogical other (the Thou).

Encounter, Meeting (*Begegnung*): "All actual life is encounter"[16]—in which one responds to the unanticipated address of another human being calling for confirmation as a Thou. Each encounter is unique and thus requires a spontaneous response, a response that cannot be "demanded": it is not an ethical imperative. "And how can the life of dialogue be demanded? . . . It is not that you *are* to answer but that you are *able*. . . . The life of dialogue is no privileged activity like dialectic. It does not begin with the upper story of humanity. It begins where humanity begins. There is gifted and ungifted here, only those who give themselves and those who withhold themselves."[17]

Experience (*Erfahrung*): Derived from the philosophical lexicon of Kant, "experience" denotes the world as it "appears" to us through our senses, principally that of sight. The images of the world we receive through our senses are mentally ordered on the "principle of individuation," the a priori "intuitions" of time and space that allow us to distinguish between distinctive, temporally and spatially individuated units, and their interaction, "causality." Kant describes "the principle of individuation" as "the necessary condition of experience" of the world of appearance, and, indeed, as "the ultimate foundation of the [general] unity of experience." Buber characterizes the *Erfahrungswelt* as the world of It. Following Arthur Schopenhauer, Buber holds that the world apprehended through the principle of individuation also individuates—isolates—individual human beings one from the other. When so perceived, individuals are given to comparison and measurement; they are thus regarded as mere objects (*Gegenstande*). In dialogue, however, "I do not find the human being to whom I say You [Thou] in any Sometime and Somewhere. I can place him there and have to do this again and again, but he immediately becomes a He or a She, an It, and no longer remains my You.... The human being to whom I say You I do not experience."[18]

Faith (*Glaube*): "There are two, and only two, types of faith [...] the one form the fact that I trust someone [*zu jemand Vertrauen*]"; the other form is "I acknowledge a thing to be true."[19] Accordingly Buber distinguished between what he regarded to be the primal Hebrew concept of faith, *emunah*—trust, faith in someone—and the Greek concept of faith, *pistis*, faith that something is true. Cf. "The great trust [...] expressed with unconditional clarity in Psalm 73, is a personal trust of the person as such."[20] Hence, when asked if he believes in God, Buber concluded, "If to believe in God is to be able to talk about him in the third person, then I do not believe in God. [But] if to believe in him means to be able to talk to him [in mutual trust], then I believe in him."[21] Nota bene, "Buber would undoubtedly admit that there are also other types [of faith] but these he would classify as types of wisdom (Buddha, Confucius, Lao-Tze) rather than types of faith."[22]

God and Revelation (*Gott, Offenbarung*): "I do not believe in God's naming himself or in God's defining himself before man. The word of revelation is: I am there as whoever I am there. That which reveals is that which reveals. That which has being, nothing more." In the first edition of *Ich und Du*, Buber presented God's reply to Moses's query in Exodus 3:14 of what his name was with the then generally accepted translation, "I am that I am what I am" (*Ich bin der ich bin*). In the subsequent editions of the book, he gave God's reply in accordance with the translation of the Hebrew Bible he undertook with Franz Rosenzweig: "I shall be present as I shall be present" (*Ich bin da als der ich da bin*). God is the Eternal Thou who is always *there*, forever present. He is thus "the eternal source..., the eternal touch" of "trust" as one navigates the uncertain waters of one's terrestrial journey.[23] Hence, Buber's formulation of biblical faith as trust (*Vertrauen*)—a trust that prompts one to take the "holy risk" of meeting the other as a Thou.[24]

Inborn Thou (*das eingeborene Du*): Cf. "The prenatal life of the child is pure natural association, a flowing toward each other [i.e., the mother and the child in embryo], a bodily reciprocity; and the life horizon of the developing being appears uniquely inscribed, and yet also not inscribed, in the being that carries it; for the womb in which it dwells is not solely that of the mother. [...] In the beginning is the relation [*Im Anfang ist die Beziehung*]—as the category of being, as readiness, as a form that reaches out to be filled, as a model of the soul; the a priori of relation; the innate You [Thou]."[25]

Intentionality: The dialogical relationship is "passive and active at once."[26] Buber's concept of passive action is informed by the Taoist concept of *wúwéi*—a nonaction, nonintentional, noncalculating, nondeliberative manner of being in the world. In adhering to the "path" of *wúwéi*, one is spontaneously and wholly open to the moment, unencumbered by the intentional reflexes of the It-World, to meet the address of a fellow human being turning to you to meet in an I-Thou dialogue.[27]

Mode of existence (*Bestand*): "Basic words [I-It; I-Thou] do not state something outside them; by being spoke[n] they establish [*stiften sie*] a mode of existence."[28]

Person and Ego (*Person und Eigenwesen*): "The I of the basic word I-It appears as an ego [*Eigenwesen*] and becomes conscious of itself as a subject (of experience and use). The I of the basic word I-You appears as a person and becomes conscious of itself as subjectivity (without any dependent genitive)—that is, without a dependent object." *Eigenwesen*, literally "self-being," denotes one who is self-centered, hence indifferent to the other. "The ego occupies himself with his My: my manner, my race, my works."[29] Person, in contrast to the *Eigenwesen*, who is conscious of itself as independent subjectivity of the It-World and its objects of experience and use.

Presence (*Gegenwart*): In contrast to a *Gegenstand*, an object that "stands over against one," *Gegenwart* denotes someone who "waits opposite" one, waiting in its singularity for an I-Thou before response. Our intersubjective life is determined by how we respond to whomever we face (*Gegenüber*) at a given moment or situation, relating to that person either as a *Gegenstand*, an It, or an existential presence (*Gegenwart*), a Thou.

Relation (*Beziehung, Verhältnis*): Buber distinguishes between *Beziehung*, denoting the mutual intersubjective relation, and *Verhältnis*, a condition, a situational relationship. *Beziehung*, derived from the verb *ziehen*, "to pull," denotes a dynamic interaction. I-Thou relations (*Ich-Du Beziehungen*) are thus said to be reciprocal. Though not consistent, in contrast to Smith, Kaufmann distinguishes between the I-Thou *relation* and the I-It *relationship* (*Ich-Es Verhältnis*), bereft as it is of mutuality.

Religion: "It is far more comfortable to have to do with religion than to have to do with God, who sends one out of home and fatherland into restless wandering. In addition religion has all kinds of aesthetic refreshments to offer its cultivated adherents.... For this reason at all times the awake spirits have been vigilant and have warned of the diverting force hidden in religion."[30] Wary of institutional religion, in his earliest writings Buber thus distinguished between institutional religion and religiosity, "man's sense of wonder and adoration, and ever new becoming, an ever-new articulation and formulation of his feeling that, transcending his conditioned being yet bursting from his very core, there is something unconditioned."[31] As such, religiosity is not confined to formal religious practice (ritual and liturgy) but embraces all of everyday life. Nor is it an expression of mere spiritual emotion but necessarily gains expression in *deeds*. In his later writings, Buber incorporated his concept of religiosity into that of a dialogical *response* to a Thou.

Thou (*Du*): The German second-person pronoun *Du* has for Buber a distinctive semantic valence not captured by "you." In consultation with Buber, Ronald Gregor Smith, the first translator of *Ich und Du*, rendered the pronoun with the old "churchly" Thou, for in the dialogical relation one "stands" in the relation to an other with the "sacred basic word [Thou]."[32] Buber thus speaks of the "sacrament of dialogue,"[33] for in every Thou one addresses the "eternal Thou," God.

Notes

1. Martin Buber, *Knowledge of Man*, ed. Maurice Friedman, trans. Maurice Friedman and Ronald Gregor Smith (New York: Harper Torchbooks, 1965), 197.
2. Martin Buber, *Israel and the World: Essays in a Time of Crisis*, trans. Greta Hort, O. Marx, and I. M. Lask (New York: Schocken Books, 1948), 209.
3. Martin Buber, *Meetings: Autobiographical Fragments*, ed. Maurice Friedman (London: Routledge, 1973), 53.
4. Martin Buber, "Replies to My Critics," in *The Philosophy of Martin Buber*, Library of Living Philosophers, vol. 12, ed. Paul Arthur Schilpp and Maurice Friedman (LaSalle, IL: Open Court, 1967), 693.
5. Michael Theunissen, "Bubers negative Ontologie des Zwischen," *Philosophisches Jahrbuch* 71, no. 2 (1964): 319–30. Also see Michael Theunissen, "The Philosophy of Dialogue as the Counter Project to Transcendental Philosophy: The Dialogic of Martin Buber," in Theunissen, *The Other: Studies in the Social Ontology of Husserl, Heidegger, Sartre, and Buber*, trans. Christopher Macann (Cambridge, MA: MIT Press, 1984), 257–344.
6. Robert E. Wood, *Martin Buber's Ontology: An Analysis of "I and Thou"* (Evanston, IL: Northwestern University Press, 1969), 41. The English collection of essays in which Buber elaborated on his philosophy of dialogue was judiciously entitled *Between Man and Man* (trans. R. G. Smith [Boston: Beacon Press, 1961]).
7. Martin Buber, *Pointing the Way*, ed. and trans. Maurice Friedman (Boston: Beacon Press, 1963), 225.
8. Martin Buber, "What Is Common to All," in Buber, *Knowledge of Man*, ed. Maurice Friedman, trans. M. Friedman and R. G. Smith (New York: Harper Torchbooks, 1965), 108–9. Cf. "Collectivity is based on the organized atrophy of personal existence, community on its increase and conformation in life lived towards one another" (*Between Man and Man*, 37).
9. Martin Buber, *I and Thou*, trans. Walter Kaufmann (New York: Simon & Schuster, 1996), 94.
10. Buber, *Knowledge of Man*, 71.
11. Buber, *Israel and the World*, 16. Cf. "In the beginning is relation" (Buber, *I and Thou*, trans. Kaufmann, 69).
12. Cf. "Each of us is encased in an armor whose task is to ward off signs [calling for us to respond dialogically to others]. Signs happen to us without respite, living means being addressed, we need only to present ourselves. [. . .] But the risk is too dangerous for us, the soundless thunderings seem to threaten us with annihilation, and from generation to generation we perfect the defense apparatus. [. . .] Each of us is encased in an armor we soon out of familiarity, no longer notice." Buber, *Between Man and Man*, 12.
13. Buber, *I and Thou*, trans. R. G. Smith (New York: Charles Scribner's Sons, 1958), 53. Walter Kaufmann translates *Schicksal* as "fate" and *Verhängnis* as "doom."
14. Buber, *I and Thou*, trans. Kaufmann, 59.
15. Buber, *Between Man and Man*, 45.
16. Buber, *I and Thou*, trans. Kaufmann, 62. Cf. "The You [das Du, the Thou] encounters me by grace—it cannot be found by seeking."
17. Buber, *Between Man and Man*, 35.
18. Buber, *I and Thou*, trans. Kaufmann, 59–60.
19. Buber, *Two Types of Faith*, trans. Norman P. Goldhawk (New York: Harper & Brothers, 1951), 7.

20. "Interrogations of Martin Buber," conducted by Maurice Friedman, in *Philosophical Interrogations*, ed. Sydney Rome and Beatrice Rome (New York: Holt, Reinhart & Winston, 1964), 109.

21. Buber, *Meetings: Autobiographical Fragments*, ed. Maurice Friedman (London: Routledge, 1967), 53.

22. R. J. Twi, "Reflections on Buber's Two Types of Faith," *Journal of Jewish Studies* 39, no. 1 (2012): 97.

23. Buber, *I and Thou*, trans. Kaufmann, 160.

24. See Martin Buber, *Two Types of Faith*, trans. Norman P. Goldhawk (New York: Harper Torchbooks, 1951), who thus contrasted the Hebrew concept of faith, *emunah*, as "a perseverance in trust in the guiding and covenanting Lord" (10) with the Greek *pistis*, faith that denotes a confessional, doctrinal affirmation.

25. Buber, *I and Thou*, trans. Kaufmann, 22–24.

26. Buber, *I and Thou*, trans. Kaufmann, 10.

27. See Martin Buber, "The Teaching of the Dao," in Buber, *Pointing the Way: Collected Essays*, trans. M. Friedman (London: Kegan & Paul, 1957), 31–36.

28. Buber, *I and Thou*, trans. Kaufmann, 53.

29. Buber, *I and Thou*, trans. Kaufmann, 113, 114.

30. Martin Buber, "Religion in God's Rule," in Buber, *A Believing Humanism: My Testimony, 1902–1965*, trans. M. Friedman (New York: Simon & Schuster, 1967), 110–11.

31. Martin Buber, "Jewish Religiosity" (1923), in Buber, *On Judaism*, ed. Nahum Glatzer, trans. Eva Jospe (New York: Schocken Books, 1967).

32. Buber, *I and Thou*, trans. Kaufmann, 60.

33. Buber, *Between Man and Man*, 17.

Contributors

HENRY ABRAMOVITCH is the founding president and senior training analyst at the Israel Institute of Jungian Psychology in Honor of Erich Neumann and professor emeritus at the Department of Medical Education, Tel Aviv University Medical School. He is also past president of the Israel Anthropological Association and has published extensively on mourning rituals, the cultural context of dreams, on Buber, and on transcultural psychotherapy. His recent books include *Why Odysseus Came Home as a Stranger . . . Panic Attacks in Pistachio: A Psychological Detective Story*. He has coauthored plays including *The Analyst and the Rabbi*, *My Lunch with Thomas*, and *Speaking of Friendship*, all available on YouTube.

ASHER D. BIEMANN is professor of modern Jewish thought and intellectual history at the University of Virginia. He is the author of *Inventing New Beginnings: On the Idea of Renaissance in Modern Judaism* (2009) and *Dreaming of Michelangelo: Jewish Variations on a Modern Theme* (2012), which appeared in German as *Michelangelo und die jüdische Moderne* (2016). He is also the editor of the *Martin Buber Reader* (2001), Martin Buber's *Sprachphilosophische Schriften* (*Martin Buber Werkausgabe*, vol. 6), and, together with Richard I. Cohen and Sarah E. Wobick-Segev, *Spiritual Homelands: The Cultural Experience of Exile, Place and Displacement among Jews and Others* (2020). He is currently completing a book entitled *Enduring Modernity: Judaism Eternal and Ephemeral*.

MICHAL BIZOŇ received his PhD in systematic philosophy in 2016 from the Faculty of Arts, Comenius University, Bratislava, Slovakia. He is currently an assistant professor at the Department of Ethics and Civic Education at the Faculty of Education of Comenius University. His research focuses on philosophical anthropology and ethics with emphasis on the philosophical legacy of Martin Buber. He is the author of *Mutuality between I and Thou—Dialogical Philosophy of Martin Buber* (2017).

DOMINIQUE BOUREL earned a Doctorat ès lettres at the Sorbonne in 1995. He served as the director of the Centre de Recherche Français de Jérusalem (1996–2004). His research focuses on German Jewish intellectual history. Among his many publications are *Moses Mendelssohn. Fondateur du Judaïsme moderne* (French 2004, German 2007, Prix Parlementaire Franco-allemand) and *Martin Buber, sentinelle de l'humanité* (French 2015, German 2017, Prix de l'Académie Française).

SAMUEL HAYIM BRODY is associate professor in the Department of Religious Studies at the University of Kansas. He is the author of *Martin Buber's Theopolitics* (2018) and the editor or coeditor of two volumes of the *Martin Buber Werkausgabe*. His research focuses on the intersections of Jewish thought with politics and economics. His articles have been published in *Religions*, the *Jewish Quarterly Review*, the *Journal of Religious Ethics*, the *Journal of Jewish Ethics*, and the *Journal of the American Academy of Religion*.

DAVID BARZILAI is professor of Jewish studies at San Diego State University. He is the author of the Hebrew monograph *Homo Dialogicus: Martin Buber's Contribution to Philosophy* (2000) and articles on modern Jewish thought.

MANUEL DUARTE DE OLIVEIRA received his PhD in Jewish thought with a dissertation written under the supervision of Paul Mendes-Flohr at the Hebrew University of Jerusalem. Later, he did a Juris Doctor at Yeshiva University's Benjamin Cardozo School of Law in New York. He was a senior fellow at Harvard's Center for the Study of World Religions, Center for Jewish Studies, and the Kennedy School of Government. He was also a fellow at Columbia University's School of Law, and later taught at the University of California, Berkeley, and Stanford University. Recently he was invited to teach Jewish thought at the Portuguese Catholic University in Lisbon, where he is a research member at CITER, and has been asked to develop the area of Jewish thought in a recently created chair of Jewish and Christian biblical studies.

MICHAEL FISHBANE is the Nathan Cummings Distinguished Service Professor of Jewish Studies Emeritus at the University of Chicago. He is the author of many scholarly works on Jewish thought and interpretation as well as two books of original theology, *Sacred Attunement: A Jewish Theology* and *Fragile Finitude: A Jewish Hermeneutical Theology*. Fishbane is a fellow of both the American Academy of Jewish Research and the American Academy of Arts and Sciences.

KHALED FURANI is professor of anthropology at Tel-Aviv University, on the lands of al-Sheikh Muwannis. He published *Silencing the Sea: Secular Rhythms in Palestinian Poetry* (2012) and *Redeeming Anthropology: A Theological Critique of a Modern Science* (2019). His most recent book, *Inside the Leviathan: Palestinian Experiences at Israeli Universities*, was published in 2022 (in Arabic) by the Van Leer Jerusalem Institute Press and Dar Leila.

CONTRIBUTORS   383

YEMIMA HADAD holds the junior Professur für Judaistik at the University of Leipzig. Dr. Hadad teaches modern Jewish thought, German Jewish philosophy, and rabbinic literature. She is a research fellow at the Bucerius Institute for Research of German Contemporary History and Society at the University of Haifa. Her research interests focus on Continental philosophy, political theology, feminism, and twentieth-century Jewish thought.

AMAL JAMAL is Romulo Betancourt Chair in political science in the School of Political Science, Government and International Affairs and vice dean in the Faculty of Social Sciences at Tel Aviv University. He is currently the head of the Walter Lebach Institute for the Study of Jewish-Arab Coexistence and editor-in-chief of the Hebrew journal *The Public Sphere*. His scholarly interests focus on political theory and culture, political communication, civil society, and postcolonial studies. He has published over one hundred articles in five languages in leading academic journals and books and over twenty books that include *Reconstructing the Civic: Palestinian Civil Activism in Israel* (2020).

STEVEN KEPNES is professor of world religions and Jewish studies and director of Chapel House at Colgate University, Hamilton, New York. He is the author of eight books, among them *Reviving Jewish Theology: Metaphysics, Hermeneutics, Ethics* (2023); *The Future of Jewish Theology* (2013); *Jewish Theological Reasoning* (2007); and *The Text Is Thou: Buber's Theological Hermeneutics* (1993). He is editor of the *Cambridge Companion to Jewish Theology* (2020).

ASLAUG KRISTIANSEN is a professor of education at the University of Agder, Kristiansand, Norway. Her 2004 doctoral dissertation at the University of Oslo, "On Trust and Trusting the Educational Setting," was inspired by Buber's philosophy of dialogue. Her continued interest in pedagogy and trust is amplified by studies in the ethics of education and the teaching of democratic values, especially as they bear on confronting xenophobia in everyday life. She is also currently engaged in developing programs to support teachers in cultivating a caring and inclusive classroom environment.

KARL-JOSEF KUSCHEL served as professor for theology of culture and interreligious dialogue at the Faculty of Catholic Theology at the University of Tübingen and as codirector of the Institute for Ecumenical and Interreligious Research from 1995 to 2013. His research and publications focus on world religions in the mirror of literature, and on the "theology of interreligious dialogue"—Judaism, Christianity, Islam. Among his many books on the theology of culture are *Jesus im Spiegel der Weltliteratur. Eine Bilanz des Jahrhunderts* (1999/2010); *Im Ringen um den wahren Ring. Lessings "Nathan der Weise"—eine Herausforderung der Religionen* (2011); and *Im Fluss der Dinge. Hermann Hesse und Bertolt Brecht im Dialog mit Buddha, Laotse und Zen* (2018). Among his publications on interfaith dialogue are *Streit um Abraham. Was*

Juden, Christen und Muslime trennt—und was sie eint (1995/2001); *Juden-Christen-Muslime: Herkunft und Zukunft* (2007); *Weihnachten und der Koran* (2008); *Martin Buber—seine Herausforderung an das Christentum* (2015); and *Die Bibel im Koran. Grundlagen für das interreligiöse Gespräch* (2017).

BERNHARD LANG, emeritus professor of Old Testament and religious studies at the University of Paderborn, Germany, has also taught at the Sorbonne (Université de Paris IV) and the University of St. Andrews, Scotland. His many publications include *Heaven: A History* (coauthored with Colleen McDannell, 1988); *Sacred Games: A History of Christian Worship* (1997); *The Hebrew God: Portrait of an Ancient Deity* (2002); and *Joseph in Egypt: A Cultural Icon from Grotius to Goethe* (2009). He has also published an annotated edition of Martin Buber's *Ich und Du* (2021).

HUNE MARGULIES is the founder and director of the Martin Buber Institute for Dialogical Ecology (New York and Goa, India), an independent scholarly institution that studies the relationship between Buber's philosophy of dialogue and Zen Buddhism. Margulies is the author of *Martin Buber and Eastern Wisdom Teachings: The Recovery of the Spiritual Imagination* (2020), *Will and Grace: Meditations on the Dialogical Philosophy of Martin Buber* (2017), and *The Social Structure of the Hasidic Polity: A New Utopia* (2000). He coined the term "dialogical ecology" to indicate the distinctive existential perspectives that emerge from the encounter between the philosophy of Martin Buber and the enlightenment practices of Zen Buddhism. He currently lectures on philosophy at the Universities of Goa and Mumbai.

PAUL MENDES-FLOHR was professor emeritus at the Divinity School, the University of Chicago, and the Hebrew University of Jerusalem. He was the editor in chief (with Peter Schäfer and Bernd Witte) of the twenty-one-volume *Martin Buber Werkausgabe*, a comprehensive critical edition of Buber's writings published by the Gütersloher Verlagshaus, 2000 to 2021. He was the author of *Martin Buber: A Life of Faith and Dissent* (2021), which has also appeared in German and Hebrew.

CORNELIA MUTH is professor of education at the University of Applied Science, Bielefeld, Germany, since 2001. On the basis of Buber's philosophy of dialogue, she has developed a phenomenology of pedagogy and the learning experience. See, among others, her *Der Andere ist der Weg: Martin Buber* (2001); *Zwischen Gut und Böse: mit Martin Bubers sechs Schritten nach der chassidischen Lehre das eigene Leben gestalten* (2001); *Willst du mit mir gehen, Licht und Schatten verstehen? Eine Studie zu Martin Bubers Ich und Du. Dialogisches Lernen* (2005); *Hilfe, ich bin mobil und heimatlos! Zur Hauslosigkeit postmoderner Menschen* (2008); *Erwachsenenbildung als transkulturelle Dialogik* (2011); *Von der interkulturellen Erfahrung zur transkulturellen Begegnung—und zurück* (2013); *Ein Wegweiser zur dialogischen Haltung* (2015); and *Phänomenologische Praxisentwicklungsforschung* (2019). She is the editor of the book series *Dialogisches Lernen* (ibidem-Verlag, Stuttgart).

CONTRIBUTORS

JOACHIM OBERST is principal lecturer in the Department of Philosophy at the University of New Mexico, where he teaches philosophy of religion, modern Christian thought (theology), existentialism, ancient Greek philosophy, and phenomenology. He is the author of *Heidegger on Language and Death: The Intrinsic Connection in Human Existence* (2009).

FUMIO ONO received his PhD from Kyoto University and is professor of philosophy and European studies at Doshisha University, Kyoto, Japan. He is the author of *Ethics of "Non-existence": Philosophy of Hospitality for the Sake of Mere Life* [Japanese edition] (2022). His articles on Buber include "The Tragedy of the Messianic Dialectic: Buber's Novel *Gog and Magog*," in *Martin Buber: His Intellectual and Scholarly Legacy*, ed. Sam Berrin Shonkoff (2018), and "Morphology of the Voice in the Hermeneutics of Martin Buber: An Inquiry into the Form of the Unformed," in *50 Jahre Martin Buber Bibel: Beiträge des Internationalen Symposiums der Hochschule für jüdische Studien Heidelberg und der Martin Buber-Gesellschaft Heidelberg 2012*, ed. Daniel Krochmalnik and Hans Joachim-Werner (2014). He is also the editor of the special issue "Martin Buber: The Echo of His Dialogical Thought" [Japanese edition], *Journal of Kyoto Association of Jewish Thought* 2, no. 7 (2019).

INKA SAUTER is a research associate at the Buber-Rosenzweig Institute at Goethe University Frankfurt, Germany. In 2019–20, she was a fellow at the Franz Rosenzweig Minerva Research Center at the Hebrew University of Jerusalem. In her dissertation, "Offenbarungsphilosophie und Geschichte: Über die jüdische Krise des Historismus" (published 2022), she analyzes the conception of history of Franz Rosenzweig, Hermann Cohen, and Walter Benjamin. Her current research is dedicated to Martin Buber's use of the German language in his *Verdeutschung* of the Hebrew scriptures.

CHRISTOPH SCHMIDT teaches at the Departments of Philosophy, Comparative Religion, and German Literature at the Hebrew University. His main research fields are modern forms of political theology, phenomenology, and philosophy as a therapeutic practice. Among his publications are *Israel und die Geister von 68—Eine Phänomenologie* (2018); *Die Legitimität der jüdischen Moderne: Zwischen Hermann Cohen und Jacob Klatzkin* (2023); *Die zwei Körper des Subjekts: Vom Gottmensch zum Subjekt* (2023) and *Zwischen Marx und Kierkegaard* (2023).

SARAH SCOTT is professor of philosophy at Manhattan College. She is the editor of *Martin Buber: Creaturely Life and Social Form* and has published on Buber's ethics, aestheticism, and forgotten influences.

SAM S. B. SHONKOFF is Taube Family Assistant Professor of Jewish Studies at the Graduate Theological Union, Berkeley, California. His scholarship focuses on modern Jewish theology, particularly in Hasidic, German Jewish, and neo-Hasidic contexts. He is coeditor with Ariel Mayse of *Hasidism: Writings on Devotion, Community* and *Life in the Modern World* (2020), and is currently completing a book on themes of embodiment in Buber's interpretations of Hasidic sources.

JOHAN SIEBERS is professor of philosophy of language and communication at Middlesex University London and director of the Ernst Bloch Centre for German Thought at the School of Advanced Study, University of London. His main research interests are in philosophy of communication; Ernst Bloch's utopian philosophy of hope; futurity and anticipation. He has published widely on these topics, recently among others *Working with Time in Qualitative Research* (2022) and a special issue on Ernst Bloch of *Revue internationale de philosophie* (2019). He is founding editor of the *European Journal for Philosophy of Communication* and series editor of Routledge Research in Anticipation and Futures.

CLAUDIA WELZ is professor of ethics and philosophy of religion at Aarhus University. She is the principal investigator of the interdisciplinary project "Epistemological Aspects of 'Dialogue': Exploring the Potential of the Second-Person Perspective" and the codirector of the research unit for Kierkegaard studies. Her work focuses on questions of existential orientation and draws mainly on Continental philosophy (particularly hermeneutics, phenomenology, philosophy of dialogue and of emotion), systematic theology in an interreligious context, modern Jewish thought, religious motifs in contemporary literature, environmental ethics, and arts-based research. She has authored *Love's Transcendence and the Problem of Theodicy* (2008); *Vertrauen und Versuchung* (2010); *Humanity in God's Image: An Interdisciplinary Exploration* (2016); and a collection of essays, *SinnSang: Theologie und Poesie* (2019), about the work of the poet Elazar Benyoëtz. She is currently working on an ethical, theological, and psychological phenomenology of listening.

ELLIOT R. WOLFSON, a fellow of the American Academy of Jewish Research and the American Academy of Arts and Sciences, holds the Marsha and Jay Glazer Endowed Chair in Jewish Studies and Distinguished Professor of Religion at the University of California, Santa Barbara. He is the author of many publications, including most recently *Heidegger and Kabbalah: Hidden Gnosis and the Path of Poiēsis* (2019); *Suffering Time: Philosophical, Kabbalistic, and Ḥasidic Reflections on Temporality* (2021); *The Philosophical Pathos of Susan Taubes: Between Nihilism and Hope* (2023); and *Nocturnal Seeing: Hopelessness of Hope and Philosophical Gnosis in Susan Taubes, Gillian Rose, and Edith Wyschogrod* (2024).

Index

Abgrund (the abyss), 54–55, 63n6
Abraham, 159, 290–91
"Abraham the Seer" (Buber), 159
Absolute Thou, 56–57
abyss, the (Abgrund), 54–55, 62–63, 63n6
actuality (Wirklichkeit), 59, 63, 67, 72
Adelung, Johann Christoph, 313
Adler, Alfred, 208
Adler, Rachel, 337
Aesthetics (Cohen), 45
aesthetics, 102, 104–7
affinity, elective (Wahlverwandtschaft), 41, 309–10
aḥizat einayim (optical illusion), 76–77
Aida (Kimura), 363
aida (the between), 363, 364, 367
Aidagara-teki Sonzai (interhumanity), 363
Allah, 257
allegory of the cave (Plato), 101
alterity, 4, 232–33
Alte und neue Gemeinschaft (Buber), 309–10
Amos (prophet), 161, 265–66
"amour de Dieu et l'amour du prochain dans le Hassidisme, L'" (Buber), 357
anarchistic theopolitics, 27–28
"An den Leser" (Werfel), 144
Andreas-Salomé, Lou, 338
Anointed One, The (Buber), 361
anthropological hour, the, 36–37
anthropology, philosophical, 33–46
Anthropology from a Pragmatic Point of View (Kant), 37, 38
apocalypse, 299
apocalyptic and prophecy, 305–6
Arendt, Hannah, 45, 106, 344
Ariga, Tetsutaro, 365–66
Armin-Brentano, Bettina, 339

Aufhebung (sublation), 29, 368
Augustine, Saint, 197–98
Auschwitz, 263, 287, 288
authentic dialogue, 59, 60–62
avodah (service), 276, 277

Ba'al Shem Tov (Israel ben Eli'ezer), 62, 76, 271, 274, 278
Bachelard, Gaston, 172, 356–57
Balint, Michael, 207
Barlach, Ernst, 142
Barth, Karl, 33, 360
Barukh of Mezhbizh, 278
Basho (poet), 242
Batnitzky, Leora, 341
Bavarian Soviet Republic, 371
Beauvoir, Simone de, 98, 345
becoming, ontology of, 364–66
Begegnung (encounter), 67, 70, 323–34. *See also* I-It relation; I-Thou relation
Bein 'Am le-Artzo: Iykarei Toledotav shel Raiyon (Buber), 267
being (Wesen), 312–15, 317–19
Being and Time (Heidegger), 38, 174, 199
being with (Miteinandersein), 42, 58
belonging, 170, 172, 314, 319
Benjamin, Mara, 342–43
Bergen-Belsen, 287
Berlin Alexanderplatz (Döblin), 142
Besht, the (Ba'al Shem Tov), 62, 76, 271, 274, 278
Besinnung (introspection), 35, 43, 45
Bestimmung (destiny), 39, 40, 43, 170
Between (Kimura), 363
between, the (das Zwischen): and the Absolute Thou, 56–57; and the abyss (Abgrund), 54–55; and community, 41; defined, 2; and dialogue,

between, the (*das Zwischen*) (*cont.*)
134, 136, 178–79; and duality, 241; and the eternal Thou, 57, 59, 62, 174–78; and feminism, 340, 344, 346–47; and *Grundworte* (primary words), 132; inquiry into, 53–54; and the interhuman, 59–60, 98–99; and the I-Thou relation, 20–21, 57–58, 174–75, 247n3; and the It-World (*Es-Welt*), 21–23; Japanese thought and, 362–64; later conception of, 58–62; and listening, 172; Maggid of Mezritch on, 62–63; and mental health, 206; and psychotherapy, 207; and theology, 25; and the Word of God, 177; as the Zen of God, 247. *See also* interhuman, the (*Zwischenmenschliche*); other, the
Between Person and Person (Kimura), 363
Between the People and Its Land (Buber), 267
Beziehung (relationship), 67, 70, 72, 169, 316–17
Bialer rebbe, the, 280–82
Bialik, Mossad, 357–58
Bible, Hebrew: Buber-Rosenzweig translation of, 93, 168, 169, 300; Harnack's rejection of, 92; Isaak's interpretations of, 234; Katsumura on the, 362; ontology of, 365; and the Word of God, 116
Bible, the: and Hasidism, 158; hermeneutical biblical theology, 156; and I-It analysis, 160; and the I-Thou relation, 157–58; Katsumura on, 362; as literature, 159–60, 163; Rosenzweig on, 93; as scripture, 161; as spoken word, 159; and the Word of God, 161, 176–77
biblical humanism, 44–45, 254
biblical theology, 156–65
biblical theopolitics, 20, 27–28
Bikkhu, Buddhadasa, 248n19
Bildung (self-transformation), 121–23, 161
binationalism, 324–26, 331–34, 371
Binswanger, Ludwig, 207, 363
Bleuler, Eugen, 206
Bloch, Jochanan, 177
Bodhisattva, 246, 249n24
Böhme, Jakob, 6n4, 102–4, 167, 273
Bologna Process of 1999, 215, 219
Boman, Thorleif, 365
Boszormenyani-Nagy, Ivan, 208
Brague, Rémi, 1
British Palestinian mandate, 327
Brod, Max, 355
Brunner, Emil, 360
Būbā: Hito to shisō (Hiraishi), 361
Buber, Carl, 272
Buber, Paula (née Winkler). *See* Winkler, Paula
"Buber and Japanese Thought" (Hiraishi), 360
Buber: The Person and His Ideas (Hiraishi), 361
Buddha, 239, 241
Buddhadharma, 243
Buddhism: and the ego (*Eigenwesen*), 245; Heynicke on, 145; humanist, 244; *I and Thou* and, 241, 361; *Jōdo* Buddhism, 361; and lemmatic reasoning, 367; Mahayana, 361, 367; and political activism, 248–49n22; Pure Land, 248n19, 361; and socialism, 248n19; socially engaged, 245; and *wu-wei*, 239; Zen, 239, 241, 242–45, 361
Buddhist Prajnaparamita, 243
Butler, Deidre, 346
Butler, Judith, 81n30, 331, 344–45, 371

Cahan, Jean, 252
Cahiers du Sud, 357
Calvin, John, 176
Campe, Joachim Heinrich, 313–14
Camus, Albert, 357
Cassirer, Ernst, 43–44
Catholicism, 49, 145, 356, 357
Celebration of Peace (Hölderlin), 30n5
Center for the Interdisciplinary Study of the Monotheistic Religions, 362
Ch'an Pure Land Buddhism, 244–45, 248n18
charisma (*charis*), 27–28
chassidischen Bücher, Die (Buber), 369
"China and Us" (Buber), 240
Chouraqui, André, 357
Christ, Jesus, 20, 25, 75, 227–28, 230–31
Christianity: and expressionism, 148; God of, 257; Heynicke on, 145; and image of God, the, 75; interfaith dialogue, and, 227–37; and the It-World (*Es-Welt*), 93; and Judaism, 73, 257; Man of Sorrows and, 146; and messianism, 303; and modernity, 29
Christology, 230
Church Dogmatics (Barth), 33
Claudel, Paul, 355–56
Cohen, Albert, 356
Cohen, Hermann, 45, 72–73, 306, 341, 358
coherence (*Zusammenhang*), 311
Cohn, Margot, 355
coincidentia oppositorum (Nicholas of Cusa), 368–69
colonialism, 325, 327, 331, 371
Columbia University, 287–89
communication: and authenticity, 59; dialogical, 19–20, 29; and *I and Thou*, 58; and I-It/I-Thou relations, 133–34; and language, 118; and *soliloquy*, 119; telepathic, 281. *See also* between, the (*das Zwischen*); other, the; speech; spokenness (*Gesprochenheit*)
communication, philosophy of, 129–39
communication theory: and binationalism, 332–33; Buber's influence on, 134–35; and dialogue, 19, 115; and phenomenology, 131, 134–35; and rhetoric, 130–31, 134
"Communication Theory as a Field" (Craig), 134–35

community (*Gemeinschaft*): and authenticity, 41–42; and biblical humanism, 45; concepts of, 309–19; crisis of, 39–40; and dialogue, 102; and the divine, 55–56, 72; and God, 316; and isolation, 194–95; and the I-Thou relation, 44, 317–18; and the It-World (*Es-Welt*), 146; and mental health, 138–39; and messianism, 300, 306; and "over against," 138–39; and philosophy of dialogue, 311; and relation, 318–19; rural vs. urban, 143; and the single one, 198; and society (*Gesellschaft*), 170, 312, 316–17; and solitude, 194–95, 196, 201; and the word of God, 176; and Zen Buddhism, 246. *See also* society (*Gesellschaft*)
Community and Society (Tönnies), 309, 315–16
confirmation, 104–5
congregation (*Gemeinde*), 41, 45
connection (*Zusammenhang*), 54–55, 311
consciousness and ego, 57–58
contextual family therapy, 208
"Conversation, A" (Buber), 209–10
conversion, 147–49
Corinthians (New Testament), 146, 192
covenant, divine, 20, 267
Craig, Robert T., 134–35, 137–38
"Crisis of European Man, The" (Husserl), 36, 39
crisis of humanity, 36–37, 40
crisis of spirit, 54–55
Critique of Judgment (Kant), 105
Culture and Civilisation (Buber), 310
Cusa. *See* Nicholas of Cusa

Daimon (periodical), 144
Dalai Lama, 248n19
Daniel: Dialogues on Realization (Buber), 54–55, 88–90, 142, 146, 149, 338
dasein, 2, 34, 36
dative, the, 60, 62
Day of Atonement, 272
Dazwischen (in between), 54–55, 62–63, 63n6
"Dead Church, The" (Trakl), 145
Décades de Pontigny, 356
Demian: The Story of Emil Sinclair's Youth (Hesse), 142, 148, 149
Descartes, René, 131–32
Desjardins, Paul, 43, 356
destiny (*Bestimmung*), 39, 40, 43, 170
Deuteronomy, 265
Deutscher Soziologentag (German sociologists' conference), 311
Deutsches Volksthum (Jahn), 314
dharmic socialism, 245, 248n19
dialectical theology, 360–61
dialogical action, 27–28
dialogical communication, 19–20, 29
dialogical event, the, 26–27

dialogical feminism, 346–47
"Dialogical Feminism" (Merrill), 346
dialogical listening, 166–79
dialogical politics, 28
dialogical relations: and Buddhism, 241; Japanese thought and, 362–64; Jews and Palestinians, between, 324, 331–32; and the Single-One, 29; and solitude, 195; and spirituality, 242; and utopia, 29
dialogical response, 26
Dialogue (Buber), 127n34, 280–82, 318
dialogue (*Gespräch*): authentic/inauthentic, 59, 60–62, 340; Bachelard on, 172; and the between, 178–79; and communication theory, 19, 115; and community (*Gemeinschaft*), 102; and epistemology, 100; and the eternal Thou, 178, 179; Hebrew, 218; and hermeneutics, 166; and I-It/I-Thou relations, 133–34; and individuation, 102; and intersubjectivity, 115; and I-Thou relation, 115–16, 133; as method, 100–101; and mysticism, 127n34, 276; and the other, 18, 107, 172, 347; phenomenology of, 27, 59–60; and the soul, 190. *See also* speech; spokenness (*Gesprochenheit*); word of God, the
dialogue, interfaith, 227–38, 239–50, 251–59
dialogue, philosophy of. *See* philosophy of dialogue
"Dialogue between God and Man in the Bible, The" (Buber), 288
"Dialogues on Realization" (Buber), 54
Dictionary of the High German Dialect (Adelung), 313
Dilthey, Wilhelm, 36, 55, 84–87, 275
Discours de la méthode (Descartes), 131
"Distance and Relation" (Buber), 42, 67, 69, 137, 208, 210, 335
"Disturbing Boundaries" (Butler, D.), 346
divine, the, 55–56, 72, 311–12
divine covenant, 20, 267
divine election, 263, 265–67, 268
divinity, 121–23
Döblin, Alfred, 142
Dogen, 239, 241, 243–45, 248n15
Dohrn, Wolf, 356
Doshisha University in Kyoto, 362
"dream of the double cry," 126–27n33
"Drei Reden" (Buber), 300
dualism, 89–90, 240–44
Duwelt (the Thou-World), 69, 151–52, 364

Eastern wisdom, 154n33, 239–50
Ecclesia-Synagoga (iconography), 235–36
"echte Gespräch und die Möglichkeiten des Friedens, Das" (Buber), 178
Eckardt, Meister, 67–68, 72
Eclipse of God (Buber), 28–29, 73, 75, 253, 287–88

eclipse of God, 288, 290
École Biblique et Archéologique de Jérusalem, 355
École Normale Israélite Orientale, 358
ecstasy (*hitlahavut*), 276–77
Ecstatic Confessions (Buber), 67, 200, 252
Edschmid, Kasimir, 149–50
education: Bologna Process of 1999 and, 215, 219; of character, 217–18; and the ego (*Eigenwesen*), 217; fundamentals of, 216; and humanism, 215–20; and inclusion, 218–19; and the It-World (*Es-Welt*), 217, 220; and self-transformation, 121–22; and trust, 216–20
Education toward Community (Buber), 318
ego, the (*Eigenwesen*): and Buddhism, 245; and consciousness, 57–58; and duality, 241; and education, 217; and the I-It relation, 98, 170, 171, 241–43; and the I-Thou relation, 67; and the other, 3; and *wu-wei*, 239. *See also* between, (*das Zwischen*); other, the; self, the
Ehyeh asher ehyeh (name of God), 74–75
Eigenwesen (individual ego). *See* ego, the (*Eigenwesen*)
Einsamkeit (lonesomeness). *See* loneliness
Ekstatische Konfessionen (Buber), 338
election, divine, 263, 265–67
"Election of Israel: A Biblical Inquiry (Exodus 3 and 19; Deuteronomy), The" (Buber), 265–66
elective affinity (*Wahlverwandtschaft*), 41, 309–10
Elements of the Interhuman (Buber), 41–42, 59–60, 133–34, 208, 362
Eli'ezer, Israel ben (Ba'al Shem Tov), 62, 76, 271, 274, 278
Elijah, 201–2
Elijah and the Mystery Play (Buber), 201–2
Emmet, Dorothy, 174
encounter (*Begegnung*), 67, 70, 144, 323–34. *See also* I-It relation; I-Thou relation
Engendering Judaism (Adler), 337
enlightenment, 101, 241, 243–45, 246–47, 248n15, 248–49n22
Enlightenment, the, 272–73
epistemology: and binationalism, 325; and dialogue, 100; of Dilthey, 85–86; and expressionism/impressionism, 150–51; and imagination, 69; and socialism, 104–5; and the soul, 190
Erasmus of Rotterdam, 44
erasure, locutionary, 252–54
Erfahrung/Erlebnis (experience), 86, 87–88, 274, 275
Erotik, Die (Andreas-Salomé), 337–38
Erziehung zur Gemeinschaft (Buber), 318
eschatology, 20, 26, 28–29, 299, 301, 305–6
Essay on Man (Cassirer), 43–44
Es-Welt (It-World, the). *See* It-World, the (*Es-Welt*)
eternal Thou, the: and the between, 57, 59, 62, 174–78; and the death of God, 290; and dialogue, 178–79; God as, 19–20, 25, 74; and the Holocaust, 287, 288, 291; and the imageless God, 17–18; and imagination, 69, 71–72; and the individual, 196; and interconnection, 56; and the I-Thou relation, 86, 115, 167; and I-Thou relation, 263; and the It-World, 187; and lemmatic reasoning, 368–69; and the other, 26, 28; and philosophy of dialogue, 317; prayer and, 169; relationship to humans, 291n1. *See also* God; word of God, the
ethics: of care, 339–41, 342; and Jewish-Palestinian relations, 323–34; phenomenology of, 3; and philosophy of dialogue, 339–41
Ethics (Cohen), 45
Ethics as the Study of Inter-Humanity (Ningen no Gaku toshite no Rinrigaku) (Watsuji), 363
everyday, the, 256
existentialism, 33, 98–99, 195, 361
Exodus (Old Testament), 160, 26
Exodus, the, 26–27, 162, 265–66, 365
experience (*Erfahrung/Erlebnis*), 86, 87–88, 274, 275
expressionism, 142–54, 155n33

Fackenheim, Emil L., 81n40, 292n17
"failure of real meeting" (*Vergegnung*), 208, 209–10, 217, 231
Faktum Mensch, das, 33
family therapy, 208
Fanon, Frantz, 98
Farber, Leslie, 208
Faust (Goethe), 85
Fear and Trembling (Kierkegaard), 24, 30–31n21
Feminine Mystique, The (Friedan), 336
feminism: academic, 345–46; alterity, feminine, 4; and the between, 344; dialogical, 346–47; and ethics of care, 339–41, 342; and gender, 341, 342, 343–47; and the interhuman, 336–37, 340, 347; and the I-Thou relation, 342, 346–47; and minor voices, 336–38; and the other, 345; and the parent-child relation, 342–43; and philosophy of dialogue, 297–98, 335–50. *See also* gender; humanism
Feuerbach, Ludwig, 20, 29, 42, 87
Fichte, Johann Gottlieb, 39, 314
Fischer, Jean, 357
Fishbane, Michael, 169
form (*Gestalt*), 69, 103, 105, 364
Frankfurt University, 169
Frau Kirche/Synagoge (iconography), 236
Frauenbewegung, Die (Key), 337–38
Freies Jüdisches Lehrhaus, 90–91
Freire, Paulo, 218
French reception, 355–59
Freud, Sigmund, 206
"Freundschaft" (Heynicke), 144
Friedan, Betty, 336

INDEX   391

"Friedensfeier" (Hölderlin), 176–77
Friedman, Maurice, 208, 219
Friedrichstrasse (Grosz), 143–44
"Friendship" (Heynicke), 144
From Mysticism to Dialogue (Mendes-Flohr), 167, 309
"From Religion as Presence" (Buber), 69
Fumet, Stanislas, 356
Furani, Khaled, 225–26

Gadamer, Hans-Georg, 161, 166, 332
Gandhi, Mahatma, 325, 327, 328
Ganzheit (wholeness), 34, 70
gegenüber ("over against"), 90, 136–139
Geist/Geistern (spirit), 27–28
Gemeinde (congregation), 41, 45
Gemeinschaft (Buber), 315–316
Gemeinschaft (community). See community (*Gemeinschaft*)
Gemeinschaft und Gesellschaft (Tönnies), 309, 312, 313, 315–16
gender, 341, 342, 343–46, 347. See also feminism
Gender Trouble (Butler), 344
Genesis (Old Testament), 77, 116, 129, 136
Genesis, 159
"Genuine Dialogue and the Possibilities of Peace" (Buber), 178
Gesalbte, Der (Buber), 301–2, 303, 304
Gesellschaft (society). See society (*Gesellschaft*)
Gesellschaft, Die (ed. Buber), 36, 41, 86–87, 311, 337–38
Gespräch (dialogue). See dialogue (*Gespräch*)
Gesprochenheit (spokenness), 61, 62, 116, 121, 158–59
Gestalt (form), 69, 103, 105, 364
Gideon (judge), 20, 27, 28
Gilligan, Carol, 337, 339–40
gnosticism, 29, 39, 92, 93, 149
God: and the between, 175–76; of Christianity/Islam/Judaism, 257; and community (*Gemeinschaft*), 316; and conversion, 147–49; covenant of, 233–37; of creation, 163, 167; death of, 25–26, 129; dialogical relations and, 195; and divine election, 263, 265–67, 268; eclipse of, 288, 290; essential relation to, 202; as the eternal Thou, 19–20, 26, 74; and expressionism, 145–47; and hermeneutics, 156–57; hiddenness of, 162, 169; and the Holocaust, 287–91; and Israel, 266; and the It-World, 21–22; kairological, 127n37; mystery of, 232–33; personhood of, 72–73; Protestant Lutherans and, 24; and religiosity, 225, 263; silence of, 289; and the single one, 198, 203n30; and solitude, 196; of sufferers, 162; as Thou, 163, 164n5; and *wu-wei*, 239. See also eternal Thou, the; word of God, the
Godhead, the, 67–68, 71, 72
God of sufferers, the, 162

Goethe, Johann Wolfgang von, 85, 121, 122, 167
Gogarten, Friedrich, 28, 360
Gog und Magog (Buber), 292n17
Golan, Joe, 355
Good and Evil (Buber), 77
Gordon, Mordechai, 172
Gospel of John, 115, 173
Great Maggid and His Succession, The (Buber), 275–76
Groethuysen, Bernhard, 42–44
Grosz, George, 143–44
Grundworte (primary words), 132, 135, 136
guilt, 211
"Guilt and Guilt Feelings" (Buber), 208
Gurion, David Ben, 28
Gush Emunim (Zionist movement), 305

Habermas, Jürgen, 332–33
habitation, epochs of, 197
Hajathologia (Hayathology), 365–66
Hakuin (Zen master), 244
Hall, Michael, 219
Hammarskjöld, Dag, 99–100, 355
Hanazaki, Kohei, 370–71
Hanh, Thich Nhat, 242–43
Harnack, Adolf/Adolph von, 29, 92–93
Hart, Heinrich and Julius, 40
Hasidism: and the Bible, 158; central aspects of, 276; decline of, 278, 279; defined, 271; divine covenant and, 20; and dualism, 240; in France, 356; and Islam, 253; and Judaism, 271–286; and mystical experience, 88; and nationalism, 263; and Neoplatonism, 102; as response to Spinoza, 78; and the soul, 192; spirituality of, 277; tales of, 273, 275–76; translation of texts, 164n18. See also Israel; Judaism; Zionism
Hayathology (*Hajathologia*), 365–66
Healing through Meeting (Trueb), 207
Heart Sutra, 242
Hebraische Denken im Vergleich mit dem Griechischen, Das (Boman), 365
Hebrew Bible: Buber-Rosenzweig translation of, 93, 168, 169, 300; and the dialogical event, 26–27; and the It-World, 93; Katsumura on the, 362; ontology of, 365; and the Word of God, 116
"Hebrew Humanism" (Buber), 267
Hebrew Thought Compared with Greek (Boman), 365
Heidegger, Martin: on appearance (*Erscheinung*), 80n28; Kimura and, 363; on language, 124, 127–28n41; and *Lebenswelt* (lifeworld), 158; and ontology, 174; and philosophical anthropology, 34, 38; and solitude, 199–200; on the They-self, 125n7
heilige Weg, Der (Buber), 55–56, 58
Heine, Heinrich, 231

Heraclitus, 100–101
Herder, Johann Gottfried von, 39, 44
hermeneutics, 160, 169, 275
hermeneutics, biblical, 156–65, 362, 365
Hesse, Herman, 142, 148, 149
Hestar Panim, 162
Heynicke, Kurt, 145–46
hierocracy, 303
Hiob (Susman), 40
Hiraishi, Yoshimori, 360, 361
hitlahavut (ecstasy), 276–77
Hito to Hito to no Aida (Kimura), 363
Hölderlin, Friedrich: on dialogue, 176–77; eschatology of, 26, 28, 29; influence of, 19, 30n5; on salvation, 23; and theopolitics, 20
Holocaust, the, 263–64, 287–91, 327
"Holy Way: A Word to the Jews and to the Peoples, The" (Buber), 304, 311
homme révolté, L' (Camus), 357–58
hooks, bell, 218
"Hope for This Hour" (Buber), 104–5
"Horse, The" (Buber), 209
human crises (twentieth century), 36–37
humanism: Buddhist, 244; and education, 215–20; Hebrew, 44–45, 163, 244, 267; and philosophical anthropology, 44–46; in Zen Buddhism, 244. See also feminism
Humanität, 39, 44–45
Human Place in the Cosmos, The (Scheler), 36, 38
human relations, 171–72
Humboldt, Wilhelm von, 39
humility (*shiflut*), 276–77
Husserl, Edmund, 36, 39, 158

I and Thou (Buber): on "actuality of faith, the," 72; and authentic community, 41; and the between, 56; and the Bible, 157; and Buddhism, 241, 243, 361; and *coincidentia oppositorum*, 368–69; and community (*Gemeinschaft*), 316; and conversion, 148–49; and crisis of community, 37; on dialogical relationship, 194; and *Discours de la méthode*, 131–32; and ethics of care, 340; and expressionism, 143, 152–153; on *Hinduism*, 241; and the Holocaust, 288; on imagination, 69–71; and interspecies dialogue, 140n31; Irigaray on, 345; Isozaki on, 364; and the It-World, 91–92; Japanese translations of, 361; and lemmatic reasoning, 366–68; and Löwith, Karl, 42; on metaphors, 170; moral philosophy of, 97–100; on Neoplatonism, 104; and philosophical anthropology, 34, 46n16; on prayer, 169; on primary words, 132–33; on religion, 146–47; on solitude, 196; on the soul, 191; and *Taoism*, 239; on the Word of God, 176; and the You relation, 166
Ich und Du (Buber). See *I and Thou* (Buber)

Idea of Man, The (Scheler), 38
I-It relation: and being, 242; and the Bible, 160; and binationalism, 325; and dialogue, 133–34, 135–36; and dualism, 241, 243; and education, 187; and the ego (*Eigenwesen*), 170, 171, 241–43; explained, 7n8; and feminism, 342; and *Gestalt*, 103; and hermeneutics, 156; and the I-Thou relation, 170, 171; and moral philosophy, 98–99; and the other, 67; and psychoanalysis, 206; and psychotherapy, 187, 209; Rosenzweig on, 91–92; and scripture, 161; and the self, 21–22; and solitude, 194; and the soul, 190–91; and *wu-wei*, 243
I Love to You (Irigaray), 345
imagination: and aesthetics, 106; and dialogical thinking, 67–69; and the eternal Thou, 71–72; and idolatry, 73–74; and the interhuman, 106; and the It-World (*Es-Welt*), 69; and the real, 105–7
impressionism, 150–51
In a Different Voice (Gilligan), 337
inclusion, 106, 218–19
individual, the, 22–23
Individual and Person—Masses and Community (Buber), 318
Individual in the Role of the Fellow Human Being, The (Löwith), 42
individuation, 1–2, 6n4, 102–5
Individuum und Person—Masse und Gemeinschaft (Buber), 318
Institut International d'Études Hébraïques, 355, 357
intention (*kavanah*), 276, 277
interfaith dialogue, 229–37
interhuman, the (*Zwischenmenschliche*): and the between, 59–60, 98–99; Dilthey and, 86–87; and feminism, 336–37, 340, 347; and imagination, 106; ontology of, 170–74, 178; and the other, 104; and philosophy of anthropology, 41–42; and philosophy of communication, 134; and speech, 178; suppositions of, 100–101; and Watsuji, 363. See also between, the (*das Zwischen*); other, the
intersubjectivity, 99, 115, 341, 342–43, 364
"Intersubjectivity Meets Maternity" (Benjamin), 342–43
introspection (*Besinnung*), 35, 43, 45
Irigaray, Luce, 344–45
Isaak, Rabbi Salomon Ben (*Rashi*), 234
Isaiah (prophet), 162, 167, 266, 289, 357
Islam: founding of, 255; God of, 257; and Hasidism, 253; interfaith dialogue and, 251–58; and philosophy of dialogue, 226; and Western philosophy, 256; and wisdom, 256–57
isolation: and community, 194–95; and enlightenment, 101; and experience (*Erfahrung*), 89; and expressionism, 143–44; and the It-World (*Es-Welt*), 87–88; and mental health, 101; and the

self, 196; social, 143, 152; and solitude, 197. See *also* loneliness; solitude
Isozaki, Arata, 363
Israel: chosenness of, 268; and Christianity, 201–2, 227–37; covenant with God, 27; divine election of, 265–69; and the eternal God, 163; God of, 160; God-time of, 235–36; and I-Thou relation, 156, 157, 163; and messianism, 299, 301; and Palestine, 297–98, 325–26, 329–31; and the prophets, 23, 24, 201–2; Spinoza and, 369; and theopolitics, 302–3, 306; and visibility of God, 74, 158; and the word of God, 116. *See also* Hasidism; Zionism
Israel ben Eli'ezer (Ba'al Shem Tov), 62, 76, 271, 274, 278
Israel National Library, 355
I-Thou relation: and attachment, 245; Bachelard on, 172; and the between, 20–21, 57–58, 174–75, 247n3; and the Bible, 157–58; and binationalism, 324–25, 331; Camus on, 357–58; and *coincidentia oppositorum*, 368–69; and community (*Gemeinschaft*), 44, 317–18; and dialogue, 133–36, 166; duality of, 241, 243; and education, 122; and enlightenment, 246–47; and the eternal Thou, 86, 115, 167, 263; and ethics of care, 340; and feminism, 346–47; Gordon on, 172; and hermeneutics, 156; and the I-It relation, 170, 171; and interspecies communication, 139; and the It-World (*Es-Welt*), 91–92, 342; and Japanese thought, 361–64; and lemmatic reasoning, 366–71; Levinas critique of, 3–4; and moral philosophy, 98–99; and mystical experience, 200; and the ontology of becoming, 366; and the other, 67, 297; and "over against," 136; and psychotherapy, 207–12; reciprocal nature of, 130; and religiosity, 225, 263; and the self, 21–22; and solitude, 194; and the soul, 190; spheres of, 167; and spirituality, 242, 247–48n8; and the Word of God, 158; and World War One, 309–11; and *wu-wei*, 243; and Zen Buddhism, 244, 247; and Zionism, 329
It-World, the (*Es-Welt*): and the between, 21–23; and Christianity, 93; and community (*Gemeinschaft*), 146; and duality, 89–90; and education, 217, 220; and expressionism, 143; hallowing of, 84–96; and the Holocaust, 263–64; and imagination, 69; and isolation, 87–88; and the I-Thou relation, 91–92; and lemmatic reasoning, 366; and loneliness, 72; and mysticism, 88, 367–368; Plaskow on, 342; and religion, 146; and the soul, 187, 190–91; and the Thou-world, 364; and tree metaphor, 151–52

Jacobi, Friedrich Heinrich, 130
Jacobson, Victor, 356
Jahn, Friedrich Ludwig, 314

Japanese architecture, 363–64
Japanese reception, 360–74
Jerubbaal. *See* Gideon (judge)
Jerubbesheth. *See* Gideon (judge)
Jesus Christ, 20, 25, 75, 227–28, 230–31
Jesus of Nazareth. *See* Jesus Christ
Jewish-Arab state. *See* binationalism
Jewish monotheism, 77–78
Jewish-Palestinian relations, 323–34
"Jewish renaissance," 40, 102, 273
Jewish Retreat Home, 169
Jewish state. *See* Israel
"Jewish Woman, The" (Winkler), 338
Jikan to Jiko (Kimura), 363
Job (Old Testament), 162–63, 290–91
Jodl, Friedrich, 87
Jōdo Buddhism, 361
John, Gospel of, 115, 173
John the Baptist, 202
Judaism: and the between, 56; and Christianity, 73, 228–37, 257; and divine election, 265–70; and feminism, 336; God of, 257; and Hasidism, 271–86; and the Holocaust, 287–93; and the image of God, 75; and Islam, 251–52; and Jesus Christ, 20, 25, 227–28; and messianism, 230–31; as "Oriental faith," 240; and Palestine, 329–30; and philosophy of dialogue, 26; and religiosity, 263; and Zen Buddhism, 244. *See also* Hasidism; Israel; Zionism
Jude, Der (ed. Buber), 311
Judges(Old Testament), 300, 302
Jüdisch Leben (Buber), 314–15
Jüdische Renaissance (Buber), 310
Jüdische Würdigkeit (Jewish worthiness), 48n52
Jung, Carl Gustav, 206

Kabbalah, 191–92, 274, 277–78
kairological God, 127n37
Kant, Immanuel, 35, 37–38, 177
Katsumura, Hiroya, 361–62
Kaufmann, Walter, 168
kavanah (intention), 276, 277
Kenmyo, Takagi, 248n19
Key, Ellen, 336, 337–38
Kierkegaard, Søren, 20, 24–25, 30–31n21, 197–98
Kimura, Bin, 363
King, Martin Luther, Jr., 97–98, 104
Kingdom of God (Buber), 25, 361
Kings (Old Testament), 158
Kingship of God (Buber), 93, 301–2, 303
Kirisutokyō Shisō ni Okeru Sonzairon no Mondai (Ariga), 365
Knevels, Wilhelm, 147
Knowledge of Man, The (Buber), 208
Kokoschka, Oskar, 142
Kommende, Das (Buber), 301–2

Koren, Israel, 78–79n5
Kotsk, Menahem Mendel of, 278
Krasner, Barbara, 208
"Kriegsbuber," 311
Kristallnacht, 265
Kultur und Zivilisation (Buber), 310
Kyoto Association of Jewish Thought, 362
Kyoto school, 360–61, 363

Lagerlöf, Selma, 336
Laing, R. D., 208
Landauer, Gustav: on Buber, 4; and community (*Gemeinschaft*), 311; death of, 371; eschatology of, 26, 28; on feminine thought, 338–39; influence of, 19–20, 55, 297; and theopolitics, 20
Lang, Bernhard, 171, 177
Lang, Fritz, 142
language, 117–27, 127–28n41, 317
"Language of the Birds, The" (Buber), 278–79
Lao-Tzu, 239, 243
Lasker-Schüler, Elsa, 337
Lebenswelt (lifeworld), 158, 164n19
Legend of the Baal-Shem, The (Buber), 273, 276, 277, 278
Leibowitz, Yeshayahu, 338
Leitwort, 159–60
lemmatic reasoning, 366–71
Lenin, Vladimir, 192
Lessing, Gotthold Ephraim, 19, 20, 26, 28
Lessing, Theodor, 154n33
"Letter from Birmingham Jail" (King), 97–98
Letters for the Advancement of Humanity (Herder), 39
Levels of Organic Life and the Human (Plessner), 36
Levinas, Emmanuel, 3–4, 72–73, 131, 243, 341, 358
Leviticus (Old Testament), 3, 254
Levy, Jakob, 144
Liady, Shneur Zalman of, 279
liberation theology, 244
lifeworld (*Lebenswelt*), 158, 164n19
Lifton, Robert J., 211
listening, dialogical, 166–79
Living Jewishly (Buber), 314–15
locutionary erasure, 252–54
Logic (Kant), 37
Logic of the Humanities (Cassirer), 44
Logos and Lemma (Yamauchi), 367
loneliness: existential, 195; and expressionism, 142, 143–47; and the It-World (*Es-Welt*), 72; Kierkegaard on, 197–98; and the Single-One, 25; and solitude, 201–202, 202n2. *See also* isolation; solitude
lonesomeness (*Einsamkeit*). *See* loneliness
Lorenz, Kuno, 44
"Losung, Die" (Buber), 311, 312

Louys, Renée, 357
Löwith, Karl, 42
Ludwig, Paula, 142, 144
Luther, Martin, 176, 229

Maggid of Mezhrech/Mezritch, 62–63, 241, 247n5
Magnes, Jehuda, 357
Mahayana Buddhism, 361, 367
making present (*Vergegenwärtigung*), 60, 69, 70, 119–20
Malkhut Shamayim, 306
"Man and His Image-Work" (Buber), 70, 208
Mann, Thomas, 40
Man of Sorrows, 146
Marcion: Das Evangelium von dem fremdem Gott (Harnack), 92–93
Maria Verkündigung (Claudel), 355–56
Martin Buber: The Echo of His Dialogical Thought (journal special issue), 362
Martin Buber's Ontology: An Analysis of "I and Thou" (Wood), 174
Massignon, Louis, 357
Mediterranean Encounters, 355
Meetings (Buber), 208–9
Meister Eckhart, 67–68
memory, 105, 312
Menahem Mendel of Kotsk, 278
Menasce, Jean de, 356
Mendel of Kotsk, Menahem, 278–82
Mendel of Vurke, Rebbe, 278–82
Mendes-Flohr, Paul, 167, 168–70, 309, 338, 367
Mensch, der neue (the new man), 142–43, 147–52
mental health, 101, 138–39
Merrill, Barbara, 346
Merton, Thomas, 244–45
messianism, 29, 230–31, 299–301, 303, 304–6
Metropolis (Lang), 142
Mezhbizh, Barukh of, 278
Mezhrech/Mezritch, Maggid of, 62–63, 241, 247n5
Micah (Old Testament), 266
Midrash, 272
minor voices, 336–38
mismeeting (Vergegnung), 208, 209–10, 217, 231
Miteinandersein (being with), 42, 58
Mitgefühl, Das (Groethuysen), 42
Mittelstelle für jüdische Erwachsenenbildung, 169
Miyamoto, Hisao, 365
moral philosophy, 98–99, 106
Mosaic revelation, 28
Moses, 28, 201, 266, 302
Moses: The Revelation and the Covenant (Buber), 74–75, 82n46, 302, 361
motherhood, 339, 342, 343
Muhammad, 255
Mūlamadhyamakakārikā (Nagarjuna), 366–67
Munk, Georg. *See* Winkler, Paula

INDEX 395

Muth, Cornelia, 177
mysticism: and dialogue, 276; early conception of, 87–89; experience of, 135; and *I and Thou*, 367–68; and the It-World (*Es-Welt*), 88; Muslim, 252; solitude of, 200–201; and the soul, 191; study of, 273
"Myth in Judaism" (Buber), 77–78

Nagarjuna, 242, 366
Nathan, prophet, 304
nationalism, 40, 263, 267, 331. *See also* binationalism
National Socialism, 229, 265, 287
"Nature of Man, The" (Buber), 254–55
Nazism, 229
negative solitude, 197–98, 199, 200–201
Neher, André, 357
Neoplatonic philosophy, 102–103, 104, 107
Neue Erde (journal), 145
Neue Gemeinschaft, 40
neue Mensch, der (the new man), 142–43, 147–52
New Testament. *See* Bible, the
New York Times, 99–100, 104–5
Nicholas of Cusa, 1, 6n4, 102–3, 105, 167, 273, 368
Nietzsche, Friedrich, 20, 54, 121, 290
Ningen no Gaku toshite no Rinrigaku (Ethics as the Study of Inter-Humanity), 363
Nishida, Kitaro, 361, 363
Noddings, Nel, 340–41, 342
"Note for Bible Courses, A" (Buber), 169
Nussbaum, Martha, 345–46

Old and New Community (Buber), 309–10
Old Testament. *See* Hebrew Bible
Olsen, Regina, 198
Ong, Walter, 139
On the Different Races of Human Beings (Kant), 37
"On the History of the Problem of Individuation: Nicholas of Cusa and Jakob Böhme" (Buber), 1
ontology: of becoming, 364–66; of the between, 2, 17; and the eternal Thou, 174–78; existential, 168; and existentialism, 117–24; of the Hebrew Bible, 365; interhuman, of the (*Zwischenmenschliche*), 86, 170–74, 178; and Jewish-Palestinian encounter, 323–24; relational, 166–84
other, the: acceptance of, 335; and *Begegnung* (encounter), 70, 323–34; and the between, 60–61, 174–75; and *Beziehung* (relationship), 70; and Christian exclusivism, 231; and community (*Gemeinschaft*), 138; dialogical response to, 26; and dialogue, 18, 107, 172, 347; and education, 219; and the ego (*Eigenwesen*), 3, 67, 217; and the eternal Thou, 26; and existentialism, 99; experience of, 209; and feminism, 345; and imagination, 67–78; and the interhuman, 104; and I-Thou relation, 67, 98, 190; and the mystery of faith, 233; Palestinian other, the, 323–34; and philosophy of dialogue, 335–36; presupposition of, 137; and relationship (*Beziehung*), 67; and the self, 21–22; and self-becoming, 118–21; and the Single-One, 23; and solicitude, 199; and speech, 124; and *wu-wei*, 239; and Zen Buddhism, 242–44, 245. *See also* between, the (*das Zwischen*); interhuman, the (*Zwischenmenschliche*); self, the
"over against" (*gegenüber*), 90, 136–39
Ozick, Cynthia, 151, 155n34

"Pagan Rabbi" (Ozick), 151, 155n34
Palestine, 253–54, 297–98, 324–35, 371
pantheism, 148–49, 167–68
Pappenheim, Bertha, 337
parent-child relation, 342–43
Pascal, Blaise, 197–98
Passover Haggadah, 268
Paths in Utopia (Buber), 28, 40, 305, 319
"Patient as Therapist to His Analyst, The" (Searles), 207
Paul, Saint, 146, 192
Paul VI (pope), 99
"Peace Celebration" (Hölderlin), 176–77
Pentateuch, 20, 159–60
perception, ethics of, 97–111
performative gender, 344–45
perlocutionary/locutionary acts, 252–54
Phaedrus (Plato), 130
phenomenology, 27, 35, 59–60, 131, 135
philosophical anthropology, 33–46
Philosophie de la Révolution française (Groethuysen), 42
Philosophische Anthropologie (Groethuysen), 42, 43
philosophy, moral, 98–99, 106
philosophy and rhetoric, 130–31
Philosophy of Anuśaya (Yamauchi), 367
philosophy of communication, 129–39
philosophy of dialogue: anthropology, and philosophical, 33–52; and the between, 53–63; and Buddhism, 244, 246; development of, 1–6; and Eastern thought, 241–42; and ethics of care, 339–41; and ethics of perception, 97–111; and feminism, 335–50; and gender, 343–46; and the It-World, 84–96; Japanese reception of, 360–74; and Jewish-Palestinian relations, 323–34; modernity, and monological, 19–32; and the other, 67–83, 335–36. *See also* communication; communication, philosophy of; communication theory; dialogue (*Gespräch*)
Philosophy of the Future (Feuerbach), 42
Pindar, paradox of, 118–21, 124
Pira, Giorgio La, 355
Plaskow, Judith, 339, 342
Plato, 101

Platonic theory, 102–3, 130
Plessner, Helmuth, 36, 40–41
Poetry and Truth (Goethe), 121
Point of View of My Work as an Author, The (Kierkegaard), 30–31n21
political theology, 20, 27–28, 93, 95n37
politics: community (*Gemeinschaft*), 309–22; feminism, 335–47; Israel and Palestine, 323–34; theopolitics, 299–308
positive solitude, 195, 201–202
Practice of Christianity (Kierkegaard), 30–31n21
prayer, 74, 168–169, 174, 178, 202
prefixes/suffixes and semantics, 312–15, 317
"Presence" (Buber), 56
presence, the, 56–57
Presses universitaires de France, 357
"primally Jewish, the," 273
primary words (*Grundworte*), 132, 135, 136
primordial spirituality, 241–44, 247, 247–48n8
Pritzker Architecture Prize, 363
Problem des Menschen, Das (Buber), 58–59
Problem of Man, The (Buber), 34, 35–36, 37, 38, 43
Problem of Ontology in Christian Thought, The (Ariga), 365
"Prophecy, Apocalyptic, and the Historical Hour" (Buber), 305
prophecy and apocalyptic, 305–6
Prophetic Faith, The (Buber), 302
prophetic voice, 161
prophets: and the divine covenant, 20; Elijah, 201–2; Isaiah, 162, 266, 289; Muhammad, 255; Nathan, 304; and philosophical anthropology, 45; Samuel, 20, 27, 303–4; solitude of, 201–2; and theopolitics, 20
Protestant Theological Faculty of the University of Bonn, 229
"Psalm" (Ludwig), 144
Psalms (Old Testament), 82, 288, 291
Psychiatry, 208
psychoanalysis, 135, 206, 208
psychology: and humanism, 215–22; and psychotherapy, 206–12; and solitude, 194–205; and the soul, 189–93
psychotherapy, 206–12
Pure Land Buddhism, 248n19, 361
Putnam, Hilary, 3

Quand Israel aime Dieu (Buber), 356
question, unasked, 209–10
"Question to the Single One" (Buber), 99, 197–98
Qur'an, the, 255, 257

Ragaz, Leonard, 26, 28
Rakats, Yoëts Kim Kadish, 280–81
Rashi (Rabbi Salomon Ben Isaak), 234
"Raumproblem der Bühne, Das" (Buber), 356

reality, everyday. *See* It-World, the (*Es-Welt*)
Realm of Things. *See* It-World, the (*Es-Welt*)
Realm of Thou. *See* Thou-World, the (*Duwelt*)
Realphantasie (the real), 69, 106–7
Realpolitik, 2
reasoning, lemmatic, 366–71
Rebbe Mendel of Vurk, 278–82
reception of teachings: France, in, 355–59; Japan, in, 360–74
redemption, 299, 300
relation, 318–19
Relational Approach to Ethics and Moral Education, A (Noddings), 340–41
relationality: and anthropology, 34, 42; and the between, 174; and communication, 132; and community (*Gemeinschaft*), 58; and feminism, 339–40, 342; and I-Thou relation, 173
relationship (*Beziehung*), 67, 70, 72, 169, 316–17. *See also* between, the (*das Zwischen*); interhuman, the (*Zwischenmenschliche*); other, the
"Religion als Gegenwart" ("Religion as Presence") (Buber), 90–91, 191–92
religiosity, 77–78, 242, 263, 273, 274
Renik, Owen, 207
"Reply to My Critics" (Buber), 33, 291
resonance, 171
response/responsibility, 281–82
Revue juive, 356
rhetoric, 129, 130–31, 134
Ricoeur, Paul, 156, 160, 164n19
Rilke, Rainer Maria, 54
Robinson, Marie, 155n38
Rogers, Carl, 206–7
Rogosu to Renma (Yamauchi), 367
Romanzero (Heine), 231
Root Verses on the Middle Way (Nagarjuna), 366–67
Rosa, Hartmut, 171
Rosenstock-Hussy, Eugen, 332
Rosenzweig, Franz: and biblical scripture, 158–60; critique of Harnack, 92–93; and feminism, 341; and the Hebrew Bible, 93, 157, 168, 169, 177; on *Humanität*, 45; on the I-It relation, 91–92; influence of, 90–91; on Islam, 252
Roshi, Daido, 245
Ross, Tamar, 339

Saint-Thomas Church, 168
Salzmann, Alexander von, 356
Sämmtliche Werke (Feuerbach), 87
saṃsāra, 242–44, 246
Samuel (Old Testament), 1, 20, 27, 300, 303–4
Sarahs, Aryeh Leib, 247n5
Sartre, Jean-Paul, 98
Schaeder, Grete, 44
Scheler, Max, 36, 38–40

INDEX 397

Schicksalsgemeinschaft (communities of destiny), 41, 45
Schmidt, Karl Ludwig, 229–30
Schmitt, Carl, 28, 330
Scholem, Gershom, 274
Schwartz, Eliezer, 209
Scott, Sarah, 6n4
scripture, Biblical, 158–59, 161–62, 169–70, 289
Searles, Harold F., 207
Selbstbesinnung (self-reflection), 35, 43, 45
self, the: and duality, 241; and freedom, 370; and guilt, 211; and the I-It relation, 21–22, 103; and isolation, 196; and the I-Thou relation, 21–22; and the It-World (Es-Welt), 89; Kierkegaard on, 118–19; and language, 123–24; and mystical experience, 88; and the other, 77; and presence, 56; and psychotherapy, 207; and wu-wei, 240. See also between, the (das Zwischen); interhuman, the (Zwischenmenschliche); other, the
self-becoming, 118–21
self-other dualism, 240–41
self-realization (Verwirklichung), 39, 42, 54–55, 71
self-reflection (Selbstbesinnung), 35, 43, 45
self-transformation (Bildung), 121–23, 161
Serouya, Henry, 355
Sheng-Yen, 244, 245, 248n18
shiflut (humility), 276–77
Shneur Zalman of Liady, 279
Shoah, the (Holocaust), 263–64, 287–91, 327
Shobogenza (Dogen), 245
Siaḥ Sarfei Qodesh (Rakats), 280–81
Sichel, Betty A., 340
Silent Tsaddik, the, 278–82
Simmel, Georg, 36, 86–87, 258n7
"Sinai" collection, 357
Sinai covenant, 302, 303
Single-One, the: and community (Gemeinschaft), 198; and dialogical relations, 28, 29; and essential relationships, 203n30; existential nature of, 23–24; and Gideon, 27; Heidegger on, 199–200; Kierkegaard on, 24–25, 125n5, 198, 199; and loneliness, 25; and solitude, 197–200. See also self, the
Sitte, Die (Tönnies), 311
Sixteenth Zionist Congress (1929), 44, 71
Social Democratic Party, 229
"Social Dimension of Man, The" (Buber), 255
socialism, 104–5, 246, 248n19, 300
social isolation, 143, 152
social philosophy, 35–36
society (Gesellschaft), 143–47, 170, 312, 316–17
sociology, 34, 86, 134
Socratic dialogue, 130, 218
Sogaku, Harada, 244
solitude: and community (Gemeinschaft), 194–95, 196, 201; and dialogical relations, 196; the epochs of, 197; in human life, 202; and the I-It relation, 195; and isolation, 197; and loneliness, 201–2, 202n2; negative, 195, 197–98, 199, 200–201; and one's essence, 197; positive, 195, 201–2; and the single one, 197–200; synthesized forms of, 196–97; and Zen Buddhism, 246. See also isolation; loneliness
Sorbonne, 358
soul, the, 67–68, 187, 189–93
Space of Darkness (Isozaki), 363–364
speech: crisis of, 178; dialogical, 115; and imagination, 69; and the interhuman, 178; and the I-Thou relation, 172; and language, 118, 120; and the natural world, 138; and the other, 124; and the primary words, 132–33, 135; and recognition, 123; and truth, 129–30; and the Word of God, 133. See also spokenness (Gesprochenheit)
Sphäre des Zwischen, die. See between, the (das Zwischen)
Spinoza, Baruch, 78, 369
spirit, 39–40
spirituality, 241–42, 277
spokenness (Gesprochenheit), 61, 62, 116, 121, 158–59. See also speech
Star of Redemption, The (Der Stern der Erlösung) (Rosenzweig), 252
Stern, Daniel, 207
Stirner, Max, 24
Strauss, Leo, 75–76
Stuttgart dialogue (1933), 229–37
sublation (Aufhebung), 29, 368
suffixes/prefixes and semantics, 312–15, 317
Sufism, 252
Susman, Margarete, 40, 337, 339
Sustainer of All Peoples / All Universes, the, 253, 257
Suurmond, Jean-Jacques, 217
Szilagyi, Ernsz, 287, 290, 292n3

Tagore, Rabindranath, 242
"Tales and Parables of Zhuangzi" (trans. Buber), 240
tales of Hasidism, 62, 273, 275–76
"Tales of Liao-Chai" (trans. Buber), 240
Tales of Rabbi Nachman (Die Geschichten des Rabbi Nachman), 62, 273
Tales of the Hasidim (Buber), 241, 278, 369
Taoism, 239–40
teaching, 217–20
"Teaching and Deed" (Buber), 253
telepathic communication, 281
ten thousand things, the, 248n15
"terre retrouvée, La" 357
theocracy, 302–3
theological anthropology, 33
theologoumenon, 33

theology: atheistic, 75; Christian, 229, 360, 365; dialectical, 360-61; and the eclipse of God, 20; and ethics of care, 339; and feminism, 343; Hasidic, 274, 279, 282; hermeneutical, 156-65; liberation, 244; monarchic political, 28; and moral philosophy, 92; political, 93; post-traditional, 25-26, 29; supersessionist, 225, 228
theopolitics, 20, 23, 27, 299-308
therapy, family, 208
Theravada Buddhist tradition, 245-46, 248n19
They-self, the, 125n7
Thomas Aquinas, Saint, 68
Thou, Absolute, 56-57
Thou, the. *See* eternal Thou, the; God
Thou, the eternal. *See* eternal Thou, the
Thou of God, 56
Thou-World, the (*Duwelt*), 69, 151-52, 364
Three Addresses on Judaism (Buber), 287, 310-11
Thus Spoke Zarathustra (Nietszche), 54
tikkun, 29, 211
Tillich, Paul, 26, 28
Time and the Self (Kimura), 363
Toller, Ernst, 142, 147-48, 149
Tönnies, Ferdinand, 37, 309, 311, 312-18
"To Paula" (Buber), 124
Torah, the, 160, 267, 302
"tote Kirche, Die" (Trakl), 145
"To the Reader" (Werfel), 144
Trakl, Georg, 142, 145
Transformation, The (Toller), 147-48, 149
tree metaphor, the, 150, 151
Trueb, Hans, 207
trust and education, 216-20
tsaddikim, 271, 274, 278
Turnbewegung (gymnastics movement), 314
Turner, Victor, 44
"Turning Point" (Isozaki), 363-64
Twelfth Zionist Congress (Karlsbad), 268
Two Types of Faith (Buber), 73, 227, 228, 366

"Über Jakob Boehme" (Buber), 86
unasked question, 209-210
Union des intellectuels juifs de France, 357
Union mondiale des étudiants juifs, 357
Universal Declaration of Human Rights (1948), 45
University of Frankfurt China Institute, 240
University of Leipzig, 168
Urdistanz (primal distance), 84
"Urdistanz und Beziehung" (Buber), 137

Van Eyck, Aldo, 363-64
Varnhagen, Rachel, 339
Vaux, Pater Roland de, 355
Veck, Wayne, 219
Verantwortung ist der Nebelsrang der Schöpfung (Buber), 93

Vergegenwärtigung (making present), 60, 69, 70, 119-20
Vergegnung (mismeeting), 208, 209-10, 217, 231
Verwirklichung (self-realization), 55, 71
vindication, perlocutionary, 254-58
voices, minor, 336-38, 339
"volonté du mal, La" (Buber), 356
Vurke, Rebbe Mendel of, 278-82

Wahlverwandtschaft (elective affinity), 41, 309-10
Wajdi al-Tabari, Farid, 254
Walter, James, 339
Wandlung, Die (Toller), 147-48, 149
Washington School of Psychiatry, 208, 211
Waßmer, Johannes, 155n38
Watakushi to Nanji (Nishida), 361
Watsuji, Tetsuro, 363
Weber, Max, 27, 37, 272, 303
Weigand, Karl, 314
Weimar Republic, 92, 93
Weizsäcker, Victor von, 363
Werfel, Franz, 142, 144
Wesen (being), 312-15, 317-19
Wesenwille (will of the self), 312, 313
"What Is Common to All" (Buber), 100-101, 208
"What Is Man?" (Buber), 28-29, 102, 197
"What Is to Be Done?" (Buber), 194
Whitehead, Alfred North, 140-41n32
wholeness (*Ganzheit*), 34, 70
Wilhelm, Richard, 240
Winkler, Paula, 82n46, 93, 338, 344
Winnicott, Donald W., 208
Wirklichkeit (actuality), 59, 63, 67
wisdom, Eastern. *See* Eastern wisdom
women. *See* feminism
women-thinking (*Frauendenken*), 338-39, 340
Wood, Robert E., 174-75
word of God, the: and the between, 25; and Biblical scripture, 161, 176-77; and community, 176; and *halacha*, 244; and the Hebrew Bible, 116; and hermeneutical theology, 156; and the I-Thou relation, 158; and speech, 133; and the Torah, 160. *See also* speech; spokenness (*Gesprochenheit*)
"Word That Is Spoken, The" (Buber), 61-62, 208
Worms Cathedral, 233-36
Worte an die Zeit: Gemeinschaft (Buber), 45, 317
Wörterbuch der hochdeutschen Mundart (Adelung), 313
wu-wei, 239-41, 243, 246

Ya, U Kay Tha, 248-49n22
Yamauchi, Tokuryu, 367
Yami no Kūkan (Isozaki), 363-64
YHVH, 74-75, 302-4, 306

INDEX 399

Zalman of Liady, Shneur, 279
Zaoui, Rabbi André, 355
Zen Buddhism, 239, 241, 242–47, 361
Zinner, Samuel, 155n38
Zionism: and binationalism, 324–26, 328–29, 371; and colonialism, 331; and divine election, 267; Gurion on, 28; and the "Jewish Renaissance," 273; and Jewish-Arab state, 28; and messianism, 304–5; and nationalism, 267; and Palestine, 324–26, 335; political theology of, 28; and State of Israel, 330. *See also* Hasidism; Israel; Judaism

"Zionism and Nationalism" (Buber), 71
Zionist-Arab conflict, 324–26, 328–29
"Zion of the Jewish Woman, The" (Buber), 335–36
Zuimen no Tetsugaku (Yamauchi), 367
Zusammenhang (connection), 54–55, 311
Zusya of Hanipoli, 103, 192, 277, 284n29
Zwei Glaubensweisen (Buber), 366
Zwiesprache (Buber), 58, 176, 318
Zwiesprache (dialogue). *See* dialogue (*Gespräch*)
Zwischen. See between, the (*das Zwischen*)
Zwischenmenschliche (interhuman, the). *See* interhuman, the (*Zwischenmenschliche*)

www.ingramcontent.com/pod-product-compliance
Lightning Source LLC
Chambersburg PA
CBHW022025290426
44109CB00014B/747